SKILLS-BASED
HEALTH EDUCATION

MARY CONNOLLY, MED, CAGS
CAMBRIDGE COLLEGE
CURRY COLLEGE

JONES & BARTLETT
LEARNING

World Headquarters
Jones & Bartlett Learning
40 Tall Pine Drive
Sudbury, MA 01776
978-443-5000
info@jblearning.com
www.jblearning.com

Jones & Bartlett Learning books and products are available through most bookstores and online booksellers. To contact Jones & Bartlett Learning directly, call 800-832-0034, fax 978-443-8000, or visit our website, www.jblearning.com.

Substantial discounts on bulk quantities of Jones & Bartlett Learning publications are available to corporations, professional associations, and other qualified organizations. For details and specific discount information, contact the special sales department at Jones & Bartlett Learning via the above contact information or send an email to specialsales@jblearning.com.

Some images in this book feature models. These models do not necessarily endorse, represent, or participate in the activities represented in the images.

Production Credits
Publisher, Higher Education: Cathleen Sether
Senior Acquisitions Editor: Shoshanna Goldberg
Senior Associate Editor: Amy L. Bloom
Associate Production Editor: Julia Waugaman
Associate Marketing Manager: Jody Sullivan
V.P., Manufacturing and Inventory Control: Therese Connell
Composition: DataStream Content Solutions, LLC
Cover Design: Kristin E. Parker
Photo Research and Permissions Supervisor: Christine Myaskovsky
Associate Photo Researcher: Sarah Cebulski
Cover Images: Abstract chalkboard © Jeff Metzger/Dreamstime.com; students in classroom © Nicu Mircea/Dreamstime.com
Printing and Binding: Courier Corporation
Cover Printing: Courier Corporation

To order this product, use ISBN: 978-1-4496-3020-1

Library of Congress Cataloging-in-Publication Data
Connolly, Mary.
  Skills-based health education / Mary Connolly.
    p. cm.
  Includes bibliographical references and index.
  ISBN 978-0-7637-7366-3
  1. Health education.   2. Health education—Study and teaching.   3. Health promotion.   I. Title.
  RA440.C66 2012
  613--dc22
                                                                                              2010046075

6048

Printed in the United States of America
17 16 15 14 13   10 9 8 7 6 5 4 3 2

Dedicated to my personal editor, soul mate, and best friend—
my husband, Richard.

Brief Contents

Contents

Chapter 9   Teaching National Health Education Standard 5   245

Chapter 10   Teaching National Health Education Standard 6   297

On the Website

Appendix A: Similarities Between the *Healthy People 2020* Leading Health Indicators and the CDC Risk Factors

Appendix B: Some Similarities Between *Healthy People 2020* and the Health Education Content Areas

Appendix C: The Alignment of ASCD Whole Child, 21st Century Skills, and the National Health Education Standards

Appendix D: Blank Map and Worksheet of Topics and Performance Indicators

Appendix E: Lesson Plan Template

Appendix F: Grade Span Checks for Teaching the Performance Indicators

Appendix G: Performance Task Template

Appendix H: Review Questions

Preface

Scenario I

"Mr. Editore, what happened to your arm?" asked Chris, a student at the Trafficanto Middle School. "Were you in an accident?"

"I am fine; I'll tell you in class."

"When I broke my arm, the doctor gave me a cast. What doctor did you go to? Yours is sticks and bandages!"

Mr. Editore smiled and said, "I'll see you inside."

When the bell rang, Mr. Editore entered the classroom and observed the students looking at the splints, bandages, and blankets placed at each of five stations. They were curious and eager to begin class.

"So, you are all wondering what happened to me?" Mr. Editore said as he removed the bandages and splints. "Actually, I thought it would be a good way to start the Practicing Healthy Behavior unit on first aid."

"I need a volunteer for a role-play. Anyone? OK. Thanks Neil.

"Here is the set-up. Neil, you and I are mountain biking, and you tried to jump over a tree trunk but didn't make it. Your lower arm looks broken, and you are screaming in pain! Ready?"

Teacher: It's a good thing I know first aid! Give me your arm.

Neil: (Neil moans in pain.)

Teacher: First, I'll place these two straight pieces of wood on either side of the break and secure them with strips of an old T-shirt. How are you doing, Neil?

Neil: (Neil moans in pain.) I thought I could make it over that log.

Teacher: The bone did not come through the skin, so it's a closed fracture. That's good news. I'll make a sling with my jacket to immobilize your arm. I can walk both bikes out of the woods.

Neil: Thanks. Can you call my mom? Man, this really hurts.

After the story and demonstration, students applauded and eagerly went to their stations to practice the skill of splinting. To help them remember how to splint, Mr. Editore prepares pictures of the sequence. He also includes an analytical rubric to show students how they are assessed.

Mr. Editore coaches the students by comparing their performance to the pictures and the rubric. He determines from this formative assessment that the students understand how to splint. As he walks from station to station, students ask questions, and Mr. Editore offers suggestions for improvement.

A summative assessment, given at the end of the unit, consists of students demonstrating first aid in response to a variety of scenarios. Mr. Editore uses an analytical rubric to grade their performance and a written test for the content.

Scenario II

At the Hightower Middle School, Mrs. Adams began her first aid class by distributing a worksheet and directing the students to complete it during her multimedia presentation on fractures and splinting. Mrs. Adams frequently stops the presentation to correct Kyle and Amy, who are misbehaving. Students are assessed on how accurately they complete the worksheet and answer questions on a written test.

Skills-Based Health Education

What is the difference in pedagogy between these two scenarios? If you broke your arm, which student would you want to administer first aid? One who has learned content and skill, or one who has learned only content?

To be prepared for the 21st century, students must be knowledgeable about their health, have skills, avoid risky behaviors, and develop and maintain healthy behaviors. In other words, they must experience comprehensive, PreK–12, skills-based health education.

Using the National Health Education Standards as the foundation of a comprehensive PreK–12 health education program is an art and a skill that takes time to perfect. This book provides teachers with the pedagogical foundation and tools to accelerate the process.

Chapters 1–4 of *Skills-Based Health Education* present the benefits of coordinated school health; national initiatives from the Centers for Disease Control and Prevention, such as *Healthy People 2020*, and The Whole Child; along with 21st Century Skills, theory, research, curriculum, and assessment. The remaining chapters provide guidance to plan, implement, and assess performance tasks. The interactive website to accompany this title, http://health.jbpub.com/Skills, includes lessons, units, helpful appendices to the text, and other support materials to enhance teaching and learning. PowerPoint presentations and a TestBank are available for instructor download. Accompanying this book is an access code to a secure PDF which contains valuable teaching tools, tables, and figures from the text which make this book even more practical in the classroom.

During the last 3 years of my 34-year career in public schools, I discovered the National Health Education Standards and used them in my classroom. The transformation was remarkable. No longer did I stand and deliver, as the old model required. Instead, I researched, prepared, and distributed packets of information (performance tasks). Students worked individually or in groups as I monitored and coached them to achieve. They were involved in learning through presentations, demonstrations, and advocacy. The change invigorated them and me.

In teaching college courses, I incorporate skills into my undergraduate and graduate classes. Here, as with my younger students, teaching both knowledge and skill energized their learning.

Use this new model and embrace skills-based health education, as I have, because it is effective, rewarding, and enjoyable.

Acknowledgements

As a new author, I entered the publishing world not knowing or understanding how to translate an idea into a textbook.

I could not have completed the book without the guidance and encouragement of the Jones & Bartlett Learning staff.

Many thanks are extended to the editors, proofreaders, graphic designers, artists, and support staff who made this experience exciting and rewarding.

I also extend thanks to my family, friends, and colleagues who supported me throughout this extraordinary endeavor.

Reviewers

Thank you to the reviewers of this *First Edition*. Your voices, suggestions, and critiques truly made this a better text.

Martin Ayim, PhD, MPH, Grambling State University

Steven P. Dion, EdD, Salem State College

Nanette Tummers, EdD, Eastern Connecticut State University

Timothy P. Winter, PhD, CHES, PAPHS, Louisiana State University, Shreveport

Health Education for the 21st Century

"Skills-based health education can be effective in the more difficult task of achieving and sustaining behavior change."[1]

Introduction

We want our children to have healthy, happy, and productive lives, but how can we make it happen? Achieving this goal requires a group effort that includes family, friends, community, and schools. With sufficient resources, support, and partnerships, schools provide an excellent environment for students to acquire the knowledge and skills to become wholesome, achieving citizens of the 21st century.

Education in America is interwoven with national legislation that mandates state and local accountability, increased flexibility, local control, expanded options for parents, and proven research-based methods of instruction. Our national educational goals include promoting student achievement and preparing students for global competition. Health education advances these goals by empowering students to be physically, mentally, and emotionally healthy and by equipping them to learn, achieve, and succeed.[2]

Why Is Comprehensive Skills-Based Health Education Important?

Without our health, life poses many unwelcome challenges because it may be more difficult to concentrate, stay on-task, or care about things other than our own feelings. We do learn to be healthy, but the question is how? Some of us learn from our parents, friends, family, media, the Internet, and other sources. While a modicum of this information is valid and reliable, a good portion is hearsay, folklore, or plainly incorrect.

Dr. Pat Cooper, the former superintendent of the McComb School District in Mississippi, has said, "Students need to be healthy to learn and must learn to be healthy." To realize this vision that all children learn how to be healthy and receive information and skills that prepare them for personal and academic success in the 21st century, schools provide quality skills-based health education from pre-kindergarten through Grade 12 (PreK–12).

Quality school-based health education, according to the American Cancer Society, uses the National Health Education Standards as the foundation for curriculum development. They concentrate on increasing **functional health knowledge** and the skills needed for healthy living. They include identifying the influence of family, peers, culture, media, and technology on behavior, accessing and using valid health information, communicating, goal setting, practicing healthy behaviors, and advocating for self and others.[3]

If our children learn to be healthy at a young age, consider the positive impact on their personal, social, and academic lives as they mature and prepare for their future. A comprehensive, PreK–12 skills-based health education program incorporating the National Health Education Standards helps students establish healthy behaviors that stay with them into adulthood.

Comprehensive school health education also serves as a funnel through which local, state, and national health programs reach all children in a coordinated, organized, and sequential manner. Each child in every school at all grades has access to a high-quality program and learns the knowledge and skills needed for a healthy and productive adulthood.

The National Health Education Standards

The foundation of comprehensive skills-based health education is the National Health Education Standards

(NHES), Second Edition, Achieving Excellence (see **Table 1.1**). The standards were revised and published in 2007 and embrace the current science of what knowledge and skills students need to acquire, maintain, and promote healthy behaviors. These standards provide a framework for curriculum, instruction, assessment, and accountability.

The first standard addresses concepts related to health promotion and disease prevention to enhance health. The standards do not specify the content school districts include in a comprehensive PreK–12 health program but do provide districts with the flexibility to choose material from the common health education content areas according to the needs of their students.

Standards two through eight are skills: analyzing influences; accessing valid information, products, and services; using interpersonal communication; making decisions; setting goals; practicing healthy behaviors; and advocating for personal, family, and community health. They are sequenced to show progression from knowledge to the application of skills.

Performance indicators accompany each standard and clarify what a student needs to know and do for each grade span of the standard (PreK–2, 3–5, 6–8, 9–12) (see **Figure 1.1**). To reach proficiency, a student demonstrates expertise in all the performance indicators for that grade span.

The numbers that precede the performance indicator signify the standard, the last year of the grade span, and the number of the performance indicator in the sequence.

Common Health Education Content Areas

Community Health
Consumer Health
Environmental Health
Family Life
Mental/Emotional Health
Injury Prevention/Safety
Nutrition
Personal Health
Prevention/Control of Disease
Substance Use/Abuse[4, p11]

The performance indicators are developmentally appropriate for each grade span and include all six levels of Bloom's original taxonomy of the cognitive domain: knowledge, comprehension, application, analysis, synthesis, and evaluation (see **Figure 1.2**).

The knowledge level expects students to retrieve information. When they take in new information, understand, and use it, students have reached the comprehension level. The application level requires them to use knowledge to solve problems without much prompting. On the analysis level, students deconstruct a complex problem into smaller parts in order to understand it better. To syn-

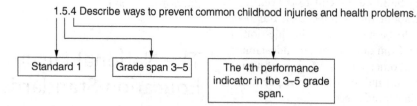

FIGURE 1.1   Performance Number Indicator Numbers

FIGURE 1.2   Bloom's Taxonomy

thesize, students organize individual ideas or parts into a new product. They make judgments based on specific criteria or evidence[5] on the evaluation level.

As students gain knowledge in content and proficiency in skill from elementary to the middle and upper grades, they progress to more difficult tasks, such as examining, analyzing, predicting, comparing, and proposing. Even though elementary students are challenged with simpler tasks, they learn to achieve at higher levels with the appropriate instruction from a skilled health educator.

The Power of Coordinated School Health

The effectiveness of school health education increases when the members of each component cooperate, collaborate, communicate, and coordinate efforts to support the health of students, staff, and the school community.

Districts and school administrators conduct team meetings for the same reasons. Likewise, to meet the health requirements of our students, we need a coordinated effort.

If asked, many schools would probably say that they already provide for student needs and would list the many services in place, such as counseling, nutrition, after-school programs, social services, mental health services, smoking cessation programs for staff and students, and crime prevention programs. Upon a closer look, we might find that these programs and services are offered but perhaps not coordinated. One department may be unaware of what another provides. Two separate departments may service one student, but neither may be aware of the other's efforts.

Community resources—local hospitals, recreational organizations, and businesses—may have services to offer schools. A lack of coordination, collaboration, cooperation, or communication between the community and the school may, however, result in their underutilization.

If the educational goal is to help students develop healthy behaviors and, consequently, improve academic achievement, the **coordinated school health model** must provide the structure through which the school and community work together towards that common goal. The Centers for Disease Control and Prevention (CDC) designed the Coordinated School Health Program (CSHP), which provides the framework for planned, sequential, integrated courses, services, policies, and interventions to meet the health needs of students in kindergarten through Grade 12. The model organizes school, community, and parent resources to marshal the full potential of the community in improving the health, well-being, and academic achievement of students.[4,p4]

As seen in **Figure 1.3**[4,p5], the CSHP has eight components: comprehensive health education; physical education; school health services; school nutrition services; school counseling, psychological, and social services; healthy school environment; school-site health promotion for staff; and family and community involvement in school health.[4,p5] The eight components, when working in unison, improve the health and well being of our students by providing an efficient, organized delivery of instruction and services. When representatives of each component meet regularly to assess student needs, curriculum, and instruction, as well as design and implement local, state, and national programs and policies, they improve the health and academic achievement of students.

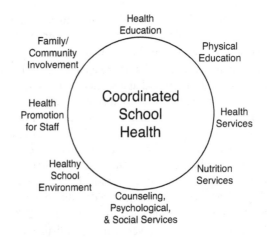

FIGURE 1.3   Coordinated School Health Model
Source: Centers for Disease Control and Prevention, A Coordinated School Health Program: The CDC Eight Component Model of School Health Programs. Available: http://www.cdc.gov/healthyyouth/cshp/. Accessed October 4, 2010.

The CDC currently provides funding to selected states to help implement coordinated school health programs. The goal is to increase the effectiveness of policies, programs, and practices that promote physical activity, nutrition, and tobacco use prevention.[6,p3]

Research published in the *Journal of School Health* demonstrates how the coordinated school health model results in positive behaviors and academic achievement. An examination of the components and the research that supports them follows.

HEALTH EDUCATION

Comprehensive PreK–12 skills-based health education is instruction that complies with state and national standards and the characteristics of effective health education. It encompasses the physical, mental, emotional, and social dimensions of health and promotes knowledge, attitudes, and skills. Assessment of student progress in the attainment of standards is continuous and reported. The effectiveness of the program increases when it is a part of a coordinated model, offers equitable access to school resources, and engages local and state partners in the implementation of standards.[6,p4]

The November 2007 edition of the *Journal of School Health* presented research on how health education contributes to improved academic outcomes.

- Academic grades for low-income minority students, aged 8–11, improved when they participated in an asthma self-management program that included health education and parent involvement. Another asthma self-management program that included health education for asthmatic children and their classmates, an orientation for school principals and counselors, and communication with and education of custodians, caretakers, and clinicians resulted in students' demonstrating higher grades in science.[7,p591-599]

- Elementary or high school students who participated in social skills training that also included teacher training experienced improved achievement. In a six-year follow-up study of high school students who had received the training in elementary school, researchers found they had improved attendance and achieved higher scores on standardized tests than members of a control group. Students who received the highest level of training exceeded the control group for scores in language arts and math.[7,p591-599]

- In a study of how to prevent adolescent drug abuse and reduce high school dropout rates through a school social network program, researchers found that ten months after participating in a five-month Personal Growth course that taught social skills and included teacher training, students demonstrated an increase in their grade point average, school bonding, and perception of school performance as compared to a control group.

- Researchers also found that academic success improved when social skills training included parents and community members and was incorporated into health education, breakfast programs, physical education, and mental and general health services.[7,p591-59]

PHYSICAL EDUCATION

Physical education is planned sequential instruction that promotes life-long physical activity. This component teaches basic movement, sports skills, and physical fitness, and enhances mental, social, and emotional capabilities.[6,p4]

Current research shows a link between participation in physical education and increased academic performance.

- Project SPARK (Sports, Play, and Active Recreation for Kids), a PreK–12 program, provides evidence-based physical activity, nutrition programs, curriculum, staff development, follow-up support, and equipment. Researchers completed a rigorous evaluation of SPARK and found significant gains in reading performance. The academic functioning of participating students was not compromised, even though time for physical education was taken out of the school day.

- In an era of high stakes testing, some worry that time is better spent in academics than physical education. One study examined physical education programs that offered classes in fitness or skill training for seventy-five minutes each day, and its researchers found no significant decrease in test scores and reported that physical education does not detract from academic achievement on standardized tests.[7,p597]

- The National Association for Sport and Physical Education & Council of Physical Education for Children found in 2001 that "students who participate in daily physical education have better attendance, a more positive attitude toward school, and superior academic performance."[8]

SCHOOL HEALTH SERVICES

School health services include preventive services, education, emergency care, referral, and management of acute and chronic health conditions. This component promotes and ensures the health of students and identifies and prevents health problems and injuries. Although not much research about the relationship between school health services and academic achievement has been undertaken, some data does show positive outcomes for students who use school health services.[6,p4]

- Students in Grades 6–12 who utilized their school health clinics showed reduced absenteeism and a significant, positive correlation with school graduation or grade promotion. African-American male students who used the clinics were three times more likely to stay in school than their peers who did not.[7,p598]

SCHOOL NUTRITION SERVICES

School nutrition services consist of nutritious, affordable, appealing meals accompanied by nutrition education in an environment that promotes healthy eating behaviors for all children. They maximize each child's education and health potential for a lifetime. Furthermore, abundant research demonstrates the connection between good nutrition and positive academic and behavioral outcomes.[6,p4]

- One study used a pre/post test to examine the food and nutrition services in the Pennsylvania and Maryland schools. Results showed that African-American and low-income students who participated in the school breakfast program for four months or longer showed a significant increase in math scores and a decrease in absence and tardiness rates.[7,p598]

- A study on the relationship between a school breakfast program and academic performance conducted in six Massachusetts schools found that students who participated had an increase in total scale scores and language scores. Researchers also found "positive trends for mathematics and reading and decreases in tardiness."[7,p598]

- In a six-month inner city, pre/post study examining diet, breakfast, and academic performance, researchers found that children who decreased their nutrition risk showed improvements in reading, math, social studies, science, and attendance.[7,p598]

SCHOOL COUNSELING AND PSYCHOLOGICAL AND SOCIAL SERVICES

School counseling and psychological and social services incorporate activities that stress the cognitive, emotional, behavioral, and social needs of individuals, groups, and families. These services prevent and address problems, facilitate positive learning and healthy behavior, and enhance healthy development. Emerging research shows a connection between increased psychological services and positive academic behaviors.[6,p4]

- In a study on the utility of psychosocial screening among 13- to 18-year-old public school students at a school clinic, researchers found that after two months of receiving school-based mental health and counseling services, absenteeism decreased by 50% and tardiness by 25%.[7,p598]

HEALTHY SCHOOL ENVIRONMENT

A **healthy school environment** encompasses the physical, emotional, and social climate of the school. It provides a safe physical building, as well as a wholesome and supportive social and academic climate that fosters learning. One way to provide a healthy school environment is to expand the classroom management skills of the teacher.[6,p4]

- Grade 1 teachers were trained in classroom-centered intervention that focused on improved management of child aggression, shyness, on-task behavior, and curriculum to improve critical thinking, composition, listening, and comprehension skills. Researchers found that students in this program had fewer behavioral problems at age twelve, which reduced the need for mental health services.[7,p598]

SCHOOL-SITE HEALTH PROMOTION

School-site health promotion includes assessment, education, and fitness activities for faculty and staff. It maintains and improves the health and well-being of school staff, thereby providing healthy role models for students. Limited research regarding worksite health promotion for school faculty and staff has been conducted.[6,p4]

- One study showed significant improvements in self-reported health status and reduced absenteeism among school employees who participated in a "personalized aerobics lifestyle system program." This program was an intensive, ten-week intervention of health education, peer support, behavior management, and supervised exercise sessions held one day a week after school.[7,p598]

FAMILY AND COMMUNITY INVOLVEMENT

The **family and community involvement** component includes partnerships among schools, families, community groups, and individuals. It focuses on the healthy development of children, youth, and their families by sharing and maximizing family and community resources and expertise.[6,p4] Research is uncovering the benefits of training parents as part of prevention programs.

- The Seattle Social Development Project is a school program that tries to prevent academic failure, drug use, and delinquency among low-income children. Training included teachers and parents to ensure that children received the same information and behavioral messages at school and home. Teachers received specific training in classroom management and social skills. Results of the program included increased class participation and more commitment to school. Girls showed lowered rates of substance abuse and boys increased their social and schoolwork skills.[9]

- Academic grades for low-income minority students, aged 8–11, increased when they participated in an asthma self-management program that included health education and parent involvement. Academic success improved when social skills training for parents and the community was incorporated into health education, breakfast programs, physical education, mental health services, and health services.[7,p591-599]

The advantages to implementing a coordinated school health program are many. School districts use staff, resources, and time more efficiently to address the needs of their students. Representatives of each component collaborate to assess needs and data collected from various tools, such as the School Health Index, Health Education Curriculum Assessment Tool, the Physical Education Curriculum Assessment Tool, and the Youth Risk Behavior Survey. They use the results of these assessments to share information and expertise, set goals, meet the needs of the students and district, implement programs that help the school and community, and coordinate local, state, and national resources.

Community agencies and institutions assist districts in providing programs and services. With community and district partners collaborating, barriers to learning decrease, while academic success increases. The coordinated school health program also provides an efficient and effective infrastructure to implement and organize national initiatives such as those from the Association for Supervision and Curriculum Development (ASCD), Action for Healthy Kids, and The U.S. Child Nutrition and WIC Reauthorization Act of 2004.

NATIONAL ORGANIZATIONS SUPPORT COORDINATED SCHOOL HEALTH

Several national organizations also recognize the importance of coordinating the efforts of the school to improve the health and academic performance of students.

In its position statement regarding the whole child, ASCD explains that the current trend in education is academic achievement. ASCD believes in a comprehensive approach to education and defines successful students as "knowledgeable, emotionally and physically healthy, motivated, civically inspired, engaged in the arts, prepared for work and economic self-sufficiency, and ready for the world beyond their own borders."[10]

According to the ASCD, schools should provide challenging and engaging curricula and adequate professional development with collaborative planning time within the school day. They should also offer a safe, healthy, orderly, and trusting environment; high-quality teachers and administrators; a culture that sustains strong relationships between adults and students; and support for coordinated school health councils or other collaborative structures that are active in the school.

Lastly, ASCD believes teachers should provide proven assessment and instructional practices, rich content, and an engaging learning climate that supports student and family connectedness, effective classroom management, and modeling of healthy behaviors.[10]

This ASCD position is consistent with the goals of the Coordinated School Health Program for several reasons. The CSHP is also a comprehensive approach to education dedicated to improving student knowledge as well as emotional and physical health. The CSHP components of health and physical education provide a challenging, engaging, and proven curriculum built on national standards. The component of a healthy school environment works to provide a safe, healthy, orderly, and trusting learning and social environment.

ASCD recognizes the importance of the CSHP when it affirms support for the coordinated school health councils and other collaborative school structures. The members of these committees collaborate, coordinate, cooperate, and communicate with each other to improve school programs, policies, and services that affect the health and well-being of the students.

Another national organization likewise dedicated is Action for Healthy Kids. It is a public-private partnership consisting of more than sixty national and government agencies that represent education, health, fitness, and nutrition. Action for Healthy Kids addresses the problems of youth who are overweight, sedentary, and undernourished by recommending that schools improve nutrition and increase physical activity.

In its report *Progress or Promises?*, Action for Healthy Kids acknowledges the importance of collaboration among the CSHP components of food services, physical and nutrition education, parents, school, and community to improve the nutrition and physical activity of students. The report cites evidence that "poor nutrition, physical inactivity, and obesity are associated with lower student academic achievement and poorer health."[11,p3]

Through a coordinated school health program, each district assesses student needs and sets goals to meet them. The coordinated school health team reviews the data presented by the Action for Healthy Kids and, when appropriate, proposes policies and programs to improve poor nutrition, increase physical inactivity, address obesity, and improve academic achievement.

Another national initiative, The U.S. Child Nutrition and WIC Reauthorization Act of 2004, required every U.S. school district participating in the national school lunch or breakfast program to create a local school district wellness policy by June 2006. The policy must include goals for nutrition education, physical activity, and other wellness promotion activities.

Nutrition guidelines for all food available in each school are mandatory, and the guidelines cannot be less restrictive than those set by the U.S. Department of Agriculture (USDA). Plans must also be in place to measure progress towards reaching established goals. One person is responsible for monitoring the development and implementation of the plan. A local committee that includes representatives of schools, parents, and other community members is also required.[11,p17]

Once again, we see a national organization recognizing the importance of collaboration to address the needs of students. Rather than establishing a separate group, the wellness committee easily merges with the coordinated school health committee to address the specific needs of wellness, nutrition education, and physical activity, as well as other school health issues.

FIGURE 1.4   Maslow's Hierarchy of Needs

COORDINATED SCHOOL HEALTH IN ACTION

One district that has embraced the coordinated school health model is the McComb School District in Mississippi. The district added a component, Academic Opportunity, to its model and believes that all children can learn if given the opportunity.

McComb uses Maslow's hierarchy (**Figure 1.4**) to show how basic needs must be met before potential is reached. Its coordinated school health model is the mechanism that helps students work their way up the hierarchy. The former superintendent of the McComb district, Dr. Pat Cooper, said, "Students must be healthy to learn, but they must also learn to be healthy."

In each school in the McComb district, a school-based Health and Wellness Team, led by a case manager, meets weekly to identify students with problems. Members work together to develop solutions and strategies that help the student, whom they then follow until reaching a resolution.

The McComb model has increased test scores and decreased negative behaviors. Teachers are teaching, and students learning more effectively. McComb has experienced a decrease in crime and pregnancy rates, special education, dropouts, suspensions, and expulsions as a result of implementing the coordinated school model.

Skills-Based Health Education Research

There is now increasing evidence that in tackling individual behavior, social and peer pressure, cultural norms, and abusive relationships, a skills-based approach to health education works, and is more effective than teaching knowledge alone.[1]

Focusing Resources on Effective School Health (FRESH), with assistance from the international organizations UNESCO, UNICEF, and WHO, recommends the following to strengthen school health:

- Schools develop health related school policies
- Provide safe water and sanitation for a safe and secure learning environment
- Skills-based health education
- School-based health and nutrition services[12]

FRESH has ascertained that, when school prevention programs include knowledge, attitudes, values, and life skills needed to make and act on decisions concerning health, incidences of HIV/AIDS risk decreased.[12]

After analyzing numerous studies, researcher, J. Hubley concluded that when teachers limit teaching to information about sex, sexually transmitted diseases, and human immunodeficiency virus (HIV), it is not enough to produce a healthy behavioral change.[13,p1]

A more effective way is to teach such content through a skill. When sexuality content is taught through Standard 2, students analyze the influences that cause them to behave in a certain way. Alternatively, Standard 3 teaches students how to access valid and reliable sexuality information. If taught through Standard 4, students learn how to communicate with partners effectively and use refusal skills, if needed. Standard 5 helps them make health-enhancing decisions about sexuality. Standard 6 teaches students how to think about their future and set goals concerning their sexuality. Standard 7 helps them learn to practice health enhancing sexual behaviors, and in Standard 8, students learn to advocate for human sexuality issues.

Walter and Vaughn researched AIDS reduction strategies among a multiethnic sample of New York high school students. The strategies included content and skills:

- Facts about AIDS
- Cognitive skills to assess transmission risk
- Changing perceptions of risk-taking behavior
- Personal values clarification
- Understanding external influences on their behavior
- Providing AIDS prevention resources
- Understanding external influences on behavior
- Skills to delay intercourse or consistently use condoms

After three months, the researchers found a "decrease in intercourse with high risk partners, an increase in monogamous relationships, and an increase in consistent condom use."[13,p4]

G. J. Botvin analyzed the research conducted on a control group of 3,000 junior high school students who participated in a drug abuse prevention program that taught skills for life and resisting social influences to use drugs. In a follow-up study six years later, he found significant reductions in drug use among these students. Botvin concluded that drug abuse prevention programs conducted during junior high school could produce significant reductions in tobacco, alcohol, and marijuana use if students are taught a combination of social resistance and general life skills.[13,p3]

Life skills training implemented in a Grade 7–12 Thai school had a positive effect on improving knowledge and attitudes about tobacco and drugs and on the development of decision-making and problem solving skills. The study concluded that a life skills program is effective in reducing tobacco and drug use among students.[14]

Research examining the effectiveness of a life skills program delivered in the physical education class found an increase in knowledge about life skills, goal setting, and strategies to successfully cope with life. These results indicate that students, with training in skills, increase their chances of becoming better students and concerned and productive community members.[15]

This research strongly suggests that skills-based health education is effective in equipping youth with the knowledge, attitudes, and competence needed to help them avoid or decrease risk-taking behavior and choose a healthier lifestyle.

Knowing that skills-based health education helps students develop healthy behaviors, and being healthy enhances academic achievement, our challenge is to advocate for our discipline. To do so, we must promote the value of the coordinated school health program, educate educational partners about the role of health education as a vital component of CSHP, write skills-based curriculum, plan instruction that focuses on developing and maintaining healthy behaviors, develop curriculum and instruction that embraces the national standards and the characteristics of effective health education, and promote the discipline as an existing tool to implement the many local, state, and national programs that are concentrating on health and wellness. By coordinating, collaborating, cooperating, and communicating with educational and community leaders, we position comprehensive skills-based health education as the foundation of health and wellness programs.

How Skills-Based Health Education Supports the National Initiatives of the Centers for Disease Control and Prevention and Healthy People 2020

A student with healthy behaviors is better equipped to cope with personal and academic challenges and, upon reaching adulthood, has the knowledge and skills to navigate life, work, and the responsibilities of citizenship successfully.

School-based skills instruction is based upon student need, which, in turn, is established by local, state, and national data. The Centers for Disease Control Youth Risk Behavior Survey (YRBS) is an excellent data source (**Table 1.2**). The CDC conducts the bi-annual survey in public and private schools, Grades 9–12. Survey questions relate to **health risk behaviors**, which are the leading causes of death, disability, and social problems in the high school population. The CDC risk factors are:

- Alcohol and other drug use
- Injury and violence (including suicide)
- Tobacco use
- Poor nutrition
- Inadequate physical activity
- Sexual risk behaviors.[4,p11]

Once the surveys are collected, data are analyzed to determine the health status and trends of youth. The CDC posts the results on their website. For example, the 2007 CDC data reported that many risk behaviors among high school students nationwide have decreased since 1991. This good news was tempered by data that also showed students continue to engage in behaviors that place them at risk for the leading causes of **mortality** and **morbidity**.[16,p1] Consequently, resources are directed to reduce the behaviors most youth experience.

State Departments of Education also conduct the same survey in randomly selected high schools. The results are posted on their website and the CDC site where state agencies use the data to plan intervention strategies, collaborate with other state agencies to meet student needs, and write grants. The public also has access to this information.

Individual school districts implement the middle and high school YRBS questionnaire to determine their own student risk behaviors and use the data to:

- Compare their own information to state and national data to determine whether to adjust curriculum and instruction to meet the emerging needs of students.
- Report student risk factors to the district and community and explain how comprehensive health education addresses them.
- Apply for Safe and Drug Free Schools grants, which are awarded to individual school districts and can be used for drug, alcohol, tobacco, and violence prevention education.
- Address social norms in health classes. When students are asked what is the percentage of drug or alcohol use and other risk factor usage, they usually overestimate. Using the actual data from a district helps to inform students that they are probably in the

TABLE 1.2   Youth Risk Behavior Surveillance System[16]

Category	Female		Male		Total	
	%	CI[§]	%	CI	%	CI
Race/Ethnicity						
White[¶]	21.5	18.4–25.1	35.6	31.2–40.2	**29.0**	**26.3–32.0**
Black[¶]	32.3	27.1–38.1	35.0	30.9–39.3	**33.7**	**30.1–37.6**
Hispanic	24.0	21.9–26.2	32.2	29.3–35.4	**28.1**	**26.1–30.2**
Grade						
9	24.6	21.7–27.7	35.6	32.7–38.7	**30.5**	**28.4–32.7**
10	23.2	20.4–26.3	34.6	29.6–40.1	**29.2**	**26.3–32.2**
11	21.3	18.8–24.1	35.2	32.2–38.4	**28.5**	**26.1–30.9**
12	23.8	20.4–27.6	32.7	29.3–36.3	**28.3**	**25.5–31.4**
Total	**23.3**	**21.0–25.8**	**34.6**	**31.7–37.5**	**29.2**	**27.2–31.2**

Percentage of high school students who drank a can, bottle, or glass of soda or pop* at least one time/day,[†] by sex, race/ethnicity, and grade — United States, Youth Risk Behavior Survey, 2009
* Not including diet soda or diet pop.
[†] During the 7 days before the survey.
[§] 95% confidence interval.
[¶] Non-Hispanic.
Source: Centers for Disease Control and Prevention. (MMWR 2009, 59 SS-5). *Surveillance Summaries.* Atlanta: Centers for Disease Control and Prevention. p.115.

majority, not the minority, if they do not participate in risky behaviors.

- Develop comprehensive skills-based health education and health promotion goals.
- Propose policies and programs to meet the needs of students.
- Advocate for a coordinated school health program.[16,p35]

Healthy People 2020 is a consortium of national agencies and organizations working since 1979 to improve the health of the nation by increasing the quality and years of healthy life and eliminating health disparities. It has developed national health objectives that identify preventable risk factors and set national goals to reduce them.

The consortium identifies ten leading health indicators that are important public health issues likely to motivate action and provides data to measure progress.[17] These indicators are similar to the CDC risk factors (see **Appendix A**). The consortium has also developed thirty-eight health areas of concentration.[17] **Appendix B** shows how these foci correspond to traditional health education content.

Comprehensive health education supports the efforts of the Centers for Disease Control and Prevention and the Healthy People 2020 initiative. It uses valid and reliable data supplied by these organizations to establish student need and teaches health education content through the national health education standards, with the goal of reducing risk factors and developing and maintaining healthy behaviors.

Health Education for the 21st Century

Preparing students for the 21st century is a daunting task. Fortunately, education and national organizations are collaborating to meet this challenge.

THE PARTNERSHIP FOR 21ST CENTURY SKILLS

Preparing students for the 21st century is a significant challenge. The Partnership for 21st Century Skills has identified and defined skills students need to be successful in the workforce and is working with educational partners, such as the Association for Supervision and Curriculum Development, to infuse these skills into K–12 education.

Comprehensive skills-based health education already encompasses many of the skills the partnership recommends. Health education and the other components of the coordinated school health program embrace this initiative and implement it fully. A closer look at the relationship between 21st century skills and the National Health Education Standards follows.

The partnership states that today's schools must "bring together rigorous content and real world relevance."[18,p6] Standard 1 of the National Health Education standards provides the framework for districts to develop health content that is rigorous and relevant. Functional health knowledge is taught through skills, with depth being preferred over breadth.

Information literacy is a 21st century skill. Although many of our students have grown up with technology, they may not fully understand the impact it and the media have on their lives. Standard 2, analyzing the influence of family, peers, culture, media, technology, and other factors on health behaviors, helps students apply critical thinking skills to these subjects. In this standard, students identify, describe, explain, and analyze the different factors that influence their decisions and behavior.[4,p26-27]

Standard 3, accessing valid and reliable information, products, and services, is also similar to the 21st century skill, information literacy. This standard teaches students how to identify, access, locate, and evaluate information, products, and services that impact their health.[4,p28-29]

The Partnership believes that the foundation of accomplishment is the ability to communicate and collaborate. Standard 4, interpersonal communication skills, provides students with the training they need to meet this goal.[4,p30-31]

Collaboration skills, according to the Partnership, are vital to success. Collaboration is embedded in skills-based health education projects because students work in groups to create a product that will show proficiency in content and skill. The Partnership also recommends project-based learning because it helps students understand content through real life scenarios. Skills-based health education incorporates **performance tasks** whereby students work in groups to respond to a challenge. Students take time to collect information and practice the skill, and, when ready, show how they have met the challenge by demonstrating their proficiency.

Health literacy is one of four interdisciplinary themes in the Partnership. The Joint Committee on Health Education Terminology defines health literacy as "the capacity of an individual to obtain, interpret, and understand basic health information and services, and the competence to use such information and services in ways that are health enhancing."[18,p10] Through skills-based health education, students learn functional health knowledge and demonstrate it through a skill. Health literacy increases as students progress from mere knowledge acquisition to the highest order skills of self-management and advocacy.

The Partnership asserts that the themes are most effective when taught through the core subject areas. Health education is closely intertwined with English language arts because students use their English skills to prepare and present projects to the class. They include research, writing, creating a variety of presentations, performing role-plays and skits, and oral presentations. Moreover, it is common for English teachers to learn of personal health concerns through a student's journal entries or research papers. Collaboration between the two disciplines improves the health and academic performance of students.

Critical Thinking and Problem Solving, Creativity and Innovation, and Communication and Collaboration are the Partnership's Learning and Innovation Skills.[18,p10] Throughout skills-based health education, students are challenged to think critically. In the decision-making standard, students are challenged to think, solve problems, and be creative and innovative in their interpretation of prompts. The Partnership assumes that critical thinking skills can be taught and aligned with Bloom's Taxonomy (Figure 1.2), which includes six levels of increasing difficulty: "knowledge, understanding, application, analysis, synthesis, and evaluation."[18,p12] All the performance indicators of the National Health Education Standards are based on Bloom's Taxonomy. This concurrence offers another example of how a comprehensive skills-based health education program can support and promote the goals of the Partnership.

In the America Diploma Project, professors and employers examine the skills necessary for success in the workforce. They agree that working in teams and presenting one's work orally are critical to success.[18,p22] Skills-based health education supports that concept because each performance task concludes with students presenting their work to the class collaboratively.

The Partnership supports emotional literacy. When schools teach how to be emotionally healthy, students are less violent, better controlled, and more productive. They get along better with other students and adults. Documented evidence suggests that emotional intelligence contributes to academic success.[18,p22] Emotional health is a content area of health education mapped into curricula from pre-kindergarten through Grade 12. In a skills-based health program, emotional health is taught through the seven national health education skills and reinforced throughout the grade levels.

The Partnership also recognizes the relationship between social and cognitive skills. Research has demonstrated that students perform at a higher level when they show self-control, delay gratification, empathize, and take responsibility for their own actions. Effective health education includes instruction according to the social cognitive and inoculation theories, and also addresses individual values and group norms, coping with social pressures, and building personal and social competence.[18,p22]

Consequently, skills-based health education teaches these qualities throughout its program, especially during a decision-making unit. Students learn that basing decisions on positive values usually results in a good choice and basing on negative values results in a poor one.

ASSOCIATION FOR SUPERVISION AND CURRICULUM DEVELOPMENT

The Association for Supervision and Curriculum Development (ASCD) has joined with the Partnership for 21st Century Skills to focus on educating the whole child and preparing our children to be skilled members of the 21st century global society and workforce. The ASCD Whole Child initiative encourages schools and communities to work together to ensure that each student has access to a challenging curriculum in a healthy and supportive climate.[10]

Comprehensive skills-based health education provides an excellent implementation framework for these two important programs. **Appendix C** shows the relationship among the ASCD Whole Child Initiative, 21st Century Skills, and the Comprehensive School Health Program.

A comprehensive health education program makes this preparation available to each student on all grade levels in every school and results in knowledge and skills to become a healthy adult who can contribute to the welfare of the family, community, nation, and world.

Review Questions

1. Explain how health education is an essential contributor to the national education goals.

2. Why is it important to provide comprehensive skills-based health education?

3. Give examples of research from two CSHP components that demonstrate the effectiveness of coordinated school health.

4. List the national health education standards and categorize them as either content or skill.

5. Explain how to demonstrate proficiency in a standard.

6. Why is it important for health education to be included in the coordinated school health model?

7. Explain the ASCD's Whole Child initiative and how skills-based health education supports it.

8. Explain one example of research that demonstrates how skills-based health education contributes to healthy behavior.

9. Explain how YRBS data can be used to improve skills-based health education.

10. Explain how skills-based health education supports the Partnership for 21st Century Skills.

References

1. Focusing Resources on Effective School Health. (n.d.). *Skills Based Health Education.* Retrieved May 16, 2010, from FRESH Focusing Resources on Effective School Health: www.fresh schools.org/Pages/SkillsBasedHealthEducation.aspx

2. The Council of Chief State School Officers. (2004). *How the CCSSO~SCASS HEAP Supports the Intent of the No Child Left Behind Act.* CCSSO.

3. American Cancer Society, American Diabetes Association, American Heart Association. (2009). *Facts Learning for Life Health Education in Schools.* p. 2. Retrieved March 1, 2009, from the American Cancer Society: www.cancer.org/down loads/PED/Healthy_Ed_Learning_for_Life_Fact_Sheet.pdf

4. Joint Committee on National Health Education Standards. (2007). *National Health Education Standards, Second Edition, Achieving Excellence.* American Cancer Society.

5. Marzano, R. J., & Kendall, J. S. (2007). *The New Taxonomy of Educational Objectives.* (2nd ed.). Thousand Oaks: Corwin Press.

6. Eva Marx, S. F. (1998). *Health is Academic.* New York, NY: Teachers College Press.

7. Murray, D. N. (2007). Coordinated School Health Programs and Academic Achievement: A Systematic Review of the Literature. *Journal of School Health,* 77(9), 589–600.

8. Satcher, D. (2005). Healthy and Ready to Learn. *Educational Leadership,* 63(1), 26–30.

9. O'Donnell, J., Hawkins, J. D., Catalano, R. F., Abbott, R. D., & Day, L. E. (1995, January). Preventing school failure, drug use, and delinquency among low-income children: Long-term intervention in elementary schools. *American Journal of Orthopsychiatry,* 65(1), 87–100.

10. Eisner, E. (2005). Back to Whole. *Educational Leadership,* 63(1), 14–18.

11. Action for Healthy Kids. (Fall 2008). *Progress or Promises? What's Working For and Against Healthy Schools.* Skokie, IL: Action for Healthy Kids.

12. Gillespie, A. D. (2000). *Focusing Resources on Effective School Health: A Fresh Start to Enhancing HIV/AIDS Prevention.* p1. Retrieved October 20, 2010, from FRESH Schools: http://www .freshschools.org/Documents/FRESHandAIDS-English.doc

13. WHO, UNICEF, UNESCO, World Bank. (2000, April). *Focusing Resources on Effective School Health.* Retrieved September 2, 2008, from Fresh Schools: www.freshschools .org/Pages/SkillsBasedHealthEducation.aspx

14. Seal PhD, R. N. (2006). Preventing Tobacco and Drug Use Among Thai High School Students Through Life Skills Training. *Nursing and Health Sciences,* 8, 164–168.

15. Goudas, M. D. (2006). The Effectiveness of Teaching a Life Skills Program in a Physical Education Context. *European Journal of Psychology of Education,* 434–435

16. Centers for Disease Control and Prevention. (MMWR, 57 SS-4) *Surveillance Summaries.* Atlanta: Author.

17. Office of Disease Prevention & Health Promotion, U.S. Department of Health and Human Services. (October 30, 2009). *Proposed Healthy People 2020 Objective-List for Public Comment.* Retrieved May 15, 2010, from Healthy People 2020-Proposed Objectives: http://healthypeople .gov/HP2020/Objectives/TopicAreas.aspx

18. Partnership for 21st Century Skills. (2007). *The Intellectual and Policy Foundations of the 21st Century Skills Framework.*

Theoretical Foundations 2

Introduction

A well-developed theoretical premise for skills-based health education provides the foundation to apply available research to improve program design, implementation, and evaluation.[1,p50] Knowledge of the different behavioral theories and the particular needs of our students makes us better equipped to develop effective strategies for students to overcome their unhealthy behaviors.

Our challenge as skills-based health educators is to use all resources available to develop curricula and instruction that produces healthy behaviors.

The Role of Self-Efficacy in Changing Behavior

One of the most important factors that contribute to behavior is **self-efficacy**. Albert Bandura describes it as our beliefs about our capabilities to produce designated levels of performance that exercise influence over events that affect our lives.[2,p1] In other words, it is the confidence we have in ourselves to cope with life's challenges in a positive manner. The central questions we should ask ourselves are, "How does self-efficacy develop? Why are some people, but not others, highly efficacious?"

A person with high self-efficacy has a sense of control over life and the confidence to meet and overcome challenges. For example, the newborn Marla, a fictional character, develops self-efficacy when she learns that her actions bring results, such as a parent who responds to her crying. Marla soon recognizes that her behavior affects the environment to her advantage. This awareness of her control gives Marla more confidence to find other ways to get the same response.

In order to develop a sense of personal self-efficacy, however, Marla must understand that she is distinct from others. For example, she learns that feeding herself results in positive feelings, but watching someone else eat does not. As her relationships and experiences with others expand, Marla eventually sees herself as an individual.[2,p8]

Parents have a profound effect on efficacy because a child's first experiences generally occur within the family. Children explore their everyday lives by challenging their physical, social, and cognitive limits. When children engage in experiences parents provide through a nurturing environment, they increase their efficacy and enjoy accelerated social and cognitive development. In turn, the more the parents observe this development, the more likely they are to provide additional opportunities for their children.

As children understand language, they think about what they experience and how it makes them feel. They also respond to how others communicate about their abilities. Language helps Marla understand the value society places on her accomplishments, which, in turn, affect her efficacy.

School expands Marla's environment and her opportunities to experience efficacy-challenging events. As she grows older, her peers become important in the development of this self-efficacy. She develops more capabilities—from modeling a behavior observed in others to being social and socialized—and evaluates and compares her self-efficacy to others.

This experience explains why children are overly sensitive to their peer group ranking with regard to who is respected or popular. A child with high social efficacy will have confidence in her relationships with peers, but one with low social efficacy may withdraw, feel unaccepted, and experience low self-worth.[2,p9]

The school provides the stage for learning academic and social skills, such as problem solving, communication, and relationship development. Marla continuously compares to others what she knows and has learned in school. As she masters skills and demonstrates proficiency according to the teacher's expectations, her cognitive and social self-efficacy evolves.[2,p10]

Coping with the risk factors inherent in adolescence provides a particular challenge to children and, when done in a healthy way, enhances self-efficacy. Marla must learn and practice new skills to prepare for adolescence and adulthood. Her adult self-efficacy is a result of navigating personal, higher education, life, and career choices successfully.[2,p11]

Throughout the school years, the role of the health educator and goal of comprehensive skills-based health education are the same: increase students self-efficacy by teaching the knowledge and skills to develop and maintain healthy behaviors that engender the confidence to face life's challenges.

Students need to:

- Have a foundation of knowledge to promote and enhance their health, and prevent disease.
- Understand how their health behaviors are influenced by family, peers, culture, media, technology, etc.
- Access valid information, products, and services to enhance their health.
- Practice healthy behaviors to avoid or reduce risks.
- Advocate for themselves, their family, and the community.

Students need to use:

- Interpersonal communication skills to improve their health and avoid or reduce health risks.
- Decision making skills to augment their health.
- Goal-setting skills to increase their health.[3,p8]

This process begins in pre-kindergarten and continues through Grade 12. A comprehensive program—with the support of the coordinated school health team and district administration—supports the efforts of the family in helping children and young adults be efficacious, academically successful, and prepared for the 21st century.

Theories of Behavior Change

This section discusses eight of the best-known theories of behavioral change, and includes full descriptions, examples of classroom utilization, research conducted, and coordinated school health applications for each. The discussion begins with Attribution Theory, and moves on to Health Locus of Control Theory, Unrealistic Optimism Theory, Trans-Theoretical Model of Health Behavior Change, Health Belief Model, Protection Motivation Theory, Theory of Planned Behavior, and Social Cognitive Theory.

ATTRIBUTION THEORY

The attribution theory originated with Fritz Heider (1896–1988), an Austrian-American who was born and educated in Europe and immigrated to the United States in the early 1930s. The Clarke School for the Deaf in Northampton, Massachusetts, offered him a research position, and it was there that he met his wife. In 1947, the University of Kansas recruited him to continue the research begun in Massachusetts. In 1958, while at the university, he published his most famous work, *The Psychology of Interpersonal Relations*,[4] from which the Attribution Theory emanated. It argues that people want to understand the cause and effect of what happens in their lives in order to see their social world as a predictable and controllable place.[5,p19]

As educators, we use the attribution theory when we struggle with why students exhibit certain behaviors. "Why is Erin, a preschooler, calling Marissa names? Why is Connor, a middle school student, bullying Tom? Why does Katie, a high school junior, still go out with Evan, even though he is abusive?" By attributing a cause to these problem behaviors and explaining them to ourselves, we gain a sense of control over our environment that helps us cope.

Harold H. Kelley (1921–2003), a professor emeritus of psychology at UCLA,[6] developed the attribution theory further in the 1960s and 1970s by suggesting the cause of the behavior, which is:

- Particular to the person carrying out the behavior (distinctiveness). For example, Erin is a name-caller, unlike any of her siblings or friends.
- Shared by others (consensus). All the teachers agree that Erin's name-calling causes problems in the classroom and on the playground.
- Consistent long term (consistency over time). Erin has been a name-caller since preschool but does not do it as frequently as she did in earlier grades.
- The same in different situations (consistency over modality). Erin name-calls in the classroom, on the playground, and on the bus.

Kelley explained that attributions are made according to the above criteria and rated with regard to the influence.[5,p19] Erin may be rated as high distinctiveness, since she always exhibits this behavior, but may also be rated low consistency over time because she is not demonstrating that behavior as often as she did as a preschooler.

The attribution theory has evolved further to redefine the dimensions of attributions.[5,p19]

- *Internal vs. external. The reason for the failure is personal rather than the person who is judging the performance.* "I didn't make the soccer team because my skills were not good enough," rather than, "I didn't make the soccer team because the coach doesn't like me."

- *Stable vs. unstable. The reason for the failure will always be present rather than the failure was specific to that one attempt.* "I'll never be an athlete, every time I try out for a team, I am rejected," versus, "My skills are usually good but during tryouts, I couldn't control the ball and as a result, I didn't make the team."
- *Global vs. specific. The cause of the failure influences other areas of my life rather than the failure only influenced that one event.* "I didn't make the soccer team, so why should I try out for the lacrosse team?" as opposed to, "Oh well, just because I didn't make the soccer team doesn't mean I won't make the lacrosse team."

If our fictional character, Marla, was experiencing the above, how could a health educator help her? Understanding why she interpreted the results of a situation as she did is important. A skills-based health educator listens to her students, is empathetic to needs, and offers suggestions to resolve problems. Coaching Marla to improve communication, decision-making, and advocacy skills and practicing health-enhancing behaviors improves her efficacy.

When Domingos, another fictional student, describes an attribution, it may be helpful to discuss personal actions in contrast to ones he cannot control. The coach did not select him as the soccer team goalie and he is very upset. He may need encouragement to improve his skills to be more competitive or try a different activity. With increased skill development, self-efficacy will improve, and Domingos may have the confidence to try again. He should understand the reason for the rejection: the coach did not need his skill, his performance notwithstanding.

Attribution Theory—Example From Research

The following research shows how the Attribution Theory was applied to decrease aggressive behavior and increase the academic performance of elementary school children.

Researchers Cynthia Hudley from the University of California, Santa Barbara; Sandra Graham from the University of California, Los Angeles; and April Taylor from California State University, Northridge, studied the relationship between decreasing the drive to be aggressive and increasing the motivation to achieve academically among elementary children in Grades 3–6. They utilized an intervention curriculum, BrainPower and Best Foot Forward, which is organized around the principle of the Attribution Theory.[7,p252]

According to these researchers, youth aggression and violence are a significant problem in school that distracts the teacher from instruction and makes learning difficult. Students who display this behavior are more at risk to drop out of school and experience poor school adjustment and more delinquency in childhood and adoles-

cence. Aggression is a powerful predictor of low achievement and motivation, poor adjustment, and dropping out of high school.[7,p251]

Attribution theorists are interested in why certain behaviors and events occur. One factor is locus of control, whereby the cause of the behavior or event is attributed to internal or external causes. Another is stability, meaning the cause is either constant or changes. The third element, controllability, asserts that the cause is either under the control of the individual or not.[7,p252]

Christopher demonstrates attribution bias when he overestimates harmful intent in others when, in fact, the behavior or event was accidental or non-existent. He perceives that he has been wronged and retaliates with inappropriate aggression, which causes others to respond accordingly. The intervention curriculum used in the study helps children recognize accidental events and, in so doing, become less likely to demonstrate angry aggressive responses.[7,p252]

This curriculum, listed as a promising program from the Substance Abuse and Mental Health Services Administration, contains twelve lessons that teach students to distinguish between accidental causes of an event and deliberate intentions to do them harm. The first component explored intent, understanding feelings, social cues, and internal and external causes of behavior. Students learned skills to respond appropriately to different situations.[8]

While a second component taught students how to take personal responsibility for the success or failure of their interactions with other peers, a third focused on academics. It helped students recognize the value of undertaking a task of intermediate difficulty, setting long- and short-term goals, accenting improvement rather than result. They learned to concentrate on controllable factors, such as effort, when performing an unfamiliar task and not to attribute failure to uncontrollable factors, such as bad luck.[7,p257]

The study demonstrated that a child's attribution of success or failure in social and academic arenas improved with educational strategies. Socially, the children learned to presume that some ambiguous situations, such as books falling off a desk, have a non-hostile intent, to select nonaggressive responses to situations, to take personal responsibility for social transgressions, and to accept the explanation and apology from peers for any so presumed.

Academically, the students learned to take risks, choose more difficult tasks, set realistic goals, consider improvement over performance, and attribute failures to circumstances under their control. These social and academic motivation skills were perceived as improved behavior in the eyes of teachers and parents.[7,p258]

This study is consistent with the goals of the National Health Education Standards to increase or maintain healthy behaviors by learning knowledge and skills. Through Standard 1, Core Concepts, students describe the relationship between healthy behaviors and personal health,[3,p24] learn about their emotions and feelings, and understand behavioral intent, causation, and social cues.

The program used for the study evidenced several National Health Education skills when the students:

- Interacted with one another in a respectful manner, which enhanced health and an avoidance or reduction in the risks associated with aggression: Standard 4, Interpersonal Communication.
- Set short and long-term academic goals and strived to achieve them: Standard 6, Goal Setting.
- Learned how to respond non-aggressively and took responsibility for their own actions rather than blaming others: Standard 7, Practicing Healthy Behaviors.

Classroom Application of the Attribution Theory

Mr. Shultz is a fourth grade teacher at the Intervale Elementary School and is upset by the increased student aggression. He asked his assistant principal if she had noticed an increase in fighting, and her data did indicate an uptick from the prior year. Mr. Shultz checked the Centers for Disease Control and Prevention Youth Risk Behavior Survey and learned that 40.9% of 9th grade students had been in a physical fight one or more times during the previous year. He did not want his students in the 40% range when they reached high school and decided to investigate programs that decreased aggressive behavior.

His district received the Safe and Drug Free Schools and Communities Grant. Upon examining the list of Promising Programs since 2004, Mr. Shultz discovered BrainPower and thought it would be a good fit for his students. The grant administrator agreed to fund its purchase and train school staff, including the coordinated school health team.

In his goal-setting unit, Mr. Shultz designed a performance task that challenged his students to help a friend who was always getting into fights and blaming everyone else for his problems. In light of Standard 1, the students described the relationship between healthy behaviors (honesty, non-violence, etc.) and personal health.[3,p24] They then used Standard 6 to set a personal health goal of coping with anger in a healthy way and track progress toward its achievement.[3,p34]

In his interpersonal communication unit, Mr. Shultz challenged students to help a friend who was threatening other students because he felt threatened by them. The students used Standard 1 to describe ways to prevent common childhood injuries and health problems by using passive, assertive, and aggressive communication.[3,p24] Thereupon, they used Standard 4 to develop a role-play in which they demonstrated nonviolent strategies to manage or resolve conflict.[3,p30]

After a year of implementation, aggressive behavior decreased with fewer fights, more positive peer interac-

tions, and in improvement in the academic success of the students who participated in the program. The district plans to extend the program to all its elementary schools in the next school year.

Implications for Coordinated School Health

Members of a coordinated school health team could each utilize the Attribution Theory. The following examples illustrate how the theory, along with the specialized expertise of each team member, could be applied in planning curriculum and teaching activities.

Health Education

- Provide instruction regarding feelings and how to understand and respond to social cues.
- Teach violence prevention content through Core Concepts (Standard 1), Interpersonal Communication (Standard 4) and Goal Setting (Standard 6).
- Model healthy ways of resolving conflict and aggression.

Physical Education

- Display posters that encourage respect, responsibility, and self-control.
- Model healthy ways of resolving conflict and aggression.

Health Services

- Refer aggressive students to counselors or administration.
- Provide information regarding feelings, respect, responsibility, and self-control.

Nutrition Services

- Provide nutritious meals that contribute to overall health.
- Display posters that encourage respect, responsibility, and self-control.

Counseling, Psychological & Social Services

- Identify at-risk students who would benefit from knowledge and skills that decrease aggressive behavior and increase academic success.

Healthy School Environment

- Display posters that illustrate respect for others and encourage peaceful problem solving.
- Monitor student behavior.
- Enforce student behavior policy.

Health Promotion for Staff

- Provide training to identify children who would benefit from an intervention program that targets aggressive behavior.
- Provide training to staff members interested in leading an intervention group.

Family/Community Involvement

- Invite parents to participate in training to help their children decrease aggressive behavior and increase their motivation to succeed academically.

HEALTH LOCUS OF CONTROL

The Health Locus of Control theory advances the internal versus the external dimensions of the Attribution theory. If Jamal perceives that he is responsible for the events in his life, he has an internal locus of control. If Jamal blames others, fate, destiny, luck, or society for an event, he has an external locus of control.[9] Some people experience a combination of both.

An internal locus of control is an advantage when changing behavior or managing lifestyle because it empowers us and reinforces motivation and commitment.[10,p19] A person with an external locus of control can feel powerless to change. Jamal may have a genetic predisposition to diabetes, believe there is nothing he can do about developing the disease, and, therefore, choose to lead a sedentary life and eat an unhealthy diet. On the other hand, Courtney, a student with an internal locus of control, may learn as much as she can about the disease and change the risk factors under her control in order to delay or prevent the onset of the diabetes.

Rachel, who has an external locus of control, learns to change or moderate it by researching the behavior she wants to confront, listing all the ways change enhances her health, determining which contributing factors to modify, making a plan to change, and then acting upon it. Success increases Rachel's self-efficacy to make other changes and nudges her locus of control closer to internal.[10,p19]

Kenneth Wallston, associate professor of psychology at Vanderbilt University, was one of the original developers of the Health Locus of Control theory. He also created a self-test that measures the beliefs a person has about who controls his or her health. The results show whether Rachel, to wit, believes she controls her health, it is a matter of chance, or controlled by powerful others, presumably doctors.

To help students take personal responsibility for their health, it may be worthwhile for them to discover whether they have an internal or external locus of control. Older students can complete the Wallston Multidimensional Health Locus of Control Scale,[11] and younger students can take the Discovery Health Locus of Control and Attribution Style Test.[9]

Health Locus of Control—Example From Research

Vanessa Malcarne and Amy Drahota from San Diego State University, and Nancy Hamilton from Southern Methodist University, studied multiethnic children of both genders from different income levels and examined the relationship between health-related locus of control and health beliefs as predictors of positive or negative health behaviors.

Malcarne and Drahota examined the sub-constructs of internal locus of control, such as health knowledge and attitudes, and psychological adjustment. External loci, such as those undefined powerful others and the role of chance, were explored to determine their effects on health outcomes and behavior. The evidence indicates that external locus of control correlates to negative health behaviors and poor psychological adjustment.[12,p48]

This study included children between the ages of 9 and 14. The researchers found that age was a factor in the development of health locus of control beliefs. Older children were less likely to see external factors as responsible for their health, whereas younger children believed the opposite. Caucasian and African American children demonstrated a decrease in external locus of control as they became older, but age was not related to health locus of control for Latin American children.[12,p55]

Latin American children were more likely to believe that fate, luck, or chance (external locus) controlled their health than were Caucasian American children. African American children also displayed a trend toward powerful others as an external locus of control when compared to Caucasians.

The role of family income and ethnicity had a varying effect on health beliefs. The higher income group of African American children had stronger beliefs in chance and powerful others controlling their health behaviors than did children from lower income families.

Although previous studies have indicated that boys exhibited a stronger belief in powerful others than girls,[12,p56] Malcarne and Drahota detected no such gender differences among the various ethnic groups.

As skills-based health educators, we help students develop an internal locus of control by designing prompts that challenge students to discover the relationship between their behavior and its effects on their health. We examine and teach the benefits of being in control of one's health and behavior rather than believing someone else is.

Classroom Application of Health Locus of Control

Mr. Olivera has been the health teacher in a multiethnic, low- to middle-income elementary school for several years. Consequently, he knows many of the children and their families. He has observed that numerous younger students believe that their overall health is not a result of their behaviors but a consequence of external factors, such as parents, teachers, the school, the community, and unpredictable factors, such as chance.

When Marina came to school with a bruise on her head, Mr. Olivera asked her about the injury. She told him that it was her brother's fault because he left one of his toy cars on the steps, she slipped on it, fell, and hit her head. Knowing that unintentional injuries are a leading cause of death for children, he planned a performance task that would challenge his students to examine their role in protecting their health.

Mr. Olivera selected Standard 1, list ways to prevent common childhood injuries,[3,p24] to gather information about seat belts, bicycle helmets, and accidents. He chose Standard 7, demonstrate behaviors that avoid or reduce health risks,[3,p35] and distributed three prompts, back-up information, and the presentation rubric. One prompt contained the story of Melina who hated to wear her seat belt because it was uncomfortable. In another, Carlos wanted to go biking but could not find his helmet. The third described a child who lived in a house under renovation where ladders and tools were not safely secured at the end of the day.

The students were challenged to identify the hazard in the prompt, determine who controls it, and explain ways to prevent common childhood injuries. During the assessment, students demonstrated their knowledge of injuries and role-played the scenario by showing the hazard, who controlled it, and steps they could take to protect their own health.

Mr. Olivera was so pleased with the results that he showed parents a videotape of the students' work during a school-wide Safety Week presentation. Parents became more aware of the danger of childhood injuries and told Mr. Olivera that they would be more vigilant about their child's safety.

Implications for Coordinated School Health

Individual members of a coordinated school health team could each utilize the Health Locus of Control Theory. The following examples illustrate how the theory, along with the specialized expertise of each team member, could be applied in planning curriculum and teaching activities.

Health Education

- Knowing that external locus of control has an adverse effect on health behaviors, design performance tasks that challenge children to modify that belief and direct them towards developing an internal locus.
- Realize that children have a variety of health beliefs that predict their health behavior.

- Focus internal locus of control instruction to young children and reinforce it through the grades to help students understand that their own behavior influences their health status.[12,p57]
- Reinforce the principle that each student is in control of his own behavior.

Physical Education

- Reinforce self-control over behavior.
- Demonstrate the relationship between behavior choices and their effect on health.

Health Services

- Emphasize that each student is responsible for her own health.
- Display safety posters to encourage students to protect their health.

Nutrition Services

- Display posters that encourage healthy eating practices.
- Maintain a clean and safe environment for eating.

Counseling, Psychological & Social Services

- Reinforce that each student is in control of his own behavior.
- Stress personal responsibility for health.
- Emphasize importance of accepting responsibility for actions rather than blaming others.

Healthy School Environment

- Display posters that illustrate personal responsibility for actions.
- Recognize students who take personal responsibility for their behavior.

Health Promotion for Staff

- Provide in-service training that shows teachers how to empower students with a sense of personal responsibility for their health.
- Model personal safety.

Family/Community Involvement

- Develop a parent education program that explains the importance of teaching children to take personal responsibility for their actions.
- Reinforce parental and school efforts by encouraging community businesses to focus on personal responsibility for health.

UNREALISTIC OPTIMISM

In 1983 and 1984, Neil Weinstein, a professor at Rutgers University, explained that people continue unhealthy behaviors because they think they are not at risk or susceptible to the dangers. He conducted research in which people examined a list of health problems and were asked if their chances of developing the problem were the same as or less than people their own age and sex. The results indicated that most people thought they were less likely to develop the problem.[5,p21] This viewpoint is called unrealistic optimism.

In 1987, Weinstein described four factors and beliefs, which when present, contribute to unrealistic optimism.

1. Lack of experience with the problem.

2. The problem can be prevented by personal action.

3. If the problem has not yet appeared, it will not in the future.

4. The problem does not occur very often.[5,p21]

People who smoke misjudge the risks involved. Weinstein, along with Stephen Marcus, an epidemiologist for the National Cancer Institute, and Richard Moser, a research psychologist for the National Cancer Institute, conducted a telephone survey that examined smokers' beliefs about the risks involved. The results showed that smokers underestimated their risk of tobacco related illness compared to non-smokers and believed they had a lower risk of developing lung cancer than the average smoker. Likewise, smokers who believed the risks of developing cancer or lung cancer did not rise with an increased number of cigarettes smoked daily also illustrates unrealistic optimism.[13,p55]

Skills-based health education may overcome unrealistic optimism by helping students understand the consequences of risk behaviors and how they affect health. Actively engaging them through performance tasks helps students discover information to resolve a challenge presented in the prompt. When planning the tasks, a skilled teacher makes the challenge appropriate to the age of students and concentrates on risks students actually experience. When presenting their projects, students reinforce the information that connects the risk to personal health and demonstrate the skill that overcomes the risk.

Unrealistic Optimism—Example from Research

Lennart Sjoberg from the Stockholm School of Economics, Lars-Erik Holm from the Swedish Radiation Protection Authority in Sweden, and Henrik Ullen and Yvonne Brandberg from the Department of Oncology, Karolinska Hospital in Sweden, used a questionnaire to investigate the attitude of Swedish teenagers, aged 13, 15, and 17, towards exposure to ultraviolet radiation, protective behavior, and risk perception of tanning.

According to the researchers, unrealistic optimism occurs when people perceive their risk-taking as less dangerous than someone else's. Documented examples include smoking, alcoholism, and food risks. Not surprisingly, extreme levels of unrealistic optimism have been found among teenagers.[14,p83]

The researchers reported that tanning increases the risk of malignant melanoma. They found that commercial tanning facilities have made tanning more accessible and younger people expose themselves to radiation more frequently and are, therefore, more at risk. Even though children and youths in the study had full knowledge of the associated dangers, they frequently tanned.[14,p82]

This study demonstrated clear evidence of unrealistic optimism regarding tanning and melanoma for all age groups and both genders. Although females usually avoid risk, the girls in this study believed that a suntan made them more attractive and, thus, continued to tan, the risks notwithstanding. Unrealistic optimism remained constant, regardless of improved knowledge and greater risk awareness among the older respondents. Students exemplified unrealistic optimism when they perceived their personal risk of melanoma as less than the risk assumed by others.[14,p81]

The study suggests that increased knowledge does not always result in healthy behavior. Older students with enhanced risk awareness still believed that others were more at risk than they were (unrealistic optimism) for developing health problems due to sun exposure and tanning. This perception of the norm has dangerous consequences for students: they may engage in increased sun exposure to be accepted, thinking the behavior is expected and believing it is not overly dangerous.[14,p91]

In this research, knowledge was not sufficient to change behavior. The challenge to the skills-based health educator is to combine Standard 1 content about sun safety with Standard 7, practicing health-enhancing behaviors, and challenge students to decrease sun exposure and increase sunscreen use. A unit addressing this problem includes a variety of prompts, like modeling, verbal persuasion, consequences, experiments, technology, overcoming impediments to use, and personal stories.

Classroom Application of the Unrealistic Optimism Theory

Mrs. Gomez is a middle school wellness teacher. She teaches health and physical education to her students both indoors and out.

Youth Risk Behavior data for 2009 indicates that only 9.3% of 9th grade students routinely use sunscreen.[15,p139] Although Mrs. Gomez always applies sunscreen before going outdoors, her students rarely do. Their excuses include not having time to put on sunscreen or none in their lockers. They also think it is not cool to be seen putting it on or the issue is unimportant; they are young, and only older people get skin cancer.

In her Standard 2 unit, analyzing influences, Mrs. Gomez designs a performance task using Standard 1 to examine the likelihood of injury or illness if engaging in unhealthy behaviors, such as exposure to ultraviolet radiation.[3,p25] She asks the students to examine how peers influence healthy (using sunscreen) and unhealthy behaviors (not using sunscreen)[3,p26] and challenges them to design a peer-led program that would make it cool to use sunscreen when outside for physical education.

For the final assessment, students created posters that showcased their knowledge of the consequences of sun exposure, the influence peers have on their decisions, and a five-step, teen sun-safety program. They also videotaped public service announcements (advocacy) to influence and support others to make the positive health choice[3,p36] of using sunscreen. They showed how to apply sunscreen and why it is important to use it, encouraged friends to use it, and conveyed the message that they will feel healthy, confident, and more attractive by protecting themselves. The principal ran the video on the school television throughout the day and displayed the posters in the school foyer.

To support her students, Mrs. Gomez persuaded a local store to donate sunscreen so that every student had access to it. The program changed the social norm: nearly all students now use sunscreen before going outdoors.

Implications for Coordinated School Health

Individual members of a coordinated school health team could each utilize the Unrealistic Optimism Theory. The following examples illustrate how the theory, along with the specialized expertise of each team member, could be applied in planning curriculum and teaching activities.

Health Education

- To demonstrate the sun's damage, invite a guest speaker from the American Lung Association to demonstrate April Age, the software program that shows students how the sun damages the skin, a condition that worsens over time.
- Provide instruction, case studies, and performance tasks and teach skills to challenge the social norm that tanning is healthy and attractive.

Physical Education

- Encourage students to bring sunscreen to school and apply it before going outdoors for class.
- Provide information about the sun protecting factor (SPF) ratings of sunscreen.
- Offer positive role modeling by applying sunscreen before conducting class outdoors.

Health Services

- Provide sun safety posters and handouts for students.

Nutrition Services

- Display sun safety posters in the cafeteria.

Counseling, Psychological & Social Services

- Provide sun safety promotional material in the waiting area.

Healthy School Environment

- Implement a school-wide sun safety program.
- Broadcast public service announcements throughout the day that promote sun safety.

Health Promotion for Staff

- Implement an in-service sun safety program to educate staff.
- Model sun safety behavior.

Family/Community Involvement

- Engage the community in a sun safety promotion.
- Seek community donations for sunscreen and dispensers.
- Provide sun safety education to parents because their attitudes about sun safety are decisive in a younger child's use of sunscreen.[14,p91]

PROCHASKA'S TRANS-THEORETICAL MODEL OF HEALTH BEHAVIOR CHANGE

James Prochaska is the director of the Cancer Prevention Research Center and professor of clinical and health psychology at the University of Rhode Island. Carlo DiClemente is Professor and Chair of the Department of Psychology for the University of Maryland. Together, they created the Trans-Theoretical Model of Health Behavior Change.[16,p2988] This theory identifies the stages a person travels through when trying to change an unhealthy behavior. It recognizes that change is a process and is used around the world for substance abuse prevention and treatment.[16,p2919]

In 1982, while studying thousands of people who were attempting to change a behavior, Prochaska and DiClemente observed that although they used different strategies, all participants in the study passed through six consistent stages of change (see **Figure 2.1**).[17]

The *pre-contemplative* stage occurs when Julio, a teen smoker, has no plans to change his behavior. He may deny that smoking has any real risks for him or be unaware of the hazards. Perhaps he has tried to quit, failed, believes he cannot succeed, and blames others for his defeat. To

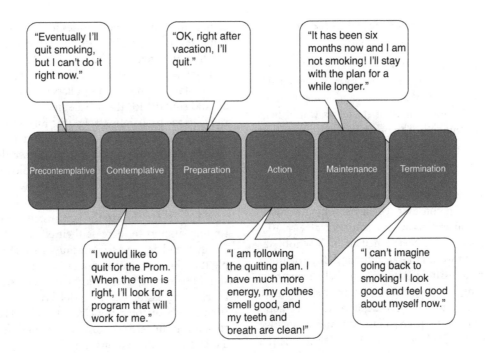

FIGURE 2.1 Trans-Theoretical Model of Health Behavior Change

move beyond this stage, Julio must think about how his smoking affects him and others. He can challenge himself to think about why a previous attempt to quit failed and how he could overcome it.[10,p20]

Progress begins when Julio moves into the *contemplative stage* where he becomes aware of his problem, thinks, and learns about it. He understands the benefits of changing but weighs the difficulties of doing so. Julio considers where he could go for help and what he could do to overcome the behavior but is unsure of how to proceed.

At this point, it is helpful to examine the pros and cons of changing the behavior. When thinking about why change did not occur, Julio could enlist help, such as the American Lung Association, to find a way of overcoming the obstacle. As mentioned previously, the person must believe that the benefits of change are greater than status quo. This self-efficacy will help Julio move to the next stage. Perhaps he will envision himself as a non-smoker, which may help him pursue the resources to quit.

In the *preparation stage*, Julio plans to take action within a month and may have made small changes in his behavior. He creates a plan that details how the change will occur, sets a date and realistic goals, establishes rewards for meeting his short and long-term objectives, and engages family and friends for support.

During the *action stage*, he changes his behavior. Julio is vulnerable to relapse at this point and needs all the plans, strategies, and help he designed during the preparation stage. It is wise for him to have a plan of action when tempted by the old behaviors. Visualization helps

him view himself as a non-smoker. Julio can review the quit plan and its rewards and remind himself of why he wanted to change, knowing how much better he will feel, if successful.

In the *maintenance stage*, Julio has successfully maintained the non-smoking behavior for six months. To increase his self-efficacy, he reviews his plan, enjoys his rewards, envisions himself demonstrating healthy behaviors, and is proud of his accomplishment. This stage can last six months to five years.

When his new habits are well established and the effort to change complete, Julio has entered the *termination stage*. Here, he is no longer tempted to return to smoking. Julio regards himself as a healthier person and has confidence he will not relapse.[10,p20]

Although the stages are listed as occurring one after another, Julio may stay in the preparation stage a long time then relapse into the contemplative stage if he does not find the help he needs to change. Once in the action stage, Julio may find the changes too difficult and revert to a previous stage.[5,p22] Lapses can occur during any of the stages, and when they do, Julio must reexamine why he wanted to change, adjust his plan of action, seek additional support, and recommit.[10,p21]

A skills-based health educator helps students realize the need for behavioral change by using Standard 1 to gather information about the effects of risky behavior on health and encouraging them to take personal responsibility for their actions, and uses Standards 2–8 to teach the skills needed to overcome unhealthy behaviors.

Trans-Theoretical Model of Health Behavior Change—Example From Research

The study *Helping Adolescents Quit Smoking: A Needs Assessment of Current Former Teen Smokers* compared the survey responses of current and former adolescent smokers, aged 15 to 17, to learn what strategies would help adolescents quit smoking. The needs of the smokers and former smokers were consistent with Prochaska and DiClemente's Trans-Theoretical Model of Health Behavior Change.[18,p192]

The authors note that the Centers for Disease Control and Prevention consider teenage smoking a major public health concern. Boys are smoking at age 10.7 years, and girls by 11.4. Nearly half of high school seniors who smoke would like to quit, and 40% of them have tried unsuccessfully. Attempts to help teens quit smoking have been unsuccessful because smoking gives teens a sense of autonomy, independence, intimacy, identity, bonding with peers, maturity, and a positive social image, all of which fulfill their developmental needs. Teens who are motivated to quit smoking want to be involved in the treatment decisions, set their own goals, and progress at their own pace.[18,p184] The stages of change model as a process to quit smoking seems consistent with the needs of the teens. **Table 2.1** describes the attitude that teens in the study had towards quitting, based on their stage of change.[18,p193]

For the pre-contemplators, we can direct instruction to addiction, the hazards of smoking, and the difficulties in quitting. Former teen smokers share quitting techniques (Standard 7, Practicing Healthy Behaviors) and the importance of receiving support from others. They may explain the impediments to quitting and how to change them into opportunities to succeed. They can remind the teens that despite the difficulties of quitting, reaching that goal is highly satisfying.

Contemplators need confidence to move toward the action stage. Former teen smokers might act as role models and support for them. To empower contemplators to move to the preparation stage, the former smokers could share useful quitting strategies (Standard 7, Practicing Healthy Behaviors) and how to plan rewards for successfully moving to the next stage. They could also share how to cope with stress, sadness, anger, and worry without using cigarettes (Standard 1).

Preparers are close to the action stage and require continuing support to increase their efficacy. Teachers, staff, family members, and friends must assure the young people that they can quit and that support is at hand. They should be encouraged to find a cigarette substitute, such as chewing gum, watching television, and talking to friends, to overcome the cigarette void. The researchers then asked the teens to rank what would help them quit. **Table 2.2** lists these motivating factors.

To help teens quit, it is important to know what motivates them. From the smokers who quit, we learn the importance of family and friend support. The health educator can use the information from **Table 2.3** to plan an intervention that would include the skills of interpersonal communication, stress management, healthy ways to cope with emotion, visualization, positive self-talk, and securing support from family and friends.

Knowing what teen smokers are thinking at each stage of behavioral change and what motivates them to quit is important planning information for the health teacher and the facilitator of a teen smoking cessation program. Not all smoking teens believe that cessation is an urgent

---

TABLE 2.1 Teen Attitudes Towards Quitting, Based on Prochaska's Trans-Theoretical Stages

Pre-contemplative
- Do not take quitting seriously.
- Predict that other people will not be very supportive.
- Think they can quit when they want to.
- Believe that nothing will help them quit.

Contemplators
- Think they may need new friends or to be with a new group in order to change.
- Least likely of the three groups to feel that they could quit successfully.
- Focused on external rewards and internal emotional issues.
- Did not see that help from others would be as useful as those who were in the action stage or those who have quit.

Preparers
- Confident in their ability to quit.
- Focused on people and situations that will help them quit.
- Less likely than other current smokers to say they smoke when relaxing, talking on the phone, after eating, at parties, and outside at home.
- Agree that talking to friends, watching television, chewing gum, and fiddling with their hands would substitute for smoking.

TABLE 2.2   What Would Help a Teen Smoker Quit?

1. Receiving a reward, such as money or a gift certificate
2. A friend wanted to quit smoking with me.
3. Learning ways to cope with cigarette cravings.
4. Learning ways to deal with stress.
5. Learning ways to deal with sadness, anger, or worry.
6. Knowing more about how to keep my mind off smoking.
7. My friends/brothers/sisters believed I could quit smoking.
8. My parents/guardian/adult family member stopped buying me cigarettes.
9. My friends/brothers/sisters did things with me where I couldn't smoke.

need, and they are on different cognitive and emotional levels from one another.[18,p193]

Classroom Application of the Theoretical Model of Health Behavior Change

Mr. DiFranza is a 9th grade health teacher and cross-country coach at Holton High School. He has caught a few students smoking after school and during meets. He

TABLE 2.3   What Helped a Former Smoker to Quit?

1. Parents/guardian/adult family member encouraged me to quit.
2. Learned ways to deal with stress.
3. My parents/guardian/family member believed I could quit.
4. My friends/brothers/sisters did things with me where I couldn't smoke.
5. My parents/guardian/adult family member did things with me where I couldn't smoke.
6. My friends/brothers/sisters stopped asking me if I want a cigarette.
7. Learned about the effects of smoking on my health.
8. Learned ways to deal with sadness, anger, or worry.
9. A friend wanted to quit with me.
10. My parents/guardian/adult family member stopped buying me cigarettes.

checked the school Youth Risk Behavior Survey data and found that 20% of his 12th grade students are current frequent cigarette users as compared to 11.2% of the students surveyed nationally.[15,p65]

When he talked to his students in class, many of the smokers told him that they had tried to quit several times but could not do it. Mr. DiFranza designs a performance task that challenges the students to devise a smoking cessation program for teens. The requirements include predicting how healthy behaviors (quitting smoking) affect health status[3,p25] and using resources from home, school, and community that provide valid health information about quitting.[3,p29] Students must design a multi-faceted approach to quitting (Standard 7, Practicing Healthy Behaviors) that explains how a student moves through the stages of behavior change, and receives rewards for progress to reduce the health risks of smoking.[3,p35]

When assessed, the students provided public service announcements explaining the benefits of quitting smoking, where teens can access help to quit, and incentives to keep working their way through the stages of behavior change. A post test showed that 10% teens who smoked stated they were ready to quit.

Mr. DiFranza has agreed to facilitate the first teen smoking cessation program, using Prochaska's Stages of Change Theory as the foundation.

Implications for Coordinated School Health

Individual members of a coordinated school health team could each utilize Prochaska's Stages of Change Theory. The following examples illustrate how the theory, along with the specialized expertise of each team member, could be applied in planning curriculum and teaching activities.

Health Education

- Explain the Trans-Theoretical Model of Health Behavior Change and how it is used to quit smoking.
- Design performance tasks that challenge students to use information about cessation (Standard 1 Health Concepts) to design a multi-approach quit program for teens. (Standard 7, Practicing Healthy Behaviors).
- Be a positive anti-tobacco role model.

Physical Education

- Display posters and information that illustrate how smoking affects physical performance.
- Display the smoking cessation program information and encourage smokers to sign up.
- Be a positive anti-tobacco role model.

Health Services

- Provide informational pamphlets that promote being smoke free.

- Offer a smoking cessation program for teens and family members.
- Design motivational rewards for students and staff who successfully quit.
- Be a positive anti-tobacco role model.

Nutrition Services

- Display posters that encourage students to eat healthy as a way of coping with the craving to smoke.

Counseling, Psychological & Social Services

- Supply students who would like to quit smoking with a list of community resources.
- Provide referrals to smoking cessation programs.
- Be a positive anti-tobacco role model.

Healthy School Environment

- Display posters that show students having fun without using cigarettes or show friends quitting smoking together.
- Enforce the smoking policy.

Health Promotion for Staff

- Provide smoking cessation programs.
- Supply information on how to refer a student for cessation.

Family/Community Involvement

- Offer a smoking cessation program for family members.
- Invite medical professionals in the community to provide smoking cessation.
- Be a positive anti-tobacco role model.

THE HEALTH BELIEF MODEL

Irwin Rosenstock initially designed The Health Belief Model in 1966, but Marshall Becker and his colleagues later modified it in the 1970s and 1980s. The model explains that the core beliefs of Tyler, a high school student, predict whether he will make a behavior change.[5,p25] Tyler is more likely to change an unhealthy behavior, such as being overweight, if certain beliefs are present.

He must:

1. Perceive that his present behavior will have serious health consequences. The more he perceives that the effects of the behavior are serious, the more likely Tyler will be to change his behavior. To wit, he must acknowledge that being overweight has a negative impact on his life.[1,p50]

2. Recognize that he is susceptible to the harmful effects of the behavior. For example, Tyler must believe that being overweight can make him susceptible to developing diabetes.

3. Acknowledge that his taking action to lose weight has beneficial effects. Tyler might say to himself, "I will look much better and be more physically active without getting winded and tired!"

4. Be aware of the barriers to changing behavior but realize that the benefits of change outweigh the hurdles. Tyler might say to himself, "It will be difficult going to a fast food restaurant with my friends and staying on my diet so I will check the menu online, make my choice, and be prepared with my order when I get there. I'll feel better knowing I made a good choice."[1,p62]

5. Identify specific internal and external cues to action associated with the change.[5,p23] An external cue occurs when Tyler sees his friends and family having fun eating high calorie, high fat foods. An internal cue occurs when he wants to join them.

The Health Belief Model is cognitive. Each of the five elements above can be overcome with information provided by Standard 1, Health Concepts, of the National Health Education Standards. This standard provides information to people engaged in unhealthy behaviors to help them comprehend their personal susceptibility and understand that changing is beneficial to their health. Moreover, they may examine the barriers to change and available supports and identify the internal and external cues for change.

The model does not include, however, the skills that help the person use the information to overcome the problem behavior. Whereas Standard 3, Accessing Valid Information, teaches how to access valid and reliable sources of information, products, and services for healthy dieting,[3,p29] Standard 7, Practicing Healthy Behaviors, provides the framework to demonstrate a variety of healthy practices, such as choosing healthy foods.[3,p35] This combination of knowledge and skill equips Tyler to confront his unhealthy behavior and uproot it.

The Health Belief Model—Example from Research

A 2003 study on the results of a large-scale trial of Project ALERT in middle schools indicated that the prevention program curbs cigarette and marijuana initiation, current and regular cigarette use, alcohol misuse, and inhalant abuse.[19,p1830]

Project ALERT is an evidence-based program, designated as exemplary by the Department of Education, and a model program by the Center for Substance Abuse Prevention. It seeks to motivate students not to use drugs by giving them skills to demonstrate resistance behavior.

The program attempts to change student beliefs about drug norms and the social, emotional, and physical consequences of using drugs. It also helps teens identify and resist pro-drug pressures from parents, peers, the media, and others and build resistance self-efficacy. Project ALERT utilizes question, answer, and small-group activities that contribute to its effectiveness.[19,p1831]

The Project ALERT curriculum utilizes three theories of behavior change: The Health Belief Model, the Social (Cognitive) Learning Model, and the Self-Efficacy Theory of behavior change. The Health Belief Model concentrates on cognitive factors that motivate healthy behavior. The Social (Cognitive) Learning Model emphasizes social norms and significant others as key determinants of behavior. The Self-Efficacy Theory proposes that a person can accomplish a task if he or she believes in succeeding.[19,p1831]

The Project ALERT lessons were taught to 7th and 8th grade students with booster lessons administered in the 9th grade. According to the data collected, Project ALERT curbed cigarette initiation by 19%, reduced current and regular smoking by 23%, and curtailed marijuana initiation by 24%. Alcohol misuse was lower than a control group, as was drinking that resulted in negative consequences.[19,p1833]

Project ALERT is consistent with the Characteristics of Effective Health Education and the National Standards. **Table 2.4** shows the correlation between Project ALERT and the National Health Education Standards.

Classroom Application of the Health Belief Model

The number of students who smoke marijuana in the Josiah Frances Middle School in Wisconsin is increasing. Those who choose to smoke feel it is a rite of passage and think it will not become a permanent habit or result in any harm. Mrs. Becker, the health teacher, knows that 21.2% of

TABLE 2.4   Correlation Between Project ALERT and the National Health Education Standards

Project ALERT	Standard 1	Standard 2	Standard 3	Standard 4	Standard 5	Standard 6	Standard 7	Standard 8
Consequences of smoking cigarettes, marijuana, and drinking alcohol	X							
Healthy alternatives	X							
How the environment affects personal health	X							
Dangers of inhalants	X							
Recognizing how peers influence one another		X						
Comprehending that pressures are internal and external		X						
Understanding social norms related to drug use		X						
Resistance skills to cope with peer pressure				X				
Refusal skills				X				
Communication skills				X				
Smoking cessation							X	
Practicing behaviors that avoid or reduce health risks[20]							X	

8th graders have tried marijuana at least once,[21] 36.8% of the high school population has tried it, and 20.8% of them are current users.[15,p77] She is worried that her students will become regular users unless she intervenes.

During an in-service, Mrs. Becker learned about an evidence-based curriculum founded upon the Health Belief Model and decided to use it in the interpersonal communication unit. She always teaches both content and skill to her students. Learning a skill increases a student's confidence to cope with challenging situations in a healthy way.

Mrs. Becker began her unit by examining the likelihood of injury or illness when engaging in unhealthy behaviors,[3,p25] such as smoking marijuana. She informed her students about the hazards and consequences of marijuana because she wants them to know how dangerous it is to the body and mind. Mrs. Becker also wants them to know that their bodies are susceptible to damage every time they smoke. She introduced the skill of interpersonal communication by asking the students what they could do to resist peer pressure when asked to smoke weed. They brainstormed many ideas, including refusal, using "I" messages, asking for help from an adult, and walking away.[3,p3]

Wanting to make the topic more personal, Mrs. Becker contacted the American Lung Association and invited to class a guest speaker who brought pigs lungs. The speaker inflated the lungs with a pump. While one lung was blackened by cigarette smoke, damaged by emphysema, and barely inflated, the other was healthy and inflated easily and fully. The students were amazed at the damage smoking did to the lungs. They became even more distressed, however, when they learned that marijuana smoke damages the lungs more than cigarette smoke.

The guest speaker also shared several stories about middle school students who smoked marijuana and how it interfered with relationships and school achievement and how difficult it was for them to quit. Angela, one of Mrs. Becker's students, was shocked by one of the stories because it sounded just like her. For the first time, she thought about quitting and liked the idea of people thinking of her as a non-user, but worried that she might have the same difficulty quitting as some of the young people in the stories.

After school, Angela and some of her friends from Mrs. Becker's class went to the park. As Angela's friends lit up, she knew she had to resist the pressure to smoke and refused when offered the weed. She remembered the damaged pig's lungs and the stories read by the guest speaker, and decided to stand with her friends who did not smoke. "It will be easier not to smoke if I hang with non-smokers," she thought. This step was her first in changing an unhealthy behavior.

Implications for Coordinated School Health

Individual members of a coordinated school health team could each utilize the Health Belief Model. The following examples illustrate how the model, along with the specialized expertise of each team member, could be applied in planning curriculum and teaching activities.

Health Education

- Develop instruction using evidence-based curriculum.
- Utilize social norms to help students understand that most teens do not use drugs, alcohol, tobacco, and inhalants.
- Collaborate with Physical Education teachers to provide a consistent message about drug use.
- Teach National Standards skills to increase a student's efficacy in refusing drugs, alcohol, tobacco, and inhalants.

Physical Education

- Collaborate with Health Education teachers to provide a consistent message about drug use.
- Display wellness posters that show students involved in healthy behaviors.

Health Services

- Provide training to the health service staff so that they can be attentive to the signs and symptoms of substance abuse.

Nutrition Services

- Display posters showing children eating healthy snacks and having fun.

Counseling, Psychological, and Social Services

- Provide a list of community resources for students who need help with substance use/abuse.

Healthy School Environment

- Enforce the alcohol, drug, and tobacco policy.
- Provide safe, fun, and healthy enrichment activities before and after school.

Health Promotion for Staff

- Provide staff training to teachers implementing evidence-based instruction.
- Train staff to identify signs and symptoms of drug use or abuse.

Family/Community Involvement

- Provide parent/community training for evidence-based substance abuse education so that students are hearing a consistent message from parents, school, and community.
- Train family and community members to identify signs and symptoms of drug use or abuse.

THE PROTECTION MOTIVATION THEORY

Ronald W. Rogers, Professor at the University of Alabama, developed the Protection Motivation Theory (**Figure 2.2**). It expands the Health Belief Model and suggests that a person is motivated to protect himself by assessing the threat of a potentially harmful behavior against how well he thinks he can cope with the behavior.[5,p29]

The Protection Motivation Theory states that health related behaviors are a result of:

- How a person assesses the severity of the problem.
- How susceptible he feels he is to the problem.
- How effective the change will be to solve the problem.
- His confidence in performing the risk-reducing behavior.
- Fear resulting from being educated about the problem.[5,p27]

The model states that there are two sources of information that influence a person making a decision about changing behavior: environmental and intrapersonal. The environmental source includes verbal persuasion and learning by observing. The intrapersonal includes the person's prior experience.

These sources of information influence the five components of the Protection Motivation Theory and result in either an adaptive response—making positive choices to change behavior—or a maladaptive response that results in no change.[5,p28] **Figure 2.2** illustrates how these sources of information influence an individual's health behavior choices.

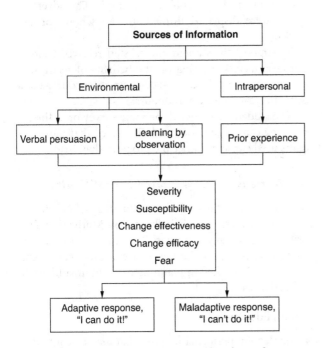

FIGURE 2.2   Protection Motivation Theory

Skills-based health education can use the Protection Motivation Theory in planning for successful behavioral change in students. Standard 1, Health Concepts, provides the information needed to persuade a student to think about changing an unhealthy behavior. It offers a framework for learning about the severity and susceptibility of a harmful behavior,[3,p25] a process that may instill enough fear to motivate change. The model may also illustrate that change can occur and be effective.

Standards 2 through 8 provide the skills a student needs to develop the confidence to make a change. When one student observes another modeling a healthy behavior, he begins to believe he can also perform this behavior. He recalls practicing healthy behaviors and this contributes to his efficacy in skill building. To use skills, students must understand why the skill is important, teachers must explain the steps of the skills, show what the skill looks like in action, provide time to practice and show proficiency, and use formative assessments for feedback and improvement.[3,p14] Building efficacy for change occurs when a student uses information and skills to prevail over the unhealthy behavior.

Protection Motivation Theory—Example from Research

In the article, *What to Convey in Antismoking Advertisements for Adolescents: The Use of Protection Motivation Theory to Identify Effective Message Themes*, the authors revealed that certain advertisement themes increased the adolescents' nonsmoking intentions by enhancing their perceptions that smoking poses severe social disapproval risks.[22,p1-18]

The 7th and 10th grade students examined advertisements with the following message themes: Disease and Death, Endangers Others, Cosmetics, Smokers' Negative Life Circumstances, Refusal Skills Role Model, and Marketing Tactics. After viewing the advertisements, the students completed a survey about how these advertisements affect their intention to smoke.

The Death and Diseases message discussed how smokers suffer from serious disease and oftentimes die prematurely. According to the protection motivation theory, the goal was to increase perceptions of health risk severity.[22,p3]

The Endangers Others message stressed the severe risks of smoking by showing the harmful effects of cigarettes on others and the strong social disapproval that smokers may experience from nonsmokers. According to the Protection Motivation Theory, these messages seek to increase the perceived severity of the health and social disapproval risks of smoking.[22,p4]

The Cosmetics message emphasized that smokers must cope with unattractive and annoying side effects of smoking, such as bad breath, smelly clothes, and stained teeth. Researchers found this theme ineffective because the respondents believed they could use various products to counteract the side effects.[22,p4]

The Smokers' Negative Life Circumstances message portrayed smokers as losers of whom other teens would disapprove because of their smoking. According to the Protection Motivation Theory, this strategy enhances the perception of the severe social disapproval risked by smokers.[22,p5]

The Marketing Tactics message argued that tobacco firms use powerful marketing devices, such as image advertising, to influence teens to smoke. According to the Protection Motivation Theory, this approach increases an adolescents' knowledge of marketing practices so they will have increased efficacy to resist them.[22,p6]

Those researching the Protection Motivation Theory discovered that:

- The messages of Endangers Others, Refusal Skills Role Model, and Smokers' Negative Life Circumstances increased adolescents' intentions not to smoke by conveying that smoking cigarettes poses severe social disapproval risks (susceptibility portion of the Protection Motivation Theory).
- The Cosmetic message sought to influence social risk severity perceptions but failed because the adolescents believed that they could use breath sprays, toothpaste, or mouthwash to decrease the unpleasant side effects of cigarettes.
- The Refusal Skills Role Model did not increase an adolescent's self-efficacy to refuse cigarettes, but was predictive of behavioral intentions not to smoke.
- Adolescents did not indicate that the Disease and Death and the Selling Disease and Death messages contributed to their perception of the severity of disease. Few of the respondents felt vulnerable to the health risks of smoking.
- Marketing Tactics and Selling Disease and Death messages failed to influence the teens' self-efficacy at resisting tobacco marketing tactics and did not contribute to the intention not to smoke.

The researchers found that self-efficacy perceptions had twice as much influence over the adolescents as did the risk of severity. To increase self-efficacy, the researchers recommend that schools implement a media literacy program that gives students time to examine advertisements and practice refusing skills. This approach is consistent with the performance indicators of Standard 2, Analyzing Influences; Standard 4, Interpersonal Communication; and Standard 7, Practicing Healthy Behaviors.

The researchers discovered that stressing the severity of long-term health risks is not an effective strategy, whereas emphasizing that teens are highly vulnerable to the health risks of smoking may be a better method. For example, advertisements could show Courtney explaining how quickly she became addicted to cigarettes and how much she has suffered as a result.

Classroom Application of the Protection Motivation Theory

Steuban High School is located in southern California. Mr. Mascierello, the health teacher, is overwrought about the potential for melanoma because his students are always outdoors and knows that only 9.3% of high school students routinely use sunscreen.[15,p139] After studying various theories of behavior change for his Master's degree, he selects the Protection Motivation Theory for his Standard 2 unit, Analyzing Influences. Standard 1, Health Concepts, includes information on the dangers of sun exposure and the benefits of using sunscreen.

Mr. Mascierello begins the unit by teaching about the dangers of melanoma and proposing ways to reduce or prevent injuries and health problems[3,p25] by using sunscreen. He explains the sun protection factor (SPF) of sunscreen and models, along with other students who routinely use it, how quick and easy it is to apply.

Mr. Mascierello designed a performance task that directed the students to design a survey with two goals: discover the number of Steuban High School students who use sunscreen versus those who do not and analyze the influence personal values and beliefs about sunscreen have on their decision.[3,p27] Based on that information, the students would create an advertisement that would influence high school students to use sunscreen. The advertisement had to explain the five hazards of sun exposure, susceptibility to danger without using sunscreen, ease of application, and how cool it is to use it. The advertisements were displayed throughout the school for two weeks.

To support the student efforts, staff received training during a faculty meeting on the benefits of using sunscreen, and the principal asked them to encourage students to wear sunscreen outdoors.

The students conducted the same survey once the advertising campaign ended and discovered that more students used sunscreen after the program than before.

Implications for Coordinated School Health

Individual members of a coordinated school health team could each utilize the Protection Motivation Theory. The following examples illustrate how the theory, along with the specialized expertise of each team member, could be applied in planning curriculum and teaching activities.

Health Education

- Implement performance tasks that include content and skill.

- Use verbal persuasion, modeling, and a student's prior experience to teach new content and skills.
- Increase student self-efficacy so he or she has the confidence to practice health-enhancing behaviors.

Physical Education

- Display posters that promote teens using sunscreen.
- Model the application of sunscreen.

Health Services

- Display posters that show students using sunscreen.
- Display posters that encourage students to take personal responsibility for their health.

Nutrition Services

- Display foods that are good for healthy skin.
- Hang posters that show young people enjoying a picnic in the shade of a tree.

Counseling, Psychological & Social Services

- Encourage students to take personal responsibility for their health.

Healthy School Environment

- Develop a school-wide sunscreen campaign
- Provide sunscreen dispensers and samples of sunscreen for student and faculty use.
- Plant trees for esthetics and shade from the sun.

Health Promotion for Staff

- Provide information and training about the dangers of sun exposure and the role of sunscreen in protecting the skin.

- Be a positive role model by always using sunscreen before going outdoors.

Family/Community Involvement

- Send home information about the importance of applying sunscreen on children before they go outdoors.

THEORY OF PLANNED BEHAVIOR

In 1989, Icek Ajzen, a professor of psychology at the University of Massachusetts, developed the Theory of Planned Behavior, which attempts to predict how a person's attitudes about a behavior are indicators that he or she intends to engage in it (see **Figure 2.3**). Ajzen proposed that behavior is best established by intention, which, in turn, is determined by attitude toward the behavior (favorable or unfavorable), subjective norm (perception of social pressures to either perform or not perform the behavior), and perceived behavioral control (perception of ease or difficulty in performing the behavior).[23,p276]

Before Estella gets to the point where she intends to change, three factors will influence her decision: her attitude toward the change, the subjective norms of friends and family, and whether or not Estella believes she has control over the process and the outcome.[24]

Her attitude toward the change depends on whether she believes the outcome of the change will result in what she wants to happen.[24] If Estella is trying to lose weight, she must believe that eating healthy and exercising results in weight loss. She must also believe that when she evaluates the potential outcome, the results will be positive. For example, losing weight will result in her looking and feeling healthy.

Another factor that influences Estella's intention to change is how subjective norms affect her decision-making

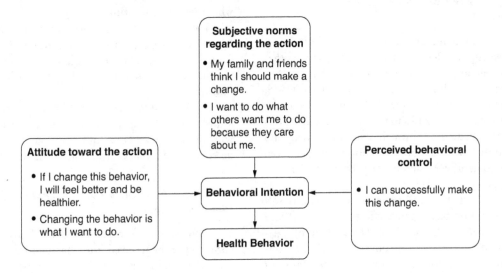

FIGURE 2.3 Theory of Planned Behavior

and how much she feels she must comply with them.[24] Estella may have health-conscious friends and family whom she respects and admires. If she believes that they want her to lose weight, the influence of those norms will affect her decision to eat healthy and exercise more.

The third factor that influences Estella's intent to change is her perceived control of the behavior change. Estella must feel that she is capable of making the desired change and that, if made, the result will be what she intended.[24] For Estella to eat healthy and establish how much exercise she needs to lose weight, she must first learn about nutrition and exercise. Going to MyPyramid.gov and completing the MyPyramid Tracker[25] will help Estella make a self-assessment that serves as the foundation for examining her eating habits and level of exercise. The Pyramid Tracker makes suggestions on how to improve diet and adjust exercise. Having the knowledge of how to make the change and the skills to do it empowers Estella by increasing her efficacy to complete the task successfully.

Skills-based health educators can use this theory when planning health instruction. Standard 1, Health Concepts, provides the framework for predicting how healthy behaviors affect health status[3,p25] and ensures that the results, such as losing weight and increasing exercise, are desirable.

The health teacher can effectively use social norms[3,p27] to demonstrate that many students do not engage in risky behaviors and that non-participants are in the majority. In addition, using social norms helps students understand that the people who care about them support a change in their behavior. These factors help Estella increase her behavioral intent and efficacy to change.

The health educator then infuses the content into Standards 2 through 8 so that students will have the skills and knowledge to change.

Theory of Planned Behavior—Example from Research

The research conducted by Nada O. Kassem from Loma Linda University, and Jerry W. Lee, identified factors that influenced regular soda consumption by North Los Angeles County male high school students, aged 13–18. They used the Theory of Planned Behavior to predict the intention to drink soft drinks in the future among a population that already did. Through a survey, Kassem and Lee learned that attitude, subjective norm, and perceived behavioral control were significant predictors of intention to drink regular soda.[23,p273]

The researchers chose this topic because excessive soft drink consumption has negative effects on the health of children. In 1996, the United States Department of Agriculture found that adolescent boys, aged 12–19, consumed an average of 1.78 twelve-ounce cans of carbonated soft drinks per day. Drinking soft drinks instead of milk may have an adverse impact on adolescent bone development or contribute to possible fractures due to a decreased intake of the bone building nutrients, calcium, magnesium, riboflavin, Vitamin A, and ascorbic acid. A correlation exists between the consumption of sugar-sweetened drinks and obesity in schoolchildren. In fact, the largest source of added sugars in the American diet is carbonated soft drinks. Dental caries, decreased esophageal pH, increased periods of duodenal acidification, possible urinary stone disease, and increased caffeine intake are also consequences of soft drink consumption.[23,p274-275]

Three facts predicted attitudes toward drinking soft drinks. The students reported that they enjoyed the taste of the drink, believed it quenched their thirst, and thought it was not unhealthy.

The most independent predicting factor of subjective norm was the parent. This influence is not surprising, considering the parent provides available food, acts a role model, and contributes to the frequency of eating out where soda is often part of the meal. Friends, teachers, coaches, doctors, and fast food restaurant owners are influential to a lesser extent.[23,p290]

The strongest predictor of perceived behavioral control was the availability of regular soda at home. Students reported that having ready access to soda made drinking it easy. The second predictor was their seeing advertisements that encourage drinking soda. Students reported that they have access to many advertisements that encourage soda consumption.[23,p291]

Although this research used the theory to predict behavior, it would be interesting to consider how it did. To affect a change in attitude toward drinking soda, health educators can explain the consequences of drinking soda on health, in particular, weight gain. A Standard 7, Practicing Health-Enhancing Behaviors, unit concentrates on substituting soda with a healthier, low-calorie drink and determines whether the change results in a decrease in weight. This tactic encourages the students to change what they chose to drink.

To affect a change in subjective norms, parents and friends support a change that substitutes drinking soda for a lower calorie, healthier drink. Doing so encourages the student to change because the people who care about him want it.

For a student to perceive that he can change, he needs knowledge and skill to choose healthier drinks and the will power to do so. Once his self-efficacy is increased and he believes he can alter his behavior, he will try.

Classroom Application of the Theory of Planned Behavior

Mr. Donellen is concerned about the Body Mass Index (BMI) report he received from the nurse during the coordinated school health meeting. The nurse informed the group that, according to the CDC, 29.2% of high school students drank a can, bottle, or glass of soda or pop at least one time during the seven days prior to the Youth Risk Behavior Survey (YRBS).[15,p115] The nurse explained the negative effects soda has on health and asked the group to think of what the school could do to help students decrease consumption.

In planning his Standard 5 unit on decision-making, Mr. Donellen challenged his students to make good decisions about healthy eating. He developed a performance task that asked students to help a friend who had a moderately overweight BMI, did not exercise much, and drank a lot of soda. The challenge was to help the friend make healthy choices about exercise, food, and drinks.

Mr. Donellen explained that for anyone to make a change in behavior, three elements must be present. Their classmate, Vaniece, for example, would need a positive attitude, a belief she can change, and a recognition that people who care about her want her to change.

The students applied Standard 1, which describes the relationship between healthy behaviors and personal health[3,p24] by explaining BMI and food input versus energy output, and providing examples of healthy drinks. The students would also utilize Standard 5, Decision Making, by determining how to balance calorie intake with energy output, predict the outcome of each solution, make a healthy choice, then analyze the result.[3,p32-33] In addition, students had to tell a story about a young person who readied himself to make a behavior change to improve diet and exercise by addressing the three Theory of Planned Behavior elements.

At the next coordinated school health team meeting, the group planned the foyer exhibits for the spring Open House. The exhibits highlighted ways to improve family wellness. They planned for several exhibits, such as quick, healthy meals; family fun exercises; portion sizes for children and adults; and healthy snacks.

Mr. Donellen brought examples of the students' projects to the meeting. Knowing that parents have a powerful influence over the food choices available to their children, the team asked if the class would present their projects in the school foyer during Open House. Parents enjoyed learning about the decision-making model and reading the student stories about behavior change. A few students role-played their stories and were a big hit with the parents!

Implications for Coordinated School Health

Individual members of a coordinated school health team could each utilize the Theory of Planned Behavior. The following examples illustrate how the theory, along with the specialized expertise of each team member, could be applied in planning curriculum and teaching activities.

Health Education

- Teach information about the health effects of drinking soda (Standard 1, Health Concepts) and the skills to make healthier choices (Standard 5, Decision Making) as well as analyzing media messages (Standard 2, Analyzing Influences) about soda consumption.
- Introduce a variety of drinks that taste good and are healthy.
- Use Standard 8 to teach students how to advocate for healthier drink choices.

Physical Education

- Teach students how to hydrate and emphasize that drinking soda furthers dehydration in thirsty people.[23,p290]

Health Services

- Provide information about the hazards of drinking soda along with ways to decrease consumption.
- Talk to students about the health effects of drinking soda, including weight gain and dental caries.

Nutrition Services

- Make delicious and healthy drinks available.
- Post the nutritive value of different types of drinks.

Counseling, Psychological, and Social Services

- Provide information about healthy eating and the effects of drinking soda.
- Healthy School Environment
- Stock the vending machines with healthy drinks.
- Promote physical activity and healthy eating.

Health Promotion for Staff

- Encourage staff to model use of thirst-quenching healthy drinks.

Family/Community Involvement

- Solicit family and community members to donate healthy drinks to the school.
- Encourage parents to adopt healthy eating behaviors by providing parent education programs that teach knowledge and skills for healthy eating.
- Lobby community organizers to provide healthy drinks during community events.
- Advocate the local media to decrease their promotion of soda and increase the promotion of healthier drinks.

SOCIAL COGNITIVE LEARNING THEORY

The Social Cognitive Theory developed by Albert Bandura, professor at Stanford University, explains the initiation, adoption, and maintenance of health behaviors. There are two key components to this theory: self-efficacy and outcome expectancies. Both have a significant effect on the goals we set for ourselves and how we pursue them.[26,p127]

According to this theory, behavior change occurs because a person—in this case Kevin—believes he can take action and have a successful outcome. Self-efficacy is enhanced by personal accomplishment/mastery, vicarious experience, verbal persuasion, and emotional arousal.

Although personal accomplishment/mastery is the greatest source of self-efficacy, Kevin must believe that he alone was responsible for the accomplishment and can repeat it.[26,p129] Vicarious experience occurs when we believe we can complete a difficult task because we have observed someone who is like ourselves be successful in the same situation. Our efficacy is also enhanced through verbal persuasion, when respected others assure us that we can perform a certain task. Emotional arousal influences efficacy when Kevin confronts a situation and determines he has the skills to resolve it.[26,p130]

Self-efficacy influences all other components of the Social Cognitive Learning Theory and has a powerful effect upon behavior. Without self-efficacy, Kevin will not meet his goals and make behavioral changes. With high self-efficacy, he has confidence to face challenges and believes he has the skills to respond and the outcomes will be favorable. Self-efficacy is also associated with better social integration and a strong sense of being able to cope with life's challenges. Low self-efficacy is associated with depression, apprehension, or helplessness.[26,p128]

The other key component of the theory is outcome expectancies, or what people expect to happen as a result of the action they take. Kevin uses this component to decide if he can set a realistic goal for behavior change. If he expects success, Kevin will continue; if not, the process will end.

Outcome expectancies have three dimensions: area of consequences, positive or negative consequences, and short or long-term consequences. Area of consequences includes physical outcomes, such as withdrawal when quitting smoking; social outcomes, such as family members and friends being proud of the quit attempt; and self-evaluative outcomes that occur when the person anticipates experiences related to the behavior change—being uncomfortable with friends who continue to smoke, for example.[26,p131]

Goal setting is central to the Social Cognitive Learning Theory. Goal setting affects a person's self-efficacy and ability to reach the goal, and whether he or she thinks the pros and cons of completing it are worth the effort. As mentioned earlier, outcome expectancy is crucial to changing, and self-efficacy is vital to completing change. However, even though setting a goal is a predictor of behavior change, it is not a guarantee that the goal will actually be reached.

Socio-structural factors are the conditions in Kevin's life that act as barriers or supports to reaching his goal. A person with high self-efficacy will recognize opportunities to overcome barriers to goals, whereas someone with

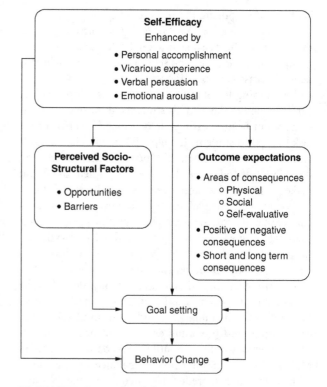

FIGURE 2.4 Social Cognitive Learning Theory

low self-efficacy may be unable.[26,p132] **Figure 2.4** illustrates the various factors that affect self-efficacy.

Skills-based health education augments self-efficacy by increasing knowledge about health promotion and disease prevention, teaching life skills that enhance one's personal and academic life, and preparing students for work in the 21st century. PreK–12 skill development provides students with personal accomplishment, vicarious experience, verbal persuasion from the teacher to perform and demonstrate proficiency, and emotional arousal to act in a health enhancing manner. Students learn to weigh the consequences of their actions and set goals that enhance their health. Through performance tasks and age appropriate prompts, they learn how to use knowledge and skills to help others and themselves change an unhealthy behavior.

The Social Cognitive Learning Theory—Example from Research

Kimberly Rinderknecht and Chery Smith used the Social Cognitive Learning Theory to demonstrate that a nutrition intervention program implemented for seven months during an after school program was an effective way to improve the dietary self-efficacy of urban Native American children, aged 5–10, and adolescents, aged 11–18. Data was gathered by administering a pre and post test designed and approved by The University of Minnesota's Institutional Review Board for Human Subjects.[27,p299]

The intervention was based on the constructs of the Social Cognitive Learning Theory: performance accomplishments, vicarious experience, verbal persuasion, and emotional arousal. One 30 to 60 minute lesson was taught each month. Self-efficacy was improved by exposing the children and adolescents to healthier foods, giving them the opportunity to choose such foods, discussing how to maintain an energy balance of food intake versus energy output, and conducting learning activities with peer groups that included modeling.

Researchers and after-school staff reviewed lessons and provided verbal reinforcements and practice to the participants regarding how to choose healthier foods when in a different environment, such as a fast food restaurant. By focusing on personal and environmental factors, the researchers hypothesized that the participants would improve their dietary self-efficacy and selected dietary behaviors.[27,p300]

The results showed that children were open to a program that helped them with their weight. The dietary self-efficacy of the 5–10-year-old boys and girls in the study increased, and the overweight 5–10-year-old children significantly improved their dietary self-efficacy as compared to their normal-weight and at-risk, overweight peers. The self-efficacy of the 11–18-year-old adolescents did not significantly increase. Their lack of progress may have been influenced by verbal persuasion and decreasing peer support for healthful eating.[27,p302]

This study links strongly with the National Standards. Rinderknecht and Smith used Standard 1, Health Concepts, when they taught the relationship between healthy eating and personal health,[3,p24-25] such as maintaining an energy balance. They incorporated Standard 2 (Analyzing the Influence of Family, Peers, Culture, Media, Technology) when they influenced the students by modeling healthy behaviors;[3,p26-27] Standard 5 (Decision-Making) when teaching how to choose healthy foods;[3,p32-33] Standard 7 (Practicing Healthy Behaviors) when demonstrating healthy practices[3,p35] when eating out with others at fast food restaurants; and Standard 4 (Interpersonal Communication) when teaching how to refuse unhealthy foods and communicate needs.[3,p30-31]

Classroom Application of the Social Cognitive Theory

Ms. Bloom, a high school health teacher, was apprehensive about beginning her CPR unit in the Standard 7, Practicing Healthy Behaviors unit. Before class, she asked her students how many of them would give CPR, if they knew how. Only a few students said they would. The rest said they would be afraid or thought it was gross. She needed a way to change their attitudes.

She knew that her students would be curious but intimidated by the manikins. To address this concern, she lined the manikins up in front of the classroom and held one in her arms as the students entered. As they passed,

Ms. Bloom used her ventriloquist skills to have the manikin welcome the students. When all were in class, she allowed them to examine the manikins by tilting the head and compressing the chest. In this way, she increased student efficacy.

Ms. Bloom began her unit by predicting how healthy behaviors, such as knowing how to administer CPR, affect health status.[3,p25] She explained the function of the heart, lungs, and circulatory system. When the students had confidence in that knowledge, she read them a scenario (emotional arousal) about a teen who had collapsed on the athletic field. She challenged them to analyze the role of individual responsibility in enhancing health[3,p35] by assessing pulse and breathing of the injured person and administering CPR. She modeled the skill so that the students could observe how to do it.

She placed mats on the floor, lined up eight manikins, and directed one row of students to the front of the room while others worked on CPR assignments. She taught the class how to clean the manikin face with isopropyl alcohol and place their face masks over the mouth to offset any fear of contamination. Ms. Bloom then talked the students through performing each step of CPR. They practiced repeatedly until they were ready to exhibit the skill. On cue, the students demonstrated the skill from assessing pulse and breathing to a reassessment after compressions. In time, the students embraced the unit and enjoyed the final assessment where they read different prompts and had to assert their skills by responding appropriately.

Ms. Bloom successfully used the Social Cognitive Theory in planning and implementing this unit. She increased the self-efficacy of her students through personal mastery, vicarious experience, verbal persuasion, and emotional arousal. She persuaded them that they could accomplish this challenge and the outcomes would be positive. She helped students overcome any impediments they had toward working with the manikins and reach the goal of being competent in performing CPR. She also was able to change their behavior from not wanting to learn the unit skills to being eager to demonstrate them.

Implications for Coordinated School Health

Individual members of a coordinated school health team could each utilize the Social Cognitive Theory. The following examples illustrate how the theory, along with the specialized expertise of each team member, could be applied in planning curriculum and teaching activities.

Health Education

- Plan and implement skills-based health education to increase the self-efficacy of students.
- Model skills to students so they can see how they are done and visualize themselves performing them.

- Encourage student performance by assuring them they can perform a skill.
- Provide prompts that are personal and evoke an emotional arousal.
- Use information from the American Heart Association to explain the positive consequences of performing CPR.
- Provide positive feedback when students have completed the skill.

Physical Education

- Display posters showing how to give CPR.

Health Services

- Train staff on CPR skills.

Nutrition Services

- Provide heart-healthy food choices.

Counseling, Psychological & Social Services

- Increase student efficacy by congratulating them on completing their CPR training.

Healthy School Environment

- Provide defibrillators throughout the school.
- Display posters illustrating heart-healthy practices.
- Display posters showing teens giving CPR.
- Broadcast public service announcements that promote heart health.

Health Promotion for Staff

- Provide CPR training.
- Provide defibrillator training.

Family/Community Involvement

- Invite parents to view students completing their final assessment in CPR.
- Have students demonstrate CPR during parent's night.
- Provide CPR training for parents and community members.

Review Questions

1. Why is it important to use theories of behavior change in planning skills-based health education?

2. How can health educators help students improve their self-efficacy?

3. Why do humans like to attribute behavior?

4. How can a health educator help a student develop an internal locus of control?

5. What is the value of students completing self-assessments such as MyPyramid and TestWell?

6. Develop a teen smoking cessation program using the Trans-Theoretical Model of Behavior.

7. What classroom strategies consistent with the Health Belief Model could you use to help students change an unhealthy behavior?

8. Using the Protection Motivation Theory, develop a plan to reduce marijuana use among students.

9. Using the Theory of Planned Behavior, develop a plan to decrease dating violence.

10. Use the Social Cognitive Theory to target and reduce a risk factor.

References

1. Gilbert, G. G. (2000). *Health Education Creating Strategies for School & Community Health* (2nd ed.). Sudbury, MA: Jones and Bartlett.

2. Bandura, A. (1994). In V. S. Ramachaudran (Ed.), *Encyclopedia of human behavior* (Vol. 4, pp. 71–81). New York: Academic Press. (Reprinted in H. Friedman [Ed.], *Encyclopedia of mental health*. San Diego: Academic Press, 1998).

3. Joint Committee on Health Education Standards. (2007). *National Health Education Standards, Second Edition, Achieving Excellence*. Atlanta: American Cancer Society.

4. New World Encyclopedia. (2008, July 20). *Heider, Fritz*. Retrieved June 26, 2009, from New World Encyclopedia, Organizing knowledge for happiness, prosperity, and world peace: http://www.newworldencyclopedia.org/entry/Fritz_Heider. p. 2

5. Ogdon, J. (2004). *Health Psychology*. GBR: McGraw-Hill Education.

6. Raven, B. H. (n.d.). *In Memoriam*. Retrieved October 20, 2010, from University of California: http://www.universityofcalifornia.edu/senate/inmemorium/HaroldH.Kelley.htm

7. Hudley, C. G. (2007). Reducing Aggressive Behavior and Increasing Motivation in School: The Evolution of an Intervention to Strengthen School Adjustment. *Educational Psychologist*, 42(4), 251–260.

8. The Brainpower Program. (2009). *The Brainpower Program*. Retrieved June 6, 2009, from The Brain Power Program—The Curriculum: http://brainpowerprogram.com/index-1.html. p. 2

9. Discovery Health. (2009). *Discovery Health Tools*. Retrieved May 22, 2009, from Discovery Health: http://discovery-health.queendom.com/cgi-bin/tests/short_test.cgi

10. Insel, P. M. (2008). *Core Concepts in Health, 10th Edition Update*. New York: McGraw-Hill.

11. Wallston, Kenneth A. P. (2007, June 15). *Greetings Fellow Health Researchers from Kenneth A. Wallston, PhD*. Retrieved May 22, 2009, from Multidimensional Health Locus of Control Scales: www.vanderbilt.edu/nursing/kwallston/mhlcscales.htm

12. Malcarne, V. L. (2005). Children's Health-Related Locus of Control Beliefs: Ethnicity, Gender, and Family Income. *Children's Health Care*, 34(1), 47–59.

13. Weinstein, N. D, Marcus, S. M, & Moser, R. P. (2005). Smokers' Unrealistic Optimism About their Risk. *Tobacco Control*, 14(1), 55–59.

14. Sjoberg, L. H.-E. (2004). Tanning and Risk Perception in Adolescents. *Health, Risk & Society*, 6(1), 81–94.

15. Centers for Disease Control and Prevention. (MMWR 2009, 59 SS-5). *Surveillance Summaries*. Atlanta: Author.

16. Johns Hopkins University. (2009, June 23). *James O. Prochaska, PhD*. Retrieved June 26, 2009, from: http://innovators awards.org/innovators

17. Hahn, D. B., Payne, W. A., & Lucas, E. B. (2009). *Focus on Health* (9th ed.). New York: Mc-Graw Hill Companies, Inc. p.13.

18. Pingree, S. B. (2004). Helping Adolescents Quit Smoking: A Needs Assessment of Current and Former Teen Smokers. *Health Communications*, 16(2), 185–194.

19. Ellickson, P. P.-D. (2003). New Inroads in Preventing Adolescent Drug Use: Results From a Large-Scale Trial of Project ALERT in Middle Schools. *American Journal of Public Health*, 93(11), 1830–1836.

20. Project ALERT.com. (n.d.). *Curriculum Components*. Retrieved June 2009, from: www.projectalert.com

21. Centers for Disease Control and Prevention (CDC). 1995-2009 Middle School Youth Risk Behavior Survey Data. Retrieved June 14, 2010, from: http://apps.nccd.cdc.gov/youthonline.

22. Pechmann, C. Z. (2003). What to Convey in Antismoking Advertisements for Adolescents: The Use of Protection Motivation Theory to Identify Effective Message Themes. *Journal of Marketing*, 67, 1–18.

23. Kassem, N. O. (2004). Understanding Soft Drink Consumption Among Male Adolescents Using the Theory of Planned Behavior. *Journal of Behavioral Medicine*, 27(3), 273–296.

24. Taylor, S. E. (2006). *Health Psychology*. (6th Ed.). Boston: McGraw-Hill, p 57.

25. United States Department of Agriculture, Center for Nutrition Policy and Promotion. (n.d.). *MyPyramidTracker*. Retrieved June 1, 20009, from: USDA - CNPP - MyPyramid Tracker: http://www. mypyramidtracker.gov/

26. Conner, M. N. (2005). *Predicting Health Behavior*. (2nd Ed.). Boston: McGraw-Hill.

27. Rinderknecht, K. R. (2004). Social Cognitive Theory in an After-School Nutrition Intervention for Urban Native American Youth. *Journal of Nutrition Education and Behavior*, 36(6) 298–304.

Curriculum and Instruction 3

Developing comprehensive PreK–12 skills-based curriculum and instruction is a challenge.
How do you decide what goes where? How do you plan?

Let us begin with the end in mind. The goal of health education is for students to adopt and maintain healthy behaviors.[1,p5] To do so, we must reduce their risk-taking behaviors by equipping them with health knowledge and positive coping skills (see **Figure 3.1**).[1,p11]

The eight National Health Education Standards and performance indicators provide the framework for planning. The box highlights Standard 1 and its performance indicators.

Health Education Standard 1

Students will comprehend concepts related to health promotion and disease prevention to enhance health.

Health Education Standard 1 Performance Indicators PreK–Grade 2

1.2.1 Identify that healthy behaviors affect personal health.
1.2.2 Recognize that there are multiple dimensions of health.
1.2.3 Describe ways to prevent communicable diseases.
1.2.4 List ways to prevent common childhood injuries.
1.2.5 Describe why it is important to seek health care.[1,p24]

Standard 1 contains the foundation for promoting health-enhancing behaviors by acquiring basic health

Standards		Risk Factors
Increase knowledge and skill	Standard 1—Common Health Education Content	Alcohol and Other Drug Use
	Standard 2—Analyzing Influences	Injury and Violence, Including Suicide
	Standard 3—Accessing Information, Products, and Services	Tobacco Use
	Standard 4—Communication	Poor Nutrition
	Standard 5—Decision Making	Inadequate Physical Activity
	Standard 6—Goal Setting	Risky Sexual Behavior
	Standard 7—Practicing Healthy Behaviors	
	Standard 8—Advocacy[2]	

FIGURE 3.1 Decreasing Risk Factors and Increasing Health Knowledge and Skill

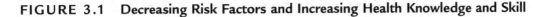

concepts and functional health knowledge from the Common Health Education Content Areas.[1,p11] Standards 2 through 8 establish the framework for skill development that gives students the confidence to cope with life's challenges in a healthy way.

The Big Picture

Planning begins with a look at the big picture and asking, "What health knowledge do we want students to know, and what skills do we want them to have when they graduate?"

To begin, the health education curriculum must be aligned to the National Health Education Standards. An undertaking this large requires the collaboration of leadership, dedicated staff, and sufficient resources. District leaders must set clear expectations and time lines, encourage and support staff, and ensure that the project meets goals and deadlines. Administrators monitor tasks and provide time and resources to maintain forward momentum.[2]

To start the alignment, analyze data from the Youth Risk Behavior Survey (YRBS) or other valid and reliable data sources—then develop curriculum goals to meet the needs identified therein. Curriculum goals should support and be consistent with district goals (see **Figure 3.2**).

Once the goals are established, the PreK–2, 3–5, 6–8, and 9–12 health educators determine the content to include in the district curriculum (see **Table 3.1**).

Mapping

Mapping is a process, accomplished in a variety of ways. The purpose is to align an item to two criteria much like using longitude and latitude to find a place on a map.

In the following examples, health content is first mapped to a grade level, then to performance indicators. The result is a PreK scope and sequence based on targeted content and performance indicators.

MAPPING CONTENT TO GRADE LEVEL— KEEPING THE END IN MIND

The first step requires staffers to identify each topic taught in their grade level.

The completed map indicates the scope and sequence of the current curriculum. The group should reflect on the diagram and decide if it meets the assessed needs of the students. If it does not, revise the map before proceeding.

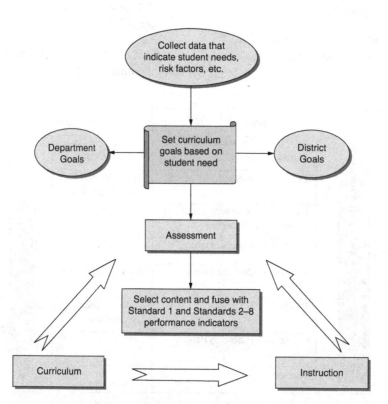

FIGURE 3.2   Planning and Aligning Skills-Based Health Education

TABLE 3.1 Mapping Content to Grade Level (Keeping the end in mind)

Directions

- What do you want your students to know and be able to do as a result of your PreK–12 comprehensive skills-based health education curriculum?
- Your goal is to meet the needs of your students, based on collected data, by teaching them the knowledge and skill they need to develop and maintain healthy behaviors.
- List your topics in the left-hand column, then place a check mark under the grade it is taught.

Topic	PreK	K	1	2	3	4	5	6	7	8	9	10	11	12

MAPPING CONTENT TO STANDARDS 1–8 PERFORMANCE INDICATORS

Once the PreK–12 district content is established, grade-level teachers map their content to the performance indicators of Standard 1 and Standards 2–6 (see **Table 3.2** and **Appendix D**).

In the sample PreK–2 map, Grade 2 teachers, collaborating with the grade span team, listed their topics, chose the performance indicators from Standard 1 and Standards 2–8 that support that topic, and then placed the topic with the skills indicator under the appropriate standard. This procedure is complex because the planning is limited to the performance indicators of Standard 1 (content) and Standards 2–8 (skills), rather than diagramming the contents of an approved text over a term, semester, or year.

Keep the end in mind. The standards are based on research and provide the framework for the development of healthy practices and behaviors.[1,p13] Effective curriculum is correlated with skill acquisition and functional health knowledge, not learning extensive content.

SAMPLE GRADE 2 MAP

Interpreting Table 3.2

To interpret Table 3.2, look at the topic in *italics* to see how it connects to the Standard 1 performance indicator and the skill performance indicator. By narrowing the topics to the essence of the performance indicator, you teach functional health knowledge rather than extensive information that may not contribute to meeting the standards. Once the correlation is complete, fuse the content into the performance indicator then rewrite it.

For example, for the topic of seat belt safety, we selected the Standard 1 performance indicator 1.2.4 – List ways to prevent common childhood injuries.[1,p24] When rewritten, it reads, "List ways, such as wearing a seat belt, to prevent childhood injuries." The Standard 2 analyzing influences performance indicator 2.2.3 states, "Describe how the media can influence health behaviors."[1,p26] When rewritten, it reads, "Describe how media can influence using a seat belt."

Here is another example. On the map, Standard 1 performance indicator 1.2.3 states, "Describe ways to prevent communicable diseases."[1,p24] The content is hand washing. When rewritten, it says, "Describe how hand washing prevents communicable disease." Standard 7 practicing healthy behaviors performance indicator 7.2.2 states, "Demonstrate behaviors that avoid or reduce health risks."[1,p35] When rewritten, it reads, "Demonstrate how hand washing helps avoid or reduce health risks."

This procedure is repeated for all the performance indicators so that content becomes an integral part of the performance indicators. Its significance to backward design as a strategy to plan assessment, instruction, and curriculum is evident later in this chapter.

TABLE 3.2   Map of Grade 2 Topics and Performance Indicators

Directions

1. How many classes do you have for Grade 2 health education? _____ 30 hours _____

2. List the Grade 2 topics:

   sun safety, personal safety, bullying prevention, hydration, bystander skills to prevent bullying, talking to adults about feelings, getting enough exercise, activity based recess, personal strategies to prevent the spread of disease, hand washing techniques, hand sanitizers, seat belt safety, bicycle safety, household injury prevention, telling an adult when not feeling well

3. Match the topic to a Standard 1 performance indicator and a skills performance indicator.

4. Follow the Standard 1 performance indicator row across to the skill column then write the skill performance indicator in that box with the topic.

Standard 1	Standard 2	Standard 3	Standard 4	Standard 5	Standard 6	Standard 7	Standard 8
Performance Indicators	Analyzing Influences	Accessing Information	Communication Skills	Decision Making	Goal Setting	Practicing Healthy Behaviors	Advocacy
Performance indication 1.2.1 — Identify that healthy behaviors affect personal health.[1,p24]	*Sun safety* 2.2.1 How the family influences personal health practices and behaviors.[1,p26]	*Personal safety* 3.2.1 Identify trusted adults and professionals who can help promote health.[1,p28]	*Bully prevention* 4.2.4 Demonstrate ways to tell a trusted adult if threatened or harmed.[1,p30]			*Hydration* 7.2.1 Demonstrate healthy practices and behaviors to maintain or improve personal	*Bystander skills to prevent bullying* 8.2.2 Encourage peers to make positive health choices.[1,p36]
Performance indicator 1.2.2 — Recognize that there are multiple dimensions of health.[1,p24]			*Talking to adults about feelings—emotional health* 4.2.1 Demonstrate healthy ways to express needs, wants, and feelings.[1,p30]		*Getting enough exercise each day—physical health* 6.2.1 Identify a short-term goal and take action toward achieving the goal.[1,p30]	*Making friends—social health* 7.2.1 Demonstrate healthy practices and behaviors to maintain or improve personal health.[1,p35]	*Activity based recess—physical health* 8.2.1 Make requests to promote personal health[1,p36]
Performance indicator 1.2.3 — Describe ways to prevent communicable diseases.[1,p24]					*Personal strategies to prevent the spread of disease* 6.2.1 Identify a short-term goal and take action toward achieving the goal.[1,p34]	*Hand washing* 7.2.2 Demonstrate behaviors that avoid or reduce health risks.[1,p35]	*Asking for hand sanitizers in the lavatories* 8.2.1 Make requests to promote personal health.[1,p36]

Performance indicator 1.2.4 — List ways to prevent common childhood injuries. [1,p24]

Wearing a seat belt
2.2.3 Describe how the media can influence health behaviors. [1,p26]

Medication safety
3.2.1 Identify trusted adults and professionals who can help promote health [1,p28]

Bicycle safety, including wearing a helmet
5.2.1 Identify situations when a health-related decision is needed. [1,p32]

Injury prevention
7.2.2 Demonstrate behaviors that avoid or reduce health risks. [1,p35]

Performance indicator 1.2.5 — Describe why it is important to seek health care. [1,p24]

Telling a adult you do not feel well
4.2.1 Demonstrate healthy ways to express needs, wants, and feelings. [1,p30]

5. Rewrite the pairs of performance indicators to include the content.

Example—Sun Safety

Standard 1 performance indicator 1.2.1—Identify that healthy behaviors affect personal health. [1,p24]

Performance indicator 1.2.1 with infused content—Identify that using sun safety strategies affects personal health. [1,p24]

Standard 2 performance indicator 2.2.1—How the family influences personal health practices and behaviors. [1,p26]

Standard 2 performance indicator 2.2.1 with infused content—How the family influences personal health practices and behaviors such as using sun safety procedures.

6. Reflection

Can you teach the amount of content listed in the allotted time? _____

If not, what adjustments are you going to make? _____

DEVELOPING SKILLS-BASED UNITS

When the map is complete, teachers organize units by skills (Standards 2–8), teaching the content through the skill. For example, a unit on goal setting (Standard 8) includes teaching the skill of goal setting then using the skill to set goals about getting enough exercise and preventing the spread of disease. Students demonstrate proficiency in the content and skill according to the requirements of the performance task (Chapters 6–12). The teacher uses formative and summative assessments to determine proficiency (Chapter 4). This pedagogy emphasizes the skill rather than content because proficiency in skill helps students develop and maintain healthy behaviors.

Standard 8–Goal Setting Unit Progression

1. Teach the skill of goal setting (Standard 8)

2. Teach the content: importance of sufficient exercise (Standard 1).

3. Teach the content: preventing the spread of disease (Standard 1).

4. Introduce the prompts: a challenge to set goals for exercising; a challenge to prevent the spread of disease.

5. Students practice their skills.

6. The teacher develops and utilizes formative and summative assessments.

7. Students demonstrate proficiency in the skill and its related content.

8. Teachers use summative assessments to score or grade the student product.

Lesson Plans

Once the unit is established, a template (**Appendix E**) is used to write the lesson plan. A well-designed lesson enhances teaching and learning. The planning is deliberate and based on student needs and standards. Assessment reflects the standard performance indicators and generates the student-centered instruction. When the lesson is completed, the teacher reflects and makes adjustments.

Lesson plans help the teacher stay on task. If distracted during instruction, the teacher returns to the plan and continues. With all the instructions written and the back-up materials (exemplars, completed worksheets, quizzes, and tests, directions, pictures, sample work, etc) in one place, the teacher does not have to remember every detail or where things are. Should the same lesson be taught to several classes, following the plan results in continuity of instruction.

Organizing lessons into unit binders gives the teacher a library of resources and provides the scaffolding that binds the units and curriculum together. Sample units, including lesson plans, are found on the book's website.

When writing a lesson plan, select the state and national standards and the time allotted for the class and grade level. Think of an **essential question** that frames the lesson and connects it to the larger goals and objectives of the curriculum.

Ask four backward-design questions:

1. *What do I want the students to know and do?* List Standard 1 (content) and Standards 2–6 (skills) performance indicators that reflect the needs of the students targeted in curriculum mapping.

2. *How will I know when my students have achieved the goal?* Explain the assessment strategies and the formative and summative assessment tools used in the lesson. (Chapter 4)

3. *What will I do to achieve my goal?* Begin the instruction by explaining the agenda. Review the previous lesson, initiate instruction, and engage the students throughout. Formatively assess for learning and reserve a few minutes at the end of class to review the content and skills.

4. *How can I improve this lesson?* This is the teacher's formative assessment. Ask, "Does the lesson need to be adjusted?" "Was there enough time?" "Were the students actively involved?" "Is it a "keeper?" This self-assessment results in continuous improvement of instruction.

After the reflection, list the homework, cite interdisciplinary connections, opportunities for parent or community involvement, and the required teacher and student resources.

GRADE SPAN GOALS

The goal for students is to achieve proficiency in content and skill standards by the end of the grade span. They do so by demonstrating all the performance indicators (Standards 1–8) for the grade span. Therefore, planners must incorporate all performance indicators into grade span planning.

Each grade span spirals to the grade span below and above so that the end-product is a comprehensive, PreK–12, skills-based health education curriculum.

Checking Grade Span Performance Indicators

Proficiency in a standard occurs when students can demonstrate the knowledge and skill represented by all of the grade span performance indicators.[1,p10]

Table 3.3 is a tool used at the end of planning to determine whether all the PreK–2 performance indicators are taught within the grade span. Teachers indicate the performance indicators taught in their grade, review the results as a grade span team, and, if some performance indicators are not taught, they develop an action plan to resolve the omission.

This table and the remaining grade span tables are in **Appendix F.**

ACCESSING MAPPING RESOURCES[1,p37-39]

Curriculum resources are available to help teachers select health topics by grade level and skill. The Health Education Curriculum Analysis Tool from the CDC examines health education curriculum to determine strengths and weaknesses and to make it more effective. The tool utilizes the Characteristics of Effective Health Education, the National Health Education Standards, and health education content to analyze the curriculum.[3]

The eight national standards are listed by grade span for each content area. Therein, planners check off the topics that are included in their curriculum. Scores are tabulated and summarized before curriculum goals are set to improve the curriculum. The topics listed under each standard are used as a guide for choosing suitable content for each grade span.

The CDC's School Health Education Resources (SHER) (http://apps.nccd.cdc.gov/sher/) is a website that provides health education resources from the U.S. Department of Health and Human Services' Centers for Disease Control and Prevention.[4] Teachers select topics, grade levels, and resource types, then view the results, noting which of the National Health Education Standards and characteristics of effective health education curriculum are referenced.

Be mindful when planning skills-based health education that you must plan for content and skill. Some of the SHER resources are content only. If you use them, plan how to teach the content within a skill.

Assessment Tools for School Health Education is a useful book published by the Council of Chief State School Officers (CCSSO), State Collaborative on Assessment and Student Standards (SCASS), and the Health Education Assessment Project (HEAP). It includes an assessment framework of content and skill organized by elementary, middle, and high school levels. The book trains teachers how to assess health literacy and emphasizes the use of performance-based assessment. The framework provides content descriptors, such as the short and long-term benefits and risks of medicinal drugs (elementary level), and links them to a skill. The content descriptors assist in matching age-appropriate content to performance indicators.[5]

Comprehensive School Health Education, Totally Awesome Teaching Strategies for Teaching Health, 7th edition, provides a K–12 Health Education[6,p701-720] and a K–12 Scope and Sequence Chart aligned to the National Health Education Standards.[6,p721-816] These documents are comprehensive and useful in planning.

TABLE 3.3   PreK–2 Grade Span Check for Teaching All the Performance Indicators[1,p37-39]

Directions

Circle PreK (PreKindergarten), K (Kindergarten), G1 (Grade 1), or G2 (Grade 2) in the space in front of the performance indicator if you have included this performance indicator in your planning.

The results indicate if all the performance indicators are taught by the end of the grade span. If they are not, adjustments are needed; develop an action plan to remediate.

	Standard 1 Content		Standard 2 Analyzing Influences
PreK, K,G1, G2	1.2.1 Identify that healthy behaviors affect personal health.	PreK, K,G1, G2	2.2.1 Identify how the family influences personal health practices and behaviors.
PreK, K,G1, G2	1.2.2 Recognize that there are multiple dimensions of health.	PreK, K,G1, G2	2.2.2 Identify what the school can do to support personal health practices and behaviors.
PreK, K,G1, G2	1.2.3 Describe ways to prevent communicable diseases.	PreK, K,G1, G2	2.2.3 Describe how the media can influence health behaviors.
PreK, K,G1, G2	1.2.4 List ways to prevent common childhood injuries.		
Reflection		Reflection	

(continues)

TABLE 3.3   PreK–2 Grade Span Check for Teaching All the Performance Indicators[1,p37-39] *(continued)*

	Standard 3 Accessing valid information		Standard 4 Using interpersonal communication skills
PreK, K,G1, G2	3.2.1 Identify trusted adults and professionals who can help promote health.	PreK, K,G1, G2	4.2.1 Demonstrate healthy ways to express needs, wants, and feelings.
PreK, K,G1, G2	3.2.2 Identify ways to locate school and community health helpers.	PreK, K,G1, G2	4.2.2 Demonstrate listening skills to enhance health.
		PreK, K,G1, G2	4.2.3 Demonstrate ways to respond when in an unwanted, threatening, or dangerous situation.
		PreK, K,G1, G2	4.2.4 Demonstrate ways to tell a trusted adult if threatened or harmed.
Reflection		Reflection	

	Standard 5 Decision making		Standard 6 Goal setting
PreK, K,G1, G2	5.2.1 Identify situations when a health-related decision is needed.	PreK, K,G1, G2	6.2.1 Identify a short-term personal health goal and take action toward achieving the goal.
PreK, K,G1, G2	5.2.2 Differentiate between situations when a health-related decision can be made individually or when assistance is needed.	PreK, K,G1, G2	6.2.2 Identify who can help when assistance is needed to achieve a personal health goal.
Reflection		Reflection	

	Standard 7 Practicing Healthy Behaviors		Standard 8 Advocacy
PreK, K,G1, G2	7.2.1 Demonstrate healthy practices and behaviors to maintain or improve personal health.	PreK, K,G1, G2	8.2.1 Make requests to promote personal health.
PreK, K,G1, G2	7.2.2 Demonstrate behaviors that avoid or reduce health risks.	PreK, K,G1, G2	8.2.2 Encourage peers to make positive health choices.
Reflection		Reflection	

Results

_____

_____

_____

_____

Action Plan

_____

_____

_____

Backwards Design

"Once I had a way of clearly defining the end in mind, the rest of the unit 'fell into place'"[7,p24]

Backwards design is a planning strategy that causes us to think about what content students should know and the skill they should perform at the end of a unit. Utilization begins by identifying what standards/performance indicators the students should know and be able to do. This first step in utilization is already completed by the mapping exercises above.

To illustrate, the topic is health care and healthcare providers in the school and community. We want our

PreK–2 students to know why it is important to seek health care—performance indicator 1.2.5—and how to access the services of healthcare helpers—3.2.2, accordingly. The performance indicators are rewritten as follows:

- *Performance indicator 1.2.5 with infused content*—Describe three reasons why it is important to seek health care from healthcare helpers in the school and community.[1,p24]

- *Performance indicator 3.2.2 with infused content*—Identify three ways to locate school and community health helpers.[1,p28]

Next, identify the assessments that require evidence of students' achievement of the concepts and skills.[8] Ask two questions: "What evidence can students produce that shows they can describe three reasons why it is important to seek health care from healthcare helpers in the school and community?".[1,p24] and "What evidence can students produce that shows they can identify three ways to locate school and community health helpers?"[1,p28]

The teacher specifically asks students for *three* reasons why it is important to seek health care and to identify *three* ways to locate school and community health helpers. (ask a parent, guardian, school nurse, etc.). He may require them to explain how they get to the health helper office, if needed, or take them on an in-school field trip to identify a way to locate the school helper. It is important to tell students the amount of information required before they begin to plan and practice so they successfully fulfill the requirements.

Finally, plan the learning and instruction.[8] To do so, identify the theory-based curriculum and instruction that helps students learn and master health-related concepts and skills.[1,p92] The Characteristics of Effective Health Education, found later in the chapter, examine this topic. The instruction for performance indicator 1.2.5 could include reading a story about healthcare providers, the help each provides and reasons why it is important to seek their help. Likewise, Standard 3, Accessing Valid Information, 3.2.2 respectively, may include teaching students how to identify ways to locate school and community helpers, such as asking a trusted adult. The teacher may invite various professionals to class to explain the importance of seeking health care and ways to locate them in school and the community.

The teacher checks for understanding during class (formative assessment) and, in light of the results of the assessment, moves the instruction forward or makes adjustments by reviewing or reinforcing it. Assessments at the end of the unit (summative) include a performance task that challenges students to demonstrate three reasons why it is important to seek health care and identify three ways to locate school and community health helpers. A quiz or test with an assessment of all the content taught in the unit completes the package. The teacher

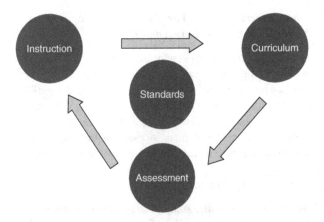

FIGURE 3.3 Continuous Cycle of Curriculum Improvement

uses the results of the summative assessment to adjust planning, instruction, and curriculum.

The link between assessment, curriculum, and instruction is a continuous cycle in which the assessment of standards informs instruction, instruction informs curriculum, and curriculum informs assessment, thereby closing the loop[1,p91] (see **Figure 3.3**). Chapter 4 also provides more information about assessment and assessment systems.

Curriculum and Instruction

Once backwards design is complete and instruction and curriculum are forming, the Characteristics of Effective Health Education complete the curriculum planning. These characteristics, if utilized properly, produce a curriculum that helps students develop and maintain healthy behaviors. This goal is important for academic success and a productive, fulfilling life in the 21st century.

Research tells us that less effective curricula concentrate on teaching facts and increasing student knowledge. Skills-based health educators, on the other hand, should emphasize teaching functional health information (essential concepts), shaping personal values that support healthy behaviors, shaping group norms that value a healthy lifestyle, and developing the essential health skills to adopt, practice, and maintain health-enhancing behaviors.[3]

CHARACTERISTICS OF EFFECTIVE HEALTH EDUCATION CURRICULUM

The fourteen Characteristics of Effective Health Education Curriculum below were developed by the Centers for Disease Control and Prevention. Planners refer to them as they develop curriculum to help students adopt and maintain health behaviors.

Characteristic One: The Curriculum Focuses on Specific Behavioral Outcomes[1,p13]

One of the first steps in developing curriculum is deciding which performance indicator meets the needs of the students. The planner selects one or more Standard 1 performance indicators for content, then one or more from the skills standards (Standard 2–8) and infuses content. These indicators keep the planner focused on behavioral outcomes, which help students develop healthy behaviors.

Classroom Application

When Mrs. Connolly, a 2nd grade teacher, writes objectives for her health class, she refers to the performance indicators of the National Health Education Standards and infuses the targeted content into the indicator. She is currently teaching about bicycle safety through performance indicator 1.2.1, which states, "Identify that healthy behaviors affect personal health"[1,p24] and 7.2.2, "Demonstrate behaviors that avoid or reduce health risks."[1,p35] She infuses the content into 1.2.1, and it now reads, "Identify how using bicycle safety procedures affects personal health" and 7.2.2 reads, "Demonstrate appropriate use of a bicycle safety, including the use of a helmet to avoid or reduce health risks."

To continue her backwards design planning, Mrs. Connolly considers how her students can explain and demonstrate bicycle safety and the appropriate use of a helmet. She invites to class a local bicycle business owner to explain bicycle safety, the safety features of a helmet, and how to fit one. She provides information from the National Highway Traffic Safety Administration that lists bicycle safety tips and how to fit a helmet properly.[9] She encourages her students to bring their helmets to class to check the size and fit. Finally, the performance task challenged them to explain and demonstrate bicycle safety tips, including wearing a properly fitting bicycle helmet.

The students enjoyed the performance task and were successful in achieving the behavioral outcome (see **Figure 3.4**).[1,p24,35]

Characteristic Two: The Curriculum is Research Based and Theory Driven[1,p13]

Instructional strategies and learning experiences are built on theory, such as the **Social Cognitive Theory**, because they have effectively influenced health-related behaviors among youth. The most promising curricula address the social influences, attitudes, values, norms, and skills that influence specific health-related behaviors.

Classroom Application

Mr. Souza is a member of the middle school health education curriculum revision committee and is using the National Health Education Standards and the Characteristics of Effective Health Education as the foundation of the revision. Mr. Souza and the other committee members want to design instructional strategies and learning experiences according to the social cognitive and inoculation theories since they effectively influence health-related behaviors among youth.

The Social Cognitive Theory explains how people change, acquire, and maintain certain behavior patterns and provides a basis for the design of intervention strategies.[10,p1] Being a middle school teacher, Mr. Souza found an interesting case study, predicated on the Social Cognitive Theory, that prevented and reduced alcohol use among students from middle school to high school. The three-year middle school program was based on a behavioral health curriculum and included input from parents and the involvement of a community task force. Because of observational learning, knowledge of the negative consequences of alcohol use, and an increased ability to com-

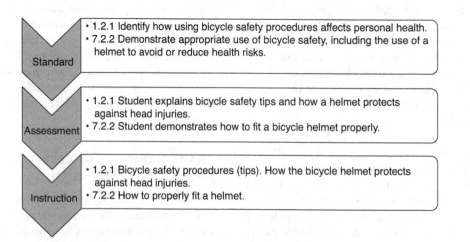

FIGURE 3.4 **Sample of Backward Design Planning**

municate with parents, students in the program said they were less likely to drink alcohol than others not so exposed. However, by the end of 9th grade, the results were insignificant.

The results of the study prompted an additional program in the 11th grade that reduced underage access to alcohol and changed community norms so that it was no longer acceptable for high school students to use alcohol. By the 12th grade, the results were significant and showed that alcohol use decreased, access to it was reduced, and parental norms of acceptance of teen alcohol use lessened.

The initiatives implemented were:

- The community was engaged and became attentive to the problem of underage alcohol use.
- Parents received alcohol education training.
- The school and community supported alcohol-free events.
- Media presentations in town no longer provided alcohol.
- Classroom discussions were held about the consequences of drinking alcohol.

The study reinforced Mr. Souza's belief that a comprehensive effort does result in a decrease in alcohol use among teens, a reduction in access to alcohol, and a change in parental norms that is less accepting of teen drinking.[10,p3] He wants to use this study to garner support from parents, the Coordinated School Health Advisory Committee, and his district for a skills-based comprehensive health program.

He noticed in the national standards book, *Achieving Excellence*, a section on the essential role of partners in the implementation of the national standards. After reading that portion, he believes his district and community will support a new skills-based curriculum because they currently support the health education program and want to see data that indicates a decrease in alcohol use.

Mrs. Parker, also a member of the revision committee, is skilled at writing real-life, engaging prompts. Her students enjoy solving these authentic problems by roleplaying because it gives them a chance to demonstrate their knowledge of a particular topic and reinforces the skills of the National Health Education Standards. By designing these student-centered activities, Mrs. Parker helps her students develop confidence, skills, and healthy behaviors to face life's challenges.

Characteristic Three: The Curriculum Targets Individual Values and Group Norms That Support Health-Enhancing Behaviors

Using group norms as part of instructional strategies and learning experiences helps students accurately assess the level of risk-taking behavior among their peers, correct misconceptions of peer and social norms, and reinforce health-enhancing behaviors.[1,p13]

Classroom Application

Mrs. Rodriquez is a high school health teacher. Her district administered the Youth Risk Behavior Survey (YRBS) to middle and high school students for the past five years. She likes to use the survey results to introduce her Standard 7 unit on practicing health-enhancing behaviors and avoiding or reducing health risks.

She reprints several questions from the Youth Risk Behavior Survey and asks students to guess what the actual responses were. In most cases, students assigned a much higher participation rate than was actually reported in the results. They all were surprised that fewer peers were engaged in risky behaviors.

The information learned from this social norms approach increased student awareness and caused them to be more open to learning the content and skills that will help them continue positive behaviors and avoid or reduce risky ones.

Characteristic Four: The Curriculum Focuses on Increasing the Personal Perception of Risk and the Harmfulness of Engaging in Specific Health-Risk Behaviors While Reinforcing Protective Factors

Effective curricula give students opportunities to assess their susceptibility to health-risk behaviors, health problems, and exposure to unhealthy situations. It also provides the opportunity to affirm health-promoting beliefs, intentions, and behaviors.[1,p13]

Classroom Application

Mr. Sym is a 3rd grade teacher who cleverly integrates health education into his daily classes. During English language arts, he reads scenarios to his students and asks them, "How would you respond to this problem?" The scenarios give him the opportunity to teach health education content and skills.

One scenario describes a group of students walking home from school when a van pulls up, and the driver asks for directions. Mr. Sym asks. "Is it safe or not to talk to the stranger or go into the van to provide the person with directions to his destination?"

This personal assessment helps the students clarify that it is unsafe to talk to a stranger or get into a car with one. Mr. Sym then teaches the students assertive communication skills and gives them time to practice. He rereads the scenario and asks them to role-play how they would respond using their new skills. This technique provides skill practice and reinforcement of content.

Mr. Sym's principal supports health education by promoting a climate that increases protective factors and encourages resiliency. He urges his faculty and staff to make personal connections with students in class and during various school activities. To reinforce health instruction, promote self-esteem, and increase a connection to the school, he gives students the opportunity to advocate for themselves by reciting safety tips on the morning announcements.

Characteristic Five: The Curriculum Addresses Social Pressure and Influences

Effective curricula help students deal with relevant personal and social pressures, such as the influence of the media, peer pressure, and social barriers that influence risky behaviors.[1,p14]

Classroom Application

Mrs. Clark, a middle school health teacher, is upset that the Youth Risk Behavior Survey (YRBS) for her district indicates that the smoking rate among students is increasing. She also loves the movies and has noticed that smoking is more common now on the big screen. Mrs. Clark is designing a Standard 2 unit on analyzing the influence of family, peers, culture, media, technology, etc., on health behaviors. She concentrates on how the media influences smoking behaviors.

Her students watched movie and television clips and tracked the number of times the actors smoked and whether they showed any adverse reaction to smoking. Then students rewrote the scene. They acted out the realistic effects of smoking, such as being burned by the match or cigarette, coughing, wearing clothes that smell like tobacco smoke, etc. They also reenacted the same scene without tobacco products and discussed whether there was any difference in the effectiveness of the scene.

In another lesson, she cites the YRBS data that indicate smoking rates in the district are lower than the national rates but rising nonetheless. She directs the students to list the internal and external factors that influence teens to smoke then analyzes the factors by discussing the positive and negative effects on behavior. Mrs. Clark also teaches refusal skills as a strategy to cope with these pressures. She gives students time to practice the skills through role-plays so they will have the confidence needed to refuse tobacco products.

Characteristic Six: The Curriculum Builds Personal and Social Competence

Effective curricula build the essential skills of analyzing influences, assessing accurate information, communicating effectively, refusing, decision-making, goal setting, self-management, and advocacy. These skills help students build personal confidence, cope with social pressures, and avoid or reduce risky behaviors.

To teach skills effectively:

- Discuss the importance of the skill and its relevance and relationship to the other skills.
- Present steps for practicing the skill.
- Model the skill.
- Practice and rehearse the skill by using real-life, relevant scenarios.
- Provide feedback and reinforcement.[1,p14]

Classroom Application

Mrs. Grinnell recently aligned her high school health curriculum to the National Health Education Standards. She adjusted her teaching techniques because she originally was trained to teach content over a specific number of lessons then give quizzes or tests to grade the student. With her new strategies, however, she discovered that her students are engaged more in their learning, enjoy class more, and achieve the national standards with the help of formative and summative assessments.

When Mrs. Grinnell begins her decision-making unit, she tells her students, "Describe several decisions you make and the process you use to make them." She anticipates that some students make decisions impulsively while others weigh them. Mrs. Grinnell also challenges the students to think about how friends, family, school leaders, politicians, corporate leaders, banks, and other businesses make important decisions.

She asks students, "Why is it important to talk about how people make decisions?" They realize that their decisions may have little or substantial impact on their lives, depending on the problem. After this discussion, the students understand the importance of making good decisions and are ready to learn how to do it.

Mrs. Grinnell demonstrates the skill of decision-making:

1. Identify the problem.

2. Determine the decision to be made.

3. Brainstorm three healthy solutions to solve the problem.

4. Evaluate the pros and cons of each solution.

5. Act on the best solution.

6. Assess its consequences.

While practicing the skill, students pretend they made the decision, acted on it, and reflected. Mrs. Grinnell notes, "You should always reflect on your decisions to see if the choice was, indeed, the correct one."

Mrs. Grinnell thereupon reads a prompt that asks students to decide about snack choices. She models the decision-making skill and checks for understanding by asking questions about the content and skill. When Mrs. Grinnell determines that the students are ready, she distributes several prompts and directs them to practice the skill in groups. She provides feedback as she walks from one group to another. The feedback, a formative assessment, helps the students adjust their work so that their presentations will reflect proficiency in content and skill.

Characteristic Seven: Provides Functional Health Knowledge That Is Basic, Accurate, and Directly Contributes to Health Promoting Decisions and Behaviors.[1,p14]

Functional health knowledge enables students to assess risk, analyze social norms, cope with risky situations, understand influences on behavior, make health-enhancing decisions, and increase competence.

Classroom Application

Mrs. Bartlett received training in the National Health Education Standards over the summer and implemented a new pedagogy in the fall. Instead of only teaching content, she now targets her instruction to student need and combines content and skills. Previously, she found the students unmotivated, despite many creative lessons. Now students are writing, practicing, and performing skits, creating public service announcements, analyzing and reporting on websites, and analyzing and reporting on social norms and risky behaviors. She still teaches basic and accurate content but instead of just teaching content with worksheets and a book, she teaches the content and the skill together and students demonstrate what they learn through a performance.

When students take the district YRBS, Mrs. Bartlett anticipates an increase in competency along with healthier decisions and behaviors.

Characteristic Eight: The Curriculum Uses Strategies to Personalize Information and Engage Students[1,p14]

Effective curricula provides student-centered, interactive, and experiential instructional strategies, such as group discussions, cooperative learning, problem solving, role playing, and peer led activities that are consistent with cognitive and emotional development. These strategies help students personalize information, increase their interest and motivation, and accommodate various learning styles and abilities.

When planning instructional strategies and learning experiences, be mindful to:

- Personalize information when writing prompts and presenting scenarios.
- Engage the students in learning.
- Address key health-related concepts and skills.
- Encourage creative expression.
- Share personal thoughts, feelings, and opinions.
- Develop critical thinking skills.[1,p14]

Classroom Application

Mr. Carney is an exceptionally creative middle school health educator. Students often request to be in his classroom because he is fun and effective. When planning his lessons, Mr. Carney thinks of ways to engage students while they learn health content and practice skills.

One of his favorite techniques is to present a prompt in which students prepare a presentation for a school committee meeting to advocate some cause. He likes to use this technique because it requires students to research information, design creative props, and practice their communication and advocacy skills. For the mock presentation, he invites parents and school staff to participate as the audience and prepares stimulating questions for them. The students must respond by using their communication and advocacy skills, correcting misinformation, and adding information to clarify their positions.

Mr. Carney also serves on the Coordinated School Health Wellness Committee, which is trying to meet one of the goals of their Wellness Policy: provide healthier snacks and increase the physical activity of students. He involves his students in this goal with a prompt that engages them to advocate for healthier snacks and more physical activity.

The prompt directs the students to form a committee and research ways to provide healthy snacks to students in school and after school and increase physical activity. Students use their talents and interests to choose their role in the project: presenter, researcher, writer, or prop designer. They demonstrate their knowledge and skills with a mock presentation to the Coordinated School Health Wellness Committee, parents, and school staff. To reach a larger audience, the presentation is taped and shown to the community via the educational television channel.

Characteristic Eight: The Curriculum Provides Age-Appropriate Information, Learning Strategies, Teaching Methods, and Materials

Effective curricula should be relevant to a student's daily life and address their needs, interests, concerns, developmental and emotional maturity, and knowledge and skills.[1,p15]

Classroom Application

In his Grade 4 goal-setting unit (Standard 6), Mr. Vazquez helps his students learn to set a personal health goal, track its progress, identify resources to achieve it, and evaluate the process and results.

Mr. Vazquez notices considerable arguing amongst his students and wants to help them improve their relationships. Because the students are young, he gives them the goal statement: "By the end of three weeks, I intend to improve my relationships with my classmates."

He asks the students to brainstorm things they can do in school to get along better with peers. As the students respond, he places long-term and short-term strategies on the left and right sides of the board, respectively. When the list is complete, Mr. Vazquez explains the difference between a long-term goal and a short-term goal. He chooses one long-term and two short-term goals that would help his students improve relationships. He offers this challenge: "Think of someone at home or at school who could help you reach this goal."

Mr. Vazquez then explains why it is so important for them to think about their goal each day and reflect on its progress. He asks the students, "How could you track your progress to complete the goal by a certain date?" Depending on the response, he gives examples of using a calendar with stickers, a journal, or a check-off list.

After three weeks, the students reflect on reaching their goal, tracking progress, the barriers experienced, and the support that helped them succeed. As the school year continues, Mr. Vazquez urges the students to set another personal goal and be prepared to share the results.

Characteristic Nine: The Curriculum Incorporates Learning Strategies, Teaching Methods, and Materials That Are Culturally Inclusive

Effective curricula materials do not include culturally biased information. They contain information, activities, and examples of cultural diversity and lifestyles such as gender, race, ethnicity, religion, age, physical/mental ability, and appearance. Learning activities promote values, attitudes, and behaviors that support student diversity, celebrate multiple cultures, strengthen skills that engage intercultural interactions, and build on the resources of families and the community.[1,p15]

Classroom Application

Mrs. Marina Spinoza came to this country when she was ten years old and knew little English. Her parents emigrated from the Azores to have a better life for themselves and their family. School was difficult for her because she did not understand what was being taught, could not read the textbooks, and did not understand her peers.

Marina's teacher was experienced at providing immigrants with the extra support needed to succeed. She believed that an inclusive classroom was necessary to make students feel comfortable, welcomed, and valued. She was deliberate about acknowledging and celebrating how each of her students, and herself, were different from one another.

In a short time, Marina was speaking English and succeeding in school. As she grew older and contemplated her life's goals, she decided to become a teacher. She wanted to work in a diverse school where she could contribute to the physical, mental, emotional/social, environmental, occupational/leisure, and spiritual health of young people. She became, of course, a health educator.

Mrs. Spinoza obtained a position teaching in a large, urban middle school. She organized and designed an inclusive classroom where all students are welcome and their diversity is valued. Students work as a team and support one another through tutoring, peer mediation, collaborative learning, and problem solving. They use information, activities, and examples of cultural diversity to learn health content and practice national health education skills.

Mrs. Spinoza designs prompts that help her students learn the content and skills needed to deal with their personal struggles. They often focus on "real life" scenarios, such as making friends, giving compliments, coping with teasing, excluding individuals or groups, and bullying. As such, her students learn to cope in a healthy way with their lives in school, at home, and in their community.

To increase further a sense of community, Mrs. Spinoza offers a special course called Health Education for Parents. In this class, she teaches parents the same content and skills also taught to her students so that school and home can be mutually supportive. The course is always filled and provides a wonderful support system and sense of community for the parents. Being involved in the school helps the parents feel welcome and results in additional support for school initiatives.

When Mrs. Spinoza retired, several of her former students wrote to her and explained that, as a result of her teaching strategies, they learned the skills to develop healthy behaviors, be comfortable with people who are different, advocate for themselves and others, be more open to relationships with people who are different, live harmoniously with many different people, and be productive members of society.[11,p49-53]

Characteristic Ten: The Curriculum Provides Adequate Time for Instruction and Learning

Because change requires an intensive, sustained effort, effective curricula provide adequate time for students to understand key concepts and practice skills. Short-term or one-shot curricula that devote only a few hours of instruction per grade level do not provide sufficient time to support the adoption and maintenance of healthy behaviors.[1,p15]

Classroom Application

Superintendent John Gallo asked Mr. DiLorenzo, a curriculum coordinator, to recommend a comprehensive skills-based health education curriculum. District Youth Risk Behavior Survey data show the current program has not decreased student risk behaviors. The program does not begin until Grade 6 and relies on outdated textbooks and high school assemblies.

Mr. DiLorenzo was trained in the National Health Education Standards and knows that to reach the goal of health education—"to learn the knowledge and skills necessary to develop healthy behaviors"[1,p5]—students need sufficient time to learn content and practice skills. Consequently, he recommends a comprehensive and co-ordinated program in which students in PreK–2 receive a minimum of 40 hours of instruction, and Grades 3–12 receive 80 hours. These times were chosen because they are recommended by the National Health Education Standards and supported by Healthy People 2010 and the National School Boards Association.[1,p63]

Assembly programs were common in the old curriculum but now, instead of being stand-alone programs, they are coordinated and aligned with the curriculum. Mr. DiLorenzo also recommends that the health curriculum be revised to incorporate the Characteristics of Effective Health Education. One of the first tasks of the revision is to align standards, curriculum, instruction, and assessment from PreK–12.

The revised curriculum:

- Actively involves students in their learning.
- Uses a variety of learning strategies.
- Utilizes formative and summative assessment to improve teaching and learning.
- Engages parents and community members to reinforce healthy behaviors and enhance school health.[1,p63]

Through collaboration, the project was completed, and the school committee and administration approved the revised, comprehensive skills-based health education curriculum. They recognized that it contributes to the health and well-being of the school community and the academic success of students.

Characteristic Eleven: The Curriculum Provides Opportunities to Reinforce Skills and Positive Health Behaviors.

Effective curriculum builds on previously learned concepts and skills and reinforces health-promoting skills across health content areas and grade levels. To accomplish this, teachers plan for frequent skill practice in booster sessions in health or interdisciplinary classes.

To achieve long-lasting results, curriculum addresses age-appropriate determinates of behavior across grade levels and reinforces and builds upon previous learning.[1,p15]

Classroom Application

To build effective curriculum, Mrs. Marks engaged the help of her curriculum committee and the support of her coordinated school health council to design a district-wide PreK–12 comprehensive health curriculum aligned to the National Health Education Standards.

Mrs. Marks and the committees began by purchasing a curriculum listed as a Department of Education Exemplary Program. It provided a specific number of lessons per grade level and booster lessons. Because the program addressed only social skills, drugs, alcohol, tobacco, and safety, they added other content and skills to make the curriculum comprehensive. Teachers had sufficient time to teach the science-based program with fidelity because students in PreK–2 receive 40 hours of instruction and Grades 3–12 receive 80 hours.

They then mapped content and skills over the grade levels to ensure that students would receive common language, appropriate content, and consistent skill building. They also wanted students to use successfully in later years the concepts and skills they learned in earlier grades. The committee provided a scope and sequence for teachers that stated what the students should know and do across grade levels. They folded practice and demonstration time into instruction so that students could gain proficiency in content and skill.

Finally, the committees provided professional development in designing varied instructional strategies and assessment for teachers to become skilled in delivering and assessing the National Health Education Standards.

They allowed flexibility in case the district YRBS indicated that a certain risk factor needed to be addressed.

Characteristic Twelve: The Curriculum Provides Opportunities to Make Connections With Other Influential Persons.

Effective curriculum links students to other influential persons who support and reinforce health-promoting norms, beliefs, and behaviors.[1,p16] Instructional strategies build on protective factors, such as caring and school connectedness, because students who feel connected to their school are less likely to use tobacco, alcohol, or drugs, or be involved in violence, gangs, and early sex.[12]

Classroom Application

Mr. Wooley is the social worker for his school and a member of the coordinated school health (CSH) team. Because of his research on protective factors, he wants his colleagues to understand their importance in helping students develop healthy behaviors and be successful in school.

During a CSH meeting, he explained that one common thread in the study, Protective Factors in Individuals, Families, and Schools: National Longitudinal Study on Adolescent Health Findings, was that students thrive when they feel a sense of connectedness with family, school, and their community.[13,p2] According to the study, students must have caring relationships, high expectations, and opportunities for participation in order to enhance their health and healthy behaviors in the school.[13,p5]

Mr. Woolsey recommended that the members of the coordinated school health team design programs that foster connectedness and the opportunity to master and apply skills, such as peer helpers, cross-age tutoring, mentoring, volunteers in the classroom, cooperative learning, and community service learning. The team agreed to examine programs currently in place that connect students to the school and investigate other programs as well.

Mrs. Ramos, the health educator, mentioned that her curriculum is aligned to the National Health Education Standards, skills-based, utilizes cooperative learning, and provides the opportunity to master and apply content and skills. The peer leader advisor volunteered to initiate a peer helper and tutoring component in her program to increase protective factors.

The physical educator welcomed the idea of using peer leaders in the gym to help with warm-ups, managing equipment, and planning student activities. Mr. Woolsey volunteered to set up a mentoring program, and the Rotary Club president, Mr. Andrews, offered to manage a community service program.

At the meeting, the team also learned that students working more than 20 hours per week, appearing older than their peers, having same-sex attraction, and anticipating early death were characteristics that are associated with the six Centers for Disease Control and Prevention risk factors. These factors include use of alcohol and other drugs, injury and violence (including suicide), tobacco use, poor nutrition, inadequate physical activity, and risky sexual behavior.

The parent members of the team recommended supplementing existing programs with special presentations that addressed these risk factors and ways to cope with them healthfully. Mrs. Ramos reminded the team that stand-alone assemblies do not contribute to the adoption and maintenance of healthy behaviors, but she would include them as part of a comprehensive program to reinforce classroom instruction.

Characteristic Thirteen: The Curriculum Includes Teacher Information and Plans for Professional Development and Training to Enhance Effectiveness of Instruction and Student Learning.[1,p15]

Effective curriculum depends on well-trained instructors who are knowledgeable, competent, and committed to teaching content and skills. Training is continuous and takes many forms, such as comprehensive professional development in a district, courses on skills-based pedagogy, online instruction and training, professional reading, and using information learned at conferences and other special events.

Classroom Application

As the wellness curriculum coordinator in her district, Mrs. Butler was asked to make recommendations for professional development for the next school year. Mrs. Butler's department consists of PreK–12 health, family and consumer science, and physical education teachers. Their professional training and experience vary, and it is Mrs. Butler's challenge to prepare them to deliver effectively to students a new skills-based health education curriculum.

Mrs. Butler and her curriculum team revised the PreK–12 wellness curriculum, based on the National Standards in Health, Physical Education, and Family and Consumer Science. To train the staff to deliver skills-based curriculum, she surveyed the staff to determine their training needs. Staffers responded that they needed training in pedagogy, teaching skills, assessment, updates on current content, and time to practice implementation strategies.

Mrs. Butler contacted the state department of education, colleges that train teachers, and professional organizations to explore available resources. She discovered that the Department of Education provides a two-day workshop on skills-based health education and assessment with a one-day follow-up in which teachers return with evidence of student work. Mrs. Butler found a professor from the local college who teaches a mini-course on skills-based pedagogy and assessment and is willing to teach it in the district.

Mrs. Butler contracted with both institutions, reserved six professional development days for the staff to learn how to implement skills-based health education, use formative, and summative assessment strategies, practice skills, discuss their experiences in trying out these strategies, and integrate these skills into their daily teaching.

To ensure support from the district administrators, the superintendent and administrators from each school were invited to the professional development series. Mrs. Butler also asked for time at an administrator's meeting to explain the new curriculum and the plans for professional development.

Using the Characteristics of Effective Health Education while planning curriculum and instruction is vital for a quality program that helps students develop and maintain healthy behaviors and prepare for life in the 21st century.

Training Health Educators

"The most important factor affecting student learning is the teacher"[14]

Training for health educators begins during the preservice years of undergraduate studies. In addition to course work, many states require candidates to pass the Praxis assessment as part of the licensure and certification process. The Praxis I measures basic academic skills, and Praxis II measures general and subject knowledge and teaching skills.[15]

Training continues into post-service as the educator completes graduate courses to increase knowledge and skill. Once in the field, in-service professional development is provided by the state department of education, consultants, or the teacher's own district.

The National Health Education Standards, Achieving Excellence, contains a section on the essential role of partners in implementing the National Health Education Standards and examines how each can contribute to improving teacher education skills. For example, institutions of higher education can prepare future teachers to use a variety of instructional methods, strategies, technologies, and resources in health instruction to meet the learning styles, interests, and needs of a diverse student population.[1,p72]

CERTIFICATION

Individuals seeking additional credentials apply to become a Certified Health Education Specialist (CHES) or the Master Certified Health Education Specialist (MCHES). Candidates obtain this certification by passing a 150 question multiple choice examination based on the Seven Areas of Responsibilities,[16] similar to the college accreditation standards of the American Association for Health Education and the National Council for Accreditation of Teacher Education (AAHE/NCATE).[17] In addition, the MCHES meets academic eligibility in health education and is practicing at the advanced level, has passed the written exam, and has an ongoing commitment to professional development.[18] The National Commission for Health Education Credentialing administers the national competency-based examination, provides standards for professional preparation, and continuing education programs for health education professionals.[19]

There are several advantages to being a CHES or MCHES. All certified specialists are held to the same standard and have pride in their accomplishments. Achieving this level of certification also confirms a specialist's knowledge and skill and assists employers who seek highly qualified health educators. Because of the recertification requirements, quality professional development is promoted and available nationally.[20]

After initial certification, the specialist renews annually by payment or annual fee and recertifies every five years. Requirements for recertification include 75 hours of continuing education contact hours, 45% of the hours from a preapproved designated provider. If a CHES does not earn enough continuing education contact hours within a five-year span and is not granted an extension, recertification occurs by retaking the examination. Failure to pass the examination results in the ex-

piration of the certification at the end of the five-year period.[21]

ELEMENTARY TEACHER PREPARATION STANDARDS

Elementary teachers have the daunting responsibility of teaching all disciplines to their students. The training they receive, pre-service and in-service, is vital to their confidence to provide quality instruction that meets the needs of the students and the requirements of the district and the state.

Teaching health education to elementary students is challenging because it requires planning, resources, time, and training. Although most states require health to be taught on the elementary level, only a little more than half mandate elementary teachers to complete coursework in health education to qualify for certification as an elementary teacher. Teachers who finish at least one formal health education course are more likely to teach health education as part of their weekly lessons than teachers who have not. Also, the more coursework completed, the more health content areas they teach, and they do so more thoroughly.[22]

Training standards ensure quality teacher preparation programs. The Association for Childhood Education International provides the Elementary Education Standards and Supporting Explanation, 2007. These standards establish the criteria to train elementary teachers to teach health education. The standard states that the "candidate know, understand, and use the major concepts in health education to create opportunities for student development and the practice of skills that contribute to good health."[23]

To fulfill this requirement, the teacher must:

- Have an understanding of the foundations of good health, including the structure and function of the body and its systems, and the importance of physical fitness and sound nutrition.
- Help students understand the benefits of a healthy lifestyle for themselves and others.
- Know and teach the dangers of diseases and the activities that contribute to disease.
- Be alert to the major health issues pertaining to children and the social forces that affect them.
- Know how to deliver health information with sensitivity.
- Help students recognize potentially dangerous situations, clarify misconceptions, and find reliable sources of age-appropriate information for them.[23]

Completing coursework that meets the above standard ensures that elementary teachers are prepared, competent, and confident to teach health education content as an integral part of their overall instruction.

SECONDARY TEACHER PREPARATION STANDARDS

Just as there are eight national standards for health education, there are eight national health education program standards that provide the framework for what a secondary school health education teacher must know and do at the completion of the pre-service program. These national standards, discussed below, are a collaboration between the American Association for Health Education and the National Council for Accreditation of Teacher Education.[24]

Standard I, like the National Health Education Standards, is the content standard and says the candidate demonstrates the knowledge and skills of a health literate educator by describing the theoretical foundations of health behavior and principles of learning, the National Health Education Standards, practices that promote health or safety, behaviors that might compromise health or safety, disease etiology and prevention practices, and demonstrate the health literacy skills of an informed consumer of health products and services.[24]

In Standard II, the candidate assesses student needs and uses this knowledge to set priorities for school health education. The standard requires accessing reliable data sources related to health, such as from the Centers for Disease Control and Prevention's Youth Risk Behavior Survey. The ability to collect data and make inferences for the health education program based on that information is also vital.[24]

For Standard III, the aspiring teacher plans effective school health education curricula and programs. She designs strategies for involving key individuals and organizations in program planning for School Health Education. She designs a logical scope and sequence of learning experiences that accommodate all students. She learns to create appropriate and measureable learner objectives that align with the assessments and scoring guides. Developmentally appropriate strategies are selected to meet learning objectives. Health education curricula is aligned with needs assessment data and the National Health Education Standards. Finally, candidates analyze the feasibility of implementing selected strategies.[24]

In Standard IV, the candidate implements health education instruction. She demonstrates multiple instructional strategies that reflect effective pedagogy, health education theories, and models that facilitate learning for all students. She uses technology and resources that provide instruction in a challenging, clear, and compelling way and engages diverse learners. She exhibits competence in classroom management, reflects on implementation practices, adjusts objectives, instructional strategies, and assessments as necessary to enhance student learning.[24]

Standard V addresses the ability of a candidate to assess student learning. She develops assessment plans, analyzes available assessment instruments, develops instruments to assess student learning, implements plans to assess student learning, and utilizes assessment results to guide future instruction.[24]

Standard VI requires administration and coordination skills. Candidates plan and coordinate a school health education program by developing a plan for comprehensive school health within a coordinated school health program, explaining how a health education program fits the culture of a school and contributes to the school's mission, and designs a plan to collaborate with others such as school personnel, community health educators, and students' families in planning and implementing health education programs.[24]

Potential health educators are trained to serve as a resource in Standard VII. Candidates use health information resources, respond to requests for health information, select educational resource materials for dissemination, and describe ways to establish effective consultative relationships with others involved in CSHPs.[24]

Communicating and advocating for health and school health education are vital skills for health educators according to Standard VIII. Candidates analyze and respond to factors that impact current and future needs in comprehensive school health education. This standard calls for the application of a variety communication methods and techniques, advocating for school health education, and demonstrating professionalism.[24]

Professional Development

"Continuous, high-quality professional development is essential to the Nation's goal of high standards of learning for every child."[25]

According to the American Federation of Teachers, teachers are a school district's most important asset. To maintain and cultivate these assets, districts must invest in high quality, continuous professional development that results in improved instructional practice and student learning.[25,p1]

What defines high quality professional development? Teachers find value in professional development programs that connect an increase in knowledge and improvement in pedagogical skills to their everyday teaching responsibilities. When a district provides continuous training in the implementation of the National Health Education Standards with scheduled follow-ups, these criteria are fulfilled because the instruction targets a special population, increases knowledge to teach the standards, and provides the practice in skill development to implement them in the classroom.

High quality professional development offers clear directions to implement new knowledge and skill pedagogy, such as the implementation of the National Health Education Standards, and provides time to practice the new skills in a non-threatening environment with support from colleagues and administrators.[26,p134] Teachers need to know that they can experiment with the goal of improving teaching and learning. Colleagues and administrators show their support by encouraging experimentation but with the understanding that pedagogy that does not work is eliminated and those methods that do will be shared and continued.

Teachers move forward with a new pedagogy when they see its value. They are motivated by observing students actively engaged in a health performance task, working effectively as a member of a group, and using information taught in class to resolve an age-appropriate problem. Although it takes considerable time to plan a performance task, once the students receive their prompt, back-up information, and rubrics, they independently complete the assignment. At that point, their teacher is a coach who exhorts students to proficiency using various formative assessments. This new role is rewarding and stimulating for the teacher.

A teacher implementing the National Health Education Standards should be encouraged to collaborate with colleagues rather than develop lessons, assessments, and performance tasks in isolation. Observing and learning from teachers who successfully use new pedagogy, such as writing and implementing performance tasks, can improve the quality of skills-based health education lessons.

Professional development is usually a reflection of state, district, and school goals. If administrative follow-up to training is lacking, teachers may not comply with changes. The principal and other building administrators should make it clear that they expect to see the new pedagogy, will ask about the progress of its implementation, and intend to provide feedback on observational or invited walk-throughs.[26,p136]

Quality district-wide professional development is driven by data that identifies a need. It is coordinated and planned for multiple-year support that includes job-embedded coaching, reflection, feedback, administrative follow-up, and accountability planning.[27,p3]

Professional development:

- *Deepens and broadens knowledge and content.*[25,p1]

    Because teachers provide high quality instruction that results in students' meeting district, state, and national standards, they must have a deep and broad knowledge of health education content and be proficient in teaching the national skills. Given that health education content is always changing and skill pedagogy varies, teachers must receive updated information and ongoing training to maintain quality instruction.

    When hiring health teachers, districts know that pre-service training varies, and they may require a

physical educator or a teacher from another discipline to implement health education instruction. Consequently, the national standards recommend that districts provide high quality, continuous professional development in health education content and pedagogy to promote consistent, quality instruction.[1,p.65]

- *Provides a strong foundation in the pedagogy of particular disciplines.*[25,p1]

    Although some teaching strategies are common to all disciplines, health education has its own uniqueness. Skills-based health education embodies a distinctive pedagogy whereby content is taught through a skill. Teachers must have access to valid and reliable health education information and learn how to model and teach skills. Students demonstrate proficiency in content and skills through an authentic assessment, such as a performance task.

    Educators need knowledge of health content, craft in formulating and implementing authentic assessment strategies, specific training in skills-based teaching techniques, and the ability to design and use formative and summative assessments, as well as holistic and analytical rubrics.

- *Imparts knowledge about teaching and learning processes.*[25,p1]

    The implementation of the National Health Education Standards requires training in health content, the teaching of skills, and assessment. For a teacher to be a successful practitioner, he must have teaching skill and understand how learning occurs. Initially, he learns how to teach during pre-service, and once in the field, perseveres through exposure to continuing education and in-service.

    Pre-service training advocates using learning theories to promote student learning. In-service professional development uses various theories for teachers to improve their instruction and student achievement. The professional development trainer adapts instruction to accommodate the various learning styles of the teachers and demonstrates styles unfamiliar to the teacher but inherent in the learner.

    To provide knowledge about teaching and learning, the trainer models the strategies the teachers eventually implement. Sufficient time exists for the teachers to practice the new strategies and skills and receive feedback (formative assessment) to improve.[28]

    Professional development trains teachers to understand student cognitive and social/emotional characteristics in order to provide developmentally appropriate curriculum and instruction. During training, teachers learn strategies to engage the strengths and interests of the students. This approach helps the learner absorb meaningful and relevant content and skills to maintain a healthy lifestyle and enhance academic achievement.[29]

- *Is rooted in and reflects the best available research*[25,p1]

Professional development research suggests that training is more successful when narrow in scope.[30] It should concentrate on specific educational elements, such as analyzing data to establish student need, planning instructional strategies or performance tasks, learning about and implementing skills-based pedagogy, and using formative and summative assessments to improve student achievement.

State education agencies have access to professional development research and best practices. They must provide all teachers with leadership in regards to best practices for health education instruction. One way of accomplishing this is to promote PreK–12 health education curricula and programs that are consistent with best practice recommendations of federal agencies or professional education and health organizations.[1,p69] States also guide local education associations to adopt research-based health education curricula and programs that are aligned with the National Health Education Standards.

The United States Department of Education publishes a list of exemplary and promising programs that are research based. It may be found at: http://www.ed.gov/admins/lead/safety/exemplary01/exemplary01.pdf.[31]

The Centers for Disease Control and Prevention posts School Health Education Resources (http://apps.nccd.cdc.gov/sher/) that reference the Characteristics of Effective Health Education and the National Health Education Standards.[4]

- *Is aligned with the standards and curriculum teachers use.*[25,p1]

The National Health Education Standards, Achieving Excellence, Second Edition, recommends that districts implement a PreK–12 comprehensive health education curriculum aligned with the national and state standards.[1,p65] As such, teachers receive professional development that trains them how to teach and implement skills-based health education.

To assist the professional development efforts of local education agencies and individual teachers, state education agencies must provide curricular and instructional support materials, such a state standards, scope and sequence, alignment and mapping tools, and frameworks to meet the National Health Education Standards or state standards.[1,p69]

- *Contributes to measurable improvement in student achievement.*[25,p1]

Professional development increases the knowledge and skill of the teacher by providing training in health education content and skills through research-based instructional strategies. The goal of professional development is practical: the teacher uses the new knowledge and skill to increase student achievement.[32]

Barriers to student achievement include behavioral risk factors such as alcohol and other drug use, injury, and violence, including suicide, tobacco use, poor nutrition, inadequate physical activity, and risky sexual conduct. Therefore, teachers deliver health education content and skills to decrease such risks.

Health teachers are trained to analyze and interpret data, establish the needs of the students based on the data (Youth Risk Behavior Survey, state and district assessments, police reports, and community surveys), forge appropriate assessment instruments, implement formative and summative assessments, and develop instruction and curriculum that decreases risky behaviors and develops and maintains healthy behaviors.

In evaluating the effectiveness of professional development, teachers assess the relationships between training and changes made in pedagogy, the decrease in student risk factors, and improvement in learning. Positive results encourage teachers to continue implementing the new strategies.[33]

- *Is engaging intellectually and addresses the complexity of teaching.*[25,p1]

Professional development, as skills-based instruction, engages the mind and reflects the complexity of teaching. It does so by inviting teachers to participate in a summer workshop that continues with follow-up sessions throughout the school year. Another example is training teachers as content leaders in a summer program and then asking them to facilitate in-service workshops during the school year. Teachers are engaged and learn about the complexities of teaching by becoming an intern with various health organizations, take electronic or traditional courses, participate in health education networks and study groups, receive or provide classroom coaching, watch demonstrations of high performing skilled teachers and engage in a follow-up discussion thereafter, collegial conversations, shared decision-making groups, reflective journals, and parent forums.

- *Provides sufficient time, support, and resources for teachers to master new content and pedagogy and integrate this knowledge and skill into their practice.*[25,p3]

Because The No Child Left Behind Act (2002) requires school districts to position highly qualified teachers in every classroom, excellent professional development is essential to teacher training. Proper time, support, and resources are mandatory for teachers to master new content and skill then integrate it into their instruction.

The scheduling of adequate and convenient time for professional development is an important topic of discussion in the management of schools. The 2005 National Education Commission on Time and Learning recommended that districts find adequate time for professional development by extending the contract year, lengthening the teacher day, releasing teachers during the school day by hiring well-prepared substitute teachers, providing summer training institutes, offering intercession training opportunities, and designing schedules with common planning opportunities.[27]

The National Staff Development Council recommends that at least 25% of a teacher's time be allocated for professional development. This amount is essential to learn, practice, and incorporate complicated strategies into daily practice.[27] District leaders, who are committed to quality professional development, understand the relationship between the professional learning of teachers and improved student performance. They develop and implement policies that support ongoing professional learning, including collaboration time, equitable resources for all departments to reach school and district goals, and the evaluation of staff development effectiveness in helping students achieve learning goals.[34]

■ *Is designed by teachers in cooperation with experts in the field.*[25,p1]

Districts have a responsibility to set educational goals based on student needs. All professional development is aligned with district goals. Although some training is district-wide, time is scheduled for department and building specific training through in-service, department meetings, building meetings, or other creative models.

Teachers have an active role in the planning of discipline training, including developing the goals and agenda, accessing experts in the field, and establishing the training and assessment pedagogy. For example, during the first year of implementing skills-based instruction, teachers request time for collegial planning of performance tasks, prompts, and assessments. After implementing them, the teachers request that colleagues observe their teaching, provide feedback, and make suggestions for improvement. If colleagues believe an expert in the field is needed for additional training or support, the district provides the resources from a variety of venues including businesses, community, state agencies, organizations, and institutions.[1,p78]

When teachers are recognized in this professional capacity, it empowers them to participate more fully in the development and implementation of staff training. They become comfortable and competent to continue the design and implementation of skills-based lessons, share those ideas, and participate in discussions about best practices and improved student performance.[35]

State education agencies are authorities in the field. Their expertise and training are accessible to all professional staff, including teachers, curriculum specialists, and district leaders.[1,p69] National organiza-

tions are also an excellent resource. They provide high-grade professional development programs for local and state education agencies as well as institutions of higher learning who, in turn, can offer that training to districts.[1,p75]

■ *Takes various forms, including some we have not typically considered.*[25,p1]

Professional development uses the same variety of research-based instructional strategies that teachers are expected to implement with students. The learning strategies are based on intended outcomes and an analysis of staff needs. Strategies may vary, focusing on the individual teacher or a group. They include peer coaching, action research, study groups, collaboration with a content expert, an extended summer institute with follow-up sessions throughout the school year, collaborative assessment and lesson planning to align instruction to standards, group examination and discussion of student work, a course on the development of formative and summative assessments, virtual learning communities, video models of new instructional strategies, and demonstrations of skills-based assessment and instruction.[36]

Learning teams are a unique aspect of ongoing professional development. Four to eight health education team members work together to improve the teaching and learning of their group by taking responsibility for the learning of their students. They examine the strategies needed for the mastery of the National Health Education Standards, develop assessments, plan effective skills-based lessons and performance tasks, analyze student work, and solve common instructional and skills-based implementation problems. The team decides what professional development training is required for their professional needs. They research resources, attend workshops or courses, observe each other to improve instruction, and request consultant help, when needed, to increase knowledge and skill.[37]

Another type of professional development is **action research**, whereby a teacher or colleagues develop strategies to improve instruction and student achievement. The process begins when staff identifies a problem that commonly occurs in the classroom or school. Information and data about the issue and possible solutions are collected, analyzed, and discussed. Teachers develop an action plan and implement it with the support of the school and district administration. Over time, the plan is reviewed for its impact on improved student achievement, and the subsequent feedback directs the future course of the project.[38] This procedure is an effective professional development strategy because it is initiated, researched, and implemented by the teachers with support from school administrators. The results impact student performance.

Another alternative form is the study group, which focuses on depth of content and skill rather than breadth. For example, the study group designs a long-term plan that includes teaching a certain number of standards each year rather than implanting all the national health standards in one year. They design and implement performance tasks and assessments for the chosen standards, evaluate the implementation at the end of the year, and use that information to improve the process for the following year.[7,p317]

- *Is job-embedded and site specific.*[25,p1]

To embed professional development into ongoing contractual requirements, districts use in-service time and a portion of department and principal meetings. For example, during the summer, educators from all disciplines rewrite curriculum. Health educators write several age-specific performance tasks that include Standard 1 content and targeted skills. The performance tasks are implemented over the school year, and teachers meet to discuss them during a portion of the monthly department meetings. Time at principal meetings is set aside for all disciplines to discuss the implementation of new curriculum and receive feedback to improve their work. The new tested and revised curriculum is placed online so that any colleague in the district can use the materials.[7,p318] This strategy is sound, practical professional development because the work is relevant and embedded in the norms and values of the school. Time is provided for colleagues to work with one another within disciplines and at their schools to improve their knowledge and skills.[35]

Knowing how to assess student need; map; select content and skill performance indicators; design skills-based units; access curriculum resources; align assessment, curriculum, and instruction to the performance indicators; and use the Characteristics of Effective Health Education to plan instruction and curriculum are skills that take a long time to develop. The foundation for learning and practicing these skills occurs during pre-service training and continues in the field with graduate courses, advanced degrees, and district professional development. When preparing for a teaching career, be prepared to be not only the purveyor of knowledge and skills but also a life-long learner yourself.

Review Questions

1. Explain how to use the performance indicators to map content to the National Health Education Standards.

2. How does a teacher know when instruction should continue or whether reviewing and re-teaching is necessary?

3. Choose a performance indicator and explain how you would use Backwards Design to develop curriculum and instruction.

4. Explain how the standards are the foundation of assessment and curriculum development.

5. Choose two Characteristics of Effective Health Education and explain how they contribute to developing and maintaining healthy behaviors.

6. Why is it important to use curriculum that is research based and theory driven?

7. Explain how two of the standards established by the Association of Childhood Education International prepare candidates to teach elementary health education.

8. Explain how two of the standards established by the American Association of Health Education and the National Council of Accreditation of Teacher Education prepare candidates to teach middle and high school health education.

9. Choose one American Federation of Teachers criteria for professional development and explain how it improves teacher competence and enhances student learning.

10. Explain one professional development pedagogy or style and explain why teachers would want to participate in it.

References

1. Joint Committee on National Health Education Standards. (2007). *National Health Education Standards, Second Edition, Achieving Excellence.* Atlanta: American Cancer Society.
2. Jacobs, H. H. (2004). *Getting Results with Curriculum Mapping.* Alexandria: Association for Supervision and Curriculum Development, p. vii.
3. Centers for Disease Control and Prevention. (2007). Health Education Curriculum Analysis Tool. Atlanta, GA: Centers for Disease Control and Prevention.
4. Center for Disease Control and Prevention. (2008, December 10). *CDC's School Health Education Resources (SHER).* Retrieved May 1, 2009, from Healthy Youth!: http://apps.nccd.cdc.gov/sher/
5. CCSSO~SCASS Health Education Project. (2006). *Assessment Tools for School Health Education, Pre-service and In-service edition.* Santa Cruz, CA: ToucanEd Inc., p. 6.
6. Meeks, L. H. (2011). *Comprehensive School Health Education, Totally Awesome Strategies for Teaching Health.* (7th ed.). New York: McGraw-Hill.
7. Wiggins, G. M. (2005). *Understanding by Design, Expanded.* (2nd ed.). Alexandria, VA: Association for Supervision and Curriculum Development.
8. Tomlinson, C. A. (2006). *Integrating Differentiated Instruction + Understanding by Design.* Alexandria, VA: Association for Supervision and Curriculum Development, p. 28.

9. National Highway Traffic Safety Administration. (2006, September). *Easy Steps to Properly Fit a Bicycle Helmet*. Retrieved March 18, 2009, from National Highway Traffic Safety Administration: http://www.nhtsa.dot.gov/people/injury/pedbimot/bike/EasyStepsWeb/index.htm

10. University of Twente. (2004, September 09). *Social Cognitive Theory*. Retrieved September 28, 2008, from University of Twente, The Netherlands: http://www.tcw.utwente.nl/theorieenoverzicht/Theory%20clusters/Health%20Communication

11. Sapon-Shevin, M. (2008, September). Learning in an Inclusive Community. *Educational Leadership*, pp. 49–53.

12. Centers for Disease Control and Prevention. (2009, March 10). *Strategies for Increasing Protective Factors Among Youth, School Connectedness*. Retrieved April 9, 2009, from National Center for Chronic Disease Prevention and Health Promotion, Healthy Youth!: http://www.cdc.gov/Healthy Youth/AdolescentHealth/connectedness.htm

13. Benard, B., & Marshall, K. (2001). *Protective Factors in Individuals, Families, and Schools: National Longitudinal Study on Adolescent Health Findings*. National Resilience Resource Center, University of Minnesota, College of Continuing Education.

14. Marzano, R. J., Pickering, D. J., & Pollock, J. E. (2001). *Classroom Instruction that Works*. Alexandria: Association for Supervision and Curriculum Development, p. 3.

15. Educational Testing Service. (2008). *The Praxis Series: Teacher Licensure & Certification*. Retrieved May 13, 2010, from ETS – The Praxis Series. http://www.ets.org/portal/site/ets/menuitem.fab2360b1645a1de9b3a0779f1751509/?vgnextoid=48c05ee3d74f4010VgnVCM10000022f95190RCRD&WT.ac=Praxis+Brochure+and+Front+Door

16. National Commission for Health Education Credentialing, Inc. (2006). *Areas of Responsibility and Competencies for Health Educators*. Whitehall: Author.

17. Hillman K. W. (2010). *Guidelines for 2008 AAHE/NCATE Health Education Teacher Preparation Standards*. Reston: American Association of Health Education.

18. National Commission for Health Education Credentialing. (2008). *Overview*. Retrieved May 14, 2010, from NCHEC: http://www.nchec.org/exam/overview/

19. National Commission for Health Education Credentialing. (2008). *Mission and Purpose*. Retrieved May 14, 2010, from NCHEC: http://www.nchec.org/aboutnchec/mission/

20. National Commission for Health Education Credentialing. (2008). *Health Education Credentialing*. Retrieved May 14, 2010, from NCHEC: http://www.nchec.org/credentialing/credential/

21. National Commission for Health Education Credentialing. (2008). *Renewal and Recertification Requirements*. Retrieved May 14, 2010, from NCHEC: http://www.nchec.org/renew_recert/recertification/

22. Seabert, D. M.-H. (2002). The Influence of Preservice Instruction in Health Education Methods on the Health Content Taught by Elementary Teachers in Indiana. *Journal of School Health*, p. 425.

23. Association for Childhood Education International. (2007). *Elementary Education Standards and Supporting Explanation, 2007*. Retrieved August 31, 2009, from National Council for Accreditation of Teacher Education: www.ncate.org/public/programStandards.asp?ch=4. p. 96.

24. Hillman, K., Wooley, S., Muller, S., Fortune, D., Patterson, S., Wengert, D., et al. (2010). Guidelines for 2008 AAHE/NCATE Health Education Preparation Standards. Reston, VA: AAHPERD.

25. American Federation of Teachers. (n.d.). *Professional Development for Teachers*. Retrieved September 9, 2009, from AFT—Hot Topics—Teacher Quality—Professional Development for Teachers: www.aft.org/topics/teacher-quality/prodev.htm. p. 1.

26. O'Shea, M. R. (2005). *From Standards to Success*. Alexandria, VA: Association for Supervision and Curriculum Development.

27. Central Regional Educational Laboratory. (2004). *Critical Issue: Providing More Time for Professional Development*. Retrieved September 6, 2009, from Providing More Time for Professional Development: www.ncrel.org/sdrs/areas/issues/educatrs/profdevl/pd600.htm.p3

28. National Staff Development Council. (n.d.). *Learning*. Retrieved September 9, 2009, from: www.nsdc.org/standards/learning.cfm

29. National Staff Development Council. (n.d.). *Equity*. Retrieved September 9, 2009, from: www.nsdc.org/standards/equity.cfm

30. Reeves, D. (2006). *The Learning Leader, How to Focus School Improvement for Better Results*. Alexandria: Association for Supervision and Curriculum Development, p. 79.

31. U.S. Department of Education, Safe, Disciplined, and Drug-Free Schools Expert Panel. (2002, April). *Exemplary & Promising Safe, Disciplined & Drug Free Schools Programs, 2001*. Jessup, MD. Retrieved from: http://www.ed.gov/admins/lead/safety/exemplary01/exemplary01.pdf

32. National Staff Development Council. (n.d.). *Quality Teaching*. Retrieved September 9, 2009, from: www.nsdc.org/standards/qualityteaching.cfm

33. National Staff Development Council. (n.d.). *Data-Driven*. Retrieved September 9, 2009, from: www.nsdc.org/standards/datadriven.cfm

34. National Staff Development Council. (n.d.). *Leadership*. Retrieved September 9, 2009, from: www.nsdc.org/standards/leadership.cfm

35. Danielson, C. (2002). *Enhancing Student Achievement, A Framework for School Improvement*. Alexandria: Association for Supervision and Curriculum Development, p. 9.

36. National Staff Development Council. (n.d.). *Designs and Strategies*. Retrieved September 9, 2009, from: www.nsdc.org/standards/design.cfm

37. National Staff Development Council. (n.d.). *Learning Communities*. Retrieved September 9, 2009, from: www.nsdc.org/standards/learningcommunities.cfm?printPage=1&

38. Ferrance, E. (2000). *Themes in Education. Action Research*. Providence: Brown University, p. 6.

Assessment 4

"If it is worth teaching, it is worth assessing." [1,p78]

Assessment is a continuous cycle of establishing clear, measurable outcomes of student learning, providing time for the students to practice, then gathering, analyzing, and interpreting evidence to determine whether student learning matches performance indicators, and then using those results to improve teaching and learning (**Figure 4.1**).[2,p4]

Purpose of Assessment

Assessment improves teaching and learning. Assessment strategies are based on the targeted performance indicators of Standard 1 and Standards 2–8. Once established, the teacher develops the instruction.

At the beginning of a unit, the teacher explains the performance indicators, assessments, grading, and how the student demonstrates proficiency. Throughout the unit, the teacher uses **formative assessments** and provides feedback from the assessments to inform students of their progress in reaching the performance indicators.[1,p36]

Consequently, the teacher may re-teach or review a portion of the instruction that is unclear. Students receive time to practice and revise their performance or product prior to the summative assessment. As the teacher analyzes the formative and summative assessments, he improves upon the delivery of content and skill instruction. This assessment cycle results in improvements to teaching and learning.

The word assess *is derived from Latin and means "to sit with" the student.*[3,p337] To assess, therefore, we monitor our students' learning and their practice of content and skills, compare those observations to the established criteria, then we "sit with them" (provide thoughtful feedback) to help them achieve the standard.

Assessment Versus Grading

Assessment is especially valuable because it identifies student progress in reaching the National Health Education Standards. Formative assessment is not graded, occurs through a variety of classroom tools during instruction, and takes many forms, such as observation, conversations, and self-assessments.[3,p6] It provides feedback to help students understand their progress in meeting the criteria of the performance indicators and helps teachers determine if instruction needs review or can move forward. Assessment that occurs at the end of an instructional unit, quarter, semester, or year is **summative assessment** and is usually graded.

Grading measures what students have achieved on a quiz or test, not their learning. We can assume that if a

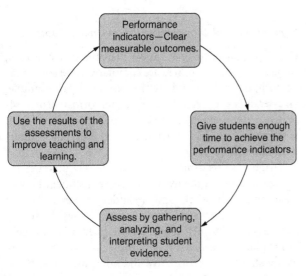

FIGURE 4.1 Assessment Cycle

student scored a 95% on the test, she has learned the content of the unit. Unless the questions on the test represent the targeted standards and performance indicators, however, the teacher learns only the ability of the student to recall facts or information, not how well she has reached the high expectations of the standard. The grade is also a result of the student's reading, writing, and test-taking ability, not just her recall of information.

Sometimes a final grade includes a student's attendance, effort, class participation, and a grade adjustment due to tardiness, etc. These elements, although important, have little to do with how much the student learns and do not contribute significantly to standards accountability. A final grade also does not account for what the student learns during an ungraded classroom activity. [2,p10-11]

Teachers are accountable to their students, administrators, and parents based on student grades. The accountability is substantive, however, when it is rooted in evidence of student learning, such as meeting the performance indicators through a performance task. [2,p11]

Using Assessment in the Classroom

To improve teaching and learning, the teacher continuously assesses by observing students as they talk in groups, ask or answer questions, work on performance tasks and class assignments, sit quietly, look confident, or look confused. Based on these assessments, the teacher gives feedback to the student to help her achieve the performance task and adjusts instruction to improve learning, as necessary. [4]

Assessment is a mutual responsibility and collaborative effort between the teacher and the students. The teacher provides information, direction, and coaching for success. The students take more responsibility for their learning because they understand the expectations, assessments, and grading. They are motivated to complete assignments and know to ask for help when needed. In fact, assessment increases student ownership of learning and results in increased self-efficacy and self-regulation skills. [5] Assessment is a win-win situation for teaching and learning.

We plan assessments as soon as the performance indicators are infused with the targeted content. Using the backwards design model, we ask the assessment question, "What can my students do or produce to show me that they are proficient in this content (Standard 1) or that skill (Standards 2–6)?

Once we have that answer, the direction of the instruction is clear. We assess students as they learn content and skill (formative), provide feedback for their improve-ment, make adjustments to instruction when needed, coach them to proficiency, then assess a final product that produces a grade (summative). Classroom assessment also enhances student achievement on written quizzes and tests because students are better prepared to succeed on a graded assessment as they increase their knowledge and skill through practice and formative assessment.

The power of assessment lies in using the information gathered from different assessments to improve teaching and learning. Throughout a skills unit, the teacher reflects on the lesson and asks, "Is there a more effective way I can teach this content and skill?" Sometimes an idea comes from training, professional development, colleagues, or even the students themselves. Regardless of the source, a good teacher continuously improves instruction to enhance learning.

Using a variety of assessment tools gives the teacher different perspectives regarding what the student knows and can do. Assessments may range from informal checks of understanding such as observations and dialogues to more formal graded tests, quizzes, performance tasks, and projects. [3,p152] The students benefit because they have numerous ways to show what content they have learned and the proficiency with which they can perform and explain a skill.

FORMATIVE AND SUMMATIVE ASSESSMENT

Assessment *for* learning is formative and ongoing and occurs during each lesson to determine what the students know as compared to the content and skill taught.

Summative assessment is an evaluation *of* learning that takes place at the end of instruction. It represents the status of the student at a given time regarding her proficiency of a standard. Summative assessment tools, such as tests, exams, and performance tasks, help the teacher assign grades and communicate student progress to families and school administrators.

Formative and Summative Assessment Tools

Of the various assessment tools available to the teacher, some are formative, others are summative, and some may be both, depending on how they are used. For example, an assessment conference can be either formative or summative. If used during instruction to improve learning, it is formative. If held following a test to explain the grade, it is summative.

Diagnostic assessment (pre-test) usually precedes instruction, informs the teacher of current student knowledge and skill level, and includes surveys, content questions, and skills checks. The teacher uses the results to plan and guide instruction and to differentiate instructional plans as needed. Because these pre-assessments are diagnostic, they are formative and not summative. [6,p12]

Student self-assessment and teacher observation occur during instruction and are generally formative, meaning ungraded. Their purpose is to improve learning. Constructed response, selected response, and quizzes or tests that are ungraded are also formative. If graded, these instruments are summative.

A demonstration, oral report, performance task, or essay are usually products of a project and, consequently, summative assessments. If done for practice and feedback, however, they are formative.

Portfolios show evidence of a student's progress over time in achieving the national standards. The portfolios may contain various media, such as electronic, paper, or video. If the items are terminal projects or performances and graded, the portfolio is summative. If the purpose of the portfolio is to examine how learning has progressed, it is formative.

Formative Assessment

"Formative assessment includes all those activities undertaken by teachers and/or by students which provide information to be used as feedback to modify the teaching and learning activities in which they engage."[7,p9]

Formative assessment is evaluation *for* learning. It measures student progress toward achieving the content and skill performance indicators. By using a variety of formative assessment tools and strategies, the teacher learns how the students are progressing. Once she ascertains student status, the teacher shares that information with the students so they can move forward with confidence or make corrections. These assessments are formal or informal and include ungraded quizzes, oral questioning, teacher observation, draft work, think-out-louds, student constructed concept maps, learning logs, and portfolio reviews.[6,p12]

Assessment *for* learning benefits the teacher and the student. Paul Black and Dylan William concluded from their research that formative assessment improves learning. In fact, the gains made by using formative assessment are "among the largest ever reported for educational interventions."[7,p2] Whereas teachers use the results of these assessments to advance instruction, students employ them to improve learning.

Formative Assessment Tools

A variety of formative assessment tools are available to assess the status of student learning. These tools are fun, easy, and interactive and provide immediate feedback for teachers to polish instruction while helping students improve their learning. The tools can be divided into two categories, group or individual.

Thumbs Up/Thumbs Down[8,p49]

While explaining the skill of goal setting, Mrs. Waters asks the students to show a thumbs up if they understand, thumbs to the side if not sure, or a thumbs down if confused. The thumbs are held close to the body so that Mrs. Waters can assess whether to continue her instruction, reteach a portion of the lesson, or work with individual students to uncover their source of confusion and correct it.

Pictures of thumbs are a variation of thumbs up/thumbs to the side/thumbs down. Students place the pictures on their desks and, when the teacher asks a question, they hold up the appropriate picture.

If the department has popsicle sticks, paste each picture to a stick. When the teacher asks a question, the students raise the appropriate stick picture.

"Give Me Five"[8,p48]

Mr. Erickson and his students like hand signals, and he uses them to check for understanding. After teaching content or skill, he instructs them:

"Show me five fingers if you understand and can demonstrate all of what we have just learned."

"Show me four fingers if you understand and can demonstrate most of what we have just learned."

"Show me three fingers if you understand and can demonstrate some of what we have just learned."

"Show me two fingers if you are confused about what we have just learned."

"Show me one finger if you do not understand what we have just learned."

Stop Lights[9,p61]

Mrs. Desperato returned from a formative assessment, professional development training determined to put into action some of the assessment strategies she learned. That evening, she used Microsoft Word to draw three circles, filling one with green, another yellow, and a third, red. She made one set for each of her students.

In the morning, she explained to the class that the purpose of the circles was to check for understanding. "If you understand the lesson, show me the green circle. If you are uncertain, use yellow, if you do not understand, flash red."

After teaching the 4.5.2 performance indicator, "Demonstrate refusal skills that avoid or reduce health risks,"[10,p30] she directed her students to place the green circles up if they understood how to demonstrate refusal skills, the yellow one up if they were not sure, and the red up if they did not understand.

Mrs. Desperato was pleased to see almost all green circles on the students' desks. During skill practice, she approached the students who showed a yellow circle and clarified their confusion. As the students were leaving, she asked them to write a note (one minute essay) expressing how they felt about the colored circles. All the students enjoyed using them because they did not have to say aloud whether they understood the instruction or not. The students who did understand also liked the formative assessment because they did not have to listen to repeated instruction that they already knew.

Green, Yellow, Red Rectangles[5,p54]

Mr. Stenberg, a middle school health educator, has been a member of the Association for Supervision and Curriculum Development for ten years. Every month he looks forward to receiving *Educational Leadership* because it has such timely and interesting articles about teaching. He was keenly interested in an article in the November edition titled, "Formative Assessment that Empowers,"[5,p54] because it showed how to use a simple, formative assessment tool.

During a unit on decision making, Mr. Stenberg taught about the hazards of alcohol, tobacco, and other drugs. He wanted his students to be knowledgeable about the dangers of drugs so they would make healthy decisions.

While teaching the skill of decision making and the different content areas that would be required in the performance task, Mr. Stenberg planned to check for understanding. He made each pair of students a packet that contained a piece of green, yellow, and red construction paper and questions on 3 × 5 cards about the skill of decision making and the hazards of using alcohol, tobacco, and other drugs.

Mr. Stenberg paired the students, and they took turns asking and answering the questions. If the students answered correctly, they placed the card on the green paper. If they were unsure or wrong, the students placed their cards on either the yellow or the red paper. They then reviewed the cards on the yellow and red papers and continued answering until correct. Mr. Stenberg's goal was to have all the cards on the green paper by the end of the session.

The students loved this activity because they worked with a peer and reviewed the questions in a fun way. As Mr. Stenberg walked around the classroom, all the students were actively involved. He effectively and efficiently checked for understanding.

Letter-Card Responses[9,p58-59]

To engage every student in checking for understanding, Mrs. W. James likes to use the Letter-Card Response activity. She has prepared sets of seven index cards, each one with the following: A, B, C, D, T, F, and a question mark symbol.

Mrs. W. James asks a question about health content or skill and gives four choices, A, B, C, D, and the students raise the card with the correct answer. This immediate feedback tells Mrs. W. James whether she should continue instruction or review. She can also ask questions with a true (T) or false (F) answer or allow students to show uncertainty by raising their question mark.

Random Response Question and Answer[9,p59]

Mr. Jackson has devised a clever system to engage his class in checking for understanding. He distributed tongue depressors to the students and asked them to put their names on it and decorate with pictures or words that are meaningful to them. Mr. Jackson made a stick to model the procedure and explained his pictures of dancing, swimming, and walking along the beach. The students liked learning about what Mr. Jackson does in his leisure time.

The sticks were placed in a bag. When Mr. Jackson was ready to check for understanding, he asked a question and then picked a stick from the bag. This strategy kept all his students attentive because they did not know what question would be asked or who would be called to answer.

If a student gave an incorrect response, another stick was pulled from the bag, and a different student had the opportunity to answer. The personal messages on the sticks also gave Mr. Jackson an easy way to open communication with students about hobbies, interests, etc.

At the end of the assessment, Mr. Jackson determines whether his students understood the content and adjusts his instruction accordingly. He sorted the sticks as students answered correctly or incorrectly. By doing so, he knows where each student stands.

Whiteboard Responses[9,p60]

Mrs. Shute is always looking for innovative ways to check for understanding. During one of the district's professional development days, she received training on how to use mini-white boards to formatively assess student learning and decided to try it. The district bought a class set of white board and markers for each teacher completing the training.

Mrs. Shute's students were learning how to advocate for healthy snacks, so she taught content about nutrition and physical activity. She distributed the boards and markers and said, "Draw the equation that represents how to maintain weight." She likes this technique because it is not limited to an A, B, C, D answer.

Most of the students drew food on one side, an equal sign in the middle, and exercise on the other side. She was pleased that the students had such a good grasp of the content and felt she moved forward in the unit. Mrs. Shute worked with the students who did not get the correct answer and clarified the input vs. output equation.

When Mrs. Shute was at the grocery store, she spotted disposable plates that had a hard coating, much just like the white boards. She wrote on them with a dry erase marker and found they worked just as well as the white boards but cost a lot less!

The Traffic Light Signal[9,p62]

Visuals have always worked well in Mr. Donaldson's 3rd grade class. One of his favorite strategies for checking for understanding is to use traffic light cups, so he gives each student a green, yellow, and red cup. When instruction begins, the students stack their cups open end down with the green on top.

Thereafter, Mr. Donaldson asks questions that will demonstrate to him whether his students understand the concept. If the student thinks she knows the information enough to explain it to another student, she keeps the green cup on top. If unsure, she puts the yellow cup on top. If she does not understand, she places the red one on top.

To verify that anyone who placed a green cup on top really knows the answer, Mr. Donaldson occasionally asks a green cup student to explain a concept.

Rate It

Rate It, developed by Central Michigan University and distributed by the Educational Materials Center, is an excellent formative assessment tool to determine the status of the class.

Students place green, yellow, or red chips into a box in response to a question asked by the teacher. If the students are confident about their answer, they place a green chip in the box; if uncertain, a yellow chip. If they do not know, they place a red one.

When the students are engaged in another activity or have left the classroom, the box is checked for the color distribution. This rating system allows the students to respond anonymously and informs the teacher regarding the scope of understanding about a topic, question, or opinion.

There, Almost There, Not Even Close[11]

While taking a course for her master's degree, Mrs. Perry learned the power of formative assessment and was required to create a formative assessment tool she could use with her students.

Knowing that her high school students needed an anonymous way to communicate their understanding,

FIGURE 4.2   There, Almost There, Not Even Close (Horizontal)

she designed a simple but effective tool. On a piece of paper, she wrote "There" in one rectangle, "Almost There" in another, and "Not Even Close" in a third. She folded the paper into thirds so that one message displayed on each of the sections, thereby forming three sides (**Figure 4.2**).

When checking for understanding, Mrs. Perry asked a question, then told the students to turn their triangles towards her so that one of the indicators, "There," "Almost There," "Not Even Close," was facing front. The students liked this strategy because no one else could see their answers. Mrs. Perry received a clear message about the status of the class.

Mrs. Perry varies this formative assessment by printing all three rectangles one on top of another on one sheet of paper (see **Figure 4.3**). She asks students to hold up the paper and use their finger as the mercury in a thermometer. If they understand, meaning There, the finger rises to the top; Almost There, hovers in the middle; and Not Even Close, sends their finger to the bottom.

Bull's Eye[12]

While teaching the skill of analyzing influences, Mr. Suarez wanted to ascertain whether his students understood its components before continuing instruction. He

FIGURE 4.3   There, Almost There, Not Even Close (Vertical)

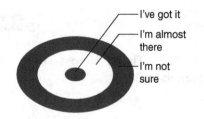

FIGURE 4.4　Bull's Eye

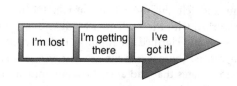

FIGURE 4.6　Learning Continuum

placed the Bull's Eye on the wall (**Figure 4.4**) and, while the students were involved in a class activity, asked them to put a check mark in the appropriate ring.

By the time the class activity was over, Mr. Suarez had a good idea how many students did or did not understand the skill. He reviewed the skill before continuing to bring everyone to the same level. He repeated the formative assessment as the students were leaving, and all hit the Bull's Eye!

The students liked this formative assessment because it was anonymous and they could see how the other students responded.

Stop/Go[12]

The elementary students in Mrs. Martin's class like to use the Stop and Go popsicle stick signs the teacher made for them (**Figure 4.5**). When Mrs. Martin wants to check her students' confidence about the lesson and determine if they are ready to continue instruction or need review, she asks them to pick up either the Stop or Go stick. The students like this activity because they would rather hold up a stick sign than raise their hand and tell Mrs. Martin they do not understand, which can be embarrassing.

Learning Continuum

Mrs. Federico challenged her 5th grade students to design a way to communicate their understanding of a skill or concept. Manny, a math-lover, created a two-way arrow (**Figure 4.6**). While a check mark on the right side of the arrow indicated the students understood, one on the left meant they did not. If checked in the middle, they were unsure.

Students presented their ideas, and Manny's classmates chose his model to implement in the classroom. The students liked to place their marks on the arrow be-

cause they could see how they compared to others without having to put their names on the paper. Mrs. Federico liked Manny's model because she could check the class for understanding simply by looking at the arrow.

3-2-1

Mrs. Simpson likes to give her students a ticket to leave at the end of class. She asks them to record three things they learned, two things they still have questions about, and one thing they can use to improve their health.

The 3-2-1 helps Mrs. Simpson identify what content and skills the students are confident about, what they are unsure of, and the practical application of the instruction. The results are helpful in determining what needs to be reviewed and how the instruction can be improved.

Self Sorting[12]

This formative assessment consists of placing red, yellow, or green magnets, Post-its, an X, or a checkmark under headings (**Table 4.1**). Once the students have placed a mark, it is easy to see the distribution of their understanding and progress.

When the students complete the activity, their progress is clear. Students can compare themselves to others, and this awareness can motivate them to continue or ask for help. The teacher uses this information to ascertain the status of the class as it meets the performance indicators.

Index Card Summaries/Questions[3,p248]

Mrs. Morrissey links her health education class to English language arts by using a writing exercise as one of her formative assessment tools.

She distributes blank index cards and instructs the students to write a sentence about the content and skill in their performance task that they fully understand on one side and on the other side write something that they still do not understand. She examines the student responses and decides whether to re-teach a portion of the instruction, work with confused students individually or in small groups, or proceed.

One-Minute Essay[3,p248]

At the end of class, Mr. Reams asks his students to write a one-minute essay summarizing their understanding of

FIGURE 4.5　Stop and Go

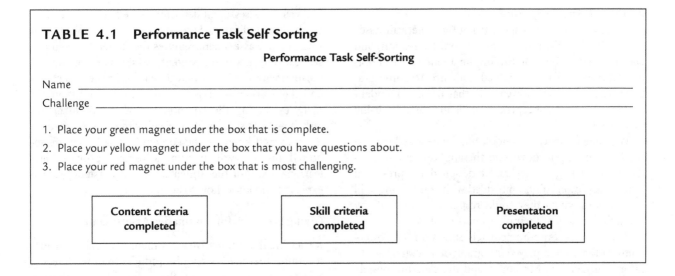

TABLE 4.1   Performance Task Self Sorting

Performance Task Self-Sorting

Name _____

Challenge _____

1. Place your green magnet under the box that is complete.
2. Place your yellow magnet under the box that you have questions about.
3. Place your red magnet under the box that is most challenging.

Content criteria completed	Skill criteria completed	Presentation completed

the key ideas he presented that day. He reviews the essay, reports the results to his students, and adjusts instruction to help them move forward in their learning.

Question Box[3,p248]

Mrs. Delgado places a question box in the classroom where students can leave questions about content, skill, projects, and resources, etc. This technique helps anyone who does not want to ask for help in front of other students but needs it.

Visual Representation (Web, Concept Map, or Graphic Organizer)[3,p248]

To assist his visual learners, Mr. Alphonse asks them to represent content or skill by drawing a web, concept map, or graphic organizer. During the analyzing influences unit, students use a Venn diagram to illustrate the relationships between the internal and external factors that influence smoking. The students enjoy this technique because it is different and creative and helps them under-

stand influences in a visual manner rather than simply talking about them.

Misconception Check[3,p249]

Mr. Cunio checks for understanding frequently. He printed and distributed the words "Agree" and "Disagree", and gave his students time to color and decorate them. This approach helped the students establish ownership and pride in their work, and Mr. Cunio expected them to keep the words in their desks or folders. During class, he asks quick questions about content and skill, and students respond by raising either Agree or Disagree. Sometimes, students develop questions and pair with a classmate to ask them, or for variety, Mr. Cunio collects the questions and uses them as a class review.

Performance Task Reflection[12]

Students may struggle as they work on their performance task. Ms. Lahani addresses that problem with a reflection whereby students communicate their progress or ask for help (**Table 4.2**).

TABLE 4.2   Performance Task Reflection

Performance Task Reflection

Name _____

Challenge _____

1. Circle the number that represents how your challenge is progressing.

    Poor   1   2   3   4   5   Excellent

2. This is what I accomplished today _____

3. I am stuck.   No   Yes

Audience Response Systems[8]

Mr. Sophe loves technology. During the American Association for Health, Physical Education, Recreation, and Dance (AAPHERD) convention, he attended a technology workshop that highlighted audience response systems. The presenter showed data that indicated student understanding of concepts and skills increased by using this system.

When he returned to school, Mr. Sophe asked for and received funding to download the application and purchase the interactive clickers. He designed and presented to his class PowerPoints embedded with content and skill questions to which they could respond interactively by using the clickers or their own smart phones.

The class response immediately shows on the PowerPoint and may be displayed in a graph or analyzed later to inform instruction. Mr. Sophe and the class thoroughly enjoy this formative assessment, which is fun and quickly uncovers the level of content and skill understanding. Mr. Sophe uses this information to refine his instruction and coach his students to achieve the performance indicators.

Summative Assessment

Summative assessment is assessment *of* learning. It measures student achievement of local curriculum, state, and National Health Education Standards. It occurs at the end of an instructional unit, a quarter, course, semester, school year, etc. and measures progress towards course, grade level, or grade span performance indicators. Grading instruments vary and may include an analytical rubric, selected response, or constructed response quizzes and tests.

When a teacher applies the backwards design model to plan standards, assessment, and instruction, she knows— prior to instruction—what her students should accomplish at its end to demonstrate their proficiency. For them to reach that goal, the teacher must explain the final product and written assessment before instruction begins.

For example, at the beginning of the goal-setting unit, Mrs. Logan explains the content and skill performance indicators, and how students show their proficiency through a performance task. To help students understand how she scores the task, she provides examples of poor, average, and well-done final projects based on the criteria of a rubric.

Knowing how they will be assessed helps students focus on what they are expected to learn (content) and do (skill).[6,p12] Mrs. Logan also gives an overview of the skill and content that is included in the unit written test so students understand the scope of the summative assessment.

This strategy has three advantages. First, the performance indicators are identified at the beginning of the unit, and the teacher explains how the performance task and written assessment determine whether students have reached the indicators. Secondly, the performance task as a summative assessment requires the students to demonstrate proficiency of the content and skill performance indicators with the intent that they transfer the knowledge and skill learned in class to a real world application. Finally, explaining the components of the performance task, how to be successful in reaching the performance indicators, and knowing the content and skill that are required on the written summative test, provide clear learning goals for the students. They understand what is expected and know how to achieve it.

Giving Feedback for Summative Assessments

Reviewing the summative assessment is valuable because it reinforces student strengths and identifies weaknesses. Summative assessment feedback should be **criterion**, rather than **norm, referenced**.

The grade in each box of the rubric reflects the degree of student proficiency in reaching the criteria as compared to the requirements of the standard.

Written quizzes, tests, or exams should also reference Standards 1–8 performance indicators so that feedback is specific to the standard. This information helps students understand their progress in reaching the standard.

In addition to criteria-referenced feedback, effective summative assessment compares a student's work with his or her previous work. This analysis informs students of a lack of improvement, some improvement, or much improvement over previous summative assessments.[13,p24]

Norm referenced feedback, on the other hand, compares a student's performance to that of others. After grading all the decision-making performance tasks, Mrs. Baldwin placed the grade distribution (A - 5, B - 3, C - 10, D - 7, F - 4) on the board so students could see their standing in the classroom. Rather than thinking about whether they met the performance indicators of the standard, they focused on the grade and their standing in the class. This technique did not encourage them to continue their good work or motivate them to improve. In fact, the students became very quiet, and those individuals that performed poorly became unmotivated.[13,p23] Mrs. Baldwin does not use this technique any more.

To reflect on a summative assessment, students identify strengths and weaknesses on the performance task rubric and the written exam. They record an area of difficulty then think of ways to improve the next time.[13,p68] This reflection provides time for students to think about their demonstration of content and skill criteria on the performance task, their achievement on the written test, and an understanding of how to improve.

To help students improve, provide suggestions on how to demonstrate proficiency in the performance criteria, study for a written exam, use problem solving strategies, and use mnemonic devices.[13,p69]

Summative Assessment Tools

Summative assessment tools have advantages and disadvantages. In a selected response assessment, the teacher provides students with several possible answers to a question, and they select the one they think is correct. This assessment uses one class and the teacher scores answers as correct or not. The assessment may cover extensive content, but not its depth, and is objective. It makes clear what the student does not know.

Selected response is easy to design and quick and simple to grade. In fact, many texts include an assessment DVD that contains worksheets, quizzes, and chapter tests. The disadvantages of selected response are that it does not reveal what the students have learned during instruction and may not be consistent with a student's learning style. Some students may, therefore, score poorly because they do not perform well on such a test.[1,p47]

Constructed response assessments may be short, extended, or take the form of a performance task. In a constructed response assessment, the students respond to a question by writing a short answer or an extended response that may also include an interpretation of charts or diagrams. It requires one class period and can assess content and skill. This assessment does not cover as much content as the selected response and challenges the student to answer questions with some depth, both of which are advantages. It also provides students a limited opportunity to demonstrate what they know and can do.[1,p48]

The disadvantages of constructed response include its subjectivity and a reliance on writing skills to demonstrate proficiency. Without a rubric, students have no expectations for a complete answer, and, consequently, the teacher may assign partial credit. The students may not understand why they received partial credit, disagree with this subjective score, and become sufficiently frustrated to believe that they cannot succeed on this assessment. Special needs students or students learning English as a second language suffer a disadvantage because their grade is dependent upon how well they express themselves through language.

A performance task is a curriculum-embedded project that provides students with an opportunity to display what they know and can do by creating a product or giving a demonstration.[1,p49] It requires several days and assesses what a student knows about specific content and how well he can demonstrate that knowledge through a skill.

The advantages of using a performance task for summative assessment include engaging all students in learning, scoring both content and skills, requiring higher order thinking skills embedded in the performance indicators, and developing valuable workplace habits, such as time management, individual responsibility, honesty, persistence, and working cooperatively with others.[14]

Additionally, performance tasks use different learning styles to demonstrate proficiency. As such, the students are not reliant solely on their writing skills to achieve a good grade but can also demonstrate proficiency in a way that highlights a particular strength. For example, an artist may choose to show what she knows and can do by drawing a comic strip rather than writing paragraphs about a topic. As long as the student fulfills the content and skill requirements on the rubric, the performance mode may be flexible.

The disadvantages of a performance task include time and content because it takes several days to prepare the students, and more time still for the students to complete the task. Less class time is available for teaching content.

A performance task does, however, target instruction to student need while concentrating on functional health knowledge, not simply coverage of a chapter. When students learn content they use every day and acquire skills that improve their confidence and competence, they are well on their way towards developing and maintaining healthy behaviors.

Rubrics

A rubric is a scoring guide based on the criteria stated in the performance indicators. It has a fixed measurement scale that can be numbers, words, letters, etc., and describes degrees of quality, proficiency, or understanding of each performance indicator.[3,p173] They take many forms, such as checklists, rating scales, and descriptive, holistic, and structured observation guides.[2,p138]

ADVANTAGES OF USING RUBRICS

Rubrics provide advantages to the teacher and the student. Because the teacher must thoroughly research and think through a project in order to design a rubric, learning goals are clear; teaching, learning, and communication are improved; grading is consistent; and instructional adjustments are made, when needed.

Students receive criterion-based feedback from the teacher to improve performance, know what is needed to achieve, and are better able to communicate with teachers and parents regarding their grade.

Clear Learning Goals

Rubrics identify the content and skill requirements of the performance indicators, thereby making the learning goals clear to the students. In short, they help students understand what is expected.[2,p139]

The teacher distributes the rubrics at the beginning of a unit along with the performance task. This material helps the student understand the content and skill criteria required by the task, makes clear what they are expected to know and do at the completion of the project, and shows them the range of scores to which they should aspire. Rubrics help students stay focused on the criteria rather than diverting their attention to something that is interesting but not pertinent to the project.

Self-Improvement

Using a rubric can help students improve.[2,p139] When students use the rubric criteria to reflect on the quality and completeness of their work before it is performed and graded, it gives them the opportunity to improve their products to meet the learning goals.

Rubrics motivate students to perform better.[2,p139] By reading and understanding the prompt and rubrics, the students know exactly what content and skill criteria the teacher expects and how they will be graded. This awareness empowers the students to perform better because they have all the information to be successful and a better understanding of the project or performance.

Feedback

Feedback is one of the best ways to improve learning. After scoring the criteria boxes of the rubric, the teacher provides feedback to the student. It may be a note written in the criteria box or a space on the rubric. The advantage of doing so is that the student connects the feedback to the specific criteria, which facilitates correcting a precise part of the project.

Feedback is most valuable to the student when given shortly after the task is completed.[15,p17] If the teacher is using the rubric formatively, the students will recognize where they need to improve and have time to make changes. When graded with the same rubric, their grade reflects the improvements made since the formative assessment.

Grading

Because the teacher explains the scoring and criteria before the performance task begins and the students use the rubric as they develop their projects, fewer arguments about scoring and grading occur.[2,p139] Students see the score in the criteria box, read the feedback, and understand their grade better.

Rubrics make scoring and grading easier, faster, and more consistent. When students read the rubric for the required content and skill criteria for the performance, they know what is expected and how the teacher plans to score or grade the project. Since every project uses criteria, scoring/grading is more accurate, unbiased, and consistent.[2,p139]

Communication Tool

Rubrics are a good communication tool when explaining a student's grade to parents, faculty, and administrators.[2,p139] If questioned about a grade, the teacher presents the student's work, the rubric, the criterion-referenced feedback, and the formative and summative assessments. Because this system is objective, it is easier to justify a grade.

Support staff also benefits when a rubric is used to score and grade a performance task because it clarifies what the student is expected to know and do to meet the performance indicators.[15,p24] Consequently, the staff member can efficiently and effectively supply the help to succeed.

When teachers in a school, department, or district use the same rubric, it is easier to analyze and compare the results of student assessments and use that data to improve teaching and learning.[15,p25] The rubric aids instructional quality control.

Adjusting Instruction

Rubrics also help the instructor assess teaching. If the students consistently score poorly on certain criteria, the teacher adjusts instruction in that area. When the task is repeated, the rubric score indicates whether the adjustment succeeded.[15,p25;6,p10-17]

TYPES OF RUBRICS

Checklist Rubric

A checklist rubric is a list of criteria required for a task. It helps the students organize their work and check it for completeness.

A checklist rubric reflects on progress made at the end of a specific time period. The teacher distributes the checklist at the end of a week or any other time and asks the students to reflect on the progress of their projects, based on the criteria of the performance task.

This rubric is also a self-assessment tool. When the students complete their final performance or product, they place a grade or a check next to each criterion, then compare it to the teacher's score. This technique provides a foundation for conversation about criteria, expectations, and meeting the performance standards.[6,p16]

Elementary Example

In a PreK–2 unit on healthy self-management, the teacher targets healthy food choices. She selected performance indicators 1.2.1, "Identify that healthy behaviors affect personal health,"[10,p24] and 7.2.1 "Demonstrate healthy practices and behaviors to maintain or improve personal health."[10,p35]

The task shows four boxes, each filled with different food items, their number stated so students can trace it, thereby connecting the health class to math. One box has an unhealthy food. The student challenge is to color the food, trace the number in each of the boxes, and draw an X through an unhealthy food.[16,p481] To organize her students and check for completeness, the teacher designs a check list that includes each of the above criteria.

Color the food. _____

Trace the number. _____

Draw an X through the unhealthy food._____

Middle School Example

In the middle and high schools, the checklist includes the performance task criteria. The student checks whether he has included all the criteria in his performance or product (**Table 4.3**).

High School Example

As high school students are preparing to practice healthy behaviors, the teacher develops a checklist rubric for them to reflect on their progress (**Table 4.4**).

The website http://rubistar.4teachers.org provides teachers with a free, project-based, learning checklist tool for K–12 writing, science, oral presentations, and multimedia projects that is adaptable for performance tasks. The template provides five categories—content, delivery, organization, presentation aids, and resources. For each category, there is a pull-down list of responsibilities to check off or you can write your own.[17] This self-assessment tool is good to use when preparing products for presentation.

Rating Scales

This rubric provides a quick and easy way to provide feedback to students on the progress of their projects.[2,p142]

A rating scale rubric resembles a checklist but has one exception. Instead of only one column to check, there are several, and they include a scale from high to low (**Table 4.5**). They allow the teacher to show gradations in the level of performance. To score accurately and effectively using the rating scale, show students examples of previously scored products and the reasons why they received a particular score. This approach helps them understand the difference between an excellent, good, fair, or poor score. Students may also use this rubric to score peer performances.

Use the rating scale formatively to improve performance or summatively by assigning points to the scale.

TABLE 4.3 Performance Task—Resolving Conflict

Criteria	Yes	No
Performance indicator 4.8.3—Demonstrate effective conflict management, or resolution strategies.[11,p30]		
The student:		
■ Stayed calm.		
■ Attempted to talk about the conflict.		
■ Suggested several ways to resolve the conflict.		
■ Talked about the pros and cons of each suggestion.		
■ Agreed on a way to settle the conflict.[20,p786]		
Feedback		

TABLE 4.4 Performance Task Checklist—Help Friends Not Drive While Under the Influence of Alcohol

1.12.5 Propose ways to reduce or prevent injuries and health problems.[11,p25]

Check if included in the project	Status as of . . .

- Ten facts about how alcohol affects driving ability.

7.12.3 Demonstrate a variety of behaviors that avoid or reduce health risks to self and others.[11,p35]

Check if included in the project	Status as of . . .

- Three strategies to avoid drinking at a party.
- Three ways to prevent a friend from driving while under the influence.

Feedback

TABLE 4.5 Performance Task Rating Scale—Help Friends Not Drive While Under the Influence of Alcohol

Criteria	Scale			
1.12.5 Propose ways to reduce or prevent injuries and health problems.[11,p25]				
	Excellent	Good	Fair	Poor

- Ten facts about how alcohol affects driving ability

Feedback

7.12.3 Demonstrate a variety of behaviors that avoid or reduce health risks to self and others.[11,p35]				
	Excellent	Good	Fair	Poor

- Three strategies to avoid drinking at a party
- Three ways to prevent a friend from driving while under the influence

Feedback

The scale in Table 4.5 was modified from the checklist format in Table 4.4. To score, a check is placed under the appropriate rating.

To give a grade using this scale, designate points for excellent, good, fair, and poor. Add the total possible score (4 [excellent] × 3 [criteria] = 12) then divide the actual score by the total points possible.

Descriptive/Analytical Rubric

A descriptive/analytical rubric contains a scale that shows level of achievement through numbers or words listed across the top of the rubric and the dimensions (content and skill criteria) placed in a column on its left side with each criteria in a separate box scored independently. The descriptions of each level of criterion performance are placed horizontally.[15,p6] This rubric layout provides the teacher and student with a specific list of criteria and levels of achievement to score/grade a product or performance.

When writing the descriptions of the level of achievement, vary them from high to low. The differences in levels should be clear because if the descriptions are too similar, the product will be difficult to score. Some rubrics use the lowest level to emphasize what might have been accomplished, rather than score the evidence. This procedure is a prerogative of the user.[15,p11]

The levels of achievement at the top of the rubric can show considerable variety in numbers or words. The choice is the designer's.

Here are a few examples:

- 5-4-3-2-1
- 4-3-2-1
- 3-2-1
- Well Done, Satisfactory, Needs Improvement, and Incomplete
- Excellent, Competent, Needs Work
- Excellent, Good, Fair, Poor
- Mastery, Partial Mastery, Progressing, Emerging[15,p8]
- Always, Usually, Sometimes, Rarely, Never
- Always, Sometimes, Rarely, Never
- Consistently, Usually, Rarely, Never
- Accurate, Mostly Accurate, A Few Inaccuracies, Mostly Inaccurate
- Thoroughly, Adequately, Inadequately, Poorly
- Appropriate, Mostly Appropriate, A Few Inappropriate Items, Mostly Inappropriate

To grade a rubric that uses words as the scale, assign a single number to each word. For example, score excellent as 4, good as 3, fair as 2, and needs work as 1. To determine the grade, add the score for each criterion and divide the total by the highest possible score, with the result being a percentage. If there are six criteria listed on the side of the rubric and the numbers 4-3-2-1 are listed across the top, there is a possibility of 6 × 4 = 24 total points. If the student scores 4, 2, 3, 4, 4, 3, for a total of 20/24, his or her grade is 83%.

Should the teacher want to emphasize the importance of one criterion over another, she can assign weight. For example, in the rubric below, the first three performance indicators are 25% of the grade, and the last two, 15% and 10%. In order to calculate a grade, we must first establish the perfect score for the project. Perfect scores for each criterion are

- PI 1.12.7—4, multiply the 4 by .25 =   1.0
- PI 5.12.4—4, multiply the 4 by .25 =   1.0
- PI 5.12.5—4, multiply the 4 by .25 =   1.0
- PI 5.12.6—4, multiply the 4 by .15 =   .6
- PI 5.12.7—4, multiply the 4 by .10 =   <u>.4</u>
- Total   4.0

The perfect weighted score for this assignment is 4.0 points.

To calculate a grade from this rubric, multiply the score for each criterion by the weight. Add all the weighted grades and divide by the perfect score (4.0)

For example, if the score for

- PI 1.12.7 was 4, multiply the 4 by .25 =   1.0
- PI 5.12.4 was 3, multiply the 3 by .25 =   .75
- PI 5.12.5 was 2, multiply the 2 by .25 =   .5
- PI 5.12.6 was 2, multiply the 2 by .15 =   .3
- PI 5.12.7 was 2, multiply the 2 by .10 =   <u>.2</u>
- Total   2.75/4=68.7%

The weighted grade is 68.7%, or 69%, if rounded.

The following is an example of an analytical rubric for a high school decision-making prompt whereby the student is trying to decide how to attend a party and not smoke. The project or performance is always scored for content and skill. Whereas the first performance indicator is the content, the remaining indicators are the skill (**Table 4.6**).

The levels of achievement are placed across the top of the rubric and scaled from 4–1. The performance criteria (dimensions) are listed on the left. The descriptions of the level criteria are listed across the criteria row under the level of achievement.

If designing an analytical rubric seems daunting, it need not be. Rubistar provides free tools to design rubrics for making a brochure or poster, puppet show, debate, letter writing, story writing, and many other projects.[18] The rubric templates are easily adaptable, may be added to, and result in a custom rubric that meets the needs of the teacher and student.

When developing a rubric for a performance task, however, the performance indicator criteria must be listed as found in the National Health Education Standards,

TABLE 4.6 Weighted Analytical Rubric

Analytical Rubric for a High School Decision-Making Prompt

Criteria	4	3	2	1
Performance indicator 1.12.7 with infused content—Compare and contrast the benefits and barriers to practicing a variety of healthy behaviors such as not smoking.[10,p25] Weight—25%	The student thoroughly compares and contrasts three benefits and barriers to practicing a variety of healthy behaviors such as not smoking.	The student adequately compares and contrasts three benefits and barriers to practicing a variety of healthy behaviors such as not smoking.	The student inadequately compares and contrasts three benefits and barriers to practicing a variety of healthy behaviors such as not smoking.	The student poorly compares and contrasts three benefits and barriers to practicing a variety of healthy behaviors such as not smoking.
Performance indicator 5.12.4 with infused content—Generates alternatives to health-related issues or problems such as not smoking at a party where friends are smoking.[10,p33] Weight—25%	The student generates three appropriate solutions explaining how he will not smoke when attending a party where friends smoke.	The three solutions generated explaining how he will not smoke when attending a party where friends smoke are mostly appropriate.	A few of the three solutions generated explaining how he will not smoke when attending a party where friends smoke are inappropriate.	The three solutions generated explaining how he will not smoke when attending a party where friends smoke are mostly inappropriate.
Performance indicator 5.12.5 with infused content—Predicts the potential short-term and long-term impact of each nonsmoking alternative on self and others.[10,p33] Weight—25%	The student appropriately predicts the short and long-term impact of each non-smoking alternative on self and others.	The student's prediction of the short and long-term impact of each nonsmoking alternative on self and others are mostly appropriate.	The student predicts the short and long-term impact of each nonsmoking alternative on self and others. Few are appropriate.	The student inappropriately predicts the short and long-term impact of each nonsmoking alternative on self and others.
Performance indicator 5.12.6 with infused content—Defend the healthy nonsmoking alternative when making a decision.[10,p33] Weight—15%	The student thoroughly defends the healthy nonsmoking alternative when making a decision.	The student adequately defends the healthy nonsmoking alternative when making a decision.	The student inadequately defends the healthy nonsmoking alternative when making a decision.	The student poorly defends the healthy nonsmoking alternative when making a decision.
Performance indicator 5.12.7 with infused content—Evaluate the effectiveness of health-related decisions.[10,p33] Weight—10%	The student thoroughly evaluates the effectiveness of the health-related decision not to smoke.	The student adequately evaluates the effectiveness of the health-related decision not to smoke.	The student inadequately evaluates the effectiveness of the health-related decision not to smoke.	The student poorly evaluates the effectiveness of the health-related decision not to smoke.

Feedback

with the content infused into it, since they are the foundation of accountability. Rubistar, however, offers criteria for creativity, time-management, works with other, etc.

Holistic Rubric

A **holistic rubric** makes a judgment on the overall impression one receives when comparing student work to all the performance indicators required.[3,p173]

When performance-based assessment is scored holistically, the product or performance is recorded for content and skill, as on an analytical rubric. When developing a holistic rubric, however, the teacher chooses the performance indicators for the content, lists them together, and assigns a score to the performance level. The process is repeated for the skill. The score can be expressed in words or numbers, depending on the designer's preference.

Scoring high on a holistic rubric assists the student in scoring well on an analytical rubric because that instrument takes each of the criteria listed together on the holistic rubric and scores them separately. When students understand this connection, it motivates them to use the feedback from the holistic rubric to improve their project or performance.

Grade 4 Example

The following are examples of content and skill holistic rubrics for a Grade 4 performance task. The Standard 1 and Standard 6 holistic rubrics reflect the performance indicator(s), which challenge the students to increase physical activity.

> Performance indicator 1.5.1—Describe the relationship between healthy behaviors and personal health.[10,p24]
> 4—The student thoroughly describes the relationship between increasing physical activity and personal health. The response is comprehensive, accurate, and draws a valid conclusion regarding increasing physical activity and personal health.[1,p209;19,p426]
> 3—The student adequately describes the relationship between increasing physical activity and personal health. The response shows some comprehensiveness, is accurate or mostly accurate, and draws a mostly valid conclusion regarding increasing physical activity and personal health.
> 2—The student inadequately describes the relationship between increasing physical activity and personal health. The response is not comprehensive, has some accurate facts but is mostly inaccurate, and draws a mostly valid

> conclusion regarding increasing physical activity and personal health.
> 1—The student poorly describes the relationship between increasing physical activity and personal health. The response is incomplete, inaccurate, and draws an invalid conclusion regarding increasing physical activity and personal health.

> Performance indicator 6.5.1—Set a personal health goal and track progress toward its achievement.[10,p34]
> Performance indicator 6.5.2—Identify resources to assist in achieving a personal health goal.[10,p25] (Since goal setting is a progressive skill, both indicators must be used.)
> 4—The student sets an appropriate personal health goal to increase physical activity, thoroughly tracks progress toward achievement, and identifies appropriate resources to assist in increasing physical activity.
> 3—The student sets a personal health goal to increase physical activity that is mostly appropriate, tracks progress toward achievement, and identifies resources to assist in increasing physical activity that are mostly appropriate.
> 2—The student sets a personal health goal to increase physical activity that has some inappropriate parts, inadequately tracks progress toward achievement, and identifies few appropriate resources to assist in increasing physical activity.
> 1—The student sets a mostly inappropriate personal health goal to increase physical activity, poorly tracks progress toward achievement, and identifies inappropriate resources to assist in increasing physical activity.

High School Example

The performance indicator 1.12.7 states, "Compare and contrast the benefits of and barriers to practicing a variety of healthy behaviors."[10,p25] The content of the task may challenge the students to compare and contrast the benefits and barriers to living smoke-free.

The teacher includes the content that best meets the needs of her students and places the criteria for the task on the prompt. As the students develop their project, the teacher scores them according to the required content criteria. If using the holistic rubric as a formative assessment tool, the teacher provides students with feedback that gives them the opportunity to improve their work before they are summitively graded on an analytical rubric.

The following are examples of content and skill holistic rubrics for a high school performance task. The Standard 1 and Standard 5 holistic rubrics reflect the performance indicators that challenge students to make a decision about smoking.

Standard 1 performance indicator 1.12.7—Compare and contrast the benefits and barriers to practicing a variety of healthy behaviors.[10,p25]

4–The student thoroughly compares and contrasts five benefits and five barriers to not smoking. The response is comprehensive, accurate, and draws a valid conclusion regarding the benefits and barriers to not smoking.[1,p209;19,p426]

3–The student adequately compares and contrasts five benefits and five barriers to not smoking. The response shows some comprehensiveness, is accurate or mostly accurate, and draws a mostly valid conclusion regarding the benefits and barriers to not smoking.

2–The student inadequately compares and contrasts five benefits and five barriers to not smoking. The response is not comprehensive, has some accurate facts but is mostly inaccurate, and draws a mostly valid conclusion regarding the five benefits and barriers to not smoking.

1–The student poorly compares and contrasts five benefits and five barriers to not smoking. The response is incomplete, inaccurate, and draws an invalid conclusion regarding the benefits and barriers to not smoking.

The Standard 5 decision-making skill performance indicators for the high school level span 5.12.4 to 5.12.7 and provide a framework for decision-making. The teacher may add additional criteria but should include each of these four performance indicators:

5.12.4—Generate alternatives to health-related issues or problems.

5.12.5—Predict the potential short-term and long-term impact of each alternative on self and others.

5.12.6—Defend the healthy choice when making decisions.

5.12.7—Evaluate the effectiveness of health-related decisions.[10,p33]

4–The problem is accurately stated, the decision to be made is appropriate and based on the problem, five appropriate solutions that directly relate to the decision to be made are stated, the short- and long-term impacts of each solution on self and others refer to the stated solution and are appropriate, the values are accurate, the choice is thoroughly defended, and a thorough evaluation of the effectiveness of the decision is stated.

3–The problem stated is mostly accurate, the decision stated is mostly appropriate, five mostly appropriate solutions are given, the short- and long-term impacts of each solution on self and others are mostly appropriate, the values each solution represents are mostly accurate, the choice is adequately defended, and an evaluation of the effectiveness of the decision is adequate.

2–The problem stated has few accurate facts; the decision to be made is inaccurate; five solutions are given, but few are appropriate; the short- and long-term impacts of each solution on self and others are predicted, but few are appropriate; few of the values each solution represents are accurate; the choice is inadequately defended; and an evaluation of the effectiveness of the decision is inadequate.

1–The problem is inaccurately stated, the decision to be made is inaccurate, five inappropriate solutions are given, the short- and long-term impacts of each solution on self and others are inappropriate, the values each solution represents are inaccurate, the choice is poorly defended, and an evaluation of the effectiveness of the decision is poorly stated.

The advantage of using a holistic rubric is that it allows a quick assessment and, if used formatively, can provide feedback to students to improve their performance. One disadvantage is that the score may be inaccurate.[2,p145] In the high school rubric above, for example, a student may adequately state the problem (Score of 2) but does a poor evaluation of the effectiveness of the decision (Score of 1). A score of 1.5 is not permitted. The teacher must decide which score is more reflective of product or presentation.

Structured Observation Guides

In a structured observation guide, the teacher lists the performance criteria required in the performance task, and rather than develop a rating scale, simply leaves room for notes. This rubric is subjective and qualitative but it is also direct and valid.[2,p146]

Designing and using rubrics is a skill and, like any skill, requires practice. Skills improve as one gains experience in designing different types of rubrics, and the diligent teacher discovers the best words and design for students. Use the performance indicators as the foundation of the rubric because they keep the students focused on what to know and do to demonstrate proficiency.

Performance Tasks

A performance task, based on the National Health Education Standards performance indicators, is a multifaceted age-appropriate challenge presented through a prompt. Students utilize the content and skills learned in class to resolve the challenge then present the project or performance to the class to demonstrate their proficiency of the performance indicators.

Performance tasks are examples of **authentic assessment** because students demonstrate their proficiency of the content and skills performance indicators[10,p89] rather than simply answer questions about them on a written test. This form of authentic assessment is grounded in a real-world, age-appropriate prompt to which students relate. It requires them to use knowledge and skill to solve a problem, and asks the students to explore ways of solving a problem rather than merely reciting content taught in class. Performance tasks place students in realistic situations, similar to their personal lives, where they must resolve a situation by using knowledge and skill. The process assesses student ability to use knowledge and skill to resolve a complicated task. Performance tasks allow appropriate time to practice, consult resources, and improve a performance or product based on teacher feedback.[3,p154]

When reflecting on the National Health Education Standards, we see that only one of the eight standards is content. Standard 1 includes all the health education content areas traditionally taught and assessed in comprehensive health education. If we refer to **Figure 4.7**, however, we see that the seven skill-related standards demand attention because they tilt the seesaw in their direction.

In skills-based comprehensive health education, we emphasize skill by designing skills-based units and teaching content through skill. Students reveal their understanding of the performance indicators when they demonstrate knowledge and skills through a challenging task in a variety of situations.[3,p153]

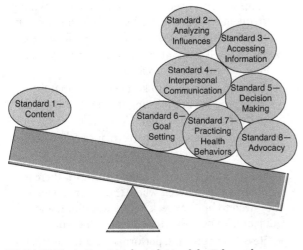

FIGURE 4.7 National Health Education Content and Skills

4. Assess the practice using a content and skill holistic rubric and other formative assessment tools.

Next few days

1. Students present their projects to the class.
2. Assess students with an analytical rubric.

Final day

1. Administer a selected response or constructed response assessment to evaluate all the content taught in the unit as well as questions about the skill.

Peformance tasks are an integral part of skills-based health education. After skill and content instruction, the teacher distributes the performance task. Students then have the opportunity to practice and demonstrate what they have learned by solving a real life problem.[18,p3] Depending on the level of the students, information to solve the challenge is explained, distributed with the prompt, or students must access the appropriate information. In all cases, the students must plan how to use the information to resolve the challenge.[2,p26]

ASSESSING PERFORMANCE TASKS

Performance-based assessment is an example of authentic assessment. The students are assessed on performing or demonstrating knowledge of content and proficiency in a skill. They do not simply write about what they know and can do; rather, they show us.

Students begin the performance-based assessment by reading the prompt, which directs them to solve an age-appropriate challenge, targeting certain content and a particular skill. To meet the challenge, they must think critically, solve a complex problem, and communicate effectively.[2,p26;1,p59]

For example, during a healthy self-management unit on CPR, a student reads a prompt with a real-life challenge, such as assessing a collapsed victim. The student explains the procedure for assessing a collapsed victim to fulfill the content requirements then demonstrates how to perform CPR to complete the skill.

While the students are preparing the project and practicing the presentation, the teacher assesses their progress by using a holistic rubric and formative assessment tools. The more the students achieve the criteria during practice, the higher they score on the analytical rubric for a grade. This pedagogy places the teacher as a coach, helping the student reach proficiency in the content and skill performance indicators.

To help students learn to use assessment information, they ask themselves three questions.

1. *Where am I going?*[20] For students to understand where they are going, they must see the big picture. To help the students understand where they are going:
   - Design performance tasks that allow for authentic assessment of a product or performance through demonstration of knowledge of content and the performance of a skill.
   - Show students, through exemplars, examples of work that meets or does not meet the criteria for proficiency in a performance indicator. Explain why each example received its assigned score or grade.
   - Provide clear, age-appropriate assessment criteria, including the number of facts required in a performance, the skill components, and any other mandatory items.
   - Provide the holistic and analytical rubrics at the beginning of instruction along with an explanation of the written exam so students understand how they are assessed.
   - Allow students to practice scoring sample projects so they understand how the performance indicators and rubrics interrelate and guide the student to proficiency.[10,p89]

2. *Where am I now?*[20] Engage in ongoing formative assessment so students learn their status, strengths and weaknesses as they work on their projects. To help the students understand where they are now:
   - Identify and reinforce student strengths. This procedure builds confidence and motivation to achieve the performance indicators.
   - Support a student's effort to achieve proficiency by coaching him or her toward performance of content and skill.
   - Help students overcome weaknesses by providing frequent and specific feedback. This information helps them learn ways to improve performance.
   - Provide self-assessment tools so that students can monitor their own progress.[10,p89]
   - Encourage students to keep a journal that lists their progress in achieving the content and skill performance indicators.
   - Provide a check list of performance criteria. As students complete the criteria, they check it.[20]

3. *How can I close the gap?*[20] If students learn there is a significant gap between where they are and where they need to be, they seek help, suggestions, and guidance. To help the students close the gap:
   - Review the prompt, performance indicators, and assessment criteria and compare it to the current status of the students' project.

- Develop a step-by-step plan to move forward and close the gap. With redirection, the students are on their way to achieving the performance indicators.[20]
- Provide frequent and timely feedback to monitor progress and give encouragement.
- Provide multiple opportunities for students to learn, practice, and apply health content and skills.[10,p89]

At the conclusion of the performance task, students reflect on their process. Did I understand how to reach the performance indicators? What were my successes? What were the barriers? How did I overcome the barriers? Did I seek help? What can I do better next time? What did I learn about myself because of this project?[20]

For example, performance indicator 8.5.1 states, "Express opinions and give accurate information about health issues."[10,p36] If the 5th grade teacher observes that a group of students has collected several opinion statements about an issue but have not collected accurate information to support their position, she needs to adjust her instruction to remind the students that they are being assessed on being able to "express opinion and give accurate information."[10,p36] She reminds the students what an opinion statement is and what accurate information is and where to access it. She then provides time for the students to make improvements to their work and move forward in reaching the performance indicator.

DESIGNING PERFORMANCE ASSESSMENTS

Designing performance assessments is a skill that improves with practice. To facilitate the development of this skill, use the following guidelines.

Goals and Objectives

When designing a performance task, align its goals and objectives with the national and state standards.[1,p60] For example, if the Grade 4 teacher wants her students to advocate for hand sanitizers in school, she targets Standard 1 performance indicator 1.5.1—Describe the relationship between healthy behaviors and personal health[10,p24] and the advocacy performance indicator 8.5.1—Express opinions and give accurate information about health issues.[10,p36] She infuses the performance indicators with the content, so they now read:

Describe the relationship between using hand sanitizers and personal health (content)

and

Express opinions and give accurate information about the benefits of using hand sanitizers to prevent the spread of germs. (Skill-advocacy)

Evaluation and Synthesis of Knowledge and Skill

The performance task requires evaluation and synthesis of knowledge and skills.[1,p60] Decide how to combine the content and skill so that the students can demonstrate their proficiency through a task. For example, the students in the example above are advocating. The teacher requires a certain amount and quality of content once the students explain the relationship between using hand sanitizers and personal health, as well as when they express opinions and give accurate facts while advocating. To assess the quality of content and degree of skill, the teacher uses holistic rubrics and other formative assessment tools during instruction and practice, then analytical rubrics for the summative assessment.

Higher Order Thinking Skills

The performance task must emphasize higher order thinking skills.[1,p60] These skills, which reflect the work of Benjamin Bloom, are embedded in the performance indicators and progress from knowledge, comprehension, application, analysis, and synthesis to the highest level, evaluation.[21,p5] When planning the performance task, build on previous lower level performance indicators so that the students are proficient by the end of the grade span in all the performance indicators and challenged with progressively higher order thinking skills to solve real life problems.

Directions

The performance task prompt clearly indicates what the students must do to fulfill the requirements. It does not, however, always explain specifically how the task should be completed, encouraging the students to use their own skills and creativity.[1,p60] For example, one student meets the challenge through a demonstration and another with a video. This open-ended problem solving causes the students to think ahead and use content knowledge and skill expertise to resolve the challenge. Students work together or individually, but the procedure is the same: they must figure out how to solve the problem. The analytical rubric provides guidance regarding the content and skill requirements.

Reading Levels

Writing a prompt at an appropriate reading level is important[1,p60] because there may be a variety of reading levels in one classroom. In the differentiated or a regular classroom, design prompts with different reading levels to meet the needs of all the students.

Prompt

An effective performance task relies on a well-written **prompt**, which is an age-appropriate, open-ended question, problem, or challenge that requires students to think critically and use health content and skills to produce a solution.[3,p153] The prompt reflects the learning goals of the performance indicator and presents a challenge that inspires students to give their best effort.[2,p156] Students present the solution to the challenge as a product or performance.

When writing the prompt, refer to the performance indicators for the content (Standard 1) and the skill (Standards 2–6). An effective prompt is challenging and age-appropriate and requires students to demonstrate knowledge and skills through a realistic scenario. To capture the attention of the student, personalize the opening lines. For example, "You are a HIV/AIDS research scientist investigating how to prevent the spread of HIV." Set the hook by giving more information then explain the challenge.[2,p157]

The prompt should include:

- Specific required content, especially amount and quality, obtained from the performance indicator.
- Specific required skill components, obtained from the performance indicator(s).
- Holistic rubrics for scoring and other formative assessment tools. (formative assessment)
- Analytical rubric for grading (summative assessment)
- Content back-up information or directions to access the information.
- Project options, such as role-play, demonstration, comic strip, etc. At first, the teacher may decide how the task is presented, thereby eliminating a student option. As he becomes more experienced in writing and implementing performance tasks and the students more experienced in completing them, the teacher may choose other options to make the demonstration of the same content and skill more interesting.

Scoring

Students are scored and graded in a performance task. While they are learning and practicing their content and skill, use a holistic rubric and other formative assessment tools. The holistic score represents a big picture of how the students are meeting all the assessment criteria of the prompt and, in turn, helps students understand what they need to do to improve their performance.[1,p60] The prompt must state how much content and what type is required, the quality of the written work (grammar,

spelling, etc.), and the specific elements of the skill. When students present their project or give their demonstration, they are graded according to an analytical rubric that evaluates each criterion of the content and skill. A higher score on the holistic rubric corresponds with a higher grade on the analytical rubric.

To see how a teacher constructs a prompt with clear criteria for scoring, let us look at a Grade 4 prompt that includes the performance indicators cited previously.

The performance indicators cited previously are:

Standard 1 performance indicator 1.5.1 with infused content—Describe the relationship between using hand sanitizers and personal health. (Content)[10,p24]

and

Standard 8 performance indicator 8.5.1 with infused content—Express opinions and give accurate information about the benefits of using hand sanitizers to prevent the spread of germs (skill-advocacy).[10,p36]

Achoo!

You are looking forward to school vacation. Your family is traveling to Disneyworld, and you are very excited. There is a problem! Cold and flu season is upon us! Everyone in school seems to be coughing and sneezing. If you get sick, you can't go on vacation!

Wait! What if the school put hand sanitizers around the building? That would help!

Your challenge is to advocate for hand sanitizers to be installed throughout the school.

1. Content criteria for performance indicator 1.5.1

   To educate yourself, write four paragraphs about viruses. In the first paragraph, explain four types of viruses, two of which are the flu and cold virus. Include a picture and diagram of each. In the second paragraph, explain how each virus makes us sick. In the third paragraph, explain how each is spread. In the fourth paragraph, explain four healthy behaviors that help prevent the spread of a virus and contribute to personal health. Include hand sanitizers as one of the behaviors.

   There can be no spelling or grammar errors in the paragraphs.

2. Skill criteria for performance indicator 8.5.1

   To advocate, write one paragraph expressing your opinion on how healthy behaviors, including using hand sanitizers, help prevent the spread of a virus and contribute to personal health.

   You can choose from the following project options:

- Create a poster that expresses your opinion on how healthy behaviors, including using hand sanitizers, help prevent the spread of a virus and contribute to personal health. Support your opinion with ten facts from the content criteria.

- Write ten public service announcements (PSAs). Start with your opinion on how healthy behaviors, including using hand sanitizers, help prevent the spread of a virus and contribute to personal health. On each PSA, include three facts from the content criteria about virus transmission.

- Write a letter to the principal that illustrates how healthy behaviors, including using hand sanitizers, help prevent the spread of a virus and contribute to personal health. Include ten facts from the content criteria.

When distributing the prompt, include the holistic rubric for assessing, back-up information on viruses and hand sanitizers, and an analytical rubric for grading.

Engaging the Student

Performance tasks must engage students and be relevant to their lives.[1,p60] The Characteristics of Effective Health Education encourage curriculum planners to use strategies to personalize information and engage the student.[10,p14]

The prompt for the performance task engages the learner by proposing thought provoking, exciting, captivating, mysterious, and relevant problems. Solving these problems and presenting a solution in the form of a product or presentation fully involves the students' intellect and energy.[3,p195]

The following performance task challenges are examples of how to engage students.

- Advocate through a letter, poster, PSA, newsletter, etc.
- Conduct a panel discussion, survey, or interview.
- Create a brochure, fitness calendar, wellness plan, or advertisement.
- Design a brochure, bumper sticker, or T-shirt.
- Film a video.
- Role play.
- Teach a lesson to younger students that includes performing a skit or creating a puppet show.
- Write a comic strip, dialogue, law, rap song, poem, or PSA.[1,p230]

Link to Ongoing Instruction

The performance task should align with and be embedded in ongoing instruction.[1,p60] The teacher accomplishes this end when she maps content and skill in such a manner that all the performance tasks support and correlate to the current, previous, and following year's instruction. Continuity matters.

"The most powerful single modification that enhances achievement is feedback."[7,p5]

Feedback

As the students develop a product or demonstration, provide feedback to improve their performance.[1,p60] Give effective feedback through various formative assessment strategies as students strive to achieve the performance indicators.[22,p96]

Effective feedback occurs immediately after observation so that the students connect the information to the task and apply the information to improve. It is criterion-referenced and refers to the required content and skill criteria of the performance task.[22,p97-98]

Students provide their own feedback by charting their progress as they learn new content and skill and think about ways to improve.[22,p99] They use the content and skill criteria on the rubric to check if they have included each in their performance. They then score themselves, comparing their own to their teacher's score.

Real World Challenges

To engage the student, the performance task prompt needs to mirror situations that occur in the lives of the students.[1,p60] Use information learned by listening to student stories, knowing their needs, interests, concerns, maturity levels, and current knowledge and skills[10,p15] to develop scenarios that are interesting and relevant and reflect the challenges they face each day.

Using Skills and Knowledge

When planning, emphasize the application of skills and knowledge.[1,p60] Designing prompts with current knowledge and skill that are age-appropriate and relevant prepares the students to use what they learn in class to meet the challenges faced outside school.

Provide a reflection day where students explain how they applied their knowledge and skill to solve a problem. This activity is an excellent technique to highlight how to transfer learning to a real life application.

RUBRICS AND PERFORMANCE TASKS

Rubrics list the content and skill criteria of the performance indicators and indicate the levels of achievement for each criterion. The rubrics are custom made for each performance task. Use holistic rubrics and formative assessment tools while the students are learning and practicing content and skill as a way to check for understanding and monitor progress towards the performance indicators. Use analytical rubrics to grade the final product.

The teacher distributes both holistic and analytical rubrics at the beginning of a skills unit in order that students know how to meet the requirements of the performance task and set their goals for success. The teacher may also administer a written quiz or test at the end of the skills unit that includes content and questions about the application of the skill.

To aid student understanding of the connection between rubrics and success on a performance task, show them **anchor papers,** samples of 4, 3, 2, 1 work. Explain why each received its score. This procedure helps translate the language of the rubric into specific, concrete, and understandable student terms.[6,p14]

It is also worthwhile to show **exemplars,** which are the highest scoring examples in the anchor paper range.[3,p336] Anchors and exemplars help the students understand what is expected because they can reference a previous example.

The rubric also includes a space for teacher feedback and rewritten goals and action steps. Consequently, the rubric becomes a vehicle not only for scoring or grading a student on a performance or product but also a place for feedback, self-assessment, and setting goals for improvement.[6,p16]

Assessment Guidelines

The publication of the National Health Education Standards, Achieving Excellence, Second Edition, provides assessment guidelines for teachers, school administrators, and state and national stakeholders to plan and implement assessment to improve teaching and learning.

Understanding these guidelines facilitates the use of appropriate classroom, school, and district assessments.

ASSESSMENT PROMOTES STUDENT LEARNING[10,p88]

Assessment measures student achievement of the national standards, how well they have learned them, and whether adjustments are needed to instruction and curriculum to enhance learning.

Before instruction begins, assess a student's knowledge of content and skill through a non-graded pre-assessment. Use the results to scaffold current knowledge and skill to the planned instruction. Because students may start the unit with a range of content and skills, it may be necessary to group them and proceed with differentiated instruction.[6,p14] To determine the status of student learning at the end of a unit, administer the same assessment and compare it to the pre-assessment or ask students to discuss and summarize what they have learned.[23,p66]

Show anchor examples of completed and scored performance tasks so students can examine a range of assessment scores and understand why each example received the assigned score.[10,p89] Exemplars, the highest range of the anchor examples, provide a tangible product students can look at to understand how to interpret the directions, prompt, and rubrics and plan their next step.[10,p89]

For assessment to promote student learning, give clear evaluation criteria for content and skill.[10,p89] Content criteria reflect the selected content and performance indicators in Standard 1 but also include the amount and quality of information required, such as the grammar and spelling expectations, how information is displayed, performed, etc. Skill criteria echo the selected performance indicators in Standards 2–8. Students show proficiency as they demonstrate their knowledge of content through demonstration of the skill.

Teachers must also provide ample time for students to learn, practice, and apply content and skills.[10,p89] Just as an athlete must practice her skills repeatedly, so must a health education student practice the skills of the national standards to be proficient.

It is vital to provide support to the student while he assumes responsibility for learning content and skills.[10,p89] In the standards-based classroom where students are working on authentic assessment projects, the teacher offers support by continually checking for understanding according to the various formative assessment tools. Using the data gathered, the teacher reinforces instruction, redirects a student, and gives suggestions for improvement. Because formative assessments are not graded, the suggestions for improvement are non-threatening and support the student.

> *"Self-understanding is the most important facet of understanding for lifelong learning"*[3,p215]

The most effective learners establish personal learning goals, use learning strategies that succeed, and assess their own work,[6,p16] which has a positive effect on learning.[7,p92] Self-assessment is formative and provides a way for students to clarify their understanding and see what was accomplished or remains to be done.

Successful people self-assess in a timely and effective way (**Figure 4.8**). They monitor their progress and

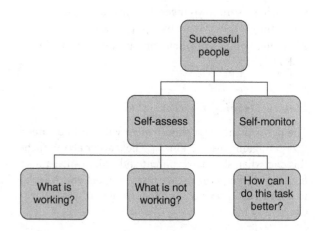

FIGURE 4.8　How Successful People Self-Assess

ask themselves whether their strategies are working or need improvement.[3,p216]

There are a variety of ways for students to use formative assessment to self-assess.

- When self-assessing, students ask, "What learning strategies help me reach my goal?" "What strategies are not working and why aren't they working?" "How can I improve my performance on this task?" By answering these questions, students improve their skills.

- As students complete a performance task, they score the content and skill criteria on the rubric and make comments about why they should receive the mark. After the teacher does the same, the students compare the scores. This self-assessment helps students become more responsible for their learning and makes scoring and grading a collaboration between the teacher and the student.[23,p69]

- Student reflection occurs after receiving the teacher's grade. The students ask, "Why did I get this grade?" "What do I need to do to improve?" This questioning is used to discuss the grade with the teacher and set goals to improve performance during the next performance task.

ASSESSMENT STRATEGIES ARE ALIGNED WITH STANDARDS, CURRICULUM, AND INSTRUCTION[10,p88]

The National Health Education Standards and state and local standards are the foundation of assessment. District leaders, curriculum coordinators, and teachers select performance indicators from each grade span and map them to determine the scope and sequence of the local curriculum. This process results in a comprehensive, skills-based health education program.

Once the alignment is in place, formative and summative assessment strategies are established by drawing on a variety of assessment tools. When planning them, ask, "What can the students do to show that they are proficient in this performance indicator?" Formative assessment strategies occur during instruction and improve teaching and learning. Summative strategies transpire at the end of instruction and determine how well the students achieved the performance indicators.

Once the assessments are established, plan the instruction. The lessons of the instructional plan, when organized, result in the curriculum, which is written last and affirms the alignment of assessment and instruction with the standard.

ASSESSMENTS MUST BE EQUITABLE, VALID, AND RELIABLE[10,p88]

Assessments are **equitable** when students are assessed through methods that are most suitable to them, taking into consideration their prior knowledge, cultural experience, and learning style. *Assessments should be flexible enough to meet the needs of all students.*[10,p88] Fair and equitable assessments:

- Match what is taught. If the performance task is assessing smoking cessation as a topic and practicing healthy behaviors as the skill, you must teach the elements of cessation and the criteria of the skill. Assessing based on an assumption of what the students know is not fair or equitable.

- Occur when teachers use many assessments rather than one or two per unit and vary them to include quizzes, tests, presentations, role-plays, brochures, public service announcements, posters, etc.

- Teach students how to do an assessment task before they are summatively assessed. The teacher explains the challenge issued by the prompt, the amount and quality of content required, the criteria of the skill, and how the holistic and analytical rubrics are used.

- Engage and encourage the students to proficiency of the standards by using formative assessments.

- Interpret the assessment results by comparing student achievement on the rubric to the requirements of the performance indicators.[2,p1-3]

Validity refers to the inferences made about student achievement as the result of an assessment. If it measures what is intended, the assessment is valid. A performance task is sound when the criteria on the rubric reflect the requirements of the performance indicator and specify the differences in quality for each score.[3,p354]

An assessment is **reliable** if a grade or score remains the same when retaken or the student earns the same score with a different scorer. One way of achieving reliability is to assign numerous tasks measuring the same outcome and have them scored by well-trained staff who use clear rubrics and refer to specific anchor papers or performances.[3,p348]

STUDENTS RECEIVE CLEAR ASSESSMENT INFORMATION REGARDING WHAT PERFORMANCE EVIDENCE IS EXPECTED[10,p88]

Before instruction begins, the teacher explains the learning outcomes so the students understand what they are expected to know and do.[2,p2] She selects performance indicators that address the needs of the students then plans the assessment, the performance task, and the instruction. Students receive a list of the required concepts, skill criteria, and holistic and analytical rubrics to assess their product along with backup information to complete the task.

The teacher shows the students examples of work that meet all the requirements of the performance indicator, do not meet the requirements, or meet some of them.

These exemplars help the students understand how to achieve proficiency in the performance indicator. While the teacher is showing examples, she explains why the work meets or does not meet the standard based on the rubric criteria. This strategy gives the students clear assessment information and helps them formulate a plan to complete the task and meet the performance indicators.

As the students prepare evidence of their work, the teacher assesses it by comparing what the student has produced to the performance indicators and the criteria on the rubric. This comparison will help her determine what the students have learned, what they are able to do, and whether to adjust instruction to improve their performance.[10,p86]

FEEDBACK FROM THE INSTRUCTOR HELPS STUDENTS IMPROVE THEIR PERFORMANCE. IF NECESSARY, STUDENTS SHOULD HAVE MORE THAN ONE OPPORTUNITY TO DEMONSTRATE WHAT THEY KNOW AND ARE ABLE TO DO[10,p88]

The function of assessment is to improve teaching and learning. If students are not proficient in the content and skill by end of a unit, they should have additional opportunities to revise their performance and be assessed again because assessment should focus on how well a student demonstrates knowledge and skill rather than when she performs it.[6,p17] Students may need more time, and if they are willing to revise and redo a task, the assessment score or grade should reflect their effort.

Feedback

> "The most powerful single modification that enhances achievement is feedback."[7,p5]

Feedback is essential for learning. It is ungraded, nonthreatening, and perceived as helpful hints to succeed. Feedback is frequent and timely in order for students to improve performance on the current task. It gives students a clear picture of the progress they are making toward achieving the performance indicators, explains how they can improve, and provides encouragement.[7,p11] Feedback does not need to be lengthy because abundant feedback does not translate into better. It can be written or oral and is specific to the individual or a group, depending on the assignment.

Performance task feedback targets the quality of content, the level of performance of the skill, and suggestions for improvement, all based on the criteria in the rubric. To motivate students, frame the feedback with positive words, pointing out the successes of the performance and giving suggestions for improving parts that do not meet the criteria.[17,p10-25]

When providing feedback to encourage a student who has received a poor assessment, the teacher helps the student interpret the score so as not to think he has failed but rather has been given an opportunity to improve.[7,p8]

Feedback is notably effective when students use it to improve their performance. Feedback should be:

- Timely: the student can connect the comments to a recent particular task.
- Specific: highlighting and commenting on the criteria of the task rather than general comments once the task is complete.
- Understandable: students know what they did well or should do to improve.[6,p16]

Using a videotape of a group presentation, speech, skit, and other performances or practices is an effective feedback strategy that increases student learning. The teacher and students watch the tape together and discuss the presentation and how it compares to the content and skill requirements on the rubric.[24]

Videotape is also a self-assessment tool because the students observe the practice performance, compare it to the content and skill criteria, and make adjustments for improvement. After viewing the tape, the students set immediate goals for improvement and monitor their long-term progress.[13,p51] For visual learners, this formative assessment can be more beneficial than written feedback.

STUDENTS AND PARENTS/GUARDIANS RECEIVE INFORMATION REGARDING ACHIEVEMENT OF THE STANDARDS[10,p88]

Parents and guardians are the primary health educators of our children. Most parents want their children to have the knowledge and skills to be healthy, successful in school, and prepared for the 21st century. In order to be informed and supportive of the comprehensive health program, parents, guardians, and community members must receive information about student progress in achieving the national standards, summative grades, assessment practices, and how assessment results are used to improve teaching and learning.

When classroom assessment occurs frequently and is shared with students, performance improves. Assessment takes the form of oral and written feedback as gathered from various assessment tools such as rubrics, self-assessments, etc.

Parents learn of assessment results through report cards, progress reports, and conferences. The community learns of results through parent information evenings, newspapers, radio news, and school and community websites. States communicate assessment results through school report cards and data posted to their websites.[25,p66]

INSTRUCTORS CONTINUALLY REVIEW AND ADJUST THEIR ASSESSMENTS AND ASSESSMENT SYSTEMS, WHEN NECESSARY[10,p88]

Assessments, as strategies to enhance learning, vary according to the performance task and learning goal. A teacher may prefer one assessment over another because it is easier to administer or manage. Remember, however, that students have different learning styles, and a variety of assessment strategies is more beneficial to them.

Frequent formative classroom assessments inform the teacher what the students know and are able to do. Classroom assessment informs the teacher when concepts or skills are learned, not learned, or should be re-taught. The teacher learns whether the assessment accurately measured what was taught, if the task was challenging, and if the directions were clear.[2,p3]

Should some students grasp the lesson while others do not, the teacher responds by forming groups and differentiating instruction. She then continues the formative assessment to determine progress toward reaching the standard.

Assessment Systems

A comprehensive skills-based health education assessment system includes classroom, school, district, and state assessments that are aligned with standards, curriculum, and instruction. The assessment data compiled provides information to stakeholders about student progress in achieving the standards and makes districts accountable for improving curriculum and instruction.[10,p90]

Authentic assessment is central to evaluation of the National Health Education Standards. Whereas the classroom provides more opportunity for authentic assessment, the district and school have less opportunity because of the numbers of students being assessed. State health education assessment has the least opportunity for authentic assessment and relies mostly on selected response or open-ended response questions (**Figure 4.9**).

CLASSROOM ASSESSMENT

The classroom provides more opportunities than local or state assessments for performance-based, authentic assessment. The teacher designs performance tasks that provide students with the opportunity to demonstrate knowledge and skill. As students apply what they learn, the teacher formatively assesses and uses that information to help the student achieve proficiency in the standards.[10,p90]

Assessment data gathered in the classroom improves teaching and learning by providing evidence of what the students know and are able to do. The data is used to adjust instruction and communicate progress in achieving

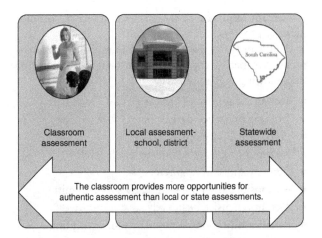

FIGURE 4.9 Authentic Assessment and Assessment Systems

standards to students, parents, teachers, administrators, the community, and the state.[25,p63]

SCHOOL AND DISTRICT ASSESSMENTS

School and district health education assessments are summative but may contain some authentic assessment in combination with traditional, state, or nationally developed assessments. Because of the scope of the assessment and the number of students involved, less authentic assessment occurs on this level.

The data collected from district assessments is reported to students, educators, parents, community members, and policymakers.[25,p14] The district assessment report includes an analysis of the results and an action plan to improve. The scheme may include plans for program evaluation, scheduling, professional development, curriculum revision, staffing, and funding for the comprehensive program.[25,p66]

STATE ASSESSMENTS

The state has a vital role in the implementation and assessment of comprehensive health education. When a state commits itself to fostering the health and well-being of its children by legislating comprehensive health education, districts must comply. State standards provide districts with what the students should know and do at the end of a grade span. Assessments based on these standards result in districts developing curriculum and instruction that reflect the state requirements.

A state may place comprehensive health questions into other state assessments or administer a separate health education assessment. Results measure the level of standards proficiency achieved by students.

States use assessment data to develop policy and regulatory decisions as well as generate information about districts.[25,p62] State education agencies (SEAs) post district assessment results on their websites as a way of communicating progress.

A SEA provides leadership and commitment to comprehensive health education by providing or requiring the following:

- Technical support for the district
- Training on policy development
- Professional development
- Minimum time allocations by grade level
- Content and skill requirements
- A coordinated school health advisory committee
- A comprehensive health advisory committee
- Parent notification requirements for exempting a child from sexuality classes
- An annual district report
- Penalties for non-compliance
- State assessments[26]

HEALTH EDUCATION ASSESSMENT PROJECT

The Council of Chief State School Officers (CCSSO) and the State Collaborative on Assessment and Student Standards (SCASS) created The Health Education Assessment Project (HEAP) in 1993 (http://scassheap.org).

HEAP's mission is "to develop effective health education assessment resources through a collaborative process, and to increase members' capacity to align curriculum, instruction, and assessment to improve student health literacy through improved health instruction."[27]

Member states pay an annual membership fee to pool their fiscal resources to develop products and services to support the implementation of standards-based health education and assessment, receive professional development, and share innovations. The states that have joined HEAP have access to an assessment bank of items used in the classroom for school, district, and state assessments. The National Health Education Standards are the foundation in aligning curriculum, instruction, and assessment, and for all products and services developed by the HEAP and support states.[1,p6]

HEAP's assessment system includes an Assessment Framework, professional development modules, CDs, and posters, exemplar binders, rubrics cards and skill posters, anchor and scoring practice sets, and assessment tools for teachers. The web-based assessment system can be used as classroom, school, district, or state assessment and consists of an online item bank and online student testing. Other available resources improve students' health and reading literacy or offer distance learning courses.[1,p39]

Review Questions

1. What is the purpose of assessment?

2. What is the difference between assessment and grading?

3. Explain the assessment cycle.

4. Explain the difference between formative and summative assessment.

5. Choose five formative assessment tools and explain how to use each to check for understanding.

6. Why should a teacher tell students how they are being assessed formatively and summatively at the beginning of a unit?

7. What is the difference between norm referenced and criterion referenced?

8. Compare the structure and use of holistic vs. analytical rubrics.

9. Why are performance tasks examples of authentic assessment?

10. What is the difference between equitable, valid, and reliable?

References

1. CCSSO~SCASS Health Education Project. (2006). *Assessment Tools for School Health Education, Pre-service and In-service edition.* Santa Cruz, CA: ToucanEd Inc.

2. Suskie, L. (2009) *Assessing Student Learning.* (2nd ed.). San Francisco: John Wiley & Sons.

3. Wiggins, G. M. (2005). *Understanding by Design.* (Expanded 2nd ed.). Alexandria, VA: Association for Supervision and Curriculum Development.

4. Leahy, S. L. (2005). Classroom Assessment, Minute by Minute, Day by Day. *Educational Leadership.* p. 19.

5. Brookhart, S. M. (2008). Formative Assessment that Empowers. *Educational Leadership.* p. 53.

6. McTighe, J. O. (2005, November). Seven Practices for Effective Learning. *Educational Leadership.*

7. Marzano, R. J. (2006). *Classroom Assessment & Grading that Work.* Alexandria, VA: Association for Supervision and Curriculum Development.

8. Fisher, D. F. (2007). *Checking for Understanding.* Alexandria: Association for Supervision and Curriculum Development.

9. Popham, W. J. (2008). *Transformative Assessment.* Alexandria, VA: Association for Supervision and Curriculum Development. p. 61.

10. Joint Committee on National Health Education Standards (2007). *National Health Education Standards, Second Edition, Achieving Excellence.* Atlanta, GA: American Cancer Society.

11. Perry, M. (2008). *Interpersonal Communication.* Unpublished manuscript.

12. Stempinski, D. (2007). Classroom Assessments Tell the Real Story. *MegaSCASS.* New Orleans, LA: CCSSO.

13. Brookhart, S. M. (2008). *How to Give Effective Feedback to Your Students.* Alexandria, VA: Association for Supervision and Curriculum Development.

14. Hibbard, K. M. (1996). *Teachers's Guide to Performance-Based Learning and Assessment.* Middlebury, CT: Association for Supervision and Curriculum Development. p. 3.

15. Stevens, D. D. (2005). *Introduction to Rubrics.* Sterling, PA: Stylus Publishing, LLC.

16. Meeks, L. H. (2009). *Comprehensive School Health Education, Totally Awesome Strategies for Teaching Health.* (6th ed.). New York: McGraw-Hill.

17. ALTEC at the University of Kansas. (2009). *Project Based Learning.* Retrieved October 26, 2009, from Project Based Learning Checklists: http://pblchecklist.4teachers.org

18. ALTEC at the University of Kansas. (2009). *Choose a Customizable Rubric Below:.* Retrieved October 26, 2009, from Create a New Rubric: http://rubistar.4teachers.org/index .php?screen=NewRubric&module=Rubistar

19. Telljohann, S. K. (2009). *Health Education Elementary and Middle School Applications.* New York: McGraw-Hill. p. 426.

20. Chappuis, S. C. (2008). The Best Value in Formative Assessment. *Educational Leadership.* p. 15.

21. Marzano, R. J., & Kendall, J. S. (2007). *The New Taxonomy of Educational Objectives.* (2nd ed.). Thousand Oaks, CA: Corwin Press. p. 5.

22. Marzano, R. J., Pickering, D. J., & Pollock, J. E. (2001). *Classroom Instruction that Works.* Alexandria, VA: Association for Supervision and Curriculum Development.

23. Shepard, L. A. (2005, November). Linking Formative Assessment to Scaffolding. *Educational Leadership.*

24. Dicks, M. J. (2005, November). Show Me the Way. *Educational Leadership.* p. 80.

25 Carr, J. F. (2001). *Succeeding with Standards.* Alexandria, VA: Association for Supervision and Curriculum Development. p. 66.

26. South Carolina Department of Education. (n.d.). *South Carolina Academic Standards for Health and Safety Education.* Retrieved November 16, 2009, from http://www.ed .sc.gov/agency/Standards-and-Learning/Academic-Standards/ CHE/documents/2009HealthEducationStandards.pdf

27. Health Education Assessment Project. (n.d.). *Advancing Student Health Literacy Through the CCSSO~SCASS Health Education Assessment Project (HEAP).* Retrieved November 16, 2009, from Council of Chief State School Officers: www.ccsso.org

Teaching National Health Education Standard 1

Students will comprehend concepts related to health promotion and disease prevention to enhance health.[1,p24]

Standard 1

One of the Characteristics of Effective Health Education Curriculum is that curricula should provide functional health knowledge. Standard 1 is the foundation for accurate, reliable, and credible health concepts and functional health knowledge that students should know and use to adopt or maintain healthy behaviors.

A curriculum that includes only content is inadequate to change behavior. Although acquiring knowledge is important, applying it to analyze influences on behavior, access valid information, communicate effectively, make good decisions, set goals, practice healthy behaviors, advocate, and build competence and confidence is more so because these skills facilitate the acquisition of health enhancing behaviors.

The concepts in Standard 1 are based on established behavior theories and models that explain why human beings behave the way we do. The performance indicators embrace these health theories and models and focus on health promotion and risk reduction.[1,p24] When a student demonstrates all the performance indicators in a grade span to a proscribed level, he is proficient in them.

By pairing Standard 1 with a skill standard (Standards 2–8) and using the Characteristics of Effective Health Education to design and implement curriculum, districts provide students with an educational environment that has a positive influence on their health behaviors and practices.[1,p13]

Choosing Content

The National Health Education Standards help students acquire the knowledge and skills needed to adopt and maintain healthy behaviors. Standards are not a curriculum but rather a framework for planning instruction to include content and skills. Performance indicators from

Standard 1 are paired with a skills standard so that students gain the knowledge and skill needed to cope with a particular need (see **Figure 5.1**). Planners choose content from the common health education content areas. Examples of valid and reliable content are found at the end of the chapter.

Common Health Education Content Areas

- Community Health
- Consumer Health
- Environmental Health
- Family Life
- Mental/Emotional Health
- Injury Prevention/Safety
- Nutrition
- Personal Health
- Prevention/Control of Disease
- Substance Use/Abuse[1,p11]

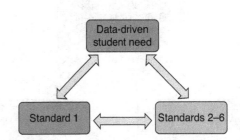

FIGURE 5.1 **Relationship Between Data-Driven Student Need, Standard 1 Performance Indicator, and Skills Standard Performance Indicator**

IF THE STANDARDS ARE A FRAMEWORK, HOW ARE THEY USED TO BUILD CURRICULUM AND INSTRUCTION? HOW DOES ONE CHOOSE CONTENT?

1. Determine the needs of the students via data analysis. Obtain data through a school, community, state, national surveys, or reports.

2. From a skill standard, choose one or more performance indicators that target the student need.

3. Select a Standard 1 performance indicator(s) that provides a framework for content.

Planning skill and content to meet a specific student need is **targeted instruction**. Students learn the knowledge and skill needed to overcome a particular problem and to develop and maintain healthy behaviors. Targeted instruction is also an efficient use of time because it targets needs, content, and skill rather than spending time on content that is good to know but not essential to the needs of the students.

For example, if school, community, state, or national data indicate that middle school students are physically inactive, the curriculum planner may choose the Standard 7 performance indicator 7.5.2—Demonstrate a variety of healthy practices and behaviors to maintain or improve personal health[1,p35] and Standard 1 performance indicator 1.5.1—Describe the relationship between healthy behaviors and personal health[1,p24] (see **Figure 5.2**).

The instructor first teaches Standard 7—Students will demonstrate the ability to practice health-enhancing behaviors and avoid or reduce health risks.[1,p35] She accomplishes this by discussing why the standard is important and relevant to students, then how it relates to all other standards. The teacher presents and models the steps of the skill so students can see what it looks like. The students then practice and rehearse the skill through a realistic prompt and receive feedback (formative assessment) and reinforcement from the teacher for self-improvement.[1,p14]

Standard 7 includes a multitude of skills from hand washing, sneezing in one's arm, and administering first aid to the correct way to use a condom. Due to the nature of this middle school data-driven problem, the skill selected by the teacher is, "Decrease inactivity through a walking program." The skill of walking includes knowing how much time to walk; how to increase and decrease intensity; the appropriate arm, elbow, fist, and feet form; and steps completed per session.[2] The teacher may also include instructions to use a pedometer, fill out a walking log, and determine benchmarks for accomplishments and a reward plan.

Standard 1 performance indicator 1.5.1 directs the teacher to show the relationship between being physically active (healthy behaviors) and personal health. Content includes the benefits of being physically active and how walking improves personal health. The teacher accesses content through a variety of valid and reliable sources from national organizations, such as the Centers for Disease Control and Prevention and the American Cancer Society, to textbook publishers.

The product for the above instruction may be a poster or demonstration that displays the skill of walking, the benefits of being physically active, benchmarks of accomplishment, and rewards for completing the program.

When planning for skills-based health education, develop a performance task based on the state and national standards, student needs, targeted content, and skill. Examples of performance tasks, prompts, and rubrics are in the skills chapters.

CONTENT RESOURCES

When instructional time is limited, use content that addresses reduction of the CDC's adolescent risk factors. They are the foundation of the data collected by the Centers for Disease Control and Prevention through the Youth Risk Behavior Survey (YRBS). The CDC conducts this high school survey every two years in randomly selected schools across the country.[3] Many states and some local districts also administer the YRBS to their middle and high school students, gaining the capability to compare their results to state and national data.

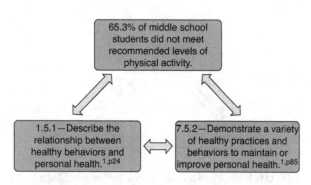

FIGURE 5.2 Targeting Instruction by Choosing Performance Indicators That Will Help Reduce Student Needs

Centers for Disease Control and Prevention Adolescent Risk Behaviors

- Alcohol and Other Drug Use
- Injury and Violence (including suicide)
- Tobacco Use
- Poor Nutrition
- Inadequate Physical Activity
- Risky Sexual Behavior[1,p11]

Table 5.1 shows the relationship among the content areas, national standards, and CDC adolescent risk factors. The national standards are in the center of the page because they are the foundation of planning. To reduce risk factors, access appropriate information through the content areas then plan instruction through Standard 1, the content standard, and Standards 2–8, the skills standards.

PreK–Grade 2

When planning a PreK–2 unit, determine student need based on collected data. Once the need is established, decide which skill standard to use to address the need. Next, examine the Standard 1 performance indicators and select one or more that complements the skills standard and gives students the knowledge needed to overcome behavioral health problems (see **Figure 5.3**).

We must teach and assess how to describe, identify, and list functional health knowledge to help students

PreK–Grade 2 Performance Indicators

1.2.1 Identify that healthy behaviors affect personal health.
1.2.2 Recognize that there are multiple dimensions of health.
1.2.3 Describe ways to prevent communicable diseases.
1.2.4 List ways to prevent common childhood injuries.
1.2.5 Describe why it is important to seek health care.[1,p24]

reach proficiency in this standard. During instruction, assess student progress formatively and adjust accordingly.

Students *identify* different healthy behaviors (performance indicator 1.2.1) that affect personal health. To teach them how to identify healthy behaviors, show pictures of a child wearing a helmet while riding a bike,

---

TABLE 5.1 How the National Health Education Standards Collaborate with the Health Content Areas to Reduce Risk Behaviors

Health Education Content Areas		National Health Education Standards		Adolescent Risk Behaviors
Community Health		**Standard 1**—Students will comprehend concepts related to health promotion and disease prevention to enhance health.		Alcohol and Other Drug Use
Consumer Health				
Family Life				Injury and Violence (Including suicide)
Mental and Emotional Health		**Standard 2**—Students will analyze the influence of family, peers, culture, media, technology, and other factors on health behaviors.		Tobacco Use
Injury Prevention and Safety				Poor Nutrition
Nutrition	Taught through	**Standard 3**—Students will demonstrate the ability to access valid information and products and services to enhance health.	Reduce	Inadequate Physical Activity
Personal Health				Risky Sexual Behavior
Prevention and Control of Disease		**Standard 4**—Students will demonstrate the ability to use interpersonal communication skills to enhance health and avoid or reduce health risks.		
Substance Use and Abuse				
Community Health		**Standard 5**—Students will demonstrate the ability to use decision-making skills to enhance health.		
		Standard 6—Students will demonstrate the ability to use goal-setting skills to enhance health.		
		Standard 7—Students will demonstrate the ability to practice health-enhancing behaviors and avoid or reduce health risks.		
		Standard 8—Students will demonstrate the ability to advocate[1,p11] for personal, family, and community health.		

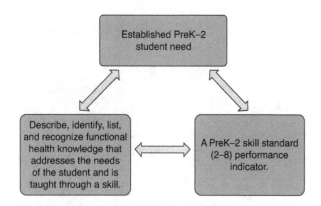

FIGURE 5.3 Planning for PreK–2

holding an adult's hand while crossing the street, taking medicine from an adult, eating healthy foods for breakfast, brushing teeth, washing hands, etc., and explain why the behavior is healthy. The information taught should be functional and appropriate in comprehensiveness to the age of the student, refer to an established need, and complement the skill being taught.

To assess, show pictures of healthy and unhealthy behaviors and ask the students to *identify* the healthy behaviors and explain why they have a positive effect on personal health. Students also *identify* unhealthy behaviors and explain why they have a negative effect on personal health.

To teach how to *recognize* the multiple dimensions of health (performance indicator 1.2.2), read a story about a PreK–2 child who is sick, upset about being bullied, excited to go on vacation, proud of an accomplishment, etc. Ask the students how those events make the child feel. As the children respond, categorize the responses into the dimensions of health. After explaining them, read a scenario and ask the children to *recognize* which dimension of health is affected.

Students also *describe* ways of preventing communicable disease. When performance indicator 1.2.3 is paired with Standard 7, the students demonstrate hand-washing techniques and *describe* how doing so removes the virus from their hands and prevents the spread of the common cold. They demonstrate sneezing into their sleeves instead of their hands and opening a door using a paper towel or their sleeve rather than a bare hand. They then *describe* how those behaviors prevent the spread of germs.

Instruction includes information about a virus and how it is transmitted or makes us sick. To demonstrate proficiency, students demonstrate the skill and *describe* how that behavior prevents the spread of communicable disease.

Ask the children to *list* different ways to prevent injury (performance indicator 1.2.4). Hold up pictures of common PreK–2 recreation items such as a bicycle, scooter,

skateboard, and baseball bat and explain how to use them safely. To show proficiency, students *list* different ways to safely use recreational equipment to prevent injury.

To show proficiency in the PreK–2 performance indicators of Standard 1, students must provide accurate, specific, and complete information related to:

- Healthy behaviors
- Dimensions of health
- Preventing disease and injuries
- Importance of seeking health care.[1,p24]

The following Standard 1 analytical rubrics offer guidance to score a student in each performance indicator. When the scope of the performance task is established, the teacher fuses content to the performance indicator and uses the rubric to assess it (see **Table 5.2**).

For example: performance indicator 1.2.1—Identify that healthy behaviors affect personal health.[1,p24]

Performance indicator 1.2.1 with infused content— Identify that washing hands affects personal health.[1,p24]

Remember, a student is assessed not only on functional knowledge but also a demonstration of it through a skill. Consequently, a rubric for a performance task includes criteria for both Standard 1 and a skills standard. Examples are found in Chapters 6–12.

Modify the rubric to accommodate differences in age and ability. It is important that students know how they are assessed before completing the performance task. Explain the assessment criteria verbally, through pictures, or as written instructions. Distribute the rubric to the older students who can read, making the language consistent with the reading level.

WHAT DOES STANDARD 1 LOOK LIKE IN THE PREK–2 CLASSROOM?

The Westchester Community Risk Behavior Survey indicates that the children in the community are overweight. In response, the Grade 1 health teacher selects a performance indicator from a skill standard that helps the students understand what influences them to make food choices at school. The teacher next selects a performance indicator from Standard 1 to target healthy eating.

Standard 2—Students will analyze the influence of family, peers, culture, media, technology, and other factors on health behaviors.[1,p26]

Performance Indicator 2.2.2—Identify what the school can do to support personal health practices and behaviors.[1,p26]

Performance Indicator 2.2.2 with infused content— Identify what the school can do by providing healthy food choices, to support personal health practices and behaviors.[1,p26]

TABLE 5.2   Sample Analytical Rubric for Performance Indicators 1.2.1 to 1.2.5

Criteria	4	3	2	1
Sample Analytical Rubric for Performance Indicator 1.2.1				
Performance indicator 1.2.1 with infused content—Identify that washing hands affects personal health.[1,p24]	Student accurately identifies that washing hands affects personal health.	Student's identification that washing hands affects personal health is mostly accurate.	Student's identification that washing hands affects personal health has a few inaccuracies.	Student's identification that washing hands affects personal health is mostly inaccurate.
Sample Analytical Rubric for Performance Indicator 1.2.2				
Performance indicator 1.2.2 with infused content—Recognize that there are multiple dimensions of health.	Student accurately recognizes three examples of each dimension of health.	Student's recognition of three examples of each dimension of health is mostly accurate.	Student's recognition of three examples of each dimension of health has a few inaccuracies.	Student's recognition of three examples of each dimension of health is mostly inaccurate.
Sample Analytical Rubric for Performance Indicator 1.2.3				
Performance indicator 1.2.3 with infused content—Describe how hand washing prevents communicable diseases.	Student thoroughly describes three ways hand washing prevents communicable disease.	Student adequately describes three ways hand washing prevents communicable disease.	Student inadequately describes three ways hand washing prevents communicable disease.	Student poorly describes three ways hand washing prevents communicable disease.
Sample Analytical Rubric for Performance Indicator 1.2.4				
Performance indicator 1.2.4 with infused content—List ways to prevent common childhood injuries.[1,p24]	Student accurately lists three ways to prevent a bicycle injury.	Student's list of three ways to prevent a bicycle injury is mostly accurate.	Student's list of three ways to prevent a bicycle injury has a few inaccuracies.	Student's list of three ways to prevent a bicycle injury is mostly inaccurate.
Sample Analytical Rubric for Performance Indicator 1.2.5				
Performance indicator 1.2.5 with infused content—Describe why it is important to seek health care when sick with the flu.	Student accurately describes three reasons why it is important to seek health care when sick with the flu.	Student's description of three reasons why it is important to seek health care when sick with the flu is mostly accurate.	Student's description of three reasons why it is important to seek health care when sick with the flu has a few inaccuracies.	Student's description of three reasons why it is important to seek health care when sick with the flu is mostly inaccurate.

In this performance indicator, students identify what the school does to support healthy nutrition practices and behaviors.

Students examine the internal and external factors that influence their school food choices and whether they have a positive or negative effect on their health. If the effect is positive, the behavior is encouraged. Otherwise, students brainstorm ways to overcome the influence.

Standard 1 performance indicator 1.2.1—Identify that healthy behaviors affect personal health.[1,p24]

Performance Indicator 1.2.1 with infused content—Identify that healthy behaviors, such as healthy food choices, affect personal health.[1,p24]

This performance indicator requires students to identify that eating healthy foods is good for personal health. Content may include the food guide pyramid[4] and why following the pyramid's recommendations is good for health.

By selecting the above performance indicators of Standard 2 and Standard 1, instruction is targeted to help students understand the factors that influence their eating choices at school and recognize that making healthy food choices affects personal health.

In the above example, content is paired with Standard 2 but could also be coupled with any of the other skills.

To Teach Students How Healthy Food Choices Affect Personal Health and How to Identify Trusted Adults Such as Parents and Food Service Providers Who Could Help to Provide the Healthy Food Choices, Pair Standard 3 with Standard 1.

Standard 3—Students will demonstrate the ability to access valid information and products and services to enhance health.[1,p28]
> Performance indicator 3.2.1—Identify trusted adults and professionals who can help promote health.[1,p28]
> > *Performance indicator 3.2.1 with infused content—* Identify trusted adults and professionals, such as parents and food service providers, who can help promote health.[1,p28]
> > > and pair it with
> Standard 1 performance indicator 1.2.1—Identify that healthy behaviors affect personal health.[1,p24]
> > *Performance Indicator 1.2.1 with infused content—* Identify that healthy behaviors, such as healthy food choices, affect personal health.[1,p24]

OR

To Learn to Communicate Feelings About Being Teased or Bullied as a Result of Being Overweight and That When One Dimension of Health Is Out of Balance, it Affects All the Other Dimensions, Pair Standards 4 and 1.

Standard 4—Students will demonstrate the ability to use interpersonal communication skills to enhance health and avoid or reduce health risks.[1,p30]
> Performance indicator 4.2.1—Demonstrate healthy ways to express needs, wants, and feelings.[1,p30]
> > *Performance indicator 4.2.1 with infused content—* Demonstrate healthy ways to express needs, wants, and feelings about being bullied because of being overweight.[1,p30]

and pair it with
Standard 1 performance indicator 1.2.2—Recognize that there are multiple dimensions of health.[1,p24]
> *Performance indicator 1.2.2 with infused content—* Recognize that there are multiple dimensions of health affected by being bullied and being overweight.[1,p24]

OR

To Teach Children to Ask for Professional Help to Decrease Their BMI, Pair Standards 5 and 1.

Standard 5—Students will demonstrate the ability to use decision-making skills to enhance health.[1,p32]
> Performance indicator 5.2.1—Identify situations when a health-related decision is needed.[1,p32]
> > *Performance indicator 5.2.1 with infused content—* Identify situations, such as needing to decrease BMI, when a health-related decision is needed.[1,p32]
> > > and pair it with
> Standard 1 performance indicator 1.2.5—Describe why it is important to seek health care.[1,p24]
> > *Performance indicator 1.2.5 with infused content—* Describe why it is important to ask for help from a healthcare provider to decrease BMI.[1,p24]

OR

To Set a Short-Term Nutrition Goal and Learn How Reaching That Goal Affects Personal Health, Pair Standards 6 and 1.

Standard 6—Students will demonstrate the ability to use goal-setting skills to enhance health.[1,p34]
> Performance indicator 6.2.1—Identify a short-term personal health goal and take action toward achieving the goal.[1,p34]
> > *Performance indicator 6.2.1 with infused content—* Identify a short-term personal health goal, such as decreasing BMI, and take action toward achieving the goal.[1,p34]
> > > and pair it with

Standard 1 performance indicator 1.2.1—Identify that healthy behaviors affect personal health.[1,p24]

Performance indicator 1.2.1 with infused content—Identify that healthy behaviors, such as decreasing BMI, affect personal health.[1,p24]

For Students to Learn About Healthy Eating and How Good Nutrition Keeps Them Healthy and Better Prepared to Fight Infections, Pair Standards 7 and 1.

Standard 7—Students will demonstrate the ability to practice health-enhancing behaviors and avoid or reduce health risks.[1,p35]

Performance indicator 7.2.1—Demonstrate healthy practices and behaviors to maintain or improve personal health.[1,p35]

Performance indicator 7.2.1 with infused content—Demonstrate healthy practices and behaviors, such as eating healthy to maintain or improve personal health.[1,p35]

and pair it with

Standard 1 performance indicator 1.2.3—Describe ways to prevent communicable diseases.[1,p24]

Performance indicator 1.2.3 with infused content—Describe ways to prevent communicable diseases by eating healthy.[1,p24]

OR

To Learn to Advocate for Healthy Snack Choices with Friends, Then Explain How Healthy Snack Choices Affect Overall Wellness, Pair Standard 8 with Standard 1.

Standard 8—Students will demonstrate the ability to advocate for personal, family, and community health.[1,p36]

Performance indicator 8.2.2—Encourage peers to make positive health choices.[1,p36]

Performance indicator 8.2.2 with infused content—Encourage peers to make positive health choices, such as eating healthy snacks.[1,p36]

and pair it with

Standard 1 performance indicator 1.2.2—Recognize that there are multiple dimensions of health.[1,p24]

Performance indicator 1.2.2 with infused content—Recognize that there are multiple dimensions of health affected by friendship and eating healthy snacks.[1,p24]

The above examples demonstrate how Standard 1 can be paired with any of the skills standards to meet the needs of the students. After selecting performance indicators, plan the unit.

By linking the skill and content performance indicators, you will have a clear idea of how to plan the unit lessons.

The first step in planning is to think through the unit by completing the performance task template. Upon completion, you will have most of the information to introduce the prompt to students.

When planning for the prompt, also include all the back-up information, holistic rubrics, analytical rubrics, and worksheets the students need to complete the task. Designing skills-based lessons requires considerable preparation, but once you distribute it and explain the task, the students are responsible for the results. Students learn with good coaching (formative assessments) to demonstrate proficiency in content and skill.

How Does the Coordinated School Health Team Contribute to Increasing Functional Health Knowledge Related to Health Promotion and Disease Prevention to Enhance Health?

Health Education

- Refocus instruction on skill building and healthy eating.
- Model healthy practices and behaviors.

Physical Education

- Promote after-school physical activity.
- Encourage students to increase their physical activity at home and in the community.

Health Services

- Provide nutrition referrals.
- Make nutrition pamphlets available to students and staff.

Nutrition Services

- Provide healthy foods and snacks in the school.
- Encourage students to make healthy food choices at home, school, and the community.

Counseling, Psychological, and Social Services

- Provide nutrition counseling.
- Provide referrals to community nutrition counselors.

Healthy School Environment

- Examine youth risk behavior data to determine student needs.
- Provide healthy snacks in the vending machines.

Health Promotion for Staff

- Be good role models when snacking in front of the children.
- Provide professional development on nutrition and physical activity.

Family/Community Involvement

- Encourage families to provide healthy snacks to children.
- Provide workshops on nutrition and physical activity.

Grades 3–5

To plan a Grade 3–5 unit, determine student need from collected data. Once the need is established, decide which skill standard best addresses it. Examine the Standard 1 performance indicators for Grades 3–5 and select one or more that complements the skills standard and gives students the functional knowledge needed to overcome the behavioral health problem (see **Figure 5.4**).

Students describe and identify functional health knowledge to reach proficiency in this standard. During instruction, formatively assess student progress and adjust accordingly.

On this level, students *identify* examples of emotional, intellectual, physical, and social health (1.5.2). Instruction includes an explanation of each dimension plus how they interrelate (see **Figure 5.5**). Assess by showing pictures, reading stories, performing role-plays, etc., and ask the students to *identify* the dimension and explain how one affects the other.

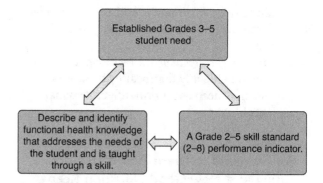

FIGURE 5.4   Planning for Grades 3–5

Performance indicator 1.5.1 pairs with many skills performance indicators since it asks students to *describe* the relationship between healthy behaviors and personal health.

Because planning starts with a student need, use this performance indicator to show the benefits of the healthy behavior vs. unhealthy behavior. For example, if the nurse has collected data that shows students have poor dental health, pair Standard 7 with performance indicator 1.5.1 to provide instruction about caring for teeth and gums and how dental health relates to personal health. Assessment includes a student demonstrating flossing and brushing and a *description* of how healthy teeth affect personal health. Furthermore, include performance indicator 1.5.2 which identifies how dental health affects emotional, intellectual, physical, and social health.

Students also *describe* ways in which safe and healthy school and community environments promote personal health (1.5.3). This performance indicator pairs nicely with performance indicator 2.5.4—Describe how the school and community can support personal health practices and behaviors,[1,p26] and performance indicator 3.5.2—Locate resources from home, school, and community that provide valid health information.[1,p28] Doing so gives the teacher a complementary pair to address skill

Grades 3–5

1.5.1 Describe the relationship between healthy behaviors and personal health.

1.5.2 Identify examples of emotional, intellectual, physical, and social health.

1.5.3 Describe ways in which safe and healthy school and community environments can promote personal health.

1.5.4 Describe ways to prevent common childhood injuries and health problems.

1.5.5 Describe when it is important to seek health care.[1,p24]

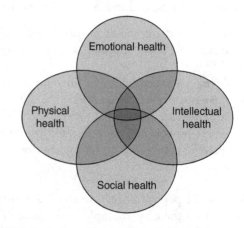

FIGURE 5.5   Dimensions of Health

and content relating to school and community resources. The assessment strategy depends on the content and how the child *describes* the information. The performance task may require a certain number of facts, a sequence, pictures, etc. The scoring rubric reflects the content, skill, and any other criteria required by the performance task.

Students *describe* in performance indicator 1.5.4, ways to prevent common childhood injuries and health problems.[1,p24] This performance indicator is broad enough to include the prevention of injuries and childhood health problems, such as accidents, falls, cuts, bruises, communicable disease, etc. To demonstrate proficiency, students *describe* ways to prevent the targeted injury or childhood health problem through a skill standard by creating explanatory posters, performing a role-play, writing and reading a poem, writing and performing a public service announcement, etc.

Students *describe* when it is important to seek health care in performance indicator 1.5.5. During instruction, explain what health care is, who provides it, and where they can go to access it. To assess, read an open-ended story and let the students *describe* whether a character should seek health care and why.

To assess the Grades 3–5 performance indicators of Standard 1, students must provide accurate, relevant, specific, and complete information related to

- Healthy behaviors
- Dimensions of health
- Healthy environments
- Preventing injuries and health problems
- Importance of seeking health care.[1,p24]

The Standard 1 analytical rubrics (**Table 5.3**) offer guidance to scoring a student in each performance indicator. When the scope of the performance task is established, the teacher adds specific criteria to the rubric.

Remember, a student is assessed not only on functional knowledge but also a demonstration of it through a skill. Consequently, a rubric for a performance task includes criteria for both Standard 1 and a skills standard. Examples are found in Chapters 6–12.

The teacher may modify the rubric in recognition of age and varying ability. It is important that students know how they are assessed before completing the performance task. Provide the assessment criteria verbally, through

---

TABLE 5.3 Sample Analytical Rubrics for Performance Indicators 1.5.1 to 1.5.5

Criteria	4	3	2	1
Sample Analytical Rubric for Performance Indicator 1.5.1				
Performance indicator 1.5.1 with infused content—Describe the relationship between brushing teeth and personal health.[1,p24]	Student thoroughly describes three facts about the relationship between brushing teeth and personal health.	Student adequately describes three facts about the relationship between brushing teeth and personal health.	Student inadequately describes three facts about the relationship between brushing teeth and personal health.	Student poorly describes three facts about the relationship between brushing teeth and personal health.
Sample Analytical Rubric for Performance Indicator 1.5.2				
Performance indicator 1.5.2 with infused content—Identify examples of emotional, intellectual, physical, and social health.[1,p24]	Student accurately identifies pictures of the emotional, intellectual, physical, and social dimensions of health.	Student's identification of pictures of the emotional, intellectual, physical, and social dimensions of health is mostly accurate.	Student's identification of pictures of the emotional, intellectual, physical, and social dimensions of health has a few inaccuracies.	Student's identification of pictures of the emotional, intellectual, physical, and social dimensions of health is mostly inaccurate.
Sample Analytical Rubric for Performance Indicator 1.5.3				
Performance indicator 1.5.3 with infused content—Describe ways in which safe and healthy school and community environments can promote personal health by preventing the spread of germs.[1,p24]	Student accurately describes three ways the safe and healthy school and community environments can promote personal health by preventing the spread of germs.	Student's description of three ways the safe and healthy school and community environments can promote personal health by preventing the spread of germs is mostly accurate.	Student's description of three ways the safe and healthy school and community environments can promote personal health by preventing the spread of germs has a few inaccuracies.	Student's description of three ways the safe and healthy school and community environments can promote personal health by preventing the spread of germs is mostly inaccurate.

(continues)

Criteria	4	3	2	1
Sample Analytical Rubric for Performance Indicator 1.5.4				
Performance indicator 1.5.4 with infused content—Describe ways to prevent common childhood injuries and health problems that occur in the home.[1,p24]	Student accurately describes three ways to prevent common childhood injuries and health problems that occur in the home.	Student's description of three ways to prevent common childhood injuries and health problems that occur in the home is mostly accurate.	Student's description of three ways to prevent common childhood injuries and health problems that occur in the home has a few inaccuracies.	Student's description of three ways to prevent common childhood injuries and health problems that occur in the home is mostly inaccurate.
Sample Analytical Rubric for Performance Indicator 1.5.5				
Performance indicator 1.5.5 with infused content—Describe when it is important to seek health care for communicable illnesses.[1,p24]	Student accurately describes when it is important to seek health care for communicable illnesses.	Student's description of when it is important to seek health care for communicable illnesses is mostly accurate.	Student's description of when it is important to seek health care for communicable illnesses has a few inaccuracies.	Student's description of when it is important to seek health care for communicable illnesses is mostly inaccurate.

pictures, or as written instructions. Distribute the rubric to the older student who can read, making the language consistent with the reading level.

WHAT DOES STANDARD 1 LOOK LIKE IN THE GRADES 3–5 CLASSROOM?

Goddard Elementary School is experiencing an outbreak of the common cold. Many children and teachers are sick. The school has decided to highlight the importance of hand washing to combat the spread of the virus.

Pair Standard 7 with Standard 1 to Target Hand Washing as a Healthy Practice That Maintains or Improves Personal Health by Preventing the Spread of Germs.

Standard 7—Students will demonstrate the ability to practice health-enhancing behaviors and avoid or reduce health risks.[1,p35]

Performance indicator 7.5.2—Demonstrate a variety of healthy practices and behaviors to maintain or improve personal health.[1,p35]

Performance indicator 7.5.2 with infused content—Demonstrate a variety of healthy practices and behaviors to maintain or improve personal health, such as how to wash hands.[1,p35]

Using this performance indicator, students learn how to wash their hands as a way to demonstrate a variety of health practices and behaviors that maintain or improve personal health. A very good source of information on this topic for adults and children is the Centers for Disease Control and Prevention. On BAM! Body and Mind,[5] on the page *The Buzz on Scuzz*, students learn about germs and when and how to wash their hands.[6]

and link with

Standard 1 performance indicator 1.5.1—Describe the relationship between healthy behaviors and personal health.[1,p24]

Performance indicator 1.5.1 with infused content—Describe the relationship between healthy behaviors and personal health such as how hand washing prevents the spread of a virus.[1,p24]

In the above example, content is paired with Standard 7, but it could also be coupled with other skills. For example, a teacher could choose Standard 2 to describe how the school keeps children healthy.

Standard 2—Students will analyze the influence of family, peers, culture, media, technology, and other factors on health behaviors.[1,p26]

Performance indicator 2.5.4—Describe how the school and community can support personal health practices and behaviors.[1,p26]

> *Performance indicator 2.5.4 with infused content—* Describe how the school and community can support personal health practices and behaviors by providing soap for the dispensers in all lavatories.[1,p26]

> > and pair it with

Standard 1 performance indicator 1.5.3—Describe ways in which safe and healthy school and community environments can promote personal health.[1,p24]

> *Standard 1 performance indicator 1.5.3 with infused content—Describe ways in which safe and healthy school and community environments can promote personal health by combating the spread of germs.[1,p24]*

OR

To Learn How to Access Valid Information About the Flu and When to Seek Health Care, Pair Standard 3 with Standard 1.

Standard 3—Students will demonstrate the ability to access valid information and products and services to enhance health.[1,p28]

> Performance indicator 3.5.1—Identify characteristics of valid health information, products, and services.[1,p28]

> > *Performance indicator 3.5.1 with infused content—* Identify characteristics of valid health information, products, and services that treat the flu.[1,p28]

> > > and pair it with

Standard 1 performance indicator 1.5.5—Describe when it is important to seek health care.[1,p24]

> *Standard 1 performance indicator 1.5.5 with infused content—Describe when it is important to seek health care when sick with the flu.[1,p24]*

OR

To Teach Refusal Skills if a Friend Is Offering Medicine to Treat a Cold, Pair Standard 4 with Standard 1.

Standard 4—Students will demonstrate the ability to use interpersonal communication skills to enhance health and avoid or reduce health risks.[1,p30]

Performance indicator 4.5.2—Demonstrate refusal skills that avoid or reduce health risks.[1,p30]

> *Performance indicator 4.5.2 with infused content—* Demonstrate refusal skills that avoid or reduce health risks such as taking cold medicine from a friend.[1,p30]

> > and pair it with

Standard 1 performance indicator 1.5.4—Describe ways to prevent common childhood injuries and health problems.[1,p24]

> *Standard 1 performance indicator 1.5.4 with infused content—Describe ways to prevent common childhood injuries and health problems by only taking medicine from a trusted adult.[1,p24]*

OR

To Teach Decision-Making to Show Students How to Cope with a Friend Who Wants to Give Them Cold Medicine, Pair Standard 5 with Standard 1.

Standard 5—Students will demonstrate the ability to use decision-making skills to enhance health.[1,p32]

> Standard 5 performance indicators 5.5.1–5.5.6—the decision making process.[1,p32]

> > *Performance indicator 5.5.1 with infused content—* Identify health-related situations that might require a thoughtful decision, such as being offered medicine by a friend.[1,p32]

> > *Performance indicator 5.5.2 with infused content—* Analyze when assistance is needed in making a health-related decision about taking medicine from a friend.[1,p32]

> > *Performance indicator 5.5.3 with infused content—* List healthy options to the health-related issue or problem of taking medicine from a friend.[1,p32]

> > *Performance indicator 5.5.4 with infused content—* Predict the potential outcomes of each option when making a health-related decision.[1,p32]

> > *Performance indicator 5.5.5 with infused content—* Choose a healthy option when making a decision about taking medicine from a friend.[1,p32]

> > *Performance indicator 5.5.6 with infused content—* Describe the outcomes of a health-related decision about taking medicine from a friend.[1,p32]

> > > and pair it with

Standard 1 performance indicator 1.5.1—Describe the relationship between healthy behaviors and personal health.[1,p24]

Standard 1 performance indicator 1.5.1 with infused content—Describe the relationship between healthy behaviors such as making healthy decisions and personal health.[1,p24]

OR

To Teach Children How to Set a Goal of More Frequent Hand Washing or Hand Sanitizing During the School Day as a Way of Preventing the Transmission of the Cold Virus, Pair Standard 6 with Standard 1.

Standard 6—Students will demonstrate the ability to use goal-setting skills to enhance health.[1,p34]

Standard 6 performance indicator 6.5.1—Set a personal health goal and track progress toward its achievement.[1,p34]

Standard 6 performance indicator 6.5.1 with infused content—Set a personal health goal to sneeze into the sleeve and use hand sanitizers, and track progress toward its achievement.[1,p34]

and pair it with

Standard 1 performance indicator 1.5.4—Describe ways to prevent common childhood injuries and health problems.[1,p24]

Standard 1 performance indicator 1.5.4 with infused content—Describe ways to prevent common childhood injuries and health problems such as sneezing into the sleeve and using hand sanitizers.[1,p24]

OR

To Advocate Friends to Wash or Sanitize Their Hands More Frequently, Pair Standard 8 with Standard 1.

Standard 8—Students will demonstrate the ability to advocate for personal, family, and community health.[1,p36]

Performance indicator 8.5.2—Encourage others to make positive health choices.[1,p36]

Performance indicator 8.5.2 with infused content—Demonstrate how to encourage others to make positive health choices such as more frequent hand washing and using hand sanitizers.[1,p36]

and pair it with

Standard 1 performance indicator 1.5.3—Describe ways in which safe and healthy school and community environments can promote personal health.[1,p24]

Performance indicator 1.5.3 with infused content—Describe ways in which safe and healthy school and community environments, such as people washing hands more frequently and using hand sanitizers, can promote personal health.[1,p24]

The above examples demonstrate how Standard 1 can be paired with the skills standards to meet the needs of the students.

By linking the skill and content performance indicators, the teacher has a clear idea of how to plan the unit lessons.

The first step in planning is to think through the unit by completing the performance task template. Upon completion, the teacher has most of the information to introduce the prompt to the students.

When planning for the prompt, also include all the back-up information, holistic rubrics, analytical rubrics, and worksheets the students need to complete the task. Designing skills-based lessons requires considerable preparation, but once the teacher distributes it and explains the task, the students are responsible for the results. Students learn with good coaching (formative assessments) to demonstrate proficiency in content and skill.

How Does the Coordinated School Health Team Contribute to Increasing Functional Health Knowledge Related to Health Promotion and Disease Prevention to Enhance Health?

Health Education

- Refocus instruction on skill building and how to prevent the spread of germs.
- Place hand-washing posters in the classroom.

Physical Education

- Promote hand-washing before and after class.
- Model hand washing and the use of hand sanitizers.

Health Services

- Provide instruction on how to wash hands properly.
- Encourage students to wash or sanitize hands before leaving the office.

Nutrition Services

- Provide antibacterial lotion in several locations in the cafeteria.
- Hang posters that encourage students not to share food or utensils.

Counseling, Psychological, and Social Services

- Display posters that show proper hand-washing techniques.
- Display health promotion posters and flyers that explain the importance of personal health.

Healthy School Environment

- Display hand-washing posters around the school and in the lavatories.
- Provide antibacterial lotion dispensers in the school.

Health Promotion for Staff

- Be good role models for frequent hand washing or use of antibacterial lotion.
- Sneeze and cough into sleeves to demonstrate good health practices.

Family/Community Involvement

- Encourage families to wash their hands frequently and be good role models for their children.
- Advocate for antibacterial lotion dispensers in town offices and businesses.
- Provide children with small containers of hand sanitizers for their personal use throughout the day.

Grades 6–8

To plan a Grade 6–8 unit, determine student need from collected data. Once the need is established, decide which skill standard to use to address it. Examine the Standard 1 performance indicators for Grades 6–8 and select one or more that complements the skills standard and gives students the functional knowledge needed to overcome behavioral health problems (see **Figure 5.6**).

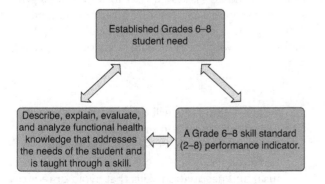

FIGURE 5.6 Planning for Grades 6–8

Grades 6–8

1.8.1 Analyze the relationship between healthy behaviors and personal health.

1.8.2 Describe the interrelationships of emotional, intellectual, physical, and social health in adolescence.

1.8.3 Analyze how the environment affects personal health.

1.8.4 Describe how family history can affect personal health.

1.8.5 Describe ways to reduce or prevent injuries and other adolescent health problems.

1.8.6 Explain how appropriate health care can promote personal health.

1.8.7 Describe the benefits of and barriers to practicing healthy behaviors.

1.8.8 Examine the likelihood of injury or illness if engaging in unhealthy behaviors.

1.8.9 Examine the potential seriousness of injury or illness if engaging in unhealthy behaviors.[1,p25]

Students learn how to describe, explain, examine, and analyze functional health knowledge to reach proficiency in this standard. During instruction, assess student progress formatively and summatively and adjust accordingly.

In Grades 6–8, students *describe* interrelationships, ways of reducing injuries and health problems, and the benefits and barriers to practicing healthy behaviors in performance indicators 1.8.2, 1.8.4, 1.8.5, and 1.8.7.[1,p25] Instruction includes a *description* of how each dimension of health relates to the other, how heredity affects personal health, and how to reduce inherited risk factors.

Common teen injuries and health problems are targeted, and students learn to *describe* ways to reduce them. They also learn to *describe* the benefits of healthy behaviors and what factors interfere with healthy behaviors. Assessment of these performance indicators includes *describing* relationships and ways to reduce injury and health problems.

Depending on the skill that is paired with the Standard 1 performance indicator, evidence includes a *description* of a health poster, a book *describing* how family health history affects health, a public service announcement that *describes* the benefits and barriers to practicing healthy behaviors, and a role-play that *describes* ways to prevent injuries or health problems.

In addition, students *explain* how appropriate health care can promote personal health in performance indicator 1.8.6.[1,p25] Instruction includes an *explanation* of appropriate health care from the school nurse, a pediatrician, and specialist. It also includes asking a teacher a health question, talking to a parent, attending a clinic, researching health topics online, using the services of a hospital, and exploring how all of these resources contribute to personal health.

Assessment of this performance indicator and its paired skill occurs when the student, presented with a variety of personal health problems, *explains* how to access appropriate health care for each of the problems. Evidence may include a call-in teen-health radio program, the production of a community-health resource card, a teen health column in the school newspaper, public service announcements in the school, and interviews with a variety of health specialists.

Performance indicators 1.8.8 and 1.8.9 ask students to *examine* the likelihood of injury and illness from unhealthy behaviors. To *examine* them, students use the information they learned about unhealthy behaviors and connect it to potential injury or illness. Access to school data from the nurse and administrators provides a good picture of high priority, unhealthy behaviors of students.

Access district, community, state, and national data in order to gather a wider picture of specific risk behavior statistics and related injury and illness. A good place to start is the Centers for Disease Control and Prevention's Adolescent Risk Behaviors.[1,p11]

Instruction begins with and *examination* of unhealthy behaviors vs. healthy behaviors to ensure that students understand the difference.

Students *examine* by demonstrating how one uses knowledge to think through consequences. For example, choose a risk factor, such as tobacco use, and ask the students to *examine* how using tobacco contributes to injury and illness. To assess them, have students demonstrate their knowledge of the consequences of unhealthy behaviors.

Students learn in performance indicators 1.8.1 and 1.8.3 to *analyze* the relationship between healthy behaviors and personal health as well as how the environment affects personal health. Students *analyze* the individual parts of an issue, and then examine how one affects the other. The teacher assesses these performance indicators by asking the students to demonstrate their knowledge of content by showing how one factor affects the other.

To assess the Grades 6–8 performance indicators of Standard 1, students must provide accurate, relevant, specific, and complete information related to

- The relationship between healthy behaviors and personal health
- Interrelationships among the dimensions of health (see **Figure 5.7**)
- How the environment affects personal health
- How family history can affect personal health

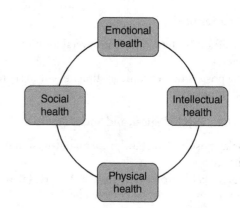

FIGURE 5.7   Dimensions of Health

- Preventing injuries and health problems
- Appropriate health care
- Positive outcomes of and barriers to practicing healthy behaviors
- The likelihood and potential seriousness of injury or illness if engaging in unhealthy behaviors. [1,p25]

The following Standard 1 analytical rubrics offer guidance to scoring a student in each performance indicator. When the scope of the performance task is established, the teacher adds specific criteria to the rubric (**Table 5.4**).

Remember to assess students not only on functional knowledge but also on a demonstration of it through a skill. Consequently, a rubric for a performance task includes criteria for both Standard 1 and a skills standard.

WHAT DOES STANDARD 1 LOOK LIKE IN THE GRADES 6–8 CLASSROOM?

The students at Eisenhower Middle School spend considerable time on social networking websites. Drennon was curious about them, so he opened an account and posted all his information. He was happy to receive many e-mails from people he knew and others who wanted to meet him. One day an online "friend" asked if he would like to meet.

Since the social networking sites are based on communication, Standard 4 is a good place to begin planning. By selecting Standard 4 and Standard 1 performance indicators, the planner targets the knowledge and skill Drennon needs to cope with the health and safety risks of meeting a stranger.

Standard 4—Students will demonstrate the ability to use interpersonal communication skills to enhance health and avoid or reduce health risks.[1,p30]

  Performance indicator 4.8.2—Demonstrate refusal and negotiation skills that avoid or reduce health risks.[1,p30]

Criteria	4	3	2	1
Sample Analytical Rubric for Performance Indicator 1.8.1				
Performance indicator 1.8.1 with infused content—Analyze the relationship between healthy behaviors such as being a non-smoker and personal health.[1,p25]	Student thoroughly analyzes the relationship between healthy behaviors such as being a non-smoker and personal health.	Student adequately analyzes the relationship between healthy behaviors such as being a non-smoker and personal health.	Student inadequately analyzes the relationship between healthy behaviors such as being a non-smoker and personal health.	Student poorly analyzes the relationship between healthy behaviors such as being a non-smoker and personal health.
Sample analytical rubric for performance indicator 1.8.2				
Performance indicator 1.8.2 with infused content—Describe the interrelationships of emotional, intellectual, physical, and social health in adolescence when being bullied.[1,p25]	Student thoroughly describes three facts about the interrelationships of emotional, intellectual, physical, and social health in adolescence when being bullied.	Student adequately describes three facts about the interrelationships of emotional, intellectual, physical, and social health in adolescence when being bullied.	Student inadequately describes three facts about the interrelationships of emotional, intellectual, physical, and social health in adolescence when being bullied.	Student poorly describes three facts about the interrelationships of emotional, intellectual, physical, and social health in adolescence when being bullied.
Sample analytical rubric for performance indicator 1.8.3				
Performance indicator 1.8.3 with infused content—Analyze how the environment affects personal health.[1,p25]	Student accurately analyzes three facts about how noise affects personal health.	Student's analysis of three facts about how noise affects personal health is mostly accurate.	Student's analysis of three facts about how noise affects personal health has some inaccuracies.	Student's analysis of three facts about how noise affects personal health is mostly inaccurate.
Sample analytical rubric for performance indicator 1.8.4				
Performance indicator 1.8.4 with infused content—Describe how a family history of alcoholism can affect personal health.[1,p25]	Student thoroughly describes five facts about how a family history of alcoholism can affect personal health.	Student adequately describes five facts about how a family history of alcoholism can affect personal health.	Student inadequately describes five facts about how a family history of alcoholism can affect personal health.	Student poorly describes five facts about how a family history of alcoholism can affect personal health.
Sample analytical rubric for performance indicator 1.8.5				
Performance indicator 1.8.5 with infused content—Describe ways to reduce or prevent skate board injuries and other adolescent health problems.[1,p25]	Student accurately describes five ways to reduce or prevent skate board injuries and other adolescent health problems.	Student's description of five ways to reduce or prevent skate board injuries and other adolescent health problems is mostly accurate.	Student's description of five ways to reduce or prevent skate board injuries and other adolescent health problems has a few inaccuracies.	Student's description of five ways to reduce or prevent skate board injuries and other adolescent health problems is mostly inaccurate.
Sample analytical rubric for performance indicator 1.8.6				
Performance indicator 1.8.6 with infused content—Explain how appropriate mental health care for depression can promote personal health.[1,p25]	Student thoroughly explains five facts about how appropriate mental health care for depression can promote personal health.	Student adequately explains five facts about how appropriate mental health care for depression can promote personal health.	Student inadequately explains five facts about how appropriate mental health care for depression can promote personal health.	Student poorly explains five facts about how appropriate mental health care for depression can promote personal health.

(continues)

TABLE 5.4 Sample Analytical Rubrics for Performance Indicators 1.8.1 to 1.8.9 *(continued)*

Criteria	4	3	2	1
	Sample analytical rubric for performance indicator 1.8.7			
Performance indicator 1.8.7 with infused content—Describe the benefits of and barriers to practicing healthy behaviors such as not smoking marijuana.[1,p25]	Student thoroughly describes five benefits of and barriers to practicing healthy behaviors such as not smoking marijuana.	Student adequately describes five benefits of and barriers to practicing healthy behaviors such as not smoking marijuana.	Student inadequately describes five benefits of and barriers to practicing healthy behaviors such as not smoking marijuana.	Student poorly describes five benefits of and barriers to practicing healthy behaviors such as not smoking marijuana.
	Sample analytical rubric for performance indicator 1.8.8			
Performance indicator 1.8.8 with infused content—Examine the likelihood of injury or illness if engaging in unhealthy behaviors such as not using a seat belt.[1,p25]	Student thoroughly examines five facts about the likelihood of injury or illness if engaging in unhealthy behaviors such as not using a seat belt.	Student adequately examines five facts about the likelihood of injury or illness if engaging in unhealthy behaviors such as not using a seat belt.	Student inadequately examines five facts about the likelihood of injury or illness if engaging in unhealthy behaviors such as not using a seat belt.	Student poorly examines five facts about the likelihood of injury or illness if engaging in unhealthy behaviors such as not using a seat belt.
	Sample analytical rubric for performance indicator 1.8.9			
Performance indicator 1.8.9 with infused content—Examine the potential seriousness of injury or illness if engaging in unhealthy behaviors such as not wearing a bicycle helmet.[1,p25]	Student thoroughly examines five facts about the potential seriousness of injury or illness if engaging in unhealthy behaviors such as not wearing a bicycle helmet.	Student adequately examines five facts about the potential seriousness of injury or illness if engaging in unhealthy behaviors such as not wearing a bicycle helmet.	Student inadequately examines five facts about the potential seriousness of injury or illness if engaging in unhealthy behaviors such as not wearing a bicycle helmet.	Student poorly examines five facts about the potential seriousness of injury or illness if engaging in unhealthy behaviors such as not wearing a bicycle helmet.

Performance indicator 4.8.2 with infused content— Demonstrate refusal and negotiation skills that avoid or reduce health risks by refusing to meet an online "friend."[1,p30]

and pair it with

Standard 1 performance indicator 1.8.7—Describe the benefits of and barriers to practicing healthy behaviors.[1,p25]

Standard 1 performance indicator 1.8.7 with infused content—Describe the benefits of and barriers to practicing healthy behaviors such as refusing to meet an online "friend."[1,p25]

Content in the above example is paired with Standard 4 but may also be coupled with other skills.

To Teach How Posting Information to the Social Networking Site Affects Personal Health, Pair Standard 2 with Standard 1.

Standard 2—Students will analyze the influence of family, peers, culture, media, technology, and other factors on health behaviors.[1,p26]

Standard 2 performance indicator 2.8.6—Analyze the influence of technology on personal and family health.[1,p27]

Standard 2 performance indicator 2.8.6 with infused content—Analyze the influence of technology on personal and family health when teens post personal information on social networking sites.[1,p27]

and pair it with

Standard 1 performance indicator 1.8.9—Examine the potential seriousness of injury or illness if engaging in unhealthy behaviors.[1,p25]

> Standard 1 performance indicator 1.8.9 with infused content—Examine the potential seriousness of injury or illness if engaging in unhealthy behaviors such as posting personal information on social networking sites.[1,p25]

OR

To Teach Students How to Use Decision Making for Healthy Choices About Meeting a Stranger from the Internet, Pair Standard 5 with Standard 1.

Standard 5—Students will demonstrate the ability to use decision-making skills to enhance health.[1,p32]

Performance indicator 5.8.1—Identify circumstances that can help or hinder healthy decision-making.[1,p32]

> Performance indicator 5.8.1 with infused content—Identify circumstances, such as a stranger from the Internet wants to meet me, that can help or hinder healthy decision-making.[1,p32]

Performance indicator 5.8.2—Determine when health-related situations require the application of a thoughtful decision-making process.[1,p32]

> Performance indicator 5.8.2 with infused content—Determine when the health-related situation of a stranger from the Internet wanting to meet me requires the application of a thoughtful decision-making process.[1,p32]

Performance indicator 5.8.3—Distinguish when individual or collaborative decision-making is appropriate.[1,p32]

> Performance indicator 5.8.3 with infused content—Distinguish when individual or collaborative decision-making is appropriate when deciding how to respond to a stranger from the Internet who wants to meet me.[1,p32]

Performance indicator 5.8.4—Distinguish between healthy and unhealthy alternatives to health-related issues or problems.[1,p33]

> Performance indicator 5.8.4 with infused content—Distinguish between healthy and unhealthy alternatives when deciding how to respond to a stranger from the Internet who wants to meet me.[1,p33]

Performance indicator 5.8.5—Predict the potential short-term impact of each alternative on self and others.[1,p33]

> Performance indicator 5.8.5 with infused content—Predict the potential short-term impact of each alternative on self and others when deciding how to respond to a stranger from the Internet who wants to meet me.[1,p33]

Performance indicator 5.8.6—Choose healthy alternatives over unhealthy alternatives when making a decision.[1,p33]

> Performance indicator 5.8.6 with infused content—Choose healthy alternatives over unhealthy alternatives when making a decision regarding how to respond to a stranger from the Internet who wants to meet me.[1,p33]

Performance indicator 5.8.7—Analyze the outcomes of a health-related decision.[1,p33]

> Performance indicator 5.8.7 with infused content—Analyze the outcomes of the health-related decision of how to respond to a stranger from the Internet who wants to met me.[1,p33]

Standard 1 performance indicator 1.8.1—Analyze the relationship between healthy behaviors and personal health.[1,p25]

> Standard 1 performance indicator 1.8.1 with infused content—Analyze the relationship between healthy behaviors, such as safety with strangers and personal health.[1,p25]

OR

To Help Students Realize That Meeting a Stranger from a Social Networking Site Could Be Very Dangerous and, by Refusing to Meet, the Risk of Personal Injury or Other Potential Health Problems Is Reduced, Link Standard 6 with Standard 1.

Standard 6—Students will demonstrate the ability to use goal-setting skills to enhance health.[1,p34]

Performance indicator 6.8.2—Develop a goal to adopt, maintain, or improve a personal health practice.[1,p34]

> Performance indicator 6.8.2 with infused content—Develop a goal to adopt, maintain, or improve a personal health practice, such as not meeting strangers from the Internet.[1,p34]

> Performance indicator 6.8.3 with infused content—Apply strategies and skills needed to attain a personal health goal of not meeting strangers from the Internet.

and pair it with

Standard 1 performance indicator 1.8.5—Describe ways to reduce or prevent injuries and other adolescent health problems.[1,p25]

Standard 1 performance indicator 1.8.5 with infused content—Describe ways to reduce or prevent injuries and other adolescent health problems by refusing to meet strangers from the Internet.[1,p25]

OR

To Teach Students to Describe and Demonstrate Behaviors to Avoid the Health Risk of Meeting a Stranger from a Social Networking Site, Pair Standard 7 with Standard 1.

Standard 7—Students will demonstrate the ability to practice health-enhancing behaviors and avoid or reduce health risks.[1,p35]

Performance indicator 7.8.3—Demonstrate behaviors that avoid or reduce health risks to self and others.[1,p35]

Performance indicator 7.8.3 with infused content—Demonstrate behaviors that avoid or reduce health risks to self and others, such as refusing to meet a stranger from the Internet.[1,p35]

with

Standard 1 performance indicator 1.8.5—Describe ways to reduce or prevent injuries and other adolescent health problems.[1,p25]

Standard 1 performance indicator 1.8.5 with infused content—Describe ways to reduce or prevent injuries and other adolescent health problems by refusing to meet a stranger from the Internet.[1,p25]

OR

To Teach Students How to Advocate for Internet Safety, Pair Standard 8 with Standard 1.

Standard 8—Students will demonstrate the ability to advocate for personal, family, and community health.[1,p36]

Performance indicator 8.8.1—State a health-enhancing position on a topic and support it with accurate information.[1,p36]

Performance indicator 8.8.1 with infused content—State a health-enhancing position on a topic, such as Internet safety, and support it with accurate information.[1,p36]

and pair it with

Standard 1 performance indicator 1.8.2—Describe the interrelationships of emotional, intellectual, physical, and social health in adolescence.[1,p25]

Standard 1 performance indicator 1.8.2—Describe the interrelationships of emotional, intellectual, physical, and social health in adolescence.[1,p25]

Standard 1 performance indicator 1.8.2 with infused content—Describe the interrelationships of emotional, intellectual, physical, and social health in adolescence as a result of advocating for Internet safety.[1,p25]

The above examples demonstrate how Standard 1 can be paired with the skills standards to meet the needs of the students.

By linking the skill and content performance indicators, the teacher has a clear idea of how to plan the unit lessons.

The first step in planning is to think through the unit by completing the performance task template. Upon completion, the teacher has most of the information to introduce the prompt to the students.

When planning for the prompt, also include all the back-up information, holistic rubrics, analytical rubrics, and worksheets the students need to complete the task. Designing skills-based lessons requires considerable preparation, but once the teacher distributes it and explains the task, the students are responsible for the results. Students learn with good coaching (formative assessments) to demonstrate proficiency in content and skill.

HOW DOES THE COORDINATED SCHOOL HEALTH TEAM CONTRIBUTE TO INCREASING FUNCTIONAL HEALTH KNOWLEDGE RELATED TO HEALTH PROMOTION AND DISEASE PREVENTION TO ENHANCE HEALTH?

Health Education

- Refocus instruction on the skills that help students stay safe while using the Internet.
- Implement an Internet safety program for students, staff, and parents.

Physical Education

- Display posters that encourage Internet safety.
- Reinforce Internet safety when discussing the use of the Internet.

Health Services

- Provide information about Internet safety.

Nutrition Services

- Display Internet safety posters.

Counseling, Psychological, and Social Services

- Provide Internet safety counseling.
- Display Internet safety posters.

Healthy School Environment

- Develop and implement an Internet safety policy.
- Display Internet safety tips throughout the building.

Health Promotion for Staff

- Be good Internet safety role models.
- Ensure that personal social networking accounts are appropriate.

Family/Community Involvement

- Implement an Internet safety program for students, staff, and parents.

Grades 9–12

To plan a Grade 9–12 unit, determine student need from collected data. Once established, decide which skill standard to use to address that need. Examine the Standard 1 performance indicators for Grades 9–12 and select one or more that complements the skills standard and gives students the functional knowledge needed to overcome behavioral health problems (see **Figure 5.8**).

To reach proficiency in this standard, students describe, compare, analyze, propose, and predict functional health knowledge. During instruction, formatively assess student progress and adjust accordingly.

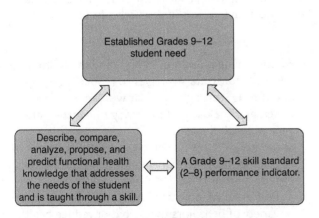

FIGURE 5.8   Planning for Grades 9–12

Grades 9–12

1.12.1 Predict how healthy behaviors can affect health status.
1.12.2 Describe the interrelationships of emotional, intellectual, physical, and social health.
1.12.3 Analyze how environment and personal health are interrelated.
1.12.4 Analyze how genetics and family history can affect personal health.
1.12.5 Propose ways to reduce or prevent injuries and health problems.
1.12.6 Analyze the relationship between access to health care and health status.
1.12.7 Compare and contrast the benefits of and barriers to practicing a variety of healthy behaviors.
1.12.8 Analyze personal susceptibility to injury, illness, or death if engaging in unhealthy behaviors.
1.12.9 Analyze the potential severity of injury or illness if engaging in unhealthy behaviors.[1,p25]

As in previous grade spans, Grades 9–12 students *describe* the interrelationships of the dimensions of health through performance indicator 1.12.1. Instruction includes an explanation of each dimension, why it is important, and how each interrelates when meeting life's challenges. A sample assessment includes an age-appropriate story of a student coping with a common Grade 9–12 challenge and *describing* how each of the components is affected. Another example is to complete a personal wellness questionnaire, then explain the results through each component.

In performance indicator 1.12.7, students use a T bar to compare and contrast the benefits and barriers of practicing a variety of healthy behaviors (see **Table 5.5**).

Depending on the skill, sample student assessments include:

- A comparison of the benefits and barriers to practicing healthy behaviors illustrated on a poster
- Two students role-playing a conversation wherein the benefits of practicing healthy behaviors are *compared* to the barriers and ending it with a positive health message
- A clothes hanger collage in which the students place a picture of a healthy behavior on the hanger then *compare* the benefits and barriers to practicing that behavior, which are pictured hanging from the horizontal bar.

Students *analyze* how the environment and personal health are interrelated and how genetics and family history affect personal health, the relationship between

TABLE 5.5   Benefits and Barriers of Practicing a Variety of Healthy Behaviors

Benefits and Barriers of Not Talking on a Cell Phone While Driving

Benefits	Barriers

access to health care and health status, and the consequences of engaging in unhealthy behaviors in performance indicators 1.12.3, 1.12.4, 1.12.6, 1.12.8, and 1.12.9. To *analyze*, students learn information about the individual parts of a problem then examine how one affects the other. Students show proficiency in a performance indicator by demonstrating their knowledge of content and showing how one factor affects another.

In the performance indicator 1.12.5, students *propose* ways to reduce or prevent injuries and health problems.[1,p25] To do so, they must have an understanding of common injuries and teen health problems and then *propose* ways to reduce them. An engaging assessment for this indicator, paired with a Standard 7 performance indicator, is a performance task that challenges students to determine the injuries and health problems that result each spring during the prom and propose ways to reduce them.

In performance indicator 1.12.1, students *predict* how healthy behaviors affect health status.[1,p25] To do so, teach the benefits of having healthy behaviors and how they have a positive effect on individuals. This indicator may be combined with 1.12.4 because, even though a person practices healthy behaviors, genetics may interfere with achieving a positive health status. To show proficiency, students demonstrate their ability to *predict* how healthy behaviors, such as choosing to be a non-smoker, affect their future health status.

To assess the Grades 9–12 performance indicators of Standard 1, students provide information or analysis that evidence breadth and depth, accuracy, and relevance and relate specifically to:

- The relationship between healthy behaviors and health
- Interrelationships among the dimensions of health
- How environment and personal health are interrelated
- How genetics and family history affect personal health

- Reducing or preventing injuries and health problems
- The relationship between access to health care and health status
- Benefits and barriers to practicing healthy behaviors
- The personal susceptibility and potential severity of injury, illness, or death if engaging in unhealthy behaviors[1,p25]

The Standard 1 analytical rubrics (**Table 5.6**) offer guidance in scoring each performance indicator. When the scope of the performance task is established, the teacher adds specific criteria to the rubric.

Remember to assess a student on functional knowledge and a demonstration of it through a skill. Consequently, a rubric for a performance task includes criteria for both Standard 1 and a skills standard.

WHAT DOES STANDARD 1 LOOK LIKE IN THE GRADES 9–12 CLASSROOM?

Tucson High School found that 19.3% of 12th grade male students drove a car while drinking alcohol, and 27.9% of 12th grade females rode in a car with someone who had been drinking alcohol.[6] The high school administrators and staff want to implement instruction and strategies to decrease the number of students who drink and drive.

By combining Standard 7 and Standard 1, students demonstrate strategies to reduce drinking and driving, getting into a car with an impaired driver, and the dangers of driving under the influence of alcohol.

Standard 7—Students will demonstrate the ability to practice health-enhancing behaviors and avoid or reduce health risks.[1,p35]

Performance indicator 7.12.3—Demonstrate a variety of behaviors that avoid or reduce health risks to self and others.[1,p35]

TABLE 5.6 Sample Analytical Rubrics for Performance Indicators 1.12.1 to 1.12.9

Criteria	4	3	2	1
Sample Analytical Rubrics for Performance Indicator 1.12.1				
Performance indicator 1.12.1 with infused content—Predict how healthy behaviors, such as choosing abstinence, can affect health status.[1,p25]	Student accurately predicts five ways a healthy behavior, such as choosing abstinence, can affect health status.	Student's prediction of five ways a healthy behavior, such as choosing abstinence, can affect health status is mostly accurate.	Student's prediction of five ways a healthy behavior, such as choosing abstinence, can affect health status has a few inaccuracies.	Student's prediction of five ways a healthy behavior, such as choosing abstinence, can affect health status is mostly inaccurate.
Sample Analytical Rubric for Performance Indicator 1.12.2				
Performance indicator 1.12.2 with infused content—Describe the interrelationships of emotional, intellectual, physical, and social health when a teen becomes pregnant.[1,p25]	Student thoroughly describes five facts about the interrelationships of emotional, intellectual, physical, and social health when a teen becomes pregnant.	Student adequately describes five facts about the interrelationships of emotional, intellectual, physical, and social health when a teen becomes pregnant.	Student inadequately describes five facts about the interrelationships of emotional, intellectual, physical, and social health when a teen becomes pregnant.	Student poorly describes five facts about the interrelationships of emotional, intellectual, physical, and social health when a teen becomes pregnant.
Sample Analytical Rubric for Performance Indicator 1.12.3				
Performance indicator 1.12.3 with infused content—Analyze how environment and personal health are interrelated.[1,p25]	Student thoroughly analyzes five facts about how environment and personal health are interrelated when breathing polluted air.	Student adequately analyzes five facts about how environment and personal health are interrelated when breathing polluted air.	Student inadequately analyzes five facts about how environment and personal health are interrelated when breathing polluted air.	Student poorly analyzes five facts about how environment and personal health are interrelated when breathing polluted air.
Sample Analytical Rubric for Performance Indicator 1.12.4				
Performance indicator 1.12.4 with infused content—Analyze how genetics and family history can affect personal health.[1,p25]	Student thoroughly analyzes five facts about how genetics and a family history of alcoholism or drug abuse can affect personal health.	Student adequately analyzes five facts about how genetics and a family history of alcoholism or drug abuse can affect personal health.	Student inadequately analyzes five facts about how genetics and a family history of alcoholism or drug abuse can affect personal health.	Student poorly analyzes five facts about how genetics and a family history of alcoholism or drug abuse can affect personal health.
Sample Analytical Rubric for Performance Indicator 1.12.5				
Performance indicator 1.12.5 with infused content—Propose ways to reduce or prevent injuries and health problems from binge drinking.[1,p25]	Student appropriately proposes five ways to reduce or prevent injuries and health problems from binge drinking.	Student's proposal of five ways to reduce or prevent injuries and health problems from binge drinking is mostly appropriate.	A few of the five ways proposed to reduce or prevent injuries and health problems from binge drinking are inappropriate.	Student's proposal of five ways to reduce or prevent injuries and health problems from binge drinking is mostly inappropriate.
Sample Analytical Rubric for Performance Indicator 1.12.6				
Performance indicator 1.12.6 with infused content—Analyze the relationship between access to health care, such as school health clinics, and health status.[1,p25]	Student thoroughly analyzes five facts about the relationship between access to health care, such as school health clinics, and health status.	Student adequately analyzes five facts about the relationship between access to health care, such as school health clinics, and health status.	Student inadequately analyzes five facts about the relationship between access to health care, such as school health clinics, and health status.	Student poorly analyzes five facts about the relationship between access to health care, such as school health clinics, and health status.

(continues)

TABLE 5.6   Sample Analytical Rubrics for Performance Indicators 1.12.1 to 1.12.9 *(continued)*

Criteria	4	3	2	1
Sample Analytical Rubric for Performance Indicator 1.12.7				
Performance indicator 1.12.7 with infused content—Compare and contrast the benefits of and barriers to practicing a variety of healthy behaviors, such as using a condom.[1,p25]	Student accurately compares and contrasts five benefits of and barriers to practicing a variety of healthy behaviors, such as using a condom.	Student's comparison and contrast of five benefits of and barriers to practicing a variety of healthy behaviors, such as using a condom is mostly accurate.	Student's comparison and contrast of five benefits of and barriers to practicing a variety of healthy behaviors, such as using a condom has a few inaccuracies.	Student's comparison and contrast of five benefits of and barriers to practicing a variety of healthy behaviors, such as using a condom is mostly inaccurate.
Sample Analytical Rubric for Performance Indicator 1.12.8				
Performance indicator 1.12.8 with infused content—Analyze personal susceptibility to injury, illness, or death if engaging in unhealthy behaviors, such as driving under the influence.[1,p25]	Student thoroughly analyzes five ways a person is susceptible to injury, illness, or death if engaging in unhealthy behaviors, such as driving under the influence.	Student adequately analyzes five ways a person is susceptible to injury, illness, or death if engaging in unhealthy behaviors, such as driving under the influence.	Student inadequately analyzes five ways a person is susceptible to injury, illness, or death if engaging in unhealthy behaviors, such as driving under the influence.	Student poorly analyzes five ways a person is susceptible to injury, illness, or death if engaging in unhealthy behaviors, such as driving under the influence.
Sample Analytical Rubric for Performance Indicator 1.12.9				
Performance indicator 1.12.9 with infused content—Analyze the potential severity of injury or illness if engaging in unhealthy behaviors, such as riding in a car with someone under the influence.[1,p25]	Student thoroughly analyzes five facts about the potential severity of injury or illness if engaging in unhealthy behaviors, such as riding in a car with someone under the influence.	Student adequately analyzes five facts about the potential severity of injury or illness if engaging in unhealthy behaviors, such as riding in a car with someone under the influence.	Student inadequately analyzes five facts about the potential severity of injury or illness if engaging in unhealthy behaviors, such as riding in a car with someone under the influence.	Student poorly analyzes five facts about the potential severity of injury or illness if engaging in unhealthy behaviors, such as riding in a car with someone under the influence.

Performance indicator 7.12.3 with infused content—Demonstrate a variety of behaviors that avoid or reduce health risks to self and others from drinking and driving.[1,p35]

and pair it with

Performance Indicator 1.12.8—Analyze the personal susceptibility to injury, illness, or death if engaging in unhealthy behaviors.[1,p25]

Performance Indicator 1.12.8 with infused content—Analyze the personal susceptibility to injury, illness, or death if engaging in unhealthy behaviors such as drinking and driving.[1,p25]

In the above example, content is paired with Standard 7, but it could also be coupled with other skills.

To Teach About the Positive and Negative Effects of Peer Pressure and How Positive Peer Pressure Can Help Reduce Teen Drinking and Driving, Link Standard 2 with Standard 1.

Standard 2—Students will analyze the influence of family, peers, culture, media, technology, and other factors on health behaviors.[1,p26]

Standard 2 performance indicator 2.12.3—Analyze how peers influence healthy and unhealthy behaviors.[1,p27]

Performance indicator 2.12.3 with infused content—Analyze how peers influence healthy and the unhealthy behavior of drinking and driving.[1,p27]

and pair it with
Standard 1 performance indicator 1.12.5—Propose ways to reduce or prevent injuries and health problems.[1,p25]

Standard 1 performance indicator 1.12.5 with infused content—Propose ways to reduce or prevent injuries and health problems from drinking and driving.[1,p25]

To Design a Pre-Prom Program that Includes Representatives from Police, Fire, Mothers Against Drunk Driving, and Local Drug Treatment Centers, Pair Standard 3 with Standard 1.

Standard 3—Students will demonstrate the ability to access valid information and products and services to enhance health.[1,p28]
Performance indicator 3.12.4—Determine when professional health services may be required.[1,p29]

Performance indicator 3.12.4 with infused content—Determine when professional health services may be required to promote a pre-prom program.[1,p29]

paired with
Standard 1 performance indicator 1.12.8—Analyze personal susceptibility to injury, illness, or death if engaging in unhealthy behaviors.[1,p25]

Standard 1 performance indicator 1.12.8 with infused content—Analyze personal susceptibility to injury, illness, or death if engaging in unhealthy behaviors, such as drinking and driving after the prom.[1,p25]

OR

To Teach Students the Refusal, Negotiation, and Collaboration Skills to Cope with the Pressure to Ride in a Car with an Impaired Driver, Pair Standard 4 with Standard 1.

Standard 4—Students will demonstrate the ability to use interpersonal communication skills to enhance health and avoid or reduce health risks.[1,p30]
Performance indicator 4.12.2—Demonstrate refusal, negotiation, and collaboration skills to enhance health and avoid or reduce health risks.[1,p31]

Performance indicator 4.12.2 with infused content—Demonstrate refusal, negotiation, and collaboration skills to enhance health and avoid or reduce the health risks associated with riding in a car with an impaired driver.[1,p31]

and pair it with
Standard 1 performance indicator 1.12.1—Predict how healthy behaviors can affect health status.[1,p25]

Standard 1 performance indicator 1.12.1 with infused content—Predict how healthy behaviors, such as refusing to ride with an impaired driver, can affect health status.[1,p25]

OR

To Challenge Students to Analyze the Potential Dangers to Themselves and Others When Driving While Impaired, Pair Standard 5 with Standard 1.

Standard 5—Students will demonstrate the ability to use decision-making skills to enhance health.[1,p32]
Performance indicator 5.12.2—Determine the value of applying a thoughtful decision-making process in health-related situations.[1,p33]

Performance indicator 5.12.2 with infused content—Determine the value of applying a thoughtful decision-making process in health-related situations, such as driving while impaired.[1,p33]

Performance indicator 5.12.3—Justify when individual or collaborative decision-making is appropriate.

Performance indicator 5.12.3 with infused content—Justify when individual or collaborative decision-making is appropriate if deciding to drive impaired.

Performance indicator 5.12.4—Generate alternatives to health-related issues or problems.

Performance indicator 5.12.4 with infused content—Generate alternatives to health-related issues or problems such as driving impaired.

Performance indicator 5.12.5—Predict the potential short-term and long-term impact of each alternative on self and others.

Performance indicator 5.12.5 with infused content—Predict the potential short-term and long-term impact of each alternative on self and others if driving impaired.

Performance indicator 5.12.6—Defend the healthy choice when making decisions.

Performance indicator 5.12.6 with infused content—Defend the healthy choice when making decisions about driving impaired.
Performance indicator 5.12.7—Evaluate the effectiveness of health-related decisions.

Performance indicator 5.12.7 with infused content—Evaluate the effectiveness of health-related decisions related to driving impaired.
and pair it with
Standard 1 performance indicator 1.12.9—Analyze the potential severity of injury or illness if engaging in unhealthy behaviors.[1,p25]

Standard 1 performance indicator 1.12.9 with infused content—Analyze the potential severity of injury or illness if engaging in unhealthy behaviors, such as driving while impaired.[1,p25]

OR

To Teach How to Set a Personal Safety Goal for Prom Night, Link Standard 6 with Standard 1.

Standard 6—Students will demonstrate the ability to use goal-setting skills to enhance health.[1,p34]
Performance indicators 6.12.1–6.12.4 help to set goals to be safe during prom season.[1,p34]

Performance indicator 6.12.1 with infused content—Assess personal health practices and overall health status regarding how to stay safe on prom night.[1,p34]

Performance indicator 6.12.2 with infused content—Develop a plan to attain a personal health goal of staying safe on prom night that addresses strengths, needs, and risks.[1,p34]

Performance indicator 6.12.3 with infused content—Implement strategies and monitor progress in achieving a personal health goal of staying safe on prom night.[1,p34]

Performance indicator 6.12.4 with infused content—Formulate an effective long-term personal health plan to be safe when driving with another person after a school event.[1,p34]
and pair it with
Standard 1 performance indicator 1.12.2—Describe the interrelationships of emotional, intellectual, physical, and social health in adolescence.[1,p25]

Standard 1 performance indicator 1.12.2 with infused content—Describe the interrelationships of emotional, intellectual, physical, and social health in adolescence when coping with personal safety on prom night.[1,p25]

OR

To Teach Students How to Advocate for a Safe Prom Program to Reduce or Prevent Injuries and Health Problems, Link Standard 8 with Standard 1.

Standard 8—Students will demonstrate the ability to advocate for personal, family, and community health.[1,p36]
Performance indicator 8.12.4—Adapt health messages and communication techniques to a specific target audience.[1,p36]

Performance indicator 8.12.4 with infused content—Adapt health messages and communication techniques to the safe prom program target audience.[1,p36]
and pair it with
Standard 1 performance indicator 1.12.5—Propose ways to reduce or prevent injuries and health problems.[1,p25]

Standard 1 performance indicator 1.12.5 with infused content—Propose ways to reduce or prevent injuries and health problems by implementing a safe prom program.[1,p25]

The above examples demonstrate how Standard 1 can be paired with the skills standards to meet the needs of the students.

By linking the skill and content performance indicators, the teacher has a clear idea of how to plan the unit lessons.

The first step in planning is to think through the unit by completing the performance task template. Upon completion, the teacher has most of the information to introduce the prompt to the students.

When planning for the prompt, also include all the back-up information, holistic rubrics, analytical rubrics, and worksheets the students need to complete the task. Designing skills-based lessons requires considerable preparation, but once the teacher distributes it and explains the task, the students are responsible for the results. Students learn with good coaching (formative assessments) to demonstrate proficiency in content and skill.

HOW DOES THE COORDINATED SCHOOL HEALTH TEAM CONTRIBUTE TO INCREASING FUNCTIONAL HEALTH KNOWLEDGE RELATED TO HEALTH PROMOTION AND DISEASE PREVENTION TO ENHANCE HEALTH?

Health Education

- Refocus instruction on skill building to prevent drinking and driving.

- Reinforce assertive skills to discourage passengers from getting into a car with an impaired driver.
- Highlight the importance of positive peer pressure to keep friends safe.

Physical Education

- Promote safe driving.
- Provide equipment for the safe prom program.

Health Services

- Provide information about the hazards of drinking and driving.
- Attend the safe prom program.

Nutrition Services

- Display posters that show high school students having fun without alcohol.
- Advertise the food available at the safe prom program.

Counseling, Psychological, and Social Services

- Provide alcohol counseling.
- Provide intervention and referral services to students and families with alcohol problems.

Healthy School Environment

- Display health promotion posters.
- Display, watch, and listen to student generated public service announcements that promote health.
- Provide access to the school facility for a safe prom program.

Health Promotion for Staff

- Provide professional development that informs staff of the student survey data and ways of promoting safe driving.
- Promote the safe prom program by participating and leading various activities.

Family/Community Involvement

- Implement an awareness program that encourages the community not to drink and drive.
- Encourage family and community support for a safe prom program.
- Develop community-sponsored events that promote healthy living.
- Ask for volunteers and donations to support the safe prom program.

Content Resources

Health education resources are abundant in print and electronic form. The following is a review of government, private, and paid resources that teachers use to plan skills-based units and lessons. The list is continuously updated on the book's website.

CENTERS FOR DISEASE CONTROL AND PREVENTION

The Centers for Disease Control and Prevention has several excellent resources for health teachers. A good place to start is the Healthy Schools Healthy Youth! It is divided into four sections: School Health, Data and Statistics, Health topics, and Our Funded Partners.[7]

The School Health section under Adolescent and School Health Tools offers six resources, all free, downloadable, and very helpful in planning. Several are appropriate activities for the Coordinated School Health Team. Health education is one component of the team whose decisions have a direct impact on classroom instruction.[8]

- The Food–Safe Schools Action Guide (FSSAG) is used by nurses, administrators, and parents to develop a response to food borne illness.
- The Health Education Curriculum Analysis Tool (HECAT) is an excellent instrument to analyze curriculum to determine its alignment to the National Health Education Standards and meet the Characteristics of Effective Health Education.
- "Improving the Health of Adolescents and Young Adults: A Guide for States and Communities" is a good source for state and local coalitions to locate data to define problems, identify solutions, and evaluate the impact of their work.
- Making It Happen! examines the nutritional quality of the food and beverages sold to children outside the regular school meals offered. Success stories model how to achieve this goal.
- The School Health Index (SHI): A Self-Assessment and Planning Guide is a tool to assess and improve the school's health and safety policies through the coordinated school health model.

The same page contains a good explanation of the Coordinated School Health Program (CSHP) and its components. Together with the resources above, a teacher has available a multitude of tools that can be used in the school to improve the health, well-being, and academic success of students.[9]

School Health Education Resources (SHER) is an excellent resource for health educators. After choosing a topic, grade level, resource type, and language, a teacher is presented with lessons that are aligned with the National Health Education Standards (NHES) and the Characteristics of Effective Health Education. The resource sometimes references only Standard 1, however, so the teacher will need to choose a skill through which to teach the content.[10]

Often health educators need information that explains their role in the academic success of their students. The Health and Academics link presents research that shows the relationship between health and academics.

PowerPoints of the 2007 Youth Risk Behavior Survey are also downloadable and used for presentations to a variety of audiences. This page also contains a link to School Connectedness. This document presents the research that found students who feel connected to their schools are less likely to become involved in risky behaviors.[11]

Make a Difference at Your School is a program that provides ten strategies consistent with the Coordinated School Health Team components to reduce obesity in the schools.[12]

The program evaluation resource on this page is for the CDC's funded partners. It is a road map the states follow when evaluating their state-wide, coordinated school health programs. Although not for classroom teachers, this resource is useful for educators who want to know what their state is doing in coordinated school health, as well as a great resource for districts and teachers who are trying to develop programs.[13]

The School Health Policy section provides CDC-funded states the information, tools, and resources to support districts that need school policy, program development, implementation, and evaluation. This information is useful because an informed health educator can enlighten district administrators about federal laws and policies regarding child and adolescent health that may result in an improved health education program.[14]

In the Data and Statistics section of the page, the health educator can access data from several federal surveys.

- The Youth Risk Behavior Surveillance System (YRBSS) is a report of biannual risk factor data from high schools across the country. Health teachers use this information to see how their school and state compare with national data.[15]

- The School Health Profile Surveys provides data from biennial assessments of school health policies and programs. The survey is conducted by state and local education and health agencies among middle and high school principals and lead health education teachers. Health educators use this data to compare their health programs with others in their state and the nation.[16]

- The School Health Policies and Programs Study (SHPPS) is a national survey that assesses school health policies and practices at the state, district, school, and classroom levels. The survey reports

information about health education programs and identifies who is responsible for them, the amount of collaboration that occurs between the school and outside agencies and organizations, and how policies and practices have changed over the years. Health educators use this information to compare their program with other states, districts, and schools.[17]

In the Health Topics portion of the page, asthma, obesity, crisis preparedness, injury, violence, physical activity, nutrition, sexual risk behaviors, and tobacco use are highlighted. Each section includes an overview of the topic, including links to other resources, a section on data and statistics, science-based strategies, policy guidance, national, state, and local programs, and references. This section is very useful for health educators because it provides valid and reliable information to use with students, colleagues, administrators, and the community.

In the Funded Partners section of the page, the CDC lists the states, territories, local agencies, and tribal governments funded to provide asthma management, coordinated school health programs, HIV prevention, professional development, and the Youth Risk Behavior Survey. Health educators use this information to determine if their state, agency, or territory has been funded by the CDC, the programs offered, and any success stories.[18]

The CDC provides free videos that address many health education issues, such as how to wash your hands, immunizations, HIV, the importance of getting the flu vaccine, fluoridation, carbon monoxide, dating violence, and several elementary stories about respecting the ways of parents, participating in physical activity, and eating healthy.[19]

OTHER FEDERAL RESOURCES

The "Safe, Disciplined, and Drug Free Schools Program, 2001" from the United States Department of Education lists exemplary and promising programs that have proven their effectiveness in promoting safe, disciplined, and drug-free schools. The document explains how the curriculum is evaluated and provides a list of programs, their emphases, targeted grade level, duration/intensity, and cost. These programs are approved for purchase with the Safe and Drug Free Schools and Community Grant.[20]

The Substance Abuse and Mental Health Services Administration (SAMSHA) website examines a registry of evidence-based programs and practices. The user can find peer reviewed interventions for substance use, mental health, and other topics. Some of the interventions cited are also located on the USDOE list of exemplary and promising programs.[21]

The National Highway Traffic Safety Administration is dedicated to saving lives, preventing injury, and reducing vehicle related crashes. Its website provides access to valid information about bicycle, car, motorcycle, pedestrian, and school bus safety.[22]

AMERICAN CANCER SOCIETY

The American Cancer Society has shown its support of comprehensive health education by publishing the National Health Education Standards. Its website contains valuable information about cancer and position papers on comprehensive school health.[23]

WEBSITES

Action for Healthy Kids is a non-profit organization dedicated to addressing the problems of overweight, undernourished, and sedentary youth. The organization works collaboratively with state-based teams and partner organizations to develop and distribute innovative programs to create schools that support health and academic achievement. Although this organization is national, it has teams across the nation and can help an individual health educator by providing tools to improve instruction or the coordinated school health program, such as the Wellness Policy Tool.[24]

The Alliance for a Healthier Generation is a partnership between the American Heart Association and the William J. Clinton Foundation. It addresses prevention of childhood obesity and creation of healthier lifestyles for children. The Healthy Schools Program encourages schools to increase the opportunities children have to exercise and play, place healthy foods in vending machines and cafeterias, and increase resources to teachers and staff to become healthy role models.[25]

The American Heart Association website provides information on a variety of topics. The Children and Youth page has links to information about the following programs

- Childhood Obesity
- Jump Rope for Heart
- Hoops for Heart
- Heartpower!
- Heart Defects[26]

The American Lung Association provides excellent information about an assortment of topics. Under "School Programs," it offers information on the Asthma-Friendly School Initiative and Indoor Air Quality Tools for Schools.[27]

The mission of the American School Health Association (ASHA) is to protect and promote the health of children and youth by supporting coordinated school health programs as a foundation for school success. The site contains information about school health, best practices, and various publications that support comprehensive school health.[28]

As mentioned, the Healthy Schools Program advocates for policies and practices that promote a healthy school for students, teachers, and staff by increasing school wellness, improving the food available at school, increasing physical activity, teaching good nutrition, encouraging staff wellness, and engaging parents. This website is a valuable resource to health educators in that it provides an advocacy model for developing or maintaining a healthy school.[29]

The Guttmacher Institute is an excellent source of information about sexual and reproductive health. Teachers can link to an adolescent site that includes fact sheets, state policies, policy articles, in brief articles, research articles, reports, statistics, slide shows, memos and statements, and audio clips.[30]

Sexuality Information and Education Council of the United States (SIECUS) provides extensive information on comprehensive sexuality education, the effectiveness of abstinence-only programs, adolescent sexuality, teen pregnancy, sexually transmitted diseases, sexual orientation, sexual and reproductive health, international topics, and publications.[31]

WebMD contains information about a variety of health topics. It is an excellent resource for a Standard 3 performance task where students determine if the site is a valid and reliable source of information then use the information to meet a student challenge.[32]

Electronic Classroom Resources

The following websites contain specific information and resources that teachers use in their classrooms. Some contain more content than skills, and others have both. The skilled teacher extracts the information needed and combines it with a skill standard to develop a targeted lesson or unit.

- Discovery Education has a classroom resources link on its home page that has excellent information for teachers, including lesson plans and Kathy Schrock's Guide for Educators.[33]
- KidsHealth.org is an accredited health website that includes health information for parents, kids, teens, and teachers. A link from the parents tab leads to PreK–12 lesson plans, some with content only, while others contain both content and skills.[34]
- Rubistar is a website that helps teachers develop rubrics for project-based learning activities. Rubric templates are available for oral projects, multimedia, products, and research and writing that can be adapted for performance tasks.[35]
- Bam! Body and Mind is a CDC interactive website that presents information about disease, food and nutrition, physical activity, your safety, your life, and your body for children ages 9–13. There is also a teacher's corner, Bam! Classroom, where educators can access activities, downloads, and related materials.[5]

- McGruff.org is a safety interactive website sponsored by the National Crime Prevention Council. It targets middle school children and contains games, stories, videos, advice, and materials about safety. There is also a link for parents and educators.[36]
- PBS.org has a link for standards-based teacher resources in health and fitness. Grade ranges include preschool to Grade 12, and topics can be selected from many of the traditional health education content areas.[37]
- MyPyramid.gov is an excellent source of information about healthy eating for all ages. It explains the basics of the food guide pyramid, provides interactive tools, podcasts, PSAs, etc. A major feature of the site is the Pyramid Tracker where students record their food intake to determine if they are following the recommended daily food allowances and then compare their food intake to their energy output. This activity aligns with Standard 6, goal setting, because students can set goals to improve their health after reviewing the results of the survey.[38]
- Lesson Planet is a search engine for teachers. To access the lesson plans, the teacher must register and pay a fee. Lessons are rated from five stars to one, based on source authority, credibility, authenticity, accuracy, objectivity, and lack of bias, quality, design, structure, comprehensiveness, readability, creativity, and innovation. The lessons are aligned with *Content Knowledge: A Compendium of Standards and Benchmarks for K–12 Education, 2nd Edition,* not the National Health Education Standards.[39]
- HealthTeacher.com is another site that requires registration and a fee. A free trial, however, is available. The website offers lesson plans aligned to the National Health Education Standards, resources, and items for purchase.[40]

PROFESSIONAL ORGANIZATIONS

The following professional organizations provide excellent information and support for health educators.

- The American Association for Health Education (AAHE) encourages, supports, and assists health educators and other health professionals who work to promote health through education or other systemic changes. The site provides current news items, professional development information, AAHE areas of interest, programs and events, issues and actions, and publications.[41]
- The American Association of Health, Physical Education, Recreation, and Dance (AAHPERD) is an alliance of five national associations, American Association for Physical Activity and Recreation, American Association for Health Education, National Association for Girls & Women in Sport, National Association for Sport & Physical Education, and the

National Dance Association. The website explains the role of AAHPERD and provides links to each of the national associations and information about conventions, publications, community, and career resources.[42]
- The Association for Supervision and Curriculum Development (ASCD) is a membership organization that develops programs, products, and services that teachers need to learn, teach, and lead.[43]
  - The magazine, *Educational Leadership,* is a bimonthly publication that contains many articles that deal directly with health education instruction and assessment.
  - ASCD also supports the Whole Child Initiative with its own website, which includes pertinent information, such as school health councils, student health screenings, lifetime healthy behaviors, healthy food choices, research, facts and stats, tools, and other resources.[44]
  - Healthy School Report Card helps schools meet state guidelines and standards and the USDA wellness policy requirements, establish the World Health Organization's (WHO) concept of health-promoting schools, and use the best practices and methods for a high-quality school.[45]
- Rocky Mountain Center for Health Promotion and Education is another excellent resource for teachers. It provides an electronic newsletter, resources for coordinated school health training for CDC funded partners, tobacco prevention, a prevention information center, and professional development.[46]
- The National Commission for Health Education Credentialing supports health education by certifying health education specialists, promoting professional development, and strengthening professional preparation and practice. Health education news, credentialing, exam information, continuing education, renewal, and recertification, and approved education providers are all found on its website.[47]
- Society for Public Health Education (SOPHE) is an independent, international professional organization consisting of health education professionals and students. The organization promotes healthy behaviors, healthy communities, and healthy environments through the organization's membership, local chapters, and partnerships. SOPHE is a leader in setting standards for professional preparation, research and practice, professional development, and public outreach.[48]

Review Questions

1. How does a student demonstrate proficiency in a standard?

2. Explain why Standard 1 is paired with a skills standard.

3. In building skills-based curriculum, how does the teacher choose content?

4. How do the Standard 1 performance indicators help target instruction?

5. Explain the benefits of targeted instruction.

6. Explain how to modify a Standard 1 rubric so it will be more specific to the performance task.

7. What should a performance task focus on?

8. What topics should be addressed when instructional time is limited?

9. What local, state, and national resources provide student risk factor data?

10. The district Youth Risk Behavior Survey indicates that students are beginning to smoke in Grade 5 and continue to smoke through Grade 12. Choose one performance indicator from each Standard 1 grade span and pair it with one performance indicator of the same grade span from each skills standard. Propose content and skill to address this student smoking problem.

References

1. Joint Committee on National Health Education Standards.(2007). *National Health Education Standards, Second Edition, Achieving Excellence.* Atlanta: American Cancer Society. p24.
2. Zamora, D. (2003, June 30). *Step by Step: Walking for Fitness.* Retrieved April 9, 2009, from WebMD: www.webmd.com
3. Centers for Disease Control and Prevention. (2008, June 6). Morbidity and Mortality Weekly Report. Atlanta, GA.
4. U.S. Department of Agriculture. (2005, April). *MyPyramid, Steps to a Healthier You.* Retrieved March 18, 2009, from U.S. Department of Agriculture: www.mypyramid.gov
5. Centers for Disease Control and Prevention. (n.d.). *Bam! Body and Mind.* Retrieved April 28, 2009, from Centers for Disease Control and Prevention: http://www.bam.gov/index.html
6. Centers for Disease Control and Prevention. (n.d.). *The Buzz on Scuzz. BAM! Body and Mind.* Retrieved April 16, 2009, from BAM! Body and Mind, Your Body: http://www.bam.gov/sub_yourbody/yourbody_buzz_how.html
7. Centers for Disease Control and Prevention. (2009, April 27). *Healthy Schools.* Retrieved April 28, 2009, from Healthy Youth!: http://www.cdc.gov/HealthyYouth/index.htm
8. Centers for Disease Control and Prevention. (2008, November 24). *Summary of Adolescent and School Health Tools.* Retrieved May 1, 2009, from Healthy Youth!: http://www.cdc.gov/HealthyYouth/SchoolHealth/tools.htm
9. Centers for Disease Control and Prevention. (2008, September 24). *Coordinated School Health Program.* Retrieved May 1, 2009, from Healthy Youth!: http://www.cdc.gov/HealthyYouth/CSHP/

10. Centers for Disease Control and Prevention. (2008, December 10). *CDC's School Health Education Resources (SHER).* Retrieved May 1, 2009, from Healthy Youth!: http://apps.nccd.cdc.gov/sher/
11. Centers for Disease Control and Prevention. (2009, March 10). *Student Health and Academic Achievement.* Retrieved May 1, 2009, from Healthy Youth!: http://www.cdc.gov/HealthyYouth/health_and_academics/index.htm
12. Centers for Disease Control and Prevention. (2008, October 20). *Make a Difference at Your School.* Retrieved May 1, 2009, from Healthy Youth!: http://www.cdc.gov/HealthyYouth/keystrategies/index.htm
13. Centers for Disease Control and Prevention. (2008, March 5). *Program Evaluation.* Retrieved May 1, 2009, from Healthy Youth!: http://www.cdc.gov/HealthyYouth/evaluation/index.htm
14. Centers for Disease Control and Prevention. (2008, October 2). *School Health Policy.* Retrieved May 1, 2009, from Healthy Youth!: http://www.cdc.gov/HealthyYouth/policy/index.htm
15. Centers for Disease Control and Prevention. (2008, October 16). *YRBSS: Youth Risk Behavior Surveillance System.* Retrieved April 28, 2009, from Healthy Youth!, Data and Statistics: http://www.cdc.gov/HealthyYouth/yrbs/index.htm
16. Centers for Disease Control and Prevention. (2008, October 16). *School Health Profiles.* Retrieved April 28, 2009, from Healthy Youth!, Data and Statistics: http://www.cdc.gov/HealthyYouth/profiles/index.htm
17. Centers for Disease Control and Prevention. (2008, October 16). *SHPPS 2006, School Health Programs and Policy Study.* Retrieved April 27, 2009, from Healthy Youth!, Data and Statistics: http://www.cdc.gov/HealthyYouth/shpps/index.htm
18. Centers for Disease Control and Prevention. (2009, April 30). *Healthy Schools Healthy Youth!* Retrieved May 1, 2009, from Healthy Schools Healthy Youth!: http://www.cdc.gov/HealthyYouth/
19. Centers for Disease Control and Prevention. (2009, April 20). *CDC-TV.* Retrieved April 28, 2009: http://www.cdc.gov/cdctv/
20. U.S. Department of Education, Safe, Disciplined, and Drug-Free Schools Expert Panel. (2002, April). Exemplary & Promising Safe, Disciplined & Drug Free Schools Programs, 2001. Jessup, MD. Retrieved November 1, 2010, from http://www.ed.gov/admins/lead/safety/exemplary01/exemplary01.pdf
21. SAMSHA. (2008, February 25). *SAMSHA's Registry of Evidence-based programs and Practices.* Retrieved April 29, 2009, from NREPP: www.nrepp.samsha.gov/index.asp
22. National Highway Safety Traffic Administration. (n.d.). *Traffic Safety.* Retrieved May 1, 2009, from Traffic Safety: http://www.nhtsa.dot.gov/
23. American Cancer Society. (2009). Retrieved April 28, 2009, from http://www.cancer.org/docroot/home/index.asp
24. Action for Healthy Kids. (n.d.). *Action for Healthy Kids.* Retrieved April 28, 2009: http://www.actionforhealthykids.org/
25. Alliance for a Healthier Generation. (n.d.). *Alliance for a Healthier Generation.* Retrieved May 1, 2009: http://www.healthiergeneration.org/default.asp

26. American Heart Association. (2009). *Children and Youth!* Retrieved May 1, 2009: http://www.americanheart.org/presenter.jhtml?identifier=3003754

27. American Lung Association. (2009). *School Programs.* Retrieved May 1, 2009, from Treatment Options and Support: http://www.lungusa.org/site/c.dvLUK9O0E/b.23014/k.A096/School_Programs.htm

28. American School Health Association. (2009). Retrieved November 1, 2010, from American School Health Association: http://www.ashaweb.org/i4a/pages/index.cfm?pageid=1

29. *Healthy Schools Campaign.* (2008). Retrieved April 28, 2009, from: http://healthyschoolscampaign.org/programs/wellness/cd/

30. Guttmacher Institute. (n.d.). *Guttmacher Institute.* Retrieved April 28, 2009: www.guttmacher.org

31. Sexuality Information and Education Council of the United States. (n.d.). *Sexuality Information and Education Council of the United States.* Retrieved May 1, 2009: http://www.siecus.org/

32. WebMD, LLC. (2005–2009). *WebMD, Better Information. Better Health.* Retrieved April 28, 2009: http://www.webmd.com/

33. Discovery Education. (2008). *Classroom Resources.* Retrieved April 28, 2009: http://school.discoveryeducation.com/index.html

34. Nemours. (1995–2009). *Kids Health.* Retrieved April 28, 2009, from Kids Health: http://kidshealth.org/

35. ALTEC at University of Kansas. (2000–2008). *Rubistar.* Retrieved April 28, 2009, from http://rubistar.4teachers.org/index.php

36. National Crime Prevention Council. (2008). *McGruff's.org Milstein Child Safety Center.* Retrieved April 28, 2009: http://www.mcgruff.org/

37. Public Broadcasting Service. (1995–2009). *PBS Teachers.* Retrieved April 28, 2009: http://www.pbs.org/teachers/healthfitness/

38. United States Department of Agriculture. (2009, April 15). *MyPyramid.gov.* Retrieved April 28, 2009: http://www.mypyramid.gov/

39. *Lesson Planet, The Search Engine for Teachers.* (1999–2009). Retrieved April 28, 2009, from http://www.lessonplanet.com/

40. *HealthTeacher, Good Health is Contagious!* (2000-2009). Retrieved April 28, 2009, from http://www.healthteacher.com/dashboard

41. American Association of Health Education. (n.d.). *American Association of Health Education.* Retrieved April 28, 2009, from American Association of Health Education: http://www.aahperd.org/aahe/

42. American Association of Health, Physical Education, Recreation and Dance. (n.d.). *American Association of Health, Physical Education, Recreation and Dance.* Retrieved April 28, 2009: http://www.aahperd.org/

43. Association for Supervision and Curriculum Development. (2009). *ASCD Learn. Teach. Lead.* Retrieved May 1, 2009: http://www.ascd.org/

44. Association for Supervision and Curriculum Development. (n.d.). *The Whole Child.* Retrieved April 28, 2009: http://www.wholechildeducation.org/clearinghouse/healthy/

45. Association for Supervision and Curriculum Development. (2007). Creating a Healthy School using the Healthy School Report Card. *Creating a Healthy School using the Healthy School Report Card.* Alexandria, VA. Association for Supervision and Curriculum Development.

46. Rocky Mountain Center for Health Promotion. (2006). *RMC Health.* Retrieved May 1, 2009, from Welcome to RMC!: http://www.rmc.org/

47. The National Commission for Health Education Credentialing. (2008). *Welcome.* Retrieved May 11, 2010 from: www.nchec.org

48. Society for Public Health Education (n.d.) *About SOPHE.* Retrieved May 11, 2010, from: www.sophe.org

Teaching National Health Education Standard 2

"Students will analyze the influence of family, peers, culture, media, technology, and other factors on health behaviors."[1,p8]

Standard 2

Causes of behavior are baffling because so many factors influence it. For example, family, friends, music, television, movies, culture, and technology are external factors (**Figure 6.1**). Others, such as personal values, beliefs, how we perceive social norms, curiosity, interests, desires, fears, and likes or dislikes, are internal (**Figures 6.2**). While some of these factors are a positive influence on behavior, others are negative.[1,p28]

Standard 2 challenges students to examine how influences affect health behavior and practices. Health behaviors require thought and change in response to a situation, knowledge, or training. Health practices are habits, things that we do without giving them much thought.

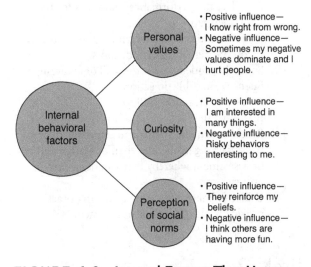

FIGURE 6.2 Internal Factors That Have a Positive or Negative Effect on Behavior

Sample performance tasks for examining influences include:

- Analyzing print and broadcast advertising
- Designing a how-to-stay-healthy book that identifies the influence of healthy behaviors, explains why they are important, and shows how to achieve them
- Writing, reading, or performing—depending on the age of the student—a skit
- Rewriting or retelling a story focused on negative influences into one portraying positive influences on behavior
- Surveying students regarding the norms of the student body and how those perceptions affect personal health behaviors.[2,p229]

To show proficiency in this standard, students identify, describe, explain, examine, analyze, and evaluate external

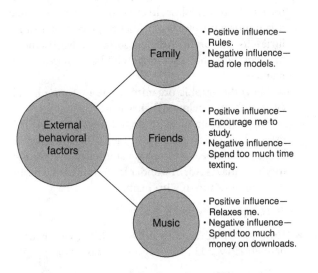

FIGURE 6.1 External Factors That Have a Positive or Negative Effect on Behavior

and internal factors and how they influence health behavior.

Teaching the Skill

Teaching and learning the national health education skills standards is a process. When planning, follow these steps:

I. Discuss the importance of understanding how internal and external factors influence behavior, why these influences are relevant to the health and well-being of the student, and how understanding them relates to other skills. For example, we make decisions (Standard 5) based on how we are influenced.

II. Explain the steps to reaching proficiency in analyzing influences.
  A. Select the performance indicators for the grade span.
  B. Teach the skill of analyzing influences based on the performance indicators.

III. Show the students what the skill of analyzing influences looks like in action.
  A. Demonstrate the skill.
  B. Model the skill.

IV. Provide adequate time for the students to practice analyzing influences, then design an authentic assessment whereby they can demonstrate proficiency.

V. Utilize formative assessments during practice to provide feedback and encouragement.[1,p14]

PreK–2

To achieve proficiency in Standard 2, PreK–2 students identify the influences of family, describe the influence of the media, and explain how the school can support personal health practices and behaviors.[1,p26]

Students initially recognize the external (family, media, and school) and internal influences (personal values, beliefs, perceived norms, curiosity, interests, desires, fears, and likes or dislikes) that affect behavior. Next, they determine whether these factors have a positive or negative effect on health practices (habits) and behavior.

PreK–Grade 2

2.2.1 Identify how the family influences personal health practices and behaviors.

2.2.2 Identify what the school can do to support personal health practices and behaviors.

2.2.3 Describe how the media can influence health behaviors.[1,p26]

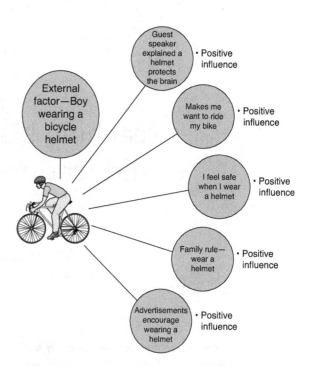

FIGURE 6.3   External Factor Having a Positive Influence on a PreK–2 Child

For example:

Show the graphic organizer of Adam, a PreK–2 child (**Figure 6.3**).

Ask the children, "Does this picture make you want to ride your bike?" Explain that the picture of the boy wearing a helmet while riding his bicycle is an external factor and has many positive influences on behavior. For example, Adam wears his helmet because it is a family rule. It also makes him feel safe, so he enjoys riding more.

Adam's health teacher invited Mr. Hooper, the owner of a bicycle shop, to class, and he explained that it is important to wear a helmet to protect against injuries to the brain. Adam also sees advertisements on television that encourage children to wear their helmets.

Show the graphic organizer of a boy riding his bicycle without a helmet (**Figure 6.4**).

Some of Adam's friends do not wear a helmet. This external factor is a negative influence on behavior because Adam's peers do not get injured, and have fun, too. This makes Adam wonder if he should ride his bicycle without wearing his helmet.

To reflect, ask the students:

- How does Adam's family influence him to wear his helmet? (PI 2.2.1) (*Wearing a helmet is a family rule.*)
- Is Adam's family an internal or external factor? (*External*)

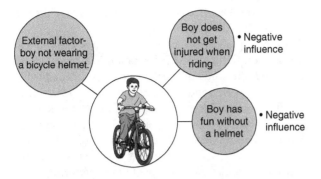

FIGURE 6.4   Boy Riding His Bicycle Without a Helmet Exerting Negative Influence

- How does Adam's school support health practices and behaviors? (PI 2.2.2) *(His health teacher invited Mr. Hooper, the owner of a bicycle shop, to class, and he explained that it is important to wear a helmet to protect against injuries to the brain.)*
- Is Adam's school an internal or external factor? *(External)*
- How did the media influence Adam's choice to wear a helmet? (PI 2.2.3) *(The media was a positive influence. Adam saw advertisements on television that encourage children to wear their helmets.)*
- Wearing a helmet makes Adam feel safe, so he enjoys riding more. Is this factor internal or external? *(Internal)*
- Adam sees his friend ride his bicycle without a helmet. Is this an internal or external factor? *(Both)*
- Does Adam's friend exert a positive or negative influence? *(Both. His friend does not wear a helmet and he still has fun.)*

When the students demonstrate an understanding of the skill, as assessed formatively, it is time to practice. Select a story, show pictures or a video clip, model a behavior, and ask the students to use the analyzing influences graphic organizer to identify the external and internal factors that cause the person to behave in a particular way.

Ask if the factors have a positive or negative influence on the person's health behavior. Students use the smiley/frown hand signs to indicate a positive or negative effect. To reinforce mathematics, use a + or a − sign. This procedure is also a good way to assess formatively whether the students understand.

If the students determine an influence is good, reinforce the positive health influence and behavior. Otherwise, discuss coping strategies to deal with the influence in a healthy way.

Once the students demonstrate the skills, teach the health content. Design a prompt that allows the students to showcase their knowledge of health content by analyzing influences. As the students practice their content and skill, use formative assessments to redirect, reinforce, and encourage them.

WHAT DOES THE SKILL OF ANALYZING INFLUENCES LOOK LIKE IN THE PREK–2 CLASSROOM?

Mr. Harrison, a Grade 2 teacher at the Washington Elementary School, recently completed the district's school bus safety policies and procedures training. Following the training, he teaches bus safety to his class. He has a very spirited group of second graders and always reminds them to think before they act and be aware of why they are behaving in a certain way. In particular, he wants his students to think about, practice, and follow the bus safety rules.

As Thanksgiving approaches, the students have completed several art and history projects. Mr. Harrison makes sure all the projects are in their backpacks before the children leave the classroom and says, "Do not open your backpacks until you are safely off the bus and in your home."

A few years ago on a dark November afternoon, a student was hit by the school bus and injured as she picked up papers she had dropped. The driver had not seen her.

In planning, Mr. Harrison chooses performance indicators that focus on specific skill and content.

Standard 2—Students will analyze the influence of family, peers, culture, media, technology, and other factors on health behaviors.[1,p26]
> Performance Indicator 2.2.2—Identify what the school can do to support personal health practices and behaviors.[1,p26]
>> *Performance indicator 2.2.2 with infused content—* Identify what the school can do to support personal health practices and behaviors about school bus safety.[1,p26]

After selecting the appropriate performance indicator for the skill, choose a Standard 1 performance indicator for bus safety.

Standard 1—Students will comprehend concepts related to health promotion and disease prevention to enhance health.[1,p24]
> Performance Indicator 1.2.1—Identify that healthy behaviors affect personal health.[1,p24]
>> *Performance indicator 1.2.1 with infused content—* Identify that healthy behaviors, such as school bus safety rules, affect personal health.[1,p24]

By linking the skill and content performance indicators, the teacher has a clear idea of how to plan the analyzing influences unit.

The first step in planning is to think through the unit by completing the performance task template (**Appendix G**). Upon completion, the teacher has a good idea of the lessons that precede this culminating activity, the information and back-up materials necessary to introduce the prompt to the students, and the assessment strategies.

When distributing the prompt, include back-up information, worksheets, and holistic and analytical rubrics. The latter are included with the prompt so that the students know how they are being assessed before beginning their project. The rubrics act as a guide and help the students attain proficiency in the standards.

Designing a performance task requires considerable preparation but once the information is distributed and explained, the students create a product independently. They learn with good coaching (formative assessment) how to demonstrate proficiency in content and skill.

The following is an example of a Grade 2 analyzing influences performance task that focuses on school bus safety. The first section demonstrates how the teacher plans for an authentic assessment of the performance indicators 2.2.2 and 1.2.1. The second section extracts some of the information from the performance task and transforms it into the student prompt and support materials.

Performance Task Name: Grade 2—School Bus Safety

I. Which state standard(s) does this performance task address?

II. Topic: What areas of health does this project assess? Why is it important? What is the focus of the project?[2,p237]

  A. This performance task assesses Injury Prevention/Safety

  B. This topic is important because:

   1. According to the National Highway Traffic Safety Administration (NHTSA), 50% of all school-age pedestrians killed in school transportation-related crashes were between the ages of 5 and 7.

   2. 32% of transportation-related fatalities (74) occur between 3:00 P.M. and 3:59 P.M., followed by crashes (52) that occur between 7:00 A.M. and 7:59 A.M.

   3. An average of 23 school-aged children die in school transportation-related traffic crashes each year, 5 as occupants of the school bus and 18 as pedestrians.[3]

  C. The focus of the project is to help students identify the factors that influence following school bus safety procedures.

III. Key Concepts: What basic concepts should students know?[2,p237]

  Standard 1—Students will comprehend concepts related to health promotion and disease prevention to enhance health.[1,p24]

  Performance indicator 1.2.1 with infused content—Identify that healthy behaviors, such as school bus safety rules, affect personal health.[1,p24]

  A. Exiting the bus

   1. If you forget something on the bus, tell your teacher the next day. Do not return by yourself because the driver may not see you.

   2. Make sure your book bag or equipment is secure as you get off the bus. Loose drawstrings may become caught on the bus equipment.

   3. The Danger Zone is 10 feet around the bus. Stay ten steps away from it so that you are outside the Danger Zone and the driver can see you.

   4. Cross the street in front of the bus. If you drop something, tell the driver so he or she will know where you are.

   5. Never speak to strangers at the bus stop or get into a car with one. Leave quickly! Tell an adult if a stranger tries to talk to you or asks you to get into his or her car.[4]

  (continues)

122   CHAPTER SIX   TEACHING NATIONAL HEALTH EDUCATION STANDARD 2

IV. Skills: Which of the seven National Health Education Standards skills does this performance task address?[2,p237]

Standard 2—Students will analyze the influence of family, peers, culture, media, technology, and other factors on health behaviors.[1,p26]

Performance indicator 2.2.2 with infused content—Identify what the school can do to support personal health practices and behaviors about school bus safety.[1,p26]

A. Demonstrate five school bus safety rules.

V. Curricular connections: What other subject areas does this project support?[2,p237]

English Language Arts

Art

VI. Student Directions and Assessment Criteria[2,p238]

A. Project Description: Write and attach an engaging prompt that draws the student into the project.[2,p238]

It was the week before Thanksgiving and the students at Washington Elementary School were excited about the holiday. Being November, it was dark in the afternoon when the students got off the bus.

Sam was tired and looking forward to going home but was also excited to show his mother the turkey model he made. While riding home, his friend asked to see the model. While showing his model to a friend, Sam suddenly realized that it was time to get off the bus. He grabbed his model and backpack and quickly moved to leave.

As he turned to walk in front of the bus, Sam dropped his turkey model but could not see it because it was dark. He put his backpack down to find it.

B. Your Challenge: Provide a challenge or mission statement that describes the project.[2,p238]

Your challenge is to help Sam understand the influences on his behavior and to follow the school bus safety rules in the future.

C. Assessment Criteria[2,p239]

You are assessed on the following key concepts: (List the concepts)

Performance indicator 1.2.1 with infused content—Identify that healthy behaviors, such as school bus safety rules, affect personal health.[1,p24]

1. If you forget something on the bus, tell your teacher the next day. Do not return by yourself because the driver may not see you.
2. Make sure your book bag or equipment is secure as you get off the bus. Loose drawstrings may become caught on the bus equipment.
3. The Danger Zone is 10 feet around the bus. Stay ten steps away from it so that you are outside the Danger Zone and the driver can see you.
4. Cross the street in front of the bus. If you drop something, tell the driver so he or she will know where you are.[4]

You are assessed on the following skills: (List the skills)

Performance indicator 2.2.2 with infused content—Identify what the school can do to support personal health practices and behaviors around school bus safety.[1,p26]

1. Demonstrate five school bus safety procedures.

Student project must include the following. (List the project components)

1. Describe factors that influenced Sam to put down his backpack in front of the bus to look for his model. Use the graphic organizer.
2. A poster that includes five school bus safety rules and one picture for each rule.
3. A role-play demonstrating the five bus safety procedures.

Prompt and assessment criteria (Distribute this information to students who are readers. For non-readers, read the prompt and explain the assessment.)

Washington Elementary School

Name _____

It was the week before Thanksgiving and the students at Washington Elementary School were excited about the holiday. Being November, it was dark in the afternoon when the students got off the bus.

Sam was tired and looking forward to going home but was also excited to show his mother the turkey model he made. While riding home, his friend asked to see the model. While showing his model to a friend, Sam suddenly realized that it was time to get off the bus. He grabbed his model and backpack and quickly moved to leave.

As he turned to walk in front of the bus, Sam dropped his turkey model but could not see it because it was dark. He put his backpack down to find it.

Your challenge is to help Sam understand the influences on his behavior and to follow the school bus safety rules in the future.

Your project must include:

1. Describe factors that influenced Sam to put down his backpack in front of the bus to look for his model. Use the graphic organizers.

2. A poster that includes five school bus safety rules and one picture for each rule.

3. A role-play demonstrating the five bus safety procedures.

ASSESSMENT MATERIALS

Graphic organizer to analyze external factors that influence behavior (**Figure 6.5**)

Graphic organizer to analyze internal factors that influence behavior (**Figure 6.6**)

Analytical rubric to assess the external and internal factors graphic organizers (**Table 6.1**)

Analytical rubric to assess the bus safety rules poster (**Table 6.2**)

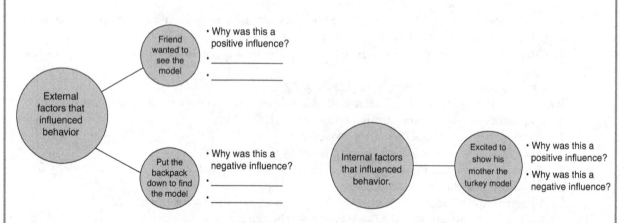

FIGURE 6.5 Graphic Organizer that Analyzes External Factors that Influence Behavior

FIGURE 6.6 Graphic Organizer that Analyzes Internal Factors that Influence Behavior

(continues)

TABLE 6.1 Analytical Rubric to Assess the External and Internal Factors Graphic Organizers

Criteria	4	3	2	1
External factors graphic organizer	Student accurately describes the positive and negative influences of each external factor in the graphic organizer.	Student's description of the positive and negative influences of each external factor in the graphic organizer is mostly accurate.	Student's description of the positive and negative influences of each external factor in the graphic organizer has a few inaccuracies.	Student's description of the positive and negative influences of each external factor in the graphic organizer is mostly inaccurate.
Internal factors graphic organizer	Student accurately describes the positive and negative influences of the internal factor in the graphic organizer.	Student's description of the positive and negative influences of the internal factor in the graphic organizer is mostly accurate.	Student's description of the positive and negative influences of the internal factor in the graphic organizer has a few inaccuracies.	Student's description of the positive and negative influences of the internal factor in the graphic organizer is mostly inaccurate.

Name _____

Total possible points – 4   Your points - _____   Your grade - _____

TABLE 6.2 Analytical Rubric to Assess the Bus Safety Rules Poster

Criteria	4	3	2	1
Performance indicator 1.2.1 with infused content—Identify that healthy behaviors, such as following school bus safety rules, affect personal health.[1,p24]	Student accurately identifies what to do if a belonging is left on the bus.	Student's identification of what to do if a belonging is left on the bus is mostly accurate.	Student's identification of what to do if a belonging is left on the bus has a few inaccuracies.	Student's identification of what to do if a belonging is left on the bus is mostly inaccurate.
Performance indicator 1.2.1 with infused content—Identify that healthy behaviors, such as following school bus safety rules, affect personal health.[1,p24]	Student accurately identifies how to secure a backpack before leaving the bus.	Student's identification of how to secure a backpack before leaving the bus is mostly accurate	Student's identification of how to secure a backpack before leaving the bus has a few inaccuracies.	Student's identification of how to secure a backpack before leaving the bus is mostly inaccurate.
Performance indicator 1.2.1 with infused content—Identify that healthy behaviors, such as following school bus safety rules, affect personal health.[1,p24]	Student accurately identifies how to stay outside the danger zone.	Student's identification of how to stay outside the danger zone is mostly accurate.	Student's identification of how to stay outside the danger zone has a few inaccuracies.	Student's identification of how to stay outside the danger zone is mostly inaccurate.

(continues)

TABLE 6.2   Analytical Rubric to Assess the Bus Safety Rules Poster *(continued)*

Criteria	4	3	2	1
Performance indicator 1.2.1 with infused content—Identify that healthy behaviors, such as following school bus safety rules, affect personal health.[1,p24]	Student accurately identifies how to cross the street in front of the bus.	Student's identification of how to cross the street in front of the bus is mostly accurate.	Student's identification of how to cross the street in front of the bus has a few inaccuracies.	Student's identification of how to cross the street in front of the bus is mostly inaccurate.
Pictures	The five pictures accurately depict each safety rule.	The five pictures depicting each safety rule are mostly accurate.	The five pictures depicting each safety rule have a few inaccuracies.	The five pictures depicting each safety rule are mostly inaccurate.

Name _____

Total possible points – 20   Your points - _____   Your grade - _____

Analytical rubric to assess the role-play of the bus safety rules (**Table 6.3**)

TABLE 6.3   Analytical Rubric to Assess the Role-Play of the Bus Safety Rules

Criteria	4	3	2	1
Performance indicator 2.2.2 with infused content—Identify what the school can do to support personal health practices and behaviors around school bus safety.[1,p26]	Student accurately demonstrates what to do if a belonging is left on the bus.	Student's demonstration of what to do if a belonging is left on the bus is mostly accurate.	Student's demonstration of what to do if a belonging is left on the bus has a few inaccuracies.	Student's demonstration of what to do if a belonging is left on the bus is mostly inaccurate.
Performance indicator 2.2.2 with infused content—Identify what the school can do to support personal health practices and behaviors around school bus safety.[1,p26]	Student accurately demonstrates how to secure a backpack before leaving the bus.	Student's demonstration of how to secure a backpack before leaving the bus is mostly accurate.	Student's demonstration of how to secure a backpack before leaving the bus has a few inaccuracies.	Student's demonstration of how to secure a backpack before leaving the bus is mostly inaccurate.
Performance indicator 2.2.2 with infused content—Identify what the school can do to support personal health practices and behaviors about school bus safety.[1,p26]	Student accurately demonstrates how to stay outside the danger zone.	Student's demonstration of how to stay outside the danger zone is mostly accurate.	Student's demonstration of how to stay outside the danger zone has a few inaccuracies.	Student's demonstration of how to stay outside the danger zone is mostly inaccurate.

(continues)

TABLE 6.3 Analytical Rubric to Assess the Role-Play of the Bus Safety Rules *(continued)*

Criteria	4	3	2	1
Performance indicator 2.2.2 with infused content—Identify what the school can do to support personal health practices and behaviors about school bus safety.[1,p26]	Student accurately demonstrates how to cross the street in front of the bus.	Student's demonstration of how to cross the street in front of the bus is mostly accurate.	Student's demonstration of how to cross the street in front of the bus has a few inaccuracies.	Student's demonstration of how to cross the street in front of the bus is mostly inaccurate.
Voice projection	Projection of voice is excellent.	Projection of voice is good.	Projection of voice is fair.	Projection of voice is poor.

Name _____

Total possible points – 20   Your points - _____   Your grade - _____

HOW THE COORDINATED SCHOOL HEALTH TEAM CONTRIBUTES TO BUS SAFETY AND THE SKILL OF ANALYZING INFLUENCES

Health Education

- Focus instruction on the skill of analyzing influences and the content of bus safety.
- Review school bus safety policies and procedures with students.
- Teach healthy coping strategies.

Physical Education

- Promote bus safety in the gymnasium through posters and demonstrations.

Health Services

- Provide bus safety information.
- Provide first aid training to bus drivers.

Nutrition Services

- Display posters that promote bus safety.
- Display reminders that peanut products cannot be consumed on the bus.

Counseling, Psychological, and Social Services

- Provide counseling to cope with problems that may occur at the bus stop, while riding the bus, exiting it, or crossing the street.

Healthy School Environment

- Post bus safety procedures throughout the school.
- Provide bus safety practice.
- Develop bus safety policy and procedures.

Health Promotion for Staff

- Provide staff training in school bus safety so that staff is better prepared to help students.
- Utilize bus safety training when monitoring students.

Family/Community Involvement

- Organize and implement a parent program to explain the bus safety policies and procedures.
- Provide a bus safety workshop for parents and the community that includes the following data from the National Highway Traffic Safety Administration (NHTSA).
  - 50% of all school-age pedestrians killed in school transportation-related crashes were between the ages of 5 and 7.
  - 32% of transportation-related fatalities (74) occur between 3:00 P.M. and 3:59 P.M., followed by crashes (52) that occur between 7:00 A.M. and 7:59 A.M.
  - An average of 23 school aged children die in school transportation-related traffic crashes each year, 5 as occupants of the school bus and 18 as pedestrians.[3]

Grades 3–5

To achieve proficiency in Standard 2, Grade 3–5 students must describe, identify, and explain how the influences of family, culture, peers, media, technology, thoughts, and feelings affect their behavior. They also identify how the school supports personal health practices and behaviors.[1,p26]

To teach Standard 2, explain why it is important to understand how health behavior is influenced externally and internally, positively and negatively. Present a scenario (prompt) and demonstrate the skill so that the students can see what analyzing influences looks like.

For example:

Classmates at school bully Daniel by calling him names and making fun of him when the teacher is not looking. Daniel does not respond to the bullies but when he gets home, calls his little brother names and makes fun of him.

Daniel's parents told him to stand tall, look the bully in the eye, and tell him, "Stop! I don't like it when you talk to me like that!" Sometimes it works; sometimes not.

Daniel asked his friend, Devin, to help him cope with the bully. "Stand next to me and help me speak up and walk away." Devin was happy to help because the same boys had bullied him.

Daniel's parents encouraged him to tell his teacher, which he did. The teacher spoke to the other boys and

Grades 3–5 Performance Indicators

2.5.1 Describe how the family influences personal health practices and behaviors.

2.5.2 Identify the influence of culture on health practices and behaviors.

2.5.3 Identify how peers can influence healthy and unhealthy behaviors.

2.5.4 Describe how the school and community can support personal health practices and behaviors.

2.5.5 Explain how media influences thoughts, feelings, and health behaviors.

2.5.6 Describe ways that technology can influence personal health.[1,p26]

told them she was reporting them and the behavior must stop.

The bullies did not think they were doing anything wrong because they see that behavior in the movies and on YouTube and television.

After reading the report, the principal required the boys to participate in an online bullying intervention program. The boys stopped bullying after participating in the program.

See **Table 6.4** for a graphic organizer that analyzes Daniel's experience. Other graphic organizers, such as

---

TABLE 6.4   Analyzing Influences Graphic Organizer

Analyzing Influences on Behavior

Event – Daniel is being bullied by his peers at school

External factor	■ Yes □ No	Internal factor	■ Yes □ No
What is the positive influence?	**What is the negative influence?**	**What is the positive influence?**	**What is the negative influence?**
■ When Daniel told the teacher, she told the boys to stop and reported them to the principal. ■ Daniel told the teacher.	■ When he gets home, Daniel calls his little brother names and makes fun of him.	■ Daniel felt much better after telling the teacher because the bullying stopped. ■ Daniel feels good that Devin agrees to help. ■ Daniel feels good that he told the teacher because the bullying has stopped.	■ Daniel is hurt and angry and asks his friend, Devin, to help.

Reflection – What did Daniel do to cope with the negative influences?

■ He told his parents

■ He asked his friend Devin to help him.

■ He told his teacher and as a result, the bullying stopped.

---

word webs, also effectively show the relationship between the external and internal factors that influence behavior in a positive or negative way.

To reflect, ask the students:

- How did Daniel's parents influence his behavior when they learned of the bullying? (PI 2.5.1) *(Daniel's parents told him to stand tall, look the bully in the eye and tell him, "Stop! I don't like it when you talk to me like that!")*
- How did the school culture influence Devin's choice to help Daniel? (PI 2.5.2) *(It was a positive influence. Devin was happy to help because the same boys had bullied him.*
- How did the bullies influence a negative behavior in Daniel? (PI 2.5.3) *(Daniel did not respond to the bullies, but when he got home, he called his little brother names and made fun of him.)*
- How did the school support Daniel? (PI 2.5.4) *(Daniel's parents encouraged him to tell his teacher, which he did. The teacher spoke to the other boys and told them she was reporting them and the behavior must stop.)*
- How did the media influence the behavior of the bullies? (PI 2.5.5) *(The bullies did not think they were doing anything wrong because they see that behavior in the movies and on YouTube and television.)*
- How can technology influence personal health? (PI 2.5.6) *(After participating in an online bullying intervention program, the boys stopped their bullying.)*

When students demonstrate understanding of the skill, as evidenced through formative assessment, it is time to practice and introduce content.

To check for understanding, use the red and green circles. Ask clarifying questions and instruct the students to raise the green circle, if they agree with the answer, or the red if they do not.

Design a prompt that allows the students to showcase their knowledge of health content and the skill of analyzing influences. As the students practice their content and skill, continue to use formative assessments to check for understanding. Redirect and encourage students when necessary.

WHAT DOES THE SKILL OF ANALYZING INFLUENCES LOOK LIKE IN THE GRADE 3–5 CLASSROOM?

Mr. Adamson is a 5th grade teacher at the Abigail Adams Elementary School. He has noticed over the past few years that his students are becoming more and more overweight.

During class, Mr. Adamson hears the students discussing food advertisements they saw on television. Students find the ads entertaining and mention that the ad seldom talks about the nutritional content of the product.

Mr. Adamson has also discovered that many of the high-sugar foods have interactive websites with fun games to keep the attention of the children, thereby exposing them to more advertisements.

In planning his health education instruction, Mr. Adamson uses the students' interest in the Internet to improve their knowledge of nutrition and the skill of analyzing influences.

Standard 2 performance indicators help Mr. Adamson develop a unit that addresses the influence of advertisement gimmicks on good nutrition choices.

> Standard 2—Students analyze the influence of family, peers, culture, media, technology, and other factors on health behaviors.[1,p26]
> > Performance indicator 2.5.6—Describe ways that technology can influence personal health.[1,p26]
> > > *Performance indicator 2.5.6 with infused content—* Describe ways that technology gimmicks influence nutrition choices.[1,p26]

After selecting the appropriate performance indicator for the skill, choose a Standard 1 performance indicator.

> Standard 1—Students will comprehend concepts related to health promotion and disease prevention to enhance health.[1,p24]
> > Performance indicator 1.5.1—Describe the relationship between healthy behaviors and personal health.[1,p24]
> > > *Performance indicator 1.5.1 with infused content—* Describe the relationship between healthy behaviors, such as healthy food choices, and personal health.[1,p24]

By linking the skill and content performance indicators, the teacher has a clear idea of how to plan the lessons for an analyzing influences unit.

The first step in planning is to think through the unit by completing the performance task template. Upon completion, the teacher has a good idea of the lessons that precede this culminating activity, the information and back-up materials necessary to introduce the prompt to the students, and the assessment strategies.

When distributing the prompt, include back-up information, worksheets, and holistic and analytical rubrics. The latter are included with the prompt so that the students know how they are being assessed before beginning their project. The rubrics act as a guide and help the students attain proficiency in the standards.

Designing skills-based lessons requires considerable preparation, but once the information is distributed and explained, the students create a product independently. They learn with good coaching (formative assessment) how to demonstrate proficiency in content and skill.

The following is an example of a Grade 5 analyzing influences performance task that focuses on under-standing how advertising gimmicks influence healthy food choices.

The first section demonstrates how the teacher plans for an authentic assessment of the performance indicators 2.5.6 and 1.5.1. The second extracts the information from the performance task and transforms it into the student prompt and support materials.

Standard 2 Performance Task: Grade 5—Analyzing the Influences of Advertising Gimmicks on Nutrition Choices

I. Which state standard(s) does this performance task address?

II. Topic: What areas of health does this project assess? Why is it important? What is the focus of the project?[2,p237]

   A. This performance task assesses Nutrition and Consumer Health.

   B. This topic is important because:

      1. According to the National Health and Nutrition Examination Survey (NHANES), administered from 1971 to 1974 and 2003 to 2006, obesity rates have increased in children aged 2–5 from 5% to 12.4%.[5]

      2. Health consequences of childhood obesity include:

         a. Social discrimination resulting in low self esteem, psychological stress, and a negative effect on academic performance and social interaction.

         b. Cardiovascular risk factors, including high cholesterol levels, high blood pressure, and abnormal glucose levels.

         c. Asthma, hepatic steatosis, sleep apnea, and Type 2 diabetes.[6]

   C. The project focuses on helping students understand how the media can influence their food choices.

III. Key Concepts: What basic concepts should students know?[2,p237]

   Standard 1—Students will comprehend concepts related to health promotion and disease prevention to enhance health.[1,p24]

   Performance indicator 1.5.1 with infused content—Describe the relationship between healthy behaviors, such as healthy food choices, and personal health.[1,p24]

   A. The United States Department of Agriculture has designed a food guide pyramid to help students aged 6–11, learn how to make healthy food choices. The plan below is based on 1,800 calories.

      1. Six ounces of grain

      2. Two and one-half cups of vegetables

      3. One and one-half cups of fruit

      4. Three cups of milk

      5. Five ounces of meat and beans

      6. Sixty minutes of moderate to vigorous activity a day or most days.

   B. Processed sugar should be limited because it:

      1. Is low in nutrients

      2. Fills us up and makes us less likely to eat healthier foods

      3. Promotes tooth decay

      4. Can cause unhealthy weight gain.[7]

IV. Skills: Which of the seven National Health Education Standards skills does this performance task address?[2,p237]

   Standard 2—Students analyze the influence of family, peers, culture, media, technology, and other factors on health behaviors.[1,p26]

(continues)

Performance indicator 2.5.6 with infused content—Describe ways that advertising gimmicks influence nutrition choices.[1,p26]

A. According to the U.S.-based Institute of Medicine, the food industry's marketing practices are not compatible with acceptable dietary recommendations for children.

    1. Under the age of eight, children have difficulty distinguishing advertisements from reality. They do not understand that ads influence consumer choices.

    2. Commercial sites are fun but sell products through the use of gimmicks.

        a. Theme and settings mimic children's books and movies.

        b. Slogans or catchy phrases are used that can be misleading.

        c. Appealing characters are used to attract a child's attention.

        d. Activities, such as games, custom activities, and video, keep children on a site for a longer time.[8]

V. Curricular connections: What other subject areas does this project support?[2,p237]

    English Language Arts

    Technology literacy

    Art

VI. Student Directions and Assessment Criteria[2,p238]

A. Project Description: Write and attach an engaging prompt that draws the student into the project.[2,p238]

    Kaden is in the 5th grade at Abigail Adams Elementary School. While watching the Saturday morning cartoons, Kaden saw a cereal that looked like it would be fun to eat. He went to the cereal website and enjoyed playing the games based on the cereal characters.

    Later at the grocery store, Kaden asked his mother to buy the cereal he had seen on television. His mother looked at the food label and would not buy the product because it contained too much sugar and was not a good food choice. Kaden was upset and disappointed because he really wanted the cereal.

B. Your Challenge: Provide a challenge or mission statement that describes the project.[2,p238]

    Your challenge is to help Kaden understand how television advertisements and Internet websites use gimmicks to influence healthy food choices.

C. Assessment Criteria[2,p239]

You are assessed on the following key concepts: (List the concepts)

Performance indicator 1.5.1 with infused content—Describe the relationship between healthy behaviors, such as healthy food choices, and personal health.[1,p24]

    1. Explain six ways the food guide pyramid helps students make healthy food choices.

    2. Explain four reasons why processed sugar should be limited.

    You are assessed on the following skills (List the skills)

Performance indicator 2.5.6 with infused content—Describe ways that advertising gimmicks influence nutrition choices.[1,p26]

    1. Explain four gimmicks and how they influence which cereal children want to buy.

        a. Theme

        b. Slogans

        c. Characters

        d. Activities

    2. Describe why the cereal in the advertisement is not healthy.

    3. Present a healthy cereal and explain why it is healthy.

    Student project must include the following:

    1. Create a cereal advertisement

    2. Poster

Abigail Adams Elementary School

Name _____

Kaden is in the 5th grade at Abigail Adams Elementary School. While watching the Saturday morning cartoons, Kaden saw a cereal that looked like it would be fun to eat. He went to the cereal website and enjoyed playing the games based on the cereal characters.

Later at the grocery store, Kaden asked his mother to buy the cereal he had seen on television. His mother looked at the food label and would not buy the product because it contained too much sugar and was not a good food choice. Kaden was upset and disappointed because he really wanted the cereal.

Your challenge is to help Kaden understand how television advertising and Internet websites use gimmicks to influence healthy food choices.

Your project must include:

1. Nutrition poster

   a. Six ways the food guide pyramid helps students make healthy food choices

   b. Four harmful effects of processed sugar

   c. Ten pictures

2. Create a cereal poster or electronic cereal advertisement (http://www.mediaawareness.ca/english/games/coco/)

   a. Explain four gimmicks and how they influence which cereal children want to buy.

   b. Explain why the cereal in the advertisement is not healthy.

   c. Present a healthy cereal and describe why it is healthy.

ASSESSMENT MATERIALS

Analytical Rubric to Assess the Nutrition Poster (**Table 6.5**)

TABLE 6.5   Analytical Rubric to Assess the Nutrition Poster

Criteria	4	3	2	1
Performance indicator 1.5.1 with infused content—Describe the relationship between healthy behaviors, such as healthy food choices, and personal health.[1,p24]	Student accurately describes six ways the food guide pyramid helps children make healthy food choices.	Student's description of six ways the food guide pyramid helps children make healthy food choices is mostly accurate.	Student's description of six ways the food guide pyramid helps children make healthy food choices has a few inaccuracies.	Student's description of six ways the food guide pyramid helps children make healthy food choices is mostly inaccurate.
Performance indicator 1.5.1 with infused content—Describe the relationship between healthy behaviors, such as healthy food choices, and personal health.[1,p24]	Student accurately describes four reasons why processed sugar should be limited.	Student's description of four reasons why processed sugar should be limited is mostly accurate.	Student's description of four reasons why processed sugar should be limited has a few inaccuracies.	Student's description of four reasons why processed sugar should be limited is mostly inaccurate.

(continues)

TABLE 6.5 Analytical Rubric to Assess the Nutrition Poster *(continued)*

Criteria	4	3	2	1
Pictures	The ten pictures are appropriate.	Most of the ten pictures are appropriate.	A few of the ten pictures are inappropriate.	The ten pictures are mostly inappropriate.
Grammar	Grammar is excellent.	Grammar is good.	Grammar is fair.	Grammar is poor.
Spelling	Spelling is excellent.	Spelling is good.	Spelling is fair.	Spelling is poor.
Voice	Voice projection is excellent.	Voice projection is good.	Voice projection is fair.	Voice projection is poor.

Name _____

Total possible points – 24   Your points - _____   Your grade - _____

Analytical Rubric to Assess the Cereal Advertisement (**Table 6.6**)

TABLE 6.6 Analytical Rubric to Assess the Cereal Advertisement

Criteria	4	3	2	1
Performance indicator 2.5.6 with infused content—Describe ways that advertising gimmicks influence nutrition choices.[1,p26]	Student accurately describes how theme is used to influence the cereal choice.	Student's description of how theme is used to influence the cereal choice is mostly accurate.	Student's description of how theme is used to influence the cereal choice has a few inaccuracies.	Student's description of how theme is used to influence the cereal choice is mostly inaccurate.
Performance indicator 2.5.6 with infused content—Describe ways that advertising gimmicks influence nutrition choices.[1,p26]	Student accurately describes how a slogan is used to influence the cereal choice.	Student's description of how a slogan is used to influence the cereal choice is mostly accurate.	Student's description of how a slogan is used to influence the cereal choice has a few inaccuracies.	Student's description of how a slogan is used to influence the cereal choice is mostly inaccurate.
Performance indicator 2.5.6 with infused content—Describe ways that advertising gimmicks influence nutrition choices.[1,p26]	Student accurately describes how a character is used to influence the cereal choice.	Student's description of how a character is used to influence the cereal choice is mostly accurate.	Student's description of how a character is used to influence the cereal choice has a few inaccuracies.	Student's description of how a character is used to influence the cereal choice is mostly inaccurate.
Performance indicator 2.5.6 with infused content—Describe ways that advertising gimmicks influence nutrition choices.[1,p26]	Student accurately describes one activity used to influence the cereal choice.	Student's description of one activity used to influence the cereal choice is mostly accurate.	Student's description of one activity used to influence the cereal choice has a few inaccuracies.	Student's description of one activity used to influence the cereal choice is mostly inaccurate.
Performance indicator 1.5.1 with infused content—Describe the relationship between healthy behaviors, such as healthy food choices, and personal health.[1,p24]	Student thoroughly describes why the cereal in the advertisement is not a healthy food choice.	Student adequately describes why the cereal in the advertisement is not a healthy food choice.	Student inadequately describes why the cereal in the advertisement is not a healthy food choice.	Student poorly describes why the cereal in the advertisement is not a healthy food choice.

(continues)

Criteria	4	3	2	1
Performance indicator 1.5.1 with infused content—Describe the relationship between healthy behaviors such as healthy food choices and personal health.[1,p24]	Student presents an example of a healthy cereal and accurately describes why it is healthy.	Student's description of why a cereal is healthy is mostly accurate.	Student's description of why a cereal is healthy has some inaccuracies.	Student's description of why a cereal is healthy is mostly inaccurate.
Grammar	Grammar is excellent.	Grammar is good.	Grammar is fair.	Grammar is poor.
Spelling	Spelling is excellent.	Spelling is good.	Spelling is fair.	Spelling is poor.
Voice	Voice projection is excellent.	Voice projection is good.	Voice projection is fair.	Voice projection is poor.

Name _____

Total possible points – 36   Your points - _____   Your grade - _____

HOW THE COORDINATED SCHOOL HEALTH TEAM CONTRIBUTES TO GOOD NUTRITION AND THE SKILL OF ANALYZING INFLUENCES

Health Education

- Focus instruction on the skill of analyzing influences and the content of nutrition.
- Use the Internet to reinforce healthy behaviors.
- Teach healthy coping strategies.

Physical Education

- Promote good nutrition.
- Instruct the students how to analyze the influence of family, peers, culture, media, technology, and other factors that obstruct physical activity.

Health Services

- Provide nutrition information.
- Be knowledgeable as to how students influence one another's behavior.

Nutrition Services

- Provide healthy food choices for lunch and snacks.
- Hang posters that show students making healthy food choices.

Counseling, Psychological, and Social Services

- Provide counseling to cope with nutrition and Internet use issues.

Healthy School Environment

- Hang posters showing students being influenced in a positive way about nutrition.
- Provide Internet safety training.
- Create a positive school environment. When students feel connected to their school, believe their teachers care, and feel the rules are clear and fair, they are less likely to be perpetrators of **electronic aggression**.[9]

Health Promotion for Staff

- Provide staff training in healthy eating and understanding how behavior can be influenced by external and internal factors.

Family/Community Involvement

- Organize and implement a parent program to explain how to provide nutritious foods to children.
- Provide training to parents so they will understand how the Internet can influence the healthy food choices of their children.

Grades 6–8

To achieve proficiency in Standard 2, Grade 6–8 students examine, describe, analyze, and explain how the school, community, media messages, technology, perception of norms, personal values, beliefs, and health risk behaviors influence health practices (habits) and behaviors.[1,p27]

Grades 6–8

2.8.1 Examine how the family influences the health of adolescents.

2.8.2 Describe the influence of culture on health beliefs, practices, and behaviors.

2.8.3 Describe how peers influence healthy and unhealthy behaviors.

2.8.4 Analyze how the school and community can affect personal health practice and behaviors.

2.8.5 Analyze how messages from media influence health behaviors.

2.8.6 Analyze the influence of technology on personal and family health.

2.8.7 Explain how the perceptions of norms influence healthy and unhealthybehaviors.

2.8.8 Explain the influence of personal values and beliefs on individual health practices and behaviors.

2.8.9 Describe how some health risk behaviors can influence the likelihood of engaging in unhealthy behaviors.

2.8.10 Explain how school and public health policies can influence health promotion and disease prevention.[1,p27]

To teach Standard 2, explain why it is important to understand what influences health behavior, why analyzing influences is relevant to one's health and well-being, the relationship between Standard 2 and the other national health education standards, and how the skills associated with Standard 2 impact health today and in the future.

Explain how to achieve the standard, model the skill, provide practice time, and use formative assessments to improve teaching and learning.

For example,

Derek and Bill are neighbors and have been friends since elementary school. The boys were always involved in before- and after-school sports and other school activities.

Recently, Bill started hanging around with peers who smoke pot, listen to loud music that promotes drugs and alcohol, and get into a lot of trouble in school and the community. They are popular, even though they get in trouble. He thinks it is cool to be in the group because he enjoys flirting with danger but does not want to get hurt or harm anyone else. His parents do not approve, but Bill is defiant.

He is coughing more since smoking pot and does not care about his schoolwork, after-school job, or his parent's expectations. He is also putting on weight because he is eating a lot of junk food.

One day the gym teacher caught Bill with weed. The school policy says when a student is caught with drugs, he or she is suspended, and the police and parents are called. When the police arrived, they took Bill to the station where he was released to his parents.

Bill now realizes he has a problem with drugs and was influenced by his desire to be friends with a certain group of students. He is glad he was caught and that the school called the police. He is trying to reconnect with Derek, but it is hard to do so after this experience.

To reflect, ask the students:

- What healthy activities did the school offer students? (PI 2.8.1) *(Before- and after-school sports and other school activities.)*

- How do messages from the media influence health behaviors? (PI 2.8.2) *(Some songs glamorize and promote drug and alcohol use.)*

- How did norms influence Bill's choice to join a group? (PI 2.8.7) *(They are popular even though they get into trouble. He wanted to be like them.)*

- How did Bill's personal values influence his health practices and behaviors? (PI 2.8.8) *(He valued being part of the group and flirting with danger. On the other hand, his values also helped him realize he was in trouble with drugs and wanted out.)*

- How did becoming a member of the group influence Bill's likelihood of engaging in unhealthy behaviors? (PI 2.8.9) *(Bill knew that members of the group smoked weed and, if he were part of the group, it would be easy for him to smoke.)*

- How do school policies influence health promotion and disease prevention? (PI 2.8.10) *(Bill's school has a drug policy that requires suspension and a call to the police and parents. Because of his being held accountable, Bill realized he made poor choices and began trying to reconnect with his old friend Derek.)*

To reinforce learning, present other scenarios and identify the influences by referencing the performance indicators. Challenge students to identify the positive and negative influences on behavior brought on by external and internal factors. Using graphic organizers or word webs to dissect the influences, assist students who are visual learners.

As the students are learning the skill, provide adequate time for them to practice before asking them to demonstrate proficiency through an authentic assessment. While the students are practicing, use formative assessments to check for understanding. Use feedback to improve performance, thereby encouraging them.

Once the students demonstrate the skill, teach the health content. Design a prompt that allows the students to display their knowledge of health content by analyzing influences. As the students practice their content and skill, use formative assessments to improve teaching and learning.

WHAT DOES THE SKILL OF ANALYZING INFLUENCES LOOK LIKE IN THE MIDDLE SCHOOL CLASSROOM?

Mr. Carson is a health teacher at Westover Middle School. He overhears many of his students talking about what they say and do on social networking websites. He is concerned about the influence these sites have on the emotional, intellectual, physical, and social health of his students.

During the coordinated school health meeting, Mr. Carson learned that several students are victims of electronic aggression. Embarrassing pictures were posted without student knowledge, and others made derogatory remarks in chat rooms and sent offensive instant messages.

The victims expressed their frustration and anger by misbehaving in class, using drugs and alcohol to cope, and starting fights with possible perpetrators. Mr. Carson has been asked to address this problem in health class.

To plan, Mr. Carson chooses specific performance indicators that address a specific skill and content.

Standard 2—Students analyze the influence of family, peers, culture, media, technology, and other factors on health behaviors.[1,p26]

> Performance indicator 2.8.10—Explain how school and public health policies can influence health promotion and disease prevention.[1,p27]
>
> *Performance indicator 2.8.10 with infused content*—Explain how school and public health policies can influence health promotion and disease prevention.[1,p27]

After selecting the appropriate performance indicator for the skill, Mr. Carson chooses a Standard 1 performance indicator for reducing risky sexual behavior.

Standard 1—Students will comprehend concepts related to health promotion and disease prevention to enhance health.[1,p24]

Performance indicator 1.8.2—Describe the interrelationships of emotional, intellectual, physical, and social health in adolescence.[1,p25]

> *Performance indicator 1.8.2 with infused content*—Describe the effects of electronic aggression on emotional, intellectual, physical, and social health in adolescence.[1,p25]

Performance indicator 1.8.5—Describe ways to reduce or prevent injuries and other adolescent health problems.[1,p25]

> *Performance indicator 1.8.5 with infused content*—Describe ways to reduce or prevent injuries and other adolescent health problems resulting from electronic aggression.[1,p25]

By linking the skill and content performance indicators, the teacher has a clear idea of how to plan the lessons for an analyzing influences unit.

The first step in planning is to think through the unit by completing the performance task template. Upon completion, the teacher has a good idea of the lessons that precede this culminating activity, the information and back-up materials necessary to introduce the prompt to the students, and the assessment strategies.

When distributing the prompt, include back-up information, worksheets, and holistic and analytical rubrics. The latter are included with the prompt so that the students know how they are being assessed before beginning their project. The rubrics act as a guide and help the students attain proficiency in the standards.

Designing skills-based lessons requires considerable preparation, but once the information is distributed and explained, the students create a product independently. They learn with good coaching (formative assessment) how to demonstrate proficiency in content and skill.

The following example is a performance task for a Grade 8 analyzing influences unit that focuses on electronic aggression. The first section is for the teacher and demonstrates the planning process for authentic assessment reflecting the performance indicators 2.8.6, 1.8.2, and 1.8.5. The second, for the student, extracts some of the information from the performance task and transforms it into the student prompt and support materials.

Standard 2 Performance Task: Grade 8—Electronic Aggression

I. Which state standard(s) does this performance task address?

II. Topic: What areas of health does this project assess? Why is it important? What is the focus of the project?[2,p237]

   A. This performance task assesses the health area of Injury Prevention/Safety and Personal Health.

(continues)

B. It is important because:
1. 9–35% of students report being the victim of electronic aggression.[9,p4]
2. Electronic aggression peaks at the end of middle school and the beginning of high school.[9,p6]
3. 47% of victims state that the perpetrator was a student at their school.[9,p7]
4. Two-thirds of electronic aggression victims are not harassed in other environments.[10,pS1-S4]
5. Exposure to electronic violence either as a victim or a bystander increases the likelihood of becoming a perpetrator.[10,pS4]
C. The focus of the project is to help students understand the influence of technology and how to cope with electronic aggression in a healthy way.

III. Key Concepts: What basic concepts should students know?[2,p237]

Standard 1—Students comprehend concepts related to health promotion and disease prevention to enhance health.[1,p25]

Performance indicator 1.8.2 with infused content—Describe the effects of electronic aggression on emotional, intellectual, physical, and social health in adolescence.[1,p25]

A. Emotional health
1. Victims are more likely to be suspended, assigned detention, skip school, or experience in-person victimization.[9,p8]
2. When the electronic aggressor is anonymous, it is more difficult to ask for help, and the victim may feel helpless.[9,p8]
3. Feeling depressed
4. Crying without reason
5. Mood swings[11,p226]
B. Intellectual health
1. Victim has difficulty concentrating on schoolwork.
2. Victim falls behind in schoolwork.
C. Physical health
1. Use alcohol and other drugs to cope.
2. Difficulty sleeping
3. Nightmares[11,p224]
4. Feeling sick[11,p226]
D. Social health
1. Victim does not want to attend school or related events.
2. Victim may not have the support of friends.[12,p153]
3. Anti-social feelings[11,p226]

Performance indicator 1.8.5 with infused content—Describe ways to reduce or prevent injuries and other adolescent health problems as a result of electronic aggression.[1,p25]

A. Strategies to reduce or prevent electronic aggression:
1. Select a site that allows you to restrict your information to a defined group.
2. Do not post personal information or a descriptive screen name that would allow strangers to identify or locate you.
3. Post only information that you would be comfortable with any person reading. Remember, anything you post is seen by anybody who looks, including parents, teachers, police, employers, and colleges. Once information is posted, it is permanent because, even if deleted, someone may have downloaded it on his or her computer. Consider not posting your photo or choose one your parents would be proud to display publicly.
4. Do not flirt online with strangers; they may not be who they claim.
5. Research anyone who wants to meet you. If you do decide to meet:
   a. Do so in a public place during the day.
   b. Bring friends you trust with you.
   c. Tell an adult where you are going and when you will return.

(continues)

6. If you feel threatened, tell a trusted adult and report it to the police and the social networking site.[13]

IV. Skills: Which one of the seven National Health Education Standards skills does this performance task address?[2,p237]

Standard 2—Students will analyze the influence of family, peers, culture, media, technology, and other factors on health behaviors.[1,p26]

Performance indicator 2.8.10 with infused content—Explain how school and public health policies for electronic aggression can influence health promotion and disease prevention.[1,p27]

A. Develop, implement, and enforce an electronic bullying policy so students feel safe and protected in school.

B. Implement instruction that provides students with knowledge and skill to cope with electronic aggression.[9,p12-13]

C. Empower student groups to combat electronic aggression.

D. Train teachers and staff to recognize and react to electronic aggression because students are more willing to tell a teacher who is aware of the problem.[12,p153]

E. Create a positive school environment and promote health by

1. Providing activities and programs that connect students to school.
2. Showing students that their teachers care about them.
3. Developing and implementing rules that are clear and fair.[9,p12-13]

V. Curricular connections: What other subject areas does this project support?[2,p237]

English Language Arts

VI. Student Directions and Assessment Criteria[2,p238]

A. Project Description: Write and attach an engaging prompt that draws the student into the project.[2,p238]

Jamie has become aggressive at school. She is angry and suspicious and does not trust anyone. Her best friend, Jodie, is upset by Jamie's change in behavior and asked her what was wrong.

After some encouragement, Jamie told Jodie that someone posted some embarrassing pictures of her on a social networking site. Jamie has posted pictures of friends, but they have always been appropriate. She does not know who posted the picture, is angry, and thinks people are laughing and talking about her behind her back.

Jamie wants to tell her teacher, but thinks Mrs. Bass does not know very much about cyberspace and would not believe her. Plus, there are no rules against using social networking sites.

Jamie received text messages that make lewd comments about the picture. She has been suspended for fighting and is now drinking to cope with the situation. Jamie still wants to take part in social networking but not have a similar experience again.

B. Your Challenge: Provide a challenge or mission statement that describes the project.

Your challenge is to help Jamie understand the influence electronic aggression has on her behavior and what she and the school can do about it.

C. Assessment Criteria[2,p239]

You are assessed on the following content:

Performance indicator 1.8.2 with infused content—Describe the effects of electronic aggression on emotional, intellectual, physical, and social health in adolescence.[1,p25]

1. Explain

a. Four effects of electronic aggression on emotional health.
b. Two effects of electronic aggression on intellectual health.
c. Four effects of electronic aggression on physical health.
d. Three effects of electronic aggression on social health.

(continues)

Performance indicator 1.8.5 with infused content—Describe ways to reduce or prevent injuries and other adolescent health problems as a result of electronic aggression.[1,p25]

1. Explain six strategies Jamie can use to reduce or prevent electronic aggression.
   You are assessed on the following skill:

Performance indicator 2.8.10 with infused content—Explain how school and public health policies for electronic aggression can influence health promotion and disease prevention.[1,p27]

1. Explain five ways school policy and practices for electronic aggression can influence health promotion.
   Student project

1. A multimedia presentation or a poster explaining the influence of electronic aggression and strategies to prevent it

2. Role-play a presentation to the principal explaining how school policies regarding electronic aggression influence health promotion.

Westover Middle School

Name _____

Jamie has become aggressive at school. She is angry and suspicious and does not trust anyone. Her best friend, Jodie, is upset by Jamie's change in behavior and asked her what was wrong.

After some encouragement, Jamie told Jodie that someone posted some embarrassing pictures of her on a social networking site. Jamie has posted pictures of friends, but they have always been appropriate. She does not know who posted the picture, is angry, and thinks people are laughing and talking about her behind her back.

Jamie wants to tell her teacher, but thinks Mrs. Bass does not know very much about cyberspace and would not believe her. Plus, there are no rules against using social networking sites.

Jamie received text messages that make lewd comments about the picture. She has been suspended for fighting and is now drinking to cope with the situation. Jamie still wants to take part in social networking but not have a similar experience again.

Your challenge is to help Jamie understand the influence electronic aggression has on her behavior and what she and the school can do about it.

Your project must include:

1. A multimedia presentation or a poster explaining the influence of electronic aggression and strategies to prevent it

2. Role-play a presentation to the principal explaining how school policies about electronic aggression influence health promotion.

ASSESSMENT MATERIALS

Analytical rubric to assess a multimedia presentation or a poster explaining the effects of electronic aggression on behavior and how to cope in a healthy way (**Table 6.7**).

(continues)

TABLE 6.7 Analytical Rubric to Assess a Multimedia Presentation or a Poster Explaining the Influence of Electronic Aggression and How to Cope in a Healthy Way

Criteria	4	3	2	1
Performance indicator 1.8.2 with infused content—Describe the effects of electronic aggression on emotional, intellectual, physical, and social health in adolescence.[1,p25]	Student thoroughly describes four ways electronic aggression influences emotional health.	Student adequately describes four ways electronic aggression influences emotional health.	Student inadequately describes four ways electronic aggression influences emotional health.	Student poorly describes four ways electronic aggression influences emotional health.
Performance indicator 1.8.2 with infused content—Describe the effects of electronic aggression on emotional, intellectual, physical, and social health in adolescence.[1,p25]	Student thoroughly describes two ways electronic aggression influences intellectual health.	Student adequately describes two ways electronic aggression influences intellectual health.	Student inadequately describes two ways electronic aggression influences intellectual health.	Student poorly describes two ways electronic aggression influences intellectual health.
Performance indicator 1.8.2 with infused content—Describe the effects of electronic aggression on emotional, intellectual, physical, and social health in adolescence.[1,p25]	Student thoroughly describes four ways electronic aggression influences physical health.	Student adequately describes four ways electronic aggression influences physical health.	Student inadequately describes four ways electronic aggression influences physical health.	Student poorly describes four ways electronic aggression influences physical health.
Performance indicator 1.8.2 with infused content—Describe the effects of electronic aggression on emotional, intellectual, physical, and social health in adolescence.[1,p25]	Student thoroughly describes three ways electronic aggression influences social health.	Student adequately describes three ways electronic aggression influences social health.	Student inadequately describes three ways electronic aggression influences social health.	Student poorly describes three ways electronic aggression influences social health.
Performance indicator 1.8.5 with infused content—Describe ways to reduce or prevent injuries and other adolescent health problems resulting from electronic aggression.[1,p25]	Student accurately describes how to select a website that allows a restriction of information to a defined group.	Student's description of how to select a website that allows a restriction of information to a defined group is mostly accurate.	Student's description of how to select a website that allows a restriction of information to a defined group has a few inaccuracies.	Student's description of how to select a website that allows a restriction of information to a defined group is mostly inaccurate.

(continues)

TABLE 6.7 Analytical Rubric to Assess a Multimedia Presentation or a Poster Explaining the Influence of Electronic Aggression and How to Cope in a Healthy Way *(continued)*

Criteria	4	3	2	1
Performance indicator 1.8.5 with infused content—Describe ways to reduce or prevent injuries and other adolescent health problems as a result of electronic aggression.[1,p25]	Student thoroughly describes how to post information or a screen name so strangers cannot identify the poster.	Student adequately describes how to post information or a screen name so strangers cannot identify the poster.	Student inadequately describes how to post information or a screen name so strangers cannot identify the poster.	Student poorly describes how to post information or a screen name so strangers cannot identify the poster.
Performance indicator 1.8.5 with infused content—Describe ways to reduce or prevent injuries and other adolescent health problems as a result of electronic aggression.[1,p25]	Student thoroughly explains how to safely post information.	Student adequately explains how to safely post information.	Student inadequately explains how to safely post information.	Student poorly explains how to safely post information.
Performance indicator 1.8.5 with infused content—Describe ways to reduce or prevent injuries and other adolescent health problems as a result of electronic aggression.[1,p25]	Student thoroughly explains the importance of not flirting online.	Student adequately explains the importance of not flirting online.	Student inadequately explains the importance of not flirting online.	Student poorly explains the importance of not flirting online.
Performance indicator 1.8.5 with infused content—Describe ways to reduce or prevent injuries and other adolescent health problems as a result of electronic aggression.[1,p25]	Student accurately explains what to do if a stranger wants to meet.	Student's explanation of what to do if a stranger wants to meet is mostly accurate.	Student's explanation of what to do if a stranger wants to meet has a few inaccuracies.	Student's explanation of what to do if a stranger wants to meet is mostly inaccurate.
Grammar	Grammar is excellent.	Grammar is good.	Grammar is fair.	Grammar is poor.
Spelling	Spelling is excellent.	Spelling is good.	Spelling is fair.	Spelling is poor.
Voice	Voice projection is excellent.	Voice projection is good.	Voice projection is fair.	Voice projection is poor.

Name _____

Total possible points – 44   **Your points - _____**   **Your grade - _____**

Analytical rubric to assess a role-play presented to the principal explaining how school policies about electronic aggression influence health promotion (**Table 6.8**).

(continues)

TABLE 6.8 Analytical Rubric to Assess a Role-Play Presented to the Principal Explaining How School Policies Regarding Electronic Aggression Influence Health Promotion

Criteria	4	3	2	1
Performance indicator 2.8.10 with infused content—Explain how school and public health policies for electronic aggression can influence health promotion and disease prevention.[1,p27]	Student thoroughly explains the need to develop, implement, and enforce an electronic aggression policy.	Student adequately explains the need to develop, implement, and enforce an electronic aggression policy.	Student inadequately explains the need to develop, implement, and enforce an electronic aggression policy.	Student poorly explains the need to develop, implement, and enforce an electronic aggression policy.
Performance indicator 2.8.10 with infused content—Explain how school and public health policies for electronic aggression can influence health promotion and disease prevention.[1,p27]	Student thoroughly explains the need for instruction that provides students with knowledge and skill to cope with electronic aggression.	Student adequately explains the need for instruction that provides students with knowledge and skill to cope with electronic aggression.	Student inadequately explains the need for instruction that provides students with knowledge and skill to cope with electronic aggression.	Student poorly explains the need for instruction that provides students with knowledge and skill to cope with electronic aggression.
Performance indicator 2.8.10 with infused content—Explain how school and public health policies for electronic aggression can influence health promotion and disease prevention.[1,p27]	Student thoroughly explains the need to empower student groups to combat electronic aggression.	Student adequately explains the need to empower student groups to combat electronic aggression.	Student inadequately explains the need to empower student groups to combat electronic aggression.	Student poorly explains the need to empower student groups to combat electronic aggression.
Performance indicator 2.8.10 with infused content—Explain how school and public health policies for electronic aggression can influence health promotion and disease prevention.[1,p27]	Student thoroughly explains the need to train teachers and staff to recognize electronic aggression.	Student adequately explains the need to train teachers and staff to recognize electronic aggression.	Student inadequately explains the need to train teachers and staff to recognize electronic aggression.	Student poorly explains the need to train teachers and staff to recognize electronic aggression.
Performance indicator 2.8.10 with infused content—Explain how school and public health policies for electronic aggression can influence health promotion and disease prevention.[1,p27]	Student thoroughly explains the need to create a positive school environment to combat electronic aggression.	Student adequately explains the need to create a positive school environment to combat electronic aggression.	Student inadequately explains the need to create a positive school environment to combat electronic aggression.	Student poorly explains the need to create a positive school environment to combat electronic aggression.

(continues)

TABLE 6.8 Analytical Rubric to Assess a Role-Play Presented to the Principal Explaining How School Policies Regarding Electronic Aggression Influence Health Promotion *(continued)*

Criteria	4	3	2	1
Grammar	Grammar is excellent.	Grammar is good.	Grammar is fair.	Grammar is poor.
Spelling	Spelling is excellent.	Spelling is good.	Spelling is fair.	Spelling is poor.
Voice	Voice projection is excellent.	Voice projection is good.	Voice projection is fair.	Voice projection is poor.

Name _____

Total possible points – 32   Your points - _____   Your grade - _____

HOW THE COORDINATED SCHOOL HEALTH TEAM CONTRIBUTES TO COMBATING ELECTRONIC AGGRESSION AND INCREASING THE SKILL OF ANALYZING INFLUENCES

Health Education

- Implement instruction that provides students with knowledge and skill to cope with electronic aggression.
- Focus instruction on the skill of analyzing influences and the content of electronic aggression.
- Review harassment and bullying policies with students.
- Teach healthy coping strategies.

Physical Education

- Display posters that combat electronic aggression.

Health Services

- Provide electronic safety information.

Nutrition Services

- Display posters that combat electronic aggression.

Counseling, Psychological, and Social Services

- Provide counseling to cope with peer pressure to engage in unhealthy behaviors.

Healthy School Environment

- Develop and implement policy that addresses electronic aggression.
- Post procedures students can follow if they are being electronically harassed.
- Display posters that combat electronic aggression and explain where to go for help.

- Use software that blocks the social networks from school computers.
- Create a positive school environment. When students feel connected to their school, believe the teachers care, and feel the rules are clear and fair, they are less likely to be perpetrators of electronic aggression.[9,p14]

Health Promotion for Staff

- Provide staff training in electronic aggression so that staff are prepared better to help students.

Family/Community Involvement

- Organize and implement a parent program to explain electronic aggression and how to protect children from becoming victims.
- Talk to your children about what they do and where they go on the Internet.
- Develop rules about acceptable and safe behavior for electronic media.
- Explore the Internet and sites your child frequents.
- Talk with other parents/caregivers to exchange monitoring ideas.
- Encourage the school to provide a class for parents/caregivers about electronic aggression.
- Keep current with the new devices your child is using. Learn how they are being used.[9,p15]
- Learn ways to monitor the electronic media used by children.[14]

Grades 9–12

To achieve proficiency in Standard 2, Grades 9–12 students analyze and evaluate how family, culture, peers, school, community, media messages, technology, perception of norms, personal values, beliefs, and health

Grades 9–12

2.12.1 Analyze how the family influences the health of individuals.

2.12.2 Analyze how the culture supports and challenges health beliefs, practices, and behaviors.

2.12.3 Analyze how peers influence healthy and unhealthy behaviors.

2.12.4 Evaluate how the school and community can affect personal health practice and behaviors.

2.12.5 Evaluate the effect of media on personal and family health.

2.12.6 Evaluate the impact of technology on personal, family, and community health.

2.12.7 Analyze how the perceptions of norms influence healthy and unhealthy behaviors.

2.12.8 Analyze the influence of personal values and beliefs on individual health practices and behaviors.

2.12.9 Analyze how some health risk behaviors can influence the likelihood of engaging in unhealthy behaviors.

2.12.10 Analyze how public health policies and government regulations can influence health promotion and disease prevention.[1,p27]

risk behaviors influence health practices (habits) and behaviors.[1,p27]

To teach Standard 2, explain why it is important to analyze the factors that influence behavior and how this skill relates to the other National Health Education Standards.

According to the selected performance indicators, present and explain how to reach proficiency, model the skill so students see what it looks like in action, provide adequate time for students to practice, and design a performance task that highlights a student's knowledge and skill through an authentic assessment.

Use formative assessments (Chapter 4) to check for understanding and make adjustments to instruction based on the results. Timely feedback promotes student initiative to improve.

For example:

Mary and Lisa were looking through a teen magazine when an ad for weight loss caught their attention. It showed a person dressed in a doctor's white coat and holding the weight-loss product. The person was saying that the product was an easy, safe, proven way to lose weight quickly without dieting.

It seems that all of Mary's friends and relatives and successful women are slim. Most of the women on television and in the movies are slim. Mary wants to be svelte also, but dieting does not work for her. Mary's parents want to give her a membership to the local gym, but she does not have time to go. Lisa lost a lot of weight after using this weight loss product and thinks it is a good idea to try it.

Both learned in health class that the purpose of advertisements is to sell a product and the pitch one views on television may not be truthful or healthy.

Nonetheless, Mary bought the product, tried it, and lost weight but found that she was always running to the bathroom and could not sleep.

To reflect, ask the students:

- How did Mary's family try to influence her? (PI 2.8.1) (Mary's parents wanted to give her a membership to the local gym.)
- Was this a positive or negative influence? (Positive)
- What cultural messages and observations influenced Mary's decision? (PI 2.8.2) (It seems that all of Mary's friends and relatives and successful women are slim. Most of the women on television and in the movies are slim.)
- How did Lisa influence Mary's decision? (PI 2.8.3) (Lisa lost a lot of weight after using the product and thinks it is a good idea.)
- Was this a positive or negative influence? (Negative)
- What did the school provide that affects personal health practices and behaviors? (PI 2.8.4, 2.8.10) (The school has a health education program. In class, both girls learned that the purpose of advertisements is to sell a product and the pitch may not be truthful or healthy.)
- How did the message seen on television influence Mary's decision? (PI 2.8.5) (It influenced her to try the product. The person was saying that it was an easy, safe, proven way to lose weight quickly without dieting. It was just what she needed because she does not have time to exercise or go to the gym.)
- How did technology influence Mary? (PI 2.8.6, 2.8.7, 2.8.8) (When Mary sees successful women in the movies or on television, they seem to be slim. She wants to be svelte, too.)
- Taking the weight loss product was a risky behavior. What was the result? (PI 2.8.9) (Mary bought the product, tried it, and lost weight but found that she was always running to the bathroom and could not sleep.)

As students are learning the skill, provide enough time to practice before asking them to demonstrate proficiency through an authentic assessment. Use formative assessments to determine student progress. Motivate students by using feedback to show how performance might be improved.

Select a story, show pictures or a video clip, or model a behavior, and ask the students to identify the influences on behavior. Select performance indicators that align with the example and ask clarifying questions. Use the thumbs up, thumbs down, white boards, or other formative assessments to check for understanding.

As the students are learning the skill, give them time to practice before teaching the health content. Design a prompt that allows the students to display their knowledge of health content through the skill of analyzing influences. As the students practice their content and skill, continue to use formative assessments to redirect and encourage them.

WHAT DOES THE SKILL OF ANALYZING INFLUENCES LOOK LIKE IN THE HIGH SCHOOL CLASSROOM?

Mrs. Carleton recently received the results of the Massasoit High School youth risk behavior survey and found that 90% of her students rarely or never wear a bicycle helmet. She researched information available from the CDC and discovered that, according the 2009 Youth Risk Behavior Surveillance System, (YRBSS), 84.7% of students who ride bicycles rarely or never wear a helmet.[14] Of late, two Massasoit students were hit by a car while riding their bikes and suffered brain injuries. They were not wearing helmets.

Mrs. Carleton's challenge is to teach the knowledge and skill her students need to adopt helmet usage. Standard 2 performance indicators help Mrs. Carleton's students address the risk factor of unintentional injuries caused by not wearing a bicycle helmet.

To begin planning, Mr. Carleton selects a performance indicator from Standard 2 that will help the students understand why it is important to wear a helmet.

Standard 2—Students analyze the influence of family, peers, culture, media, technology, and other factors on health behaviors.[1,p26]
Performance indicator 2.12.1—Analyze how the family influences the health of the individual.[1,p27]
Performance indicator 2.12.1 with infused content—Analyze how the family influences the health of individuals by the wearing of a bicycle helmet.[1,p27]
Performance indicator 2.12.3—Analyze how peers influence healthy and unhealthy behaviors.[1,p27]

Performance indicator 2.12.3 with infused content—Analyze the influence peers exert over the choice to wear or not wear a helmet.[1,p27]

After selecting the appropriate performance indicator for the skill, choose a Standard 1 performance indicator.

Standard 1—Students comprehend concepts related to health promotion and disease prevention to enhance health.[1,p24]
1.12.5—Propose ways to reduce or prevent injuries and health problems.[1,p25]
Performance indicator 1.12.5 with infused content—Propose ways to reduce or prevent bicycle injuries and health problems by wearing a helmet.[1,p25]

By linking the skill and content performance indicators, the teacher has a clear idea of how to plan the lessons for an analyzing influences unit.

The first step in planning is to think through the unit by completing the performance task template. Upon completion, the teacher has a good idea of the lessons that precede this culminating activity, the information and supporting materials necessary to introduce the prompt to the students, and the assessment strategies.

When distributing the prompt, include back-up information, worksheets, and holistic and analytical rubrics. The latter are included with the prompt so that the students know how they are being assessed before beginning their project. The rubrics act as a guide and help the students attain proficiency in the standards.

Designing the performance task takes considerable preparation, but once the information is distributed and explained, the students create a product independently. Students learn with good coaching (formative assessment) how to demonstrate proficiency in content and skill.

The following is an example of a Grade 9 analyzing influences performance task that focuses on bicycle safety.

The first section, for the teacher, demonstrates how to plan for an authentic assessment of the performance indicators 2.12.3, 2.12.1, and 1.12.5. The second is for the student. It extracts some of the information from the performance task and transforms it into the student prompt and support materials.

Standard 2 Performance Task: Grade 9—Bicycle Safety

I. Which state standard(s) does this performance task address?

II. Topic: What areas of health does this project assess? Why is it important? What is the focus of the project?[2,p237]

    A. This performance task assesses the health area of Injury Prevention/Safety, Personal Health.

    B. It is important because:

        1. 84.7% of students who rode a bicycle rarely or never wore a bicycle helmet.[14]

        2. 12% of cyclists killed in 2008 were between the ages of 5 and 15.[15,p2]

        3. A bicycle helmet is the single most effective way to prevent head injury resulting from a crash.[15,p5]

    C. The focus of the project is to analyze how students can be influenced to use a bicycle helmet and follow safety rules of the road.

III. Key Concepts: What basic concepts should students know?[2,p237]

    Standard 1—Students comprehend concepts related to health promotion and disease prevention to enhance health.[1,p24]

    Performance indicator 1.12.5 with infused content—Propose ways to reduce or prevent bicycle injuries and health problems by wearing a helmet and following the safety rules of the road.[1,p25]

    A. A bicycle helmet is the single most effective way to prevent head injury resulting from a crash.[15,p2]

    B. Statistics about helmet usage and injury prevention

        1. 84.7 % of high school students who ride a bicycle rarely or never use a helmet.[14]

        2. 90% of Massasoit High School students do not wear a helmet.

    C. How to be fitted for a helmet:

        1. Measure the circumference of your head. Use sizing pads to make adjustments.

        2. The helmet should fit level on your head, one or two finger-widths above your eyebrow.

        3. Center the left buckle under the chin.

        4. The side straps should form a V under and slightly in front of the ear.

        5. Buckle and tighten the chinstrap until snug. No more than two fingers should fit under the strap.[15,p2]

    D. Following bicycle road safety rules can help prevent unintended injuries.

        1. Wear a helmet.

        2. Drive with traffic on the right side of the road.

        3. Check all directions before turning.

        4. Ride single file.

        5. Obey all traffic lights and signs.

        6. Use hand signals when turning.

            a. Left turn: hold left arm out, pointing left.

            b. Right turn: make a right angle with your right arm, palm facing forward, flat.

        7. Do not listen to music or text while biking.

        8. Make eye contact with drivers.

        9. Be courteous.

        10. Keep your eyes on the road for hazards such as sewer grates, potholes, etc.

        11. Wear reflective gear at night and bright colors during the day.[7,p747]

IV. Skills: Which of the seven National Health Education Standards skills does this performance task address?[2,p237]

    Standard 2—Students will analyze the influence of family, peers, culture, media, technology, and other factors on health behaviors.[1,p26]

    Performance indicator 2.12.1 with infused content—Analyze how the family influences the health of individuals by the wearing of a bicycle helmet.[1,p27]

    A. 95% of children aged 5–14 wore a helmet when riding with an adult who wore a helmet.

    B. 41% of children aged 5–14 wore a helmet when riding with an adult who did not wear a helmet.[16]

    C. Bike is grounded if the rider does not wear a helmet or follow the safety rules of the road.

(continues)

Performance indicator 2.12.3 with infused content—Analyze the influence peers exert over the choice to wear a helmet.[1,p27]

    A. 77% of children aged 5–14 wore a helmet while riding with another child who wore a helmet.

    B. 10% of children aged 5–14 wore a helmet when riding with other children who were not wearing a helmet.[16]

    C. Students and community members must wear a helmet when using the school bike trail.

V. Curricular connections: What other subject areas does this project support?[2,p237]

    English Language Arts

    Social studies

    Art

VI. Student Directions and Assessment Criteria[2,p238]

    A. Project Description: Write and attach an engaging prompt that draws the student into the project.[2,p238]

        Mike and Adam are freshmen at Massasoit High School. They are fit and enjoy riding their bikes as training for track.

        Mike usually wears his helmet but complains that it is hot and uncomfortable. Sometimes, in the summer, he does not wear it at all. He usually follows the bike safety rules of the road, but if there are no cars around, will not ride on the side of the road or use hand signals.

        Mike's parents caught him cycling without a helmet and not obeying safety rules. They grounded him from his bike riding for two weeks.

        Adam avoids wearing a helmet and following the rules of the road. He tells Mike, "Most teenagers don't wear helmets, so why should I?" He heard about two boys who died in a bike accident but thinks it will not happen to him.

        The high school recently built a bike trail through the woods. Students and community members who use the trail must wear a helmet. The boys enjoy riding there and always wear their helmets.

    B. Your Challenge: Provide a challenge or mission statement that describes the project.[2,p238]

        Your challenge is to influence Mike and Adam to wear their helmets consistently and to follow the safety rules of the road.

    C. Assessment Criteria[2,p239]

    You are assessed on the following content:

    Performance indicator 1.12.5 with infused content—Propose ways to reduce or prevent bicycle injuries and health problems by wearing a helmet and following the safety rules of the road.[1,p25]

      1. Three reasons to wear a helmet

      2. Five facts that explain how to be fitted for a helmet

      3. A chart depicting eleven bicycle safety rules for the road

    You are assessed on the following skills:

    Performance indicator 2.12.1 with infused content—Analyze how the family influences the health of individuals by the wearing of a bicycle helmet.[1,p27]

      1. Three facts about how family influences the wearing of a bicycle helmet

    Performance indicator 2.12.3 with infused content—Analyze the influence peers exert over the choice to wear or not wear a helmet.[1,p27]

      1. Three facts about how peers influence the wearing of a bicycle helmet

        Student project

      1. Poster on safety rules of the road

        a. Explain eleven bicycle safety rules for the road.

        b. Include ten pictures.

      2. Helmet demonstration

        a. Three reasons why it is important to wear a helmet

        b. Five facts to consider when fitting a helmet

(continues)

3. Story
    a. Write a story about a high school boy influenced by his parents and friend to wear a bicycle helmet.
    b. Explain three ways his parents influence him to wear his helmet.
    c. Explain three ways his friends influence him to wear his helmet.
    d. Include five bicycle safety rules of the road.
    e. Include a description of left- and right-hand turn signals.
    f. Conclusion that emphasizes the positive influences to wear a helmet
    g. Include five pictures.

Massasoit High School

Name _____

Mike and Adam are freshmen at Massasoit High School. They are fit and enjoy riding their bikes as training for track.

Mike usually wears his helmet but complains that it is hot and uncomfortable. Sometimes, in the summer, he does not wear it at all. He usually follows the bike safety rules of the road, but if there are no cars around, will not ride on the side of the road or use hand signals.

Mike's parents caught him cycling without a helmet and not obeying safety rules. They grounded him from his bike riding for two weeks.

Adam avoids wearing a helmet and following the rules of the road. He tells Mike, "Most teenagers don't wear helmets, so why should I?" He heard about two boys who died in a bike accident but thinks it will not happen to him.

The high school recently built a bike trail through the woods. Students or community members who use the trail must wear a helmet. The boys enjoy riding there and always wear their helmets.

Your challenge is to influence Mike and Adam to wear their helmets consistently and follow the safety rules of the road.

Your project must contain:

1. Poster on safety rules of the road

    a. Explain eleven bicycle safety rules for the road.

    b. Include ten pictures.

2. Helmet demonstration

    a. Three reasons why it is important to wear a helmet

    b. Five facts to consider when fitting a helmet

3. Story

    a. Write a story about a high school boy influenced by his parents and friend to wear a bicycle helmet.

    b. Explain three ways his parents influence him to wear his helmet.

    c. Explain three ways his friends influence him to wear his helmet.

    d. Include five bicycle safety rules of the road.

    e. Include a description of left- and right-hand turn signals.

    f. Conclusion that emphasizes the positive influences to wear a helmet

    g. Include five pictures

(continues)

Analytical rubric to assess the explanation of the rules of the road chart (**Table 6.9**).

TABLE 6.9 Analytical Rubric to Assess the Explanation of the Rules of the Road Chart

Criteria	4	3	2	1
Performance indicator 1.12.5 with infused content—Propose ways to reduce or prevent bicycle injuries and health problems by wearing a helmet and following the safety rules of the road.[1,p25]	Student accurately explains how to ride with traffic on the right side of the road.	Student's explanation of how to ride with traffic on the right side of the road is mostly accurate.	Student's explanation of how to ride with traffic on the right side of the road has a few inaccuracies.	Student's explanation of how to ride with traffic on the right side of the road is mostly inaccurate.
Performance indicator 1.12.5 with infused content—Propose ways to reduce or prevent bicycle injuries and health problems by wearing a helmet and following the safety rules of the road.[1,p25]	Student accurately describes how to check all directions before turning.	Student's description of how to check all directions before turning is mostly accurate.	Student's description of how to check all directions before turning has a few inaccuracies.	Student's description of how to check all directions before turning is mostly inaccurate.
Performance indicator 1.12.5 with infused content—Propose ways to reduce or prevent bicycle injuries and health problems by wearing a helmet and following the safety rules of the road.[1,p25]	Student accurately explains how to ride single file.	Student's explanation of how to ride single file is mostly accurate.	Student's explanation of how to ride single file has a few inaccuracies.	Student's explanation of how to ride single file is mostly inaccurate.
Performance indicator 1.12.5 with infused content—Propose ways to reduce or prevent bicycle injuries and health problems by wearing a helmet and following the safety rules of the road.[1,p25]	Student accurately explains how to obey all traffic lights and signs.	Student's explanation of how to obey all traffic lights and signs is mostly accurate.	Student's explanation of how to obey all traffic lights and signs has a few inaccuracies.	Student's explanation of how to obey all traffic lights and signs is mostly inaccurate.
Performance indicator 1.12.5 with infused content—Propose ways to reduce or prevent bicycle injuries and health problems by wearing a helmet and following the safety rules of the road.[1,p25]	Student accurately explains the importance of not listening to music or texting while riding.	Student's explanation of the importance of not listening to music while riding is mostly accurate.	Student's explanation of the importance of not listening to music while riding has a few inaccuracies.	Student's explanation of the importance of not listening to music while riding is mostly inaccurate.

(continues)

TABLE 6.9 Analytical Rubric to Assess the Explanation of the Rules of the Road Chart *(continued)*

Criteria	4	3	2	1
Performance indicator 1.12.5 with infused content—Propose ways to reduce or prevent bicycle injuries and health problems by wearing a helmet and following the safety rules of the road.[1,p25]	Student accurately explains the importance of making eye contact with drivers.	Student's explanation of the importance of making eye contact with drivers is mostly accurate.	Student's explanation of the importance of making eye contact with drivers has a few inaccuracies.	Student's explanation of the importance of making eye contact with drivers is mostly inaccurate.
Performance indicator 1.12.5 with infused content—Propose ways to reduce or prevent bicycle injuries and health problems by wearing a helmet and following the safety rules of the road.[1,p25]	Student presents excellent reasons to be courteous.	Student presents good reasons to be courteous.	Student presents fair reasons to be courteous.	Student presents poor reasons to be courteous.
Performance indicator 1.12.5 with infused content—Propose ways to reduce or prevent bicycle injuries and health problems by wearing a helmet and following the safety rules of the road.[1,p25]	Student thoroughly explains the importance of keeping eyes on the road for hazards.	Student adequately explains the importance of keeping eyes on the road for hazards.	Student inadequately explains the importance of keeping eyes on the road for hazards.	Student poorly explains the importance of keeping eyes on the road for hazards.
Performance indicator 1.12.5 with infused content—Propose ways to reduce or prevent bicycle injuries and health problems by wearing a helmet and following the safety rules of the road.[1,p25]	Student accurately explains the importance of wearing reflective gear at night and bright colors during the day.	Student's explanation of the importance of wearing reflective gear at night and bright colors during the day is mostly accurate.	Student's explanation of the importance of wearing reflective gear at night and bright colors during the day has a few inaccuracies.	Student's explanation of the importance of wearing reflective gear at night and bright colors during the day is mostly inaccurate.
Pictures	Ten pictures are appropriate.	Most of the ten pictures are appropriate.	A few of the ten pictures are inappropriate.	The ten pictures are mostly inappropriate.

Name _____

Total possible points – 40   Your points - _____   Your grade - _____

(continues)

Analytical rubric to assess the helmet demonstration (**Table 6.10**).

TABLE 6.10   Analytical Rubric to Assess the Helmet Demonstration

Criteria	4	3	2	1
Performance indicator 1.12.5 with infused content—Propose ways to reduce or prevent bicycle injuries and health problems by wearing a helmet and following the safety rules of the road.[1,p25]	Student thoroughly explains three reasons to wear a helmet.	Student adequately explains three reasons to wear a helmet.	Student inadequately explains three reasons to wear a helmet.	Student poorly explains three reasons to wear a helmet.
Performance indicator 1.12.5 with infused content—Propose ways to reduce or prevent bicycle injuries and health problems by wearing a helmet and following the safety rules of the road.[1,p25]	Student accurately demonstrates how to measure the head and use sizing pads to make adjustments to the fit of the helmet.	Student's demonstration of how to measure the head and use sizing pads to make adjustments to the fit of the helmet is mostly accurate.	Student's demonstration of how to measure the head and use sizing pads to make adjustments to the fit of the helmet has a few inaccuracies.	Student's demonstration how to measure the head and use sizing pads to make adjustments to the fit of the helmet is mostly inaccurate.
Performance indicator 1.12.5 with infused content—Propose ways to reduce or prevent bicycle injuries and health problems by wearing a helmet and following the safety rules of the road.[1,p25]	Student accurately demonstrates how the helmet should fit two finger-widths above the eyebrow.	Student's demonstration of how the helmet should fit two finger-widths above the eyebrow is mostly accurate.	Student's demonstration of how the helmet should fit two finger-widths above the eyebrow has a few inaccuracies.	Student's demonstration of how the helmet should fit two finger-widths above the eyebrow is mostly inaccurate.
Performance indicator 1.12.5 with infused content—Propose ways to reduce or prevent bicycle injuries and health problems by wearing a helmet and following the safety rules of the road.[1,p25]	Student accurately demonstrates how to center the left buckle under the chin.	Student's demonstration of how to center the left buckle under the chin is mostly accurate.	Student's demonstration of how to center the left buckle under the chin has a few inaccuracies.	Student's demonstration of how to center the left buckle under the chin is mostly inaccurate.
Performance indicator 1.12.5 with infused content—Propose ways to reduce or prevent bicycle injuries and health problems by wearing a helmet and following the safety rules of the road.[1,p25]	Student accurately demonstrates how the side straps should form a V under and slightly in front of the ear.	Student's demonstration of how the side straps should form a V under and slightly in front of the ear is mostly accurate.	Student's demonstration of how the side straps should form a V under and slightly in front of the ear has a few inaccuracies.	Student's demonstration of how the side straps should form a V under and slightly in front of the ear is mostly inaccurate.

(continues)

TABLE 6.10   Analytical Rubric to Assess the Helmet Demonstration *(continued)*

Criteria	4	3	2	1
Performance indicator 1.12.5 with infused content—Propose ways to reduce or prevent bicycle injuries and health problems by wearing a helmet and following the safety rules of the road.[1,p25]	Student accurately demonstrates how to buckle and tighten the chinstrap so that no more than two fingers fit under the strap.	Student's demonstration of how to buckle and tighten the chinstrap so that no more than two fingers fit under the strap is mostly accurate.	Student's demonstration of how to buckle and tighten the chinstrap so that no more than two fingers fit under the strap has a few inaccuracies.	Student's demonstration of how to buckle and tighten the chinstrap so that no more than two fingers fit under the strap is mostly inaccurate.
Voice projection	Projection of voice is excellent.	Projection of voice is good.	Projection of voice is fair.	Projection of voice is poor.

Name _____

Total possible points – 28   Your points - _____   Your grade - _____

Analytical rubric to assess the story about a high school boy influenced by his parents and friends to wear a bicycle helmet (**Table 6.11**).

TABLE 6.11   Analytical Rubric to Assess the Story About a High School Boy Influenced by His Parents and Friends to Wear a Bicycle Helmet

Criteria	4	3	2	1
Performance indicator 2.12.1 with infused content—Analyze how the family influences the health of individuals by the wearing of a bicycle helmet.[1,p27]	Story thoroughly analyzes three ways the parents influence their son to wear his helmet.	Story adequately analyzes three ways the parents influence their son to wear his helmet.	Story inadequately analyzes three ways the parents influence their son to wear his helmet.	Story poorly analyzes three ways the parents influence their son to wear his helmet.
Performance indicator 2.12.3 with infused content—Analyze the influence peers exert over the choice to wear or not wear a helmet.[1,p27]	Story thoroughly analyzes three ways peers exerted influence over their friend to wear his helmet.	Story adequately analyzes three ways peers exerted influence over their friend to wear his helmet.	Story inadequately analyzes three ways peers exerted influence over their friend to wear his helmet.	Story poorly analyzes three ways peers exerted influence over their friend to wear his helmet.
Performance indicator 1.12.5 with infused content—Propose ways to reduce or prevent bicycle injuries and health problems by wearing a helmet and following the safety rules of the road.[1,p25]	Student thoroughly weaves five bicycle safety rules of the road into the story.	Student adequately weaves five bicycle safety rules of the road into the story.	Student inadequately weaves five bicycle safety rules of the road into the story.	Student poorly weaves five bicycle safety rules of the road into the story.

(continues)

TABLE 6.11   Analytical Rubric to Assess the Story About a High School Boy Influenced by His Parents and Friends to Wear a Bicycle Helmet *(continued)*

Criteria	4	3	2	1
Performance indicator 1.12.5 with infused content—Propose ways to reduce or prevent bicycle injuries and health problems by wearing a helmet and following the safety rules of the road.[1,p25]	Student accurately explains how to signal for a right and left turn.	Student's explanation of how to signal for a right and left turn is mostly accurate.	Student's explanation of how to signal for a right and left turn has a few inaccuracies.	Student's explanation of how to signal for a right and left turn is mostly inaccurate.
Performance indicator 2.12.1 with infused content—Analyze how the family influences the health of individuals by the wearing of a bicycle helmet.[1,p27]	Story concludes by thoroughly emphasizing three positive influences to wear a helmet.	Story concludes by adequately emphasizing three positive influences to wear a helmet.	Story concludes by inadequately emphasizing three positive influences to wear a helmet.	Story concludes by poorly emphasizing three positive influences to wear a helmet.
Performance indicator 2.12.3 with infused content—Analyze the influence peers exert over the choice to wear or not wear a helmet.[1,p27]	Story concludes by thoroughly emphasizing three positive influences to wear a helmet.	Story concludes by adequately emphasizing three positive influences to wear a helmet.	Story concludes by inadequately emphasizing three positive influences to wear a helmet.	Story concludes by poorly emphasizing three positive influences to wear a helmet.
Pictures	The five pictures appropriately reflect the intent of the story.	The five pictures selected to reflect the intent of the story are mostly appropriate.	A few of the five pictures selected to reflect the intent of the story are somewhat inappropriate.	The five pictures selected to reflect the intent of the story are mostly inappropriate.
Grammar	Grammar is excellent.	Grammar is good.	Grammar is fair.	Grammar is poor.
Spelling	Spelling is excellent.	Spelling is good.	Spelling is fair.	Spelling is poor.

Name _____

Total possible points – 36   Your points - _____   Your grade - _____

HOW THE COORDINATED SCHOOL HEALTH TEAM CONTRIBUTES TO HELPING STUDENTS UNDERSTAND THE FACTORS THAT INFLUENCE THEIR BEHAVIOR

Health Education

- Focus instruction on the skill of analyzing influences and the content of bicycle safety.
- Review bicycle safety policies with students.
- Teach healthy coping strategies.

Physical Education

- Promote bicycle safety in the gymnasium through posters and demonstrations.

Health Services

- Provide bicycle safety information.

Nutrition Services

- Encourage healthy eating for an active lifestyle.

Counseling, Psychological, and Social Services

- Provide counseling to cope with peer pressure to engage in unhealthy behaviors.

Healthy School Environment

- Post procedures students can follow for bicycle safety.
- Display posters that promote bicycle safety and explain where to go for more information.
- Provide bicycle racks and places to store helmets.
- Develop policy and procedures to addresses bicycle safety.

Health Promotion for Staff

- Provide staff training in bicycle safety so that staff are better prepared better to help students.
- Be good role models and use a helmet when riding.
- Acknowledge students who wear bicycle helmets.

Family/Community Involvement

- Organize and implement a parent program to explain bicycle safety and how to protect children from injury.
- Encourage families to provide helmets to their children.
- Identify community resources, such as the fire department, where helmets can be obtained for free.

Review Questions

1. Why is it important to understand the influences on behavior?

2. Name one performance task example from each grade span.

3. If a factor has a negative influence on behavior, how does that impact instruction?

4. Give an example of a prompt for analyzing influences.

5. Why is it important to use data when planning instruction?

6. Why is it important to give students time to practice using the skills?

7. Explain how to use formative assessment during a skills-based unit.

8. How do you transfer the requirements of the performance assessment to an analytical rubric?

References

1. Joint Committee on National Health Education Standards (2007). *National Health Education Standards, Second Edition, Achieving Excellence.* Atlanta, GA: American Cancer Society.
2. CCSSO~SCASS Health Education Project. (2006). Assessment Tools for School Health Education, Pre-service and In-service edition. Santa Cruz, CA: ToucanEd Inc.
3. National Hghway Transportation Safety Administration. (2006). Traffic Safety Facts, 2006 Data. Retrieved February 14, 2009, from: www.nhta.dot.gov/portal/site/nhtsa/menu item.e712547f8daccabbbf30811060008a0c/
4. North Carolina Department of Public Instruction. (2009, January 13). School Bus Safety Tips for Students. Retrieved February 14, 2009, from North Carolina School Bus Safety: http://itre.ncsu.edu/GHSP/TipsStudents.pdf
5. Centers for Disease Control and Prevention. (2009, February 10). Overweight and Obesity> Childhood Overweight and Obesity> Obesity Prevalence. Retrieved February 12, 2009: www.cdc.gov/nccdphp/dnpa/obesity/childhood/prevalence.htm
6. Centers for Disease Control and Prevention. (2009, January 28). Overweight and Obesity>Childhood Overweight and Obesity>Consequences. Retrieved February 12, 2009: www.cdc.gov/nccdphp/dnpa/obesity/childhood/consequences.htm
7. Bronson, Mary H. P. (2009). Glencoe Health. Woodland Hills, CA: McGraw-Hill.
8. Media Awareness Network. (2007). Co - Co's AdverSmarts: an Interactive Unit on Food marketing on the Web Background information for parents and teachers. Retrieved February 12, 2009: www.media-awareness.ca
9. Hertz, M. M., & David-Ferdon, P. C. (2008). *Electronic Media and Youth Violence: A CDC Issue Brief for Educators and Caregivers.* Atlanta, GA: CDC.
10. David-Ferdon PhD, C. F. (2007). Electronic Media, Violence, and Adolescents: An Emerging Public Health Problem. *Journal of Adolescent Health,* 41(6), S1–S5.
11. Keith, S. M. (2005). Cyber-Bullying: Creating a Culture of Respect in a Cyber World. *Reclaiming Children and Youth,* 13(4), 224–228.
12. Slonje, R. P. (2008). Cyberbullying: Another Main Type of Bullying? *Scandinavian Journal of Psychology,* 153.
13. Federal Trade Commission. (2006, May). Federal Trade Commission, Protecting America's Consumers. Retrieved January 22, 2009, from Social Networking Sites:Safety Tips for Tweens and Teens: http://www.ftc.gov/bcp/edu/pubs/consumer/tech/tec14.shtm
14. Centers for Disease Control and Prevention. (MMWR 2010, 59). *Surveillance Summaries.* Atlanta, GA: Author. p. 40.
15. National Highway Traffic Safety Administration. (2006, September). Easy Steps to Properly Fit a Bicycle Helmet. Retrieved March 18, 2009: http://www.nhtsa.dot.gov/people/injury/pedbimot/bike/EasyStepsWeb/index.htm. p. 2.
16. Khambalia, A. M. (2005). Peer and Adult Companion Helmet Use is Associated With Bicycle Helmet Use by Children. *Pediatrics,* p. 940.

7

Teaching National Health Education Standard 3

"Students will demonstrate the ability to access valid information and products and services to enhance health."[1,p28]

Standard 3

Accessing valid information, products, and services is an important skill because the information learned is often the foundation of a decision that affects personal health.

Many teens ask friends, relatives, or healthcare providers for health information.[2,p817] They also use the Internet to obtain information because it provides easy access, is confidential, personalized, and less threatening.[2,p814]

In 2001, the Kaiser Family Foundation completed a study titled, "Generation Rx," and found that 75% of the 1,209 respondents, aged 15–24, had searched on the Internet for health information about sex, mental health, weight loss and gain, cancer, or diabetes.[3,p1] The survey revealed that, although many teens use the Internet to access health information, they might not search it effectively, evaluate the validity of information or legitimacy of websites, or apply the presumed knowledge to resolve a personal health need.[3,p2] In fact, a teen may assume that, simply because she has found an answer to her health question, it must be correct.[4,p25]

Standard 3 challenges students to learn how to access valid sources of information, as well as health products and services, from not only the Internet but also other resources. Furthermore, it encourages them to use that information to enhance their health by preventing health problems, detecting health issues early, and accessing appropriate treatment.

Sample performance tasks for accessing valid information and products and services to enhance health include:

- Identify community health helpers, determine how to contact them, and anticipate when their services are required.
- Highlight health information, a product, or service that enhances health and explain why the source is valid and reliable.

- Report on the validity of resources cited in a video.
- Select a variety of health products then explain why each is valid, reliable, or health enhancing.
- Select a video that contains valid sources and create a corresponding support brochure that includes their information, products, and services.
- Conduct a research project with valid sources of information, products, and services that enhance health.
- Conduct a survey based on valid sources of information, products, and services that enhance health.[5,p229]

To show proficiency in this standard, students analyze, compare, and evaluate health resources. Achieving this standard improves health literacy and the confidence to access legitimate sources of information, products, and services that enhance their health.[1,p28]

Teaching the Skill

Teaching and learning the national health education skills standards is a process. When planning, follow these steps:

I. Discuss the importance of accessing valid information, products, and services to enhance health.
   - Use of valid information, products, and services prevents illness, detects health problems early, and assists in the treatment of health problems.
   - Proficiency in this skill helps to identify or reject unproven health information, products, and services.
   - Competence in all the performance indicators contributes to health literacy.[1,p28]
II. Explain the steps to proficiency in accessing information, products, and services that enhance health.

A. Select the performance indicators for the grade span.

B. Teach the steps to achieve proficiency, such as identifying, locating, analyzing, accessing, determining, describing, evaluating, and implementing.

III. Show the students what the skill of accessing information and products and services to enhance health looks like.

A. Demonstrate the skill.

B. Model how to identify, locate, analyze, access, determine, describe, evaluate, and use valid sources of information, products, and services to enhance health.

IV. Provide adequate time for the students to practice accessing information, products, and services to enhance health.

V. Utilize formative assessments during practice for feedback and encouragement.[1,p14]

PreK–2

To achieve proficiency in Standard 3, PreK–2 students identify trusted adults and professionals who promote health and discover ways to locate school and community health helpers.

For example:

Show pictures of several adults from various occupations and their workplace. Ask students to show a thumbs up sign if the picture depicts a trusted adult who helps promote health. Ask the student to show a thumbs down if the picture depicts an adult who does not promote health. Hang the sorted pictures to reinforce the information.

Show pictures of a child talking to a parent, teacher, nurse, crossing guard, and police man/woman. Hang them on the board/wall. Tell the students that these people, when asked, help us with our health. Explain that children ask these health helpers for help, when needed.

To review, remove the pictures from the wall/board and distribute to the students. Ask the students to place the picture under the correct heading of "Helps promote health" or "Does not promote health." Place a smiley face next to "Helps promotes health" and a frown face next to "Does not promote health" to help the non-readers.

PreK–2 Performance Indicators

3.2.1 Identify trusted adults and professionals who can help promote health.

3.2.2 Identify ways to locate school and community health helpers.[1,p28]

To review ways to locate school and community health helpers, distribute these pictures and ask the child to explain different ways to locate these helpers.

Reflect by asking:

- Raise your hand if you can point to a picture of a person who helps promote health. (PI 3.2.1) (*Student goes to the wall/board and points to a picture of a trusted adult who can help promote health.*)
- Raise your hand if you can identify one way to locate a school or community health helper. (PI3.2.2) (*Student goes to the wall/board and points to a picture of a health helper then explains how to locate the health helper in the school or community.*)

Once the students demonstrate an understanding of the skill, as assessed formatively, they practice. Select a story that includes adults who promote health and other adults. After reading the story, challenge the students to identify the characters who promote health and explain where they work. Ask them to identify the other adults in the story, where they work, and why they are not health helpers.

Formatively assess the practice by observing which adults the students select as health helpers. Correct any misinformation and continue instruction when students understand the content and perform the skill.

WHAT DOES THE SKILL OF ACCESSING VALID INFORMATION, PRODUCTS, AND SERVICES TO ENHANCE HEALTH LOOK LIKE IN THE GRADE 1 CLASSROOM?

Mrs. Rupp, a Grade 1 teacher, understands the relationship between healthy students and academic achievement. She knows through her research that academic success is a strong indicator of overall health and well-being.[6,p1] Consequently, she wants her children to know how to remain healthy to be successful in school.

The school nurse notified Mrs. Rupp that she has several students who have asthma and another with a peanut allergy. The nurse told her that in 2007, 3 million children under the age of 18 (3.9%) reported a food allergy, and that those under the age of five had reported rates of food allergy higher than those reported in the older population (5–17 years).[7,p3] The nurse also told Mrs. Rupp that children with food allergies are two to four times more likely to have asthma and other allergies.[7,p2] In fact, the Centers for Disease Control and Prevention estimated in 2006 that children with asthma lost 15 million days of school each year.[8,p2] The nurse and Mrs. Rupp plan to work together to keep the children healthy and in school.

In planning her accessing information unit, Mrs. Rupp wants the children to identify the adults at school and in the community who help them stay healthy, such as their pediatrician, the allergist, and the school nurse. She expects the children to find the quickest route to the nurse's office and learn how to remain healthy to minimize illness and absences.

In planning, Mrs. Rupp targets the two performance indicators for her grade, 3.2.1 and 3.2.2.

Performance indicator 3.2.1—Identify trusted adults and professionals who can help promote health.[1,p28]

> Performance indicator 3.2.1 with infused content—Identify trusted adults and professionals who can help promote health through their knowledge of allergies and asthma.[1,p28]

Performance indicator 3.2.2—Identify ways to locate school and community health helpers.[1,p28]

> Performance indicator 3.2.2 with infused content—Identify ways to locate school and community health helpers who have knowledge and expertise in allergies and asthma.[1,p28]

After selecting the appropriate skill performance indicators, Mrs. Rupp chooses Standard 1 performance indicator for content.

Standard 1—Students will comprehend concepts related to health promotion and disease prevention to enhance health.[1,p24]

Performance indicator 1.2.1—Identify that healthy behaviors affect personal health.[1,p24]

> Performance indicator 1.2.1 with infused content—Identify that healthy behaviors, such as eating a balanced diet, being physically active, getting the proper amount of sleep and scheduled check-ups, getting dental care, and wearing seat belts and safety gear, affect personal health.[1,p24]

By linking the skill and the content performance indicators, Mrs. Rupp gains direction in planning the unit on accessing valid information, products, and services to enhance health.

The first step is to complete the performance task template. This planning helps the teacher see the big picture, especially standards, assessment, and instruction. Once done, most of the planning is complete.

Because Grade 1 students are initially non-readers, instruction and assessment are verbal and visual. To identify healthy behaviors, the teacher shows pictures of healthy vs. unhealthy behaviors. The children sort the pictures and explain how each behavior affects health and why it is important to have healthy behaviors (**Table 7.1**).

Mrs. Rupp also has collected pictures from the community and school of trusted adults and professionals, their workplaces, and samples of their tools. She divides the whiteboard into three sections and labels them: Who are these trusted adults and professionals? Where do they work? What helpful tools do they use? After explaining each piece, students practice placing the detachable figures in the correct box (**Table 7.2**).

Table 7.1 Healthy vs. Unhealthy Behaviors

Healthy	Unhealthy	Why
1 hour		

(continues)

Table 7.1 Healthy vs. Unhealthy Behaviors *(continued)*

Healthy	Unhealthy	Why

10 hours

30 minutes

5 hours

(continues)

Table 7.1 Healthy vs. Unhealthy Behaviors *(continued)*

Healthy	Unhealthy	Why
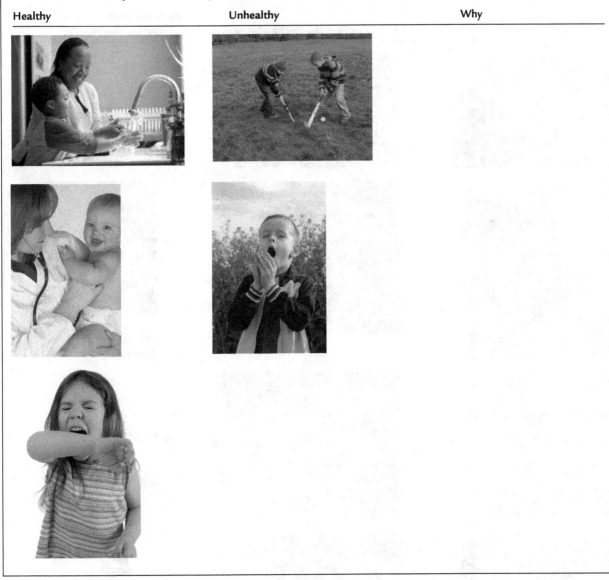		

Table 7.2 Health Helpers, Where They Work, and the Tools They Use

Health Helper	Where to Find the Health Helper	Tools the Health Helper Uses to Help Us Stay Healthy

(continues)

Health Helper	Where to Find the Health Helper	Tools the Health Helper Uses to Help Us Stay Healthy

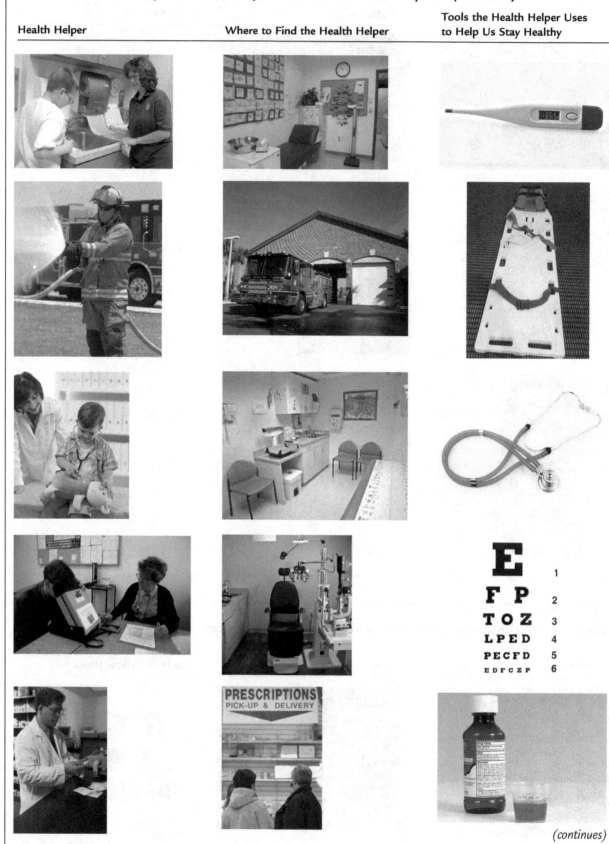

Table 7.2 Health Helpers, Where They Work, and the Tools They Use *(continued)*

Health Helper	Where to Find the Health Helper	Tools the Health Helper Uses to Help Us Stay Healthy

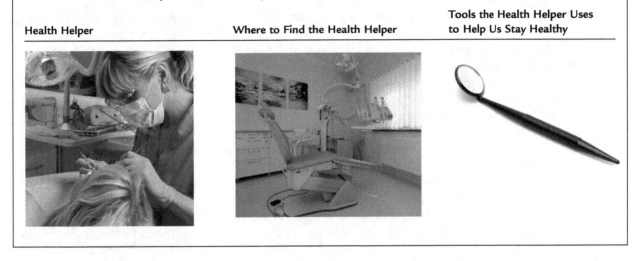

To learn how to locate the school nurse from a variety of locations within the school, Mrs. Rupp projects a map of the building on the whiteboard. She highlights the nurse's office, and the students practice finding the most direct route from three different locations (**Figure 7.1**).

The students are assessed formatively during instruction and summatively, at the end of instruction, using an analytical rubric.

The following is an example of a Grade 1 performance task for accessing information, products, and services. The first section demonstrates how the teacher plans an authentic assessment of the performance indicators 3.2.1, 3.2.2., and 1.2.1. The second extracts some of the information from the performance task and transforms it into the prompt and support materials for students.

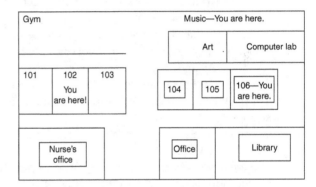

FIGURE 7.1   School Map Assessment

Performance Task Name: Grade 1—Health Helpers

I. Which state standard(s) does the performance task address?

II. Topic: What areas of health does this project assess? Why is it important? What is the focus of the project?[5,p237]

   A. This performance task assesses Personal Health.

   B. This topic is important because rates of allergies and asthma are rising and contribute to school absenteeism.

   C. The focus of the project is for students to identify health helpers, find the nurse from different locations in the school, and recognize the importance of practicing healthy behaviors.

III. Key Concepts: What basic concepts should students know?[5,p237]

   Standard 1—Students will comprehend concepts related to health promotion and disease prevention to enhance health.[1,p24]

   Performance indicator 1.2.1 with infused content—Identify that healthy behaviors, such as eating a balanced diet, being physically active, getting the proper amount of sleep, getting scheduled check-ups, getting dental care, and wearing seat belts and safety gear, affect personal health.[1,p24]

(continues)

1. Eat a well-balanced diet (grains, vegetables, fruits, milk, meat, and beans) to obtain the nutrients to grow healthy.[9]
2. Participate in moderate to vigorous physical activity for 60 minutes each day to keep your body healthy.[9]
3. Sleep 10 hours a night to meet the challenges of the day.[10]
4. Receive regular check-ups to become healthy adults.[11]
   - Physical checkup
   - Check ears, eyes, and mouth
   - Update immunizations
   - Dental checkups every 6 months
5. Brush and floss teeth to prevent tooth decay, cavities, and gum disease.
   - Brush teeth two times a day with a fluoride toothpaste, morning and night
   - Floss teeth at least once a day.[12]
6. Wear a safety belt in a car to protect you against severe injury.
   - Traffic crashes are the leading cause of death in the United States for children aged 3–15.
   - Lap/shoulder seat belts used correctly reduce the risk of fatal injury to front-seat occupants (aged 5 and older) in passenger cars by 45% and the risk of moderate to critical injury by 50%.[13]
7. Wearing safety gear that is the correct size and fits well when participating in physical activities prevents injuries.[14]
8. Wash hands frequently to prevent the spread of infectious disease.[15]
9. Always carry an EpiPen if you have a life-threatening allergy.
   a. Allergist makes a diagnosis and gives a prescription.
   b. An EpiPen injects a dose of adrenaline into the thigh to reduce the severe allergic reactions.[16]

IV. Skills: Which of the seven National Health Education Standards skills does this performance task address?[5,p237]

Standard 3—Students will demonstrate the ability to access valid information and products and services to enhance health.[1,p28]

Performance indicator 3.2.1 with infused content—Identify trusted adults and professionals who can help promote health through their knowledge of allergies and asthma.[1,p28]

1. Pediatrician
2 School Nurse
3. Dentist
4. Allergist
5. Fireman
6. Policeman
7. Optometrist
8. Pharmacist

Performance indicator 3.2.2 with infused content—Identify ways to locate school and community health helpers who have knowledge and expertise in allergies and asthma.[1,p28]

1. Locate the school nurse's office
2. Ways to locate allergy and asthma health helpers.
   a. Ask for help
      1. Parents/Guardians
      2. Teachers
      3. Nurses
   b. Access adults by
      1. Telephone
      2. Internet

V. Curricular connections: What other subject(s) does this performance task support?[5,p237]
   A. Social studies—mapping
   B. English Language Arts

(continues)

C. Physical education—walking to the nurse

D. Art—drawing and decorating the map

E. Math—measuring steps to the nurse

F. Music—safety songs, optional

VI. Student directions and assessment criteria[5,p238]

A. Write an engaging prompt that draws the student into the project.

Carson is a Grade 1 student at the Kinkaid Elementary School. He has been to many doctors but does not always know exactly what kind of doctor he is visiting.

Carson just learned that he has a peanut allergy and asthma. This awareness made him a little nervous because he knows if he has a reaction he needs help fast.

Carson lives near the fire station and visits the firemen when they are outside working on the trucks or washing them. He told them about his allergy, and the firemen showed him the emergency kit they would bring to his house if he or a family member called 911. Carson felt good that he would get help quickly in an emergency.

At home, his mom and dad make sure he eats healthy foods, exercises, gets enough sleep and regular checkups, uses safety equipment when playing, and wears a seat belt in the car.

At school, Carson's teacher and the nurse have an EpiPen for him. He needs to know how to get to the nurse's office quickly if he needs help.

B. Your challenge: Provide a challenge or mission statement that describes the project (CCSSO).[5,p238]

1. Use the chart to identify three health helpers, the tools they use to make people feel better, and where their offices are located. Put a star next to the health helpers who treat allergies and asthma.

2. Use the map to draw a path to the nurse's office from three different locations in the school.

3. Identify three healthy behaviors and explain why they are important.

C. Assessment Criteria[5,p239]

You are assessed on the following key concepts: (List the concepts)

Performance indicator 1.2.1 with infused content—Identify that healthy behaviors, such as eating a balanced diet, being physically active, getting the proper amount of sleep, getting scheduled check-ups, getting dental care, and wearing seat belts and safety gear affect personal health.[1,p24]

1. A balanced diet includes grains, vegetables, fruits, milk, meat, and beans.

2. Sixty minutes of exercise are needed each day.

3. Ten hours of sleep are necessary each night.

4. During a regular check-up, the doctor checks heart, lungs, eyes, ears, mouth, and administers immunizations.

5. A seat belt protects your body if the car is in a crash.

6. Athletic safety equipment prevents injuries.

7. An EpiPen injects a dose of adrenaline into the thigh to reduce the severe allergic reactions.[16]

You are assessed on the following skills: (List the skills)

Performance indicator 3.2.1 with infused content—Identify trusted adults and professionals who promote health through their knowledge of allergies and asthma.[1,p28]

1. Identify three health helpers, where they work, and the tools they use to keep people healthy.

Performance indicator 3.2.2 with infused content—Identify ways to locate school and community health helpers who have knowledge and expertise in allergies and asthma.[1,p28]

1. Identify how to locate the school nurse by drawing a line from three locations in the school to the nurse's office.

Student project must include the following:

1. Use the chart to identify three health helpers, the tools they use to make people feel better, and where their offices are located. Put a star next to the health helpers who treat allergies and asthma.

2. Use the map to draw a path to the nurse's office from three different locations in the school.

3. Identify three healthy behaviors and explain why they are important.

Kinkaid Elementary School

Name _____

Carson is a Grade 1 student at the Kinkaid Elementary School. He has been to many doctors but does not always know exactly what kind of doctor he is visiting.

Carson just learned that he has a peanut allergy and asthma. This awareness made him a little nervous because he knows if he has a reaction he needs help fast.

Carson lives near the fire station and visits the firemen when they are outside working on the trucks or washing them. He told them about his allergy, and the firemen showed him the emergency kit they would bring to his house if he or a family member called 911. Carson felt good that he would get help quickly in an emergency.

At home, his mom and dad make sure he eats healthy foods, exercises, gets enough sleep and regular checkups, uses safety equipment when playing, and wears a seat belt in the car.

At school, Carson's teacher and the nurse have an EpiPen for him. He needs to know how to get to the nurse's office quickly if he needs help.

You have three challenges.

1. Use the chart to identify three health helpers, the tools they use to make people feel better, and where their offices are located. Put a star next to the health helpers who treat allergies and asthma.

2. Use the map to draw a path to the nurse's office from three different locations in the school.

3. Identify three healthy behaviors and explain why they are important.

While the students prepare for the authentic assessment and to encourage them to practice, Mrs. Rupp develops a review and check-off list to formatively assess their progress.

TABLE 7.3 Self-Assessment for Health Helpers and Mapping

Kinkaid Elementary School

Name _____

Directions: Place a check in the box when you have completed the task.

My Chart Contains

Three Health Helpers	The Tools Each Helper Uses	Where to Find the Health Helper
☐	☐	☐
☐	☐	☐
☐	☐	☐

Directions: Check off one box every time you map a different way to reach the nurse's office.

My maps show three ways to get to the nurse's office.

First map	Second map	Third map
☐	☐	☐

(continues)

TABLE 7.4   Assessment-Healthy Behaviors vs. Unhealthy Behaviors

Kinkaid Elementary School

Name _____

Circle three healthy behaviors.

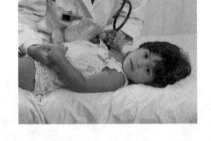  

Why are these healthy behaviors important?

(continues)

Health Helpers, Where They Work, and Their Helping Tools

Kinkaid Elementary School

Name _____

Directions: Match these two **health helpers** to their tools and office in **Table 7.5**.

Directions: Match these **tools** to the health helper and their office.

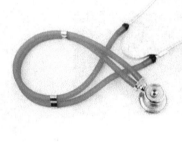

Directions: Match these two offices to the health helpers and their tools.

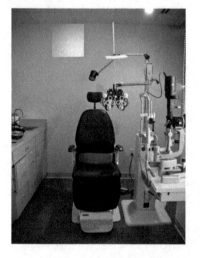

(continues)

TABLE 7.5 Health Helper Assessment

Health Helper	Where is the Health Helper's Office?	Tools the Health Helper Uses to Help Us Stay Healthy
		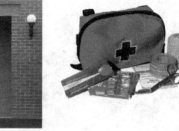

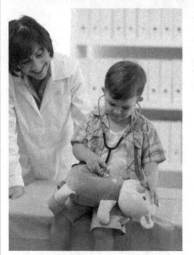		

(continues)

TABLE 7.5 Health Helper Assessment *(continued)*

Health Helper	Where is the Health Helper's Office?	Tools the Health Helper Uses to Help Us Stay Healthy

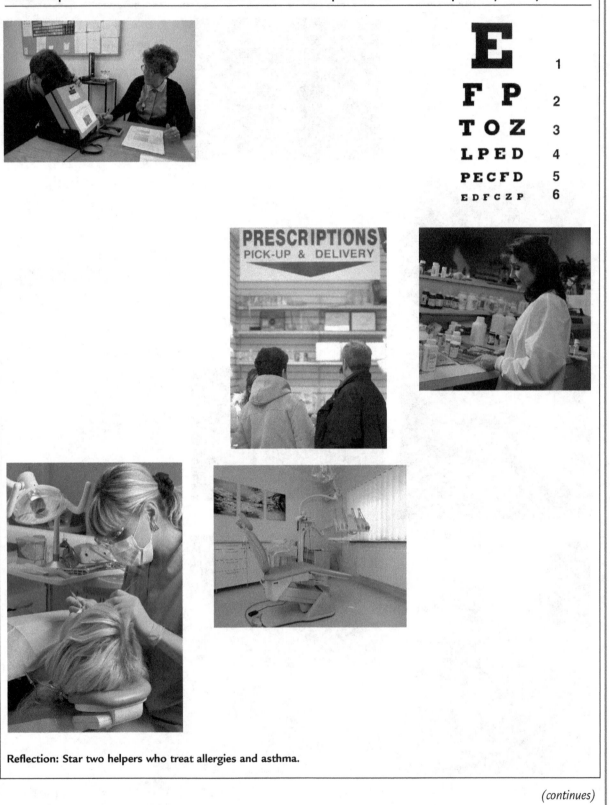

Reflection: Star two helpers who treat allergies and asthma.

(continues)

School Map

Kinkaid Elementary School

Name _____

Directions: Draw the most direct way from "You are Here" to the nurse's office (**Figure 7.1**). Draw two other ways to reach the nurse's office.

The following is a written assessment that can accompany the performance task.

Kinkaid Elementary School

Name _____

Directions: Circle the healthy behavior.

1. Balanced Diet

2. Exercise

   30 minutes   1 hour   2 hours

3. Sleep

   5 hours   10 hours   15 hours

4. Check-ups

   Only when sick   Once a year   When you have an injury

5. Teeth

6. Car Safety

7. Play Safety

(continues)

8. Hygiene

9. What to Do When You Are Sick

PreK–2 Analytical Rubric For Accessing Information Performance Task

This analytical rubric calculates a grade for all the activities of the accessing information unit. In the older grades, students receive it with the prompt so they know, in advance, how they are graded. On the PreK–2 level, the teacher also explains how the students are graded but may or may not distribute the rubric because of the reading ability of the students (**Table 7.6**).

TABLE 7.6 PreK–2 Analytical Rubric for Accessing Information Performance Task

Criteria	4	3	2	1
Performance indicator 1.2.1 with infused content—Identify that healthy behaviors, such as eating a balanced diet, being physically active, getting the proper amount of sleep, getting scheduled check-ups, getting dental care, and wearing seat belts and safety gear affect personal health.[1,p24]	Student thoroughly explains three ways healthy behaviors affect health.	Student adequately explains three ways healthy behaviors affect health.	Student inadequately explains three ways healthy behaviors affect health.	Student poorly explains three ways healthy behaviors affect health.

(continues)

Criteria	4	3	2	1
Performance indicator 3.2.1 with infused content—Identify trusted adults and professionals who promote health through their knowledge of allergies and asthma.[1,p28]	Student accurately identifies three health helpers, their tools, and offices.	Student's identification of three health helpers, their tools, and offices is mostly accurate.	Student's identification of three health helpers, their tools, and offices has a few inaccuracies.	Student's identification of three health helpers, their tools, and offices is mostly inaccurate.
Performance indicator 3.2.2 with infused content—Identify ways to locate school and community health helpers who have knowledge and expertise in allergies and asthma.[1,p28]	Student accurately identifies how to locate the nurse's office from three different locations.	Student's identification of how to locate the nurse's office from three different locations is mostly accurate.	Student's identification of how to locate the nurse's office from three different locations has a few inaccuracies.	Student's identification of how to locate the nurse's office from three different locations is mostly inaccurate.

Name _____

Total possible points – 12   Your points - _____   Your grade - _____

HOW THE COORDINATED SCHOOL HEALTH TEAM CONTRIBUTES TO HELPING STUDENTS LEARN THE SKILL OF ACCESSING VALID SOURCES OF INFORMATION, PRODUCTS, AND SERVICES

Health Education

- Identify trusted adults and professionals who enhance health, especially doctors who treat allergy and asthma.
- Develop healthy behaviors.
- Explain the importance of seeking health care.
- Ways to locate school and community health helpers

Physical Education

- Promote healthy behaviors.
- Explain how to access valid health information, products, and services.
- Provide 30 minutes of physical education each day.

Health Services

- Provide allergy support.
- Provide emergency care.
- Provide resources for valid sources of information, products, and services to enhance health.

Nutrition Services

- Provide allergen-free lunch tables.
- Provide allergen-free lunches.
- Hang posters that explain various food allergies.
- Provide healthy balanced food choices.

Counseling, Psychological, and Social Services

- Provide support for students with allergies.
- Provide health resources to families and students.

Healthy School Environment

- Hang posters that promote healthy behaviors.
- Encourage students who are sick to seek medical care.
- Provide allergy-free zone for students with food allergies.

Health Promotion for Staff

- Provide staff training about food allergies and asthma.
- Encourage staff to model healthy behaviors.

Family and Community Involvement

- Ask the community to offer family and youth programs that promote health.

- Encourage restaurants to offer a variety of foods so children with allergies can dine there.
- Provide a food allergy training for staff, parents, and community members.

Grades 3–5

To achieve proficiency in Standard 3, Grades 3–5 students must identify characteristics of valid health information, products, and services, and locate resources from home, school, and community that provide valid health information.

To teach Standard 3, provide specific characteristics of valid health information, products, and services. Challenge students to investigate resources in their home, school, and community that provide valid health information.

For example:

> Desmond was visiting Eric's house one afternoon. Eric asked if Desmond would like a snack. Desmond was very hungry, so he said, "Yes." Instead of a piece of fruit, Eric gave Desmond a candy bar saying it was a healthy snack because it had peanuts in it. Not wanting to embarrass himself or insult his friend by reading the label, he ate the candy. A short time later, he was hungry again and had another.
>
> While at the store with his mother, Desmond spied the same candy and checked out the label. He found that it was not healthy at all for it contained a lot of sugar and fat.

To reflect, ask the students:

- Was Eric a valid source of health information? (PI 3.5.1) *(No. Eric is not an expert in health or nutrition.)*
- At the grocery store, what did Desmond have that is a valid source of information? (PI 3.5.1) *(The candy wrapper nutrition information label)*
- Who is a good resource from home or school to provide valid health information? (PI 3.5.2) *(Desmond's mother, school nurse, or teacher)*

In this skill, students identify the characteristics of valid sources of information and locate them within the home, school, or community. When students demon-

Grades 3–5 Performance Indicators

3.5.1 Identify characteristics of valid health information, products, and services.

3.5.2 Locate resources from home, school, and community that provide valid health information.[1,p28]

Characteristics of Valid Sources of Information

- The source of the information is identified.
- The credentials of the author or organization demonstrate knowledge and training in health.
- The information is based on current research or scientific knowledge rather than opinion.
- Health professionals evaluate the information.
- The information informs you, rather than trying to persuade you that you need a product or service.
- The information educates you without appealing to your emotions.
- Additional information is available upon request.
- The claims are realistic.[17,p74]

strate their understanding of the skill, as determined through formative assessment, it is time to practice.

Show the students examples of valid and invalid sources of health information, products, and services. An information example may be one article that is a valid source and another that is not. A valid product example may be an advertisement for a bicycle helmet, and an invalid product, a weight control formula that promises quick and easy weight loss. A valid service example may include an advertisement for gymnastic lessons that promises fun, strength, and flexibility; the invalid service example promotes skating lessons that promise placement on the school or town hockey team.

Challenge the students to sort the above examples into valid and invalid and defend their placement. While defending, record the characteristics they mention to indicate validity.

Discuss the characteristics of valid sources of information, the importance of being able to identify them, and how to use valid information to enhance health. When students understand the skill, they brainstorm and defend their own examples of valid and invalid sources of information, products, and services.

To continue the practice, ask students to locate valid sources of information, products, and services in their homes, school, and the community. List the resource and explain why it is valid.

Once the students understand the skill, teach the content. Design a prompt that causes the student to explain content and demonstrate skill.

As the students learn and practice the skill and content, formatively assess their progress. If necessary, provide additional instruction before continuing to the performance task.

WHAT DOES THE SKILL OF ACCESSING VALID SOURCES OF INFORMATION, PRODUCTS, AND SERVICES TO ENHANCE HEALTH LOOK LIKE IN THE GRADE 4 CLASSROOM?

Mr. Handler, a Grade 4 teacher at the Ellis Elementary School, is concerned about the high rate of unintentional injuries among his students. According to data from the CDC, the leading cause of death for children aged 5–9 is unintentional injuries.[18] The school nurse corroborates those facts by saying that 5% of absences are due to injuries, mostly motor vehicle accidents and athletic injuries due to improper use or lack of safety equipment.

Mr. Handler knows product advertisements influence his students because he overhears them talking about pestering their parents to buy certain brands of athletic gear. Some students complain about using a car booster seat saying that they are uncomfortable. Others want to sit in the front seat and use a regular seat belt.

When researching "tween" marketing, Mr. Handler discovered that advertisers depend on pestering and increased their spending from $100 million in 1990 to $2 billion in 2000[19] and to over $300 billion in 2007.[20] In "tween" magazines, he saw few advertisements from valid health sources that promote products and services that enhance health. In his accessing information unit, Mr. Handler wants students to become more media literate and make safe product choices.

He has selected the following performance indicator from Standard 3:

Standard 3—Students will demonstrate the ability to access valid information, products, and services to enhance health.[1,p28]

Performance Indicator 3.5.1—Identify characteristics of valid health information, products, and services.[1,p28]

Performance indicator 3.5.1 with infused content— Identify in advertisements characteristics of valid health information, products, and services.[1,p28]

After selecting the appropriate performance indicator for the skill, choose a Standard 1 performance indicator.

Standard 1—Students will comprehend health promotion and disease prevention to enhance health.[1,p24]

Performance Indicator 1.5.1—Describe the relationship between healthy behaviors and personal health.[1,p24]

Performance indicator 1.5.1 with infused content— Describe the relationship between healthy behaviors, such as using safety equipment, and personal health.[1,p24]

By linking the skill and content performance indicators, the teacher knows how to plan the lessons for an accessing information unit.

The first step in planning is to think through the unit by completing the performance task template. Upon completion, the teacher has most of the information to introduce the prompt to the students.

For the prompt, include all the back-up information, holistic rubrics, analytical rubrics, and worksheets for the students to complete the task. Designing skills-based lessons requires considerable preparation for the performance task, but once the teacher distributes and explains the information, the students are on their own to create a product. Students learn with good coaching (formative assessment) how to demonstrate proficiency in content and skill.

The following is an example of a Grade 4 accessing information performance task that focuses on constructing an advertisement that uses valid sources of information about athletic or car safety equipment.

The first section, which is for the teacher, demonstrates how to plan for an authentic assessment of the performance indicators 3.5.1 and 1.5.1. The second section, for the student, extracts information from the performance task and transforms it into the student prompt and support materials.

When preparing for this authentic assessment, the teacher designs a worksheet and a rubric and distributes them to the students along with the prompt. It is crucial for students to know how they are being assessed before the project begins in order to produce evidence of their proficiency in the standards.

Performance Task Name: Grade 4—Accessing Valid Information About Safety Products.

I. Which state standard(s) does this performance task address? (Varies by state)

II. Topic: What areas of health does this project assess? Why is it important? What is the focus of the project?[5,p237]

(continues)

A. This performance task assesses Injury Prevention/Safety
B. This topic is important because:
  1. Advertising to "tweens" is a $300 billion dollar market.[20]
  2. Children must learn to recognize the characteristics that determine whether information, products, and services are valid and enhance health.
  3. According to data from the CDC, the leading cause of death for children aged 5–9 is unintentional injuries.[18,p2]
  4. The school nurse reports that 5% of absences are due to injuries.
C. The focus of this project is for students to identify characteristics of valid information about safety equipment and promote its use by constructing an advertisement.
III. Key Concepts: What basic concepts should students know?[5,p237]
  Standard 1—Students will comprehend concepts related to health promotion and disease prevention to enhance health.[1,p24]
  *Performance indicator 1.5.1 with infused content—*Describe the relationship between healthy behaviors such as using safety equipment, and personal health.[1,p24]
A. Athletic injury
  1. Information
    a. Injuries are more likely in a contact or collision sport
    b. Most athletic injuries involve muscle strains, sprained ligaments, fractures, contusions, and over-use syndromes.
    c. To reduce injuries, require proper athletic equipment.[21]
  2. Children under 8 years old are more susceptible to sports injuries than older children because they:
    a. Are less coordinated
    b. Have slower reaction times
    c. Are still growing and developing. The difference in height and weight among players can result in injury.[14,p1]
  3. Preventing sports injuries
    a. Be in good physical condition.
    b. Know and follow the rules.
    c. Wear protective gear
      1. Baseball—hard shell helmet when facing the pitcher, cleats
      2. Basketball—mouth guard, proper footwear, goggles
      3. Biking—helmet
      4. Field hockey—mouth guard, knee and shin pads, proper footwear
      5. Football—helmet with a facemask, body padding (jaw, neck, shoulder, rib, arm, elbow, hip, tailbone, thigh, knee), mouth guard, cup, cleats[22]
      6. Gymnastics—snuggly fitting outfits, long hair pulled back, hand guards, chalk[22]
      7. Ice hockey—helmet with face mask, body padding, mouth guard
      8. In-line skating—wrist guards, helmet, elbow and knee pads[22]
      9. Lacrosse—mouth and face guards
      10. Running—running shoes
      11. Skateboarding—wrist guards, helmet, knee and ankle pads, non-slip shoes
      12. Scooters—helmet
      13. Soccer—mouth guard, shin pads, cleats
      14. Wrestling—mouth guard
    d. Know how to use athletic equipment.
    e. Warm up 15 minutes before playing and cool down afterwards.
      1. Light jog
      2. Stretch muscles[23]
    f. Know and follow the rules of the game.
    g. Avoid playing when tired or injured.[24]

(continues)

B. Car Safety
1. The most common cause of unintentional injury in children aged 5–9 is motor vehicle occupant injury.
2. 90% of unintentional injuries can be prevented.[25]
3. Booster seats
   a. Booster seats protect a child under 4'9" who weighs between 40 and 80 pounds.
   b. Booster seats protect the child's upper body with a shoulder belt or shield.
   c. The booster seat raises the child so the lap/shoulder strap fits correctly.[26,p1]
4. How the lap belt should fit:
   a. Fit the belt low over a child's upper thighs, not the belly.
   b. The child must sit straight against the seat back.
   c. Shoulder belt should be snug to the child's chest.[26,p2]
5. Safety tips for children
   a. Always stay in the booster seat when the car is in motion.
   b. Always wear a seat belt.
   c. Keep your body parts inside the car at all times.
   d. Do not misbehave with other passengers. You may distract the driver.
   e. Do not eat foods, such as lollipops or other foods on a stick that could hurt you, if the car stopped suddenly.
   f. Always sit in the back.[27]

IV. Skills: Which of the seven National Health Education Standards skills does this performance task address?[5,p237]

Standard 3—Students will demonstrate the ability to access valid information, and products and services to enhance health.[1,p28]

Performance indicator 3.5.1 with infused content—Identify in advertisements characteristics of valid health information, products, and services.[1,p28]

A. Characteristics
1. Identify the source of the information.
2. The credentials of the author/organization demonstrate knowledge and training in health.
3. The information is based on current research or scientific knowledge rather than opinion.
4. Health professionals evaluate the information.
5. The information informs you, rather than trying to convince you that you need a product or service.
6. The information educates you without appealing to your emotions.
7. Additional information is available upon request.
8. The claims are realistic.[17,p74]

B. A valid source of information is one that provides accurate information from reputable and verifiable resources about health and health-promoting products and services.
1. BAM
2. KidsHealth
3. American Academy of Orthopaedic Surgeons
4. Centers for Disease Control and Prevention
5. Massachussetts General Hospital
6. Safe Kids USA
7. Media Awareness Network
8. Children's Car Seat Guide

C. A health product is an item that is manufactured and used for health. Examples include safety equipment, dental floss, toothpaste, sunscreen, etc.[17,p73]

D. A health service includes aid given by a person or organization that enhances health.[17,p73]

(continues)

V. Curricular connections: What other subject areas does this project support?[5,p237]

    English Language Arts

    Art

    Physical Education

    Science

VI. Student Directions and Assessment Criteria[5,p238]

  A. Project Description—Write and attach an engaging prompt that draws the student into the project.[5,p238]

> Joey is a fourth grader at the Ellis Elementary School. He and many of his friends are involved in after-school and town sports programs. They also like to go to the playground or a friend's house to play and, when they do, do not use safety equipment. Recently, many of his friends have been injured.
>
> Carolyn is also in the fourth grade. She does not like to sit in her booster seat while riding in the car. She wants to sit in the front seat and wear a regular seat belt.

  B. Your Challenge: Provide a challenge or mission statement that describes the project.[5,p238]

> Your challenge is to identify characteristics of valid information about safety and safety products, then use that information to construct an advertisement for sport or car safety equipment.
>
> You will present your advertisement to the class, identifying the characteristics of valid information used to construct your advertisement, and specifying how your product enhances personal safety and health.

  C. Assessment Criteria[5,p239]

You are assessed on the following key concepts: (List the concepts.)

Performance indicator 1.5.1 with infused content—Describe the relationship between healthy behaviors such as using safety equipment, and personal health.[1,p24]

  1. Sports Safety

    a. Explain five ways to prevent sports injuries.

    b. Illustrate how using sports safety equipment protects and enhances personal health.

  2. Car Safety

    a. Explain five ways to practice passenger safety while traveling in a car.

    b. Illustrate how a booster seat and seat belts protect and enhance personal health.

    You are assessed on the following skill:

Performance indicator 3.5.1 with infused content—Identify characteristics of valid health informaion, products, and services in advertisements.[1,p28]

  1. Complete and include the Accessing Information worksheet with your advertisement.

  2. Identify the eight characteristics of valid information you accessed to complete your advertisement.

    Student project must include the following:

  1. An advertisement for either sports or car safety equipment.

  2. Completed accessing information worksheet.

Ellis Elementary School

Name _____

Joey is a fourth grader at the Ellis Elementary School. He and many of his friends are involved in after-school and town sports programs. They also like to go to the playground or a friend's house to play and, when they do, do not use safety equipment. Recently, many of his friends have been injured.

  Carolyn is also in the fourth grade. She does not like to sit in her booster seat while riding in the car. She wants to sit in the front seat and wear a regular seat belt.

(continues)

Your challenge is to identify characteristics of valid information about safety and safety products, then use that information to construct an advertisement for sport or car safety equipment.

You will present your advertisement to the class, identifying the characteristics of valid information used to construct your advertisement and specifying how your product enhances personal safety and health.

Your project must include the following:

1. An advertisement for either sports or car safety

2. Completed worksheet on the characteristics of valid information used in the project

ASSESSMENT MATERIALS

Questions that identify the characteristics of valid information (**Table 7.7**).

Accessing Information Worksheet

TABLE 7.7   Questions That Identify the Characteristics of Valid Information

Name _____

Directions: Using the resources supplied by Mr. Handler, determine whether the source is a valid one for information about safety products.

1. Name the source of the health information. _____
   _____

2. How do you know that the author has knowledge and training in health? (Credentials)
   _____
   _____

3. Is the information based on research and scientific knowledge or on the opinion of an individual or group?
   _____

4. Name the health professionals who evaluated the source of information. _____
   _____

5. Did the information inform you or try to persuade you that you need a particular product or service?
   _____
   _____

6. Did the information educate you or simply appeal to your emotions? _____
   _____

7. Could you access additional information if you wanted it? _____
   _____

8. Were the claims stated in the information realistic?[91] For example, "Using wrist guards prevents injury."
   _____

9. Was this source a valid one for health information? _____
   Explain your answer: _____
   _____

10. State five facts about how using different safety equipment effects personal health.
   1._____
   2. _____
   3. _____
   4. _____
   5. _____

(continues)

Analytical rubric to assess the accessing information performance task (**Table 7.8**).

TABLE 7.8 Grade 4 Analytical Rubric for the Accessing Information Performance Task

Criteria	4	3	2	1
Performance indicator 1.5.1 with infused content—Describe the relationship between healthy behaviors, such as using safety equipment, and personal health.[1,p24]	The advertisement thoroughly describes five facts about how sports safety affects personal health.	The advertisement adequately describes five facts about how sports safety affects personal health.	The advertisement inadequately describes five facts about how sports safety affects personal health.	The advertisement poorly describes five facts about how sports safety affects personal health.
Performance indicator 1.5.1 with infused content—Describe the relationship between healthy behaviors, such as using safety equipment, and personal health.[1,p24]	The advertisement thoroughly describes five facts about how car safety affects personal health.	The advertisement adequately describes five facts about how car safety affects personal health.	The advertisement inadequately describes five facts about how car safety affects personal health.	The advertisement poorly describes five facts about how car safety affects personal health.
Performance indicator 3.5.1 with infused content—Identify in advertisements characteristics of valid health information, products, and services.[1,p28]	The advertisement thoroughly identified the eight characteristics of valid information accessed to complete the advertisement.	The advertisement adequately identified the eight characteristics of valid information accessed to complete the advertisement.	The advertisement inadequately identified the eight characteristics of valid information accessed to complete the advertisement.	The advertisement poorly identified the eight characteristics of valid information accessed to complete the advertisement.
Creativity	The advertisement is an excellent example of creativity.	The advertisement is a very good example of creativity.	The advertisement is a fair example of creativity.	The advertisement is a poor example of creativity.
Spelling	The spelling is always correct.	The spelling is sometimes correct.	The spelling is rarely correct.	The spelling is never correct.
Grammar	The grammar is always correct.	The grammar is sometimes correct.	The grammar is rarely correct.	The grammar is never correct.

Name _____

Total possible points – 24   **Your points - _____**   **Your grade - _____**

HOW THE COORDINATED SCHOOL HEALTH TEAM CONTRIBUTES TO DECREASING UNINTENTIONAL INJURIES AND INCREASING THE SKILL OF ACCESSING INFORMATION

Health Education

- Teach the skill of accessing information, products, and services.
- Teach how to develop healthy behaviors.
- Explain the importance of determining whether information, a product, or a service is valid and enhances health.

Physical Education

- Promote healthy behaviors.
- Explain how to access valid health information, products, and services.
- Explain the importance of determining if sports safety information, safety equipment, or a service is valid and enhances health.

Health Services

- Provide resources for valid sources of information, products, and services to enhance health.

Nutrition Services

- Hang posters about healthy food choices based on valid sources of information.

Counseling, Psychological, and Social Services

- Provide valid health resources to families and students.

Healthy School Environment

- Hang posters that promote healthy behaviors based on valid sources of information.
- Provide valid sources of information and resources that students can access in the school and community.
- Promote safety.

Health Promotion for Staff

- Provide staff training about identifying valid sources of information, products, and services.
- Model safety practices such as wearing a seat belt.

Family and Community Involvement

- Provide training on how to access valid sources of information, products, and services.
- Request that businesses display health-enhancing messages from valid sources of information.
- Model safety practices such as wearing a seat belt.

Grades 6–8

To achieve proficiency in Standard 3, Grades 6–8, students analyze, access, determine, describe, and locate valid information, products, and services to enhance health.

To teach Standard 3, explain why it is important to access valid information, why accessing valid information, products, and services is relevant to the health and well-

being of the students, and how this capacity relates to other skills. Present the performance indicators and a means to achieve them, model the skill, and provide practice time. Use formative assessments while the students are learning and practicing to improve your teaching and their learning.

For example:

The students in Mr. Anthony's classes are worried about getting the flu and other adolescent problems, such as acne and whitening their teeth. Some refuse the flu shot because they hate needles and have heard it makes them sick. Other spent considerable money trying different acne and teeth whitening products.

Mr. Anthony is planning a unit on accessing information, focusing on these issues. He explains how to analyze the validity and reliability of sources of information, products, and services in print and on the Internet.

He asks his students:

- What does validity mean? *(Truthful)*
- What does reliability mean? *(Trustworthy, dependable)*
- How can you determine if print information about a product or service is valid and reliable?
- How can you determine if a website is valid and reliable?

To determine if the students understand, he assigns them three questions to research using the Internet and the website evaluation tool.

1. How does the flu shot protect you against getting the flu?

2. How does acne medicine work?

3. How do teeth whiteners work?

At the end of class, the students explain why the website was a valid/invalid, reliable/unreliable source of information.

Website Evaluation Tool (Table 7.9)

When the students are learning the skill, provide adequate time for them to practice before they demonstrate proficiency through an authentic assessment. While practicing, use formative assessments (Chapter 4) to check for their understanding. Use the feedback to show students how to improve performance, thereby encouraging them to improve.

Once the students demonstrate the skill, teach the health content. Design a prompt that allows them to display their knowledge of health content while accessing valid sources of information and products and services. As the students practice, use formative assessments to redirect and encourage them.

> ## Grades 6–8
>
> 3.8.1 Analyze the validity of health information, products, and services.
> 3.8.2 Access valid health information from home, school, and community.
> 3.8.3 Determine the accessibility of products that enhance health.
> 3.8.4 Describe situations that may require professional health services.
> 3.8.5 Locate valid and reliable health products and services.[1,p28]

TABLE 7.9 Website Evaluation Tool

Name _____

I. Website Information

A. Title of the site _____

B. Subject of the site _____

C. Website address _____

D. What is the significance of the domain name? (.org, .gov, .edu, .com, etc.)

_____

E. Who is the intended audience? _____

F. What is the objective of the site? _____

_____

	Agree	Disagree	N/A
Directions: circle the number that best represents the site.	2	1	0
II. Website information			
A. The purpose of the site is clearly stated.	2	1	0
B. The information does not appear to be an infomercial (an advertisement posing as health information).	2	1	0
C. There is no bias (favoritism).			
D. If the site is opinionated, the author discusses all sides of the issue, respecting each point of view.	2	1	0
E. All aspects of the subject are covered sufficiently.	2	1	0
F. External links fully cover the subject. If not needed, place a 0 under N/A.	2	1	0
G. The site has been updated in the last six months.	2	1	0
Section II score _____			
III. Accuracy			
A. The information is accurate.	2	1	0
B. Sources are clearly documented.	2	1	0
C. The website states that it conforms to the Health on the Net (www.hom.ch/HONcode/Conduct.html.) code principles.	2	1	0
Section III score _____			
IV. Author			
A. The site is sponsored by or is associated with an institution or organization.	2	1	0
B. Individually created sites: author's/editor's credentials (educational background, professional affiliations, certifications, previous writing, professional experience) are clearly stated.	2	1	0
C. Contact information (e-mail, address, and/or phone number) for the author/editor or webmaster is included.	2	1	0
Section IV score _____			
V. Audience			
A. It is evident whom (academic, youth, minority, general, etc.) the author is addressing.	2	1	0
B. The level of detail is appropriate.	2	1	0
C. The reading level is appropriate.	2	1	0
D. Technical terms are appropriate.	2	1	0
Section V score _____			

(continues)

TABLE 7.9   Website Evaluation Tool *(continued)*

	Agree	Disagree	N/A
VII. Navigation			
A. Internal links increase the usefulness of the site.	2	1	0
B. Information is retrieved in a reasonable amount of time.	2	1	0
C. A search instrument is required to make this site functional.	2	1	0
D. A search instrument is provided.	2	1	0
E. The site is organized logically, making it easy to find information.	2	1	0
F. If software is needed to use the page, download links are included (For example, Adobe).	2	1	0
Section VII score _____			
VIII. External Links			
A. Links are relevant and suitable for this site.	2	1	0
B. Links function properly.	2	1	0
C. Links are current and reflect changes that occur in the field.	2	1	0
D. Links are appropriate for the audience.	2	1	0
E. Links connect to reliable information from dependable sources.	2	1	0
F. The page includes links to appropriate organizations.	2	1	0
Section VIII score _____			
IX. Structure			
A. Educational graphics and art add to the helpfulness of the site.	2	1	0
B. Decorative graphics do not significantly slow downloading.	2	1	0
C. Text-only option exits for text-only web browsers.	2	1	0
D. Usefulness of the site is unaffected when using text-only option.	2	1	0
E. Options (large print, audio) exist for disabled persons.	2	1	0
F. If audio and video components of the site cannot be accessed, the information there is still complete.	2	1	0
Section IX score _____			
Total Score _____			

To find the percentage, divide the total score by the highest possible score (70)

Total score/70=%

Percentage _____

Interpretation		
90–100%	Excellent	This website is an excellent source of information that is easy to access and understand.
75–89%	Adequate	The site has relevant information and can be navigated easily. It is a good source but may be incomplete.
0–74%	Poor	This site is not recommended for use.
		Validity and reliability of information cannot be verified.
		The site contains information that is not accessible or links do not work.[28]

Source: Courtesy of Leslie Levine, MPH.

WHAT DOES THE SKILL OF ACCESSING VALID SOURCES OF HEALTH INFORMATION, PRODUCTS, AND SERVICES LOOK LIKE IN THE MIDDLE SCHOOL CLASSROOM?

While preparing first aid lessons, Mr. Dennis researched some common causes of shock and breathing problems among middle school students. He discovered that 3 million children under the age of 18 have a food allergy, and that these allergies have increased 18% among the population under the age of 18. He also discovered that these allergy sufferers are 2–4 times more likely to have asthma.[7,p2]

Mr. Dennis also learned that 1–2% of the population is allergic to peanuts (tree nuts, 18% and cashews, 17%). In fact, reactions to these nuts are the most common cause of anaphylactic shock in children.[29,p370] Most deaths from anaphylaxis occur in individuals older than 10,[30,p1071] and a high number of victims are adolescents and young adults.[29,p370]

Mr. Dennis thought his middle school students should be informed about this problem and know what to do as first responders. He learned that most allergic reactions occur in the home and that learning how to treat those emergencies is important, especially when many of his students babysit younger siblings or neighborhood children.

Mrs. Bennett, the nurse, uses staff meetings to explain the signs and symptoms of food allergies and asthma and what to do when a student has a reaction. Over 10 million children under 18 have asthma[31,p16] and are at greater risk for fatal anaphylaxis.[30,p1074] In fact, studies in the United Kingdom showed that 60–75% of children allergic to peanuts also have asthma.[29,p369] The nurse knows who the asthmatic children are and is aware that most of them use inhalers. Her goal is to keep the children healthy and attending school.

In planning his accessing information, products, and services unit, Mr. Dennis thought the students would benefit from learning where on the Internet they can find valid and reliable information about these common health issues.

Mr. Dennis selects particular performance indicators that address a specific skill and content.

Standard 3—Students will demonstrate the ability to access valid information, and products and services to enhance health.[1,p28]

Performance indicator 3.8.1—Analyze the validity of health information, products, and services found on the Internet.[1,p28]

Performance indicator 3.8.1 with infused content— Analyze the validity of food allergy and asthma information, products, and services found on the Internet.[1,p28]

Standard 1—Students comprehend concepts related to health promotion and disease prevention to enhance health.[1,p24]

Performance indicator 1.8.5—Describe ways to reduce or prevent injuries and other adolescent health problems.[1,p25]

Performance indicator 1.8.5 with infused content— Describe ways to reduce or prevent injuries and other adolescent health problems that result from food allergies or asthma.[1,p25]

By linking the skill and content performance indicators, the teacher has a clear idea of how to plan the accessing information unit lessons.

The first step in planning is to think through the unit by completing the performance task template. Upon completion, the teacher has most of the information to introduce the prompt to the students.

When planning for the prompt, also include all the back-up information, holistic rubrics, analytical rubrics, and worksheets the students need to complete the task. Designing skills-based lessons requires considerable preparation, but once the teacher distributes it and explains the task, the students are responsible for the results. Students learn with good coaching (formative assessments) to demonstrate proficiency in content and skill.

The following is a performance task for a Grade 7 unit that concentrates on accessing valid information from the Internet about food allergies and asthma. The first section is for the teacher and demonstrates planning for authentic assessment that embodies the performance indicators 3.8.1 and 1.8.5. The second extracts information from the teacher section and transforms it into the student prompt and support materials.

When preparing for this authentic assessment, the teacher designs a rubric and distributes it to the students along with the prompt. It is crucial for students to know how they are being assessed before the project begins in order for them to produce evidence of their proficiency in the standards.

Standard 3 Performance Task: Grade 7—Accessing Information About Food Allergies and Asthma.

I. Which state standard(s) does this performance task address?

II. Topic: What areas of health does this project assess? Why is it important? What is the focus of the project?[1,p237]

    A. This performance task assesses the health area of Prevention/Control of Disease and Injury Prevention/Safety.

    B. It is important because incidents of food allergies and asthma affect the health, attendance, and academic achievement of middle school students.

    C. The focus of the project is to evaluate websites to determine whether the health information is valid.

III. Key Concepts: What basic concepts should the students know?[1,p237]

    Standard 1—Students comprehend concepts related to health promotion and disease prevention to enhance health.[1,p24]

    Performance indicator 1.8.5 with infused content—Describe ways to reduce or prevent injuries and other adolescent health problems that result from food allergies or asthma.[1,p25]

    A. Food allergies

        1. General information

            a. 1–2% of the population is allergic to peanuts; 18% and 17%, respectively, to tree nuts and cashews.

            b. Reactions to peanuts and tree nuts are the most common cause of anaphylactic shock in children.[30,p1075]

            c. Most deaths from anaphylaxis occur in people older than 10.[30,p1071]

            d. A high number of victims are adolescents and young adults.[29,p370]

            e. Most allergy reactions occur in the home.

        2. Cause

            a. The immune system mistakenly attacks a food protein.

            b. Certain foods trigger a sudden release of histamines, causing an allergic reaction.[32]

        3. Diagnosis

            a. Skin prick test or immunoassay test for antibodies.

        4. Treatment

            a. Epinephrine (EpiPen or Twinject) is the medication of choice for a severe reaction.

            b. The EpiPen injects a dose of adrenaline into the thigh to reverse the allergic reaction.[16]

        5. Prevention

            a. Be aware of the signs of allergic reactions:

                1. Tingling sensation in the mouth

                2. Swelling of the tongue and throat

                3. Difficulty breathing

                4. Hives

                5. Vomiting

                6. Abdominal cramps

                7. Diarrhea

                8. Drop in blood pressure

                9. Loss of consciousness

                10. Death

            b. Avoid foods that trigger allergy.

            c. Read all labels. If a product does not have a label, do not eat it.

            d. Contact the manufacturer if there is a question about ingredients.

        6. First aid

            a. Call 911.

            b. Ask if the person has an EpiPen and needs help.

(continues)

        c. Inject the epinephrine into the person's thigh.
        d. Lay the person on his back.
        e. Loosen tight clothing and cover the person with a blanket.
        f. If vomiting, turn the person on his side to prevent choking.
        g. If there are no signs of breathing, coughing, or movement, begin CPR.[33]
    B. Asthma
        1. General information
            a. Over 1 million children under 18 have been diagnosed with asthma.[34,p16]
            b. Students who have asthma are at greater risk for fatal anaphylaxis.[30,p1074]
            c. A study in the United Kingdom indicates that 60–70% of children allergic to peanuts also have asthma.[29,p369]
        2. Cause
            a. Inflammation and narrowing of the airways.
            b. Symptoms include recurring wheezing, tightness in the chest, shortness of breath, and coughing.[35]
        3. Diagnosis
            a. Based on medical history
            b. Results of a physical exam
            c. Results from tests
                1. Lung function
                2. Allergy test
                3. Airway sensitivity (bronchoprovocation test)
                4. Tests for conditions similar to asthma
                5. Chest x-ray
                6. Electrocardiogram[35]
        4. Treatment
            a. There is no cure.
            b. Follow an action plan to manage the asthma.
            c. Medicines
                1. Long term control
                2. Quick relief[35]
        5. Prevention
            a. Use peak flow meter to monitor and control asthma.
            b. Avoid asthma triggers.[35]
            c. Follow the asthma action plan.
            d. Use medicines prescribed by the doctor.
            e. Track asthma symptoms.
            f. Get regular check-ups.[35]
        6. First aid
            a. Call the doctor if medicine does not relieve the symptoms.
            b. Call 911 if you have trouble walking and talking from being out of breath or have blue lips or fingernails.[35]
IV. Skills: Which of the seven National Health Education Standards does this performance task address?[5,p237]

    Standard 3—Students will demonstrate the ability to access valid information and products and services to enhance health.[1,p28]

        Performance indicator 3.8.1 with infused content—Analyze the validity of food allergy and asthma information, products, and services found on the Internet.[1,p28]

    A. Evaluate two websites that provide information about food allergies and two more that provide information about asthma.

(continues)

B. Select one valid food allergy website and defend its validity based on the criteria on the evaluation worksheet.

C. Select one valid asthma website and defend its validity based on the criteria on the evaluation worksheet.

V. Curricula connections—What other subject areas does this project support?[5,p237]

    English Language Arts

    Technology education

VI. Student directions and assessment criteria[5,p238]

A. Project description—Write and attach an engaging prompt that draws the student into the project.[5,p238]

Shelly's sister, Anna, is allergic to peanuts. In the bus on the way home, some children eat peanut products and Anna is afraid of having a reaction in the afternoon and needing first aid.

Shelly watches her sister until her mother comes home and she wants to be prepared if Anna needs help.

B. Your challenge: Provide a challenge or mission statement that describes the project.[5,p239]

Your challenge is to help Shelly find valid sources of information about food allergies and asthma so she can educate herself and be prepared to administer first aid.

C. Assessment criteria[5,p239]

You are assessed on the following content:

Performance indicator 1.8.5 with infused content—Describe ways to reduce or prevent injuries and other adolescent health problems that result from food allergies or asthma.[1,p25]

1. Based on the information provided by a valid website, provide three facts each about general information, the causes, diagnosis, treatment, and prevention of food allergies.

    a. Explain how to administer first aid to a person experiencing the symptoms of a food allergy.

    b. Explain how to use an EpiPen.

2. Based on the information provided by a valid website, provide three facts each about general information, the causes, diagnosis, treatment, and prevention of asthma.

    a. Explain how to administer first aid to a person experiencing the symptoms of asthma.

You will be assessed on the following skill:

Performance indicator 3.8.1 with infused content—Analyze the validity of food allergy and asthma information, products, and services found on the Internet.[1,p28]

1. Use the website evaluation worksheet to analyze the validity of two websites that provide information about *food allergies*. Defend the most valid one.

2. Use the website evaluation worksheet to compare the validity of two websites that provide information about *asthma*. Defend the most valid one.

3. Use the website with the most validity to provide the content necessary for the assessment above.

Student Project

1. Use the website evaluation worksheet to analyze the validity of two food allergy websites and two asthma websites. (4 worksheets)

2. PowerPoint presentation or poster

    a. Analyze two websites for food allergies and two for asthma. Include a defense of the most valid food allergy and asthma websites.

    b. The presentation must contain three facts each about general information, the causes, diagnosis, treatment, and prevention of food allergies and asthma.

3. A demonstration must show how to administer first aid for food allergies and asthma, including anaphylaxis.

Eastover Middle School
Mr. Dennis

Name _____

Shelly's sister, Anna, is allergic to peanuts. In the bus on the way home, some children eat peanut products and Anna is afraid of having a reaction in the afternoon and needing first aid.

Shelly watches her sister until her mother comes home and she wants to be prepared if Anna needs help.

Your challenge is to help Shelly find valid sources of information about food allergies and asthma so she can educate herself. You must also explain how to administer first aid for food allergies and asthma, including first aid for anaphylaxis.

Your project must include the following:

1. Use the website evaluation worksheet to analyze the validity of two food allergy websites and two asthma websites. (4 worksheets)

2. PowerPoint presentation or poster

   a. Analyze two websites for food allergies and two for asthma. Include a defense of the most valid food allergy and asthma websites.

   b. The presentation must contain three facts each about general information, the causes, diagnosis, treatment, and prevention of food allergies and asthma.

3. A demonstration must show how to administer first aid for food allergies and asthma, including anaphylaxis.

ASSESSMENT MATERIALS

TABLE 7.10   Assessment—Website Evaluation Tool

Name _____

   I. **Website Information**

   A. Title of the site _____

   B. Subject of the site _____

   C. Website address _____

   D. What is the significance of the domain name? (.org, .gov, .edu, .com, etc.)

   _____

   E. Who is the intended audience? _____

   F. What is the objective of the site? _____

   _____

	Agree	Disagree	N/A
Directions: circle the number that best represents the site.	2	1	0
II. Website information			
A. The purpose of the site is clearly stated.	2	1	0
B. The information does not appear to be an infomercial (an advertisement posing as health information).	2	1	0
C. There is no bias (favoritism).			

(continues)

TABLE 7.10 Assessment—Website Evaluation Tool *(continued)*

	Agree	Disagree	N/A
D. If the site is opinionated, the author discusses all sides of the issue, respecting each point of view.	2	1	0
E. All aspects of the subject are covered sufficiently.	2	1	0
F. External links fully cover the subject. If not needed, place a 0 under N/A.	2	1	0
G. The site has been updated in the last six months.	2	1	0

Section II score _____

III. Accuracy

	Agree	Disagree	N/A
A. The information is accurate.	2	1	0
B. Sources are clearly documented.	2	1	0
C. The website states that it conforms to the Health on the Net (www.hom.ch/HONcode/Conduct.html.) code principles.	2	1	0

Section III score _____

IV. Author

	Agree	Disagree	N/A
A. The site is sponsored by or is associated with an institution or organization.	2	1	0
B. Individually created sites: author's/editor's credentials (educational background, professional affiliations, certifications, previous writing, professional experience) are clearly stated.	2	1	0
C. Contact information (e-mail, address, and/or phone number) for the author/editor or webmaster is included.	2	1	0

Section IV score _____

V. Audience

	Agree	Disagree	N/A
A. It is evident whom (academic, youth, minority, general, etc.) the author is addressing.	2	1	0
B. The level of detail is appropriate.	2	1	0
C. The reading level is appropriate.	2	1	0
D. Technical terms are appropriate.	2	1	0

Section V score _____

VII. Navigation

	Agree	Disagree	N/A
A. Internal links increase the usefulness of the site.	2	1	0
B. Information is retrieved in a reasonable amount of time.	2	1	0
C. A search instrument is required to make this site functional.	2	1	0
D. A search instrument is provided.	2	1	0
E. The site is organized logically, making it easy to find information.	2	1	0
F. If software is needed to use the page, download links are included (For example, Adobe).	2	1	0

Section VII score _____

VIII. External Links

	Agree	Disagree	N/A
A. Links are relevant and suitable for this site.	2	1	0
B. Links function properly.	2	1	0
C. Links are current and reflect changes that occur in the field.	2	1	0
D. Links are appropriate for the audience.	2	1	0

(continues)

TABLE 7.10   Assessment—Website Evaluation Tool *(continued)*

	Agree	Disagree	N/A
E. Links connect to reliable information from dependable sources.	2	1	0
F. The page includes links to appropriate organizations.	2	1	0

Section VIII score _____

IX. Structure

	Agree	Disagree	N/A
A. Educational graphics and art add to the helpfulness of the site.	2	1	0
B. Decorative graphics do not significantly slow downloading.	2	1	0
C. Text-only option exits for text-only web browsers.	2	1	0
D. Usefulness of the site is unaffected when using text-only option.	2	1	0
E. Options (large print, audio) exist for persons with disabilities.	2	1	0
F. If audio and video components of the site cannot be accessed, the information there is still complete.	2	1	0

Section IX score _____

Total Score _____

To find the percentage, divide the total score by the highest possible score (70)

Total score/70=%

Percentage _____

Interpretation

90–100%	Excellent	This website is an excellent source of information that is easy to access and understand.
75–89%	Adequate	The site has relevant information and can be navigated easily. It is a good source but may be incomplete.
0–74%	Poor	This site is not recommended for use.
		Validity and reliability of information cannot be verified.
		The site contains information that is not accessible or links do not work.[28]

Source: Courtesy of Leslie Levine, MPH.

TABLE 7.11   Analytical Rubric to Assess the Food Allergy Portion of the PowerPoint or Poster

Grade 7

Criteria	4	3	2	1
Performance indicator 1.8.5 with infused content—Describe ways to reduce or prevent injuries and other adolescent health problems that result from food allergies or asthma.[1,p25]	Student accurately describes three general facts about food allergies.	Student's description of three general facts about food allergies is mostly accurate.	Student's description of three general facts about food allergies has a few inaccuracies.	Student's description of three general facts about food allergies is mostly inaccurate.

(continues)

TABLE 7.11 Analytical Rubric to Assess the Food Allergy Portion of the PowerPoint or Poster *(continued)*

Grade 7

Criteria	4	3	2	1
Performance indicator 1.8.5 with infused content—Describe ways to reduce or prevent injuries and other adolescent health problems that result from food allergies or asthma.[1,p25]	Student accurately describes three general facts about the causes of food allergies.	Student's description of three general facts about the causes of food allergies is mostly accurate.	Student's description of three general facts about the causes of food allergies has a few inaccuracies.	Student's description of three general facts about the causes of food allergies is mostly inaccurate.
Performance indicator 1.8.5 with infused content—Describe ways to reduce or prevent injuries and other adolescent health problems that result from food allergies or asthma.[1,p25]	Student accurately describes three general facts about the diagnosis of food allergies.	Student's description of three general facts about the diagnosis of food allergies is mostly accurate.	Student's description of three general facts about the diagnosis of food allergies has a few inaccuracies.	Student's description of three general facts about the diagnosis of food allergies is mostly inaccurate.
Performance indicator 1.8.5 with infused content—Describe ways to reduce or prevent injuries and other adolescent health problems that result from food allergies or asthma.[1,p25]	Student accurately describes three general facts about the treatment of food allergies.	Student's description of three general facts about the treatment of food allergies is mostly accurate.	Student's description of three general facts about the treatment of food allergies has a few inaccuracies.	Student's description of three general facts about the treatment of food allergies is mostly inaccurate.
Performance indicator 1.8.5 with infused content—Describe ways to reduce or prevent injuries and other adolescent health problems that result from food allergies or asthma.[1,p25]	Student accurately describes three general facts about the prevention of food allergies.	Student's description of three general facts about the prevention of food allergies is mostly accurate.	Student's description of three general facts about the prevention of food allergies has a few inaccuracies.	Student's description of three general facts about the prevention of food allergies is mostly inaccurate.
Performance indicator 1.8.5 with infused content—Describe ways to reduce or prevent injuries and other adolescent health problems that result from food allergies or asthma.[1,p25]	Student accurately demonstrates first aid for food allergies.	Student's description of first aid for food allergies is mostly accurate.	Student's description of first aid for food allergies has a few inaccuracies.	Student's description of first aid for food allergies is mostly inaccurate.

(continues)

TABLE 7.11 Analytical Rubric to Assess the Food Allergy Portion of the PowerPoint or Poster *(continued)*

Grade 7

Criteria	4	3	2	1
Creativity	The student presented a poster or PowerPoint that shows excellent creativity.	The student presented a poster or PowerPoint that shows good creativity.	The student presented a poster or PowerPoint that shows fair creativity.	The student presented a poster or PowerPoint that shows poor creativity.
Speech	The student always speaks clearly.	The student sometimes speaks clearly.	The student rarely speaks clearly.	The student never speaks clearly.

Name _____

Total possible points – 32   Your points - _____   Your grade - _____

TABLE 7.12 Analytical Rubric to Assess the Asthma Portion of the PowerPoint or Poster

Grade 7

Criteria	4	3	2	1
Performance indicator 1.8.5 with infused content—Describe ways to reduce or prevent injuries and other adolescent health problems that result from food allergies or asthma.[1,p25]	Student accurately describes three general facts about asthma.	Student's description of three general facts about asthma is mostly accurate.	Student's description of three general facts about asthma has a few inaccuracies.	Student's description of three general facts about asthma is mostly inaccurate.
Performance indicator 1.8.5 with infused content—Describe ways to reduce or prevent injuries and other adolescent health problems that result from food allergies or asthma.[1,p25]	Student accurately describes three general facts about the causes of asthma.	Student's description of three general facts about the causes of asthma is mostly accurate.	Student's description of three general facts about the causes of asthma has a few inaccuracies.	Student's description of three general facts about the causes of asthma is mostly inaccurate.

(continues)

TABLE 7.12 Analytical Rubric to Assess the Asthma Portion of the PowerPoint or Poster *(continued)*

Grade 7

Criteria	4	3	2	1
*Performance indicator 1.8.5 with infused content—*Describe ways to reduce or prevent injuries and other adolescent health problems that result from food allergies or asthma.[1,p25]	Student accurately describes three general facts about the diagnosis of asthma.	Student's description of three general facts about the diagnosis of asthma is mostly accurate.	Student's description of three general facts about the diagnosis of asthma has a few inaccuracies.	Student's description of three general facts about the diagnosis of asthma is mostly inaccurate.
*Performance indicator 1.8.5 with infused content—*Describe ways to reduce or prevent injuries and other adolescent health problems that result from food allergies or asthma.[1,p25]	Student accurately describes three general facts about the treatment of asthma.	Student's description of three general facts about the treatment of asthma is mostly accurate.	Student's description of three general facts about the treatment of asthma has a few inaccuracies.	Student's description of three general facts about the treatment of asthma is mostly inaccurate.
*Performance indicator 1.8.5 with infused content—*Describe ways to reduce or prevent injuries and other adolescent health problems that result from food allergies or asthma.[1,p25]	Student accurately describes three general facts about the prevention of asthma.	Student's description of three general facts about the prevention of asthma is mostly accurate.	Student's description of three general facts about the prevention of asthma has a few inaccuracies.	Student's description of three general facts about the prevention of asthma is mostly inaccurate.
*Performance indicator 1.8.5 with infused content—*Describe ways to reduce or prevent injuries and other adolescent health problems that result from food allergies or asthma.[1,p25]	Student accurately demonstrates first aid for asthma.	Student's description of first aid for asthma is mostly accurate.	Student's description of first aid for asthma has a few inaccuracies.	Student's description of first aid for asthma is mostly inaccurate.
Creativity	The student presented a poster or PowerPoint that shows excellent creativity.	The student presented a poster or PowerPoint that shows good creativity.	The student presented a poster or PowerPoint that shows fair creativity.	The student presented a poster or PowerPoint that shows poor creativity.
Speech	The student always speaks clearly.	The student sometimes speaks clearly.	The student rarely speaks clearly.	The student never speaks clearly.

Name _____

Total possible points – 32   Your points - _____   Your grade - _____

TABLE 7.13 Analytical Rubric to Assess the Validity of Websites Portion of the PowerPoint or Poster

Criteria	4	3	2	1
Performance indicator 3.8.1 with infused content—Analyze the validity of food allergy and asthma information, products, and services found on the Internet.[1,p28]	Student accurately analyzes two websites for food allergies.	Student's analysis of two websites for food allergies is mostly accurate.	Student's analysis of two websites for food allergies has a few inaccuracies.	Student's analysis of two websites for food allergies is mostly inaccurate.
Defend allergy site	Student thoroughly defends the most valid food allergy website.	Student adequately defends the most valid food allergy website.	Student inadequately defends the most valid food allergy website.	Student poorly defends the most valid food allergy website.
Performance indicator 3.8.1 with infused content—Analyze the validity of food allergy and asthma information, products, and services found on the Internet.[1,p28]	Student accurately analyzes two websites for asthma.	Student's analysis of two websites for asthma is mostly accurate.	Student's analysis of two websites for asthma has a few inaccuracies.	Student's analysis of two websites for asthma is mostly inaccurate.
Defend asthma site	Student thoroughly defends the most valid asthma website.	Student adequately defends the most valid asthma website.	Student inadequately defends the most valid asthma website.	Student poorly defends the most valid asthma website.
Creativity	The student presented a poster or PowerPoint that showed excellent creativity.	The student presented a poster or PowerPoint that showed good creativity.	The student presented a poster or PowerPoint that showed fair creativity.	The student presented a poster or PowerPoint that showed poor creativity.
Speech	The student always speaks clearly.	The student sometimes speaks clearly.	The student rarely speaks clearly.	The student never speaks clearly.

Name _____

Total possible points – 24   **Your points - _____**   **Your grade - _____**

HOW THE COORDINATED SCHOOL HEALTH TEAM SUPPORTS WAYS TO REDUCE OR PREVENT INJURIES AND OTHER ADOLESCENT HEALTH PROBLEMS THAT RESULT FROM FOOD ALLERGIES AND ASTHMA AND ACCESS VALID INFORMATION, PRODUCTS, AND SERVICES TO ENHANCE HEALTH

Health Education

- Explain the importance of determining if information, a product, or service is valid and enhances health.
- Explain how accessing valid information, products, and services relate to other skills.
- Teach the skill of evaluating websites to access valid information, products, and services to enhance health.
- Teach how reduce or prevent injuries caused by food allergies and asthma.
- Teach first aid skills to respond to a food allergy or asthma.

Physical Education

- Explain how to be physically active if you have a food allergy or asthma.
- Explain how to access valid health physical education information, products, and services from the Internet.

Health Services

- Provide valid and reliable information about food allergies and asthma.
- Provide support for students with food allergies and asthma.
- Provide resources for valid sources of information, products, and services to enhance health.

Nutrition Services

- Hang posters about food allergies based on valid sources of information.
- Provide allergy-free lunch tables and chairs.
- Provide safe food for students with food allergies.

Counseling, Psychological, and Social Services

- Provide valid health resources to families and students.
- Provide support for students with food allergies and asthma.

Healthy School Environment

- Hang posters that promote healthy behaviors based on valid sources of information.

- Provide valid sources of information and resources that students can access in the school or community.
- Provide spaces in the school that are safe for students with food allergies and asthma.
- Provide a clean environment for students.

Health Promotion for Staff

- Provide professional development training on food allergies and asthma.
- Provide staff training for identifying valid sources of information, products, and services.

Family and Community Involvement

- Help families establish support groups in which they strategize how to help one another's children attend school safely.
- Encourage restaurants to provide a menu and environment that is safe for children with food allergies and asthma.
- Provide training on how to access valid sources of information, products, and services.
- Request that businesses display health-enhancing messages based on valid sources of information.

Grades 9–12

To achieve proficiency in Standard 3, Grade 9–12 students must learn to evaluate the validity and accessibility of sources of information, products, and services. They demonstrate how to use these resources and determine when professional health services are needed.

To teach Standard 3, explain why it is important and relevant to access valid sources of information, products, and services and how this skill relates to the other National Health Education Standards. According to the performance indicators chosen, present and explain how to reach proficiency in the skill. Model it so the students can see the skill in action. Provide adequate time for students to practice the skill and show their proficiency through an

Grades 9–12

3.12.1 Evaluate the validity of health information, products, and services.

3.12.2 Use resources from home, school, and community that provide valid health information.

3.12.3 Determine the accessibility of products and services that enhance health.

3.12.4 Determine when professional health services may be required.

3.12.5 Access valid and reliable health products and services.[1,p29]

authentic assessment. Use formative assessments (Chapter 4) to provide feedback and encouragement and to improve instruction.

For example:

Jamal and Everett are best friends and juniors at Brewster High School. Each became sexually active at age 14. Jamal always uses a condom but sometimes Everett does not. Recently, Everett has experienced a lot of pain and a burning sensation when he urinates. He told Jamal, and together they searched online to figure out what was wrong.

Jamal and Everett went to Wikipedia and found non-referenced information about Everett's symptoms. When they checked Wikipedia, they found that anyone could post information on the site, regardless of his or her knowledge or expertise so they wanted to check a more reputable site. They then went to the CDC website and found recently updated, documented information created by experts in the field.

Because of what they learned, Everett wanted to get medical help but he did not know where to go. Jamal told him that the community health center was nearby so he made an appointment there to be checked for a sexually transmitted disease.

To reflect, ask the students:

- How did Everett and Jamal determine that Wikipedia was not a valid source of information about sexually transmitted disease? (PI 3.12.1) *(When they checked Wikipedia, they found that anyone could post information on the site, regardless of his or her knowledge or expertise.)*
- What criteria made Everett and Jamal believe that the CDC website was a valid source of information? (PI 3.12.1) *(The CDC website contains updated, documented information created by experts in the field.)*
- What resources from home, school or the community did the boys use to find information about Everett's symptoms? (PI 3.12.2) *(Internet)*
- How accessible was the community health center? (PI 3.12.3) *(It was nearby)*
- Why did Everett seek professional help? (PI 3.12.4) *(Everett has experienced a lot of pain and a burning sensation when he urinates.)*
- Where did Everett seek professional help? (PI 3.12.5) *(The health clinic)*

As the students are learning the skill, provide enough time for them to practice. Use formative assessments to determine the progress of their learning. Motivate students by using feedback to show how their performance improves.

When students demonstrate understanding of the skill, teach the content. Design a prompt that allows them to showcase their knowledge of health by accessing valid sources of information, products, and services that enhance health. Use formative assessments, such as white boards (Chapter 4), during content instruction to determine student understanding.

WHAT DOES THE SKILL OF ACCESSING INFORMATION LOOK LIKE IN THE GRADE 10 CLASSROOM?

Mrs. Condon is a Grade 10 health teacher at Manston High School. In preparing for her unit on accessing valid information, products, and services, she asked her students what health information they access from the Internet. Her students told her they most often look for information about sexually transmitted diseases, diet, fitness and exercise, and sexual behaviors.[2,p1] However, when asked whether the information accessed was truthful (valid), they told her they had never thought about that issue when searching.[3,p243]

Mrs. Condon plans the unit by developing a website evaluation tool that helps students determine whether the location is valid and whether it provides accurate information about health, products, and services.

She then chooses the performance indicators for Standard 3 that meet the needs of her students.

Standard 3—Students will demonstrate the ability to access valid information and products and services to enhance health.[1,p28]

3.12.2—Use resources from home, school, and community that provide valid health information.[1,p29]

Performance indicator 3.12.2 with infused content—Students will use Internet resources from home, school, and the community to access valid information about contraception and sexually transmitted diseases.[1,p29]

After selecting the performance indicator for the skill, Mrs. Condon chooses the performance indicator for Standard 1.

Standard 1—Students will comprehend concepts related to health promotion and disease prevention to enhance health.[1,p24]

1.12.1—Predict how healthy behaviors can affect health status.[1,p25]

Performance indicator 1.12.1 with infused content—Students will predict how using contraceptives can protect against pregnancy and decrease the transmission of sexually transmitted infections.[1,p25]

By linking the skill and content performance indicators, the teacher has a clear idea of how to plan the lessons for the accessing information unit.

The first step in planning is to think through the unit by completing the performance task template. Upon completion, the teacher has most of the information to introduce the prompt to the students.

When planning the prompt, she includes all the back-up information, holistic and analytical rubrics, and worksheets that the students need to complete the task. Students use the criteria on the rubric to stay on task. Designing skills-based lessons requires considerable preparation, but once the information is distributed and explained, the students are responsible for the results. They learn with good coaching (formative assessment) to demonstrate proficiency in content and skill.

The following is an example of a performance task for a Grade 10 unit in accessing valid Internet information that focuses on using contraceptives to protect against pregnancy and decreasing the transmission of sexually transmitted infections.

The first section is for the teacher and demonstrates how to plan an authentic assessment of the performance indicators 1.12.1 and 3.12.2. The second is for the student. It extracts some of the information from the performance task and transforms it into the student prompt and support materials.

Standard 3 Performance Task: Grade 10—Accessing Valid Information About Sexuality From the Internet

I. Which state standard(s) does this performance task address?

II. Topic: What areas of health does this project assess? Why is it important? What is the focus of the project?[5,p237]

    A. This performance task assesses Personal Health and Prevention/Control of Disease.

    B. This topic is important because 46% of teens aged 15–19 in the United States have had sex at least once.[36,p1,3]

    C. Teen pregnancy rate rose 3% in 2006.

    D. Teen abortion rate increased 1%.[37]

    E. The focus of the project is for students to learn to access valid information on the Internet about contraception and sexually transmitted diseases.

        1. Accessing valid and reliable information in the health curriculum builds better health literacy skills.[3,p243]

        2. Valid and reliable information from the Internet helps teens adopt healthy behaviors and avoid unhealthy ones.[3,p243]

III. Key Concepts: What basic concepts do students need to know?[5,p237]

    Standard 1—Students will comprehend concepts related to health promotion and disease prevention to enhance health.[1,p24]

    Performance indicator 1.12.1 with infused content—Students will predict how using contraceptives can protect against pregnancy and decrease the transmission of sexually transmitted infections.[1,p25]

    A. The condom is the most common contraceptive used by teens during their first intercourse (66% females, 71% males)[36,p2]

    B. 83% of teen females and 91% of teen males used contraceptives during their most recent intercourse.[36,p2]

    C. Twenty-one states and the District of Columbia allow contraceptive services to minors without parental approval.[36,p2]

    D. The decline in teen pregnancy rates in the 1990s was due to a better use of contraceptives.[37,p1]

    E. Contraceptive use effectiveness (Effectiveness of a method in preventing conception when used by the general public) (**Table 7.14**)

(continues)

TABLE 7.14   Contraceptive Effectiveness Rates

Contraception	Use effectiveness	Protects against a sexually transmitted infection
IUD	99%	No
Depo-Provera	97%	No
Male Condom with spermicide	95%	Yes
Contraceptive ring, patch, and the pill[38,p369]	92%	No[1]

IV. Skills: Which of the seven National Health Education Standards skills does this performance task address?[5,p237]

Standard 3—Students will demonstrate the ability to access valid information and products and services to enhance health.[1,p28]

Performance indicator 3.12.2 with infused content—Students will use Internet resources from home, school, and the community to access valid information about contraception and sexually transmitted diseases.[1,p29]

A. Students evaluate websites (CDC.gov and Wikipedia.org) to determine their validity as sources of information about contraceptives and sexually transmitted infections.

V. Curricular connections—What other subject areas does this project support?[5,p237]

English Language Arts

Technology Education

VI. Student Directions and Assessment Criteria[5,p238]

A. Project Description—Write an engaging prompt that draws the student into the project.[5,p238]

Sean and Michael are tenth graders at Manston High School. They are sexually active and have had several partners. They talk to each other and read magazines but still have questions about sex, birth control, and sexually transmitted infections.

They do not feel comfortable talking to their parents or teachers and decided to use the Internet instead.

B. Your Challenge—Provide a challenge or mission statement that describes the project.[5,p238]

Your challenge is to help Sean and Michael find accurate information about contraception and sexually transmitted diseases from valid websites, predict the effectiveness of five types of contraception, and explain the causes, transmission, symptoms, effects, treatment, and prevention of five sexually transmitted infections.

C. Assessment Criteria[5,p239]

You are assessed on the following content:

Performance indicator 1.12.1 with infused content—Students will predict how using contraceptives can protect against pregnancy and decrease the transmission of sexually transmitted infections.[1,p25]

1. Predict the effectiveness of five different types of contraception as a result of analyzing information from a valid website.

2. Select five sexually transmitted infections and write one paragraph about each of the following:
   a. Pathogen that causes the infection
   b. Transmission
   c. Symptoms
   d. Effects on the body
   e. Treatment
   f. Prevention

(continues)

Manston High School

Name _____

Sean and Michael are tenth graders at Manston High School. They are sexually active and have had several partners. They talk to each other and read magazines to learn more but still have questions about sex, birth control, and sexually transmitted infections.

They do not feel comfortable talking to their parents or teachers so they have decided to use the Internet instead.

Your challenge is to help Sean and Michael find accurate information about contraception and sexually transmitted diseases from valid websites, predict the effectiveness of five types of contraception, and explain the causes, transmission, symptoms, effects, treatment, and prevention of five sexually transmitted diseases.

1. Use the website evaluation tool to evaluate two websites (CDC.gov and Wikipedia.org) to determine their validity. Be prepared to explain the validity of each site.

2. From the valid website, use the contraceptive and sexually transmitted disease worksheets to gather information about five forms of contraception and five sexually transmitted infections.

3. Present the results through a comic book or a poster.

TABLE 7.15   Website Evaluation Tool

Two copies required. One for sexually transmitted infections and one for contraception.

Name _____

Directions: Compare the validity of the http://www.cdc.gov/std/ website to www.wikipedia.org with regard to information about contraceptive devices and sexually transmitted infections.

I. **Website Information**

A. Title of the site _____

B. Subject of the site _____

C. Website address _____

D. What is the significance of the domain name? (.org, .gov, .edu, .com, etc.)

_____

E. Who is the intended audience? _____

F. What is the objective of the site? _____

_____

(continues)

TABLE 7.15   Website Evaluation Tool *(continued)*

	CDC	Wikipedia
II. Website Information	CDC	Wikipedia
A. The purpose of the site is clearly stated.		
B. The information does not appear to be an infomercial (An advertisement posing as health information.)		
C. There is no bias (favoritism).		
D. If the site is opinionated, the author discusses all sides of the issue, respecting each point of view.		
E. All aspects of the subject are covered sufficiently.		
F. External links fully cover the subject. If not needed, place a 0 under N/A.		
G. The site has been updated in the last six months.		
III. Accuracy	CDC	Wikipedia
A. The information is accurate.		
B. Sources are clearly documented.		
C. The website states that it conforms to the Health on the Net (www.hom.ch/HONcode/Conduct.html.) code principles.		
IV. Author	CDC	Wikipedia
A. The site is sponsored by or is associated with an institution or organization.		
B. Individually created sites: author's/editor's credentials (educational background, professional affiliations, certifications, prior writing, professional experience) are clearly stated.		
C. Contact information (e-mail, address, and/or phone number) for the author/editor or web master is included.		
V. Audience	CDC	Wikipedia
A. It is evident whom (academic, youth, minority, general audience, etc.) the author is addressing.		
B. The detail is appropriate for the audience.		
C. The reading level is appropriate for the audience.		
D. Technical terms are appropriate for the audience.		
VI. Navigation	CDC	Wikipedia
A. Internal links increase the usefulness of the site.		
B. Information is retrieved in a reasonable amount of time.		
C. A search instrument is required to make this site functional		
D. A search instrument is provided.		
E. The site is organized logically, making it easy to find information.		
F. If software is needed to use the page, download links are included (for example, Adobe).		
VII. External Links	CDC	Wikipedia
A. Links are relevant and suitable for this site.		
B. Links function properly.		
C. Links are current and reflect changes that occur in the field.		
D. Links are appropriate for the audience.		
E. Links connect to reliable information from dependable sources.		
F. The page includes links to appropriate organizations.		

(continues)

TABLE 7.15 Website Evaluation Tool *(continued)*

VIII. Structure	CDC	Wikipedia
A. Educational graphics and art add to the helpfulness of the site.		
B. Decorative graphics do not significantly slow downloading.		
C. Text-only option exits for text-only Web browsers.		
D. Usefulness of the site is not affected by text-only option.		
E. Options (large print, audio) exist for persons with disabilities.		
F. If audio and video components of the site cannot be accessed, the information on the site is still complete.[28]		

Reflection

Which site is valid and provides accurate information? Explain.

Source: Courtesy of Leslie Levine, MPH.

Manston High School

Contraceptive Worksheet

Name _____

Directions: Use this worksheet to gather information from a valid website about use and effectiveness of five different types of contraception (**Table 7.16**).

TABLE 7.16 Contraceptives

Website address:

Contraceptive	How Does it Work?	What is the Use Effectiveness?
1.		
2.		
3.		
4.		
5.		

Reflection

1. Which of the contraceptives provides the greatest protection against pregnancy? _____

2. Which of the contraceptives also protects against sexually transmitted infections? _____

3. Which form of contraception is very effective and protects against the transmission of sexually transmitted infections? _____

4. In your opinion, which of the contraceptives would teens prefer? Why? _____

Name _____

Directions: Use information for a valid website to examine five different sexually transmitted diseases, their causes, transmission, symptoms, effects on the body, treatment, and prevention (**Tables 7.17** and **7.18**).

TABLE 7.17   Sexually Transmitted Infection Worksheet

Website address:

	#1 STI	#2 STI	#3 STI	#4 STI	#5 STI
Pathogen that causes the infection					
How the pathogen is transmitted					
Symptoms of the infection					
Effects of the infection on the body					
Treatment of the infection					
Prevention of the infection					

TABLE 7.18   Analytical Rubric to Assess Accessing Information Comic Book or Poster

Criteria	4	3	2	1
Performance indicator 1.12.1 with infused content—Students will predict how using contraceptives can protect against pregnancy and decrease the transmission of sexually transmitted infections.[1,p25]	The student accurately predicts how five contraceptives protect against pregnancy.	The student's prediction of how five contraceptives protect against pregnancy is mostly accurate.	The student's prediction of how five contraceptives protect against pregnancy has a few inaccuracies.	The student's prediction of how five contraceptives protect against pregnancy is mostly inaccurate.
Performance indicator 1.12.1 with infused content—Students will predict how using contraceptives can protect against pregnancy and decrease the transmission of sexually transmitted infections.[1,p25]	The student accurately predicts how each contraceptive decreases the transmission of sexually transmitted infections.	The student's prediction of how each contraceptive decreases the transmission of sexually transmitted infections is mostly accurate.	The student's prediction of how each contraceptive decreases the transmission of sexually transmitted infections has a few inaccuracies.	The student's prediction of how each contraceptive decreases the transmission of sexually transmitted infections is mostly inaccurate.
Cause, transmission, symptoms, and treatment of three common sexually transmitted infections.	The student accurately explains the cause, transmission, symptoms, treatment, and prevention of five common sexually transmitted infections.	The student's explanation of the cause, transmission, symptoms, treatment, and prevention of five common sexually transmitted infections is mostly accurate.	The student's explanation of the cause, transmission, symptoms, treatment, and prevention of five common sexually transmitted infections has a few inaccuracies.	The student's explanation of the cause, transmission, symptoms, treatment, and prevention of five common sexually transmitted infections is mostly inaccurate.

(continues)

TABLE 7.18   Analytical Rubric to Assess Accessing Information Comic Book or Poster (continued)

Criteria	4	3	2	1
Performance indicator 3.12.2 with infused content—Students will use Internet resources from home, school, and the community to access valid information about contraception and sexually transmitted diseases.[1,p29]	The student thoroughly evaluates two websites to determine if they provide valid information about contraception.	The student adequately evaluates two websites to determine if they provide valid information about contraception.	The student inadequately evaluates two websites to determine if they provide valid information about contraception.	The student poorly evaluates two websites to determine if they provide valid information about contraception.
Performance indicator 3.12.2 with infused content—Students will use Internet resources from home, school, and the community to access valid information about contraception and sexually transmitted diseases.[1,p29]	The student thoroughly evaluates two websites to determine if they provide valid information about sexually transmitted infections.	The student adequately evaluates two websites to determine if they provide valid information about sexually transmitted infections.	The student inadequately evaluates two websites to determine if they provide valid information about sexually transmitted infections.	The student poorly evaluates two websites to determine if they provide valid information about sexually transmitted infections.
Validity of CDC website	Student presents five accurate reasons why the website is valid/invalid.	Student's presentation of five reasons why the website is valid/invalid is mostly accurate.	Student's presentation of five reasons why the website is valid/invalid has a few inaccuracies.	Student's presentation of five reasons why the website is valid/invalid is mostly inaccurate.
Validity of Wikipedia website	Student presents five accurate reasons why the website is valid/invalid.	Student's presentation of five reasons why the website is valid/invalid is mostly accurate.	Student's presentation of five reasons why the website is valid/invalid has a few inaccuracies.	Student's presentation of five reasons why the website is valid/invalid is mostly inaccurate.
Five appropriate/ approved graphics	The student includes five appropriate graphics.	The student includes five mostly appropriate graphics.	The student includes few appropriate graphics.	The student includes inappropriate graphics.
Creativity	Creativity of the comic book or poster is excellent.	Creativity of the comic book or poster is good.	Creativity of the comic book or poster is fair.	Creativity of the comic book or poster is poor.
Grammar	The grammar is excellent.	The grammar is good.	The grammar is fair.	The grammar is poor.

Name _____

Total possible points – 40   Your points - _____   Your grade - _____

HOW THE COORDINATED SCHOOL HEALTH TEAM CONTRIBUTES TO INCREASING KNOWLEDGE OF SEXUALLY TRANSMITTED DISEASES AND INCREASING THE SKILL OF ACCESSING INFORMATION

Health Education

- Explain the importance of determining if information, a product, or service is valid and enhances health.
- Explain how accessing valid information, products, and services relates to other skills.
- Teach the skill of evaluating websites to access valid information, products, and services to enhance health.
- Teach how to determine the use effectiveness of various forms of contraception.
- Teach the causes, effects, transmission, symptoms, treatment, and prevention of sexually transmitted infections.

Physical Education

- Promote a healthy lifestyle.
- Explain how to access valid health physical education information, products, and services from the Internet.

Health Services

- Provide valid and reliable information about contraception and sexually transmitted infections.
- Provide resources for valid sources of information about contraceptives and sexually transmitted infections.

Nutrition Services

- Hang posters that promote a healthy lifestyle.

Counseling, Psychological, and Social Services

- Provide valid health resources to families and students.
- Provide support for students who need contraceptive information and services to treat sexually transmitted infections.

Healthy School Environment

- Hang posters that promote healthy behaviors based on valid sources of information.
- Provide valid sources of information and resources that students can access in the school and community.

Health Promotion for Staff

- Provide professional development on contraception and sexually transmitted infections.

- Provide staff training about identifying valid sources of information, products, and services.

Family and Community Involvement

- Provide training on how to access valid sources of information, products, and services.
- Request that businesses display health-enhancing messages from valid sources of information.
- Provide training on how to communicate with a teen about sexuality.

Review Questions

1. Why is accessing information an important skill?

2. What is the danger of using the Internet to access health information?

3. What does Standard 3 challenge students to do with the information they learn from valid and reliable sources?

4. If the teacher assigns a nutrition project and the students are instructed to use the information on MyPyramid.com, why is this not an example of the accessing information skill?

5. What effect does having proficiency in accessing information have on an individual?

6. Why is it important to refer to the performance indicators when reviewing examples of the skill?

7. Why is it important to complete the performance task template rather than just writing the prompt and project instructions?

8. Why is it important for students to know how to access valid information, products, and services at home and in the community and not just at school?

9. Why is it important to incorporate writing, art, theater, music, poetry, etc. into performance tasks?

10. What is the relationship between health literacy, Standard 1, and Standards 2–8?

References

1. Joint Committee on National Health Education Standards. (2007). *National Health Education Standards, Second Edition, Achieving Excellence*. Atlanta: American Cancer Society.

2. Borzekowski, E. D. (2001). Adolescent Cybersurfing for Health Information. *Pediatrics & Adolescent Medicine*, 155, 813–817.

3. Gray, P. K. (2005). The Internet: A Window on Adolescent Health Literacy. *Journal of Adolescent Health*, 37(3), 243.e1–243.e7.

4. Hansen, D. D. (2003). Adolescents Searching for Health Information on the Internet: An Observational Study. *Journal of Medical Internet Research, 5*(4), e25.

5. CCSSO~SCASS Health Education Project. (2006). *Assessment Tools for School Health Education, Pre-service and Inservice edition.* Santa Cruz, CA: ToucanEd Inc.

6. Centers for Disease Control and Prevention. (2009, March 10). *Student Health and Academic Achievement.* Retrieved May 1, 2009, from Healthy Youth!: http://www.cdc .gov/HealthyYouth/health_and_academics/index.htm.

7. Centers for Disease Control and Prevention. (2009, November 18). *NCHS Data Brief, Number 9, October 2008.* Retrieved January 3, 2010, from Department of Health and Human Services, Centers for Disease Control and Prevention: http://www.cdc.gov/nchs/data/databriefs/db10.htm.

8. Merkle, S. L. (2006). Introduction: Learning From Each Other About Managing Asthma in Schools. *Journal of School Health, 76*(6), 202–204.

9. USDA. (2009, September 23). *MyPyramid Worksheet.* Retrieved December 20, 2009, from My Pyramid for Kids Worksheet: http://teamnutrition.usda.gov/resources/mpk_worksheet.pdf

10. KidsHealth. (2009). *All About Sleep.* Retrieved December 20, 2009, from KidsHealth: http://kidshealth.org/parent/general/sleep/sleep.html.

11. State of Illinois. (2005). *All Kids.* Retrieved December 20, 2009, from All Kids Member Handbook Regular Checkups: http://www.allkids.com/customers/checkups.html

12. WebMD. (2009, April 23). *Dental Care: Brushing and flossing your teeth.* Retrieved December 20, 2009, from WebMD Better Information Better Health: http://www.webmd.com/oral-health/effective-tooth-brushing-and-flossing

13. National Highway Traffic Safety Administration. (2007, February). *Traffic Safety Facts Laws.* Retrieved December 20, 2009: http://www.nhtsa.dot.gov/people/injury/TSFLaws/PDFs/810728W.pdf

14. KidsHealth. (2008, November). *Preventing Children's Sports Injuries.* Retrieved January 6, 2010: http://kidshealth.org/parent/fitness/safety/sports_safety.html

15. Centers for Disease Control and Prevention. (2009, April 27). *CDC Features Wash Your Hands.* Retrieved December 20, 2009: http://www.cdc.gov/Features/HandWashing/

16. The Children's Hospital at Westmead. (2007, October 10). *Fact Sheet.* Retrieved January 28, 2010: www.chw.edu.au/parents/factsheets/epipen_use.htm?print

17. Meeks, L. H. (2009). *Comprehensive School Health Education, Totally Awesome Strategies for Teaching Health.* (6th Ed.). New York: McGraw-Hill.

18. Centers for Disease Control and Prevention. (2009, August 20). *Ten Leading Causes of Death and Injury (Charts).* Retrieved January 5, 2010, from CDC - Scientific Data, Surveillance, & Injury Statistics - NCIPC: http://www.cdc.gov/injury/wisqars/LeadingCauses.html

19. Media Awareness Network. (2009). *How Markets Target Kids.* Retrieved January 3, 2010: http://www.media-awareness.ca/english/parents/marketing/marketers_target_kids.cfm?RenderForPrint=1. p1

20. Dakss, B. (2007, May 14). Retrieved January 29, 2010, from Marketing to "Tweens" Going Too Far? - The Early Show - CBS News: www.cbsnews.com/stories/2007/05/14earlyshow/living/parenting/main2798400.shtml

21. Massachussetts General Hospital. (2010). *Athletic Equipment.* Retrieved January 6, 2010, from MassGeneral Hospital for Children: http://www.massgeneral.org/children/adolescenthealth/articles/aa_athletic_Equipment.aspx

22. Centers for Disease Control and Prevention. (n.d.). *BAM! Body and Mind.* Retrieved November 7, 2008, from Centers for Disease Control and Prevention: http://www.bam .gov/sub_yoursafety/yoursafety_helmets.html

23. KidsHealth. (2008, October). *Five Ways to Avoid Sports Injuries.* Retrieved January 6, 2010: http://kidshealth.org/kid/watch/out/sport_safety.html

24. American Academy of Orthopaedic Surgeons . (2007, October). *A Guide to Safety for Young Athletes.* Retrieved January 6, 2010, from Your Orthopaedic Connection: A Guide to Safety for Young Athletes: http://orthoinfo.aaos.org/topic .cfm?topic=A00307

25. Safe Kids USA. (2004). Retrieved January 6, 2010, from Safe Kids USA: Preventing Accidental Injury. Injury Facts, Childhood Injury: www.use.safekids.org/tier3_printable .cfm?content_item_id_=1030&folder_id=540

26. Iannelli, MD, V. (2007, October 14). *Children's Car Seat Safety Guide.* Retrieved January 6, 2010, from How Should Preschool And School Children Ride Safely?: http://pediatrics.about.com?library/car_seats/blbooster_seats.htm?p=1

27. The Nemours Foundation/KidsHealth. (2008). *Personal Health Series.* Retrieved January 6, 2010, from Car and Bus Safety: http://classroom.kidshealth.org/prekto2/personal/safety/car_bus_safety_handout2.pdf

28. *Health-Related Website Evaluation Form.* (n.d.). Retrieved January 12, 2010, from: www.carlbring.se/form/itform_ing.pdf

29. Skripak, J. M. (2008). Peanut and tree nut allergy in childhood. *Pediatric Allergy and Immunology, 19,* 368–373.

30. de Silva, I. M. (2008). Paediatric Anaphylaxix: A 5 Year Retrospective Review. *Allergy, 63*(8), 1071–1076.

31. U.S. Department of Health and Human Services. (2008). *Vital and Health Statistics.* Hyattsville, MD: Centers for Disease Control and Prevention, p. 16.

32. The Food Allergy & Anaphylaxis Network. (2009). *About Food Allergy.* Retrieved January 16, 2010: http://www .foodallergy.org/section/about-food-allergy

33. Mayo Foundation for Medical Education and Research. (2010, January 5). *Anaphylaxis: First Aid.* Retrieved January 16, 2010: http://www.mayoclinic.com/health/first-aid-anaphylaxis/FA00003/METHOD=print

34. U.S. Department of Health and Human Services. (2008). *Vital and Health Statistics.* Hyattsville, MD: Centers for Disease Control and Prevention, p. 16.

35. U.S. Department of Health & Human Services. (2008, September). *Asthma.* Retrieved January 16, 2010: http://www .nhlbi.nih.gov/health/dci/Diseases/Asthma/Asthma_All.html

36. Guttmacher Institute. (n.d.). *Facts on American Teens' Sexual and Reproductive Health.* Retrieved January 20, 2009: http://www.guttmacher.org/pubs/fb_ATSRH.html p1,3

37. Wind, R. (2010, January 26). *Media Center News Release.* Retrieved January 30, 2010, from Following Decade - Long Decline, U.S. Teen Pregnancy Rate Increases as Both Births and Abortions Rise: http://www.guttmacher.org/media/nr/2010/01/26/index.html

38. Hahn, D. B., Payne, W. A., & Lucas, E. B. (2009). *Focus on Health.* (9th Ed.). New York: McGraw-Hill, p. 369.

Teaching National Health Education Standard 4

"Students will demonstrate the ability to use interpersonal communication skills to enhance health and avoid or reduce health risks."[1,p28]

Standard 4

"Understanding the principles of effective communication is helpful in developing and maintaining interpersonal relationships."[2,p73]

Communicating effectively is a learned skill.[1,p30] According to Healthy People 2010, health communication includes the study and use of communication strategies to inform and influence individual and community decisions that enhance health.[3]

The National Health Education Standards provide performance indicators that guide teachers for Grades PreK–12, in designing instruction in interpersonal communication skills. Students learn to demonstrate verbal and non-verbal skills and communicate information and feelings to strengthen their interpersonal relations and reduce or avoid conflict.[1,p30]

These skills are also fundamental to success in the workforce. According to a nationwide survey of 400 employers across the United States, professionalism, work ethic, oral and written communications, teamwork, collaboration, critical thinking, and problem solving are the most important skills that recently hired graduates from high school and two- and four-year postsecondary institutions need.[4]

Sample performance tasks for using interpersonal communication skills to enhance health and avoid or reduce health risks include:

- Role-play how to use verbal and nonverbal communication.

> When engaged in conversation, our blood pressure increases. However, listening and paying attention to something outside ourselves causes us to relax and decreases blood pressure.[5]

- As a health professional radio talk host, advise using interpersonal communication skills to respond to unwanted, threatening, or dangerous situations.
- Demonstrate refusal skills for sexual activity, alcohol, tobacco, and other drugs.
- Act as mediator and demonstrate how to manage or resolve conflict between two angry students.
- Be a talk show caller and ask for help from a professional health expert on how to decrease stress, improve nutrition or mental health, or increase physical activity.
- Create for a younger audience a puppet show that demonstrates using verbal and nonverbal communication skills.
- Interview a health professional about expressing needs, wants, feelings, and fears.
- Design a comic book that illustrates refusal skills.
- Write and act out a play about any two topics using interpersonal communication skills.[6,p229]

To show proficiency in this standard, students must demonstrate healthy ways to express needs, wants, and feelings; how to respond to dangerous situations; how to tell a trusted friend or adult if threatened; listening, refusal, negotiation, and collaboration skills; and nonviolent strategies to resolve conflict.[1,p30-31]

Teaching the Skill

Teaching and learning the national health education skills is a process. When planning, follow these steps:

I. Discuss the importance of understanding how to use interpersonal communication skills to enhance health and avoid or reduce health risks.

- Being able to express needs, wants, and feelings in a healthy way enhances relationships.[1,p30]
- Body language is a form of communication that may confuse.[2,p74]
- The tone of a conversation influences its meaning.[2,p74]
- Inconsistent body language and tone send mixed messages.[2,p76]
- "I" messages are a good way to communicate because they express speakers feelings.[2,p76]
- Listening skills show our involvement, interest, and commitment to the conversation.
- Assertive, passive, and aggressive communication styles are used for different purposes, depending on the situation.[2,p77]
- Communication skills, such as asking for help or responding to unwanted, threatening, or dangerous situations, add to our health and well-being.
- Refusal, negotiation, collaboration, and conflict resolution skills strengthen interpersonal relationships and enhance health.[1,p30]

II. Explain the steps to reach proficiency in interpersonal communication skills to enhance health and avoid or reduce health risks.
   A. Select the performance indicators for the grade span.
   B. Teach the steps to achieve proficiency of the selected performance indicators, such as how to ask for help; express needs, wants and feelings in a healthy way; and demonstrate the skills of listening, speaking, refusing, resolving conflict, collaborating, and negotiating.
III. Show the students what the skill of using interpersonal communication to enhance health and avoid or reduce health risks looks like.
   A. Demonstrate the skills of listening, speaking, refusing, resolving conflict, collaborating, and negotiating.
   B. Model how to express needs, wants, and feelings in a healthy way.
IV. Provide adequate time for the students to practice using interpersonal communication to enhance health and avoid or reduce health risks.
V. Utilize formative assessments during practice to provide feedback and encouragement.[1,p14]

PreK–2

To achieve proficiency in Standard 4, PreK–2 students demonstrate healthy ways to ask for help and to express needs, wants, and feelings. They demonstrate listening

Pre K–Grade 2 Performance Indicators

4.2.1 Demonstrate healthy ways to express needs, wants, and feelings.
4.2.2 Demonstrate listening skills to enhance health.
4.2.3 Demonstrate ways to respond to an unwanted, threatening, or dangerous situation.
4.2.4 Demonstrate ways to tell a trusted adult if threatened or harmed.[1,p30]

skills, as well as ways to respond to unwanted, threatening, and dangerous situations.[1,p30]

For example:

Use hand puppets to demonstrate how one puppet expresses disappointment about not being invited to a birthday party while the other listens actively.

"When you didn't invite me to your birthday party, I felt left out, and my feelings were hurt."

"Did you want to come to the party?" "Next time I will invite you."

Reflect by asking:

- What words did puppet use to express needs, wants, and feelings? (PI4.2.1) (*"When you didn't invite me to your birthday party, I felt left out, and my feelings were hurt."*)
- How could you tell the puppet was listening? (PI 4.2.2) (*The puppet maintained eye contact, nodded his head in empathy, and asked questions.*)

In another example, two students role-play a bully threatening another student. Demonstrate how to use "I" messages to respond, then turn confidently, walk away, and tell an adult.

"Stop!" "I don't care what you say!" "I'm out of here!" "Mrs. Galley, Brad just threatened me."

FIGURE 8.1   An Adult with Hand Puppets

Reflect by asking:

- What words did puppet use to express needs, wants, and feelings? (PI4.2.1) *("Stop!" "I don't care what you say!" "I'm out of here!")*
- How did the puppet respond to the bully? (PI 4.2.3) *(He confidently told the bully he didn't care what he was saying, then he walked away.)*
- How did the puppet tell an adult he needed help? (PI 4.2.4) *("Mrs. Galley, Brad just threatened me.")*

Explain that these examples show how to use communication skills to enhance health and avoid or reduce health risks.

When the students demonstrate an understanding of the skill, as assessed formatively, it is time to practice. Because these performance indicators require the skill to be demonstrated, utilize pair shares and role-plays. Present different scenarios, and then pair the students so that each has the opportunity to practice. To track their practice, students use the self-check. It can take many forms, such as a paper or numbers 1, 2, 3, 4, for the number of times practiced. To indicate proficiency, circle thumbs up on the self-check (**Table 8.1**).

Formatively assess the practice, provide feedback for students to improve their skill development, and continue instruction only when students can perform the skill.

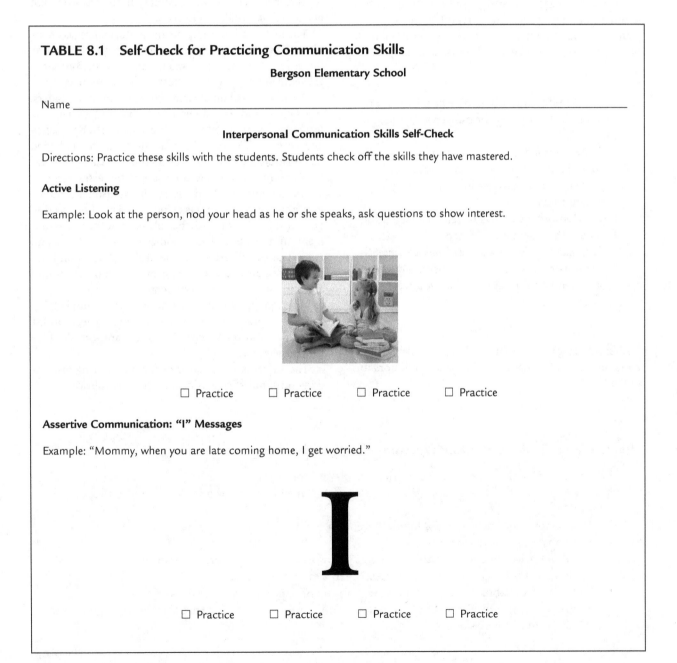

TABLE 8.1   Self-Check for Practicing Communication Skills

Bergson Elementary School

Name _____

Interpersonal Communication Skills Self-Check

Directions: Practice these skills with the students. Students check off the skills they have mastered.

Active Listening

Example: Look at the person, nod your head as he or she speaks, ask questions to show interest.

☐ Practice   ☐ Practice   ☐ Practice   ☐ Practice

Assertive Communication: "I" Messages

Example: "Mommy, when you are late coming home, I get worried."

I

☐ Practice   ☐ Practice   ☐ Practice   ☐ Practice

WHAT DOES THE SKILL OF INTERPERSONAL COMMUNICATION LOOK LIKE IN THE PREK–2 CLASSROOM?

Mrs. Conley is a Kindergarten teacher at the Court Street Elementary School. Recently, the local newspaper reported a man in a white van luring children into cars.

She was alarmed to learn that over 80,000 reported incidences of child sexual abuse occur each year, and the number of unreported cases is even greater because children are afraid to tell anyone what has happened to them.[7]

Mrs. Conley wants her students to know what to do if they are in a dangerous situation and how to use interpersonal communication skills to report an incident.

In planning the interpersonal communication unit, she targets two performance indicators: 4.2.3 and 4.2.4.

4.2.3—Demonstrate ways to respond when an unwanted, threatening, or dangerous situation arises.[1,p30]

> *Performance indicator 4.2.3 with infused content—* Demonstrate how to run away when approached by a stranger in a car or when feeling threatened.[1,p30]

4.2.4—Demonstrate ways to tell a trusted adult if you are threatened or harmed.[1,p30]

> *Performance indicator 4.2.4 with infused content—* Demonstrate ways to tell a trusted adult if a stranger asks for help or when you feel threatened.[1,p30]

After selecting the appropriate skill performance indicators, she selects Standard 1 performance indicators for content.

Standard 1—Students will comprehend concepts related to health promotion and disease prevention to enhance health.[1,p24]

Performance indicator 1.2.1—Identify that healthy behaviors affect personal health.[1,p24]

> *Performance indicator 1.2.1 with infused content—* Identify that healthy behaviors, such as identifying strangers, trusted adults, and feelings, affect personal health.[1,p24]

By linking the skill and content performance indicators, the teacher has direction in planning the unit on using interpersonal communication skills to enhance health and avoid or reduce health risks.

The first step is to complete the performance task template. This planning helps the teacher see the big picture, including standards, assessment, and instruction. Once the template is completed, most of the planning is also.

Because most kindergarten students are non-readers, instruction and assessment are verbal and visual. The teacher gives students time to learn about stranger safety and communication skills. Students practice, and then demonstrate their knowledge and skill in a class presentation accompanied by a written summative assessment.

An example of a kindergarten interpersonal communication performance task follows. The first section demonstrates how the teacher plans an authentic assessment of the performance indicators 4.2.3, 4.2.4, and 1.2.1. The second extracts some of the information from the performance task and transforms it into the prompt and support materials for students.

When preparing an authentic assessment and helping children to practice, the teacher develops a check-off list for students to track what they know and can do. (See student section.)

The students are assessed formatively during instruction and summatively using an analytical rubric.

Performance Task Name: Kindergarten—Safety with Strangers

I. Which state standard(s) does the performance task address?

II. Topic: What areas of health does this project assess? Why is it important? What is the focus of the project?[6,p237]

  A. This performance task assesses Injury Prevention/Safety.

  B. This topic is important because:

   1. 80,000 cases of child sexual abuse occur each year with many more unreported.

   2. Someone the child knows perpetrates 70–90% of child sexual abuse.[8,p10]

   3. Child sexual abusers target children with low confidence and self-esteem.[8,p10]

   4. When children receive instruction victimization prevention, they improve their knowledge and application of safety skills.[9]

(continues)

5. A range of psychological problems, such as depression, anxiety, anger, impaired sense of self, problems with sexuality, and cognitive disturbances that lead to behavioral and academic problems are more common amongst people who have been sexually abused.[8,p3]

6. Children who participate in active-learning programs that provide multiple opportunities to practice skills demonstrate higher resistance skills.[8,p5]

7. 40% of children trained in anti-victimization programs reported that they used the information or skills taught to protect themselves.[8,p5]

8. After completing a personal safety program, pre-school and school-aged children are more willing to tell an adult about inappropriate touching.[8,p5]

C. The focus of the project is to role-play scenarios during which children use interpersonal communication skills to respond to and tell a trusted adult about an unwanted, threatening, or dangerous situation.

III. Key Concepts: What basic concepts should students know?[6,p237]

Standard 1—Students will comprehend concepts related to health promotion and disease prevention to enhance health.[1,p24]

Performance indicator 1.2.1 with infused content—Identify that healthy behaviors, such as identifying strangers, trusted adults, and feelings, affect personal health.[1,p24]

A. Strangers
1. A stranger is someone you do not know at all or very well.
2. You cannot tell if a person is nice by looking at them.
3. Some strangers may try to hurt you.[10]

B. Safety
1. Always tell a trusted adult where you are.
2. Don't walk or bicycle alone.
3. Know where you can go for help while outside.[11]
4. Avoid places that are unsafe.
5. Do not talk to strangers, even if they seem nice.
6. Do not go near a stranger's car.
7. If you feel uncomfortable, run away and tell a trusted adult.

C. Examples of strangers who may make you feel unsafe
1. Someone on the street
2. A person in a car
3. Someone who knocks on the door that you do not know.

D. Feelings associated with being unsafe
1. Unsure
2. Strange
3. Scared
4. Curious[10]
5. Worried

E. Examples of trusted adults who make you feel safe
1. Mom
2. Dad
3. Guardian
4. Grandmother
5. Grandfather
6. Brothers and sisters
7. Aunts and uncles
8. Teachers[10]
9. Crossing guards

(continues)

F. Feelings associated with being safe
  1. Happy
  2. Comfortable
  3. Protected
  4. Calm[10]
G. Safe touches
  1. High fives
  2. A pat on the back for doing something well
  3. A handshake
  4. A hug from a trusted adult[10]
H. Unsafe touches that are inappropriate for anyone
  1. Uncomfortable hug
  2. Touching private parts (body parts under a bathing suit)
  3. Pulling
  4. Pushing
  5. Grabbing

IV. Skills: Which of the seven National Health Education Skills does this performance task address?[6,p237]
  Standard 4—Students will demonstrate the ability to use interpersonal communication skills to enhance health and avoid or reduce health risks.[1,p30]

  Performance indicator 4.2.3 with infused content—Demonstrate how to run away when approached by a stranger in a car or when feeling threatened.[1,p30]
    1. Demonstrate running away in the opposite direction if a stranger in a car causes you to feel threatened or unsafe.
      a. If the stranger is in a car, run away in the opposite direction.
      b. Scream
      c. Try to remember something about the person or the car.
    2. Demonstrate running away from a stranger in the library to a trusted adult.

  Performance indicator 4.2.4 with infused content—Demonstrate ways to tell a trusted adult if a stranger asks for your help or when you feel threatened.[1,p30]
    1. Demonstrate how to tell a trusted adult about a stranger in a car.
      a. "When I was walking home, a man pulled up in a van and asked me to help him look for his puppy."
      b. "I am scared."
      c. "He was driving a white van with a dent in the door."
    2. Demonstrate how to tell a trusted adult about a stranger in the library.
      a. "Mom, a man asked me to show him where the bathrooms were."
      b. "I felt uncomfortable and was scared, so I ran away!"

V. Curricular connections: What other subject(s) does this project support?[6,p237]
  English Language Arts
  Music—safety songs, optional

VI. Student directions and assessment criteria[6,p238]
  Prompt #1
  A. Project Description: Write and attach an engaging prompt that draws the student into the project.[6,p238]
    Allison was walking home by herself when a white van slowed and a man asked her if she has seen his puppy. Allison was confused because she had seen a few puppies in the neighborhood. The man held a picture of the puppy out the window and asked Allison to take a closer look.[12,p497]
  B. Your challenge: Provide a challenge or mission statement that describes the project.[6,p238]
    Allison wants to help the man find his puppy but feels uncomfortable.
    What should she do?

(continues)

Prompt #2
A. Project Description: Write and attach an engaging prompt that draws the student into the project.[6,p238]

Jeremy and his mother were at the library. His mom scanned the videos while he was looking at the books in the children's section. A stranger approached him and asked, "Can you show me where the men's room is?"

B. Your challenge: Provide a challenge or mission statement that describes the project.[6,p238]

Jeremy wants to help the man but feels uncomfortable. What should he do?

C. Assessment Criteria[6,p239]

You are assessed on the following key concepts: (List the concepts)

Performance indicator 1.2.1 with infused content—Indicate that healthy behaviors, such as identifying strangers, trusted adults, and feelings, affect personal health.[1,p24]

1. Two stranger safety tips
2. Two examples of strangers
3. Two feelings you have when you feel unsafe
4. Two examples of trusted adults
5. Two feelings you have when you feel safe
6. Two examples of safe touches
7. Two examples of unsafe touches.

You are assessed on the following skills: (List the skills)

Performance indicator 4.2.3 with infused content—Demonstrate how to run away when approached by a stranger in a car or when feeling threatened.[1,p30]

1. Role-play how to respond to a stranger in a car asking you to help find his lost puppy.
2. Role-play how to respond when a stranger in the library asks you to take him to the bathroom.

Performance indicator 4.2.4 with infused content—Demonstrate ways to tell a trusted adult if a stranger asks for help or when you feel threatened.[1,p30]

1. Demonstrate how to tell a trusted adult if a stranger asks to come close to the car to look at a picture of his lost puppy.
2. Demonstrate how to tell a trusted adult if a stranger asks if you will take him to the bathroom.

Student project must include the following. (List the project components)

1. Safety demonstration
   a. Demonstrate how to run away in the opposite direction when approached by a stranger in a car.
   b. Demonstrate how to tell a trusted adult about the stranger in the car.
   c. Demonstrate how to run away from a stranger in the library who wants you to take him to the bathroom.
   d. Demonstrate how to tell a trusted adult about the stranger in the library.
2. Complete the paper assessment selecting:
   a. Two stranger safety tips
   b. Two examples of strangers
   c. Two feelings you have when you feel unsafe
   d. Two examples of trusted adults
   e. Two feelings you have when you feel safe
   f. Two examples of safe touches
   g. Two examples of unsafe touches

Distribute this information to students who are readers. For nonreaders, read the prompt and explain the assessment.

Bergson Elementary School

Interpersonal Communication Unit

Name _____

Allison

Allison was walking home alone when a white van slowed and the driver asked her if she had seen his puppy. Allison was confused because she had seen a few puppies in the neighborhood. The man held a picture of the puppy out the window and asked Allison to take a closer look.

Allison wants to help the man find his puppy but feels uncomfortable. What should she do?

Jeremy

Jeremy and his mother were at the library. His mom scanned the videos while he was looking at the books in the children's section. A stranger approached him and asked, "Can you show me where the men's room is?"

Jeremy wants to help the man but feels uncomfortable. What should he do?

Here are your challenges:

1. Safety demonstration

   a. Demonstrate how to run away in the opposite direction when approached by a stranger in a car.

   b. Demonstrate how to tell a trusted adult about the stranger in the car.

   c. Demonstrate how to run away from a stranger in the library who wants you to take him to the bathroom.

   d. Demonstrate how to tell a trusted adult about the stranger in the library.

2. Paper assessment

   a. Two stranger safety tips

   b. Two examples of strangers

   c. Two feelings you have when you feel unsafe

   d. Two examples of trusted adults

   e. Two feelings you have when you feel safe

   f. Two examples of safe touches

   g. Two examples of unsafe touches

ASSESSMENT MATERIALS

Self-Check for Practicing Active Listening and "I" Messages (**Table 8.2**)

TABLE 8.2   Self-Check for Practicing How to Use Communication Skills to Tell a Trusted Adult About Feeling Threatened

Bergson Elementary School

Interpersonal Communication Skills Self-Check

Name _____

Directions: Practice these skills with the students. Students check off the skills they have mastered.

(continues)

TABLE 8.2 Self-Check for Practicing How to Use Communication Skills to Tell a Trusted Adult About Feeling Threatened *(continued)*

Check the box when you can demonstrate the skill.

☐ Practice running away in the opposite direction from a stranger in a car.

☐ Practice remembering something about the stranger in the car or something about the car.

☐ Practice telling a trusted adult about the stranger in the car.

☐ Practice running away from a stranger in the library to a trusted adult.

☐ Practice telling a trusted adult about the stranger in the library.

(continues)

Bergson Elementary School

Interpersonal Communication Skills Assessment

Name _____

1. Explain two stranger safety tips.

2. Circle two strangers

3. Circle two unsafe feelings.

4. Circle two trusted adults

(continues)

5. Circle two safe feelings

6. Circle two safe touches

7. Circle two unsafe touches

Analytical Rubric to Assess Interpersonal Communication Performance Task(Table 8.3)

TABLE 8.3   Analytical Rubric to Assess the Safety Demonstration

Criteria	4	3	2	1
Performance indicator 4.2.3 with infused content—Demonstrate how to run away when approached by a stranger in a car.[1,p30]	The student accurately demonstrates how to scream, run away in the opposite direction from a stranger in a car, and remember something about the car.	Student's demonstration of screaming, running away in the opposite direction from a stranger in a car, and remembering something about the car is mostly accurate.	Student's demonstration of screaming, running away in the opposite direction from a stranger in a car, and remembering something about the car has a few inaccuracies.	Student's demonstration of screaming, running away in the opposite direction from a stranger in a car, and remembering something about the car is mostly inaccurate.

(continues)

TABLE 8.3   Analytical Rubric to Assess the Safety Demonstration *(continued)*

Criteria	4	3	2	1
Performance indicator 4.2.3 with infused content—Demonstrate how to run away when feeling threatened in the library.[1,p30]	The student accurately demonstrates how to run away from a stranger to a trusted adult in the library when feeling threatened.	Student's demonstration of how to run away from a stranger to a trusted adult in the library when feeling threatened is mostly accurate.	Student's demonstration of how to run away from a stranger to a trusted adult in the library when feeling threatened has a few inaccuracies.	Student's demonstration of how to run away from a stranger to a trusted adult in the library when feeling threatened is mostly inaccurate.
Performance indicator 4.2.4 with infused content—Demonstrate ways to tell a trusted adult when approached by a stranger in a car.[1,p30]	The student accurately demonstrates using "I" messages when telling a trusted adult about being approached by a stranger in a car.	Student's demonstration of "I" messages when telling a trusted adult about being approached by a stranger in a car is mostly accurate.	Student's demonstration of "I" messages when telling a trusted adult about being approached by a stranger in a car has a few inaccuracies.	Student's demonstration of "I" messages when telling a trusted adult about being approached by a stranger in a car is mostly inaccurate.
Performance indicator 4.2.4 with infused content—Demonstrate ways to tell a trusted adult when feeling threatened in the library.[1,p30]	The student accurately demonstrates "I" messages when telling a trusted adult about feeling threatened in the library.	The student's demonstration of "I" messages when telling a trusted adult about feeling threatened in the library is mostly accurate.	The student's demonstration of "I" messages when telling a trusted adult about feeling threatened in the library has a few inaccuracies.	The student's demonstration of "I" messages when telling a trusted adult about feeling threatened in the library is mostly inaccurate.

Name _____

Total possible points – 16   Your points - _____   Your grade - _____

HOW THE COORDINATED SCHOOL HEALTH TEAM HELPS STUDENTS USE INTERPERSONAL COMMUNICATION SKILLS TO ENHANCE HEALTH AND AVOID OR REDUCE HEALTH RISKS

Health Education

- Model interpersonal communication skills.
- Show students how to develop healthy behaviors.
- Demonstrate how to practice safety with strangers

Physical Education

- Promote healthy behaviors.
- Explain and model interpersonal communication skills.

Health Services

- Be aware of signs and symptoms of child abuse.
- Report any incidents of child abuse.

Nutrition Services

- Promote healthy behaviors.

Counseling, Psychological, and Social Services

- Provide valid and reliable resources about child safety to children and families.
- Provide support to children who are victims of abuse.

Healthy School Environment

- Hang posters that promote safety.
- Hang posters that promote healthy behaviors.

Health Promotion for Staff

- Provide staff training in safety with strangers

Family and Community Involvement

- Promote web-based child sexual abuse educational programs.[8,p11]

- Provide child safety training to parents and community members.
- Promote and participate in Kids Walk-to-School programs[13]

Grades 3–5

To achieve proficiency in Standard 4, Grade 3–5, students must demonstrate verbal and nonverbal communication skills, refusal skills, nonviolent strategies to manage or resolve conflict, and how to ask for help to enhance health and avoid or reduce health risks.

To teach Standard 4, emphasize skill development through role-playing.

For example:

Andrew and Bobby are known bullies in the Ashmont Elementary School. They tried to recruit Anthony to join them on the playground where they planned to prevent Johnny from joining a game of tag.

Andrew and Bobby had bullied Anthony before, and he did not want to be a part of their plan. When bullied in the past, he did not want to go to school. While there, Anthony could not concentrate on his work. He learned from the counselor to stand up for himself and ask friends for help to stop the bullying.[14,p371] He has much more confidence now to handle Andrew and Bobby.

The next day, he stood tall in front of Andrew and Bobby and told them that he would not get involved with their plan. "When you do not let some children play, it makes them feel bad, and I don't like it."

The next day, Anthony told the teacher about the bullying and asked her to watch the boys in case he needed her help. During recess, he played with Johnny and Andrew and Bobby did not bother him.

To reflect, ask the students:

- What verbal and nonverbal communication skills did Anthony use with Andrew and Bobby? (PI 4.5.1) *(The next day, he stood tall in front of Andrew and Bobby and told them that he would not get involved*

with their plan. "When you do not let some children play, it makes them feel bad, and I don't like it.")
- What refusal skills did Anthony use with Andrew and Bobby? (PI 4.5.2) *(He told them that he would not get involved with their plan.)*
- What nonviolent strategy did Anthony use to resolve the conflict? (PI 4.5.3) *(Anthony played with Johnny during recess, and Andrew and Bobby did not bother him.)*
- How did Anthony ask for help? (PI 4.5.4) *(Anthony told the teacher about the bullying and asked her to watch the boys in case he needed her help.)*

In this skill, students demonstrate their interpersonal communication skills in a variety of scenarios. When they establish an understanding of the skill, as determined through formative assessment, instruction continues with the content.

To educate students about bullying, show them different examples of physical (pushing, hitting, shoving, name-calling, threatening, malicious teasing[14,p363]) and relational bullying (social exclusion, spreading rumors, and demanding compliance as a condition of friendship[14,p363]). Brainstorm and practice using interpersonal communication skills to combat bullying. Present students with varied scenarios and give them time to practice their skills.

As they learn and practice, formatively assess their progress. Provide additional instruction when needed before continuing to the performance task.

WHAT DOES THE SKILL OF INTERPERSONAL COMMUNICATION LOOK LIKE IN THE GRADE 3–5 CLASSROOM?

Miss Hanafin, the Hammond Elementary School counselor, is distressed over bullying occurring during recess, in the halls, and at lunch. During a staff meeting, she asked the teachers whether they had observed any bullying. Most said occurrences of pushing, hitting, shoving, name-calling, threatening, or malicious teasing were infrequent. If they did observe these behaviors, they spoke to the children and notified the office.

A small number of teachers mentioned that they had observed social exclusion, spreading rumors, or students requiring others to behave in a certain way to be friends. Because of her training in bullying prevention, Miss Hanafin knows this bullying is underreported and hurtful and leads to depression and decreased academic performance.[14,p367]

Miss Hanafin received permission to implement a bullying prevention program with major emphasis on interpersonal communication skills. She will work with classroom teachers and the health specialist, nurse, and coordinated school health team to implement instruction, staff training, and policy development, and to

---

Grades 3–5 Performance Indicators

4.5.1 Demonstrate effective verbal and nonverbal communication skills to enhance health.

4.5.2 Demonstrate refusal skills that avoid or reduce health risks.

4.5.3 Demonstrate nonviolent strategies to manage or resolve conflict.

4.5.4 Demonstrate how to ask for assistance to enhance personal health.[1,p30]

increase supervision and parent and community involvement.

The health specialist designed an interpersonal communication unit and selected the following performance indicator from Standard 4:

Standard 4—Students will demonstrate the ability to use interpersonal communication skills to enhance health and avoid or reduce health risks.[1,p30]

Performance Indicator 4.5.1—Demonstrate effective verbal and nonverbal communication skills to enhance health.[1,p30]

Performance indicator 4.5.1 with infused content— Demonstrate effective verbal and nonverbal communication skills to combat bullying and enhance health.[1,p30]

Performance Indicator 4.5.3—Demonstrate nonviolent strategies to manage or resolve conflict.[1,p30]

Performance indicator 4.5.3 with infused content— Demonstrate nonviolent strategies to manage or resolve bullying.[1,p30]

After selecting the appropriate performance indicator for the skill, choose the Standard 1 performance indicator.

Standard 1—Students will comprehend concepts related to health promotion and disease prevention to enhance health.[1,p24]

Performance Indicator 1.5.3—Describe ways in which safe and healthy school and community environments can promote personal health.[1,p24]

Performance indicator 1.5.3 with infused content— Describe ways in which safe and healthy school and community environments can promote personal health by decreasing bullying.[1,p24]

By linking the skill and content performance indicators, the teacher has a sound idea of how to plan the lessons for an accessing information unit. The first step in planning is to think through the unit by completing the performance task template. Thereupon, the teacher has most of the information to introduce the prompt to the students.

When distributing the prompt, include all the back-up information, student worksheets, and holistic and analytical rubrics, which inform students how they are being assessed before they work on their product. Rubrics act as a guide and help the students attain proficiency in the standards.

Designing the performance task takes considerable preparation. Once the teacher distributes and explains the information, the students are free to create a product. They learn with effective coaching (formative assessment) how to demonstrate proficiency in content and skill.

The following is an example of a Grade 4 interpersonal communication performance task for bullying prevention.

The first section, which is the teacher's, demonstrates how to plan an authentic assessment of the performance indicators, 4.5.1, 4.5.3, and 1.5.3. The second, for the student, extracts information from the performance task and transforms it into the student prompt and support materials.

Performance Task Name: Grade 4—Interpersonal Communication

I. Which state standard(s) does this performance task address? (Varies by state)
II. Topic: What areas of health does this project assess? Why is it important? What is the focus of the project?[6,p237]
   A. This performance task assesses Injury Prevention/Safety.
   B. This topic is important because:
      1. Bullying occurs when there is intent, the behavior repeats, and an imbalance of power exists.[14,p368]
      2. 29.9% of students in Grades 6–10 report moderate or frequent bullying, and the CDC estimates that twice as many elementary students experience bullying.[15]
      3. Bullying is the most prevalent form of violence in schools.[14,p363]
      4. The optimal age for bullying intervention is between the ages of five and six and eight and nine.[14,p369]

(continues)

5. Children who bully are more likely to smoke, drink alcohol, fight, vandalize property, skip classes, and drop out of school.[15]
6. 60% of boys who bully in middle school acquire at least one criminal conviction by the age of 24.[15]
7. Two-thirds of school shootings were committed by chronic victims of bullying. Revenge was the predominant motivator.[14,p362]
8. In classrooms that implement bullying prevention with fidelity, there are lower student-reported incidents of victimization, thereby indicating teachers are key elements of change in bullying prevention.[16]
9. Comprehensive multilevel interventions and policies, such as staff training, classroom instruction, promoting one-on-one behavior change, and parent training reduced rates of bullying and victimization.[16]

C. This project focuses on students using interpersonal communication skills to cope with bullying.

III. Key Concepts: What basic concepts should students know?[6,p237]

Standard 1—Students will comprehend concepts related to health promotion and disease prevention to enhance health.[1,p24]

Performance indicator 1.5.3 with infused content—Describe ways in which safe and healthy school and community environments can promote personal health by decreasing bullying.[1,p24]

A. Bullying
1. A bully is a person who hurts or frightens smaller or weaker people.[12,p415]
2. Physical bullying is pushing, hitting, or shoving.
3. Verbal bullying is name-calling, threatening, or malicious teasing.
4. Psychological bullying is spreading rumors, isolating a person, or threatening physical harm.[17,p213]

B. Trusted adults to whom children report bullying:
1. School
   a. Teacher
   b. Counselor
   c. Principal
   d. Recess monitor
   e. Hall monitor
   f. Lunch monitor
2. Home
   a. Parent
   b. Guardian

IV. Skills: Which of the seven National Health Education Standards skills does this performance task address?[6,p237]

Standard 4—Students will demonstrate the ability to use interpersonal communication skills to enhance health and avoid or reduce health risks.[1,p30]

Performance indicator 4.5.1 with infused content—Demonstrate effective verbal and nonverbal communication skills to combat bullying and enhance health.[1,p30]

A. Stand tall, look the bully in the eye, and say:
1. "Stop, I am out of here!"
2. "I don't like it when you talk to me like that."
3. "Leave me alone!"
4. "My friends are not leaving this table. They are having lunch with me!"

B. Report bullying to a teacher, counselor, or principal.
1. "I need some help. During recess, a classmate wouldn't let me play."
2. "When I walk by a certain group in the hallway, they call me names. I feel nervous when I have to leave the classroom."
3. "When I went to the bathroom, a girl made fun of me. I am afraid."
4. "During lunch, some girls I know made me sit alone. Then they made fun of me."

(continues)

C. Use humor to change the topic.[12,p423]

Performance indicator 4.5.3 with infused content—Demonstrate nonviolent strategies to manage or resolve bullying.[1,p30]

A. Walk away.

B. Ignore the bully.

C. Ask friends or bystanders to stand with you when bullies approach.

D. Tell a trusted adult.[18]

V. Curricular connections: What other subject areas does this project support?[6,p237]

    English Language Arts

VI. Student Directions and Assessment Criteria[6,p238]

Prompt #1

A. Project Description: Write and attach an engaging prompt that draws the student into the project.[6,p238]

Domina is a fourth grade student at the Hinsman Elementary School. She is very pretty, wears glasses, is somewhat shy, and not quite sure of herself.

She is on the community soccer team, really loves playing the flute, and was just accepted into the school band.

Some of the girls at school do not like her. They make fun of Domina by calling her names as she passes to the music room. One girl pushed her into the lavatory and held the door shut while other girls made sure no one sat with her at lunch. At recess, Domina had no one to play with.

She is not sleeping well, has a stomachache most mornings, and begs her mom to let her stay home.

B. Your Challenge: Provide a challenge or mission statement that describes the project.[6,p238]

Your challenge is to help Domina use interpersonal communication skills to get help and learn how to cope with the bullies.

Prompt #2

A. Project Description: Write and attach an engaging prompt that draws the student into the project.[6,p238]

Jonathan used to be friends with Ethan, but lately they do not play together. Jonathan spends a lot of time with Kaden because they both have Wii and enjoy playing the sports games together.

Ethan is having a birthday party at the YMCA and invited all his friends—except Jonathan. In fact, Ethan told his friends, "If you want to come to my party, you better not talk to Jonathan or Kaden."

Jonathan's feelings are hurt because he does not know why Ethan did not invite him to the party. He tried to talk to Ethan, but Ethan pretended not to hear.

B. Your Challenge: Provide a challenge or mission statement that describes the project.[6,p238]

Your challenge is to help Jonathan use his interpersonal communication skills to talk to a trusted adult and cope with the snub.

Prompt #3

A. Project Description: Write and attach an engaging prompt that draws the student into the project.[6,p238]

Darren is rather small for his age and often made fun of by the bigger boys. When in the lavatory, the bigger boys laugh at him. They often trip and laugh at him in the hall, and some call him gay. During recess, no one invites Darren to play.

Lately, he does not want to go to school. His teachers have noticed that Darren does not participate or seem very happy.

B. Your Challenge: Provide a challenge or mission statement that describes the project.[6,p238]

Your challenge is to help Darren use his interpersonal communication skills to talk to a trusted adult and cope with the bullying.

(continues)

C. Assessment Criteria[6,p239]

You are assessed on the following key concepts: (List the concepts.)

Performance indicator 1.5.3 with infused content—Describe ways in which safe and healthy school and community environments can promote personal health by decreasing bullying.[1,p24]

1. Describe three types of bullying
2. List two trusted adults you can tell about being bullied.

You are assessed on the following skill:

Performance indicator 4.5.1 with infused content—Demonstrate effective verbal and nonverbal communication skills to combat bullying and enhance health.[1,p30]

1. Demonstrate two verbal and two nonverbal communication skills to combat bullying, both verbal and nonverbal.

Performance indicator 4.5.3 with infused content—Demonstrate nonviolent strategies to manage or resolve bullying.[1,p30]

1. Demonstrate two nonviolent ways to cope effectively with a bully.

   Student project includes the following:

1. Write and role-play a puppet show.
   a. Explain three aspects of bullying
   b. Name two trusted adults to tell
   c. Demonstrate two verbal and two nonverbal communication skills to combat bullying, both verbal and nonverbal.
   d. Demonstrate two non-violent strategies to cope with a bully.

Hammond Elementary School

Name _____

Prompt #1

Domina is a fourth grade student at the Hinsman Elementary School. She is very pretty, wears glasses, is somewhat shy, and not quite sure of herself.

She is on the community soccer team, really loves playing the flute, and was just accepted into the school band.

Some of the girls at school do not like her. They make fun of Domina by calling her names as she passes to the music room. One girl pushed her into the lavatory and held the door shut while other girls made sure no one sat with her at lunch. At recess, Domina had no one to play with.

She is not sleeping well, has a stomachache most mornings, and begs her mom to let her stay home.

Your challenge is to help Domina use interpersonal communication skills to get help and learn how to cope with the bullies.

Prompt #2

Jonathan used to be friends with Ethan, but lately they do not play together. Jonathan spends a lot of time with Kaden because they both have Wii and enjoy playing the sports games together.

Ethan is having a birthday party at the YMCA and invited all his friends—except Jonathan. In fact, Ethan told his friends, "If you want to come to my party, you better not talk to Jonathan or Kaden."

Jonathan's feelings are hurt because he does not know why Ethan did not invite him to the party. He tried to talk to Ethan, but Ethan pretended not to hear.

Your challenge is to help Jonathan use interpersonal communication skills to get help and learn how to cope with the bullies.

(continues)

Prompt #3

Darren is rather small for his age and often made fun of by the bigger boys. When in the lavatory, the bigger boys laugh at him. They often trip him and laugh at him in the hall, and some call him gay. During recess no one invites Darren to play.

Lately, he does not want to go to school. His teachers have noticed that Darren does not participate or seem very happy.

Your challenge is to help Darren use his interpersonal communication skills to talk to a trusted adult and cope with the bullying.

ASSESSMENT MATERIALS

Role-Play Self-Check (**Table 8.4**)

TABLE 8.4   Role-Play Self Check

Hammond Elementary School

Interpersonal Communication Worksheet

Name _____

Directions: Check off each section you complete to help you fulfill all the requirements of the role-play.

1. Name of the characters in the play.
    a. Name of the bully _____
    b. Name of the victim _____
    c. Name of the two trusted adults you turn to for help.

        _____

        _____

2. Did you define bully?   ☐ Yes ☐ No
3. List the three types of bullying you are using in the play.

    _____

    _____

    _____

4. Explain the two examples of verbal communication skills you are using in the play.

    _____

    _____

5. Explain the two examples of nonverbal communication skills you are using in the play.

    _____

6. Explain the two non-violent strategies you use to cope with the bully.

    _____

    _____

(continues)

TABLE 8.5 **Analytical Rubric to Assess the Bullying Role-Play Portion of the Interpersonal Communication Performance Task**

Criteria	4	3	2	1
Performance indication 1.5.3. with infused content—Describe ways in which safe and healthy school and community environments can promote personal health[1,p24]	Student thoroughly describes three types of bullying.	Student adequately describes three types of bullying.	Student inadequately describes three types of bullying.	Student poorly describes three types of bullying.
Performance indicator 1.5.3. with infused content—Describe ways in which safe and healthy school and community environments can promote personal health[1,p24]	Student accurately lists two trusted adults to tell about bullying.	Student list of two trusted adults to tell about bullying is mostly accurate.	Student list of two trusted adults to tell about bullying has a few inaccuracies.	Student list of two trusted adults to tell about bullying is mostly inaccurate.
Performance indicator 4.5.1 with infused content—Demonstrate effective verbal and nonverbal communication skills to combat bullying and enhance health.[1,p30]	Student demonstrates two accurate examples of verbal communication skills to cope with bullying.	Student's demonstration of two examples of verbal communication skills to cope with bullying is mostly accurate.	Student's demonstration of two examples of verbal communication skills to cope with bullying has a few inaccuracies.	Student's demonstration of two examples of verbal communication skills to cope with bullying is mostly inaccurate.
Performance indicator 4.5.1 with infused content—Demonstrate effective verbal and nonverbal communication skills to combat bullying and enhance health.[1,p30]	Student demonstrates two accurate examples of nonverbal communication skills to cope with bullying.	Student's demonstration of two examples of nonverbal communication skills to cope with bullying is mostly accurate.	Student's demonstration of two examples of nonverbal communication skills to cope with bullying has a few inaccuracies.	Student's demonstration of two examples of nonverbal communication skills to cope with bullying is mostly inaccurate.
Performance indication 4.5.3 with infused content—Demonstrate nonviolent strategies to manage or resolve bullying.[1,p30]	Student demonstrates two accurate examples of nonviolent strategies to cope with bullying.	Student's demonstration of two examples of nonviolent strategies to cope with bullying is mostly accurate.	Student's demonstration of two examples of nonviolent strategies to cope with bullying has a few inaccuracies.	Student's demonstration of two examples of nonviolent strategies to cope with bullying is mostly inaccurate.
Creativity	The role-play is an excellent example of creativity.	The role-play is a good example of creativity.	The role-play is a fair example of creativity.	The role-play is a poor example of creativity.

(continues)

TABLE 8.5 Analytical Rubric to Assess the Bullying Role-Play Portion of the Interpersonal Communication Performance Task *(continued)*

Criteria	4	3	2	1
Grammar	The grammar is always correct.	The grammar is sometimes correct.	The grammar is rarely correct.	The grammar is never correct.
Involvement	All members of the role-play are always involved.	All members of the role-play are sometimes involved.	Some members of the role-play are rarely involved.	Some members of the role-play are never involved.

Name _____

Total possible points – 32   **Your points -** _____   **Your grade -** _____

HOW THE COORDINATED SCHOOL HEALTH TEAM HELPS STUDENTS USE INTERPERSONAL COMMUNICATION SKILLS TO ENHANCE HEALTH AND AVOID OR REDUCE HEALTH RISKS

Health Education

- Teach interpersonal communication skills.
- Teach skills to combat bullying.
- Model interpersonal communication skills with students and adults.
- Implement a bullying-prevention program in the classroom.

Physical Education

- Model interpersonal communication skills with students and adults.
- Promote healthy behaviors.
- Implement a bullying-prevention program in the gymnasium.

Health Services

- Model interpersonal communication skills with students and adults.
- Watch for signs of bully victimization.
- Communicate with administration and parents when bullying is detected.

Nutrition Services

- Model interpersonal communication skills with students and adults.
- Provide cafeteria monitors trained in bullying prevention.

Counseling, Psychological, and Social Services

- Model interpersonal communication skills with students and adults.
- Take a leadership role in implementing a bullying prevention program.
- Intervene and assist victims of bullying.

Healthy School Environment

- Use interpersonal communication skills to resolve conflict among students.
- Develop a district and school anti-bullying policy.
- Provide trained monitors for the lavatory, hallways, recess, and cafeteria to prevent bullying.

Health Promotion for Staff

- Model interpersonal communication skills with students and adults.
- Provide staff training in bullying prevention.

Family and Community Involvement

- Provide training in interpersonal communication skills and problem solving.
- Provide training in bullying prevention.

Grades 6–8

To achieve proficiency in Standard 4, Grade 6–8 students apply verbal and nonverbal communication skills; demonstrate refusal, negotiation, and effective conflict management strategies; and learn how to ask for help to enhance health and avoid or reduce health risks.

To teach Standard 4, explain the importance of communication, why communication skills are relevant to the health and well-being of the students, and how these competencies relate to other national health education skills. Present the performance indicators and the means to achieve them, model the skill, provide practice time for students, and use formative assessments while they are learning and practicing in order to improve your teaching and their learning.

For example:

Mr. Burkhead observes frequent conflicts among his students. They do not have the skills to resolve their differences peacefully and, consequently, often allow arguments to escalate into fights between classes or at lunch.

In one instance, Stephanie let Allison borrow her CD but Allison returned it damaged. Stephanie was angry and told Allison she wanted her to replace it. Allison said, "The CD was like that when I borrowed it." She refused. Name-calling and threats ensued and the girls fought in the hallway.

Both girls feel badly and would like to resolve this matter. They asked their teacher for help.

To reflect, ask the students:

- Did you hear any effective verbal or nonverbal communication skills? (PI 4.8.1) *(Effective: "The CD was like that when I borrowed it." Ineffective: Name-calling and threats ensued.)*
- Did you hear any refusal or negotiation skills? (PI 4.8.2) *(No. Stephanie was angry and told Allison she wanted her to replace the CD. Allison refused.)*
- What nonviolent strategies could the girls use to resolve their conflict? (PI 4.5.3) *(Stay calm, talk about the conflict, suggest and discuss a number of solutions to the problem, agree on a way to settle the conflict.[12,p786])*
- To whom did the girls go for help in solving the problem? (PI 4.5.4) *(They asked their teacher for help.)*

To determine whether the students understand, Mr. Burkhead offers another scenario: Two friends, Jamal and Anton, were going to the movies. Anton was late arriving at Jamal's house, and they missed the show. They argued, and Anton left angry and upset. He understood why Jamal was angry, but he is afraid their friendship is over.

Mr. Burkhead challenged the students to explore a way to resolve the conflict in a peaceful manner and rescue the friendship. The students brainstormed and made good suggestions.

When the students are learning the skill, provide adequate time for them to rehearse before they demonstrate proficiency through an authentic assessment. While they are learning, use formative assessments (Chapter 4) to check for understanding and use feedback to show how to improve their performance, thereby encouraging them.

Once the students demonstrate the skill, teach the health content. Design a prompt that allows them to display their knowledge of health content while demonstrating interpersonal communication skills. As they practice both, use formative assessments for redirection and encouragement.

WHAT DOES THE SKILL OF INTERPERSONAL COMMUNICATION LOOK LIKE IN THE MIDDLE SCHOOL CLASSROOM?

Mr. David is a health teacher in a rural district in the Midwest. He recently presented to the coordinated school health team the results of a Midwest, Northern Plains, middle school alcohol study that indicated the following:

- Students begin drinking at 9.5 years of age.[19,p61]
- Nearly half reported trying alcohol at least once.
- 15% drank within the past month.[19,p63]
- 22% of Grade 6–8 students have been drunk at least once.[19,p61]
- Eighth grade students had higher levels of lifetime and past month use than the national sample.[19,p63]
- The district's 61% lifetime alcohol use exceeded a national sample (44%).

When Mr. David shared the survey with his students, they thought more young people drank than the survey reported. He asked, "Why do so many young people drink?" The students told him: "We drink to fit in and because most teens drink." "It helps us cope with stress." "There was nothing else to do."[19,p64]

He then asked them, "Where do you obtain the alcohol?" "From our parents and friends," they answered.[19,p64]

These admissions worried Mr. David because he knows from previous advisory meetings with parents that they underestimate their children's alcohol use. Drinking by 10–12-year-old children forecasts their higher usage of alcohol in later adolescence and adulthood.[19,p59]

In planning his interpersonal communication unit, Mr. David thought the students should learn refusal skills and assertive communication to reduce their alcohol use. He selects specific performance indicators that address a particular skill and content.

Standard 4—Students will demonstrate the ability to use interpersonal communication skills to enhance health and avoid or reduce health risks.[1,p30]

Performance indicator 4.8.1—Apply effective verbal and nonverbal communication skills to enhance health.[1,p30]

*Performance indicator 4.8.1 with infused content—*Apply effective verbal and nonverbal communication skills to resist peer pressure and enhance health.[1,p30]

Performance indicator 4.8.2—Demonstrate refusal and negotiation skills that avoid or reduce health risks.[1,p30]

*Performance indicator 4.8.2 with infused content—*Demonstrate refusal skills that avoid or reduce health risks.[1,p30]

After selecting the appropriate performance indicator for the skill, choose the Standard 1 performance indicator.

Standard 1—Students comprehend concepts related to health promotion and disease prevention to enhance health.[1,p24]

Performance indicator 1.8.7—Describe the benefits of and barriers to practicing healthy behaviors.[1,p25]

*Performance indicator 1.8.7 with infused content—*Describe the benefits of and barriers to resisting the peer pressure to use alcohol and practicing healthy behaviors.[1,p25]

By linking the skill and content performance indicators, the teacher has a sound idea of how to plan the lessons for the interpersonal communication unit.

The first step in planning is to think through the unit by completing the performance task template. Thereupon, the teacher has most of the information to introduce the prompt to the students.

When distributing the prompt, include all the back-up information, student worksheets, and holistic and analytical rubrics, which inform students how they are being assessed before they work on their product. Rubrics act as a guide and help the students attain proficiency in the standards.

Designing the performance task takes considerable preparation. Once the teacher distributes and explains the information, the students are free to create a product. They learn with effective coaching (formative assessment) how to demonstrate proficiency in content and skill.

The following performance task for a Grade 8 unit on interpersonal communication focuses on resisting peer pressure to use alcohol and finding alternative healthy activities.

The first section is for the teacher and demonstrates the planning process for authentic assessment reflecting the performance indicators 4.8.1, 4.8.2, and 1.8.7. The second section, for the student, extracts information from the performance task and transforms it into the student prompt and support materials.

Standard 4 Performance Task: Grade 8—Using Interpersonal Communication to Resist Alcohol

I. Which state standard(s) does this performance task address?

II. Topic: What areas of health does this project assess? Why is it important? What is the focus of the project?[6,p237]

   A. This performance task assesses the health area of Substance Use/Abuse

   B. It is important because:

   1. Lifetime median alcohol use among middle school students is:

      a. 32.6% for 6th grade

      b. 44.9% for 7th grade

      c. 57.9% for 8th grade[20]

   2. Drinking by 10–12-year-old children forecasts their higher alcohol usage in later adolescence and adulthood.

(continues)

C. The purpose of the project is to demonstrate interpersonal communication skills that provide confidence to resist peer pressure to use alcohol.

III. Key Concepts: What basic concepts should the students know?[6,p237]

Standard 1—Students comprehend concepts related to health promotion and disease prevention to enhance health.[1,p24]

Performance indicator 1.8.7 with infused content—Describe the benefits of and barriers to resisting the peer pressure to use alcohol and practicing healthy behaviors.[1,p25]

A. Benefits of resisting peer pressure to use alcohol
   1. Increased self-respect
   2. Increased self-esteem
   3. Spend time with friends who do not use alcohol
   4. Improved family relationships
   5. Feel more in control of your life
   6. Have a high level of wellness
   7. A drug-free future[17,p287]
   8. No damage to the developing body
   9. No influence on emotional development
   10. Greater concentration in school [17,p280]
   11. Decrease in unhealthy behaviors due to alcohol

B. Barriers to resisting peer pressure to use alcohol
   1. Effect on self-respect and self-esteem
   2. Friends who drink
   3. Friends become more important than family
   4. Feel out of control of one's life
   5. Unable to cope with stress, anger, sadness, boredom, and other problems in a healthy way
   6. Accustomed to taking unhealthy risks, such as driving with a person under the influence or becoming sexually active
   7. Does not connect alcohol use to a negative school performance

IV. Skills: Which of the seven National Health Education Standards does this performance task address?[6,p237]

Standard 4—Students will demonstrate the ability to use interpersonal communication skills to enhance health and avoid or reduce health risks.[1,p30]

Performance indicator 4.8.1 with infused content—Apply effective verbal and nonverbal communication skills to resist peer pressure and enhance health.[1,p30]

A. Verbal communication skills
   1. Be prepared. Think about what needs to be said.
   2. Practice "I" messages.
      a. "I feel really uncomfortable when you pressure me."
      b. "When you talk to me like that, I feel pressured, and I don't like it."
   3. Use language from the STOP strategy that is firm but not offensive.
      a. Use clear, specific, simple statements.
      b. Use examples when you share an idea or suggestion.[17,p176]

B. Nonverbal communication skills
   1. Stand straight.
   2. Look the person in the eye.
   3. Appear confident.

Performance indicator 4.8.2 with infused content—Demonstrate refusal skills that avoid or reduce health risks.[1,p30]

(continues)

A. STOP strategy
  1. **S**ay, "No" firmly. Look the person in the eye, with shoulders back, and clearly tell him how you feel.
  2. **T**ell the person why you do not want to drink. Use "I" messages when speaking. For example, "When you pressure me, I do not like it."
  3. **O**ffer suggestions for other activities, instead of drinking alcohol.
  4. **P**romptly leave if you are uncomfortable or the pressure continues.[17,p286]
V. Curricula connections: What other subject areas does this project support?[6,p237]
   English Language Arts
VI. Student directions and assessment criteria[6,p238]
   Prompt #1
   A. Project description: Write and attach an engaging prompt that draws the student into the project.[6,p238]

      Maryann, Dorothy, and Linda have been friends through middle school. Lately, Maryann and Dorothy go to Jean's house to go on Facebook. While there, they sneak some alcohol and have fun. Jean's parents know what is happening but say nothing because they also snuck alcohol as adolescents.

      The girls are pressuring Linda to come with them. Linda's parents do not want her to drink and would be angry if she went against the family rules.

   B. Your challenge: Provide a challenge or mission statement that describes the project.[6,p238]

      Your challenge is to help Linda use interpersonal communication skills to cope with peer pressure and refuse alcohol.

   Prompt #2
   A. Project description: Write and attach an engaging prompt that draws the student into the project.[6,p238]

      Greg and Cheyenne are at Deena's house for a party. Everyone is having fun playing video games and dancing.

      When Deena's parents leave to go shopping, she goes to the liquor cabinet, takes some alcohol, and passes it around. Greg takes a big gulp and hands the bottle to Cheyenne. Cheyenne does not want to take a drink or look foolish in front of his friends.

   B. Your challenge: Provide a challenge or mission statement that describes the project.[6,p238]

      Your challenge is to help Cheyenne use interpersonal communication skills to cope with peer pressure and refuse alcohol.

   Prompt #3
   A. Project description: Write and attach an engaging prompt that draws the student into the project.[6,p238]

      Tony's older brother, Bob, invited him and his friend, Jim, to the high school football game Friday night. Tony and Jim were excited because they were interested in trying out for the team next year. They thought it would be fun hanging out with the older boys.

      During the game, some of the older boys passed around beer. Tony had tried beer before with his brother, so he took a drink. Jim does not drink but did not want Tony to be mad at him.

   B. Your challenge: Provide a challenge or mission statement that describes the project.[6,p238]

      Your challenge is to help Jim use interpersonal communication skills to cope with peer pressure and refuse alcohol.

   C. Assessment criteria[6,p239]

      You are assessed on the following content:

      Performance indicator 1.8.7 with infused content—Describe the benefits of and barriers to practicing healthy behaviors and resisting the peer pressure to use alcohol[1,p25]

      1. Describe three benefits of resisting peer pressure.
      2. Describe three barriers to resisting peer pressure.

(continues)

Performance indicator 4.8.1 with infused content—Apply effective verbal and nonverbal communication skills to resist peer pressure and enhance health.[1,p30]

1. Demonstrate three nonverbal communication skills to resist peer pressure.
2. Apply the STOP strategy to resist peer pressure.

Performance indicator 4.8.2 with infused content—Demonstrate refusal skills that avoid or reduce health risks.[1,p30]

1. Demonstrate the STOP strategy to resist peer pressure

   Student project:

1. Write and present a role-play that contains:
   a. Three verbal and three nonverbal communication skills to resist peer pressure and enhance health
   b. The STOP strategy to refuse alcohol
2. Include a poster that explains:
   a. Three benefits to resisting peer pressure and practicing healthy behaviors
   b. Three barriers to resisting peer pressure and practicing healthy behaviors and how to overcome them.

Plains Middle School

Name _____

Prompt #1

Maryann, Dorothy, and Linda have been friends through middle school. Lately, Maryann and Dorothy go to Jean's house to use Facebook. While there, they sneak some alcohol and have fun. Jean's parents know what is happening but say nothing because they also snuck alcohol as adolescents. The girls are pressuring Linda to come with them. Linda's parents do not want her to drink and would be livid if she went against the family rules.

Your challenge is to help Linda use interpersonal communication skills to cope with peer pressure and refuse alcohol.

Prompt #2

Greg and Cheyenne are at Deena's house for a party. Everyone is having fun playing video games and dancing. When Deena's parents leave to go shopping, she goes to the liquor cabinet, takes some alcohol, and passes it around. Greg takes a big gulp and hands the bottle to Cheyenne. Cheyenne does not want to take a drink or look foolish in front of his friends.

Your challenge is to help Cheyenne use interpersonal communication skills to cope with peer pressure and refuse alcohol.

Prompt #3

Tony's older brother, Bob, invited him and his friend, Jim, to the high school football game Friday night. Tony and Jim were excited because they were interested in trying out for the team next year. They thought it would be fun hanging out with the older boys.

During the game, some of the older boys passed around beer. Tony had tried beer before with his brother, so he took a drink. Jim does not drink but did not want Tony to be mad at him.

Your challenge is to help Jim use interpersonal communication skills to cope with peer pressure and refuse alcohol.

Your project must include the following:

1. A role-play that contains:

   a. Three nonverbal communication skills to resist peer pressure and enhance health

   b. The STOP strategy to refuse alcohol

(continues)

2. A poster that explains:

   a. Three benefits to resisting peer pressure and practicing healthy behaviors

   b. Three barriers to resisting the peer pressure and practicing healthy behaviors and how to overcome them

ANALYTICAL RUBRIC TO ASSESS RESISTING PEER PRESSURE TO DRINK ALCOHOL (TABLE 8.6)

TABLE 8.6 Grade 8: Analytical Rubric to Assess Resisting Pressure to Drink Alcohol

Poster

Criteria	4	3	2	1
Performance indicator 1.8.7 with infused content—Describe the benefits of practicing the healthy behavior of resisting the peer pressure to use alcohol.[1,p25]	The poster thoroughly explains three benefits of practicing the healthy behavior of resisting peer pressure to use alcohol.	The poster adequately explains three benefits of practicing the healthy behavior of resisting peer pressure to use alcohol.	The poster inadequately explains three benefits of practicing the healthy behavior of resisting peer pressure to use alcohol.	The poster poorly explains three benefits of practicing the healthy behavior of resisting peer pressure to use alcohol.
Performance indicator 1.8.7 with infused content—Describe the barriers to practicing the healthy behavior of resisting the peer pressure to use alcohol.[1,p25]	The poster thoroughly explains three barriers to practicing the healthy behavior of resisting peer pressure to use alcohol.	The poster adequately explains three barriers to practicing the healthy behavior of resisting peer pressure to use alcohol.	The poster inadequately explains three barriers to practicing the healthy behavior of resisting peer pressure to use alcohol.	The poster poorly explains three barriers to practicing the healthy behavior of resisting peer pressure to use alcohol.
Role-Play				
Performance indication 4.8.1 with infused content—Apply effective nonverbal communication skills to resist peer pressure and enhance health.[1,p30]	The students accurately demonstrate three nonverbal communication skills to resist peer pressure and enhance health.	The students' demonstration of three nonverbal communication skills to resist peer pressure and enhance health is mostly accurate.	The students' demonstration of three nonverbal communication skills to resist peer pressure and enhance health has a few inaccurate steps.	The students' demonstration of three nonverbal communication skills to resist peer pressure and enhance health is mostly inaccurate.
Performance indicator 4.8.1 with infused content—Apply effective verbal communication skills to resist peer pressure and enhance health.[1,p30]	The students accurately demonstrate the STOP strategy to resist peer pressure and enhance health.	The students' demonstration of the STOP strategy to resist peer pressure and enhance health is mostly accurate.	The students' demonstration of the STOP strategy to resist peer pressure and enhance health has a few inaccurate steps.	The students' demonstration of the STOP strategy to resist peer pressure and enhance health is mostly inaccurate.
Performance indicator 4.8.2 with infused content—Demonstrate refusal skills that avoid or reduce health risks[1,p30]				

(continues)

TABLE 8.6 Grade 8: Analytical Rubric to Assess Resisting Pressure to Drink Alcohol *(continued)*

| | Poster | | | |
Criteria	4	3	2	1
Group involvement	Group involvement in the role-play is excellent.	Group involvement in the role-play is good.	Group involvement in the role-play is fair.	Group involvement in the role-play is poor.
Speech	The students always speak clearly.	The students sometimes speak clearly.	The students rarely speak clearly.	The students never speak clearly.
Creativity	The creativity of the role-play is excellent.	The creativity of the role-play is good.	The creativity of the role-play is fair.	The creativity of the role-play is poor.

Name _____

Total possible points – 28   Your points - _____   Your grade - _____

HOW THE COORDINATED SCHOOL HEALTH TEAM HELPS STUDENTS USE INTERPERSONAL COMMUNICATION SKILLS TO ENHANCE HEALTH AND AVOID OR REDUCE HEALTH RISKS

Health Education

- Teach the consequences of alcohol use.
- Use social norms to help students understand the dangers of peer drinking.
- Discuss healthy ways to cope with depression, stress, and anxiety and how negative coping strategies, such as drinking, are hazardous to health.
- Suggest ways to cope with peer pressure
- Teach verbal and nonverbal communication skills, including refusal skills.

Physical Education

- Provide after-school activities to engage students in healthy behaviors.
- Hang health promotion posters that encourage students to abstain from alcohol.

Health Services

- Be aware of signs of alcohol use and abuse.
- Refer students to guidance or the student assistance team if you detect alcohol use/abuse.

Nutrition Services

- Offer healthy foods, including snacks.
- Hang posters that encourage abstinence from alcohol.

- Hang posters that encourage friends to make healthy decisions.

Counseling, Psychological, and Social Services

- Provide support to students experiencing alcohol related problems.
- Offer alcohol intervention services.
- Arrange alcohol counseling referrals when indicated.

Healthy School Environment

- Provide health promotion posters that encourage students to develop and maintain healthy behaviors.
- Develop after-school clubs and programs that engage students in healthy behaviors.

Health Promotion for Staff

- Provide healthy lifestyle professional development.
- Demonstrate how to be positive role models to students.
- Provide professional development in how to identify students with alcohol problems and refer them to guidance or a student assistance team.

Family and Community Involvement

- Parent workshops
  - To help parents understand the scale of the problem, present data showing alcohol use among middle school students.
  - Explain that a close relationship with parents is associated with less lifetime alcohol use.[19,p65]

- Encourage parents to set clear rules regarding alcohol use, including consequences for breaking them.[19,p64]
- Explain the legal and social ramifications of buying alcohol for teens.
- Suggest that the community provide healthy activities for teens after school, on weekends, and during the summer.

Grades 9–12

To achieve proficiency in Standard 4, Grade 9–12 students must learn to use effective communication skills and demonstrate refusal, negotiation, collaboration, and conflict resolution skills, as well as demonstrate how to ask for help to enhance health.

To teach Standard 4, explain why it is important to communicate effectively and use skills to resolve interpersonal problems. Also, explain how this skill relates to the other National Health Education Standards.

According to the performance indicators selected, present and explain how to achieve proficiency in the skill. Model it so that the students can see competence in action. Provide adequate time for the students to practice the skill and show proficiency through an authentic assessment. Use formative assessments (Chapter 4) to provide feedback and encouragement and to improve instruction.

For example:

Janeen has not been getting along with her parents lately. It seems they yell at one another rather than discuss their problems. Her father says, "You are messy! Clean up after yourself!" Janeen retorts, "You are just as messy! You leave your dishes in the sink, on the table, or in the TV room." Sometimes she would try to negotiate by saying, "If you clean up after yourself, I'll clean up after myself!" Sometimes she is passive, ignores her father, and says or does nothing.

In health class, Janeen learned that when someone starts a sentence with the word, you, it is aggressive, and people may respond in kind. Such dialogue may lead to conflict and, sometimes, violence. Janeen learned about "I" messages and tried them at home saying, "When you call me names and yell at me, it hurts my feelings. Would you please just tell me what the problem is so I can fix it?" Using similar communication helps us own our own feelings rather than blaming or showing contempt for the other person.

Janeen's parents were confused at this new way to communicate, but found that they were able to resolve their differences without yelling and fighting.

To reflect, ask the students:

- What effective communication skills did Janeen use with her parents? (PI 4.12.1) (*"When you call me names and yell at me, it hurts my feelings.)*
- What negotiation skills did Janeen use with her parents? (PI 4.12.2) (*"If you clean up after yourself, I'll clean up after myself!"*)
- What strategies did Janeen use to manage the conflict with her parents? (PI 4.12.3) (*Would you please just tell me what the problem is so I can fix it?"*)
- How did Janeen receive help to improve communication with her parents? (PI 4.12.4)(*In health class, Janeen learned that when someone starts a sentence with the word, you, it is aggressive, and people may respond in kind. Such dialogue may lead to conflict and, sometimes, violence*)

Think of a common family problem, such as a sister or brother wearing a sibling's clothing without permission. Demonstrate how to use interpersonal communication skills to resolve the problem.

As the students are learning the skill, provide enough time for them to practice. Use formative assessments to determine the progress of learning. Motivate students by using feedback to show how performance is improved.

When students demonstrate understanding of the skill, teach the content. Design a prompt that allows the students to showcase their knowledge of health by demonstrating interpersonal communication skills. Use formative assessments, such as white boards (Chapter 4), during content instruction to determine student understanding.

WHAT DOES THE SKILL OF INTERPERSONAL COMMUNICATION LOOK LIKE IN THE GRADE 11 CLASSROOM?

Mrs. Callahan is a Grade 11 health teacher at Westchester High School. Most of her students have cell phones with

---

Grades 9–12

4.12.1 Use skills for communicating effectively with family, peers, and others to enhance health.

4.12.2 Demonstrate refusal, negotiation, and collaboration skills to enhance health and avoid or reduce health risks.

4.12.3 Demonstrate strategies to prevent, manage, or resolve interpersonal conflicts without harming self or others.

4.12.4 Demonstrate how to ask for and offer assistance to enhance the health of self and others.[1,p31]

---

picture taking functionality. Despite not allowing phones in class, she saw two students showing a picture to others, then making rude remarks and sneering.

She approached the girls and noticed that they were looking at semi-nude pictures of another girl. Shocked, she ordered, "Please step into the hall," which they did. "Do you know the ramifications of your sexting and sexual harassment?"

Later that day, a group of girls supporting the student in the pictures ganged up on the two girls who were showing them. They cornered the boyfriend of one girl and sprayed him with paint. The principal suspended all offenders for a day and required them to spend time with the counselors to learn about sexual harassment of students and teachers, the legal ramifications of sexting, and battery.

That evening, Mrs. Callahan researched teens and sexting. She found a study that reported that 71% of teen girls and 67% of boys have sent or posted sexually suggestive content. In fact, 51% of teen girls say they send sexy messages or images because their boyfriends pressure them.[21,p4] They also send sexy pictures to someone else they want to date or hook up with.[21,p2] Forty-four percent of teen girls and boys say it is common to share sexually suggestive text messages with someone other than the intended recipient.[21,p3]

Mrs. Callahan wants her students to recognize the dangers of sexting and the consequences of sexual harassment, to refuse being pressured into such activity, and to learn to resolve interpersonal conflict in a non-violent manner.

She plans the unit by choosing the performance indicators for Standard 4 that meet the needs of her students.

Standard 4—Students will demonstrate the ability to use interpersonal communication skills to enhance health and avoid or reduce health risks.[1,p30]

> 4.12.2—Demonstrate refusal, negotiation, and collaboration skills to enhance health and avoid or reduce health risks.[1,p31]
>
> > *Performance indicator 4.12.2 with infused content*—Demonstrate refusal skills to enhance health and avoid or reduce health risks when asked to create and send sexually suggestive texts and pictures.[1,p31]
>
> 4.12.3—Demonstrate strategies to prevent, manage, or resolve interpersonal conflict without harming self or others.[1,p31]

> *Performance indicator 4.12.3 with infused content*—Demonstrate strategies to prevent, manage, or resolve interpersonal conflict resulting from sexting or sexual harassment without harming self or others.[1,p31]

After selecting the appropriate performance indicator for the skill, Mrs. Callahan chooses the performance indicator for Standard 1.

Standard 1—Students will comprehend concepts related to health promotion and disease prevention to enhance health.[1,p24]

> 1.12.2—Describe the interrelationships of emotional, intellectual, physical, and social health.[1,p25]
>
> > *Performance indicator 1.12.2 with infused content*—Describe the interrelationships of emotional, intellectual, physical, and social health when coping with the consequences of sexting and sexual harassment.[1,p25]

By linking the skill and content performance indicators, the teacher has a sound idea of how to plan the lessons for the interpersonal communications unit.

The first step in planning is to think through the unit by completing the performance task template. Thereupon, the teacher has most of the information to introduce the prompt to the students.

When distributing the prompt, include all the back-up information, student worksheets, and holistic and analytical rubrics, which inform students how they are being assessed before they work on their product. Rubrics act as a guide and help the students attain proficiency in the standards.

Designing the performance task takes considerable preparation. Once the teacher distributes and explains the information, the students create a product. They learn with effective coaching (formative assessment) how to demonstrate proficiency in content and skill.

The following is an example of a performance task for a Grade 11 interpersonal communication unit that focuses on the consequences of sexting and sexual harassment.

The teachers section demonstrates how to plan an authentic assessment of the performance indicators, 1.12.2, 4.12.2, and 4.12.3. The second, for the student, extracts information from the performance task and transforms it into the student prompt and support materials.

Standard 4 Performance Task: Grade 11—Using Interpersonal Communication Skills to Cope with Sexting and Sexual Harassment.

I. Which state standard(s) does this performance task address?

II. Topic: What areas of health does this project assess? Why is it important? What is the intent of the project?[6,p237]

  A. This performance task assesses the health area of Personal Health and Injury Prevention/Safety.

  B. This topic is important because:

   1. 71% of teen girls and 67% of teen boys have sent or posted sexually suggestive content.

   2. 51% of teen girls say they send sexy messages or images because their boyfriends pressure them.[21,p4]

   3. Girls send the pictures or text to boyfriends or someone they want to date or hook-up with.[21,p2]

   4. 44% of teen girls and boys say it is common to share sexually suggestive text messages with someone other than the intended recipient.[21,p3]

  C. The focus of the project is to help students learn to use interpersonal communication skills to cope with sexual harassment and the pressure of taking and sending sexually suggestive texts or pictures.

III. Key Concepts: What basic concepts do students need to know?[6,p237]

  Standard 1—Students will comprehend concepts related to health promotion and disease prevention to enhance health.[1,p24]

  Performance indicator 1.12.2 with infused content—Describe the interrelationships of emotional, intellectual, physical, and social health when coping with the consequences of sexting and sexual harassment.[1,p25]

  A. Terms

   1. Sexually suggestive pictures/videos are semi-nude or nude personal pictures taken on a cell phone or video camera that are not found on the Internet or received from a stranger.

   2. Sexually suggestive messages are personally written and sent through e-mail, text, or instant messaging to someone the person knows.[21,p5]

   3. Sexual harassment is unwanted physical contact, pressure to date someone, sexually explicit humor, sexual innuendos or remarks, offers of job advancement or better grades in exchange for sexual favors, or sexual assault.[22,p409]

  B. Consequences of sexting or sexual harassment

   1. Emotional health

    a. Post traumatic stress

    b. Broken trust[22,p408]

    c. Anger

    d. Embarrassment

    e. Frustration

    f. Scared

    g. Depressed

    h. Helpless

    i. Hopeless

    j. Decreased self-esteem[23]

   2. Intellectual health

    a. Fear that one's reputation is compromised[23]

    b. Difficulty concentrating

   3. Physical health

    a. Headaches

    b Stomachaches

    c. Sleeping problems

    d. Eating problems[23]

(continues)

4. Social health
    a. Difficulty developing new friendships
    b. Difficulty developing new relationships[22]
IV. Skills: Which of the seven National Health Education Standards skills does this performance task address?[6,p237]

Standard 4—Students will demonstrate the ability to use interpersonal communication skills to enhance health and avoid or reduce health risks.[1,p30]

Performance indicator 4.12.2 with infused content—Demonstrate refusal skills to enhance health and avoid or reduce health risks when asked to take and send sexually suggestive texts and pictures.[1,p31]

A. Refusal skills
    1. Step one
        a. Say, "No!"
        b. State your position simply but firmly.
        c. Be sure your nonverbal body language is consistent with your spoken language.
            1. Stand tall.
            2. Look the person in the eye.
        d. Give a reason for your refusal.
    2. Step two
        a. Suggest an alternative healthy activity with which you are comfortable.
        b. Suggest meeting with friends, if alone.
    3. Step three
        a. Do not allow the other person to persuade once you have refused.
        b. Make it clear you will not change your mind.
        c. Maintain eye contact, and stand tall.
    4. Step four
        a. If the pressure continues, leave.[17,p202-203]

Performance indicator 4.12.3 with infused content—Demonstrate strategies to prevent, manage, or resolve interpersonal conflict resulting from sexting or sexual harassment without harming self or others.[1,p31]
    1. Remain calm.
    2. Set a positive tone.
    3. Define the conflict.
    4. Take responsibility for personal actions.
    5. Listen to the needs and feelings of others.
    6. List and evaluate possible solutions.
    7. Agree on a solution.[12,p786]
    8. Seek adult help, if necessary.
V. Curricular connections: What other subject areas does this project support?[6,p237]
    English Language Arts
VI. Student Directions and Assessment Criteria[6,p238]
    A. Project Description: Write/attach an engaging prompt that draws the student into the project.[6,p238]
    Scenario #1

    Evan and Diane are juniors at East Meadow High School and have been dating for a few months. They have many mutual friends and often hang out with them on the weekends.

    They like to take digital pictures of themselves, exchange them and text each other about where they are and with whom. They also like receiving texts, e-mails, and pictures from friends.

    One night, Evan asked Diane to take a picture of herself in just her underwear and send it to him. The idea seemed exciting. Diane knew she should not do it, but she knew Evan would be mad at her if she refused.

(continues)

B. Your Challenge: Provide a challenge or mission statement that describes the project.[6,p238]

Your challenge, as a health professional and radio talk show host, is to help Diane to refuse to take and send a compromising picture to Evan. Give advice on how to use the interpersonal communication skill of refusing to respond to this unwanted situation.

Scenario #2

Abby is a popular 11th grader at East Meadow High School. She invited several friends to her house for a sleepover on Saturday night.

While watching a sexy movie, Abby suggested they all strip down to their underwear, take some pictures, and send them to their boyfriends. A few of the girls agreed, thinking it would be funny, but several refused.

During the evening, Daneene decided to take a shower, and, when done, opened the curtain. Some of the girls took her picture and sent it to their other friends!

On Monday, many of the girls were shocked to discover their boyfriends had sent the sleepover pictures to their friends. Daneene felt humiliated because her picture circulated the school. Each girl was called names, pinched, and ridiculed. They felt very uncomfortable, and told the students to stop harassing them.

A brawl was about to erupt!

B. Your Challenge: Provide a challenge or mission statement that describes the project.[6,p238]

Your challenge is help your friends resolve their conflict peacefully and respectfully.

C. Assessment Criteria[6,p239]

You will be assessed on the following content:

Performance indicator 1.12.2 with infused content—Describe the interrelationships of emotional, intellectual, physical, and social health when coping with the consequences of sexting and sexual harassment.[1,p25]

1. Describe two emotional, intellectual, physical, and social health consequences when coping with sexting and sexual harassment.

You will be assessed on the following skills:

Performance indicator 4.12.2 with infused content—Demonstrate refusal skills to enhance health and avoid or reduce health risks when asked to take and send sexually suggestive texts and digital pictures.[1,p31]

1. Demonstrate refusal skills

Performance indicator 4.12.3 with infused content—Demonstrate strategies to prevent, manage, or resolve interpersonal conflict resulting from sexting or sexual harassment without harming self or others.[1,p31]

1. Demonstrate conflict resolution skills

Student project must contain the following:

1. A completed refusal skill worksheet for Prompt #1 and the conflict resolution worksheet for Prompt #2.
2. A role-play that contains:
   a. Discussion of two emotional, intellectual, physical, and social health consequences of sexting and sexual harassment.
   b. Demonstration of refusal skills, or
   c. Demonstration of conflict resolution skills

East Meadow High School

Name _____

Scenario #1

Evan and Diane are juniors at East Meadow High School and have been dating for a few months. They have many mutual friends and often hang out with them on the weekends.

(continues)

They like to take digital pictures of themselves and exchange them and text each other about where they are and with whom. They also like receiving texts, e-mails, and pictures from friends.

One night, Evan asked Diane to take a picture of herself in just her underwear and send it to him. The idea seemed exciting. Diane knew she should not do it, but she knew Even would be mad at her if she refused.

Your challenge, as a health professional and radio talk show host, is to help Diane to refuse taking and sending the picture to Evan. Give advice on how to use the interpersonal communication skills of refusal and conflict resolution to respond to this unwanted situation.

Scenario #2

Abby is a popular 11th grader at East Meadow High School. She invited several friends to her house for a sleepover on Saturday night.

While watching a sexy movie, Abby suggested they all strip down to their underwear, take some pictures, and send them to their boyfriends. A few of the girls agreed, thinking it would be funny, but several refused.

During the evening, Daneene decided to take a shower, and, when done, opened the curtain. Some of the girls took her picture and sent it to their other friends!

On Monday, many of the girls were shocked to discover their boyfriends had sent the sleepover pictures to their friends. Daneene felt humiliated because her picture circulated the school. Each girl was called names, pinched, and ridiculed. They felt very uncomfortable, and told the students to stop.

A brawl was about to erupt!

Your challenge is help your friends resolve their conflict peacefully and respectfully.

Your project must contain:

1. A completed refusal skill worksheet for Prompt #1 and the conflict resolution worksheet for Prompt #2.

2. A role-play that contains:

   a. Discussion of two emotional, intellectual, physical, and social health consequences of sexting and sexual harassment

   b. Demonstration of refusal skills, or

   c. Demonstration of conflict resolution skills

ASSESSMENT MATERIALS

Refusal skill worksheet (**Table 8.7**)

TABLE 8.7   Refusal Skill Worksheet

Refusal Skill Worksheet for Prompt #1

Step 1–Skill	Your response
a. Say, "No!"	
b. State your position simply but firmly.	
c. Be sure your nonverbal body language is consistent with your verbal language.	
1. Stand tall.	
2. Look the person in the eye.	
d. Give a reason for your refusal.	

(continues)

TABLE 8.7   Refusal Skill Worksheet *(continued)*

Refusal Skill Worksheet for Prompt #1

Step 2–Skill	Your response

a. Suggest an alternative healthy activity with which you
   are comfortable.

b. Suggest meeting with friends, if alone.

Step 3–Skill	Your response

a. Do not allow the other person to persuade once you have refused.

b. Make it clear you will not change your mind.

c. Maintain eye contact, and stand tall.

Step 4–Skill	Your response

a. If the pressure continues, leave.[17,p203]

Conflict resolution worksheet (**Table 8.8**)

TABLE 8.8   Conflict Resolution Worksheet

Conflict Resolution Worksheet for Prompt #2

Skill	Your response

1. Remain calm.

2. Set a positive tone.

3. Define the conflict.

4. Take responsibility for personal actions.

5. Listen to the needs and feelings of others.

6. List and evaluate possible solutions.

7. Agree on a solution

8. Seek adult help, if necessary.[12,p786]

Grade 11 Health Education—Analytical Rubrics for Demonstrating Interpersonal Communication Skills to Cope with "Sexting" and Sexual Harassment (**Tables 8.9** and **8.10**)

(continues)

TABLE 8.9   Grade 11: Analytical Rubric to Assess a Demonstration of Refusal Skills

Criteria	4	3	2	1
Performance indicator 1.12.2 with infused content—Describe the emotional health consequences of coping with sexting and sexual harassment.[1,p25]	The students thoroughly explain two emotional health consequences of coping with sexting and sexual harassment.	The students adequately explain two emotional health consequences of coping with sexting and sexual harassment.	The students inadequately explain two emotional health consequences of coping with sexting and sexual harassment.	The students poorly explain two emotional health consequences of coping with sexting and sexual harassment.
Performance indicator 1.12.2 with infused content—Describe the intellectual health consequences of coping with sexting and sexual harassment.[1,p25]	The students thoroughly explain two intellectual health consequences of coping with sexting and sexual harassment.	The students adequately explain two intellectual health consequences of coping with sexting and sexual harassment.	The students inadequately explain two intellectual health consequences of coping with sexting and sexual harassment.	The students poorly explain two intellectual health consequences of coping with sexting and sexual harassment.
Performance indicator 1.12.2 with infused content—Describe the physical health consequences of coping with sexting and sexual harassment.[1,p25]	The students thoroughly explain two physical health consequences of coping with sexting and sexual harassment.	The students adequately explain two physical health consequences of coping with sexting and sexual harassment.	The students inadequately explain two physical health consequences of coping with sexting and sexual harassment.	The students poorly explain two physical health consequences of coping with sexting and sexual harassment.
Performance indicator 1.12.2 with infused content—Describe the social health consequences when coping with sexting and sexual harassment.[1,p25]	The students thoroughly explain two social health consequences of coping with sexting and sexual harassment.	The students adequately explain two social health consequences of coping with sexting and sexual harassment.	The students inadequately explain two social health consequences of coping with sexting and sexual harassment.	The students poorly explain two social health consequences of coping with sexting and sexual harassment.
		Refusal Skills		
Performance indicator 4.12.2 with infused content—Demonstrate refusal skills to enhance health and avoid or reduce health risks when asked to take and send sexually suggestive texts and pictures.[1,p31]	The student accurately demonstrates step one of the refusal skill.	The student's demonstration of step one of the refusal skill is mostly accurate.	The student's demonstration of step one of the refusal skill has a few inaccuracies.	The student's demonstration of step one of the refusal skill is mostly inaccurate.
Performance indicator 4.12.2 with infused content—Demonstrate refusal skills to enhance health and avoid or reduce health risks when asked to take and send sexually suggestive texts and pictures.[1,p31]	The student accurately demonstrates step two of the refusal skill.	The student's demonstration of step two of the refusal skill is mostly accurate.	The student's demonstration of step two of the refusal skill has a few inaccuracies.	The student's demonstration of step two of the refusal skill is mostly inaccurate.

(continues)

TABLE 8.9   Grade 11: Analytical Rubric to Assess a Demonstration of Refusal Skills *(continued)*

Criteria	4	3	2	1
Performance indicator 4.12.2 with infused content—Demonstrate refusal skills to enhance health and avoid or reduce health risks when asked to take and send sexually suggestive texts and pictures.[1,p31]	The student accurately demonstrates step three of the refusal skill.	The student's demonstration of step three of the refusal skill is mostly accurate.	The student's demonstration of step three of the refusal skill has a few inaccuracies.	The student's demonstration of step three of the refusal skill is mostly inaccurate.
Performance indicator 4.12.2 with infused content—Demonstrate refusal skills to enhance health and avoid or reduce health risks when asked to take and send sexually suggestive texts and pictures.[1,p31]	The student accurately demonstrates step four of the refusal skill.	The student's demonstration of step four of the refusal skill is mostly accurate.	The student's demonstration of step four of the refusal skill has a few inaccuracies.	The student's demonstration of step four of the refusal skill is mostly inaccurate.
Group involvement	Group involvement in the role-play is excellent.	Group involvement in the role-play is good.	Group involvement in the role-play is fair.	Group involvement in the role-play is poor.
Speech	The student always speaks clearly.	The student sometimes speaks clearly.	The student rarely speaks clearly.	The student never speaks clearly.
Creativity	The creativity of the role-play is excellent.	The creativity of the role-play is good.	The creativity of the role-play is fair.	The creativity of the role-play is poor.

Name _____

Total possible points – 44   Your points - _____   Your grade - _____

TABLE 8.10   Analytical Rubric for Demonstrating Conflict Resolution Skills

Criteria	4	3	2	1
Performance indicator 1.12.2 with infused content—Describe the emotional health consequences of coping with sexting and sexual harassment.[1,p31]	The students thoroughly explain two emotional health consequences of coping with sexting and sexual harassment.	The students adequately explain two emotional health consequences of coping with sexting and sexual harassment.	The students inadequately explain two emotional health consequences of coping with sexting and sexual harassment.	The students poorly explain two emotional health consequences of coping with sexting and sexual harassment.

(continues)

Criteria	4	3	2	1
Performance indicator 1.12.2 with infused content—Describe the intellectual health consequences of coping with sexting and sexual harassment.[1,p25]	The students thoroughly explain two intellectual health consequences of coping with sexting and sexual harassment.	The students adequately explain two intellectual health consequences of coping with sexting and sexual harassment.	The students inadequately explain two intellectual health consequences of coping with sexting and sexual harassment.	The students poorly explain two intellectual health consequences of coping with sexting and sexual harassment.
Performance indicator 1.12.2 with infused content—Describe the physical health consequences of coping with sexting and sexual harassment.[1,p25]	The students thoroughly explain two physical health consequences of coping with sexting and sexual harassment.	The students adequately explain two physical health consequences of coping with sexting and sexual harassment.	The students inadequately explain two physical health consequences of coping with sexting and sexual harassment.	The students poorly explain two physical health consequences of coping with sexting and sexual harassment.
Performance indicator 1.12.2 with infused content—Describe the social health consequences of coping with sexting and sexual harassment.[1,p25]	The students thoroughly explain two social health consequences of coping with sexting and sexual harassment.	The students adequately explain two social health consequences of coping with sexting and sexual harassment.	The students inadequately explain two social health consequences of coping with sexting and sexual harassment.	The students poorly explain two social health consequences of coping with sexting and sexual harassment.
		Conflict Resolution Skills		
Performance indicator 4.12.3 with infused content—Demonstrate strategies to prevent, manage, or resolve interpersonal conflict resulting from sexting or sexual harassment without harming self or others.[1,p31]	The students accurately demonstrate how to remain calm during interpersonal conflict resulting from sexting or sexual harassment without harming self or others.	The students' demonstration of how to remain calm during interpersonal conflict resulting from sexting or sexual harassment without harming self or others is mostly accurate.	The students' demonstration of how to remain calm during interpersonal conflict resulting from sexting or sexual harassment without harming self or others has a few inaccuracies.	The students' demonstration of how to remain calm during interpersonal conflict resulting from sexting or sexual harassment without harming self or others is mostly inaccurate.
Performance indicator 4.12.3 with infused content—Demonstrate strategies to prevent, manage, or resolve interpersonal conflict resulting from sexting or sexual harassment without harming self or others.[1,p31]	The students accurately demonstrate how to set a positive tone during interpersonal conflict resulting from sexting or sexual harassment without harming self or others.	The students' demonstration of how to set a positive tone during interpersonal conflict resulting from sexting or sexual harassment without harming self or others is mostly accurate.	The students' demonstration of how to set a positive tone during interpersonal conflict resulting from sexting or sexual harassment without harming self or others has a few inaccuracies.	The students' demonstration of how to set a positive tone during interpersonal conflict resulting from sexting or sexual harassment without harming self or others is mostly inaccurate.

(continues)

TABLE 8.10 Analytical Rubric for Demonstrating Conflict Resolution Skills *(continued)*

Criteria	4	3	2	1
Performance indicator 4.12.3 with infused content—Demonstrate strategies to prevent, manage, or resolve interpersonal conflict resulting from sexting or sexual harassment without harming self or others.[1,p31]	Students accurately define the conflict resulting from sexting or sexual harassment without harming self or others.	Students' definition of the conflict resulting from sexting or sexual harassment without harming self or others is mostly accurate.	Students' definition of the conflict resulting from sexting or sexual harassment without harming self or others has a few inaccuracies.	Students' definition of the conflict resulting from sexting or sexual harassment without harming self or others is mostly inaccurate.
Performance indicator 4.12.3 with infused content—Demonstrate strategies to prevent, manage, or resolve interpersonal conflict resulting from sexting or sexual harassment without harming self or others.[1,p31]	Students accurately demonstrate how to take responsibility for personal actions when resolving conflict resulting from sexting or sexual harassment without harming self or others.	Students' demonstration of how to take responsibility for personal actions when resolving conflict resulting from sexting or sexual harassment without harming self or others is mostly accurate.	Students' demonstration of how to take responsibility for personal actions when resolving conflict resulting from sexting or sexual harassment without harming self or others has a few inaccuracies.	Students' demonstration of how to take responsibility for personal actions when resolving conflict resulting from sexting or sexual harassment without harming self or others is mostly inaccurate.
Performance indicator 4.12.3 with infused content—Demonstrate strategies to prevent, manage, or resolve interpersonal conflict resulting from sexting or sexual harassment without harming self or others.[1,p31]	Students appropriately demonstrate how to listen to the needs and feelings of others when resolving conflict resulting from sexting or sexual harassment without harming self or others.	Students' demonstration of how to listen to the needs and feelings of others when resolving conflict resulting from sexting or sexual harassment without harming self or others is mostly appropriate.	Students' demonstration of how to listen to the needs and feelings of others when resolving conflict resulting from sexting or sexual harassment without harming self or others has a few inaccuracies.	Students' demonstration of how to listen to the needs and feelings of others when resolving conflict resulting from sexting or sexual harassment without harming self or others is mostly inappropriate.
Performance indicator 4.12.3 with infused content—Demonstrate strategies to prevent, manage, or resolve interpersonal conflict resulting from sexting or sexual harassment without harming self or others.[1,p31]	Students accurately demonstrate how to list and evaluate possible solutions to the conflict resulting from sexting or sexual harassment without harming self or others.	Students' demonstration of how to list and evaluate possible solutions to the conflict resulting from sexting or sexual harassment without harming self or others is mostly accurate.	Students' demonstration of how to list and evaluate possible solutions to the conflict resulting from sexting or sexual harassment without harming self or others has a few inaccuracies.	Students' demonstration of how to list and evaluate possible solutions to the conflict resulting from sexting or sexual harassment without harming self or others is mostly inaccurate.
Performance indicator 4.12.3 with infused content—Demonstrate strategies to prevent, manage, or resolve interpersonal conflict resulting from sexting or sexual harassment without harming self or others.[1,p31]	Students accurately demonstrate how to agree on a solution to the conflict resulting from sexting or sexual harassment without harming self or others.	Students' demonstration of how to agree on a solution of the conflict resulting from sexting or sexual harassment without harming self or others is mostly accurate.	Students' demonstration of how to agree on a solution of the conflict resulting from sexting or sexual harassment without harming self or others has a few inaccuracies.	Students' demonstration of how to agree on a solution of the conflict resulting from sexting or sexual harassment without harming self or others is mostly inaccurate.

(continues)

TABLE 8.10   Analytical Rubric for Demonstrating Conflict Resolution Skills *(continued)*

Criteria	4	3	2	1
Performance indicator 4.12.3 with infused content—Demonstrate strategies to prevent, manage, or resolve interpersonal conflict resulting from sexting or sexual harassment without harming self or others.[1,p31]	Students accurately demonstrate how to seek help in a conflict resulting from sexting or sexual harassment without harming self or others.	Students' demonstration of how to seek help in a conflict resulting from sexting or sexual harassment without harming self or others is mostly accurate.	Students' demonstration of how to seek help in a conflict resulting from sexting or sexual harassment without harming self or others has a few inaccuracies.	Students' demonstration of how to seek help in a conflict resulting from sexting or sexual harassment without harming self or others is mostly inaccurate.
Group involvement	Group involvement in the role-play is excellent.	Group involvement in the role-play is good.	Group involvement in the role-play is fair.	Group involvement in the role-play is poor.
Speech	The students always speak clearly.	The students sometimes speak clearly.	The students rarely speak clearly.	The students never speak clearly.
Creativity	The creativity of the role-play is excellent.	The creativity of the role-play is good.	The creativity of the role-play is fair.	The creativity of the role-play is poor.

Name _____

Total possible points – 70   Your points - _____   Your grade - _____

HOW THE COORDINATED SCHOOL HEALTH TEAM HELPS STUDENTS USE INTERPERSONAL COMMUNICATION SKILLS TO ENHANCE HEALTH AND AVOID OR REDUCE HEALTH RISKS

Health Education

- Promote skills that help students develop healthy behaviors.
- Teach about and role-play the consequences of sexual harassment.
- Teach refusal and conflict resolution skills to cope with sexting and sexual harassment.

Physical Education

- Promote a healthy lifestyle.
- Monitor locker rooms to prevent students from taking pictures while others are changing.

Health Services

- Be alert to the physical and emotional signs and symptoms of sexual harassment.
- Intervene if students reveal victimization.

Nutrition Services

- Prepare and serve special foods for students recognized for demonstrating positive values such as friendship, respect, honesty, truthfulness, integrity, etc.

Counseling, Psychological, and Social Services

- Provide support for students who are victims of sexual harassment and sexting.
- Provide resources for students and parents.

Healthy School Environment

- Hang posters that promote respect in relationships.
- Develop and enforce policies that address sexual harassment and sexting.
- Monitor the halls and lavatories to prevent inappropriate picture taking.

Health Promotion for Staff

- Model appropriate ways to communicate.
- Provide sexual harassment training.
- Provide professional development on contraception and sexually transmitted infections.

Family and Community Involvement

- Participate in sexual harassment workshops that include sexting.
- Set family rules regarding the use of cell phones.
- Encourage the community to provide healthy after-school and weekend activities to engage young people.

Review Questions

1. Why do employers prefer candidates who are proficient in interpersonal communication skills?

2. Explain two reasons why it is important to be proficient in interpersonal communication skills.

3. What are the steps to reaching proficiency in Standard 4?

4. Why is it important to model the skill for students?

5. Explain the relationship between giving students time to practice and using formative assessment tools.

6. How can a teacher assess students who do not read?

7. What is the benefit of assessing skills through role-play?

8. Why is it important to use the same rubric for different scenarios?

9. Justify assessing items that are not in the performance indicator.

10. Explain three reasons why it is important to involve the coordinated school health team in the planning of performance tasks.

References

1. Joint Committee on National Health Education Standards. (2007). *National Health Education Standards, Second Edition, Achieving Excellence.* Atlanta: American Cancer Society.

2. Page, R. M. (2007). *Promoting Health and Emotional Well-Being in Your Classroom.* Sudbury, MA: Jones and Bartlett.

3. Pettit, M. L. (2009). Greeting Cards: A Technique for Communicating Health Messages. *Journal of School Health*, p. 433.

4. Partnership for 21st Century Learning Skills. (n.d.). *A Shared vision of a 21st Century Education System.* Retrieved January 23, 2010, from: http://www.21stcenturyskills.org/documents/21st_century_skills_education_and_competitiveness_guide.pdf, p. 12.

5. Floyd, P. A. (2008). *Personal Health, Perspectives and Lifestyles* (4th ed.). Australia: Thompson Wadsworth, p. 81.

6. CCSSO~SCASS Health Education Project. (2006). *Assessment Tools for School Health Education, Pre-service and In-service edition.* Santa Cruz, CA: ToucanEd, Inc.

7. American Academy of Child & Adolescent Psychiatry. (May 2008). *Facts for Families.* Retrieved January 3, 2010 from Child Sexual Abuse, American Academy of Child & Adolescent Psychiatry: http://aacap.org/cs/root/facts_for_families/child_sexual_abuse, p1.

8. Wurtele, S. K. (2009). Preventing Sexual Abuse of Children in the Twenty-First Century: Preparing for Challenges and Opportunities. *Journal of Child Sexual Abuse*, 18(1), 1–18.

9. Sylvester, L. (1997). *Talking About Touching: A Personal Safety Curriculum Preschool to Grade 3 Curriculum Evaluation Summary.* Seattle: Committee for Children.

10. Healthteacher. (2010). *Stay Safe and Tell.* Retrieved February 5, 2010 from Health Teacher::Lessons: http://www.healthteacher.com/lesson/index/82.

11. KidsHealth. (February 2007). *Do You Know How to Be Street Smart?* Retrieved February 5, 2010: http://kidshealth.org/kid/watch/out/street_smart.html, p. 1.

12. Meeks, L. H. (2009). *Comprehensive School Health Education, Totally Awesome Strategies for Teaching Health* (6th ed.). New York: McGraw-Hill.

13. U.S. Department of Health and Human Services. (n.d.). Kidswalk to School, A Guide to Promote Walking to School. Retrieved November 1, 2010, from http://www.cdc.gov/nccdphp/Dnpa/kidswalk/pdf/kidswalk.pdf

14. Bauman, S. (2008). The Role of Elementary School Counselors in Reducing School Bullying. *The Elementary School Journal*, 108(5), 362–375.

15. Centers for Disease Control and Prevention. (2008). *Fact Sheet.* Retrieved February 6, 2010, from Understanding School Violence: www.cdc.gov/injury, p. 2.

16. Hirschstein, M. K. (2007). Walking the Talk in Bullying Prevention: Teacher Implementation Variables Related to Initial Impact of the Steps to Respect Program. *School Psychology Review*, 36(1), 3–21.

17. Bronson, P. M. (2007). *Teen Health, Course 2.* New York: McGraw-Hill Glencoe.

18. National Crime Prevention Council. (2010). *Facts and advice to help kids overcome bullying.* Retrieved February 7, 2010, from What to Teach Kids about Bullying: http://www.ncpc.org/topics/bullying/teaching-kids-about-bullying/what-to-teach-kids-about-bullying

19. de Haan, P. L. (2009). Alcohol Use Among Rural Middle School Students: Adolescents, Parents, Teachers, and Community Leaders' Perceptions. *Journal of School Health*, 79(2), 58–66.

20. U.S. Department of Health and Human Services, Centers for Disease Control and Prevention. (2005). *2005 Middle School Youth Risk Behavior Survey.* Retrieved February 7, 2010, from: www.cdc.gov/healthyyouth/yrbs/middleschool2005/pdf/YRBS_MS_fullreport.pdf, p. 9.

21. The National Campaign to Prevent Teen and Unplanned Pregnancy. (2008). *Sex and Tech, Results from a Survey of Teens and Young Adults.* Chicago: TRU Insights Program.

22. Hahn, D. B., Payne, W. A., & Lucas, E. B. (2009). *Focus on Health* (9th ed.). New York: McGraw-Hill.

23. The National Center for Victims of Crime. (2010). *Sexual Harassment.* Retrieved February 16, 2010, from Sexual Harassment Information for Teens: http://www.ncvc.org/ncvc/main.aspx?dbName=DocumentViewer&DocumentAction=ViewProperties&DocumentID=32451&UrlToReturn=http%3a%2f%2fwww.ncvc.org%2fncvc%2fmain.aspx%3fdbName%3dAdvancedSearch

Teaching National Health Education Standard 5

"Students will demonstrate the ability to use decision-making skills to enhance health.[1,p32]"

Standard 5

Decision-making skills position us to sort through problems, make a determination, identify healthy alternatives, evaluate their pros and cons, and then implement and reflect on the healthy choices. This proactive process leads to lifelong healthy behaviors.

Effective decision making is also an important component of two national initiatives:

- According to *Healthy People 2020: The Road Ahead*, the ten-year national health objectives have guided individuals toward making informed health decisions since 1979.[2]
- *Education & Competitiveness, A Resource and Policy Guide*, states that all Americans need 21st century skills, such as solving complex, multidisciplinary, open-ended problems, to increase their marketability, employability, and readiness for citizenship.[3]

"Businesses expect employees at all levels to identify problems, think through solutions and alternatives, and explore new options if their approaches don't pan out. Often, this work involves groups of people with different knowledge and skills who, collectively, add value to their organizations."[3]

Our youth see and experience decision making daily. The decisions they observe or experience, however, may not have been carefully considered. The National Health Education Standards provide us with performance indicators that guide us, PreK–12, in designing instruction in decision making. Students learn to demonstrate steps to making healthy decisions and collaborating with others, and, as a result, enhance the quality of their lives.[1,p32]

Sample performance tasks for using decision-making skills to enhance health and avoid or reduce health risks include:

- Role-play how to make decisions.
- As a professional counselor, help an adolescent work through a problem using decision-making skills.
- Write a comic strip showing the thought behind the decision.
- Be a talk show caller and ask for help from a professional health expert regarding decision making about a common teen problem.
- Create a puppet show for a younger audience that demonstrates using decision-making skills.
- Write and act out a play about making healthy decisions.[4,p230]
- Use a scenario to compare a decision based on negative versus positive values. Discuss the decision and consequences that enhance health behavior.

To show proficiency in this standard, students identify situations that require a decision, analyze when to make it alone or with an adult, list healthy options, predict their outcomes, choose a healthy option, then defend and analyze the outcome of the decision.[1,p32-33]

Teaching the Skill

Teaching and learning the national health education skills is a process. When planning, follow these steps to teach decision-making skills.

I. Discuss the importance of using decision-making skills to enhance health.
- A proactive role in making a decision gives the individual a sense of control.
- Make decisions alone or with adult help.
- Involve a trusted friend or adult to brainstorm different decision-making options.
- Weigh the positive versus negative outcomes.
- Be responsible for your own behavior.

- Recognize that decisions have positive and negative consequences.[5,p223]
- Learn not to repeat decisions with negative consequences.

II. Explain the steps to proficiency in decision-making skills to enhance health.
- Select the performance indicators for the grade span.
- Teach the steps to achieve proficiency of the selected performance indicators, such as how to:
  - Sort through a problem and identify when a decision is necessary.
  - Decide whether to involve an adult.
  - Establish the decision to be made.
  - List healthy options.
  - Weigh the pros and cons of each option.
  - Choose a healthy option.
  - Defend the option.
  - Evaluate and reflect on the effectiveness of the decision.[1,p33]

III. Show the students what the decision-making skill looks like.
- Demonstrate the steps.
- Model them in the classroom.

IV. Provide adequate time for students to practice.

V. Utilize formative assessments during practice to provide feedback and encouragement.[1,p14]

PreK–2

To achieve proficiency in Standard 5, PreK–2 students identify situations when a health-related decision is needed, and whether a decision can be made alone or requires help.[1,p32]

Distribute a Stop and Go sign to each student.

Show students pairs of pictures. Tell them to raise the Go sign if the situation requires a health-related decision. If it does, ask the students, "What is the decision to be made?" and "Can the decision be made alone or does the child need help?" If the situation does not require a health-related decision, raise the Stop sign. Discuss why not.

PreK–Grade 2 Performance Indicators

5.2.1 Identify situations when a health-related decision is needed.

5.2.2 Differentiate between situations when a health-related decision can be made individually or when assistance is needed.[1,p32]

- Bicycle
  - Riding a bicycle with a helmet.
  - Riding a bicycle without a helmet.
  - Riding a bicycle in the street with a helmet on, but not accompanied by an adult.
  - Riding a bicycle in the street with a helmet on, but accompanied by an adult.
- Snacks
  - Drinking soda.
  - Drinking juice.
- Safety
  - Crossing a street
    - Using the crosswalk to cross the street.
    - Running across the street, not in the crosswalk.
    - Crossing the street, not holding the hand of an adult.
    - Crossing the street, holding the hand of an adult.
  - Equipment[6,p471]
    - Skating, dressed in a helmet, kneepads, elbow pads, and wrist pads.
    - kating with no safety equipment.
- Responsibility
  - Taking care of clothing
    - Hanging up a coat.
    - Throwing a coat on the floor.
  - Cleaning up after dinner
    - Bringing a plate to the sink.
    - Leaving a plate on the table and walking away.
  - Keeping room clean[6,p471]
    - Putting toys away after playing with them.
    - Walking away from toys after playing with them.

When the students demonstrate an understanding of the skill, as assessed formatively, it is time to practice. Ask the students to give a few more examples of health enhancing decisions and decisions that require help. Examples include

- To brush teeth or not
- To floss teeth or not
- To wash hands or not before eating

Explain that these examples demonstrate how to use decision-making skills to enhance health.

Formatively assess the practice and provide feedback for students to improve their skill development. Continue instruction when students perform the skill.

WHAT DOES THE ABILITY TO USE DECISION-MAKING SKILLS TO ENHANCE HEALTH LOOK LIKE IN THE PREK–2 CLASSROOM?

Mrs. Gage is a preschool teacher. Because of excellent professional development, she knows that contact with cosmetics, personal care products, analgesics, and household cleaning substances is the most common cause of pediatric (ages 5 and under) exposure to poisons.[7,p911-1084] She wants her children to be safe and make good decisions about medicines and other products.

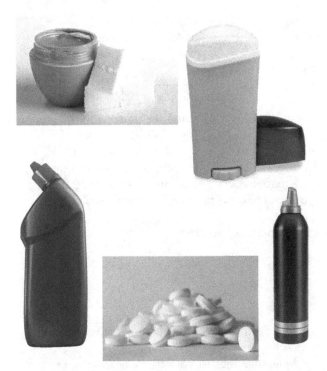

In planning the decision-making unit, she targets the performance indicator 5.2.2.

> 5.2.2—Differentiate between situations when a health-related decision can be made individually or when assistance is needed.[1,p32]

Performance indicator 5.2.2 with infused content— Differentiate between situations when a health-related decision, such as taking a medicine or ingesting other products, can be made individually or when assistance is needed.[1,p32]

After selecting the skill performance indicators, Mrs. Gage selects Standard 1 performance indicators for content.

> Standard 1—Students will comprehend concepts related to health promotion and disease prevention to enhance health.[1,p24]
> > Performance indicator 1.2.4—List ways to prevent common childhood injuries.[1,p24]
> > > *Performance indicator 1.2.4 with infused content—* List ways to prevent common childhood injuries that result from taking medicines or ingesting other products.[1,p24]

By linking the skill and the content performance indicators, the teacher has direction in planning the unit on using decision-making skills to enhance health.

The first step in planning is to think through the unit by completing the performance task template. Upon completion, the teacher has a good idea of the lessons that precede this culminating activity, the information and back-up materials necessary to introduce the prompt to the students, and the assessment strategies.

Because most PreK students are non-readers, the instruction and assessment are verbal and visual. The teacher gives students time to learn about medicine safety and decision-making skills. Students practice and then demonstrate their knowledge and skill during a class presentation followed by a written summative assessment.

The following is an example of a PreK decision-making performance task. The first section demonstrates how the teacher plans for an authentic assessment of the performance indicators 5.2.2 and 1.2.4. The second section extracts some of the information from the performance task and transforms it into the prompt and support materials for students.

The students are assessed formatively during instruction and summatively using an analytical rubric.

Performance Task Name: PreKindergarten—Being Safe with Medicine by Using Decision-Making Skills.

I. Which state standard(s) does the performance task address?
II. Topic: What areas of health does this project assess? Why is it important? What is the focus of the project? [4,p237]
   A. This performance task assesses Injury Prevention/Safety.

(continues)

B. This topic is important because of the following annual statistics that relate to children under the age of five:
1. 173,945 children were exposed to the poisonous effects of cosmetics and personal care products.
2. 125,454 children were exposed to the poisonous effects of analgesics.
3. 124,934 children were exposed to the poisonous effects of household cleaning substances.[7,p911-1084]

C. The focus of the project is for students to use safety rules and decision-making skills to identify medicines and other substances safe to put in the mouth, and determine whether they can decide by themselves or ask an adult for help.

III. Key Concepts: What basic concepts should students know?[4,p237]

Standard 1—Students will comprehend concepts related to health promotion and disease prevention to enhance health.[1,p24]

Performance indicator 1.2.4 with infused content—List ways to prevent common childhood injuries resulting from ingesting medicines or other products.[1,p24]

A. Safety rules
1. Medicine can make you sick if you take the wrong kind or too much.
2. If you do not know what something is, do not put it in your mouth. Ask a trusted adult about its safety.
3. Never take a medicine unless an adult gives it to you.
4. Always ask a grown-up if something is safe to eat.
5. Never play with a spray can or bottle.
6. Stay away from make-up, products that are used to clean your house, or things adults use for grooming.[8]

IV. Skills: Which of the seven National Health Education Skills does this performance task address?[4,p237]

Standard 5—Students will demonstrate the ability to use decision-making skills to enhance health.[1,p32]

Performance indicator 5.2.2 with infused content—Differentiate between situations when a health-related decision, such as taking a medicine or ingesting other products, can be made individually or when assistance is needed.[1,p32]

V. Curricular connections: What other subject(s) does this project support?[4,p237]

English Language Arts
Science—the digestive system
Art

VI. Student directions and assessment criteria[4,p238]

Prompt #1

A. Project Description—Write and attach an engaging prompt that draws the student into the project.[4,p238]

Nicola's older brother Nicolas is babysitting her while their mother goes to the grocery store.

When Nicola came home from day care, her head hurt, but she didn't tell anyone. Now, it hurts more. When her mommy's head hurts, Nicola sees her take the white pills in the medicine cabinet in the bathroom.

Nicola wants to take the pills to stop her headache.

B. Your challenge—Provide a challenge or mission statement that describes the project.[4,p238]

Your challenge is to help Nicola stay safe and make a good decision.

Prompt #2

A. Project Description—Write and attach an engaging prompt that draws the student into the project.[4,p238]

Ramon's throat hurts when he swallows, and he feels tired. When his daddy has a sore throat, Ramon sees him spray something into his mouth.

Daddy is mowing the lawn, and mommy is making supper.

Ramon wants to go into the bathroom, find the medicine, and spray it into his mouth.

B. Your challenge—Provide a challenge or mission statement that describes the project.[4,p238]

Your challenge is to help Ramon stay safe and make a good decision.

(continues)

C. Assessment Criteria[4,p239]

You are assessed on the following key concepts: (List the concepts)

Performance indicator 1.2.4 with infused content—List ways to prevent common childhood injuries resulting from taking medicines or ingesting other products.[1,p24]

1. Explain two safety rules.
2. Identify two items that are safe to put in the mouth.

You are assessed on the following skills: (List the skills)

Performance indicator 5.2.2 with infused content—Differentiate between situations when a health-related decision, such as taking a medicine or ingesting other products, can be made individually or only with help.[1,p32]

1. Two examples of when it is safe to make a decision by yourself.
2. Two examples of when a decision should be made with an adult.

Student project must include the following:(List the project components)

1. A completed prompt worksheet for each prompt.
2. Poster showing:
   a. Two safety rules
   b. Two items that are safe to put in the mouth
   c. Two decisions that can be made alone
   d. Two decisions that should be made with an adult
2. Explain the poster to the class.

Prompt and Assessment Criteria

(For non-readers, read the prompt and explain the directions.)

Regina Preschool

Decision Making Unit

Name _____

Prompt #1

Nicola's older brother Nicolas is babysitting her while their mother goes to the grocery store.

When Nicola came home from day care, her head hurt, but she didn't tell anyone. Now, it hurts more. When her mommy's head hurts, Nicola sees her take the white pills in the medicine cabinet in the bathroom.

Nicola wants to take the pills to stop her headache.

Your challenge is to help Nicola stay safe and make a good decision.

Prompt #2

Ramon's throat hurts when he swallows, and he feels very tired. When his daddy has a sore throat, Ramon sees him spray something into his mouth.

Daddy is mowing the lawn, and mommy is making supper.

Ramon wants to go into the bathroom, find the medicine, and spray it into his mouth.

Your challenge is to help Ramon stay safe and make a good decision.

Complete a prompt worksheet for each prompt.

1. Explain two safety rules, and two items that are safe to put into the mouth.

2. Explain two examples of when it is safe to make a decision alone.

3. Explain two examples of when a decision should be made only with an adult.

(continues)

Make a poster, color the words, and explain it to the class. Include:

1. Two safety rules.

2. Two items that are safe to put in the mouth

3. Two decisions that can be made alone.

4. Two decisions that must be made with an adult.

ASSESSMENT MATERIALS

Prompt Worksheet (Table 9.1)

TABLE 9.1   PreK Prompt Worksheet

Prompt Worksheet

Make two copies, one for each prompt.

Directions: Provide the student with a sticker when the skill is demonstrated.

1. Explain two medicine safety rules.   1.

                                                          2.

2. Explain two rules about not putting something into   1.
   the mouth.

                                                          2.

3. Explain two examples of when it is safe to make a   1.
   decision alone.

                                                          2.

4. Explain two examples of when a decision should be   1.
   made only with an adult.

                                                          2.

(continues)

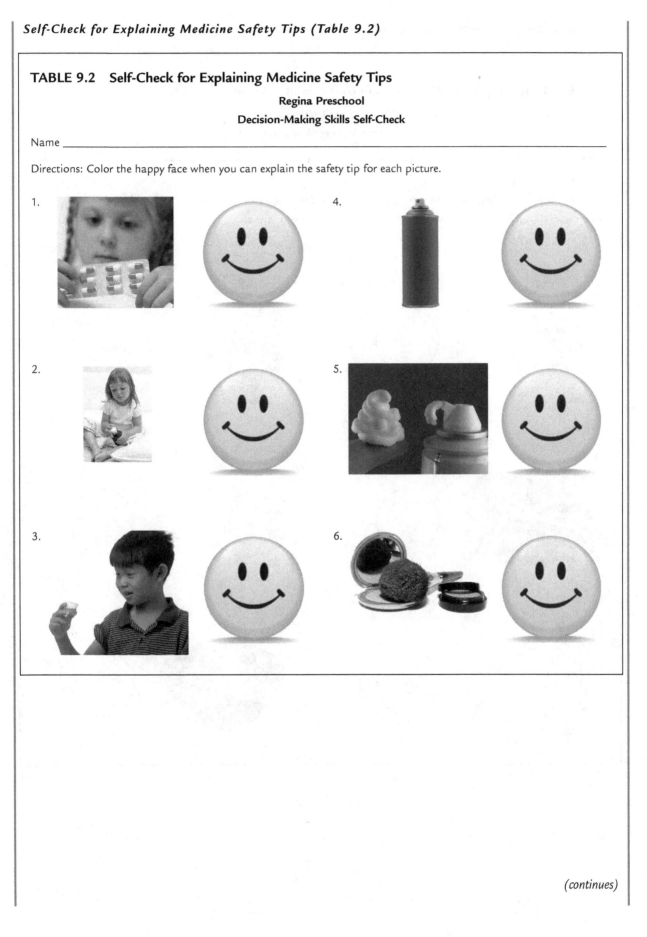

TABLE 9.2 Self-Check for Explaining Medicine Safety Tips

Regina Preschool

Decision-Making Skills Self-Check

Name _____

Directions: Color the happy face when you can explain the safety tip for each picture.

1.

4.

2.

5.

3.

6.

(continues)

TABLE 9.3   Identify Items That Are Safe to Put in the Mouth

Regina Preschool
Decision-Making Skills Self-Check

Name _____

Directions:

Color the circle green if you know the item in the picture is safe to put in your mouth.

Color the circle red if the item in the picture is not safe to put in your mouth

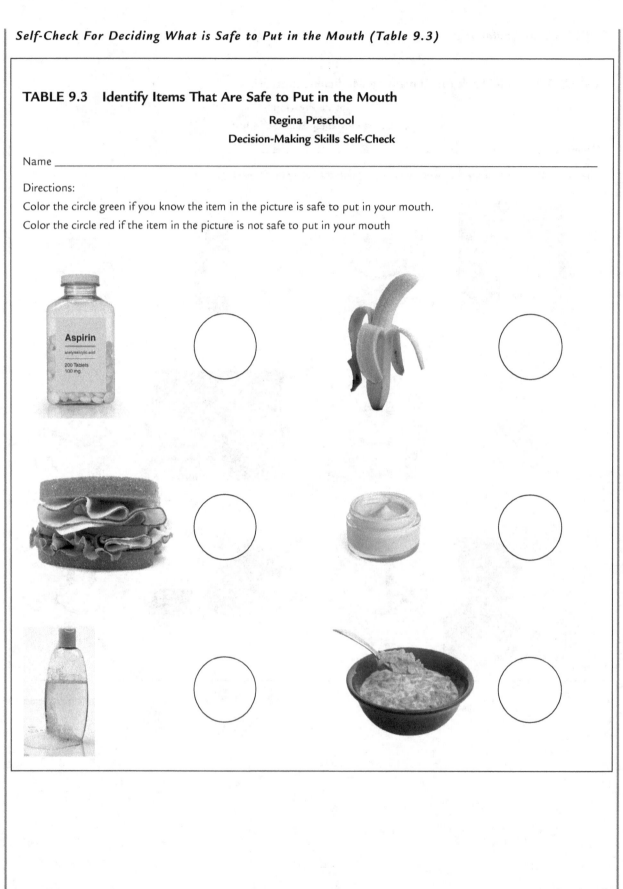

(continues)

TABLE 9.4   Self-Check for Practicing Identifying Situations Where a Decision Can be Made Alone or Must Be Made With an Adult

Regina Preschool

Decision-Making Skills Self-Check

Name _____

Directions: Color the child if he can make the decision alone. Color the child and adult if the child needs help to make the decision.

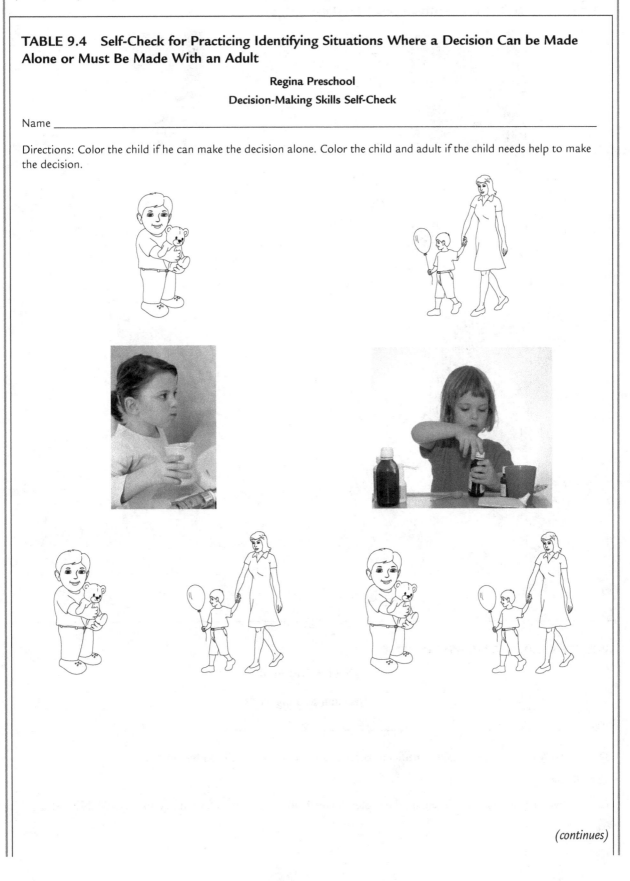

(continues)

TABLE 9.4 Self-Check for Practicing Identifying Situations Where a Decision Can be Made Alone or Must Be Made With an Adult *(continued)*

WRITTEN SUMMATIVE ASSESSMENT

Regina Preschool

Decision-Making Skills

Name _____

Directions: You are going to make a medicine safety poster. Color the words on the poster.

Explain the medicine safety rules.

Cut out two pictures and place them on the poster. Be ready to explain the safety rule to the class (**Table 9.5**).

(continues)

1.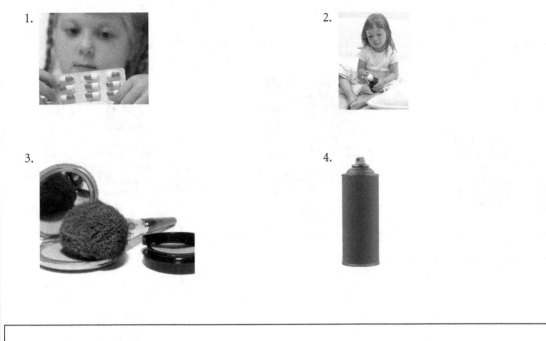

2.

3.

4.

TABLE 9.5 Items Safe to Put in the Mouth

Cut out two pictures of items that are safe to put in the mouth and paste them into the chart. Cut out the chart and paste it on the poster.

Items Safe to Put in the Mouth	

(continues)

Decisions Safe to Make Alone

Cut out two pictures that show when it is safe to make a decision alone and paste them on the chart. Cut out the chart and paste it on the poster (**Table 9.6**).

TABLE 9.6   Decisions You Can Make Alone

Decisions That Are Made With an Adult

Cut out two pictures of decisions that you make with an adult and paste them on the chart. Cut out the chart and paste it on the poster (**Table 9.7**).

TABLE 9.7   Decisions You Can Make With an Adult

(continues)

TABLE 9.8   **Poster for Showing Proficiency in Medicine Safety and Decision-Making**

Make good decisions

Two safety rules

Two things safe to put in the mouth

Decisions safe to make alone.

Decisions to make with an adult.

Analytical Rubric to Assess the Decision-Making Poster (Table 9.9)

TABLE 9.9   **Pre-Kindergarten—Analytical Rubric to Assess the Decision-Making Poster**

Criteria	4	3	2	1
Performance indicator 1.2.4 with infused content—List ways to prevent common childhood injuries caused by taking medicines or ingesting other products.[1,p24]	Student thoroughly explains two medicine safety rules or safety rules about putting objects in the mouth.	Student adequately explains two medicine safety rules or safety rules about putting objects in the mouth.	Student inadequately explains two medicine safety rules or safety rules about putting objects in the mouth.	Student poorly explains two medicine safety rules or safety rules about putting objects in the mouth.
Performance indicator 1.2.4 with infused content—List ways to prevent common childhood injuries caused by taking medicines or ingesting other products.[1,p24]	Student accurately identifies two items that are safe to put in the mouth.	Student's identification of ways to prevent common childhood injuries caused by taking medicines or ingesting other products is mostly accurate.	Student's identification of ways to prevent common childhood injuries caused by taking medicines or ingesting other products has some inaccuracies.	Student inaccurately identifies two items that are safe to put in the mouth.

(continues)

TABLE 9.9 Pre-Kindergarten—Analytical Rubric to Assess the Decision-Making Poster *(continued)*

Criteria	4	3	2	1
Performance indicator 5.2.2 with infused content—Differentiate between situations when a health-related decision, such as taking a medicine or ingesting other products, can be made individually.[1,p32]	Student accurately explains when two health-related decisions, such as taking a medicine or ingesting other products, can be made individually.	Student's explanation of when two health-related decisions, such as taking a medicine or ingesting other products, can be made individually is mostly accurate.	Student's explanation of when two health-related decisions, such as taking a medicine or ingesting other products, can be made individually has some inaccuracies.	Student's explanation of when two health-related decisions, such as taking a medicine or ingesting other products, can be made individually is inaccurate.
Performance indicator 5.2.2 with infused content—Differentiate between situations when assistance is needed when making a health-related decision, such as taking a medicine or ingesting other products.[1,p32]	Student accurately explains when two health-related decisions, such as taking a medicine or ingesting other products, should be made with an adult.	Student's explanation of when two health-related decisions such as taking a medicine or ingesting other products should be made with an adult is mostly accurate.	Student's explanation of when two health-related decisions such as taking a medicine or ingesting other products should be made with an adult has some inaccuracies.	Student's explanation of when two health-related decisions such as taking a medicine or ingesting other products should be made with an adult is inaccurate.
Presentation	Student always speaks clearly.	Student sometimes speaks clearly.	Student rarely speaks clearly.	Student never speaks clearly.
Colorful	The poster has excellent color.	The poster has good color.	The poster has fair color.	The poster has poor color.

Name _____

Total possible points – 24   Your points – _____   Your grade – _____

HOW THE COORDINATED SCHOOL HEALTH TEAM HELPS STUDENTS USE DECISION-MAKING SKILLS TO ENHANCE HEALTH

Health Education

- Teach decision-making skill.
  - Medicine safety
  - Items that can be safely put into the mouth
  - Ask for help, when needed.
- Model medicine safety.

Physical Education

- Model medicine safety.
- Encourage students to ask for help when needed.

Health Services

- Provide support for students who take medicine during the day.
- Review medicine safety with students.

Nutrition Services

- Encourage students to ask for help from an adult, when needed.
- Model food safety.

Counseling, Psychological, and Social Services

- Provide support for students who take medicine during the day.
- Help students be comfortable asking adults for help, when needed.

Healthy School Environment

- Hang posters that promote medicine safety.
- Encourage teachers to establish nurturing relationships with students.

Health Promotion for Staff

- Model medicine safety.

- Provide professional development on how to encourage students to ask for help when needed.

Family and Community Involvement

- Provide workshops on medicine safety.

Grades 3–5

To achieve proficiency in Standard 5, Grade 3–5 students identify when to make health-related decisions with or without an adult, then use the decision-making skill to enhance health.

To teach Standard 5, identify the problem and its solution. List healthy options, predict the outcome of each, choose a healthy one, and then describe the results of the decision.

For example,

Sean is sad lately because he is doing poorly in school. When he comes home in the afternoon, Sean checks Facebook and then plays video games. After supper, he talks to friends, attempts his homework and studies, but he is tired. He sets his alarm to finish his homework in the morning, but when it goes off he hits the snooze button and stays in bed.

Sean knows he can do the homework and study for exams. He is not using his time well and seems unable to change his behavior.

His friend, Ben, does his schoolwork and keeps up with friends, so Sean asks Ben for help.

Ben knew Sean was not getting his work done but he was not sure what decision Sean wanted to make. Sean said, "I want to do better in school, but I still want to keep up with my friends and be able to play my video games."

Ben helped Sean brainstorm ideas, and they talked about how easy or hard each idea was. They settled on

Sean's doing homework right after school then having the rest of the day and evening to socialize and have fun.

Sean tried the plan and feels much better. His grades are better too.

To reflect, ask the students:

- What was Sean's problem? *(He was not doing well in school and felt sad about it because he knows he can do the work.)*
- What decision did Sean have to make? (PI 5.5.1) *(How to improve his school performance)*
- Why is it a good idea to brainstorm solutions with someone you trust who has your values? (PI 5.5.2) *(They may have different ideas but are consistent with your values)*
- What was the next step for Sean in deciding? (PI 5.5.3) *(Brainstorming solutions to the problem)*
- How did Ben help Sean decide on the possible options? (PI 5.5.4) *(Whether the option was easy or hard.)*
- What healthy option did Sean decide on? (PI 5.5.5) *(Sean is going to do his homework right after school then socialize and have fun in the evening after his work is done.)*
- What was the outcome of Sean's decision? (PI 5.5.6) *(Sean tried the plan and feels much better. His grades are better too.)*
- Why is it important to reflect on the decision made? *(Sometimes the decision works; other times a different choice would have worked better.)*

In this skill, students must demonstrate their decision-making skills in a variety of scenarios. When students demonstrate an understanding of the skill, as determined through formative assessment, instruction continues with the content.

To continue the practice, ask students to brainstorm common decisions they make. Write these suggestions into prompts and give students time to practice their skill. Avoid a "yes" or "no" answer by using this phrasing: "How can I…..?"

As the students learn and practice the skill and content, formatively assess their progress. If additional instruction is needed, provide it before continuing to the performance task.

WHAT DOES THE ABILITY TO USE DECISION-MAKING SKILLS TO ENHANCE HEALTH LOOK LIKE IN THE GRADE 5 CLASSROOM?

As a seasoned Grade 5 health teacher, Mr. Rodriques works closely with the school nurse and learned through the Community Health Survey that the Body Mass Index (BMI) of his students is increasing. He knows a high BMI

Grades 3–5

5.5.1 Identify health-related situations that might require a thoughtful decision.

5.5.2 Analyze when assistance is needed in making a health-related decision.

5.5.3 List healthy options to health-related issues or problems.

5.5.4 Predict the potential outcomes of each option when making a health-related decision.

5.5.5 Choose a healthy option when making a decision.

5.5.6 Describe the outcomes of a health-related decision.[1,p32]

is dangerous and contributes to other health problems such as Type 2 diabetes, metabolic syndrome, high blood pressure, asthma, sleep disorders, liver disease, early puberty, eating disorders, and skin infections.[9,p4-5]

Upon checking the CDC figures, he found that 15% of children ages 6–11 are overweight.[10] The community survey also revealed that the adult population is overweight.

Mr. Rodriques overhears students saying that they do not like the way they look and try to lose weight by not eating. Mr. Rodriques was once overweight and realizes that keeping a healthy weight requires healthy food and exercise choices. The decision-making unit is a great place for him to start. Aware that sound decision making is a process, he selects all the Standard 5 performance indicators.

Standard 5—Students will demonstrate the ability to use decision-making skills to enhance health.[1,p32]

Performance Indicator 5.5.1—Identify health-related situations that might require a thoughtful decision.[1,p32]

Performance indicator 5.5.1 with infused content— Identify health-related situations that might require a thoughtful decision about losing weight.[1,p32]

Performance Indicator 5.5.2—Analyze when assistance is needed in making a health-related decision.[1,p32]

Performance indicator 5.5.2 with infused content— Analyze when assistance is needed in making a decision about losing weight.[1,p32]

Performance Indicator 5.5.3—List healthy options to health-related issues or problems.[1,p32]

Performance indicator 5.5.3 with infused content— List healthy options for losing weight.[1,p32]

Performance Indicator 5.5.4—Predict the potential outcomes of each option when making a health-related decision.[1,p32]

Performance indicator 5.5.4 with infused content— Predict the potential outcomes of each option when making a health-related decision about losing weight.[1,p32]

Performance Indicator 5.5.5—Choose a healthy option when making a decision about losing weight.[1,p32]

Performance indicator 5.5.5 with infused content— Choose a healthy option when making a decision about losing weight.[1,p32]

Performance Indicator 5.5.6—Describe the outcomes of a health-related decision.[1,p32]

Performance indicator 5.5.6 with infused content— Describe the outcomes of a health-related decision about losing weight.[1,p32]

After selecting the appropriate performance indicator for the skill, choose a Standard 1 performance indicator.

Standard 1—Students will comprehend concepts related to health promotion and disease prevention to enhance health.[1,p24]

Performance Indicator 1.5.1—Describe the relationship between healthy behaviors and personal health.[1,p24]

Performance indicator 1.5.1 with infused content— Describe the relationship between the healthy behaviors of eating healthy and being physically active.[1,p24]

By linking the skill and content performance indicators, the teacher has a clear idea of how to plan the lessons for the decision-making unit.

The first step in planning is to think through the unit by completing the performance task template. Thereupon, the teacher has a good idea of the lessons that precede this culminating activity, the information and back-up materials necessary to introduce the prompt to the students, and the assessment strategies.

When distributing the prompt, include all the back-up information, student worksheets, and holistic and analytical rubrics. The latter are included with the prompt so that students know how they are being assessed before beginning their product. The rubrics act as a guide and help the students attain proficiency in the standards.

Designing the performance task requires considerable preparation, but once the information is distributed and explained, the students create a product independently. They learn with good coaching (formative assessment) how to demonstrate proficiency in content and skill.

The following is an example of a Grade 5 decision-making performance task that focuses on eating healthy foods and increasing physical activity to reach and maintain a healthy weight.

The first section, for the teacher, demonstrates how to plan for an authentic assessment of the performance indicators 5.5.1 through 5.5.6, and 1.5.1. The second, for the student, extracts information from the performance task and transforms it into the student prompt and support materials.

Performance Task Name: Grade 5—Making Decisions to Eat Healthy and Increase Physical Activity

I. Which state standard(s) does this performance task address? (Varies by state).

II. Topic: What areas of health does this project assess? Why is it important? What is the focus of the project?[4,p237]

A. This performance task assesses Nutrition and Personal Health.

B. This topic is important because:

1. 15% of children aged 6–11 are overweight.[10]

2. Obesity contributes to other health problems such as:

a. Type 2 diabetes

b. Metabolic syndrome

c. High blood pressure

d. Asthma

e. Sleep disorders

f. Liver disease

g. Early puberty

h. Eating disorders

i. Skin infections.[9,p4-5]

j. High cholesterol[11]

3. Obese children and adolescents are more likely to remain obese as adults.[11]

C. The focus of this project is to demonstrate decision-making skills about healthy eating and physical activity.

III. Key Concepts: What basic concepts should students know?[4,p237]

Standard 1—Students will comprehend concepts related to health promotion and disease prevention to enhance health.[1,p24]

Performance indicator 1.5.1 with infused content—Describe the relationship between the healthy behaviors of eating healthy and being physically active.[1,p24]

A. Making smart food choices and being active every day

1. Keeps us mentally and physically fit

2. Helps us maintain a healthy weight

3. Reduces the risks of developing:

a. Heart disease

b. High blood pressure

c. Type 2 diabetes

d. Some types of cancer

4. Allows the body to grow and develop

5. Provides energy needed to learn and play[12]

B. Healthy balance for an eleven-year-old child (Note: Calories are taught prior to this performance task.)

1. Food (1800 calories)

a. 6 ounces of grains

b. 2.5 cups of vegetables

c. 1.5 cups of fruit

d. 3 cups of milk

e. 5 ounces of meat and beans

2. Exercise (Note: Calorie expenditure of different exercises is taught prior to this performance task.)

a. 60 minutes each day[13]

IV. Skills: Which of the seven National Health Education Standards skills does this performance task address?[4,p237]

(continues)

Standard 5—Students will demonstrate the ability to use decision-making skills to enhance health.[1,p32]

Performance indicator 5.5.1 with infused content—Identify health-related situations that might require a thoughtful decision about losing weight.[1,p32]

Performance indicator 5.5.2 with infused content—Analyze when assistance is needed in making a decision about losing weight.[1,p32]

Performance indicator 5.5.3 with infused content—List healthy options for losing weight.[1,p32]

Performance indicator 5.5.4 with infused content—Predict the potential outcomes of each option when making a health-related decision about losing weight.[1,p32]

Performance indicator 5.5.5 with infused content—Choose a healthy option when making a decision about losing weight.[1,p32]

Performance indicator 5.5.6 with infused content—Describe the outcomes of a health-related decision about losing weight.[1,p32]

V. Curricular connections: What other subject areas does this project support?[4,p237]

English language arts

Math

Art

VI. Student Directions and Assessment Criteria[4,p238]

Prompt #1

A. Project Description—Write and attach an engaging prompt that draws the student into the project.[4,p238]

Alana is worried about going to middle school next year because she is overweight and anxious that the older students will bully and make fun of her.

She skips lunch to lose weight, but becomes very hungry at home and eats a lot of junk food. When supper is ready, she is not hungry and snacks before going to bed.

The only exercise Alana gets is a half-hour of physical education on Tuesdays and Thursdays and recess. Alana and her friends usually just talk during recess and watch the boys run around.

B. Your Challenge—Provide a challenge or mission statement that describes the project.[4,p238]

Your challenge is to help Alana reach a healthy weight by making a decision to balance a healthy food intake with activity output.

Prompt #2

A. Project Description—Write and attach an engaging prompt that draws the student into the project.[4,p238]

Marvin wants to lose some weight but does not know what to do. He dislikes gym class because the other boys laugh when he cannot do all the activities without becoming out of breath. He tells the gym teacher that he is sick and needs to go to the nurse.

Frustrated at lunch, he buys double desserts instead of the full meal. He feels good for a few minutes but bad again when no one talks to him or walks with him to their next class.

B. Your Challenge—Provide a challenge or mission statement that describes the project.[4,p238]

Your challenge is to help Marvin reach a healthy weight by making a decision to balance a healthy food intake with activity output.

Prompt #3

A. Project Description—Write and attach an engaging prompt that draws the student into the project.[4,p238]

Pedro is among the smallest boys in the fifth grade. The others pick on him for this reason. He eats a lot of food, including junk, but he still does not gain weight.

B. Your Challenge—Provide a challenge or mission statement that describes the project.[4,p238]

Your challenge is to help Pedro reach a healthy weight by making a decision to balance a healthy food intake with activity output.

(continues)

C. Assessment Criteria[4,p239]

You are assessed on the following key concepts: (List the concepts.)

Performance indicator 1.5.1 with infused content—Describe the relationship between the healthy behaviors of eating healthy and being physically active.[1,p24]

1. Five reasons making smart food choices and being active every day improves your health
2. List each of the food groups and the appropriate serving size of each.
3. Give examples balancing input of 1800 calories with 60 minutes of physical activity.

You are assessed on the following skills:

Performance indicator 5.5.1.with infused content—Identify health-related situations that might require a thoughtful decision about losing weight.[1,p32]

Performance indicator 5.5.2 with infused content—Analyze when assistance is needed in making a decision about losing weight.[1,p32]

Performance indicator 5.5.3 with infused content—List healthy options for losing weight.[1,p32]

Performance indicator 5.5.4 with infused content—Predict the potential outcomes of each option when making a health-related decision about losing weight.[1,p32]

Performance indicator 5.5.5 with infused content—Choose a healthy option when making a decision about losing weight.[1,p32]

Performance indicator 5.5.6 with infused content—Describe the outcomes of a health-related decision about losing weight.[1,p32]

Student project must include the following:

1. A poster containing:
   a. Five reasons why making healthy food choices and being active every day improves your health
   b. A scale balancing an 1800 calorie intake from each of the food groups balanced with 60 minutes of physical activity. Insert the serving size for each group.
2. A decision-making chart for each of the prompts showing how to make a healthy decision to meet the challenge
3. A role-play, based on each prompt, showing friends helping each other to meet the challenge

---

Charlton Elementary School

Name _____

Prompt #1

Alana is worried about going to middle school next year because she is overweight and anxious that the older students will bully and make fun of her.

She skips lunch to lose weight, but becomes very hungry at home and eats a lot of junk food. When supper is ready, she is not hungry and snacks before going to bed.

The only exercise Alana gets is a half-hour of physical education on Tuesdays and Thursdays and recess. Alana and her friends usually just talk during recess and watch the boys run around.

Your challenge is to help Alana reach a healthy weight by making a decision to balance a healthy food intake with activity output.

(continues)

Prompt #2

Marvin wants to lose some weight but does not know what to do. He dislikes gym class because the other boys laugh when he cannot do all the activities without becoming out of breath. He tells the gym teacher that he is sick and needs to go to the nurse.

Frustrated at lunch, he buys double desserts instead of the full meal. He feels good for a few minutes but bad again when no one talks to him or walks with him to their next class.

Your challenge is to help Marvin reach a healthy weight by making a decision to balance a healthy food intake with activity output.

Prompt #3

Pedro is among the smallest boys in the fifth grade. The others pick on him for this reason.

He eats a lot of food, including junk, to gain weight but does not.

Your challenge is to help Pedro reach a healthy weight by making a decision to balance a healthy food intake with activity output.

ASSESSMENT MATERIALS

Self-Check (Table 9.10)

TABLE 9.10   Grades 3–5 Self-Check For the Decision-Making Performance Task

Charlton Elementary School

Decision-Making Worksheet

Name _____

Directions: Check off each section you complete to help you fulfill all the requirements of the role-play.

Poster

1. ☐ Five reasons why making healthy food choices and being active every day improves your health

2. ☐ A scale balancing food from the five food groups (1800 calories) and activity (60 minutes)

3. ☐ Foods in the balance must represent each food group and show the appropriate serving sizes

Three Decision-Making Charts

1. ☐ Prompt #1

2. ☐ Prompt #2

3. ☐ Prompt #3

Role-Play

1. Names and roles of the characters in the play

   _____

   _____

2. ☐ Identify the situation that requires a decision. (PI 5.5.1)

3. ☐ Analyze if assistance is needed in making a decision about losing weight. (PI 5.5.2)

4. ☐ List three healthy options for losing weight. (PI 5.5.3)

5. ☐ Predict the potential outcomes of each option when making a health-related decision about losing weight. (PI 5.5.4)

6. ☐ Choose a healthy option when making a decision about losing weight. (PI 5.5.5)

7. ☐ Describe or reflect on the outcomes of a health-related decision about losing weight. (PI 5.5.6)

(continues)

TABLE 9.11 Grades 3–5 Analytical Rubric to Assess the Nutrition and Physical Activity Poster

Criteria	4	3	2	1
Performance indicator 1.5.1 with infused content—Describe the relationship between the healthy behaviors of eating healthy foods and being physically active.[1,p24]	Student thoroughly explains five reasons why making healthy food choices and being active every day helps you be healthy.	Student adequately explains five reasons why making healthy food choices and being active every day helps you be healthy.	Student inadequately explains five reasons why making healthy food choices and being active every day helps you be healthy.	Student poorly explains five reasons why making healthy food choices and being active every day helps you be healthy.
Performance indicator 1.5.1 with infused content—Describe the relationship between the healthy behaviors of eating healthy foods and being physically active.[1,p24]	Student accurately explains the five food groups.	Student's description of the five food groups is mostly accurate.	Student's description of the five food groups has a few inaccuracies.	Student's description of the five food groups is mostly inaccurate.
Performance indicator 1.5.1 with infused content—Describe the relationship between the healthy behaviors of eating healthy foods and being physically active.[1,p24]	Student accurately describes the portion sizes for the five food groups.	Student's description of the portion sizes is mostly accurate.	Student's description of the portion sizes has a few inaccuracies.	Student's description of the portion sizes is mostly inaccurate.
Performance indicator 1.5.1 with infused content—Describe the relationship between the healthy behaviors of eating healthy foods and being physically active.[1,p24]	Student accurately balances an input of 1800 calories with 60 minutes of activity.	Student's balance of 1800 calories with 60 minutes of activity is mostly accurate.	Student's balance of 1800 calories with 60 minutes of activity has a few inaccuracies.	Student's balance of 1800 calories with 60 minutes of activity is mostly inaccurate.
Creativity	The poster is an excellent example of creativity.	The poster is a very good example of creativity.	The poster is a fair example of creativity.	The poster is a poor example of creativity.
Grammar	The grammar is always correct.	The grammar is sometimes correct.	The grammar is rarely correct.	The grammar is never correct.

Name _____

Total possible points – 24   **Your points – _____**   **Your grade – _____**

(continues)

Decision-Making Chart for the Prompts (Table 9.12)

TABLE 9.12 Decision-Making Chart For the Prompts

Charlton Elementary School

Decision-Making Worksheet

Name _____

1. What is the decision to be made? (Performance Indicator (PI) 5.5.1)

   _____

2. Can you make this decision alone or should you ask for adult help? (PI 5.5.2)

   _____

Solutions (PI 5.5.3)	Positive results of the solution (PI 5.5.4)	Negative results of the solution (PI 5.5.4)	Check off your choice (PI 5.5.5)
#1			
#2			
#3			

Reflection (PI 5.5.6)

Did the solution solve the problem in a healthy way? Explain.

_____

_____

Analytical Rubric For the Performance Task Role-Play (Table 9.13)

TABLE 9.13 Grade 5—Analytical Rubric to Assess the Decision-Making Role Play

Criteria	4	3	2	1
Performance indicator 5.5.1.with infused content—Identify health-related situations that might require a thoughtful decision about losing weight.[1,p32]	Student accurately identifies the situation that requires a decision.	Student's identification of a situation that requires a decision is mostly accurate.	Student's identification of a situation that requires a decision has a few inaccuracies.	Student's identification of a situation that requires a decision is mostly inaccurate.
Performance indicator 5.5.2 with infused content—Analyze when assistance is needed in making a decision about losing weight.[1,p32]	Student accurately analyzes whether assistance is needed in making a decision about reaching a healthy weight.	Student's analysis of determining whether assistance is needed in making a decision about reaching a healthy weight is mostly accurate.	Student's analysis of determining whether assistance is needed in making a decision about reaching a healthy weight has a few inaccuracies.	Student's analysis of determining whether assistance is needed in making a decision about reaching a healthy weight is mostly inaccurate.

(continues)

Criteria	4	3	2	1
Performance indicator 5.5.3 with infused content—List healthy options for losing weight.[1,p32]	Student lists three appropriate healthy options for reaching a healthy weight.	Student's list of three healthy options to reach a healthy weight is mostly appropriate.	A few of the three healthy options to reach a healthy weight are inappropriate.	Student's list of three healthy options to reach a healthy weight is mostly inappropriate.
Performance indicator 5.5.4 with infused content—Predict the potential outcomes of each option when making a health-related decision about losing weight.[1,p32]	Student accurately predicts the potential outcomes of each option when making a health-related decision about reaching a healthy weight.	Student's prediction of the potential outcomes of each option when making a health-related decision about reaching a healthy weight is mostly accurate.	Student's prediction of the potential outcomes of each option when making a health-related decision about reaching a healthy weight has a few inaccuracies.	Student's prediction of the potential outcomes of each option when making a health-related decision about reaching a healthy weight is mostly inaccurate.
Performance indicator 5.5.5 with infused content—Choose a healthy option when making a decision about losing weight.[1,p32]	Student accurately chooses a healthy option when making a decision about reaching a healthy weight.	Student's choice of a healthy option when making a decision about reaching a healthy weight is mostly accurate.	Student's choice of a healthy option when making a decision about reaching a healthy weight has a few inaccuracies.	Student's choice of a healthy option when making a decision about reaching a healthy weight is mostly inaccurate.
Performance indicator 5.5.6 with infused content—Describe the outcomes of a health-related decision about losing weight.[1,p32]	Student thoroughly reflects on the outcome of a health-related decision about reaching a healthy weight.	Student adequately reflects on the outcome of a health-related decision about reaching a healthy weight.	Student inadequately reflects on the outcome of a health-related decision about reaching a healthy weight.	Student poorly reflects on the outcome of a health-related decision about reaching a healthy weight.
Involvement	All members of the role-play are always involved.	All members of the role-play are sometimes involved.	All members of the role-play are rarely involved.	All members of the role-play are never involved.

Name _____

Total possible points – 28   Your points – _____   Your grade – _____

HOW THE COORDINATED SCHOOL HEALTH TEAM HELPS STUDENTS USE DECISION-MAKING SKILLS TO ENHANCE HEALTH

Health Education

- Model healthy decision making.
- Teach content through the decision-making skill.
- Allow ample practice time for skill development.
- Use formative assessment tools to enhance teaching and learning.

Physical Education

- Promote physical activity in school and at home.

- Provide positive support for students trying to become more active.
- Teach physical activities that students can enjoy when they are home or outside.
- Offer physical activities for adults during the evenings and on weekends.
- Offer parent/child physical education classes that promote a healthy, active lifestyle.

Health Services

- Utilize the Children's BMI Tool for Schools from the CDC to compute individual and group BMI information.[14]

Nutrition Services

- Provide healthy low-fat and low-calorie nutritious food choices, including desserts.
- Do not sell snack foods during the school day.

Counseling, Psychological, and Social Services

- Provide support for students with an unhealthy BMI.
- Provide support for families who struggle with maintaining healthy weight.
- Provide nutrition and physical activity resources to students and families.

Healthy School Environment

- Provide healthy low-fat and low-calorie snacks in school vending machines.
- Ban soft drinks from vending machines.

Health Promotion for Staff

- Model healthy eating.
- Provide staff development on nutrition.
- Provide staff development on decision making.

Family and Community Involvement

- Purchase and prepare healthy foods.
- Limit the purchase of junk foods.
- Model healthy eating habits.
- Model healthy ways of coping with stress.
- Participate in a healthy eating workshop sponsored by the local community hospital or nutritionist.
- Encourage restaurants to offer children's portions of healthy food choices.[9]
- Provide appropriate serving sizes to adults and children.[12]

Grades 6–8

To achieve proficiency in Standard 5, Grade 6–8 students demonstrate the ability to use the decision-making process to enhance health.[1,p32]

To teach Standard 5, explain why it is important to make healthy decisions, as well as how decision-making skills are relevant to one's health and well-being, relate to the other national health education skills, and impact health today and tomorrow.

Because this standard is a progression of skill, use each of the performance indicators in the grade span. Explain how to achieve the standard, model the skill, provide practice time for the students, and use formative assessments while the students are learning and practicing in order to improve teaching and learning.

Grades 6–8

5.8.1 Identify circumstances that can help or hinder healthy decision making.

5.8.2 Determine when health-related situations require the application of a thoughtful decision-making process.

5.8.3 Distinguish when individual or collaborative decision making is appropriate.

5.8.4 Distinguish between healthy and unhealthy alternatives to health-related issues or problems.

5.8.5 Predict the potential short-term impact of each alternative on self and others.

5.8.6 Choose healthy alternatives over unhealthy alternatives when making a decision.

5.8.7 Analyze the outcomes of a health-related decision.[1,p32-33]

For example,

Mr. Conolli is an art teacher and the girls lacrosse coach at Rice Junior High School. During practice, some of his students excuse themselves to visit the lavatory but return smelling of cigarette smoke.

Lilly and Kaitlyn are on the lacrosse team and have been smoking since last summer. They want to be slim for the lacrosse season, so they smoke to curb their appetite. Lately, they notice they cannot run as fast or far without becoming winded.

Many people in the community smoke, and it is common for students and parents to go behind the snack bar during athletic events to smoke, knowing that they are breaking the rules.

Mr. Canolli knows some of his students are smoking and not making good decisions, so he approached the health teacher, Mrs. Kinsler, for help in reinforcing how to make healthy decisions about smoking cigarettes and healthy weight management.

In health class, Mrs. Kinsler presents a scenario about girls on a sports team who use cigarettes to remain slim. She teaches the decision-making skill then gives the students time to work through the process.

DECISION-MAKING PROCESS (TABLE 9.14)

When the students complete the process, they understand that the decision to smoke to manage weight is unhealthy and affects themselves and others, such as teammates, coaches, friends, and family.

To reinforce the process, Mrs. Kinsler presented another scenario in which two friends, Kneve and Harrison, often spend time at each other's homes after school and on weekends. Kneve's father smokes at home and in the

TABLE 9.14   Grade 6—Decision-Making Process

Decision-Making Chart

1. What is the problem?

   I am a member of the lacrosse team and I am smoking to stay slim.

2. What is the decision to be made?

   How can I have a healthy weight without smoking?

3. (5.8.1) List two circumstances that help and two circumstances that hinder healthy decision-making.

Help	Hinder
1. *Most of the girls on the team do not smoke, so there is support not to smoke.*	1. *Smoking keeps my weight under control more easily than dieting.*
2. *It is against the rules to smoke.*	2. *If I do not smoke, I get irritable.*

4. (5.8.2) Does the situation require using a thoughtful decision-making process?

   ■ Yes   ☐ No

   Explain your answer.

   I have to think about ways to keep my weight down without smoking.

5. (5.8.3) Can the decision be made alone or should the decision be made collaboratively?

   ■ The decision can be made alone.

   ☐ The decision should be made collaboratively.

   Who can help provide healthy alternatives to the problem?

   Health teacher, nurse, parents

6. Alternatives	(5.8.4) Is this alternative healthy? *Yes or No*	(5.8.5) Short-term impact of each alternative	(5.8.6) Put an X next to your healthy choice.
a. *Use MyPyramid.gov to figure out how many calories I need for my level of activity and healthy food choices.*	Yes	*I will know how many calories I should be taking in and the healthy foods to keep me on target.*	X
b. *Cut down on the junk food but keep smoking.*	Yes and No	*It is good to cut out junk food, but smoking is bad for me and keeps me from running as fast as I can.*	
c. *Just quit smoking and don't change my diet.*	Yes and No	*Quitting smoking is healthy, but I also need to start eating healthy.*	

7. Which healthy alternative did you choose?

   Use MyPyramid.gov to figure out how many calories I need for my level of activity and healthy food choices.

8. (5.8.7) Reflection—Analyze how your decision resolved the problem in a healthy way.

   I decided to go to MyPyramid.gov to see how many calories I should have each day, rather than just eating what I want. When I started eating healthy, I didn't want to smoke anymore, so everything worked out great! I feel and look much better! The coach said I am playing much better, so he puts me in the game more often. My teammates are happy that I am running fast and scoring again. My family is proud of me for making a healthy change. Mom buys healthier foods now, and everyone is enjoying eating healthy.

car. Kneve and Harrison don't like being around the smoke because it makes them cough and their clothes smell bad. In fact, Harrison's mom asked him if he was smoking! What can they do not to breathe the smoke?

The students worked through their decision making and discovered several healthy alternatives. When Mrs. Kinsler reflected on the process, the students said they liked doing the activity because it was a problem that they face and it was good to know how to deal with the situation in a healthy way.

When the students are learning the skill, provide adequate time for them to practice before asking them to demonstrate proficiency through an authentic assessment. While they are practicing, use formative assessments (Chapter 4) to check for understanding. Use feedback to show students how to improve performance, thereby encouraging them to improve.

Once the students demonstrate the skill, teach the health content. Design a prompt that allows the students to display their knowledge of health content while demonstrating decision-making skills. As the students practice their content and skill, use formative assessments to redirect and encourage them.

WHAT DOES THE ABILITY TO DEMONSTRATE DECISION-MAKING SKILLS TO ENHANCE HEALTH LOOK LIKE IN THE GRADE 8 CLASSROOM?

The Cooper Middle School coordinated school health team recently met to learn the results of the youth risk behavior survey (YRBS). There is good and bad news. The students showed an increase in physical activity but also an increase in tobacco use and eating disorders.

Mrs. Margolis, the health teacher, reported that 6.5% of Grade 8 students smoked cigarettes on at least one out of 30 days before the survey was administered.[15] Also, 24% of the students described themselves as overweight, and 4.4% took pills to lose weight.[15]

In addition to the YRBS, Mrs. Margolis reported on a study that showed a connection between smoking and eating disorders. Students who are dissatisfied with their weight also used tobacco, which was the most significant predictor of eating disorder symptoms.[16,p1811]

Parents were interested in learning that children who do not eat meals regularly with the family or communicate poorly with family members have higher eating disorder symptoms.[16,p1808] A lively discussion focused on ways the family could eat together more regularly, despite the challenge of busy schedules.

The team is concerned about these statistics and wants to support an initiative to reduce smoking, encourage healthy weight loss, and address the symptoms of eating disorders in order to increase student health, well-being, and academic performance.

In planning her decision-making unit, Mrs. Margolis wants students to learn decision-making skills regarding tobacco, healthy weight loss, and eating disorders.

In planning, Mrs. Margolis selects specific performance indicators that address a certain skill and content. Since decision making is a process, she selects all the performance indicators.

Standard 5—Students will demonstrate the ability to use decision-making skills to enhance health.[1,p32]

5.8.1—Identify circumstances that can help or hinder healthy decision making.[1,p32]

Performance indicator 5.8.1 with infused content— Identify circumstances that can help or hinder healthy decision making about tobacco, healthy weight loss, and eating disorders.[1,p32]

5.8.2—Determine when health-related situations require the application of a thoughtful decision-making process.[1,p32]

Performance indicator 5.8.2 with infused content— Determine when health-related situations about tobacco, healthy weight loss, and eating disorders require the application of a thoughtful decision-making process.[1,p32]

5.8.3—Distinguish when individual or collaborative decision making is appropriate.[1,p32]

Performance indicator 5.8.3 with infused content— Distinguish when individual or collaborative decision making about tobacco, healthy weight loss, and eating disorders is appropriate.[1,p32]

5.8.4—Distinguish between healthy and unhealthy alternatives to health-related issues or problems.[1,p33]

Performance indicator 5.8.4 with infused content— Distinguish between healthy and unhealthy alternatives when making a decision about tobacco, weight loss, or an eating disorder.[1,p33]

5.8.5—Predict the potential short-term impact of each alternative on self and others.[1,p33]

Performance indicator 5.8.4 with infused content— Predict the potential short-term impact of each tobacco, healthy weight loss, and eating disorder alternatives on self and others.[1,p33]

5.8.6—Choose healthy alternatives over unhealthy alternatives when making a decision.[1,p33]

Performance indicator 5.8.6 with infused content— Choose healthy alternatives regarding tobacco, healthy weight loss, and eating disorders over unhealthy alternatives when making a decision.[1,p33]

5.8.7—Analyze the outcomes of a health-related decision.[1,p33]

Performance indicator 5.8.7 with infused content— Analyze the outcomes of a health-related decision regarding tobacco, healthy weight loss, and eating disorders.[1,p33]

Standard 1–Students comprehend concepts related to health promotion and disease prevention to enhance health[1,p24]

> Performance indicator 1.8.1—Analyze the relationship between healthy behaviors and personal health.[1,p25]
>
> > *Performance indicator 1.8.1 with infused content—* Analyze the relationship between healthy behaviors, such as managing weight and personal health.[1,p25]
>
> Performance indicator 1.8.4—Describe how family history can affect personal health[1,p25]
>
> > *Performance indicator 1.8.4 with infused content—* Describe how family history of tobacco use, weight, and eating disorders can affect personal health.[1,p25]
>
> Performance indicator 1.8.9—Examine the potential seriousness of injury or illness if engaging in unhealthy behaviors[1,p25]
>
> > *Performance indicator 1.8.9 with infused content—* Examine the potential seriousness of injury or illness if engaging in unhealthy behaviors such as using tobacco.

By linking the skill and the content performance indicators, the teacher has a clear idea of how to plan the decision-making unit.

The first step in planning is to think through the unit by completing the performance task template. Thereupon, the teacher will have a good idea of the lessons that precede this culminating activity, the information and back-up materials necessary to introduce the prompt to the students, and the assessment strategies.

When distributing the prompt, include all the back-up information, student worksheets, and holistic and analytical rubrics. The latter are distributed with the prompt so students know how they are being assessed before they begin work on their product. The rubrics act as a guide and help the students attain proficiency in the standards.

Designing skills-based lessons requires considerable preparation, but once the teacher distributes the information and explains the task, the students are responsible for the results. They learn with good coaching (formative assessments) how to demonstrate proficiency in content and skill.

The following is a performance task for a Grade 8 unit on decision making that focuses on tobacco, weight loss, and eating disorders. The first section is for the teacher and demonstrates the planning process for authentic assessment reflecting the performance indicators 5.8.1 through 5.8.7 and 1.8.4. The second, for the student, extracts information from the performance task and transforms it into the student prompt and support materials.

Standard 5 Performance Task: Grade 8—Making Decisions about Tobacco, Healthy Weight Loss, and Eating Disorders

I. Which state standard(s) does this performance task address?

II. Topic: What areas of health does this project assess? Why is it important? What is the focus of the project?[4,p237]

  A. This performance task assesses the health area of Substance Use/Abuse, Personal Health, and Nutrition.

  B. It is important because, in the case of:

    1. Tobacco

      a. More than 80% of adult smokers began before their 18th year.[17]

      b. Youth who want to gain or lose weight are 1.5 to 2.2 times more likely to be experimental smokers.[18,p283]

      c. Students believe that smoking contributes to weight loss and quitting leads to gain.[18,p284]

    2. Weight Loss

      a. 24% of 8th grade students describe themselves as overweight.

      b. 4.4% of 8th grade students took diet pills, powders, or liquids to lose weight or avoid gaining it.[15]

    3. Eating Disorders

      a. 6.2% of 8th grade students vomited or took laxatives to lose weight or to avoid gaining it.

      b. 4.4% of 8th grade students took diet pills, powders, or liquids to lose weight or avoid gaining it.[15]

      c. Night eating syndrome occurs in families.[19]

  C. The focus of the project is to demonstrate decision-making skills to meet the challenges of tobacco use, healthy weight loss, and eating disorders.

(continues)

III. Key Concepts—What basic concepts should the students know?[4,p237]

Standard 1—Students comprehend concepts related to health promotion and disease prevention to enhance health.[1,p24]

Performance indicator 1.8.1—Analyze the relationship between healthy behaviors and personal health.[1,p25]

> Performance indicator 1.8.1 with infused content—Analyze the relationship between healthy behaviors such as managing weight and personal health.[1,p25]

A. Managing weight healthfully
1. Determine body mass index to learn if weight needs to be maintained, lost, or gained.
2. To maintain
    a. Determine the appropriate number of calories required for age.
    b. Choose healthy foods to eat.
    c. Balance food choices with exercise.
3. To lose weight
    a. Determine the appropriate number of calories required for age.
    b. Choose healthy foods to eat.
    c. Decrease food intake; increase exercise.
4. To gain weight
    a. Determine the appropriate number of calories required for age.
    b. Choose healthy foods to eat.
    c. Increase healthy food intake; decrease exercise.

Performance indicator 1.8.4—Describe how family history can affect personal health.[1,p25]

> Performance indicator 1.8.4 with infused content—Describe how family history of tobacco use, weight management, and eating disorders can affect personal health.[1,p25]

A. Tobacco
1. Family history
    a. One reason teens use tobacco is because their parents or other family members smoke.[20,p233]
    b. A predictor of daily smoking is having a sibling who smokes.[21]
    c. Parenting that includes low warmth and high hostility has been associated with increased child behavior problems and smoking.[22,p1216]
    d. Poor parenting and family functioning is related to adolescent smoking
    e. Lack of parental nurturing and presence of hostility contribute more to adolescent smoking than peer pressure and parental smoking.[22,p1217]
    f. Girls are more likely to cope with negative parent-child relationships by smoking or acting out.[22,p1218]

B. Weight management
1. Family history
    a. An obese parent increases the risk of his or her child's becoming obese because of shared genetics and environment.[23,p1138]
    b. Obesity is caused by a combination of genetic, physiological, metabolic, environmental, and psychological factors.[24]
    c. Genes influence
        —Body size and shape
        —Body fat distribution
        —Metabolic rate
        —Ease in weight gain
        —Where body adds the extra weight
    d. If both parents are obese, the children have an 80% chance of being so.
    e. If one parent is obese, the children have a 40% chance.[25,p419]

(continues)

C. Eating disorders
1. Family history: eating orders develop
   a. when parents are controlling and dominate conversations about weight management.[26,p90]
   b. in homes where there is hostility, abuse, or lack of cohesion[25,p437]
   c. as a result of hormonal, genetic, psychological, and socio-cultural factors.[27]

Performance indicator 1.8.9—Examine the potential seriousness of injury or illness if engaging in unhealthy behaviors.[1,p25]

Performance indicator 1.8.9 with infused content—Examine the potential seriousness of injury or illness if engaging in unhealthy behaviors such as using tobacco.[1,p25]

A. Tobacco Dangers
1. Smoke damages the alveoli in the lungs, which can lead to emphysema.
2. Smoking causes cavities, gingivitis, stomach ulcers, and cancer of the mouth, throat, stomach, esophagus, pancreas, and bladder.
3. Tobacco causes less oxygen to go to the brain, thereby increasing the risk of stroke.
4. Tobacco use is linked to heart disease.[20,p233]

B. Eating disorders
1. Night Eating: syndrome
   a. is an eating disorder in which a person eats 25% of their daily calories after supper and /or gets up at night to eat at least three times a week.
   b. may be inherited.
   c. is triggered by stress.
      —Dangers
      —Obesity
      —Source of distress[28]
2. Bulimia
   a. Bulimia is an eating disorder characterized by eating large amounts of food.
   b. Food is purging by throwing up or taking laxatives.
   c. Dangers
      —Prevents nutrients from being absorbed
      —May damage the heart. colon, liver, and kidneys
      —Tooth enamel wears off due to the stomach acids passing over them.
      —Esophagus is damaged by the stomach acids
      —Dehydration[20,p133]

IV. Skills: Which of the seven National Health Education Standards does this performance task address?[4,p237]

Standard 5—Students will demonstrate the ability to use decision-making skills to enhance health.[1,p32]

Performance indicator 5.8.1 with infused content—Identify circumstances that can help or hinder healthy decision making about tobacco and eating disorders.[1,p32]

Performance indicator 5.8.2 with infused content—Determine when health-related situations about tobacco and eating disorders require the application of a thoughtful decision-making process.[1,p32]

Performance indicator 5.8.3 with infused content—Distinguish when individual or collaborative decision making about tobacco and eating disorders is appropriate.[1,p32]

Performance indicator 5.8.4 with infused content—Distinguish between healthy and unhealthy alternatives when making a decision about tobacco or an eating disorder.[1,p33]

Performance indicator 5.8.5 with infused content—Predict the potential short-term impact of each tobacco and eating disorder alternative on self and others.[1,p33]

Performance indicator 5.8.6 with infused content—Choose healthy alternatives regarding tobacco and eating disorders over unhealthy alternatives when making a decision.[1,p33]

Performance indicator 5.8.7 with infused content—Analyze the outcomes of a health-related decision about tobacco and eating disorders.[1,p33]

(continues)

V. Curricula connections—What other subject areas does this project support?[4,p237]
   English language arts
   Art
VI. Student directions and assessment criteria[4,p238]
   Prompt #1
   A. Project description—Write and attach an engaging prompt that draws the student into the project.[4,p238]
      Renee is afraid of putting on weight and has started smoking. She likes the way it makes her look and believes it will help her manage her weight. She also takes a laxative to keep down her weight.

      Renee and her mother do not get along very well. They seldom eat together as a family and rarely talk about things on her mind because an argument usually results. Because her mother smokes in the house and the car, Renee is used to cigarette smoke.

      Renee is learning about the hazards of tobacco, healthy weight management, and eating disorders in health class and now realizes she has a problem.
   B. Your challenge—Provide a challenge or mission statement that describes the project.[4,p238]
      Your challenge is to help Renee make a decision about managing her weight in a healthy way.
   Prompt #2
   A. Project description—Write and attach an engaging prompt that draws the student into the project.[4,p238]
      Nolan is stressed because his parents expect him to excel in school. He does not have much time for his friends because he must complete his paper route by dinner. On Saturdays, Nolan has family responsibilities, such as weekly chores, babysitting his little brother, and visiting his grandmother.

      Nolan's body mass index is in the high normal range. He does not eat much during the day or at supper. In the evening while doing his homework, he raids the refrigerator for snacks and other food. At least three nights a week, he gets up in the middle of the night to eat. Nolan is putting on weight, so he smokes to control it.
   B. Your challenge—Provide a challenge or mission statement that describes the project.[4,p238]
      Your challenge is to help Nolan make a decision about maintaining his weight in a healthy way.
   Prompt #3
   A. Project description—Write and attach an engaging prompt that draws the student into the project.[4,p238]
      Jessica's parents were overweight when they were children. Not wanting her to suffer the same way, they monitor Jessica carefully by weighing her a couple of times a week and showing her pictures of beautiful women who are thin.

      Jessica loves to eat but is afraid she will put on weight. To control it, she sometimes throws up her food after she has eaten it. She has also started smoking.
   B. Your challenge–Provide a challenge or mission statement that describes the project.[4,p238]
      Your challenge is to help Jessica make a decision about maintaining her weight in a healthy way.
   C. Assessment criteria[4,p239]
      You are assessed on the following content:
      Performance indicator 1.8.1 with infused content—Analyze the relationship between healthy behaviors such as managing weight and personal health.[1,p25]
      1. Managing weight healthfully
         a. How to maintain, gain, and lose weight using healthy strategies.
      Performance indicator 1.8.4 with infused content—Describe how family history of tobacco use, weight, and eating disorders can affect personal health.[1,p25]
      1. Tobacco
         a. Three facts about how family history affects tobacco use.

(continues)

2. Managing weight healthfully
    a. Three facts about how family history affects weight.
3. Eating disorders
    a. Three facts about how family history affects the development of eating disorders.

Performance indicator 1.8.9 with infused content—Examine the potential seriousness of injury or illness if engaging in unhealthy behaviors such as using tobacco.[1,p25]

1. Tobacco
    a. Two facts each of how tobacco damages the lungs, heart, digestive system, excretory system and increases the chances of stroke and different cancers.
2. Eating disorders
    a. Explain three facts about night eating syndrome and three more about bulimia.
    b. Two dangers of night eating syndrome
    c. Three dangers of bulimia.

You are assessed on the following skill:

Performance indicator 5.8.1 with infused content—Identify circumstances that can help or hinder healthy decision making about tobacco and eating disorders.[1,p32]

Performance indicator 5.8.2 with infused content—Determine when health-related situations about tobacco and eating disorders require the application of a thoughtful decision-making process.[1,p32]

Performance indicator 5.8.3 with infused content—Distinguish when individual or collaborative decision making about tobacco and eating disorders is appropriate.[1,p32]

Performance indicator 5.8.4 with infused content—Distinguish between healthy and unhealthy alternatives when making a decision about tobacco or an eating disorder.[1,p33]

Performance indicator 5.8.5 with infused content—Predict the potential short-term impact of each tobacco and eating disorder alternative on self and others.[1,p33]

Performance indicator 5.8.6 with infused content—Choose healthy alternatives about tobacco and eating disorders over unhealthy alternatives when making a decision.[1,p33]

Performance indicator 5.8.7 with infused content—Analyze the outcomes of a health-related decision about tobacco and eating disorders.[1,p33]

Student Project

1. A book with three chapters (Each chapter must contain two pictures.)
    a. Tobacco
        1. Three facts about how family history affects tobacco use
        2. Two facts each of how tobacco damages the lungs, heart, digestive system, excretory system and increases the chances of stroke and different cancers
    b. Weight Loss
        1. Three facts about how family history affects weight
        2. How to maintain, gain, and lose weight using healthy strategies
    c. Eating disorders
        1. Three facts about how family history affects the development of eating disorders
        2. Explain three facts about night eating syndrome and two more about bulimia
        3. Two dangers of night eating syndrome
        4. Three dangers of bulimia
2. Use the decision-making process to help the students in each prompt make a healthy decision about their weight.
3. Choose a prompt and use the decision-making skill to role-play how to resolve the problem and enhance health.

Cooper Middle School

Name _____

Prompt #1

Renee is afraid of putting on weight and has started smoking. She likes the way it makes her look and believes it will help her manage her weight. She also takes a laxative to keep down her weight.

Renee and her mother do not get along very well. They seldom eat together as a family and rarely talk about things on her mind because an argument usually results. Because her mother smokes in the house and the car, Renee is used to cigarette smoke.

Renee is learning about the hazards of tobacco, healthy weight management, and eating disorders in health class and now realizes she has a problem.

Your challenge is to help Renee make a decision about managing her weight in a healthy way.

Prompt #2

Nolan is stressed because his parents expect him to excel in school. He does not have much time for his friends because he must complete his paper route by dinner. On Saturdays, Nolan has family responsibilities, such as weekly chores, babysitting his little brother, and visiting his grandmother.

Nolan's body mass index is in the high normal range. He does not eat much during the day or at supper. In the evening while doing his homework, he raids the refrigerator for snacks and other food. At least three nights a week, he gets up in the middle of the night to eat.

Nolan is putting on weight, so he smokes to control it.

Your challenge is to help Nolan make a decision about maintaining his weight in a healthy way.

Prompt #3

Jessica's parents were overweight when they were children. Not wanting her to suffer the same way, they monitor Jessica carefully by weighing her a couple of times a week and showing her pictures of beautiful women who are thin.

Jessica loves to eat but is afraid she will put on weight. To control it, she sometimes throws up her food after she has eaten it. She has also started smoking.

Your challenge is to help Jessica make a decision about maintaining her weight in a healthy way.

Your project must include the following:

1. A book with three chapters (Each chapter must contain two pictures.)

   a. Tobacco

     1. Three facts about how family history affects tobacco use

     2. Two facts each about how tobacco damages the lungs, heart, digestive system, excretory system and increases the chances of stroke and different cancer

   b. Weight Loss

     1. Three facts about how family history affects weight

     2. How to maintain, gain, and lose weight using healthy strategies

   c. Eating Disorders

     1. Three facts about how family history affects the development of eating disorders

     2. Explain three facts about night eating syndrome and two more about bulimia.

     3. Two dangers of night eating syndrome

     4. Three dangers of bulimia

2. Use the decision-making process to help the students in prompt make a healthy decision about their weight.

3. Choose a prompt and use the decision-making skill to role-play how to resolve the problem and enhance health.

(continues)

TABLE 9.15   Grades 6–8 Decision-Making Process

Decision-Making Chart (One for Each Prompt)

Cooper Middle School

Name _____

Directions: For each prompt, fill in the decision-making chart.

1. What is the problem?

2. What is the decision to be made?

3. List two circumstances that help and two circumstances that hinder healthy decision-making. (PI 5.8.1)

Help	Hinder
a.	
b.	

4. Does the situation require using a thoughtful decision-making process? (PI 5.8.2)

   ☐ Yes   ☐ No

   Explain your answer.

5. Can the decision be made alone or should the decision be made collaboratively? (PI 5.8.3)

   ☐ The decision can be made alone.

   ☐ The decision should be made collaboratively.

   Who can help provide healthy alternatives to the problem?

   _____

6. Alternatives	(PI 5.8.4) Is this alternative healthy? *Yes or No*	(PI 5.8.5) Short-term impact of each alternative	(PI 5.8.6) Put an X next to your healthy choice.
a.			
b.			
c.			

7. Which healthy alternative did you choose?

8. (5.8.7) Reflection – Analyze how your decision resolved the problem in a healthy way.

(continues)

TABLE 9.16   Grades 6–8—Analytical Rubric to Assess the Tobacco, Healthy Weight Loss, and Eating Disorder Book Portion of the Performance Task

Criteria	4	3	2	1
Performance indicator 1.8.1 with infused content—Analyze the relationship between healthy behaviors such as managing weight and personal health.[1,p25]	The weight loss chapter thoroughly analyzes how to maintain, gain, and lose weight using healthy strategies.	The weight loss chapter adequately analyzes how to maintain, gain, and lose weight using healthy strategies.	The weight loss chapter inadequately analyzes how to maintain, gain, and lose weight using healthy strategies.	The weight loss chapter poorly analyzes how to maintain, gain, and lose weight using healthy strategies.
Performance indicator 1.8.4 with infused content—Describe how family history of tobacco use, weight, and eating disorders can affect personal health.[1,p25]	The tobacco chapter thoroughly describes three facts about how family history affects tobacco use.	The tobacco chapter adequately describes three facts about how family history affects tobacco use.	The tobacco chapter inadequately describes three facts about how family history affects tobacco use.	The tobacco chapter poorly describes three facts about how family history affects tobacco use.
Performance indicator 1.8.4 with infused content—Describe how family history of tobacco use, weight, and eating disorders can affect personal health.[1,p25]	The managing weight healthfully chapter thoroughly describes how to maintain, gain, and lose weight using healthy strategies.	The managing weight healthfully chapter adequately describes how to maintain, gain, and lose weight using healthy strategies.	The managing weight healthfully chapter inadequately describes how to maintain, gain, and lose weight using healthy strategies.	The managing weight healthfully chapter poorly describes how to maintain, gain, and lose weight using healthy strategies.
Performance indicator 1.8.4 with infused content—Describe how family history of tobacco use, weight, and eating disorders can affect personal health.[1,p25]	The weight loss chapter thoroughly describes three facts about how family history affect weight.	The weight loss chapter adequately describes three facts about how family history affect weight.	The weight loss chapter inadequately describes three facts about how family history affect weight.	The weight loss chapter poorly describes three facts about how family history affect weight.
Performance indicator 1.8.4 with infused content—Describe how family history of tobacco use, weight, and eating disorders can affect personal health.[1,p25]	The eating disorders chapter thoroughly describes three facts about how family history affects the development of eating disorders.	The eating disorders chapter adequately describes three facts about how family history affects the development of eating disorders.	The eating disorders chapter inadequately describes three facts about how family history affects the development of eating disorders.	The eating disorders chapter poorly describes three facts about how family history affects the development of eating disorders.
Performance indicator 1.8.9 with infused content—Examine the potential seriousness of injury or illness if engaging in unhealthy behaviors such as using tobacco.[1,p25]	The tobacco chapter thoroughly examines two facts each about how tobacco damages the lungs, heart, digestive and excretory systems, and increases the chances of stroke and different types of cancer.	The tobacco chapter adequately examines two facts each about how tobacco damages the lungs, heart, digestive and excretory systems, and increases the chances of stroke and different types of cancer.	The tobacco chapter inadequately examines two facts each about how tobacco damages the lungs, heart, digestive and excretory systems, and increases the chances of stroke and different types of cancer.	The tobacco chapter poorly examines two facts each about how tobacco damages the lungs, heart, digestive and excretory systems, and increases the chances of stroke and different types of cancer.

(continues)

TABLE 9.16   Grades 6–8—Analytical Rubric to Assess the Tobacco, Healthy Weight Loss, and Eating Disorder Book Portion of the Performance Task *(continued)*

Criteria	4	3	2	1
Performance indicator 1.8.9 with infused content—Examine the potential seriousness of injury or illness if engaging in unhealthy behaviors such as using tobacco.[1,p25]	The eating disorders chapter thoroughly examines three facts about night eating syndrome.	The eating disorders chapter adequately examines three facts about night eating syndrome.	The eating disorders chapter inadequately examines three facts about night eating syndrome.	The eating disorders chapter poorly examines three facts about night eating syndrome.
Performance indicator 1.8.9 with infused content—Examine the potential seriousness of injury or illness if engaging in unhealthy behaviors such as using tobacco.[1,p25]	The eating disorders chapter thoroughly examines two facts about bulimia.	The eating disorders chapter adequately examines two facts about bulimia.	The eating disorders chapter inadequately examines two facts about bulimia.	The eating disorders chapter poorly examines two facts about bulimia.
Performance indicator 1.8.9 with infused content—Examine the potential seriousness of injury or illness if engaging in unhealthy behaviors such as using tobacco.[1,p25]	The eating disorders chapter thoroughly examines three dangers of bulimia.	The eating disorders chapter adequately examines three dangers of bulimia.	The eating disorders chapter inadequately examines three dangers of bulimia.	The eating disorders chapter poorly examines three dangers of bulimia.
Pictures/Illustrations	Two pictures per chapter are appropriate.	Two pictures per chapter or mostly appropriate.	One of the pictures per chapters is appropriate.	The two pictures per chapter are inappropriate.
Creativity	The creativity of the book's cover is excellent.	The creativity of the book's cover is good.	The creativity of the book's cover is fair.	The creativity of the book's cover is poor.

Name _____

Total possible points – 44   Your points – _____   Your grade – _____

Analytical Rubric For the Decision-Making Role-Play Portion of the Performance Task (Table 9.17)

TABLE 9.17   Grades 6–8—Analytical Rubric to Assess the Decision-Making Process

Criteria	4	3	2	1
Performance indicator 5.8.1 with infused content—Identify circumstances that can help or hinder healthy decision-making regarding tobacco and eating disorders.[1,p32]	Student accurately identifies two circumstances that help or hinder healthy decision-making regarding tobacco and eating disorders.	Student's identification of two circumstances that help or hinder healthy decision-making regarding tobacco and eating disorders is mostly accurate.	Student's identification of two circumstances that help or hinder healthy decision-making regarding tobacco and eating disorders has a few inaccuracies.	Student's identification of two circumstances that help or hinder healthy decision-making regarding tobacco and eating disorders is mostly inaccurate.

(continues)

Criteria	4	3	2	1
Performance indicator 5.8.2 with infused content—Determine when health-related situations regarding tobacco and eating disorders require the application of a thoughtful decision-making process.[1,p32]	Student accurately determines when health-related situations regarding tobacco and eating disorders require the application of a thoughtful decision-making process.	Student's determination of when health-related situations regarding tobacco and eating disorders require the application of a thoughtful decision-making process is mostly accurate.	Student's determination of when health-related situations regarding tobacco and eating disorders require the application of a thoughtful decision-making process has a few inaccuracies.	Student's determination of when health-related situations regarding tobacco and eating disorders require the application of a thoughtful decision-making process is mostly inaccurate.
Performance indicator 5.8.3 with infused content—Distinguish when individual or collaborative decision-making regarding tobacco and eating disorders is appropriate.[1,p32]	Student accurately distinguishes when individual or collaborative decision-making regarding tobacco and eating disorders is appropriate.	Student's distinction of when individual or collaborative decision-making regarding tobacco and eating disorders is appropriate is mostly accurate.	Student's distinction of when individual or collaborative decision-making regarding tobacco and eating disorders is appropriate has a few inaccuracies.	Student's distinction of when individual or collaborative decision-making regarding tobacco and eating disorders is appropriate is mostly inaccurate.
Performance indicator 5.8.4 with infused content—Distinguish between healthy and unhealthy alternatives to health-related issues or problems.[1,p32]	Student accurately distinguishes between healthy and unhealthy alternatives to health-related issues or problems.	Student's distinction between healthy and unhealthy alternatives to health-related issues or problems is mostly accurate.	Student's distinction between healthy and unhealthy alternatives to health-related issues or problems has a few inaccuracies.	Student's distinction between healthy and unhealthy alternatives to health-related issues or problems is mostly inaccurate.
Performance indicator 5.8.5 with infused content—Predict the potential short-term impact of each alternative on self and others.[1,p32]	Student accurately predicts the potential short-term impact of each alternative on self and others.	Student's prediction of the potential short-term impact of each alternative on self and others is mostly accurate.	Student's prediction of the potential short-term impact of each alternative on self and others has a few inaccuracies.	Student's prediction of the potential short-term impact of each alternative on self and others is mostly inaccurate.
Performance indicator 5.8.6 with infused content—Choose healthy alternatives regarding tobacco and eating disorders over unhealthy alternatives when making a decision.[1,p32]	Student accurately chooses healthy alternatives regarding tobacco and eating disorders over unhealthy alternatives when making a decision.	Student's choice of healthy alternatives regarding tobacco and eating disorders over unhealthy alternatives when making a decision is mostly accurate.	Student's choice of healthy alternatives regarding tobacco and eating disorders over unhealthy alternatives when making a decision has a few inaccuracies.	Student's choice of healthy alternatives regarding tobacco and eating disorders over unhealthy alternatives when making a decision is mostly inaccurate.
Choice	Student chooses an appropriate healthy alternative.	The student's healthy alternative choice is mostly appropriate.	Parts of the healthy alternative choice are somewhat inappropriate.	The student's healthy alternative choice is mostly inappropriate.

(continues)

TABLE 9.17   Grades 6–8—Analytical Rubric to Assess the Decision-Making Process *(continued)*

Criteria	4	3	2	1
Performance indicator 5.8.7 with infused content—Analyze the outcomes of a health-related decision regarding tobacco and eating disorders.[1,p32]	Student thoroughly analyzes the outcomes of a health-related decision regarding tobacco and eating disorders.	Student adequately analyzes the outcomes of a health-related decision regarding tobacco and eating disorders.	Student inadequately analyzes the outcomes of a health-related decision regarding tobacco and eating disorders.	Student poorly analyzes the outcomes of a health-related decision regarding tobacco and eating disorders.
Participation	Student participation in the role-play is excellent.	Student participation in the role-play is good.	Student participation in the role-play is fair.	Student participation in the role-play is poor.

Name _____

Total possible points – 36   Your points – _____   Your grade – _____

HOW THE COORDINATED SCHOOL HEALTH TEAM HELPS STUDENTS USE DECISION-MAKING SKILLS TO ENHANCE HEALTH

Health Education

- Teach content and skills that promote positive body image.[18,p285]
- Explain how family history affects smoking, healthy weight, and eating disorders.
- Focus on how peers influence others to smoke.[17,p329]
- Model and teach decision making.

Physical Education

- Post a Body Mass Index chart so students can become aware of healthy weight ranges for their height and weight.
- Encourage lifetime physical activity to control and maintain weight.

Health Services

- Provide professional development to identify eating disorders.
- Screen students for eating disorders.[16,p1805]
- Intervene when eating disorders are discovered.[16,p1808]

Nutrition Services

- Provide foods low in fat and sugar.
- Monitor student purchases for possible intervention of unhealthy or imbalanced selections.

Counseling, Psychological, and Social Services

- Provide smoking cessation for teen smokers. Screen students for mental health.
- Screen students for eating disorders.
- Use data from student health surveys to plan interventions, resources, and professional development.[16,p1812]
- Provide healthy weight loss strategies.[18,p285]

Healthy School Environment

- Hang posters that encourage teens not to smoke.
- Hang posters that encourage students to be physically active in order to be healthy.
- Hang posters that encourage teens to seek help for an eating disorder.

Health Promotion for Staff

- Provide professional development in the identification of eating disorders.
- Provide healthy weight loss clinics.
- Provide smoking cessation.

Family and Community Involvement

- Encourage families to plan time to eat together.
- Encourage communication during family meals.[16,p1811]
- Since a child's initiation into smoking has a genetic and environmental component, encourage parents not to smoke when in enclosed spaces, such as a car in which children are passengers.[17,p334]

Grades 9–12

To achieve proficiency in Standard 5, Grade 9–12 students must learn to use decision-making skills to enhance health.

To teach Standard 5, explain why it is important to make healthy decisions and how this skill relates to the other National Health Education Standards.

According to the performance indicators chosen, present and explain how to reach proficiency in the skill. Model it so the students can see the skill in action. Provide adequate time for the students to practice and show proficiency through an authentic assessment. Use formative assessments (Chapter 4) to provide feedback and encouragement and to improve instruction.

For example,

Michaela and Alex have been going together for several months. All their friends are sexually active and openly talk about it. Alex has been pressuring Michaela to have sex, but she is not ready. He really cares for her, does not want to hurt her, but does not understand why she is reluctant. He told her he would wear a condom and assured her that she would be safe.

Mrs. Fuentes is aware of the sexual activities of her students because they like to talk about what they do. She knows, through the school Youth Risk Behavior Survey that 35% of the high school students are sexually active and that 39% did not use a condom during their last intercourse.[29,p1]

Mrs. Fuentes believes her students need to learn how to use decision-making skills in regard to sexual

activities and asks, "How can you cope with sexual pressure without losing your boy/girlfriend?" She encourages them to work through their decision making to find an acceptable solution.

DECISION-MAKING CHART (TABLE 9.18)

To reflect, ask the students:

- Why is it important to differentiate between the problem and the decision? *(One problem can involve many decisions.)*
- Why is it a good idea to think about the things that hinder a decision? (PI 5.12.1) *(When you identify what prevents you from making a good decision, it helps you think of effective solutions.)*
- Why is it important to apply thoughtful decision making in health-related situations? (PI5.12.2) *(Taking your time to think through solutions prevents an impulsive decision that may or may not be a healthy decision.)*
- Why is it important to determine if a decision can be made alone or collaboratively? (PI 5.12.3) *(Usually we have the ability to make a decision alone, but sometimes a trusted friend or adult suggests different alternatives that may have not occurred to us.)*
- What were some of the alternatives generated in this exercise? (PI 5.12.4) *(Tell him that I am just not ready, but I still want him as a boyfriend; We should spend more time with our friends so we won't be tempted; We should always have a plan to do something so we are busy and do not think about sex.)*
- Why should we think about the short and long-term effects of alternatives on ourselves and others? (PI 5.12.5) *(Examining the short and long-term effects of each alternative helps us consider possible consequences that lead to a better decision.)*
- Why is it important to defend the healthy choice when making decisions? (PI 5.12.6) *(Defending a healthy choice confirms our belief.)*
- Why is it important to evaluate the effectiveness of the health-related decision? (PI 5.12.7) *(Usually the alternative we choose provides us with the results we want, but sometimes it does not. If the choice was inappropriate, we need to examine why and learn from our mistake.)*

Mrs. Fuentes asks the students to brainstorm common health-related decisions they make each day. When they list several situations, she breaks the students into groups, assigns a problem, and asks the students to use the decision-making process to reach a decision.

As the students are learning the skill, provide enough time for them to practice. Use formative assessments to determine the progress of learning. Motivate students by using feedback to show how performance is improved.

Grades 9–12

5.12.1 Examine barriers that can hinder healthy decision making.

5.12.2 Determine the value of applying a thoughtful decision-making process in health-related situations.

5.12.3 Justify when individual or collaborative decision making is appropriate.

5.12.4 Generate alternatives to health-related issues or problems.

5.12.5 Predict the potential short-term and long-term impact of each alternative on self and others.

5.12.6 Defend the healthy choice when making decisions.

5.12.7 Evaluate the effectiveness of health-related decisions.[1,p33]

TABLE 9.18 Grades 9–12 Decision-Making Chart

1. What is the problem?

   My boyfriend is pressuring me to have sex.

2. What is the decision to be made?

   How can I keep my boyfriend but refuse sex?

3. List three circumstances that hinder healthy decision-making. (PI 5.12.1)

Hinder

a. *My boyfriend is tired of waiting for me to say yes.*

b. *My boyfriend might break up with me if I say no.*

c. *All my friends are sexually active and they think I should be, too.*

4. What is the value of applying a thoughtful decision-making process in health-related situations? (PI 5.12.2)

   The value of applying thoughtful decision-making in a health-related situation is that it helps me clarify my values and figure out my sexual limits.

5. Can the decision be made alone or should the decision be made collaboratively? (PI 5.12.3)

   ■ The decision can be made alone.

   ☐ The decision should be made collaboratively.

   Who can help provide healthy alternatives to the problem?

6. Alternatives (5.12.4)	(PI 5.12.5) Short-term impact of each alternative on self and others.	(PI 5.12.5) Long-term impact of each alternative on self and others.	Put an X next to your healthy choice.
a. *Tell him that I just am not ready, but I still want him as a boyfriend.*	*He might understand and stay with me.*	*He might get tired of waiting and break up with me.*	X
b. *We should spend more time with our friends so we won't be tempted.*	*He might agree.*	*He might get tired of just being with friends and not spending time with just me.*	
c. *We should always have a plan to do something so we are busy and do not think about sex.*	*It will distract him for a while.*	*He will get tired of always doing something instead of just hanging out.*	

7. Which healthy alternative did you choose?

   Tell him that I just am not ready, but I still want him as a boyfriend.

8. Reflection—Defend the healthy choice when making decisions. (PI 5.12.6)

   I am comfortable with this decision because, if he respects me, he won't pressure me.

9. Evaluate the effectiveness of the health-related decision. (PI 5.12.7)

   Well, the decision worked for two more months; then my boyfriend broke up with me. It was hard at first but then a relief not to be pressured anymore.

When students demonstrate understanding of the skill, teach the content. Design a prompt that allows the students to display their knowledge of health. Use formative assessments, such as white boards (Chapter 4), during content instruction to determine student understanding.

WHAT DOES THE SKILL OF DECISION MAKING LOOK LIKE IN THE GRADE 9 CLASSROOM?

Mr. Delgado is a Grade 9 health teacher at the Davidson High School. While preparing for his first period class, he heard students arguing in the hall and saw two 9th grade boys fighting. He brought the boys to the principal's office and discovered later that they were fighting because one boy had flirted with the other's girlfriend at a party they had attended Saturday night. Both boys were under the influence during the party, one from alcohol, the other from marijuana.

Mr. Delgado is upset about the number of fights in school. Last year 22% of the conflicts in school were between 9th grade boys, mostly due to unresolved problems at parties that they attended over the weekend. He knows that 6.6% of his freshman boys missed school because they feared for their safety.[29,p9]

In planning the decision-making unit, Mr. Delgado focuses on making decisions about alcohol and marijuana. He chooses the performance indicators for Standard 5 that meet the needs of his students. Since decision making is a process, all the performance indicators for the grade span must be selected.

Standard 5—Students will demonstrate the ability to use decision-making skills to enhance health.[1,p32]

   5.12.1—Examine barriers that can hinder healthy decision making.[1,p33]

      Performance indicator 5.12.1 with infused content—Examine barriers that hinder healthy decision making regarding alcohol and marijuana.[1,p33]

   5.12.2—Determine the value of applying a thoughtful decision-making process in health-related situations.[1,p33]

      Performance indicator 5.12.2 with infused content—Determine the value of applying a thoughtful decision-making process in health-related situations regarding alcohol and marijuana.[1,p33]

   5.12.3—Justify when individual or collaborative decision making is appropriate.[1,p33]

      Performance indicator 5.12.3 with infused content—Justify when individual or collaborative decision making is appropriate regarding alcohol and marijuana.[1,p33]

   5.12.4—Generate alternatives to health-related issues or problems.[1,p33]

      Performance indicator 5.12.4 with infused content—Generate alternatives to health-related issues regarding alcohol or marijuana.[1,p33]

   5.12.5—Predict the potential short-term and long-term impact of each alternative on self and others.[1,p33]

      Performance indicator 5.12.5 with infused content—Predict the potential short-term and

long-term impact of each alternative regarding alcohol and marijuana on self and others.[1,p33]

   5.12.6—Defend the healthy choice when making decisions.[1,p33]

      Performance indicator 5.12.6 with infused content—Defend the healthy choice in regards to coping with alcohol and marijuana.[1,p33]

   5.12.7—Evaluate the effectiveness of health-related decisions.[1,p33]

      Performance indicator 5.12.7 with infused content—Evaluate the effectiveness of health-related decisions about alcohol and marijuana.[1,p33]

After selecting the appropriate performance indicator for the skill, Mr. Delgado chooses the performance indicator for Standard 1.

Standard 1—Students will comprehend concepts related to health promotion and disease prevention to enhance health.[1,p24]

   1.12.9—Analyze the potential severity of injury or illness if engaging in unhealthy behaviors.[1,p25]

      Performance indicator 1.12.2 with infused content—Analyze the potential severity of injury or illness if engaging in unhealthy behaviors such as drinking alcohol or smoking marijuana.[1,p25]

By linking the skill and content performance indicators, the teacher has a clear idea of how to plan the lessons for the decision-making unit.

The first step in planning is to think through the unit by completing the performance task template. Thereupon, the teacher has a good idea of the lessons that precede this culminating activity, the information and back-up materials necessary to introduce the prompt to the students, and the assessment strategies.

When distributing the prompt, include all the back-up information, student worksheets, and holistic and analytical rubrics. The latter are distributed with the prompt so students know how they are being assessed before they begin working on their product. The rubrics guide and help students attain proficiency in the standards.

Designing the performance task takes considerable preparation, but once the information is distributed and explained, the students create a product independently. Students learn with good coaching (formative assessment) how to demonstrate proficiency in content and skill.

The following is an example of a performance task for Grade 12 decision making that focuses on using alcohol and marijuana.

The first section is for the teacher and demonstrates how to plan for an authentic assessment of the performance indicators 1.12.9 and 5.12.1 through 5.12.7. The second section is for the student. It extracts some of the information from the performance task and transforms it into the student prompt and support materials.

Standard 5 Performance Task: Grade 12—Using Decision-Making Skills to Cope With the Pressure to Use Alcohol and Marijuana

I. Which state standard(s) does this performance task address?

II. Topic: What areas of health does this project assess? Why is it important? What is the focus of the project?[4,p237]

   A. This performance task assesses the health area of Substance Use/Abuse

   B. This topic is important because:

      1. Alcohol

         a. 28.6% of 12th grade males and 27.9% of females rode with a driver who had been drinking alcohol during the 30 days prior to the survey.[30,p43]

         b. 19.3% of 12th grade males and 11.4% of females drove when drinking alcohol.[30,p43]

         c. 52.6% of 12th grade males and 50.7% of females had at least one drink of alcohol on at least one day during the thirty days prior to the survey.

         d. 36.6% of 12th grade males and 30.4% of females drank five or more drinks of alcohol in a row on at least one day during the thirty days before the survey.[30,p75]

      2. Marijuana

         a. 29.9% of 12th grade males and 19.1% of females used marijuana one or more times during the thirty days before the survey.[30,p77]

      3. Dangers

         a. 22.4% of 12th grade males and 16.8% of females were offered, sold, or given an illegal drug by someone on school property during the twelve months prior to the survey.[30,p20]

         b. 25.8% of 12th grade males and 15.2% of females drank alcohol or used drugs before their most recent intercourse.[30,p108]

   C. The focus of the project is to help students learn how to make healthy decisions about alcohol and marijuana.

III. Key Concepts: What basic concepts do students need to know? [4,p237]

   Standard 1—Students will comprehend concepts related to health promotion and disease prevention to enhance health.[1,p24]

   Performance indicator 1.12.2 with infused content—Analyze the potential severity of injury or illness if engaging in unhealthy behaviors, such as drinking alcohol or smoking marijuana.[1,p25]

   A. Alcohol

      1. Alcohol lowers inhibitions and impairs judgment.[31,p239]

         a. Use may result in compromising values.

         b. Users are more likely to become sexually active at a younger age.

         c. Users are more likely to engage in unprotected sexual activity.

         d. Users are twice as likely to contract a sexually transmitted infection than teens who do not drink.[31,p574]

      2. Driving

         a. An adult with a blood alcohol concentration (BAC) of .08% is considered legally drunk.

         b. There is no acceptable BAC for individuals under the age of 21.[31,p579]

(continues)

    c. Effects of alcohol
        1. Slows reflexes
        2. Reduces the ability to judge distances and speeds
        3. Increases risk-taking
        4. Reduces concentration
        5. Increases forgetfulness[31,p578]
    3. Bingeing:
        a. Occurs when five or more drinks are consumed at one sitting
        b. Can lead to alcohol poisoning
            1. Mental confusion
            2. Coma
            3. Vomiting and seizures
            4. Slow respiration
            5. Irregular heartbeat
            6. Low body temperature (hypothermia)[31,p570]
    B. Marijuana
        1. Effects
            a. Hallucinogens
            b. Impaired short-term memory, reaction time, concentration, and coordination
            c. Decreased motivation
            d. Lung damage
            e. Heart damage
            f. Increased chance of stillbirth and birth defects
            g. Risk of infertility for both males and females
        2. Driving dangers
            a. Alters depth perception
            b. Increases reaction time
            c. Causes sleepiness
            d. Impairs judgment
            e. Slows reflexes[31,p598-600]
IV. Skills: Which of the seven National Health Education Standards skills does this performance task address?[4,p237]

Standard 5—Students will demonstrate the ability to use decision-making skills to enhance health.[1,p32]

Performance indicator 5.12.1 with infused content—Examine barriers that can hinder healthy decision making regarding alcohol and marijuana.[1,p33]

Performance indicator 5.12.2 with infused content—Determine the value of applying a thoughtful decision-making process in health-related situations that concern alcohol and marijuana.[1,p33]

Performance indicator 5.12.3 with infused content—Justify when individual or collaborative decision making is appropriate regarding alcohol and marijuana.[1,p33]

Performance indicator 5.12.4 with infused content—Generate alternatives to health-related issues concerning alcohol or marijuana.[1,p33]

Performance indicator 5.12.5 with infused content—Predict the potential short-term and long-term impact of each alternative regarding alcohol and marijuana on self and others.[1,p33]

Performance indicator 5.12.6 with infused content—Defend the healthy choice in regards to coping with alcohol and marijuana.[1,p33]

Performance indicator 5.12.7 with infused content—Evaluate the effectiveness of health-related decisions regarding alcohol and marijuana.[1,p33]

V. Curricular connections: What other subject areas does this project support?[4,p237]

English language arts

(continues)

VI. Student Directions and Assessment Criteria[4,p238]

Prompt #1

A. Project Description—Write/attach an engaging prompt that draws the student into the project.[4,p238]

Malena is a popular student in her graduating class and a member of the basketball team and band. She is looking forward to college in the fall.

During the past few months, the senior parties have become more and more frequent, and the drinking at them has increased.

Last weekend, Malena and her friend, Rafaella, attended a senior party at the lake house of one of her friends. The parents were not present, and a lot of alcohol and marijuana circulated.

Malena was feeling uncomfortable and wanted to go home. When Rafaella was ready to leave, she was under the influence but insisted she could drive.

B. Your Challenge—Provide a challenge or mission statement that describes the project.[4,p238]

Your challenge is to help Malena use decision making to find a way to get home safely.

Prompt #2

A. Project Description—Write/attach an engaging prompt that draws the student into the project.[4,p238]

Ben is an all-sports star and has many friends and choice of girlfriends. He has tried alcohol but does not like getting drunk.

Many of his friends play drinking games, get drunk quickly, and often throw up or pass out. He is becoming bored with this scene, but his friends expect him to go to the parties and participate.

This weekend, there is a party for the seniors who got early acceptance into college. The parents are on vacation, and he knows there will be a lot of drinking.

B. Your Challenge—Provide a challenge or mission statement that describes the project.[4,p238]

Your challenge is to help Ben use the decision-making process to figure out how to keep his friends without becoming involved in drinking games.

Prompt #3

A. Project Description—Write/attach an engaging prompt that draws the student into the project.[4,p238]

Dick and Marilyn hang out together at school. Their friends have been smoking weed for a few years and love it. Recently, they have been pressuring Dick and Marilyn to try it. They are curious because everyone seems to have a great time when high but do not want to become involved.

During lunch one day, Larry told them, "I'm selling and will give you a good first-try price." Dick and Marilyn were shocked and upset at being approached in school.

B. Your Challenge—Provide a challenge or mission statement that describes the project.[4,p238]

Your challenge is to help Dick and Marilyn use decision making to figure out what to do about being approached in school to buy drugs.

Prompt #4

A. Project Description—Write/attach an engaging prompt that draws the student into the project.[4,p238]

Tony and Alaina have been going together for just a few months. They enjoy spending time alone and have limited their sexual activity, with some difficulty, because they respect each other.

A few weeks ago, they were together and drinking with friends at a friend's house. They had too much to drink and made a poor decision to spend time alone in one of the bedrooms.

One thing led to another, and they had intercourse. Fortunately, Alaina did not get pregnant, but she is frightened the situation will happen again. She and Tony are going to another party this weekend, and she knows there will be alcohol and marijuana. She thinks she will not have the self-control to say, "No," to Tony.

B. Your Challenge—Provide a challenge or mission statement that describes the project.[4,p238]

Your challenge is to help Alaina use decision making to prevent using alcohol and becoming intimate with Tony.

(continues)

C. Assessment Criteria[4,p239]

You will be assessed on the following content:

Performance indicator 1.12.2 with infused content—Analyze the potential severity of injury or illness if engaging in unhealthy behaviors such as drinking alcohol or smoking marijuana.[1,p25]

1. Four facts about how alcohol lowers inhibitions and impairs judgment
2. Five effects alcohol has on driving ability
3. Five effects of binge drinking
4. Five effects of marijuana on the body
5. Five effects of marijuana on driving ability

You will be assessed on the following skills:

Performance indicator 5.12.1 with infused content—Examine barriers that can hinder healthy decision making regarding alcohol and marijuana.[1,p33]

Performance indicator 5.12.2 with infused content—Determine the value of applying thoughtful decision making in health-related situations concerning alcohol and marijuana.[1,p33]

Performance indicator 5.12.3 with infused content—Justify when individual or collaborative decision making is appropriate regarding the pressure to use alcohol and marijuana.[1,p33]

Performance indicator 5.12.4 with infused content—Generate alternatives to health-related issues or problems, such as the pressure to use alcohol or marijuana.[1,p33]

Performance indicator 5.12.5 with infused content—Predict the potential short-term and long-term impact on self and others of each alternative regarding the pressure to use alcohol and marijuana.[1,p33]

Performance indicator 5.12.6 with infused content—Defend the healthy choice about coping with the pressure to use alcohol and marijuana.[1,p33]

Performance indicator 5.12.7 with infused content—Evaluate the effectiveness of health-related decisions about the pressure to use alcohol and marijuana.[1,p33]

Your project consists of:

1. A PowerPoint presentation or poster that includes:
   a. Four facts about how alcohol lowers inhibitions and impairs judgment
   b. Five effects alcohol has on driving ability
   c. Five effects of binge drinking
   d. Five effects of marijuana on the body
   e. Five effects of marijuana on driving ability
2. A completed decision-making worksheet for each prompt
3. Select one of the prompts; then design a role-play that demonstrates how to use decision making to meet the challenge of the scenario.

Brewsterville High School

Name _____

Prompt #1

Malena is a popular student in her graduating class and a member of the basketball team and band. She is looking forward to college in the fall.

During the past few months, the senior parties have become more and more frequent, and the drinking at them has increased.

Last weekend, Malena and her friend, Rafaella, attended a senior party at the lake house of one of her friends. The parents were not present, and a lot of alcohol and marijuana circulated.

Malena was feeling uncomfortable and wanted to go home. When Rafaella was ready to leave, she was under the influence but insisted she could drive.

Your challenge is to help Malena use decision making to find a way to get home safely.

(continues)

Prompt #2

Ben is an all-sports star and has many friends and choice of girlfriends. He has tried alcohol, but does not like getting drunk.

Many of his friends play drinking games, get drunk quickly, and often throw up or pass out. He is becoming bored with this scene, but his friends expect him to go to the parties and participate.

This weekend, there is a party for the seniors who got early acceptance into college. The parents are on vacation, and he knows there will be a lot of drinking.

Your challenge is to help Ben use the decision-making process to figure out how to keep his friends without becoming involved in drinking games.

Prompt #3

Dick and Marilyn hang out together at school. Their friends have been smoking weed for a few years and love it. Recently, they have been pressuring Dick and Marilyn to try it. They are curious because everyone seems to have a great time when high but do not want to become involved.

During lunch, Larry told them, "I'm selling and will give you a good first-try price." Dick and Marilyn were shocked and upset at being approached in school.

Your challenge is to help them use decision making to figure out what to do about being approached in school to buy drugs.

Prompt #4

Tony and Alaina have been going together for just a few months. They enjoy spending time alone and have limited their sexual activity, with some difficulty, because they claim to respect each other.

A few weeks ago, they were together and drinking with friends at a friend's house. They had too much to drink and made a poor decision to spend time alone in one of the bedrooms.

One thing led to another, and they had intercourse. Fortunately, Alaina did not get pregnant but is frightened the situation will happen again. She and Tony are going to another party this weekend, and she knows there will be alcohol and marijuana. She thinks she will not have the self-control to say, "No," to Tony.

Your challenge is to help Alaina use decision making to prevent using alcohol and becoming intimate with Tony. Your project includes:

1. A PowerPoint presentation or a poster that includes:

   a. Four facts about how alcohol lowers inhibitions and impairs judgment

   b. Five effects alcohol has on driving ability

   c. Five effects of binge drinking

   d. Five effects of marijuana on the body

   e. Five effects of marijuana on driving ability

2. A completed decision-making worksheet for each prompt

3. Select one of the prompts; then design a role-play that demonstrates how to use decision making to meet the challenge of the scenario.

(continues)

Grades 9–12 Analytical Rubric for a PowerPoint or Poster About Alcohol and Marijuana (Table 9.19)

TABLE 9.19   Grades 9–12 Analytical Rubric to Assess a PowerPoint or Poster About Alcohol and Marijuana

Criteria	4	3	2	1
Performance indicator 1.12.2 with infused content—Analyze the potential severity of injury or illness if engaging in unhealthy behaviors such as drinking alcohol or smoking marijuana.[1,p25]	Student thoroughly analyzes how alcohol lowers inhibitions and impairs judgment.	Student adequately analyzes how alcohol lowers inhibitions and impairs judgment.	Student inadequately analyzes how alcohol lowers inhibitions and impairs judgment.	Student poorly analyzes how alcohol lowers inhibitions and impairs judgment.
Performance indicator 1.12.2 with infused content—Analyze the potential severity of injury or illness if engaging in unhealthy behaviors such as drinking alcohol or smoking marijuana.[1,p25]	Student thoroughly analyzes five ways alcohol effects driving ability.	Student adequately analyzes five ways alcohol effects driving ability.	Student inadequately analyzes five ways alcohol effects driving ability.	Student poorly analyzes five ways alcohol effects driving ability.
Performance indicator 1.12.2 with infused content—Analyze the potential severity of injury or illness if engaging in unhealthy behaviors such as drinking alcohol or smoking marijuana.[1,p25]	Student thoroughly analyzes five effects of binge drinking.	Student adequately analyzes five effects of binge drinking.	Student inadequately analyzes five effects of binge drinking.	Student poorly analyzes five effects of binge drinking.
Performance indicator 1.12.2 with infused content—Analyze the potential severity of injury or illness if engaging in unhealthy behaviors such as drinking alcohol or smoking marijuana.[1,p25]	Student thoroughly analyzes five effects of marijuana on the body	Student adequately analyzes five effects of marijuana on the body	Student inadequately analyzes five effects of marijuana on the body	Student poorly analyzes five effects of marijuana on the body

(continues)

TABLE 9.19   Grades 9–12 Analytical Rubric to Assess a PowerPoint or Poster About Alcohol and Marijuana (continued)

Criteria	4	3	2	1
Performance indicator 1.12.2 with infused content—Analyze the potential severity of injury or illness if engaging in unhealthy behaviors such as drinking alcohol or smoking marijuana.[1,p25]	Student thoroughly analyzes five effects of marijuana on driving ability.	Student adequately analyzes five effects of marijuana on driving ability.	Student inadequately analyzes five effects of marijuana on driving ability.	Student poorly analyzes five effects of marijuana on driving ability.
Creativity	The creativity of the poster or PowerPoint is excellent.	The creativity of the poster or PowerPoint is good.	The creativity of the poster or PowerPoint is fair.	The creativity of the poster or PowerPoint is poor.
Grammar	The grammar on the poster or PowerPoint is always correct.	The grammar on the poster or PowerPoint is usually correct.	The grammar on the poster or PowerPoint is sometimes correct.	The grammar on the poster or PowerPoint is never correct.
Spelling	The spelling on the poster or PowerPoint is always correct.	The spelling on the poster or PowerPoint is usually correct.	The spelling on the poster or PowerPoint is sometimes correct.	The spelling on the poster or PowerPoint is never correct.

Name _____

Total possible points – 32   Your points – _____   Your grade – _____

Grades 9–12 Decision-Making Chart (Table 9.20)

TABLE 9.20   Grades 9–12 Decision-Making Worksheet

1. What is the problem?

2. What is the decision to be made?

3. List three circumstances that hinder healthy decision making. (PI 5.12.1)

Hinder

a.

b.

c.

4. What is the value of applying thoughtful decision making in health-related situations? (PI 5.12.2)

(continues)

TABLE 9.20   Grades 9–12 Decision-Making Worksheet *(continued)*

5. Can the decision be made alone or should the decision be made collaboratively? (PI 5.12.3)

☐ The decision can be made alone.

☐ The decision should be made collaboratively.

Who can provide healthy alternatives to the problem?

_____

6. Alternatives (PI 5.12.4)	(PI 5.12.5) Short-term impact of each alternative on self and others.	(PI 5.12.5) Long-term impact of each alternative on self and others.	Put an X next to your healthy choice.
a.			
b.			
c.			

7. Which healthy alternative did you choose?

8. Reflection—Defend the healthy choice when making decisions. (PI 5.12.6)

9. Evaluate the effectiveness of the health-related decision. (PI 5.12.7)

Analytical Rubric to Assess a Decision-Making Role Play (Table 9.21)

TABLE 9.21   Grades 9–12—Analytical Rubric to Assess the Decision-Making Role-Play

Criteria	4	3	2	1
Identification of the problem	Student accurately identifies the problem.	Student's identification of the problem is mostly accurate.	Some parts of the student's identification of the problem are inaccurate.	Student's identification of the problem is mostly inaccurate.
Identification of the decision to be made	Student accurately identifies the decision to be made.	Student's identification of the decision to be made is mostly accurate.	Some parts of the student's identification of the decision to be made are accurate.	Student's identification of the decision to be made is inaccurate.

(continues)

Criteria	4	3	2	1
*Performance indicator 5.12.1 with infused content—*Examine barriers that can hinder healthy decision making regarding alcohol and marijuana.[1,p33]	Student accurately examines the barriers that hinder healthy decision making regarding alcohol and marijuana.	Student's analysis of the barriers that hinder healthy decision making regarding alcohol and marijuana is mostly accurate.	Some of the student's analysis of the barriers that hinder healthy decision making regarding alcohol and marijuana is inaccurate.	Student's analysis of the barriers that hinder healthy decision making regarding alcohol and marijuana is mostly inaccurate.
*Performance indicator 5.12.2 with infused content—*Determine the value of applying a thoughtful decision-making process in health-related situations concerning alcohol and marijuana.[1,p33]	Student accurately determines the value of applying a thoughtful decision-making process in health-related situations concerning alcohol and marijuana.	Student's determination of the value of applying a thoughtful decision-making process in health-related situations concerning alcohol and marijuana is mostly accurate.	Some of the student's determination of the value of applying a thoughtful decision-making process in health-related situations concerning alcohol and marijuana is somewhat inaccurate.	Student's determination of the value of applying a thoughtful decision-making process in health-related situations concerning alcohol and marijuana is mostly inaccurate.
*Performance indicator 5.12.3 with infused content—*Justify when individual or collaborative decision-making is appropriate regarding alcohol and marijuana.[1,p33]	Student accurately justifies when individual or collaborative decision-making is appropriate regarding alcohol and marijuana.	Student's justification of when a decision regarding alcohol and marijuana should be individual or collaborative is mostly accurate.	Student's justification of when a decision regarding alcohol and marijuana should be individual or collaborative has a few inaccuracies.	Student's justification of when a decision regarding alcohol and marijuana should be individual or collaborative is mostly inaccurate.
*Performance indicator 5.12.4 with infused content—*Generate alternatives to health-related issues regarding alcohol or marijuana.[1,p33]	Student thoroughly generates alternatives to health-related issues regarding alcohol or marijuana.	Student adequately generates alternatives to health-related issues regarding alcohol or marijuana.	Student inadequately generates alternatives to health-related issues regarding alcohol or marijuana.	Student poorly generates alternatives to health-related issues regarding alcohol or marijuana.
*Performance indicator 5.12.5 with infused content—*Predict the potential short-term and long-term impact of each alternative regarding alcohol and marijuana on self and others.[1,p33]	Student accurately predicts the potential short-term impact of each alternative on self and others.	Student's prediction of the potential short-term impact of each alternative on self and others is mostly accurate.	Student's prediction of the potential short-term impact of each alternative on self and others has a few inaccuracies.	Student's prediction of the potential short-term impact of each alternative on self and others is mostly inaccurate.

(continues)

TABLE 9.21   Grades 9–12—Analytical Rubric to Assess the Decision-Making Role-Play (continued)

Criteria	4	3	2	1
Performance indicator 5.12.5 with infused content—Predict the potential short-term and long-term impact of each alternative regarding alcohol and marijuana on self and others.[1,p33]	Student accurately predicts the potential long-term impact of each alternative on self and others.	Student's prediction of the potential long-term impact of each alternative on self and others is mostly accurate.	Student's prediction of the potential long-term impact of each alternative on self and others has a few inaccuracies.	Student's prediction of the potential long-term impact of each alternative on self and others is mostly inaccurate.
Performance indicator 5.12.6 with infused content—Defend the healthy choice in regards to coping with alcohol and marijuana.[1,p33]	Student thoroughly defends a healthy choice in regards to coping with alcohol and marijuana.	Student adequately defends a healthy choice in regards to coping with alcohol and marijuana.	Student inadequately defends a healthy choice in regards to coping with alcohol and marijuana.	Student poorly defends a healthy choice in regards to coping with alcohol and marijuana.
Performance indicator 5.12.7 with infused content—Evaluate the effectiveness of health-related decisions about alcohol and marijuana.[1,p33]	Student thoroughly evaluates the effectiveness of health-related decisions regarding alcohol and marijuana.	Student adequately evaluates the effectiveness of health-related decisions regarding alcohol and marijuana.	Student inadequately evaluates the effectiveness of health-related decisions regarding alcohol and marijuana.	Student poorly evaluates the effectiveness of health-related decisions regarding alcohol and marijuana.
Creativity	The role-play is an excellent example of creativity.	The role-play is a very good example of creativity.	The role-play is a fair example of creativity.	The role-play is a poor example of creativity.
Involvement	All members of the role-play are always involved.	All members of the role-play are sometimes involved.	All members of the role-play are rarely involved.	All members of the role-play are never involved.

Name _____

Total possible points – 48   Your points – _____   Your grade – _____

HOW THE COORDINATED SCHOOL HEALTH TEAM HELPS STUDENTS USE DECISION-MAKING SKILLS TO ENHANCE HEALTH

Health Education

- Teach content and skills that promote responsible drug and alcohol behaviors.
- Model and teach the decision-making process.
- Explain how alcohol affects driving ability, judgment, and behavior.
- Explain the hazards of binge drinking.
- Explain the choices available if offered drugs in school.

Physical Education

- Encourage a drug and alcohol-free lifestyle.
- Hang posters that show the effect of alcohol and marijuana on physical ability and health.

Health Services

- Provide intervention for students with alcohol and marijuana use/abuse or addiction.
- Provide information about the effects of alcohol and marijuana on the body.

Nutrition Services

- Hang posters that promote a drug-free lifestyle. Hang posters that depict peer resistance skills.
- Model good decision making.

Counseling, Psychological, and Social Services

- Provide referrals to alcohol and marijuana treatment centers.
- Provide support for students who have alcohol and marijuana use/abuse or addiction.
- Refer families to resources where they can get help for alcohol and marijuana use/abuse or addiction.

Healthy School Environment

- Develop and enforce a no-tolerance alcohol and drug policy.
- Quickly remove graffiti that encourages alcohol and marijuana use.

Health Promotion for Staff

- Provide staff development that trains teachers to detect use/abuse or addiction to alcohol and marijuana.
- Model drug-free behaviors through talk and behavior.

Family and Community Involvement

- Provide training on how to increase protective factors and decrease risk factors in order to protect children from substance use/abuse.
- Request town/city officials to adopt no-tolerance alcohol and drug laws.
- Provide supervised summer and weekend activities to engage adolescents in healthy activities.

Review Questions

1. How do *Healthy People 2020* and 21st Century Skills support Standard 5?

2. How do decision-making skills enhance health?

3. What are the steps in decision making?

4. How do formative assessments help the teacher determine whether the student is progressing toward proficiency?

5. Explain the lessons that lead to the PreK–2 performance task.

6. Why is Standard 1 always linked with a skills standard?

7. How can a teacher develop prompt-writing skills?

8. Explain how to construct an analytical rubric using performance indicators.

9. Can an analytical rubric contain criteria that are not performance indicators? Explain.

10. What is the value of including a written test with the performance task?

References

1. Joint Committee on National Health Education Standards. (2007). *National Health Education Standards, Second Edition, Achieving Excellence.* Atlanta, GA: American Cancer Society.

2. Office of Disease Prevention & Health Promotion. (2009). *Healthy People 2020: The Road Ahead.* Retrieved February 18, 2010: www.healthypeople.gov/hp2020/default.asp

3. Partnership for 21st Century Skills. (2010). 21st Century Skills, Education & Competitiveness. Tucson, AZ.

4. CCSSO~SCASS Health Education Project. (2006). *Assessment Tools for School Health Education, Pre-service and In-service edition.* Santa Cruz, CA: ToucanEd, Inc.

5. Page, R. M. (2007). *Promoting Health and Emotional Well-Being in Your Classroom.* Sudbury, MA: Jones and Bartlett.

6. Meeks, L. H. (2009). *Comprehensive School Health Education, Totally Awesome Strategies for Teaching Health* (6th ed.). New York: McGraw-Hill, p. 471.

7. Bronstein, A. C. (2009). 2008 Annual Report of the American Association of Poison Control Centers' National Poison Data System (NPDS): 26th Annual Report. *Clinical Toxicology, 47*(10), 911–1084.

8. American Association of Poison Control Centers. (n.d.). *Poison Tips for Children.* Retrieved February 19, 2010: http://www.aapcc.org/dnn/PoisoningPrevention/Children/tabid/120/Default.aspx

9. Mayo Clinic Staff. (2008). *Childhood Obesity : All-Mayo-Clinic.com.* Retrieved February 28, 2010: http://www.mayoclinic.com/health/childhood-obesity/DS00698. p. 4–5.

10. Centers for Disease Control and Prevention. (2010). *FAST-STATS-Overweight Prevalence.* Retrieved February 28, 2010: www.cdc.gov/nchs/fastats/overwt.htm

11. Centers for Disease Control and Prevention. (2009). *Obesity and Overweight for Professionals: Childhood DNPAO CDC.* Retrieved March 4, 2010: http://www.ced.gov/obesity/childhood/

12. U.S. Department of Agriculture. (2007). Balancing What You Eat With What You Do.

13. U. S. Department of Agriculture. (n.d.). *MyPyramid Worksheet.* Retrieved March 2, 2010: http://teamnutrition.usda.gov/resources/mpk_worksheet.pdf

14. Centers for Disease Control and Prevention. (2009). *Children's BMI Tool for Schools.* Retrieved February 28, 2010: http://www.cdc.gov/healthyweight/assessing/bmi/childrens_bmi/tool_for_schools.html

15. U.S. Department of Health and Human Services, Centers for Disease Control and Prevention. (2005). *2005 Middle School Youth Risk Behavior Survey.* Retrieved February 7, 2010: www.cdc.gov/healthyyouth/yrbs/middleschool2005/pdf/YRBS_MS__fullreport.pdf

16. Hautala, L. A., Junnila, J. , Helenius, H., Vaananen, A-M., Liuksila, P-R., Raiha, H., et al. (2008). Towards understanding gender differences in disordered eating among adolescents. *Journal of Clinical Nursing,* 17(13), 1803–1813.

17. Seo, P. D.-C. (2008). Factors Influencing Openness to Future Smoking Among Nonsmoking Adolescents. *Journal of School Health,* 78(6), 328–336.

18. Bean, M. K. (2008). Rural adolescent attitudes toward smoking and weight loss: Relationship to smoking status. *Nicotine & Tobacco Research,* 10(2), 279–286.

19. Lundgren, P. J. (2006). Familial Aggregation in the Night Eating Syndrome. *International Journal of Eating Disorders,* 39(6), 516–518.

20. Bronson, P. M. (2007). *Teen Health, Course 2.* New York: McGraw-Hill Glencoe.

21. Tucker, J. S. (2002). Five Year Prospective Study of Risk Factors for Daily Smoking in Adolescence Among Early Non-smokers and Experimenters. *Journal of Applied Social Psychology,* 32(8), 1588–1603.

22. Shelton, H. K. (2008). Parent-Child Relations, Conduct Problems and Cigarette Use in Adolescence: Examining the Role of Genetic and Environmental Factors on Patterns of Behavior. *Journal of Youth Adolescence,* 37(10), 1216–1228.

23. Jain, M. A. (2001). Why Don't Low-Income Mothers Worry About Their Preschoolers Being Overweight? *Pediatrics,* 107(5), 1138–1146.

24. Hahn, D. B. (2011). *Focus on Health* (10th ed.). New York: McGraw-Hill. p. 134.

25. Insel, P. M. (2008). *Core Concepts in Health, 10th Edition Update.* New York: McGraw-Hill.

26. Tester, M. L. (2005). Self-Deceptive Enhancement and Family Environment: Possible Protective Factors Against Internalization of the Thin Ideal. *Eating Disorders,* 13(2), 187–199.

27. Alters, S. S. (2009). *Essential Concepts for Healthy Living* (5th ed.). Sudbury, MA: Jones and Bartlett, p. 43.

28. Stunkard, M. A. (2008). Issues for DSM-V: Night Eating Syndrome. *American Journal of Psychology,* 165(4), 424.

29. Centers for Disease Control and Prevention. (2008). *Healthy Youth! YRBSS National Trends in Risk Behaviors.* Retrieved October 23, 2008: http://www.cdc.gov/healthy youth/yrbs/trends.htm. p. 1.

30. U.S. Department of Health and Human Services, Centers for Disease Control and Prevention. (2010). *Youth Risk Behavior Surveillance—United States, 2009.* Atlanta: Centers for Disease Control and Prevention.

31. Bronson, P. M. (2009). *Glencoe Health.* Woodland Hills, CA: McGraw-Hill.

Teaching National Health Education Standard 6

"Students will demonstrate the ability to use goal-setting skills to enhance health."[1,p34]

Standard 6

"Setting and reaching goals are key skills needed for emotional well-being"[2,p87]

Goal-setting skills help students identify, adopt, and maintain healthy behaviors. The steps progress from simple in PreK–2 to more complex in Grades 9–12.[1,p34]

Setting goals empowers young people to take control of their actions and strive for healthy outcomes. When reached, a goal gives a student confidence and encouragement for continuous self-improvement.

Sample performance tasks for the goal-setting skill include:

- Role-play how to determine personal needs; set goals to meet them.
- Create wellness plans.
- Develop a puppet show for younger children on how to set goals.
- Write a journal showing progress in reaching a goal.
- Write a story showing how a young person overcame academic stress by setting and achieving goals.
- Role-play a fitness instructor identifying activity and nutrition needs and setting goals. Include strategies and rewards.
- Identify a health need within a school and develop short-term goals to meet it.
- Create a comic strip, play, poem, or song showing a young person overcoming a need by reaching a goal.[3,p229-230]

To show proficiency in this standard, students assess personal needs; set long-term and short-term goals based on a need; track progress; identify helping resources; develop strategies that adjust to time, ability, priorities, and responsibilities; and prepare an effective long-term personal health plan.[1,34]

Teaching the Skill

According to the National Health Education Standards, Achieving Excellence, the teaching and learning of skills is a process. When planning, follow these steps:

I. Discuss the importance of using goal setting to enhance health[1,p14]
   - The individual experiences empowerment and control when achieving a goal.
   - Goals do not have to be set in isolation. We can ask a trusted adult or friend for help.
   - Rather than trying to solve a large problem, the process trains us to set smaller short-term goals to reach a larger long-term objective.
   - The process identifies and rejects unrealistic goals.
   - Resources are identified and accessed to achieve a goal and used for future problem solving and goal setting.
   - Rather than abandoning a goal because a strategy does not work, we learn to make adjustments or try a different strategy.[2,p88]

II. Explain the steps to proficiency in goal-setting skills to enhance health.
   - Select the performance indicators for the grade span.
   - Teach the steps to achieve proficiency of the selected performance indicators, such as how to
     - Identify a personal need.
     - Ask for help.
     - Set short-term goals that realize the long-term goal.
     - Set a long-term goal to address a need.
     - Track progress in achieving the goal.

297

- Adjust goals when abilities, priorities, and responsibilities change.
- Design an effective long-term personal health plan[1,p34]

III. Show the students what the goal-setting skill looks like.
- Demonstrate the goal-setting steps.
- Model the goal-setting steps in the classroom.

IV. Provide adequate time for the students to practice goal-setting skills to enhance health.

V. Utilize formative assessments during practice to provide feedback and encouragement.[1,p14]

PreK–2

To achieve proficiency in Standard 6, PreK–2 students identify a short-term personal health goal and take action to achieve it. They also identify trusted adults who can help them set and achieve goals.[1,p34]

For example:

Brandon is hungry at snack and lunchtime and does not take the time to wash his hands before he eats. Consequently, the germs on his hands go into his mouth, and he keeps getting a cold.

Explain the goal-setting skill and indicate that the class is going to use it to help Brandon stay healthy. Ask the students, "What can Brandon do to keep healthy?" The ideas the students generate are short-term goals. The list provides students with many options to reach the goal.

To reflect, ask the students:

"What can Brandon do to keep healthy?" *(Goal)* Answers are short-term goals.

- *He can only get his snack or lunch from the teacher after he has washed or cleaned his hands.*
- *He can use a hand sanitizer before he eats his lunch.*
- *His parents or teacher can write a check-off list that the teacher or aide signs, indicating that Brandon washes*

or cleans his hands before eating. If Brandon has checked off a box each day, he is rewarded at the end of the week (**Figure 10.1**).

For another example, distribute the goal-setting worksheet. Ask the students to cut out and paste the picture of the need (sick child) in the first section. Determine the goal (healthy, smiling child) and paste it in the second section. Cut out and paste two things the children can do to stay healthy (short-term goal—sneeze into elbow and wash hands).

Reflect by asking:

- Did you achieve the goal?
- Did the short-term goals help?
- If the short-term goals did not help, what else could you do to achieve the goal?

PREK–2 GOAL-SETTING WORKSHEET (TABLE 10.1)

When the students demonstrate an understanding of the skill, as assessed formatively, practice the skill. Present situations that show a need and challenge the students to set a goal to address it. Brainstorm different steps (short-term goals) to take to achieve the long-term goal.

Formatively assess the practice, provide feedback for students to improve the skill, and continue instruction when students perform it.

FIGURE 10.1 **Goal Setting with Two Short-Term Goals and a Self Check.**

TABLE 10.1 PreK–2 Goal-Setting Worksheet

PreK–2 Goal-Setting Worksheet

Name _____

Goal-Setting Worksheet

Need

The child is sick.

Goal

To keep healthy

Do you need help to achieve the goal? (PI 6.2.2) ■ Yes ☐ No

Who can help you?

My parents and my teacher.

1. Short-term goal (PI 6.2.1)

   Sneeze into my elbow.

2. Short-term goal (PI 6.2.1)

   Wash my hands.

Reflection

Did you achieve the goal? *Yes*

Did the short-term goals help? *Yes*

If not, what else could you do to achieve the goal? *Ask an adult for help.*

WHAT DOES THE SKILL OF GOAL SETTING TO ENHANCE HEALTH LOOK LIKE IN THE PREK–2 CLASSROOM?

Mrs. Blanchard is a Grade 1 teacher at the Bilossi Elementary School. The school is located in the city and, like other city schools, serves a low-income socio-economic community. Mrs. Blanchard and Mrs. Dunlap, the health specialist, have read research that supports teaching goal setting to early elementary students as a way of achieving behavioral and academic objectives. The research explains when children learn the self-determination skills of decision making, problem solving, and goal setting during the elementary years, they have time to practice and improve them for use later in life.[4,p116]

Mrs. Blanchard and Mrs. Dunlap work together to determine the needs of their students and select performance indicators and content to meet those requirements. The latest data indicates their students have poor dental health and, consequently, are asking to go to the nurse more frequently because of mouth pain. The nurse corroborates this information.

The teachers also observe students with poor dental health have trouble eating their snacks and lunch and concentrating on their lessons. They also do not speak clearly, and exhibit poor self-image and self-esteem.[5,p1]

The school recognizes the need to improve the self-esteem, confidence, and motivation of all the children. The school also needs to improve the learning environment and save money on supplies. With these parameters in mind, the staff and administration designed a recycling program because it is a goal that everyone can reach and from which they can all benefit.

Mrs. Blanchard and Mrs. Dunlap want the students to learn the goal-setting skill to resolve their own problems, know when to ask for adult support, and become more confident and empowered.

In planning the goal-setting unit, they target the performance indicator 6.2.1.

> 6.2.1—Identify a short-term personal health goal and take action toward achieving the goal.[1,p34]
> *Performance indicator 6.2.1 with infused content—* Identify a short-term personal health goal for improving dental health and recycling that enhances health.[1,p34]

After selecting the appropriate skill performance indicators, the teachers select Standard 1 performance indicators for content.

Standard 1—Students will comprehend concepts related to health promotion and disease prevention to enhance health.[1,p24]

Performance indicator 1.2.1—Identify that healthy behaviors affect personal health.[1,p24]

Performance indicator 1.2.1 with infused content— Identify that healthy behaviors such as brushing and flossing teeth and recycling affect personal health.[1,p24]

By linking the skill and the content performance indicators, the teacher has direction in planning the unit on using goal-setting skills to enhance health.

The first step in planning is to think through the unit by completing the performance task template. Thereupon, the teacher will have a good idea of the lessons that precede this culminating activity, the information and back-up materials to introduce the prompt to the students, and the assessment strategies.

Because Grade 1 students are learning to read, the instruction and assessment are verbal and visual. The teacher gives students time to learn about dental health, recycling, and goal setting. Students practice and demonstrate their knowledge and skill during a class presentation.

The following is an example of a Grade 1 goal-setting performance task. The first section illustrates how the teacher plans for an authentic assessment of the performance indicators 6.2.1 and 1.2.1. The second extracts some of the information from the performance task and transforms it into the prompt and support materials for students.

The students are assessed formatively during instruction and summatively through an analytical rubric.

Performance Task Name: Grade 1—Setting Goals for Dental Health and Recycling

I. Which state standard(s) does the performance task address?

II. Topic: What areas of health does this project assess? Why is it important? What is the focus of the project?[3,p237]

A. This performance task assesses Personal Health and Environmental Health.

B. This topic is important because:

1. Dental Health

a. Dental disease is one of the leading causes of absenteeism for children.

b. Over 51 million school hours are lost each year due to dental-related illnesses.

c. *Healthy People 2010* espouses increasing the number of children receiving sealants on their molars, increasing the number of adolescents receiving preventive dental services, and increasing the number of school-based oral health programs.[5,p2]

2. Recycling

a. Recycling decreases greenhouse gas emissions.

b. Every ton of mixed paper recycled can save the energy equivalent of 185 gallons of gas.[6,p1-2]

C. The focus of the project is to use goal-setting skills to improve dental health and increase recycling.

III. Key Concepts: What basic concepts should students know?[3,p237]

*Performance indicator 1.2.1 with infused content—*Identify that healthy behaviors, such as brushing and flossing teeth and recycling, enhance personal health.[1,p24]

A. Dental Health

1. Keeping teeth healthy

a. Brush daily

b. Floss daily

c. Use fluoride

d. Eat a healthy diet

e. Wear a mouth guard when participating in sports

2. Brushing teeth

a. Purpose

1. Plaque is a sticky substance that causes cavities. Brushing removes the plaque.

2. Freshens breath

(continues)

    b. Brush and toothpaste

       1. Use a soft brush to brush after each meal.

       2. The brush must be long enough to reach all the teeth.

       3. Use toothpaste that has fluoride because it strengthens teeth and helps prevent decay.

       4. Replace toothbrushes every few months.

    c. Technique

       1. Brush the outside, inside, and chewing surface of the tooth.

       2. Brush the tongue.

       3. Use short gentle strokes.[7,p262]

  3. Flossing

    a. Helps prevent gum disease by removing plaque and bits of food between the teeth.

    b. Floss reaches places that the toothbrush cannot.

    c. Technique

       1. Wrap the floss around one finger of each hand.

       2. Move the floss gently along the tooth to the gum.

       3. Bend the floss around the tooth and slide it up and down to remove the plaque.

       4. Use a new section on different teeth to prevent spreading bacteria from one tooth to another.[7,p263]

B. Recycling

    a. Occurs when a waste product is broken down so it can be used again

    b. Benefits to health:

       1. Conserves natural resources, such as trees and water.

       2. Takes less energy to recycle than to make a new product

       3. Takes less water to recycle than to make a new product.

       4. Pollutes the air less than making a new product.

       5. Saves space in the landfill where trash is buried.

       6. Costs less money to recycle than to make a new product.

       7. Produces more jobs.

       8. Recycling one can saves enough energy to run a television for three hours.[6]

       9. Personal health

         a) Recycling increases self-esteem and pride because of the contribution to a healthier community and environment.

         b) Recycling increases self-confidence because it is an action within our capabilities.

         c) Recycling increases physical activity.

         d) Social health is enhanced because students work with each other to recycle.[8]

    c. Paper recycling process

       1. Collect waste paper.

       2. Send the paper to a recycling plant.

       3. Mix paper with water to convert it into pulp.

       4. Pass the pulp through a screen to clean it of staples and paper clips.

       5. Mix with new pulp to make recycled paper.[6,p2]

IV. Skills: Which of the seven National Health Education Skills does this performance task address?[3,p237]

Performance indicator 6.2.1 with infused content—Identify a short-term personal health goal of improving dental health and recycling and take action toward achieving the goals.[1,p34]

A. Dental health

    a. Set a goal to prevent cavities.

    b. Set two short-term goals to prevent cavities.

    c. Reflection

B. Recycling

    a. Set a goal to recycle paper.

    b. Set two short-term goals to recycle paper.

(continues)

V. Curricular connections: What other subject(s) does this project support?[3,p237]

    English language arts

    Math

    Science

VI. Student directions and assessment criteria[3,p238]

A. Project Description—Write and attach an engaging prompt that draws the student into the project.[3,p238]

Steven is a Grade 1 student at the Bilossi Elementary School. Mrs. Blanchard, his teacher, believes it is critical for him to know how to set goals in school and at home.

Steven likes his school, particularly the nurse, because he often goes to her office with a toothache and she is very kind to him. One day the nurse and a dentist came to his class and explained the importance of brushing and flossing teeth. The dentist gave everyone a toothbrush, fluoride toothpaste, and dental floss.

One thing Steven does not like about his school is that sometimes there is not enough paper for his assignments. He notices a lot of used paper on the floor, in the hallways, and around the outside of the school. Sometimes the school looks messy, and he does not like it.

B. Your Challenge—Provide a challenge or mission statement that describes the project.[3,p238]

Your challenge is to help Steven improve his dental health and increase recycling at his school.

C. Assessment Criteria[3,p239]

You are assessed on the following key concepts: (List the concepts)

Performance indicator 1.2.1 with infused content—Identify that healthy behaviors, such as brushing and flossing teeth and recycling, enhance personal health.[1,p24]

1. Dental health
   a. Five ways to keep teeth healthy
   b. Describe plaque and why we need to remove it.
   c. Three facts about a toothbrush and toothpaste
   d. Describe how to brush and floss teeth.

2. Recycling
   a. Five reasons why recycling is good for personal and communal health
   b. A poster showing the five step process of recycling paper

You are assessed on the following skills: (List the skills)

Performance indicator 6.2.1 with infused content—Identify short-term personal health goals of improving dental health and recycling and take action toward achieving them.[1,p34]

1. Brushing/Flossing
   a. One goal
   b. Two short-term goals
   c. Reflection

2. Recycling paper and plastic bottles
   a. One goal
   b. Two short-term goals
   c. Reflection

Student project must include the following: (List the project components)

1. Two goal-setting worksheets
   a. Brushing and flossing
   b. Recycling

2. Poster
   a. Dental health
      1. Five ways to keep teeth healthy
      2. What is plaque and why is it important to remove it?
      3. Three facts about a toothbrush and toothpaste

(continues)

    4. How to brush and floss teeth

    5. One goal, two short-term goals, and a reflection on personal goal of brushing and flossing teeth

  b. Recycling

    1. Five reasons why recycling is good for health

    2. The five-step recycling process

    3. One goal, two short-term goals, and a reflection on the personal goal of recycling paper in school

---

Bilossi Elementary School

Name _____

Steven is a Grade 1 student at the Bilossi Elementary School. Mrs. Blanchard, his teacher, believes it is critical for him to know how to set goals in school and at home.

Steven likes his school, particularly the nurse, because he often goes to her office with a toothache. One day the nurse and a dentist came to his class and explained the importance of brushing and flossing teeth. The dentist gave everyone a toothbrush, fluoride toothpaste, and dental floss.

One thing Steven does not like about his school is that sometimes there is not enough paper for his assignments. He notices a lot of used paper on the floor, in the hallways, and around the outside of the school. Sometimes the school looks messy, and he does not like it.

Your challenge is to help Steven improve his dental health and increase recycling at his school.

Your project must include:

1. Two goal-setting worksheets

  a. Improve dental health by brushing and flossing.

  b. Recycle paper in school.

2. Poster

  a. Dental health

    1. Five ways to keep teeth healthy

    2. A description of plaque and why it is important to remove it

    3. Three facts about a toothbrush and toothpaste

    4. How to brush and floss teeth

    5. One goal, two short-term goals, and a reflection on personal goal of brushing and flossing teeth

  b. Recycling

    1. Five reasons why recycling is good for personal and communal health

    2. The five step recycling process

    3. One goal, two short-term goals, and a reflection on the personal goal of recycling paper in school

(continues)

TABLE 10.2   Goal-Setting Worksheet—Brushing and Flossing Teeth

Goal-Setting Skill

Name _____

Goal Setting Worksheet–Brushing and Flossing

Need

Goal

Do you need help to achieve the goal? (PI 6.2.2)   ☐ Yes   ☐ No

Who can help you?

1. Short-term goal (PI 6.2.1)

2. Short-term goal (PI 6.2.1)

Reflection

Did you achieve the goal? _____

Did the short-term goals help? _____

If not, what else could you do to achieve the goal?

TABLE 10.3   Goal-Setting Worksheet—Recycling

Need

Goal

Do you need help to achieve the goal? (PI 6.2.2)   ☐ Yes   ☐ No

Who can help you?

1. Short-term goal (PI 6.2.1)

2. Short-term goal (PI 6.2.1)

Reflection

Did you achieve the goal? _____

Did the short-term goals help? _____

If not, what else could you do to achieve the goal?

(continues)

TABLE 10.4 Dental Health Goal-Setting Self-Check

1. Five ways to keep teeth healthy

   a.   d.

   b.   e.

   c.

       Yes   Not yet   No

2. Describe plaque and why it is important to remove it.

   Yes   No

3. Two facts about the toothbrush and toothpaste

   Yes   No

4. Explain how to brush teeth.

   Yes   No

5. Explain how to floss teeth.

   Yes   No

6. Goal setting

   Goal _____

       Short-term goal _____

       Short-term goal _____

Reflection _____

    Yes   No

TABLE 10.5 Recycling Poster Self-Check

1. Five reasons why recycling is good for health

   a.   d.

   b.   e.

   c.

       Yes   Not yet   No

2. Describe five-step recycling process.

   a.   d.

   b.   e.

   c.

       Yes   Not yet   No

5. Goal setting

   Goal _____

       Short-term goal _____

       Short-term goal _____

Reflection _____

    Yes   No

(continues)

TABLE 10.6   Analytical Rubric to Assess the Recycling Poster Portion of the Performance Task

| Criteria | Recycling Poster | | | |
	4	3	2	1
Performance indicator 1.2.1 with infused content—Identify that healthy behaviors such as brushing and flossing teeth and recycling, enhance personal health.[1,p24]	Student thoroughly identifies five reasons why recycling is good for health.	Student adequately identifies five reasons why recycling is good for health.	Student inadequately identifies five reasons why recycling is good for health.	Student poorly identifies five reasons why recycling is good for health.
Performance indicator 1.2.1 with infused content—Identify that healthy behaviors such as brushing and flossing teeth and recycling, enhance personal health.[1,p24]	Student thoroughly identifies the five-step recycling process and explains how it enhances health.	Student adequately identifies the five-step recycling process and explains how it enhances health.	Student inadequately identifies the five-step recycling process and explains how it enhances health.	Student poorly identifies the five-step recycling process and explains how it enhances health.
Performance indicator 6.2.1 with infused content—Identify a short-term personal health goal of improving recycling, and take action toward achieving the goal.[1,p34]	Student accurately identifies one goal, two short-term goals, and a reflection of the personal goal of recycling paper in school.	The student's identification of one goal, two short-term goals, and a reflection of the personal goal of recycling paper in school is mostly accurate.	There are a few inaccuracies in the student's identification of one goal, two short-term goals, and a reflection of the personal goal of recycling paper in school.	The student's identification of one goal, two short-term goals, and a reflection of the personal goal of recycling paper in school is mostly inaccurate.
Creativity	The creativity of the poster is excellent.	The creativity of the poster is very good.	The creativity of the poster is fair.	The creativity of the poster is poor.
Grammar	The grammar is always correct.	The grammar is sometimes correct.	The grammar is rarely correct.	The grammar is never correct.
Spelling	The spelling is always correct.	The spelling is sometimes correct.	The spelling is rarely correct.	The spelling is never correct.

Name _____

Total possible points – 24   Your points – _____   Your grade – _____

(continues)

TABLE 10.7   Analytical Rubric to Assess the Dental Health Poster Portion of the Performance Task

| Criteria | Brushing and Flossing Poster | | | |
	4	3	2	1
Performance indicator 1.2.1 with infused content—Identify that healthy behaviors such as brushing and flossing teeth and recycling, enhance personal health.[1,p24]	Student thoroughly identifies five ways to keep teeth healthy to enhance personal health.	Student adequately identifies five ways to keep teeth healthy to enhance personal health.	Student inadequately identifies five ways to keep teeth healthy to enhance personal health.	Student poorly identifies five ways to keep teeth healthy to enhance personal health.
Plaque	Student thoroughly describes plaque and why it is important to remove it.	Student adequately describes plaque and why it is important to remove it.	Student inadequately describes plaque and why it is important to remove it.	Student poorly describes plaque and why it is important to remove it.
Toothbrush/ Toothpaste	Student thoroughly explains two facts about a toothbrush and toothpaste.	Student adequately explains two facts about a toothbrush and toothpaste.	Student inadequately explains two facts about a toothbrush and toothpaste.	Student poorly explains two facts about a toothbrush and toothpaste.
Performance indicator 1.2.1 with infused content—Identify that healthy behaviors such as brushing and flossing teeth and recycling, enhance personal health.[1,p24]	Student accurately identifies how brushing teeth enhances personal health.	Student's identification of how brushing teeth enhances health is mostly accurate.	Student's identification of how brushing teeth enhances health has a few inaccuracies.	Student's identification of how brushing teeth enhances health is mostly inaccurate.
Performance indicator 1.2.1 with infused content—Identify that healthy behaviors such as brushing and flossing teeth and recycling, enhance personal health.[1,p24]	Student accurately identifies how flossing teeth enhances health.	Student's identification of how flossing teeth enhances health is mostly accurate.	Student's identification of how flossing teeth enhances health has a few inaccuracies.	Student's identification of how flossing teeth enhances health is mostly inaccurate.
Performance indicator 6.2.1 with infused content—Identify a short-term personal health goal of improving dental health, and take action toward achieving the goal.[1,p34]	Student accurately identifies one goal, two short-term goals, and a reflection of the personal goal of improving dental health.	The student's identification of one goal, two short-term goals, and a reflection of the personal goal of improving dental health is mostly accurate.	There are a few inaccuracies in the student's identification of one goal, two short-term goals, and a reflection of the personal goal of improving dental health.	The student's identification of one goal, two short-term goals, and a reflection of the personal goal of improving dental health is mostly inaccurate.

(continues)

TABLE 10.7 Analytical Rubric to Assess the Dental Health Poster Portion of the Performance Task *(continued)*

Criteria	4	3	2	1
Creativity	The creativity of the poster is excellent.	The creativity of the poster is very good.	The creativity of the poster is fair.	The creativity of the poster is poor.
Grammar	The grammar is always correct.	The grammar is sometimes correct.	The grammar is rarely correct.	The grammar is never correct.
Spelling	The spelling is always correct.	The spelling is sometimes correct.	The spelling is rarely correct.	The spelling is never correct.

Name _____

Total possible points – 36   Your points – _____   Your grade – _____

HOW THE COORDINATED SCHOOL HEALTH TEAM HELPS STUDENTS USE GOAL-SETTING SKILLS TO ENHANCE HEALTH

Health Education

- Teach goal-setting skill.
- Provide instruction in dental health.
- Provide instruction in recycling.
- Provide recycling bins in the classroom to encourage recycling.

Physical Education

- Model good dental health through healthy snacking. Hang posters that promote dental health.
- Provide recycling bins in the gymnasium to encourage recycling.

Health Services

- Screen students for dental health.
- Provide recycling bins in the office to encourage recycling.

Nutrition Services

- Promote healthy eating as a way of increasing dental health.
- Provide recycling bins in the cafeteria to encourage recycling.

Counseling, Psychological, and Social Services

- Provide dental health resources for students and families.
- Provide recycling bins in the office to encourage recycling.

Healthy School Environment

- Ensure that the vending machines contain healthy snacks that promote dental health.
- Encourage school-wide recycling.
- Provide recycling bins in the halls to encourage recycling.

Health Promotion for Staff

- Use staff meetings to introduce and encourage recycling.
- Institute a recycling campaign that encourages each classroom to recycle.
- Model good dental health through healthy snacking.

Family and Community Involvement

- Invite a community dentist to the meeting to discuss how the family can promote dental health.
- Ask a dentist to volunteer time to screen students for dental health problems.

Grades 3–5

To achieve proficiency in Standard 6, Grades 3–5 students set a personal health goal, track progress, and identify resources that assist in achieving the goal.

For example:

Ben takes karate lessons on Saturday mornings. His strength and skill are improving, and he wants to compete in the Karate Classic for the school. Tryouts are in two weeks, but his teacher thinks Ben is not ready.

To increase his skill and persuade his teacher, Ben decides to practice his skills for one half-hour each day. He is also eating healthy foods and getting plenty of sleep. Every day he feels physically and mentally stronger.

To track his progress, after practice Ben cuts out a picture of a karate competitor and pastes it into his journal (**Table 10.8**). He tracks his eating and sleeping habits by filling a chart listing the food he eats and how much sleep he gets.

Ben asked his older brother, Jerry, to help him practice the different karate movements because Jerry had also competed at Ben's age.

On the morning of the tryouts, Ben ate a nutritious breakfast and practiced his moves. He was nervous, but used his deep breathing exercises to calm down.

When it was Ben's turn, he performed each skill perfectly. He was very pleased, and so was his teacher. He selected Ben to compete!

The extra training, healthy eating, and enough sleep were the right choices for Ben to reach his goal.

To reflect, ask the students:

- What was Ben's need? (*He was not in good physical condition or skilled enough to compete.*)

- What was Ben's personal health goal? (PI 6.5.1) (*To get into good physical condition and increase his skill in order to be selected to compete.*)
- What things (short-term goals) did Ben do to help him reach his goal? (*Practiced every day, ate healthy foods, got adequate sleep, used deep breathing to reduced stress*)
- How did Ben track his progress towards his goal? (PI 6.5.1) (*Placing the picture of a competitor in his journal along with writing down what he ate and how much sleep he got.*)
- What resources did Ben use to help him reach his goal? (PI 6.5.2) (*His brother*)
- Reflection. Did Ben's goal-setting plan work? (*Yes*) Could he have made a better plan? (*Maybe. There are many ways to achieve a goal.*)

In this skill, students must demonstrate their goal-setting skills in several scenarios. When they demonstrate an understanding of the skill, as determined through formative assessment, instruction continues with the content.

To continue the practice, ask students to brainstorm goals common for students their age. Write these suggestions into prompts and give students time to practice their skill in small groups. Pair the groups and ask one to present to the other. The group that is listening uses a goal-setting check-off list to make sure all the steps of the process are complete (**Table 10.9**).

As the students learn and practice the skill and content, continue to formatively assess their progress. If additional instruction is needed, provide it before moving to the performance task.

TABLE 10.8   Weekly Journal to Record Practice, Diet, and Sleep

	Monday	Tuesday	Wednesday	Thursday	Friday	Saturday	Sunday
Picture (Practice)							
Food							
Sleep							

TABLE 10.9   Goal-Setting Self-Check

1. The need was clearly stated.   ☐ Yes   ☐ No

2. The personal health goal was clearly stated. (PI 6.5.1)   ☐ Yes   ☐ No

3. Two short-term goals were clearly stated.   ☐ Yes   ☐ No

4. The group specifically showed how they would track
   progress toward achieving the goal. (PI 6.5.1)   ☐ Yes   ☐ No

5. Resources to assist in the achieving of the goal were
   clearly stated. (PI 6.5.2)   ☐ Yes   ☐ No

Reflection

1. Was the goal reached?

2. Did the short-term goals help the person reach the goal?

3. Was the progress tracked effectively? Explain.

4. Were the resources clearly stated?

5. Would you do anything differently? Explain.

WHAT DOES THE SKILL OF GOAL SETTING LOOK LIKE IN THE GRADE 3 CLASSROOM?

Mr. Copeland, the assistant principal at the Midland Elementary School, recently read the profiles of the third grade class and found that many children have parents who are separated or divorced. Research explains that some children of divorce have few adjustment problems while others exhibit poor school achievement, depression, anxiety, physical ailments, and behavioral problems at home and school.[9,p110-112] Mr. Copeland wants his staff to think of projects for their classes that address the whole child and foster mental and emotional health.

Mr. Burke, the Grade 3 teacher, believes that young children should learn how to set goals and discover strategies and resources to help reach them. When his young students succeed, it enhances their physical, mental/emotional, and social health. This state of wellness is beneficial to the child both at home and school.

He decides to teach students how to use goal setting to improve relationships. To do so, he asked the children to list common problems they experience in relationships with family and friends. The students provided many relevant problems and gave Mr. Burke some good ideas for prompts.

He begins with Standard 6 performance indicators. Knowing that goal setting is a process, he addresses each performance indicator.

Standard 6—Students will demonstrate the ability to use goal-setting skills to enhance health.[1,p34]
  Performance Indicator 6.5.1—Set a personal goal and track progress toward its achievement.[1,p34]

Performance indicator 6.5.1 with infused content—Set a personal goal to improve relationships and track progress toward its achievement.[1,p34]

Performance Indicator 6.5.2—Identify resources to assist in achieving a personal health goal.[1,p34]

Performance indicator 6.5.2 with infused content—Identify resources to assist in achieving a personal health goal of improving relationships.[1,p34]

After selecting the appropriate performance indicator for the skill, choose a Standard 1 performance indicator.

Standard 1—Students will comprehend concepts related to health promotion and disease prevention to enhance health.[1,p24]
  Performance Indicator 1.5.2—Identify examples of emotional, intellectual, physical, and social health.[1,p24]
    Performance indicator 1.5.2 with infused content—Identify examples of emotional, intellectual, physical, and social health that result from improving relationships.[1,p24]

By linking the skill and content performance indicators, the teacher has a clear idea of how to plan the lessons for a goal-setting unit.

The first step in planning is to think through the unit by completing the performance task template. Upon completion, the teacher will have a good idea of the lessons that precede this culminating activity, the information and back-up materials necessary to introduce the prompt to the students, and the assessment strategies.

When distributing the prompt, include all the back-up information, student worksheets, and holistic and analytical rubrics. Distribute the rubrics with the prompt so students know how they are being assessed before working on their product. The rubrics act as a guide and help the students attain proficiency in the standards.

Designing the performance task takes considerable preparation, but once the information is distributed and explained, the students create a product independently. They learn with good coaching (formative assessment) how to demonstrate proficiency in content and skill.

The following is an example of a Grade 3 goal-setting performance task that focuses on setting a goal to improve relationships and identifying examples of emotional, intellectual, physical, and social health.

The first section, for the teacher, demonstrates how to plan for an authentic assessment of the performance indicators 6.5.1, 6.5.2, and 1.5.2. The second, the student's, extracts information from the performance task and transforms it into the student prompt and support materials.

Performance Task Name: Grade 3—Setting Goals to Improve Relationships

I. Which state standard(s) does this performance task address? (Varies by state)

II. Topic: What areas of health does this project assess? Why is it important? What is the focus of the project?[3,p237]

   A. This performance task assesses Family life and Mental/Emotional Health

   B. This topic is important because:

      1. Approximately 50% of marriages end in divorce.[10]

      2. The impact of divorce on a child's growth and development varies from minimal to long-term.

      3. Effects of divorce on children:

         a. Short-term depression and anxiety

         b. Behavioral problems at home and school

         c. Physical ailments[9,p111]

   C. The focus of this project is to set a goal to improve relationships and identify examples of emotional, intellectual, physical, and social health.

III. Key Concepts: What basic concepts should students know?[3,p237]

   Standard 1—Students will comprehend concepts related to health promotion and disease prevention to enhance health.[1,p24]

   Performance indicator 1.5.2 with infused content—Identify examples of emotional, intellectual, physical, and social health that result from improving relationships.[1,p24]

   A. Examples of mental and emotional health:

      1. Keep a positive attitude.

      2. Recognize strengths and improve weaknesses.

      3. Set realistic goals.

      4. Act responsibly.

      5. Retain ability to relax and have fun.

      6. Remain aware of feelings and express them in a healthy way.

      7. Empathetic towards others

      8. Acknowledge constructive feedback.

      9. Face challenges realistically and with a positive attitude.[11,p6]

   B. Examples of intellectual health:

      1. Use problem-solving skills.

      2. Use goal-setting skills.

      3. Reflect on decisions.

      4. Learn from experiences.

      5. Feel in control.[12,p3]

(continues)

C. Examples of physical health:
   1. Have energy.
   2. Physically active (60 minutes each day)[13]
   3. Choose a healthy diet.
   4. Get nine hours of sleep.
   5. Good dental health[11,p4-5]
D. Examples of social health:
   1. Friendly towards other people
   2. Support family and friends
   3. Care for family and friends
   4. Remain considerate of others
   5. Accept others for who they are
   6. Follow through on promises
   7. If an argument occurs, disagree respectfully.[11,p6-7]
IV. Skills: Which of the seven National Health Education Standards skills does this performance task address?[3,p237]

Standard 6—Students will demonstrate the ability to use goal-setting skills to enhance health.[1,p32]

Performance indicator 6.5.1.with infused content—Set a personal goal to improve relationships and track progress toward its achievement.[1,p34]
A. Determine a personal need.
B. Set a goal to meet the need.
C. Set two short-term goals that help achieve the goal.
D. Keep a daily assessment of progress for one week.
   Performance indicator 6.5.2 with infused content—Identify resources to assist in achieving a personal health goal of improving relationships.[1,p34]
A. Identify a family member or friend who can help a young person reach a goal.
B. Identify someone in school who can help a young person reach a goal.
V. Curricular connections—What other subject areas does this project support?[3,p237]
   English language arts
   Math
   Art
VI. Student Directions and Assessment Criteria[3,p238]
Prompt #1
A. Project Description—Write and attach an engaging prompt that draws the student into the project.[3,p238]

   Marjorie's parents are divorcing. Recently she and her older sister have been arguing more than ever. Marjorie wants to feel older, so she wore her sister's clothes without asking. She took her sister's iPod and forgot to do her chores, both of which also upset her mother.

   Everyone seems to be mad at everyone else, and it is making Marjorie sad and sick.
B. Your Challenge—Provide a challenge or mission statement that describes the project.[3,p238]

   Your challenge is to use the goal-setting worksheet to help Marjorie improve her relationship with her sister and her mother.
Prompt #2
A. Project Description—Write and attach an engaging prompt that draws the student into the project.[3,p238]

   Moussa has been misbehaving in school recently. He is angry all the time and fights with his classmates. He accused one student of tripping him and another of pushing him. In both cases, Moussa pushed the other boys and started a fight.

   When the teacher asked for a parent conference, she learned that Moussa's parents are divorced and that he is also misbehaving at home.

(continues)

Your challenge is to use the goal setting worksheet to help Moussa improve his relationship with his classmates and his family.

Prompt #3

A. Project Description—Write and attach an engaging prompt that draws the student into the project.[3,p238]

Danielle's mom and dad are divorced. She visits her dad every other weekend. Recently, her dad invited his new girlfriend to join them without asking Danielle first.

Danielle does not like her dad's girlfriend or sharing time with her, so she is rude and complains to her dad.

Danielle told her dad she did not want to visit anymore.

B. Your Challenge—Provide a challenge or mission statement that describes the project.[3,p238]

Your challenge is use the goal-setting worksheet to help Danielle improve her relationship with her dad.

C. Assessment Criteria[3,p239]

You are assessed on the following key concepts: (List the concepts.)

Performance indicator 1.5.2 with infused content—Identify examples of emotional, intellectual, physical, and social health that result from improving relationships.[1,p24]

1. Draw a health circle in the shape of a CD with four health components
   a. Mental and emotional health
   b. Intellectual health
   c. Physical health
   d. Social health
2. Show two ways you or the prompt person can improve health in each of the four sections of the health circle.
3. Place your picture or a picture of the prompt person in the center of the CD.

You are assessed on the following skills:

Performance indicator 6.5.1.with infused content—Set a personal goal to improve relationships and track progress toward its achievement.[1,p34]

1. Complete a goal-setting worksheet for each prompt.
2. Write a book with the following chapters based on one of the prompts or a personal need/goal.
   a. Chapter 1—Determine a personal need.
   b. Chapter 2—Set a goal to meet the need.
   c. Chapter 3—Set two short-term goals that help to achieve the goal.
   d. Chapter 4—Keep a journal for one week that shows progress toward reaching your goal.

Performance indicator 6.5.2 with infused content—Identify resources to assist in achieving a personal health goal of improving relationships.[1,p34]

   a. Chapter 5—Identify a family member, friend, or school staff member who can help you or the person in the prompt achieve the goal. Explain what they can do to help.

Student project must include the following:

1. One completed goal-setting worksheet for each prompt.
2. My Health CD Poster
   a. Draw a health circle with the four health components
      1. Mental and emotional health
      2. Intellectual health
      3. Physical health
      4. Social health
   b. Show two ways you or the person in the prompt can improve health in each of the four sections of the health circle.
   c. Place your picture or a picture of the prompt person in the middle of the CD.

(continues)

2. Book—Goal setting
   a. Chapter 1—Determine a need.
   b. Chapter 2—Set a goal to meet the need.
   c. Chapter 3—Set two short-term goals that help to achieve the goal.
   d. Chapter 4—Keep a journal for one week that shows progress toward reaching the goal.
   e. Chapter 5—Identify a family member, friend, or school staff member who can help achieve the goal. Explain what they can do to help.
   f. Chapter 6—Reflect by asking
      1. Did you or the prompt person reach the goal? Explain.
      2. Using the journal entries, summarize the experience.
   g. Book must contain two pictures per chapter.

Midland Elementary School

Name _____

Prompt #1

Marjorie's parents are divorcing. Recently she and her older sister have been arguing more than ever.

Marjorie wants to feel older, so she wore her sister's clothes without asking. She took her sister's iPod and forgot to do her chores, both of which also upset her mother.

Everyone seems to be mad at everyone else, and it is making Marjorie sad and sick.

Your challenge is:

1. Use the goal-setting worksheet to help Marjorie improve her relationship with her sister and her mother.

2. Complete a CD label for the prompt person or yourself.

3. Complete a book based on one of the prompts or on a personal goal.

Prompt #2

Moussa has been misbehaving in school recently. He is angry all the time and fights with his classmates. He accused one of tripping him and another of pushing him. In both cases, Moussa pushed the other boys and started a fight.

When the teacher asked for a parent conference, she learned that Moussa's parents are divorced and that he is also misbehaving at home.

Your challenge is:

1. Use the goal-setting worksheet to help Moussa improve his relationship with his classmates.

2. Complete a CD label for the prompt person or yourself.

3. Complete a book based on one of the prompts or on a personal goal.

Prompt #3

Danielle's mom and dad are divorced. She visits her dad every other weekend. Recently, her dad invited his new girlfriend to join them without asking Danielle first.

Danielle does not like her dad's girlfriend or sharing time with her, so she is rude and complains to her dad. Danielle told her dad she did not want to visit anymore.

Your challenge is:

1. Use the goal-setting worksheet to help Danielle improve her relationship with her dad.

2. Complete a CD label for the prompt person or yourself.

3. Complete a book based on one of the prompts or on a personal goal.

(continues)

Performance Task Self-Check (Table 10.10)

TABLE 10.10   Goal-Setting Performance Task Self-Check

Name _____

Directions: Check off each section you complete to help you fulfill all the requirements of the performance task.

Goal-Setting Worksheet

1. ☐ Prompt #1
2. ☐ Prompt #2
3. ☐ Prompt #3

CD Label

1. ☐ Two ways to improve mental emotional health
2. ☐ Two ways to improve intellectual health
3. ☐ Two ways to improve physical health
4. ☐ Two ways to improve social health.

Book

1. ☐ Chapter 1—The need
2. ☐ Chapter 2—A goal to meet the need
3. ☐ Chapter 3—Two short-terms goals that help achieve the goal
4. ☐ Chapter 4—Spaces for seven (one week) journal entries showing progress toward reaching the goal.
5. ☐ Chapter 5—Identify a family member, friend, or someone from school who can help achieve the goal. Explain how the person would help.
6. ☐ Chapter 6—Reflection

   ___ Was the goal achieved? Why or why not?

   ___ Using the journal entries, summarize the experience.

Grades 3–5 Goal-Setting Worksheet (Table 10.11)

TABLE 10.11   Grades 3–5 Goal-Setting Worksheet

Need

Goal (PI 6.5.1)

1. Short-term goal

2. Short-term goal

How can the person in the prompt track progress toward achieving their goal? (PI 6.5.1)

(continues)

TABLE 10.11   Grades 3–5 Goal-Setting Worksheet *(continued)*

Identify the resources the person in the prompt can use to help achieve their goal. (PI 6.5.2)

Reflection

Did they achieve the goal? _____

Did the short-term goals help? _____

If not, what else could you do to achieve the goal?

Were the resources helpful in achieving the goal? Why or why not?

CD Label (Figure 10.2)

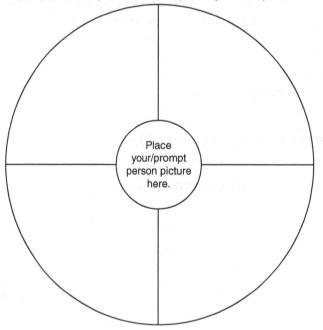

Midland Elementary School

Name _____

Health CD Label

**When we have healthy relationships, all parts
of our health are affected.**

Directions: Label quadrants emotional, intellectual, physical, and social health. Then either cut out pictures or draw two things the prompt person or you can do to keep healthy in each quadrant.

Place your/prompt person picture here.

FIGURE 10.2   My Health CD Label

(continues)

Analytical Rubric for the CD Portion of the Performance Task (Table 10.12)

TABLE 10.12   Analytical Rubric For the Performance Task CD Poster

My Health CD Label Rubric

Criteria	4	3	2	1
Labels	The student accurately labels each quadrant.	The student's labels are mostly accurate.	The student's labels have a few inaccuracies.	The student's labels are mostly inaccurate.
Performance indicator 1.5.2 with infused content—Identify examples of emotional, intellectual, physical, and social health that result from improving relationships.[1,p24]	Student accurately identifies two ways to improve emotional health.	Student's identification of two ways to improve emotional health is mostly accurate.	Student's identification of two ways to improve emotional health has a few inaccuracies.	Student's identification of two ways to improve emotional health is mostly inaccurate.
Performance indicator 1.5.2 with infused content—Identify examples of emotional, intellectual, physical, and social health that result from improving relationships.[1,p24]	Student accurately identifies two ways to improve intellectual health.	Student's identification of two ways to improve intellectual health is mostly accurate.	Student's identification of two ways to improve intellectual health has a few inaccuracies.	Student's identification of two ways to improve intellectual health is mostly inaccurate.
Performance indicator 1.5.2 with infused content—Identify examples of emotional, intellectual, physical, and social health that result from improving relationships.[1,p24]	Student accurately identifies two ways to improve physical health.	Student's identification of two ways to improve physical health is mostly accurate.	Student's identification of two ways to improve physical health has a few inaccuracies.	Student's identification of two ways to improve physical health is mostly inaccurate.
Performance indicator 1.5.2 with infused content—Identify examples of emotional, intellectual, physical, and social health that result from improving relationships.[1,p34]	Student accurately identifies two ways to improve social health.	Student's identification of two ways to improve social health is mostly accurate.	Student's identification of two ways to improve social health has a few inaccuracies.	Student's identification of two ways to improve social health is mostly inaccurate.
Picture	The picture accurately represents the student.	The student's picture is mostly accurate.	The picture has a few inaccuracies.	The picture is mostly inaccurate.
Creativity	The CD is an excellent example of creativity.	The CD is a very good example of creativity.	The CD is a fair example of creativity.	The CD is a poor example of creativity.
Grammar	The grammar is always correct.	The grammar is sometimes correct.	The grammar is rarely correct.	The grammar is never correct.

Name _____

Total possible points – 32   Your points – _____   Your grade – _____

(continues)

TABLE 10.13   Grade 3—Analytical Rubric for the Book Portion of the Goal-Setting Performance Task

| Criteria | Goal-Setting Book | | | |
	4	3	2	1
Book Cover	The book cover is an excellent example of creativity.	The book cover is a good example of creativity.	The book cover is a fair example of creativity.	The book cover is a poor example of creativity.
Chapter 1—Need	Student thoroughly describes a need.	Student adequately describes a need.	Student's description of a need is inadequate.	Student's description of a need is poor.
Chapter 2—A goal to meet the need. *Performance indicator 6.5.1.with infused content—Set a personal goal to improve relationships and track progress toward its achievement.*[1,p34]	Student accurately sets a goal to address a need.	The setting of the student's goal to address a need is mostly accurate.	The setting of the student's goal to address a need has a few inaccuracies.	The setting of the student's goal to address a need is mostly inaccurate.
Chapter 3—Two short-term goals that help achieve the goal	Student's two short-term goals are appropriate to achieve the goal.	Student's short-term goals are mostly appropriate to achieve the goal.	One of the student's short-term goals to achieve the goal is inappropriate.	Student's short-term goals to achieve the goal are mostly inappropriate.
Chapter 4— Seven journal entries that show progress toward reaching the goal. *Performance indicator 6.5.1.with infused content—Set a personal goal to improve relationships and track progress toward its achievement.*[1,p34]	Student's seven journal entries appropriately track progress toward achieving the goal.	Student's seven journal entries are mostly appropriate to track progress toward achieving the goal.	A few of the journal entries inappropriately track progress toward achieving the goal.	Most of the student's seven journal entries inappropriately track progress toward achieving the goal.
Chapter 5—Resources *Performance indicator 6.5.2 with infused content—Identify resources to assist in achieving a personal health goal of improving relationships.*[1,p34]	Student identifies appropriate resources to assist in achieving the personal health goal of improving relationships.	Student's identification of resources to assist in achieving the personal health goal of improving relationships is mostly appropriate.	A few of the resources identified by the student to assist in achieving the personal health goal of improving relationships are inappropriate.	Student's identification of resources to assist in achieving the personal health goal of improving relationships is mostly inappropriate.

(continues)

TABLE 10.13   Grade 3—Analytical Rubric for the Book Portion of the Goal-Setting Performance Task *(continued)*

Criteria	4	3	2	1
Chapter 6—Reflection	Student uses the journal entries to thoroughly reflect on achieving the goal.	Student's use of the journal entries to reflect on achieving the goal is adequate.	Student's use of the journal entries to reflect on achieving the goal is inadequate.	Student's use of the journal entries to reflect on achieving the goal is poor.
Pictures (two per chapter)	The two pictures in each chapter are appropriate.	The two pictures in each chapter are mostly appropriate.	One of the two pictures in each chapter is inappropriate.	The pictures in each chapter are mostly inappropriate.
Grammar/Spelling	The grammar and spelling are always correct.	The grammar and spelling are sometimes correct.	The grammar and spelling are rarely correct.	The grammar and spelling are never correct.

Name _____

Total possible points – 36   Your points – _____   Your grade – _____

HOW THE COORDINATED SCHOOL HEALTH TEAM HELPS STUDENTS USE GOAL-SETTING SKILLS TO ENHANCE HEALTH

Health Education

- Model the goal-setting skill.
- Teach content through the goal-setting skill.
- Allow ample practice time for skill development.
- Use formative assessment tools to enhance teaching and learning.

Physical Education

- Promote goal setting in the physical education environment.
- Hang posters that show athletes achieving a goal.
- Show pictures of current and former students achieving a physical education goal.

Health Services

- Utilize goal setting with students who arrive in the office with health concerns.
- Monitor students who are trying to achieve health goals.

Nutrition Services

- Provide motivational posters showing students achieving a healthy weight by setting a goal of healthy eating and physical activity.

Counseling, Psychological, and Social Services

- Help students set goals to increase personal health and academic achievement.
- Model goal setting with students.
- Provide motivational materials that encourage healthy goal setting.

Healthy School Environment

- Develop and enforce policies that encourage goal setting.
- Hang posters showing students achieving goals.

Health Promotion for Staff

- Provide professional development so staff can learn to use goal-setting strategies with students.
- Model goal setting with students and staff.

Family and Community Involvement

- Encourage family and community members to support students in setting goals.
- Explain how to overcome barriers to goals, reflect on the process, and provide rewards for successful completion of goals.

Grades 6–8

To achieve proficiency in Standard 6, Grades 6–8 students demonstrate the ability to assess personal health practices, develop a goal to improve them, use strategies and skills to achieve the goal, and explain how personal goals change over time.[1,p34]

To teach Standard 6, explain the importance of setting goals, their effect on current and future health, why the skill is relevant to the student, and how it relates to the other national health education skills.

Because this standard is a progression of skills, use each of the performance indicators in skill development. Explain how to achieve the standard, model the skill, provide practice time for the students, and use formative assessments while the students are learning and practicing in order to improve teaching and learning.

For example:

> The health department in the Michaels Middle School secured funding from the state department of education that requires the district to improve the nutrition of its students and increase their physical activity.
>
> Mrs. Laroche, the health teacher, is teaching her students how to set goals based on the nutrition and physical activity needs they discover from completing the MyPyramid Tracker assessment on MyPyramid.gov.[14]
>
> Upon examining the final report, students select a need and set a goal to address it. To accomplish this, the students set short-term goals that include strategies and skills to attain the goal. They track their progress for two weeks then reflect on their progress (**Table 10.14**). Many students were pleased with the results while others needed more time or wanted to adjust strategies to align with their changing abilities, priorities, and responsibilities.[1,p34]

To reflect, ask the students:

- Based on the results of your food intake inventory, name one dietary strength and one weakness. (PI 6.8.1)
  - *Strength—my eating habits are healthy.*
  - *Weakness—None*
- Based on the results of your physical activity intake inventory, name one physical activity strength and one weakness. (PI 6.8.1)
  - *Strength—I like physical activity.*
  - *Weakness—I am not getting enough physical activity each day.*
- After selecting one weakness from the food intake and physical activity results, what goal did you establish? (PI 6.8.2)
  - *Goal—Increase my physical activity to one hour each day.*

- What strategies (short-term goals) or skills did you choose to help you achieve your goals? (PI 6.8.3)
  - *Deliver newspapers to the neighborhood each day.*
  - *Take the dog for a walk each day for additional physical activity.*
- Did the strategies work? Explain.
  - *Yes, I increased my physical activity each day.*
- If the strategies did not work, what adjustments should you make to reach your goal?
  - *Develop an exercise plan that can be accomplished in the house, such as workout exercises, exercises to my favorite song, Zumba, etc.*
- Did changing abilities, priorities, or responsibilities affect your result? Explain. (PI 6.8.4)
  - *Yes, when I made physical activity a priority, I did it.*

By the time the students complete the process, they understand how to set goals based on personal need. They recognize that goals sometimes were not met initially because the accompanying strategies and short-term goals were unrealistic or unattainable. When this situation occurs, students reassess their strategies and try again.

To reinforce the goal-setting process, Mrs. Laroche asked the students to brainstorm common needs. She wrote these on the board, broke the students into groups, and challenged them to use the goal-setting skill to address the needs.

The students shared the results and said they enjoyed performing the activity because the needs listed were real. They also found it helpful to hear different ideas on how to overcome a need by setting a goal.

When the students are learning the skill, provide adequate time for them to practice before asking them to demonstrate proficiency through an authentic assessment. While they are practicing, use formative assessments (Chapter 4) to check for understanding. Use feedback to show students how to improve performance, thereby encouraging them to improve.

TABLE 10.14 Grades 6–8 Goal-Setting Worksheet

1. What strengths and needs were discovered by assessing personal health practices? (PI 6.8.1)

Eating Habits	Physical Activity
Strengths—*Eating habits are healthy*	Strengths—*I like physical activity.*
Needs—*None*	Needs—*Not enough physical activity*

2. Establish a goal based on a need. (PI 6.8.2)

   Increase my physical activity to one hour each day.

3. This goal_____ personal health practices. (PI 6.8.2)

   ___ adopts

   ___ maintains

   _X_ improves

4. Name two strategies or skills needed to reach your goal. (PI 6.8.3)

   a. *Deliver newspapers to the neighborhood each day.*

   b. *Take the dog for a walk each day for additional physical activity.*

5. **Reflection.** Did you reach your goal?

   _X_ Yes

   ___ No

6. Did changing abilities, priorities, or responsibilities affect your result? Explain. (PI 6.8.4)

   Yes, I made my physical activity a priority and as a result, I reached my goal.

7. If you did not meet your goal, name two different strategies or skills to try.

   a. *N/A*

   b.

Once the students demonstrate the skill, teach the health content. Design a prompt that allows the students to display their knowledge of health content while demonstrating goal-setting skills. As the students practice their content and skill, use formative assessments to redirect and encourage them.

WHAT DOES THE SKILL OF GOAL SETTING LOOK LIKE IN THE GRADE 8 CLASSROOM?

Mrs. Goodwin, the health teacher at Melville Junior High School, likes to start the school year with goal setting. She takes her students to the computer lab and directs them to www.TestWell.org. On this site, students can confidentially assess their health status from the social, intellectual, spiritual, physical, emotional, and occupational segments of the wellness hexagon. Thereafter, they determine needs and set goals to address them.

This activity is a great way to start the school year because the students identify their strengths and weaknesses and learn how the National Health Education Standards

help them maintain healthy behaviors and change unhealthy ones.

To begin planning, Mrs. Goodwin selects specific performance indicators that address a targeted skill and content. Since goal setting is a process, all the performance indicators are selected.

Standard 6—Students will demonstrate the ability to use goal-setting skills to enhance health.[1,p32]

   6.8.1—Assess personal health practices.[1,p34]

   Performance indicator 6.8.1 with infused content— Assess personal health practices by completing the TestWell.org teen assessment.[1,p34]

   6.8.2—Develop a goal to adopt, maintain, or improve a personal health practice.[1,p34]

   Performance indicator 6.8.2 with infused content— Develop a goal to adopt, maintain, or improve a personal health practice to meet a need.[1,p34]

6.8.3—Apply strategies and skills needed to attain a personal health goal.[1,p34]

Performance indicator 6.8.3 with infused content— Apply strategies and skills needed to attain a personal health goal based on a need.[1,p34]

6.8.4—Describe how personal health goals can vary with changing abilities, priorities, and responsibilities.[1,34]

Performance indicator 6.8.4 with infused content— Describe how personal health goals, based on needs, can vary with changing abilities, priorities, and responsibilities.[1,p34]

Standard 1—Students comprehend concepts related to health promotion and disease prevention to enhance health.[1,p24]

Performance indicator 1.8.2—Describe the interrelationships of emotional, intellectual, physical, and social health in adolescence.[1,p25]

Performance indicator 1.8.2 with infused content— Describe the interrelationships of emotional, intellectual, physical, and social health in adolescence when setting goals to address needs.[1,p25]

By linking the skill and content performance indicators, the teacher has a clear idea of how to plan the lessons for a goal-setting unit.

The first step in planning is to think through the unit by completing the performance task template. When finished, the teacher has a good idea of the lessons that precede this culminating activity, the information and back-up materials necessary to introduce the prompt to the students, and the assessment strategies.

When distributing the prompt, include all the back-up information, student worksheets, and holistic and analytical rubrics. Distribute the rubrics with the prompt so students know how they will be assessed before working on their product. The rubrics act as a guide and help the students attain proficiency in the standards.

Designing skills-based lessons requires considerable preparation, but once the teacher distributes the information and explains the task, the students are responsible for the results. Students learn with good coaching (formative assessments) how to demonstrate proficiency in content and skill.

The following is a performance task for a Grade 7 unit on goal setting that focuses on wellness.

The first section, for the teacher, demonstrates how to plan for an authentic assessment of the performance indicators 6.8.1 through 6.8.4 and 1.8.2. The second section, the student's, extracts information from the performance task and transforms it into the student prompt and support materials.

Standard 6 Performance Task: Grade 7—Setting Goals to Improve Wellness

I. Which state standard(s) does this performance task address?
II. Topic: What areas of health does this project assess? Why is it important? What is the focus of the project?[3,p237]
   A. This performance task assesses many of the common health education content areas, with particular focus on social, intellectual, spiritual, physical, emotional, and occupational/leisure health.
   B. It is important because seventh grade adolescent risk behaviors exist in all components of the wellness hexagon and need to be reduced.
      1. 16.8% never wear a seat belt when riding in a car.
      2. 31.5% rode with a driver who had been drinking alcohol.
      3. 85.7% of bicycle riders and 83% of skateboarders do not wear a helmet.
      4. 74% have been in a physical fight.
      5. 25.9% have thought of killing themselves.
      6. 5.1% currently smoke cigarettes.
      7. Lifetime alcohol and other drug use
         a. Alcohol—44.9%
         b. Marijuana—22.2%

(continues)

    c. Cocaine—4.4%

    d. Inhalant—10.3%

    e. Steroid—3.4%

    f. Injection—3.4%

  8. 25.5% ever had sexual intercourse.

  9. 10.4% have had more than three sex partners.

  10. 69.7% used a condom during their most recent intercourse.

  11. 18.1% describe themselves as overweight.

  12. 50.6% watch more than three hours of television during a school day.[15]

C. The project focuses on using goal-setting skills to improve wellness.

III. Key Concepts: What basic concepts should the students know?[3,p237]

Standard 1—Students comprehend concepts related to health promotion and disease prevention to enhance health.[1,p24]

Performance indicator 1.8.2 with infused content—Describe the interrelationships of emotional, intellectual, physical, and social health in adolescence when setting goals to address needs.[1,p25]

A. Examples of emotional health

  1. Know, share, and respond to feelings in a positive and realistic way.

  2. Face challenges realistically.

  3. Show patience when learning something new.

  4. Take action to meet goals.

  5. Make choices consistent with positive values.

  6. Take responsibility for personal actions.[11,p6]

B. Examples of intellectual health

  1. Use problem-solving skills.

  2. Use goal-setting skills.

  3. Reflect on decisions.

  4. Learn from experiences.

  5. Feel in control.[12,p3]

C. Examples of physical health

  1. Eat a well-balanced diet.

  2. Perform 60 minutes of physical activity each day.

  3. Get nine hours of sleep each night.

  4. Get regular check-ups.

  5. Brush and floss teeth daily.

  6. Always wear a seat belt when riding in a car.

  7. Always wear protective gear when involved in physical activities.

  8. Abstain from alcohol, tobacco, and other drugs.[11,p4-5]

D. Examples of social health

  1. Be friendly and open to people.

  2. Show support to family and friends.

  3. Encourage others as they are learning new skills.

  4. Demonstrate care for others.

  5. Be reliable.

  6. Be responsible.

  7. Be respectful.[11,p6]

IV. Skills: Which of the seven National Health Education Standards does this performance task address?[3,p237]

Standard 6—Students will demonstrate the ability to use goal-setting skills to enhance health.[1,p34]

Performance indicator 6.8.1 with infused content—Assess personal health practices by completing the Test-Well.org teen assessment.[1,p34]

(continues)

Performance indicator 6.8.2 with infused content—Develop a goal to adopt, maintain, or improve a personal health practice to address a need.[1,p34]

Performance indicator 6.8.3 with infused content—Apply strategies and skills needed to attain a personal health goal based on a need.[1,p34]

Performance indicator 6.8.4 with infused content—Describe how personal health goals, based on needs, can vary with changing abilities, priorities, and responsibilities.[1,p34]

V. Curricula connections: What other subject areas does this project support?[3,p237]

   English language arts

   Art

VI. Student directions and assessment criteria[3,p238]

   A. Project Description—Write and attach an engaging prompt that draws the student into the project.[3,p238]

   You have just started the seventh grade. Your body is changing, and you have made new friends and are experiencing different physical and emotional feelings. It is all very confusing.

   Mrs. Goodwin is starting her goal-setting unit, and you are going to assess your physical, social, emotional, spiritual, occupational/leisure, intellectual, and environmental health. You are looking forward to the task because it will reveal to you your strengths and weaknesses in each category. Mrs. Goodwin will teach you the goal-setting skill to help you improve your on your weaknesses.

   B. Your Challenge—Provide a challenge or mission statement that describes the project.[3,p238]

   Your challenge is to assess your personal wellness by completing the TestWell Adolescent Assessment;[16] and then use the goal-setting worksheet to set a goal to address a need. You will also design a one-month wellness calendar that includes wellness information and your plan of action.

   C. Assessment criteria[3,p239]

   You are assessed on the following content:

   Performance indicator 1.8.2 with infused content—Describe the interrelationships of emotional, intellectual, physical, and social health in adolescence when setting goals to address needs.[1,p25]

   1. Twelve ways emotional, intellectual, physical, and social health are interrelated. (Include three ways from each component.)

   You are assessed on the following skill:

   Performance indicator 6.8.1 with infused content—Assess personal health practices by completing the TestWell.org teen assessment.[1,p34]

   Performance indicator 6.8.2 with infused content—Develop a goal to adopt, maintain, or improve a personal health practice to address a need.[1,p34]

   Performance indicator 6.8.3 with infused content—Apply two weeks of strategies and skills needed to attain a personal health goal based on a need.[1,p34] Track your application of these strategies and skills on the calendar.

   Performance indicator 6.8.4 with infused content—Describe how personal health goals, based on needs, can vary with changing abilities, priorities, and responsibilities.[1,p34]

   Student project

   1. Completed TestWell.org teen assessment
   2. Completed goal-setting worksheet
   3. A wellness calendar
      a. Twelve ways emotional, intellectual, physical, and social health are interrelated. (Include three ways from each component.)
      b. Place the two weeks of strategies and skills in the calendar.
      c. Place five motivational messages in ten calendar days.
   4. A role-play discussing the results of assessing personal health needs and setting a goal to meet them

Name _____

You have just started the seventh grade. Your body is changing, and you have made new friends and are experiencing different physical and emotional feelings. It is all very confusing.

Mrs. Goodwin is starting her goal-setting unit, and you are going to assess your physical, social, emotional, spiritual, occupational/leisure, intellectual, and environmental health. You are looking forward to the task because it will reveal to you your strengths and weaknesses in each category. Mrs. Goodwin will teach you the goal-setting skill to help you address your weaknesses.

Your challenge is to assess your personal wellness then use the goal-setting worksheet to set a goal to address a need. You will also design a one-month wellness calendar that includes wellness information and your plan of action.

Your project must include the following:

1. Completed TestWell.org teen assessment

2. Completed goal-setting worksheet

3. A wellness poster and calendar

   a. Twelve ways emotional, intellectual, physical, and social health are interrelated. (Include three ways from each component.)

   b. Place the two weeks of strategies and skills in the calendar.

   c. Place five motivational messages in ten calendar days.

   d. Indicate whether the goal was met.

   e. If the goal was not met, indicate how you are adjusting the strategies and skills to meet the goal.

   f. The poster/calendar must contain five pictures.

4. A role-play discussing the results of assessing personal health needs and setting a goal to address needs

ASSESSMENT MATERIALS

Grades 6–8 Goal-Setting Worksheet (Table 10.15)

TABLE 10.15   Grades 6–8 Goal-Setting Worksheet

Name _____

Grades 6–8 Goal-Setting Worksheet

1. What strengths and needs were discovered by assessing personal health practices? (PI 6.8.1)

Strengths	Needs

2. Establish a goal based on a need. (PI 6.8.2)

3. This goal_____ a personal health practices. (PI 6.8.2)

   ___ adopts

   ___ maintains

   ___improves

(continues)

TABLE 10.15   Grades 6–8 Goal-Setting Worksheet *(continued)*

4. Name two strategies or skills needed to reach your goal. (PI 6.8.3)

   a.

   b.

5. **Reflection.** Did you reach your goal?

   ___ Yes

   ___ No

6. Did changing abilities, priorities, or responsibilities affect your result? Explain. (PI 6.8.4)

7. If you did not meet your goal, name two different strategies or skills to try.

   a.

   b.

Wellness Calendar (Table 10.16)

TABLE 10.16   Wellness Calendar

Name _____

Goal _____

Wellness Calendar

Sunday	Monday	Tuesday	Wednesday	Thursday	Friday	Saturday

Did you reach your goal?

If not, what adjustments are you going to make to reach your goal?

(continues)

Analytical Rubric for the Wellness Poster/Calendar Portion of the Goal-Setting Performance Task (Table 10.17)

TABLE 10.17   Grade 7—Analytical Rubric to Assess the Wellness Poster/Calendar

Criteria	4	3	2	1
Performance indicator 6.8.1 with infused content—Assess personal health practices by completing the TestWell.org teen assessment.[1,p34]	Student thoroughly assessed personal health practices by completing the TestWell.org teen assessment.	Student adequately assessed personal health practices by completing the TestWell.org teen assessment.	Student inadequately assessed personal health practices by completing the TestWell.org teen assessment.	Student poorly assessed personal health practices by completing the TestWell.org teen assessment.
Performance indicator 1.8.2 with infused content—Describe the interrelationships of emotional, intellectual, physical, and social health in adolescence when setting goals to address needs.[1,p25]	On the poster, the student thoroughly describes three ways emotional health is interrelated with intellectual, physical, and social health.	On the poster, the student adequately describes three ways emotional health is interrelated with intellectual, physical, and social health.	On the poster, the student inadequately describes three ways emotional health is interrelated with intellectual, physical, and social health.	On the poster, the student poorly describes three ways emotional health is interrelated with intellectual, physical, and social health.
Performance indicator 1.8.2 with infused content—Describe the interrelationships of emotional, intellectual, physical, and social health in adolescence when setting goals to address needs.[1,p25]	On the poster, the student thoroughly describes three ways intellectual health is interrelated with emotional, physical, and social health.	On the poster, the student adequately describes three ways intellectual health is interrelated with emotional, physical, and social health.	On the poster, the student inadequately describes three ways intellectual health is interrelated with emotional, physical, and social health.	On the poster, the student poorly describes three ways intellectual health is interrelated with emotional, physical, and social health.
Performance indicator 1.8.2 with infused content—Describe the interrelationships of emotional, intellectual, physical, and social health in adolescence when setting goals to address needs.[1,p25]	On the poster, the student thoroughly describes three ways physical health is interrelated with emotional, intellectual, and social health.	On the poster, the student adequately describes three ways physical health is interrelated with emotional, intellectual, and social health.	On the poster, the student inadequately describes three ways physical health is interrelated with emotional, intellectual, and social health.	On the poster, the student poorly describes three ways physical health is interrelated with emotional, intellectual, and social health.
Performance indicator 1.8.2 with infused content—Describe the interrelationships of emotional, intellectual, physical, and social health in adolescence when setting goals to address needs.[1,p25]	On the poster, the student thoroughly describes three ways social health is interrelated with emotional, intellectual, and physical health.	On the poster, the student adequately describes three ways social health is interrelated with emotional, intellectual, and physical health.	On the poster, the student inadequately describes three ways social health is interrelated with emotional, intellectual, and physical health.	On the poster, the student poorly describes three ways social health is interrelated with emotional, intellectual, and physical health.

(continues)

Criteria	4	3	2	1
Performance indicator 6.8.3 with infused content—Apply two weeks of strategies and skills needed to attain a personal health goal based on a need.[1,p34]	On a calendar, the student applied two weeks of appropriate strategies and skills needed to attain a personal health goal based on a need.	On a calendar the student applied two weeks of mostly appropriate strategies and skills needed to attain a personal health goal based on a need.	Over two weeks, the student applied onto a calendar a few inappropriate strategies and skills intended to attain a personal health goal based on a need.	On a calendar the student applied two weeks of mostly inappropriate strategies and skills intended to attain a personal health goal based on a need.
Motivational messages	Student lists five appropriate motivational messages on the calendar.	Student's five motivational messages are mostly appropriate.	A few of the five motivational messages listed are inappropriate.	Student's five motivational messages are mostly inappropriate.
Strategy adjustment	Student thoroughly explains adjustments in strategy if the goal is not met.	Student adequately explains adjustments in strategy if the goal is not met.	Student inadequately explains adjustments in strategy if the goal is not met.	Student poorly explains adjustments in strategy if the goal is not met.
Pictures/Illustrations	The five pictures on the poster/calendar are appropriate.	The five pictures on the poster/calendar are mostly appropriate.	A few of the five pictures on the poster/calendar are inappropriate.	The five pictures on the poster/calendar are mostly inappropriate.
Creativity	The creativity of the poster/calendar is excellent.	The creativity of the poster/calendar is good.	The creativity of the poster/calendar is fair.	The creativity of the poster/calendar is poor.

Name _____

Total possible points – 40   Your points – _____   Your grade – _____

Analytical Rubric for the Goal-Setting Role-Play Portion of the Performance Task (Table 10.18)

TABLE 10.18   Grade 7—Analytical Rubric to Assess the Goal-Setting Role-Play

Criteria	4	3	2	1
Performance indicator 6.8.1 with infused content—Assess personal health practices by completing the TestWell.org teen assessment.[1,p34]	Student thoroughly discusses the results of the personal assessment, including the strengths and weaknesses.	Student adequately discusses the results of the personal assessment, including the strengths and weaknesses.	Student inadequately discusses the results of the personal assessment, including the strengths and weaknesses.	Student poorly discusses the results of the personal assessment, including the strengths and weaknesses.
Performance indicator 6.8.2 with infused content—Develop a goal to adopt, maintain, or improve a personal health practice to address a need.[1,p34]	Student develops an appropriate goal to adopt, maintain, or improve a personal health practice.	The student develops a mostly appropriate goal to adopt, maintain, or improve a personal health practice.	The student develops a less than appropriate goal to adopt, maintain, or improve a personal health practice.	Student develops an inappropriate goal to meet personal health needs.

(continues)

Criteria	4	3	2	1
Performance indicator 6.8.3 with infused content—Apply two weeks of strategies and skills needed to attain a personal health goal based on a need.[1,p34]	Student thoroughly discusses how to apply two weeks of strategies or skills needed to attain a personal health goal.	Student adequately discusses how to apply two weeks of strategies or skills needed to attain a personal health goal.	Student inadequately discusses how to apply two weeks of strategies or skills needed to attain a personal health goal.	Student poorly discusses how to apply two weeks of strategies or skills needed to attain a personal health goal.
Performance indicator 6.8.4 with infused content—Describe how personal health goals, based on needs, can vary with changing abilities, priorities, and responsibilities.[1,p34]	Student thoroughly describes how personal health goals, based on needs, can vary with changing abilities, priorities, and responsibilities.	Student adequately describes how personal health goals, based on needs, can vary with changing abilities, priorities, and responsibilities.	Student inadequately describes how personal health goals, based on needs, can vary with changing abilities, priorities, and responsibilities.	Student poorly describes how personal health goals, based on needs, can vary with changing abilities, priorities, and responsibilities.
Participation	Student participation in the role-play is excellent.	Student participation in the role-play is good.	Student participation in the role-play is fair.	Student participation in the role-play is poor.

Name _____

Total possible points – 20   Your points – _____   Your grade – _____

HOW THE COORDINATED SCHOOL HEALTH TEAM HELPS STUDENTS USE GOAL-SETTING SKILLS TO ENHANCE HEALTH

Health Education

- Explain how setting and reaching goals enhances self-esteem and self-confidence.
- Teach goal-setting skills.
- Teach targeted content that assists students to overcome deficiencies.
- Model goal-setting skills.

Physical Education

- Encourage students to set physical activity goals.
- Provide opportunities for students to set and attain goals in physical education.

Health Services

- Encourage the nurse to assist students to set and achieve health goals.
- Model goal setting.

Nutrition Services

- Provide promotional materials that encourage students to set healthy eating goals.
- Encourage and reward students who consistently eat healthy foods.

Counseling, Psychological, and Social Services

- Model goal-setting.
- Assist students in setting and achieving goals for personal health and academic achievement.

Healthy School Environment

- Hang posters that encourage teens to set and attain goals.
- Set a school goal and encourage students and staff to participate in achieving the goal.
- Acknowledge and reward students and staff who work toward achieving the school goal.

Health Promotion for Staff

- Provide training in how to set and achieve goals.
- Model the goal-setting skill.

Family and Community Involvement

- Provide a goal-setting workshop that demonstrates the benefits of setting and achieving goals.
- Encourage parents and the community to establish goals that enhance health, to provide incentives to work toward the goal, and to offer rewards when the goal is reached.

Grades 9–12

To achieve proficiency in Standard 6, Grade 9–12 students must learn to use goal-setting skills to enhance health.

To teach Standard 6, explain why it is important to set goals and how this skill relates to the other National Health Education Standards.

According to the performance indicators chosen, present and explain how to reach proficiency in the skill. Model the skill so the students can see it in action. Provide adequate time for the students to practice the skill and show proficiency through an authentic assessment. Use formative assessments (Chapter 4) to provide feedback and encouragement and improve instruction.

For example:

Jeremy is a senior and looking forward to the prom, graduation, and college. He has never smoked cigarettes, but in the eighth grade, on a whim, he and his wrestling friends tried dip. He has been using ever since and is addicted to the nicotine.

Jeremy thought he and his friends were the only teens dipping but learned that 15.9% of male high school seniors are current users of smokeless tobacco.[17,p13] He was surprised that so many boys dip.

Jeremy's family, friends, and girlfriend are encouraging him to quit. They tell him, "You have bad breath, and your teeth are yellow." The spitting is particularly disgusting! His dentist told him the sores in his mouth lead to gum disease.

Not persuaded that he is addicted, Jeremy tried to quit on his own but failed. He decided to complete the HONC (Hooked on Nicotine Checklist) he found on the National Cancer Institute's website (**Table 10.19**).[18]

Jeremy answered "yes" to all ten questions on the checklist, which indicates he has a powerful tobacco addiction. He has decided to quit and wants to be free of dip by graduation.

He decides to use the goal-setting skills he learned in health class to quit (**Table 10.20**).

TABLE 10.19   The Hooked on Nicotine Checklist (HONC—National Cancer Institute)

The Hooked on Nicotine Checklist (HONC)

1. Have you tried to quit but couldn't?	Yes	No
2. Do you smoke (dip) now because it is really hard to quit?	Yes	No
3. Have you ever felt like you were addicted to tobacco?	Yes	No
4. Do you ever have strong cravings to smoke (dip)?	Yes	No
5. Have you ever felt like you really needed a cigarette (dip)?	Yes	No
6. Is it hard to keep from smoking (dipping) in places where you are not supposed to, like school?	Yes	No
When you tried to stop smoking (dipping), or if you hadn't smoked for a while . . .		
7. Did you find it hard to concentrate because you couldn't smoke (dip)?	Yes	No
8. Did you feel more irritable because you couldn't smoke (dip)?	Yes	No
9. Did you feel a strong need or urge to smoke?	Yes	No
10. Did you feel nervous, restless, or anxious?	Yes	No
Total score: Add the yes responses	10	

Source: Courtesy of Joseph DiFranza, University of Massachusetts Medical School.

TABLE 10.20 Grades 9–12 Goal-Setting Worksheet 18

1. Assess personal health practices and overall health status. (PI 6.12.1)

   According to HONC (Hooked on Nicotine Checklist), I am addicted to nicotine.

2. What is the goal?

   I want to quit smokeless tobacco.

3. Develop a plan to attain a personal health goal that addresses strengths, needs, and risks. (PI 6.12.2)

   My plan is to quit using smokeless tobacco.

   Strengths – *I am young and determined.*

   My family and my girlfriend support me.

   I won't be involved in a socially unacceptable behavior.[19,p4]

   Needs – *I need something in my mouth to replace the dip.[19,p4]*

   I need to be prepared, so I know what to expect.

   Risks – *The sores in my mouth lead to gum disease[19,p4] and I don't want to lose my teeth or develop cancer.*

   The cravings will be too strong and I will give in to them.

   If I don't stop now, I might not ever be able to quit.

4. Implement strategies to achieving a personal health goal. (PI 6.12.3)

   a. *My quit date is Friday night. I am throwing away all my dip. Friday night is a good time because I'll have all weekend to deal with the worst symptoms.*

   b. *I'll cut down on my use before Friday so quitting won't be so hard.*

   c. *Mom is buying me nicotine gum, so I'll have something to replace the dip in my mouth and ease the nicotine withdrawal. If the gum doesn't work, I'll try the nicotine lozenges.[19,p7] She is also buying me some sunflower seeds, sugarless gum, and sugarless candy so I will have something to put in my mouth to help me get over the cravings.[19,p11]*

   d. *I know being at the school games is a trigger, so I am not going to go to the next few games. I'll change some of my routines to avoid other triggers.[19,p12]*

   e. *I have written down all the successful strategies I have used in the past to quit and plan to use them again.[19,p11] I like the deep-breathing exercises, running, and playing Wii. They always helped me get over the cravings.*

   f. *I'll tell my friends I am quitting so they know why I am grumpy and can support me.[19,p11]*

   g. *I'll attend the smoking cessation class at school and ask the school nurse for support.[19,p11]*

   h. *I'll stay committed even when it gets tough and keep thinking of myself free of tobacco.*

   i. *My reward is to take my girlfriend to an expensive restaurant with all the money I saved from not buying dip.*

5. Monitor progress in achieving a personal health goal. (PI 6.12.3)

   For one month, I'll keep a journal and record my progress. If I am still not dipping at the end of each week, mom said she would reward me.

6. **Reflection**

   I made it! It has been six weeks, and I am not dipping! I slipped once but went right back to my quitting strategies. The smoking cessation class in school was good because there were a few other boys trying to quit dip. The nurse has been great. When I think I am going to slip, I go to her office, and she talks to me and reminds me of all the reasons why it is important to keep fighting.

   My family, friends, and especially my girlfriend are very proud of me. My dentist said my gums are looking better and beginning to heal!

7. Formulate an effective long-term personal health plan. (PI 6.12.4)

   a. *Prepare a strategy for experiencing a trigger, such as attending athletic events. Have a coping plan ready. Recommit to being tobacco free.*

   b. *Review my reasons for quitting and the benefits I experienced as a result of being tobacco free.*

   c. *Remind myself that there is no such thing as just one dip.*

   d. *Work through the desire to dip by using strategies that work.*

   e. *Although I don't drink, I know that alcohol decreases my ability to resist tobacco.[19,p13]*

To reflect, ask the students:

- How did Jeremy assess his health practices and overall health status? (PI 6.12.1) *He completed The Hooked on Nicotine Checklist.*

- What is Jeremy's plan, and what factors does he have to consider? (PI 6.12.2) *His plan is to quit using smokeless tobacco, and he has to consider his strengths, needs, and the risks of the plan.*

- Explain two strategies Jeremy is using to quit using smokeless tobacco? (PI 6.12.3) *Establish a quit date; throw away the dip; cut down on use before the quit day; use nicotine gum to replace the tobacco and ease the nicotine withdrawal; eat sunflower seeds; chew sugarless gum; eat sugarless candy; avoid triggers; use previous strategies that worked, such as deep breathing and exercising; ask friends for support; attend smoking cessation class; ask the school nurse for support; stay committed; and reward self when the goal is reached.*

- What is Jeremy's long-term health plan? (PI 6.12.4) *He has a plan to cope with smoking triggers and is committed to be tobacco free.*

As the students are learning the skill, provide enough time for them to practice. Use formative assessments to determine the progress of learning. Motivate students by using feedback to show how performance has improved.

When students demonstrate understanding of the skill, teach the content. Design a prompt that allows the students to display their knowledge of health. Use formative assessments, such as white boards (Chapter 4), during content instruction to determine student understanding.

WHAT DOES THE SKILL OF GOAL SETTING LOOK LIKE IN THE GRADE 12 CLASSROOM?

Mr. Fernandez is a Grade 12 health teacher at the Teton Mountain High School. He received Safe and Drug Free Schools funding to teach about the hazards of nicotine. He is concerned about the number of students, especially seniors, who smoke and how the number of smokers who have tried to quit has decreased.

He believes the data he submitted for the grant helped him to gain funding.

- 19.5% of students smoked cigarettes at least one day during the 30 days prior to the Youth Risk Behavior Survey (YRBS). The seniors had the highest percentage—27%. (Females - 22.4%, Males - 28.1%)[25,p65]

- 50.8% had tried to quit smoking during the 12 months prior to the YRBS. (Females - 54.2%, Males - 48%)[25,p67]

He overheard some of his students talk about buying the e-cigarette because they think it is safe and a good way to quit. Mr. Fernandez went to the kiosk at the mall and

asked questions about the device. The e-cigarette has refillable cartridges that contain different amounts of nicotine and other substances. When a person inhales, the tip glows red, and a mist of liquid, flavorings, and nicotine goes into the lungs and is exhaled. He checked the Food and Drug Administration and found there are no clinical trials that suggest that the e-cigarette helps a smoker quit. However, he did learn that it might contain cancer-causing substances.[20,p16-17]

In planning the nicotine cessation classes, his objective is to guide students towards setting a goal to quit nicotine. Mr. Fernandez begins by choosing the performance indicators for Standard 6 that meet the needs of his students. Since goal setting is a process, he selects all the performance indicators.

Standard 6—Students will demonstrate the ability to use goal-setting skills to enhance health.[1,p34]

> 6.12.1—Assess personal health practices and overall health status.[1,p34]
>
> *Performance indicator 6.12.1 with infused content—Assess personal health practices, such as using nicotine products, and overall health status.[1,p34]*
>
> 6.12.2—Develop a plan to attain a personal health goal that addresses strengths, needs, and risks.[1,p34]
>
> *Performance indication 6.12.2 with infused content—Develop a plan to attain a personal health goal, such as nicotine cessation, that addresses strengths, needs, and risks.[1,p34]*
>
> 6.12.3—Implement strategies and monitor progress in achieving a personal health goal.[1,p34]
>
> *Performance indicator 6.12.3 with infused content—Implement strategies and monitor progress in achieving a personal health goal, such as nicotine cessation.[1,p34]*
>
> 6.12.4—Formulate an effective long-term personal health plan.[1,p34]
>
> *Performance indicator 6.12.4 with infused content—Formulate an effective long-term personal health plan that demonstrates how to be free of nicotine products.[1,p34]*

After selecting the appropriate performance indicator for the skill, Mr. Fernandez chooses the performance indicator for Standard 1.

Standard 1—Students will comprehend concepts related to health promotion and disease prevention to enhance health.[1,p25]

1.12.5—Propose ways to reduce or prevent injuries and health problems.[1,p25]

Performance indicator 1.12.5 with infused content—Propose ways to reduce or prevent injuries and health problems by quitting nicotine.[1,p25]

By linking the skill and content performance indicators, the teacher has a clear idea of how to plan the lessons for a goal-setting unit.

The first step in planning is to think through the unit by completing the performance task template. Thereupon, the teacher will have a good idea of the lessons that precede this culminating activity, the information and back-up materials necessary to introduce the prompt to the students, and the assessment strategies.

When distributing the prompt, include all the back-up information, student worksheets, and holistic and analytical rubrics. Distribute the rubrics with the prompt so students know how they will be assessed before working on their product. The rubrics act as a guide and help the students attain proficiency in the standards.

Designing the performance task takes considerable preparation, but once the information is distributed and explained, the students create a product on their own or in a group. Students learn with good coaching (formative assessment) how to demonstrate proficiency in both content and skill.

The following is an example of a performance task for Grade 12 goal setting that focuses on quitting nicotine.

The first section is for the teacher and demonstrates how to plan for an authentic assessment of the performance indicators 1.12.5, and 6.12.1 through 6.12.4. The second, the student's, extracts some of the information from the performance task and transforms it into the student prompt and support materials.

Standard 6 Performance Task: Grade 12—Using Goal-Setting Skills to Quit Tobacco

I. Which state standard(s) does this performance task address?

II. Topic: What areas of health does this project assess? Why is it important? What is the focus of the project?[3,p237]

A. This performance task assesses the health area of Consumer Health and Substance Use/Abuse, particularly nicotine cessation.

B. This topic is important because:

1. Teen usage
   a. 26% of teens smoked cigarettes on at least one day prior to the Youth Risk Behavior Survey (YRBS).
   b. 14% of teens smoked cigars at least one day prior to the YRBS.
   c. 8.9% of teens used smokeless tobacco at least one day prior to the YRBS.[21,p90]

2. According to the U.S. Surgeon General, "Smoking cessation represents the single most important step that smokers can take to enhance the length and quality of their lives."[20,p1]

3. 50.8% of high school smokers have tried to quit during the 12 months prior to the Youth Risk Behavior Survey.
   a. Females—54.2%,
   b. Males—48%[25,p90]

C. The focus of the project is to help students learn how to set goals to eliminate nicotine use.

III. Key Concepts: What basic concepts do students need to know?[3,p237]

Standard 1—Students will comprehend concepts related to health promotion and disease prevention to enhance health.[1,p25]

Performance indicator 1.12.5 with infused content—Propose ways to reduce or prevent injuries and health problems by quitting nicotine.[1,p25]

A. Health effects of using tobacco

1. Short-term effects
   a. Brain chemistry changes as a result of addiction.
   b. Respiration and heart rate increase.
   c. Decreased sense of taste
   d. Reduced appetite

(continues)

  e. Bad breath

  f. Yellowed teeth

  g. Smelly hair, skin, personal effects, and clothes[22,p545]

 2. Long-term effects

  a. Chronic bronchitis

  b. Emphysema

  c. Lung cancer

  d. Coronary heart disease

  e. Stroke

  f. Weakened immune system[22,p545]

B. Cigar

 1. Users have the same rate of mouth, throat, larynx, and esophageal cancer as cigarette smokers.[23,p206]

C. Smokeless tobacco

 1. Nicotine is absorbed into the blood through the mucous membranes of the mouth.

 2. Effects

  a. Leukoplakia is a white, pre-cancerous spot that appears in the mouth.

  b. Erythroplakia is a red, pre-cancerous spot that appears in the mouth.

  c. Periodontal disease occurs when the gum pulls away from the tooth.

  d. Tooth enamel is damaged.

  e. Sugar in the processed tobacco contributes to tooth decay.

  f. Oral cancer[23,p207]

D. E-cigarette

 1. Nicotine is inhaled into the lungs.

 2. No published clinical trials indicate e-cigarettes help people stop smoking.

 3. No ingredients are listed, so it is not clear what substances are inhaled.

 4. Reinforces the smoking habit

 5. In 2009, the Food and Drug Administration found:

  a. Cancer-causing substances in half the samples tested

  b. Diethylene glycol, a substance found in antifreeze, was found in one tested sample.

  c. Puffs contained varying amounts of nicotine

  d. Nicotine was found in the nicotine-free cartridges.[20,p16-17]

  e. The device emitted nitrosamines, which are human carcinogens.[24]

E. Benefits of tobacco cessation

 1. Ex-smokers live longer than smokers.

 2. Freedom from addiction

 3. Quitting decreases the risk of:

  a. Lung and other cancer

  b. Heart attack

  c. Stroke

  d. Chronic lung disease

  e. Pregnant women having low weight babies.[20,p2-3]

 4. More money

IV. Skills: Which of the seven National Health Education Standards skills does this performance task address?[3,p237]

 Standard 6—Students will demonstrate the ability to use goal-setting skills to enhance health.[1,p34]

  Performance indicator 6.12.1 with infused content—Assess personal health practices, such as using tobacco products, and overall health status.[1,p34]

(continues)

A. Complete the Hooked on Nicotine Checklist to determine any addiction to tobacco[18]

Performance indication 6.12.2 with infused content—Develop a plan to attain a personal health goal, such as tobacco cessation, that addresses strengths, needs, and risks.[1,p34]

A. Prepare for quit day by setting a date.

B. Throw away all tobacco products.

C. Avoid places or people who trigger the desire to use tobacco.

D. Ask family and friends for support.

E. Seek professional help
    1. Enroll in a smoking cessation class.
    2. Obtain prescription or non-prescription nicotine replacement drugs.
    3. Join a support group.

Performance indicator 6.12.3 with infused content—Implement strategies and monitor progress in achieving a personal health goal, such as tobacco cessation.[1,p34]

A. Access national and community organizations for information and support.
    1. American Cancer Society
    2. American Lung Association
    3. Centers for Disease Control and Prevention
    4. Local hospitals

B. Replace tobacco with healthy behaviors.
    1. Relaxation techniques
    2. Exercise
    3. Good nutrition
    4. Avoid drugs and alcohol.[22,p551]

Performance indicator 6.12.4 with infused content—Formulate an effective long-term personal health plan that demonstrates how to be free of tobacco products.[1,p34]

A. Spend time with people who do not smoke and have values that promote healthy behaviors.

B. Avoid people or places that trigger the urge to smoke.

C. Have strategies ready when faced with the pressure or the urge to smoke.[22,p550]

V. Curricular connections—What other subject areas does this project support?[3,p237]
    English Language Arts
    Art

VI. Student Directions and Assessment Criteria[3,p238]

Prompt #1

A. Project Description—Write/attach an engaging prompt that draws the student into the project.[3,p238]
    Alan is graduating from school this year and wants to set a goal of becoming smoke free before the senior celebrations start. He is tired of smelling of smoke and spending all his money on cigarettes.
    Over the summer, Alan would like time to get used to being a non-smoker so that, when he enters college in the fall, his healthy habit is established.
    All Alan's friends smoke, however, and he is used to smoking wherever he goes. In addition, he doesn't have any idea of how to quit!

B. Your Challenge—Provide a challenge or mission statement that describes the project.[3,p238]
    Your challenge is to help Alan set a goal to quit tobacco.

Prompt #2

A. Project Description—Write/attach an engaging prompt that draws the student into the project.[3,p238]
    Angela is trying to quit smoking. While she was at the mall, she saw the e-cigarette kiosk. She watched the smoking demonstration and was intrigued with the product. "I can smoke without any smoke or odor!" she thought. Angela told the retailer that she was trying to quit smoking, so he sold her the system that slowly decreases the amount of nicotine inhaled.

(continues)

Angela was the hit of every party! Everyone wanted to try the new e-cigarette. When she finally got to her last cartridge, she still had the urge to smoke. She also took comfort in the feel of the cigarette, the inhaling, and knowing the pack was in her bag. This strategy was not working out the way she planned.

B. Your Challenge—Provide a challenge or mission statement that describes the project.[3,p238]

Your challenge is to help Angela set a goal to quit e-cigarettes.

Prompt #3

A. Project Description—Write/attach an engaging prompt that draws the student into the project.[3,p238]

Frank smokes cigars. He enjoys the flavor, the smell of the smoke, and the feel of the cigar in his hand.

Unfortunately, there are only a few places where he is allowed to smoke; no one else enjoys the smell of his cigar; and his habit is expensive.

Frank has decided to quit but is not very optimistic. He has tried giving up cigars several times but couldn't do it.

B. Your Challenge—Provide a challenge or mission statement that describes the project.[3,p238]

Your challenge is to help Frank set a goal to quit smoking cigars.

Prompt #4

A. Project Description—Write/attach an engaging prompt that draws the student into the project.[3,p238]

Mark has been using smokeless tobacco since the ninth grade. He uses it only with his friends or in private because when people see him spitting they think it is gross.

Mark has a new non-smoking girlfriend, and she wants him to quit using smokeless tobacco. He has tried to quit many times but always goes back to his old ways.

B. Your Challenge—Provide a challenge or mission statement that describes the project.[3,p238]

Your challenge is to help Mark set a goal to quit smokeless tobacco.

C. Assessment Criteria[3,p239]

You will be assessed on the following content:

Performance indicator 1.12.5 with infused content—Propose ways to reduce or prevent injuries and health problems by quitting nicotine.[1,p25]

1. Five facts of how tobacco affects health
2. Five facts about the dangers of smokeless tobacco
3. Five facts about the e-cigarette
4. Five benefits of quitting nicotine products

You will be assessed on the following skills:

Performance indicator 6.12.1 with infused content—Assess personal health practices, such as using nicotine products, and overall health status.[1,p34]

1. Utilize the Hooked on Nicotine Checklist

Performance indicator 6.12.2 with infused content—Develop a plan to attain a personal health goal, such as nicotine cessation, that addresses strengths, needs, and risks.[1,p34]

1. A five-step nicotine cessation plan addressing the strengths of the user, needs of the user, and the risks to the user

Performance indicator 6.12.3 with infused content—Implement strategies and monitor progress in achieving a personal health goal, such as nicotine cessation.[1,p34]

1. Explain two national or community resources that assist in nicotine cessation.
2. Implement two healthy behaviors that can replace nicotine use.
3. Construct a method, such as a calendar or journal, to monitor progress in achieving nicotine cessation.

Performance indicator 6.12.4 with infused content—Formulate an effective long-term personal health plan that demonstrates how to be free of tobacco products.[1,p34]

1. A long-term personal health plan that contains three objectives

(continues)

Your project consists of:
1. Completing the goal-setting worksheet for each prompt
2. Select one of the prompts and the corresponding goal-setting worksheet. Demonstrate the goal-setting skill by designing a role-play or a comic book in which the scenario character sets a goal to quit nicotine with the help of a cessation counselor.
3. Include the following in the dialogue:
   a. Five facts about how tobacco affects health
   b. Five facts about the dangers of smokeless tobacco
   c. Five facts about how the e-cigarette affects health
   d. Five benefits of quitting nicotine products

Teton Mountain High School

Name _____

Prompt #1

Alan is graduating from school this year and wants to set a goal of becoming smoke free before the senior celebrations start. He is tired of smelling of smoke and spending all his money on cigarettes.

Over the summer, Alan wants time to get used to being a non-smoker so that, when he enters college in the fall, his healthy habit is established.

All his friends smoke, however, and he is used to smoking wherever he goes. In addition, he doesn't have any idea of how to quit!

Your challenge is to help Alan set a goal to quit tobacco.

Prompt #2

Angela is trying to quit smoking. While she was at the mall, she saw the e-cigarette kiosk. She watched the smoking demonstration and was intrigued with the product. "I can smoke without any smoke or odor!" she thought. Angela told the retailer that she was trying to quit smoking, so he sold her the system that slowly decreases the amount of nicotine inhaled.

Angela was the hit of every party! Everyone wanted to try the new e-cigarette. When she finally got to her last cartridge, she still had the urge to smoke. She also took comfort in the feel of the cigarette, the inhaling, and knowing the pack was in her bag. This strategy was not working out the way she planned.

Your challenge is to help Angela set a goal to quit e-cigarettes.

Prompt #3

Frank smokes cigars. He enjoys the flavor, the smell of the smoke, and the feel of the cigar in his hand.

Unfortunately, there are only a few places where he is allowed to smoke; no one else enjoys the smell of his cigar; and his habit is expensive.

Frank has decided to quit but is not very optimistic. He has tried giving up cigars several times but couldn't do it.

Your challenge is to help Frank set a goal to quit smoking.

Prompt #4

Mark has been using smokeless tobacco since the ninth grade. He uses it only with his friends or in private because, when people see him spitting, they think it is gross.

Mark has a new non-smoking girlfriend, and she wants him to using smokeless tobacco. He has tried to quit many times but always goes back to his old ways.

Your challenge is to help Mark set a goal to quit smokeless tobacco.

(continues)

Your project includes:

1. Completed goal-setting worksheet for each prompt

2. Select one of the prompts and the corresponding goal-setting worksheet. Demonstrate the goal-setting skill by designing a role-play or a comic book in which the scenario character sets a goal to quit nicotine with the help of a cessation counselor.

3. Include the following in the dialogue:

   a. Five facts about how tobacco (cigarettes, cigars, smokeless tobacco) affects health

   b. Five facts about how the e-cigarette affects health

   c. Five benefits of quitting nicotine products

ASSESSMENT MATERIALS

Grades 9–12 Goal-Setting Worksheet (Table 10.21)

TABLE 10.21   Grades 9–12 Goal-Setting Worksheet

1. Assess personal health practices and overall health status. (PI 6.12.1)

2. What is the goal?

3. Develop a five-step plan to attain a personal health goal that addresses strengths, needs, and risks. (PI 6.12.2)

   a. What are the

      1) **Strengths** –

      2) **Needs** –

      3) **Risks** –

   b. **Plan**

      1)

      2)

      3)

      4)

      5)

4. Implement strategies to achieving a personal health goal. (PI 6.12.3)

   a. Two national or community cessation resources

   _____   _____

   b. Two healthy behaviors that replace nicotine use

   _____   _____

5. Monitor progress in achieving a personal health goal. (PI 6.12.3)

6. **Reflection**

7. Formulate an effective long-term personal health plan that includes three objectives. (PI 6.12.4)

   a.

   b.

   c.

(continues)

TABLE 10.22   Grade 12—Analytical Rubric to Assess a Goal-Setting Role-Play or Comic Book

Criteria	4	3	2	1
Performance indicator 1.12.5 with infused content—Propose ways to reduce or prevent injuries and health problems by quitting nicotine.[1,p25]	Student thoroughly explains five dangers each of tobacco, smokeless tobacco, and e-cigarettes to reduce health problems and encourage quitting nicotine.	Student adequately explains five dangers each of tobacco, smokeless tobacco, and e-cigarettes to reduce health problems and encourage quitting nicotine.	Student inadequately explains five dangers each of tobacco, smokeless tobacco, and e-cigarettes to reduce health problems and encourage quitting nicotine.	Student poorly explains five dangers each of tobacco, smokeless tobacco, and e-cigarettes to reduce health problems and encourage quitting nicotine.
Performance indicator 1.12.5 with infused content—Propose ways to reduce or prevent injuries and health problems by quitting nicotine.[1,p25]	Student proposes a way to prevent injuries and nicotine-related health problems by thoroughly explaining five benefits to quitting.	Student proposes a way to prevent injuries and nicotine-related health problems by adequately explaining five benefits to quitting.	Student proposes a way to prevent injuries and nicotine-related health problems by inadequately explaining five benefits to quitting.	Student proposes a way to prevent injuries and nicotine-related health problems by poorly explaining five benefits to quitting.
Performance indicator 6.12.1 with infused content—Assess personal health practices, such as using nicotine products, and overall health status.[1,p34]	Student thoroughly assesses personal health practices, such as addiction to nicotine, and overall health status.	Student adequately assesses personal health practices, such as addiction to nicotine, and overall health status.	Student inadequately assesses personal health practices, such as addiction to nicotine, and overall health status.	Student poorly assesses personal health practices, such as addiction to nicotine, and overall health status.
Goal statement	Student's goal statement is appropriate.	Student's goal statement is mostly appropriate.	A portion of student's goal statement is inappropriate.	Student's goal statement is mostly inappropriate.
Performance indicator 6.12.2 with infused content—Develop a plan to attain a personal health goal, such as nicotine cessation, that addresses strengths, needs, and risks.[1,p34]	Student develops a thorough five-step plan that explains a nicotine cessation strategy addressing the strengths, needs of the user, and the risks to the user.	Student develops an adequate five-step plan that explains a nicotine cessation strategy addressing the strengths, needs of the user, and the risks to the user.	Student develops an inadequate five-step plan that explains a nicotine cessation strategy addressing the strengths, needs of the user, and the risks to the user.	Student develops a poor five-step plan that explains a nicotine cessation strategy addressing the strengths, needs of the user, and the risks to the user.
Performance indicator 6.12.3 with infused content—Implement strategies and monitor progress in achieving a personal health goal, such as nicotine cessation.[1,p34]	Student thoroughly explains two national or community resources as a strategy to support nicotine cessation.	Student adequately explains two national or community resources as a strategy to support nicotine cessation.	Student inadequately explains two national or community resources as a strategy to support nicotine cessation.	Student poorly explains two national or community resources as a strategy to support nicotine cessation.

(continues)

TABLE 10.22   Grade 12—Analytical Rubric to Assess a Goal-Setting Role-Play or Comic Book (continued)

Criteria	4	3	2	1
Performance indicator 6.12.3 with infused content—Implement strategies and monitor progress in achieving a personal health goal, such as nicotine cessation.[1,p34]	Student thoroughly implements two healthy behaviors that replace nicotine use.	Student adequately implements two healthy behaviors that replace nicotine use.	Student inadequately implements two healthy behaviors that replace nicotine use.	Student poorly implements two healthy behaviors that replace nicotine use.
Performance indicator 6.12.3 with infused content—Implement strategies and monitor progress in achieving a personal health goal, such as nicotine cessation.[1,p34]	Student thoroughly explains how to monitor progress to achieve a personal health goal, such as nicotine cessation.	Student adequately explains how to monitor progress to achieve a personal health goal, such as nicotine cessation.	Student inadequately explains how to monitor progress to achieve a personal health goal, such as nicotine cessation.	Student poorly explains how to monitor progress to achieve a personal health goal, such as nicotine cessation.
Reflection	Student thoroughly reflects on the process of achieving the goal.	Student adequately reflects on the process of achieving the goal.	Student inadequately reflects on the process of achieving the goal.	Student poorly reflects on the process of achieving the goal.
Performance indicator 6.12.4 with infused content—Formulate an effective long-term personal health plan that demonstrates how to be free of tobacco products.[1,p34]	Student thoroughly formulates an effective long-term personal health plan that explains three ways to be free of nicotine products.	Student adequately formulates an effective long-term personal health plan that explains three ways to be free of nicotine products.	Student inadequately formulates an effective long-term personal health plan that explains three ways to be free of nicotine products.	Student poorly formulates an effective long-term personal health plan that explains three ways to be free of nicotine products.
Creativity	The creativity of the role-play or comic book is excellent.	The creativity of the role-play or comic book is good.	The creativity of the role-play or comic book is fair.	The creativity of the role-play or comic book is poor.

Name _____

Total possible points – 44   Your points – _____   Your grade – _____

HOW THE COORDINATED SCHOOL HEALTH TEAM HELPS STUDENTS USE GOAL-SETTING SKILLS TO ENHANCE HEALTH

Health Education

- Teach content and skills to promote nicotine cessation.
- Model and teach the goal-setting skill.
- Explain the effects of nicotine products on personal health.

Physical Education

- Encourage a nicotine-free lifestyle.

- Hang posters that show the effect of nicotine on physical ability and health.

Health Services

- Provide information about the effects of nicotine on the body.
- Provide intervention for students with nicotine addiction.
- Provide nicotine cessation support for students who need help.

Nutrition Services

- Hang posters that promote a drug-free lifestyle.

- Hang posters that illustrate peer resistance skills.
- Model how to set goals for healthy eating.

Counseling, Psychological, and Social Services

- Provide referrals to nicotine cessation programs.
- Provide support for students who have a nicotine addiction.
- Provide resources where families can get help for nicotine addiction.

Healthy School Environment

- Develop and enforce a no-tolerance policy for nicotine products.
- Provide healthy before and after-school activities to engage students.

Health Promotion for Staff

- Provide staff development in nicotine cessation.
- Model nicotine-free behaviors through talk and behavior.

Family and Community Involvement

- Provide training on how to help children quit nicotine.
- Request town/city officials to adopt a no-tolerance policy for nicotine products.
- Provide supervised summer and weekend activities to engage adolescents in healthy activities.

Review Questions

1. Why is it important for teens to learn how to set goals?

2. Why is it important to assess needs when goal setting?

3. What are the steps of goal setting?

4. Why is it important to distribute rubrics to students along with the prompt rather than when they are assessed?

5. Explain when to use formative and summative assessments.

6. Why is it important to provide interdisciplinary connections when planning performance tasks?

7. View the website http://www.aprilage.com/ and explain how this tool can be used to teach the skill of goal setting.

8. Explain how the coordinated school health team can promote goal setting in the school and community.

9. How do you construct an effective prompt?

References

1. Joint Committee on National Health Education Standards (2007). *National Health Education Standards, Second Edition, Achieving Excellence.* Atlanta, GA: American Cancer Society.

2. Page, R. M. (2007). *Promoting Health and Emotional Well-Being in Your Classroom.* Sudbury, MA: Jones and Bartlett.

3. CCSSO~SCASS Health Education Project. (2006). *Assessment Tools for School Health Education, Pre-service and In-service edition.* Santa Cruz, CA: ToucanEd, Inc.

4. Palmer, S. B. (2003). Promoting Self-Determination in Early Elementary School. *Remedial and Special Education,* 24(2), 115–126.

5. Jackson, D. M. (2007). Creating a Successful School-Based Mobile Dental Program. *Journal of School Health,* 77(1), 1–6.

6. The Resourceful Schools Project. (n.d.). *Fun Facts to Know and Share.* Retrieved March 15, 2010: http://www.resourceful schools.org/facts.html

7. Meeks, L. H. (2009). *Comprehensive School Health Education, Totally Awesome Strategies for Teaching Health* (6th ed.). New York: McGraw-Hill.

8. KidsPeace, The National Center for Kids Overcoming Crisis. (n.d.). *Green Means Self-Esteem.* Retrieved March 20, 2010: http://www.kidspeace.org/news.aspx?id=1796

9. Gilman, J. S. (2005). Children's Ability to Cope Post-Divorce: The Effects of Kids' Turn Intervention Program on 7 to 9 Year Olds. *Journal of Divorce & Remarriage,* 42, 109–126.

10. Malone, P. S. (2004). Divorce and Child Behavior Problems: Applying Latent Change Score Models to Life Event Data. *Structural Equation Modeling,* 11(3), 401–423.

11. Bronson, P. M. (2007). *Teen Health, Course 2.* New York: McGraw-Hill Glencoe.

12. Alters, S. S. (2009). *Essential Concepts for Healthy Living* (5th ed.). Sudbury, MA: Jones and Bartlett.

13. United States Department of Agriculture. (n.d.). *MyPyramid Worksheet.* Retrieved March 2, 2010: http://team nutrition.usda.gov/resources/mpk_worksheet.pdf

14. United States Department of Agriculture. (n.d.). *My Pyramid Tracker.* Retrieved March 20, 2010: http://www.mypyramidtracker.gov/

15. U.S. Department of Health and Human Services, Centers for Disease Control and Prevention. (2005). *2005 Middle School Youth Risk Behavior Survey.* Retrieved February 7, 2010: www.cdc.gov/healthyyouth/yrbs/middleschool2005/pdf/YRBS_MS_fullreport.pdf. p. 1–18.

16. National Wellness Institute. (2000). *Your Online Wellness Inventory.* Retrieved March 20, 2010: http://www.national wellness.org/testwell/index.htm

17. Department of Health and Human Services, Centers for Disease Control and Prevention. (2008). *Youth Risk Behavior Surveillance—United States, 2007.* Atlanta, GA: Centers for Disease Control and Prevention.

18. DiFranza, M. J. (n.d.). *NCI Measures Guide for Youth Tobacco Research.* Retrieved March 23, 2010: http://dccps.nci.nih.gov/TCRB/honc.html

19. American Cancer Society. (2010). *Smokeless Tobacco and How to Quit.* Retrieved March 23, 2010: http://www

.cancer.org/docroot/PED/content/PED_10_13X_Quitting_ Smokeless_Tobacco.asp?sitearea=&level=.

20. American Cancer Society. (2009). *Guide to Quit Smoking.* Retrieved March 25, 2010: www.cancer.org/docroot/PED/ content/PED_10_13X_Guide_for_Quittiing_Smoking.asp? sitearea=PED&viewmode=print&.

21. Department of Health and Human Services, Centers for Disease Control and Prevention. (2010). *Youth Risk Behavior Surveillance—United States, 2009.* Atlanta, GA: Centers for Disease Control and Prevention.

22. Bronson, P. M. (2009). *Glencoe Health.* Woodland Hills, CA: McGraw-Hill.

23. Hahn, D. B. (2011). *Focus on Health* (10th ed.). New York: McGraw-Hill.

24. DeNoon, D. J. (2009). *Smoking Cessation Health Center, WebMD.* Retrieved March 26, 2010: http://www.webmd .com/smoking-cessation/news/20090722/fda-ecigarettes bad-not-banned

Teaching National Health Education Standard 7

"Students will demonstrate the ability to practice health-enhancing behaviors and avoid or reduce health risks"[1,p35]

Standard 7

"Healthy or unhealthy lifestyles are developed early in life and thereafter are very difficult to change. For this reason it is very important for children to be taught how to live healthy lives during their formal schooling"[2,p682]

The goal of health education is to adopt and maintain healthy behaviors.[1,p5] Learning and practicing healthy behaviors occur in each of the skills standards—analyzing influences; accessing valid information, products, and services; interpersonal communication; decision-making; goal setting; and advocacy.

Standard 7, practicing healthy behaviors, encourages individuals to take responsibility for their health by demonstrating behaviors that reduce health risks and improve personal health.[1,p35]

Sample performance tasks for practicing health-enhancing behaviors and avoiding or reducing health risks include:

- Keep a journal.
- Write letters.
- Create a family tree.
- Create a health and fitness plan.
- Present a role-play.
- Interview family members.[3,p230]
- Write a CPR instruction book for teens.
- Write a first aid instruction book for teens.
- Design a healthy snack menu.

To show proficiency in this standard, students identify, exhibit, explain, and analyze the importance of taking personal responsibility for health. They also demonstrate healthy behaviors that avoid or reduce health risks.[1,p35]

Teaching the Skill

According to the *National Health Education Standards, Achieving Excellence,* teaching and learning skills is a process. When planning, follow these steps:

I. Discuss the importance of practicing healthy behaviors to avoid or reduce health risks.
- Learning and practicing healthy behaviors:
  - Gives students the skill and confidence they need to cope with health risks
  - Protects health because children can assume responsibility for their own well-being and develop healthy lifestyles[2,p682]
  - Such as physical activity, healthy eating, and avoiding tobacco use is correlated with the prevention of chronic disease
  - As a young person is easier than correcting unhealthy behaviors in adults[4]
II. Explain the steps to proficiency in practicing healthy behaviors to avoid or reduce health risks.
- Select the performance indicators for the grade span.
- Assume responsibility for personal health.
- Demonstrate healthy practices that maintain or improve health.
- Demonstrate healthy behaviors that help youth avoid or reduce risk factors.[1,p35]
III. Show the students what practicing healthy behaviors looks like.
- Model and practice healthy behaviors in the classroom.
- Demonstrate healthy behaviors in the school.
IV. Provide adequate time for the students to practice health-enhancing behaviors and avoid or reduce health risks.
V. Utilize formative assessments during practice to provide feedback and encouragement.

PreK–2

To achieve proficiency in Standard 7, PreK–2 students demonstrate healthy behaviors and behaviors that avoid or reduce health risks.

For example:

> In health class, Rodelle learned to stop, drop, and roll when escaping from a fire. She also learned to smother a fire by putting a blanket or a towel over the flame and to call 9-1-1.
>
> Rodelle's mother often wears her long-sleeved bathrobe when she cooks breakfast. Rodelle told her mother not to let the sleeve go near the flame because it could catch on fire. He mother was proud that her daughter knew about fire safety but didn't think she was in any danger.
>
> One morning her mother's sleeve caught fire as she was cooking. Rodelle gave her mother a towel and told her to wrap it around the sleeve to stop the fire, ran to the phone, and called 9-1-1.
>
> Rodelle knew that the police would answer and ask some questions. When asked what happened, she told the police her mother was cooking and her sleeve caught fire and that they needed help! The policeman told Rodelle that help was on the way.

To reflect, ask the students:

- What healthy behavior did Rodelle demonstrate that stopped her mother's sleeve from burning? (PI 7.2.1) *(Put a towel over the flame to smother it.)*
- What skill did Rodelle demonstrate that brought help to her home and reduced the damage of the fire? (PI 7.2.2) *(Call 9-1-1)*

For another example, ask the students to name behaviors that improve personal health. Student responses may include washing hands, brushing and flossing teeth, eating healthy foods, exercising, getting flu mist, and seeing a doctor when sick.

Instruct the students to brainstorm behaviors that cause sickness or injury. Beside each risk factor, ask the students to write a healthy behavior that decreases or avoids it (**Table 11.1**).

PreK–Grade 2 Performance Indicators

7.2.1 Demonstrate healthy practices and behaviors to maintain or improve personal health.

7.2.2 Demonstrate behaviors that avoid or reduce health risks.[1,p35]

Self-Check on Demonstrating Behaviors that Improve Personal Health and Reduce Health Risks

As the students practice, assess them formatively, provide feedback to improve the skill, and continue instruction when they demonstrate proficiency.

WHAT DOES THE SKILL OF PRACTICING HEALTH-ENHANCING BEHAVIORS LOOK LIKE IN THE PREK–2 CLASSROOM?

It is September, and Mrs. Palmieri is looking forward to her new Grade 2 students but not to cold and flu season. Before school started, the school nurse trained the staff on ways to keep the students healthy and reduce absenteeism. The training included proper hand-washing techniques, the effectiveness of using anti-bacterial gels, how to sneeze and cough without spreading germs, and how to care for a minor scrape or cut.

Mrs. Palmieri thought the best way for her students to learn these health manners[5] would be to write a book about them and act out the scenes.

In planning the practicing healthy behaviors unit, she targets the performance indicator 7.2.1.

> 7.2.1—Demonstrate healthy practices and behaviors to maintain or improve personal health.[1,p35]
> *Performance indicator 7.2.1 with infused content—* Demonstrate health manners to maintain or improve personal health.[1,p35]

After selecting the appropriate skill performance indicators, Mrs. Palmieri selects Standard 1 performance indicators for content.

> Standard 1—Students will comprehend concepts related to health promotion and disease prevention to enhance health.[1,p24]
> Performance indicator 1.2.2—Recognize that there are multiple dimensions of health.[1,p24]
> *Performance indicator 1.2.2 with infused content—* Recognize the healthy behaviors found in the multiple dimensions of health.[1,p24]

By linking the skill and the content performance indicators, the teacher has direction in planning the unit on practicing healthy behaviors.

The first step is to think through the unit by completing the performance task template. The teacher then has a good idea of the lessons that precede this culminating activity, the information and back-up materials needed to

TABLE 11.1 Self-Check on Demonstrating Behaviors That Improve Personal Health and Reduce Health Risks

Risky Behaviors		Healthy Behaviors
Risky Behavior	What is the risk?	Draw a picture of a healthy behavior that reduces the health risk. (PI 7.2.1, 7.2.2)
1.		
2.		
3.		
4.		
5.		

introduce the prompt to the students, and the assessment strategies.

The teacher uses formative assessments while the students learn content and skill to prevent illness. The summative assessment occurs when students demonstrate their knowledge and skill during a class presentation.

The following is an example of a Grade 2 practicing healthy behaviors performance task. The first section illustrates how the teacher plans an authentic assessment of the performance indicators 7.2.1 and 1.2.2. The second extracts some of the information from the performance task and transforms it into the prompt and support materials for students.

The students are assessed formatively during instruction and summatively through an analytical rubric.

Performance Task Name: Grade 2—Using Healthy Behaviors to Improve Health

I. Which state standard(s) does the performance task address?

II. Topic: What areas of health does this project assess? Why is it important? What is the focus of the project?[3,p237]

   A. This performance task assesses personal health.

   B. This topic is important because:

   1. Infections acquired at school are a significant reason for absenteeism among the elementary population.[6,p368]

   2. Hand cleansing and improved hand hygiene reduces the spread of infection.[6,p369]

   3. Anti-microbial-gel hand sanitizer is a viable alternative to soap and water.[6,p368]

   4. Antibacterial cream prevents and treats a bacterial infection in small cuts, scrapes, or burns.[7,p3]

   C. The focus of the project is to practice healthy behaviors to prevent illness.

III. Key Concepts: What basic concepts should students know?[3,p237]

   Performance indicator 1.2.2 with infused content—Recognize the healthy behaviors found in the multiple dimensions of health.[1,p24]

   A. Healthy behaviors that promote physical health

   a. Eat a well-balanced diet.

   b. Exercise one hour each day.

   c. Get ten hours of sleep each night.

   d. Have regular check-ups.

   e. Brush and floss teeth.

   f. Wear a seat belt.

   g. Use protective gear when involved in physical activities.

   h. Follow safety rules.[8,p4-5]

   B. Healthy behaviors that promote mental/emotional health

   a. Cope with changes.

   b. Solve problems.

   c. Share feelings.

   d. Face challenges.

   e. Be patient.

   f. Set and reach goals.

   g. Make healthy decisions.

   h. Keep promises.

   i. Take responsibility.[8,p6]

   C. Healthy behaviors that promote social health

   a. Maintain strong relationships.

   b. Have supportive friends and family.

   c. Show care and concern.

   d. Show the ability to listen.

   e. Follow through on promises.[8,p6]

(continues)

IV. Skills: Which of the seven National Health Education Skills does this performance task address?[3,p237]

   Performance indicator 7.2.1 with infused content—Demonstrate health manners[5] to maintain or improve personal health.[1,p35]

   A. Hand hygiene
   1. Hand washing
      a. Wet your hands with clean running water.
      b. Apply soap.
      c. Rub hands together to create a lather and scrub all surfaces of your hands for 15–20 seconds. (Sing "Happy Birthday" twice.)
      d. Rinse hands well under running water.
      e. Dry hands with a paper towel or a dryer.
      f. Turn off the faucet with the paper towel to avoid hand-to-surface contact.[9]
   2. Hand sanitizer
      a. Apply gel to the palm of one hand.
      b. Rub hands together.
      c. Rub the gel over all the surfaces of the hand and fingers until dry.[9]
   3. Sneezing and coughing
      a. Cover mouth and nose with a tissue when sneezing or coughing.
      b. Throw the tissue away when finished.
      c. If no tissue is available, sneeze or cough into upper sleeve or elbow, not your hands.[10]
   B. First aid for minor cuts, scrapes, and burns
   1. Neosporin, bacitracin, polymyxin
      a. Wash hands.
      b. Clean and dry the cut, scrape, or burn.
      c. Place a small amount of the cream on the tip of your finger.
      d. Apply to the skin and rub gently.
      e. Reapply 1–3 times a day.[7,p3]
      f. Cover the wound.

V. Curricular connections—What other subject(s) does this project support?[3,p237]

   English language arts
   Science
   Art

VI. Student directions and assessment criteria[3,p238]

   A. Project Description: Write and attach an engaging prompt that draws the student into the project.[3,p238]

   Leo is not feeling well today and his nose is stuffy. His head aches and he is very tired. Leo does not have an appetite and just wants to go home.

   In health class, Mrs. Palmieri showed everyone how to have good health manners to avoid getting sick but not everyone practices them.

   B. Your Challenge—Provide a challenge or mission statement that describes the project.[3,p238]

   Your challenge is to help the students in Mrs. Palmieri's class stay healthy by reinforcing health manners.

   C. Assessment Criteria[3,p239]

   You are assessed on the following key concepts: (List the concepts)

   Performance indicator 1.2.2 with infused content—Recognize the healthy behaviors found in the multiple dimensions of health.[1,p24]

   1. Two healthy behaviors that promote physical health
   2. Two healthy behaviors that promote mental/emotional health
   3. Two healthy behaviors that promote social health

(continues)

You are assessed on the following skills: (List the skills)

Performance indicator 7.2.1 with infused content—Demonstrate health manners to maintain or improve personal health.[1,p35]

1. Demonstrate hand washing.
2. Demonstrate how to sneeze or cough without spreading germs.
3. Demonstrate how to use a hand sanitizer.
4. Demonstrate first aid for a minor cut or scrape.

Student project must include the following. (List the project components)

1. Book
   a. Chapter 1—A drawing of the health triangle
      1. Two ways to remain physically healthy
      2. Two ways to remain emotionally/mentally healthy
      3. Two ways to remain socially healthy
   b. Health manners
      1. Chapter 2—Hand washing procedure
      2. Chapter 3—Coughing and sneezing techniques
      3. Chapter 4—How to use hand sanitizer
      4. Chapter 5—First aid for a minor cut or scrape
2. Role-play
   a. Hand washing
   b. Coughing and sneezing
   c. Use of hand sanitizer
   d. How to apply antibacterial cream

Leo is not feeling well today and his nose is stuffy. His head aches and he is very tired. Leo does not have an appetite and just wants to go home.

In health class, Mrs. Palmieri showed everyone how to have good health manners to avoid getting sick but not everyone practices them.

Your challenge is to help the students in Mrs. Palmieri's class stay healthy by reinforcing health manners.

Your project must contain the following:

1. Book with five chapters. Each chapter must contain three pictures.

   a. Chapter 1—A drawing of the health triangle

      1. Two ways to stay physically healthy

      2. Two ways to stay emotionally/mentally healthy

      3. Two ways to stay socially healthy

   b. Health manners

      1. Chapter 2—Hand washing procedure

      2. Chapter 3—Coughing and sneezing techniques

      3. Chapter 4—How to use hand sanitizer

      4. Chapter 5—First aid for a minor cut or scrape

(continues)

2. Role-play of health manners

    a. Hand washing

    b. Coughing and sneezing

    c. Use of hand sanitizer

    d. How to apply antibacterial cream

ASSESSMENT MATERIALS

Analytical Rubric to Assess the Healthy Manners Book Portion of the Performance Task (Table 11.2)

TABLE 11.2 Analytical Rubric to Assess the Healthy Manners Book

Criteria	4	3	2	1
Chapter 1 *Performance indicator 1.2.2 with infused content*—Recognize the healthy behaviors found in the multiple dimensions of health.[1,p24]	Student recognizes and thoroughly describes two healthy behaviors that promote physical health.	Student recognizes and adequately describes two healthy behaviors that promote physical health.	Student recognizes but inadequately describes two healthy behaviors that promote physical health.	Student recognizes but poorly describes two healthy behaviors that promote physical health.
Chapter 1 *Performance indicator 1.2.2 with infused content*—Recognize the healthy behaviors found in the multiple dimensions of health.[1,p24]	Student recognizes and thoroughly describes two healthy behaviors that promote mental/ emotional health.	Student recognizes and adequately describes two healthy behaviors that promote mental/ emotional health.	Student recognizes but inadequately describes two healthy behaviors that promote mental/ emotional health.	Student recognizes but poorly describes two healthy behaviors that promote mental/ emotional health.
Chapter 1 *Performance indicator 1.2.2 with infused content*—Recognize the healthy behaviors found in the multiple dimensions of health.[1,p24]	Student recognizes and thoroughly describes two healthy behaviors that promote social health.	Student recognizes and adequately describes two healthy behaviors that promote social health.	Student recognizes but inadequately describes two healthy behaviors that promote social health.	Student recognizes but poorly describes two healthy behaviors that promote social health.
Chapter 2 *Performance indicator 7.2.1 with infused content*—Demonstrate health manners to maintain or improve personal health.[1,p35]	Student accurately demonstrates the hand washing procedure.	Student's demonstration of hand washing procedure is mostly accurate.	Student's demonstration of hand washing procedure has a few inaccuracies.	Student's demonstration of hand washing procedure is mostly inaccurate.
Chapter 3 *Performance indicator 7.2.1 with infused content*—Demonstrate health manners to maintain or improve personal health.[1,p35]	Student accurately demonstrates coughing and sneezing techniques.	Student's demonstration of coughing and sneezing techniques is mostly accurate.	Student's demonstration of coughing and sneezing techniques has a few inaccuracies.	Student's demonstration of coughing and sneezing techniques is mostly inaccurate.

(continues)

TABLE 11.2   Analytical Rubric to Assess the Healthy Manners Book *(continued)*

Criteria	4	3	2	1
Chapter 4 *Performance indicator 7.2.1 with infused content*—Demonstrate health manners to maintain or improve personal health.[1,p35]	Student accurately demonstrates how to use hand sanitizers.	Student's demonstration of how to use hand sanitizers is mostly accurate.	Student's demonstration of how to use hand sanitizers has a few inaccuracies.	Student's demonstration of how to use hand sanitizers is mostly inaccurate.
Chapter 5 *Performance indicator 7.2.1 with infused content*—Demonstrate health manners to maintain or improve personal health.[1,p35]	Student accurately demonstrates first aid for a minor cut or scrape.	Student's demonstration of first aid for a minor cut or scrape is mostly accurate.	Student's demonstration of first aid for a minor cut or scrape has a few inaccuracies.	Student's demonstration of first aid for a minor cut or scrape is mostly inaccurate.
Pictures	Student provides three appropriate pictures per chapter.	Student's selection of three pictures is mostly appropriate.	A few of the three pictures the student selected are somewhat inappropriate	Student's selection of three pictures is mostly inappropriate.
Grammar	The grammar is always correct.	The grammar is sometimes correct.	The grammar is rarely correct.	The grammar is never correct.
Spelling	The spelling is always correct.	The spelling is sometimes correct.	The spelling is rarely correct.	The spelling is never correct.

Name _____

Total possible points – 40   Your points – _____   Your grade – _____

Analytical Rubric to Assess the Role-Play of Healthy Manners (Table 11.3)

TABLE 11.3   Analytical Rubric to Assess the Role-Play of Healthy Manners

Criteria	4	3	2	1
Performance indicator 7.2.1 with infused content—Demonstrate health manners to maintain or improve personal health.[1,p35]	Student accurately demonstrates the hand washing procedure.	Student's demonstration of hand washing procedure is mostly accurate.	Student's demonstration of hand washing procedure has a few inaccuracies.	Student's demonstration of hand washing procedure is mostly inaccurate.
Performance indicator 7.2.1 with infused content—Demonstrate health manners to maintain or improve personal health.[1,p35]	Student accurately demonstrates coughing and sneezing techniques.	Student's demonstration of coughing and sneezing techniques is mostly accurate.	Student's demonstration of coughing and sneezing techniques has a few inaccuracies.	Student's demonstration of coughing and sneezing techniques is mostly inaccurate.

(continues)

TABLE 11.3 Analytical Rubric to Assess the Role-Play of Healthy Manners *(continued)*

Criteria	4	3	2	1
Performance indicator 7.2.1 with infused content—Demonstrate health manners to maintain or improve personal health.[1,p35]	Student accurately demonstrates how to use hand sanitizers.	Student's demonstration of how to use hand sanitizers is mostly accurate.	Student's demonstration of how to use hand sanitizers has a few inaccuracies.	Student's demonstration of how to use hand sanitizers is mostly inaccurate.
Performance indicator 7.2.1 with infused content—Demonstrate health manners to maintain or improve personal health.[1,p35]	Student accurately demonstrates first aid for a minor cut or scrape.	Student's demonstration of first aid for a minor cut or scrape is mostly accurate.	Student's demonstration of first aid for a minor cut or scrape has a few inaccuracies.	Student's demonstration of first aid for a minor cut or scrape is mostly inaccurate.
Participation	Participation of all students is excellent.	Participation of all students is good.	Participation of all students is fair.	Participation of all students is poor.

Name _____

Total possible points – 20   Your points – _____   Your grade – _____

HOW THE COORDINATED SCHOOL HEALTH TEAM HELPS STUDENTS PRACTICE HEALTHY BEHAVIORS AND AVOID OR REDUCE HEALTH RISKS

Health Education

- Teach health manners to prevent the spread of communicable diseases.
- Model health manners.
- Teach how to promote health in each of the health triangles.

Physical Education

- Model health manners.
- Clean the surfaces of gymnasium equipment to keep them free of pathogens.

Health Services

- Provide professional development that teaches ways to prevent the spread of communicable disease.
- Monitor students and adults for communicable disease.

Nutrition Services

- Provide hand sanitizer in the lunchroom.

Counseling, Psychological, and Social Services

- Ask staff to promote health manners when counseling students.
- Encourage staff to model health manners when counseling students.

Healthy School Environment

- Develop and enforce policies to control communicable disease.
- Provide hand sanitizer for each instructional or community space and office.

Health Promotion for Staff

- Participate in professional development that teaches ways to prevent the spread of communicable disease.
- Model health manners.

Family and Community Involvement

- Send home information about preventing the spread of communicable disease.
- Urge members of the community to provide antibacterial gels in businesses to prevent the spread of communicable disease.

Grades 3–5

To achieve proficiency in Standard 7, Grade 3–5 students identify personal health behaviors, exhibit healthy practices and behaviors that maintain or improve health, and demonstrate behaviors that avoid or reduce health risks.

For example:

Evan is a busy fifth grader who works hard in school. He belongs to the after-school rocket club, where Monday through Thursday he enjoys designing and shooting rockets.

Because Evan gets home from school so late, he cannot start his homework until after supper. Sometimes it is late when he finishes, so he goes right to bed.

Evan also has family responsibilities, such as helping his mom and dad clean up after dinner, babysitting his younger sister, and keeping his room clean. He takes care of himself by brushing and flossing his teeth each day.

Lately, Evan is having trouble sleeping, is losing his appetite, and does not have time to play with his friends. He worries that he will forget one of his responsibilities and disappoint his parents or teachers.

Ask the children to list the things Evan does to maintain or improve his health. (PI 7.5.2)

- *Enjoys designing and building rockets.*
- *Brushes and flosses his teeth each day.*
- *Works on his relationship with his family by doing his chores.*

What does Evan need to do to cope with his trouble sleeping and lack of appetite? (PI 7.5.3)

- *Cut down on some activities.*
- *Make a schedule.*
- *Ask for help from his parents or teachers.*
- *Have some fun with family and friends to relax.*

After talking to his parents and rocket coach, Evan designed a weekly schedule that contains more free time and fun time with his family but still allows him to build rockets (**Table 11.4**).

Grades 3–5 Performance Indicators

7.5.1 Identify responsible personal health behaviors.

7.5.2 Demonstrate a variety of healthy practices and behaviors to maintain or improve personal health.

7.5.3 Demonstrate a variety of behaviors that avoid or reduce health risks.[1,p35]

To ease his stress, Evan's parents told him that he did not have to clean up after supper anymore. Because he now has more time at home, Evan can play with his friends in the afternoon or start his homework. This strategy gives him more time to have fun and relax before he goes to bed.

The changes are working. Evan is sleeping much better and is more relaxed and enjoying himself!

To reflect, ask the students the following questions.

- What has Evan done to maintain or improve his health? (PI 7.5.2)
  - *Decreased the amount of time he attends the rocket club.*
  - *Starts his homework earlier because he does not clean up after dinner anymore.*
  - *Still brushes and flosses his teeth every day.*
  - *Still babysits but tries to make it more fun.*
  - *Does not schedule all his time.*
  - *Makes time to play with friends.*
  - *Relaxes before he goes to bed.*

In this skill, students must exhibit practicing healthy behaviors in several scenarios. When they demonstrate an understanding of the skill, as determined through formative assessment, instruction continues with the content.

To extend practicing, ask students to brainstorm common health problems for students their age. Write these suggestions into prompts and give students time to practice their skill in small groups. Pair the groups and ask each to share with the other the healthy behaviors used to cope with common health problems (**Table 11.5**).

TABLE 11.4 Evan's Weekly Activity Schedule

Sunday	Monday	Tuesday	Wednesday	Thursday	Friday	Saturday
Nothing scheduled.	Go home	Rocket club	Go home	Rocket club	Family fun night.	Babysit sister at night but get a fun movie to watch.
Have fun.	Play with friends		Play with friends			

TABLE 11.5 Worksheet to Demonstrate How to Maintain or Improve Personal Health

Common Health Problems	Healthy Behaviors That Maintain or Improve Health

Problem – Damien often falls asleep in class. He stays up late playing electronic games.

Healthy Behavior – Get more sleep. Pre-teens need 8–10 hours of sleep each night.

Problem – Derek does not like to wear his bicycle helmet. He fell once and hit his head.

Healthy Behavior – Derek wears his bicycle helmet each time he rides so he does not injure his head if he falls.

Problem – Carlotta is often sad and lonely and has few friends.

Healthy Behavior – Carlotta talks to the school counselor and learns healthy ways to cope with problems.

Problem – Caroline is babysitting and her little sister is choking!

Healthy Behavior – Caroline learns how to use the Heimlich maneuver to help someone who is choking.

As the students learn and practice the skill and content, continue to formatively assess their progress. If additional instruction is needed, provide it before moving to the performance task.

WHAT DOES THE SKILL OF PRACTICING HEALTHY BEHAVIORS LOOK LIKE IN THE GRADE 4 CLASSROOM?

Mrs. Strickland is a Grade 4 teacher at the Joseph Richman School. She noticed that as the year progressed, her students showed signs of stress. They seemed to hurry, rushing through their work as if there was not enough time to complete it. They often say, "I am not good enough," when they are unable to remember something or do not feel they lived up to adult expectations. Students also stress over what others think about how they look or what they do. They express their dislike when they cannot change or leave a situation. They often ask to go to the nurse with symptoms of rapid eye movement, a tense face, heavy breathing, and a racing heartbeat. Students seem angry or irritated much of the time.[11,p289-291]

Budgetary restraints and more time needed for test preparation have resulted in reduced time for physical education and recess. Mrs. Strickland has shared her concerns with the school nurse and the health teacher, who confirm that middle school youth risk behavior data indicates that 17.9% of students reported being so depressed that they seriously thought about suicide.[12] Since stress overload can lead to anxiety and depression, Mrs. Strickland and Mrs. Englewood, the health teacher, decided to teach stress management strategies to their students to help them maintain or improve their health.

Planning begins with selecting Standard 7 performance indicators.

Standard 7—Students will demonstrate the ability to practice health-enhancing behaviors and avoid or reduce health risks.[1,p35]

Performance indicator 7.5.2—Demonstrate a variety of healthy practices and behaviors to maintain or improve personal health.[1,p35]

Performance indicator 7.5.2 with infused content— Demonstrate a variety of healthy practices and behaviors, including yoga, to maintain or improve personal health.[1,p35]

After selecting the appropriate performance indicator for the skill, choose a Standard 1 performance indicator.

Standard 1—Students will comprehend concepts related to health promotion and disease prevention to enhance health.[1,p24]

Performance Indicator 1.5.4—Describe ways to prevent common childhood injuries and health problems.[1,p24]

Performance indicator 1.5.4 with infused content— Describe ways to prevent common childhood injuries and health problems that are stress related.[1,p24]

By linking the skill and content performance indicators, the teacher has direction in planning the lessons for a healthy behaviors unit.

The first step is to think through the unit by completing the performance task template. Thereupon, the teacher has a good idea of the lessons that precede this culminating activity, the information and back-up materials necessary to introduce the prompt to the students, and the assessment strategies.

When distributing the prompt, include all the back-up information, student worksheets, and holistic and analytical rubrics. Distribute the rubrics with the prompt so students know how they will be assessed before working on their product. The rubrics act as a guide and help the students attain proficiency in the standards.

Designing the performance task takes considerable preparation, but once the information is distributed and explained, the students create a product independently. They learn with good coaching (formative assessment) how to demonstrate proficiency in content and skill.

The following is an example of a Grade 4 practicing healthy behaviors performance task that focuses on stress reduction.

The first section, for the teacher, demonstrates how to plan for an authentic assessment of the performance indicators 7.5.2 and 1.5.4. The second, the student's, extracts information from the performance task and transforms it into the student prompt and support materials.

Performance Task Name: Grade 3—Practicing Healthy Behaviors to Reduce Stress

I. Which state standard(s) does this performance task address? (Varies by state)

II. Topic: What areas of health does this project assess? Why is it important? What is the focus of the project?[3,p237]

    A. This performance task assesses personal and mental/emotional health.

    B. This topic is important because:

        1. Children experience stress from home, school, self, and others.

        2. Stress interferes with school functioning and relationships with family and friends.[13,p79]

        3. Children respond to stress by exhibiting anxiety, withdrawal, aggression, and drug and alcohol use.

        4. The most common physiological disorders associated with stress are obesity, cardiovascular disease, asthma, and hypertension.[13,p80]

        5. Children are able to practice and implement stress prevention skills.[13,p88]

    C. The focus of this project is to practice healthy behaviors to reduce stress.

III. Key Concepts: What basic concepts should students know?[3,p237]

    Standard 1—Students will comprehend concepts related to health promotion and disease prevention to enhance health.[1,p24]

    Performance indicator 1.5.4 with infused content—Describe ways to prevent common stress-related childhood injuries and health problems.[1,p24]

        1. Stress

            a. Types of stress

                1. Good stress

                    a. Helps to maintain focus

                    b. Helps to complete tasks

                    c. Increases physical activity[11,p291]

                2. Bad stress results in feeling

                    a. Angry

                    b. Dizzy

                    c. Irritable

                    d. A loss of self-confidence

                    e. Confusion

                    f. Powerless[11,p289-291]

            b. Identifying stressors

                1. Home

                2. School

                3. Community

            c. Effects on the body

                1. Heart rate increases.

                2. Blood pressure rises.

                3. Breathing rate increases.

                4. Senses are heightened.[8,p157]

        2. Yoga

            a. Yoga is a non-threatening and gentle way to increase fitness and enhance health.

            b. Yoga calms children, reduces obesity, reduces discipline problems, decreases anger and panic attacks, and enhances imagination, concentration, and academic performance.[14,p277]

            c. Yoga utilizes Howard Gardner's Theories of Multiple Intelligences.[15]

IV. Skills: Which of the seven National Health Education Standards skills does this performance task address?[3,p237]

    Standard 7—Students will demonstrate the ability to practice health enhancing behaviors and avoid or reduce health risks.[1,p35]

(continues)

Performance indicator 7.5.2 with infused content—Demonstrate a variety of healthy practices and behaviors, including yoga, to maintain or improve personal health.[1,p35]

    A. Strategies to manage stress

        1. Eat nutritious foods.

        2. Talk with trusted friends or adults.

        3. Plan your time.

        4. Think positively.

        5. Make time to relax.

        6. Get adequate sleep.

        7. Be physically active.

    B. Yoga

        1. Yoga warm-up

            a. Lie down, sit cross-legged on the floor, or in a chair.

            b. Close eyes, if comfortable doing so.

            c. Think of something that is worrisome; imagine throwing it away or watching it float away.[14,p280]

        2. Breathing

            a. Inhale through the nose.

            b. Exhale through the mouth saying, "Ahh."

            c. Repeat three times.[14,p280]

        3. Postures

            a. Warm up by stretching.

            b. Breathing

                1. Hold postures for a count of ten.

                2. Hold breath for four seconds.

                3. Inhale and exhale during postures.

                4. Follow each posture with one or two deep breaths.[14,p280]

            c. Examples

                1. Gentle sitting pose.

                2. Tree pose

                3. Triangle pose

                4. Cat pose

                5. Cow pose

                6. Downward dog

                7. Cobra pose

                8. Child's pose

                9. Starfish pose[16]

        4. Relaxation (under three minutes for children 3–6 years old)

            a. Lie supine on the floor with eyes shut.

            b. Concentrate on breathing and an image of something pleasant.

            c. Slowly stretch and wiggle fingers and toes.[14,p281]

V. Curricular connections—What other subject areas does this project support?[3,p237]

    English language arts

    Biology

    Art

VI. Student Directions and Assessment Criteria[3,p238]

    Prompt #1

    A. Project Description—Write and attach an engaging prompt that draws the student into the project.[3,p238]

(continues)

Diego is feeling stressed. Because his parents work, he attends the before- and after-school enrichment programs. As a result, he gets up early in the morning and does not come home until suppertime. On the weekends, Diego plays soccer in the fall, hockey in the winter, and baseball in the spring. He does not spend time with his friends because he is too busy and tired.

Lately, he feels nervous, has trouble concentrating, and gets stomachaches. Diego sometimes forgets his homework and his lunch.

B. Your Challenge—Provide a challenge or mission statement that describes the project.[3,p238]

Your challenge is to help Diego improve his personal health by demonstrating healthy practices.

Prompt #2

A. Project Description—Write and attach an engaging prompt that draws the student into the project.[3,p238]

Carla lives with her grandmother, who became sick and went to the hospital the other day. Carla has moved into her aunt and uncle's house until her grandmother is better.

Carla has to get up much earlier to be at school on time and worries all day about her grandmother. She feels her heart beating and sometimes has trouble catching her breath. She is worried about getting sick, having trouble concentrating on her school work, and falling behind.

B. Your Challenge—Provide a challenge or mission statement that describes the project.[3,p238]

Your challenge is to help Carla improve her personal health by demonstrating healthy practices.

C. Assessment Criteria[3,p239]

You are assessed on the following key concepts: (List the concepts.)

Performance indicator 1.5.4 with infused content—Describe ways to prevent common stress-related childhood injuries and health problems.[1,p24]

1. Complete the stress graphic.
   a. Identify three common stressors and explain if they are good or bad sources of stress.
   b. Explain how the heart, lungs, blood, and senses are affected by stress.
2. Complete the yoga graphic.
   a. Explain three benefits of yoga.

You are assessed on the following skills:

Performance indicator 7.5.2 with infused content—Demonstrate a variety of healthy practices and behaviors, including yoga, to maintain or improve personal health.[1,p35]

1. Posters
   a. Three strategies to manage stress
   b. Yoga posters
      Poster #1—How to stretch
      Poster #2—How to breathe
      Poster #3—Three yoga positions
      Poster #4—Relaxation techniques

Joseph Richman School

Name _____

Prompt #1

Diego is feeling stressed. Because his parents work, he attends the before- and after-school enrichment programs. As a result, he gets up early in the morning and does not come home until suppertime. On the weekends, Diego plays soccer in the fall, hockey in the winter, and baseball in the spring. He does not spend time with his friends because he is too busy and tired.

(continues)

Lately, he feels nervous, has trouble concentrating, and gets stomachaches. Diego sometimes forgets his homework and his lunch.

Your challenge is to help Diego improve his personal health by demonstrating healthy practices.

Prompt #2

Carla lives with her grandmother, who became sick and went to the hospital the other day. Carla has moved into her aunt and uncle's house until her grandmother is better.

Carla has to get up much earlier to be at school on time and worries all day about her grandmother. She feels her heart beating and sometimes has trouble catching her breath. She is worried about getting sick, having trouble concentrating on her school work, and falling behind.

Your challenge is to help Carla improve her personal health by demonstrating healthy practices.

Your project must contain the following:

1. Stress graphic organizer

   a. Identifies three common stressors and explains if they are good or bad sources of stress.

   b. Explains how the heart, lungs, blood, and senses are affected by stress.

   c. Three strategies to manage stress.

   d. Includes five pictures.

2. Yoga graphic organizer

   a. Explains three benefits of yoga.

   b. Includes three pictures.

3. Posters

   a. Yoga posters. Include two pictures on each poster.

      Poster #1—How to stretch and how stretching maintains or proves personal health

      Poster #2—How to breathe and how breathing maintains or improves personal health

      Poster #3—Three yoga positions and how they maintain or improve personal health

      Poster #4—Three relaxation techniques and how they maintain or improve personal health

ASSESSMENT MATERIALS

Stress Graphic Analysis (Figure 11.1)

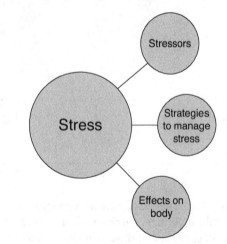

FIGURE 11.1   Identifying Sources of Stress, How Stress Affects the Body, and Strategies to Manage Stress

Yoga Graphic Organizer (Figure 11.2)

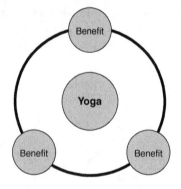

FIGURE 11.2   Yoga Graph

(continues)

TABLE 11.6   Analytical Rubric for the Stress and Yoga Graph Portion of the Performance Task

Stress and Yoga Graph

Criteria	4	3	2	1
		Stress Graphic Organizer		
Performance indicator 1.5.4 with infused content—Describe ways to prevent common childhood injuries and health problems that are stress related.[1,p24]	To prevent stress-related health problems, student accurately identifies three common stressors and explains if they are good or bad.	Student's identification of three common stressors and whether they are good or bad in order to prevent stress-related health problems is mostly accurate.	Student's identification of three common stressors and whether they are good or bad in order to prevent stress-related health problems has a few inaccuracies.	Student's identification of three common stressors and whether they are good or bad in order to prevent stress-related health problems is mostly inaccurate.
Performance indicator 1.5.4 with infused content—Describe ways to prevent common childhood injuries and health problems that are stress related.[1,p24]	To prevent stress-related health problems, student accurately describes how the heart, lungs, blood, and senses are affected by stress.	Student's description of how the heart, lungs, blood, and senses are affected by stress in order to prevent stress-related health problems is mostly accurate.	Student's description of how the heart, lungs, blood, and senses are affected by stress in order to prevent stress-related health problems has a few inaccuracies.	Student's description of how the heart, lungs, blood, and senses are affected by stress in order to prevent stress-related health problems is mostly inaccurate.
Performance indicator 7.5.2 with infused content—Demonstrate a variety of healthy practices and behaviors, including yoga, to maintain or improve personal health.[1,p35]	Student thoroughly demonstrates three strategies to manage stress.	Student adequately demonstrates three strategies to manage stress.	Student inadequately demonstrates three strategies to manage stress.	Student poorly demonstrates three strategies to manage stress.
Pictures	The five pictures on the graph are appropriate.	The five pictures on the graph are mostly appropriate.	A few of the five pictures on the graph are appropriate.	The five pictures on the graph are mostly inappropriate.
Spelling	The spelling is always correct.	The spelling is sometimes correct.	The spelling is rarely correct.	The spelling is never correct.
		Yoga Graphic Organizer		
Performance indicator 1.5.4 with infused content—Describe ways to prevent common childhood injuries and health problems that are stress related.[1,p24]	Student accurately explains three benefits of yoga.	Student's explanation of the three benefits of yoga are mostly accurate.	A few of the three benefits of yoga are inaccurate.	Student's explanation of the three benefits of yoga are mostly inaccurate.
Pictures	The three pictures on the graph are appropriate.	The three pictures on the graph are mostly appropriate.	A few of the three pictures on the graph are appropriate.	The three pictures on the graph are mostly inappropriate.
Spelling	The spelling is always correct.	The spelling is sometimes correct.	The spelling is rarely correct.	The spelling is never correct.

Name _____

Total possible points – 32   Your points – _____   Your grade – _____

TABLE 11.7   Grade 4—Analytical Rubric for Yoga Portion of the Performance Task

Yoga Posters

Criteria	4	3	2	1
Performance indicator 7.5.2 with infused content—Demonstrate a variety of healthy practices and behaviors, including yoga, to maintain or improve personal health.[1,p35]	Student thoroughly demonstrates how to stretch and how stretching maintains or improves personal health.	Student adequately demonstrates how to stretch and how stretching maintains or improves personal health.	Student inadequately demonstrates how to stretch and how stretching maintains or improves personal health.	Student poorly demonstrates how to stretch and how stretching maintains or improves personal health.
Performance indicator 7.5.2 with infused content—Demonstrate a variety of healthy practices and behaviors, including yoga, to maintain or improve personal health.[1,p35]	Student thoroughly demonstrates how to breathe and how breathing maintains or improves personal health.	Student adequately demonstrates how to breathe and how breathing maintains or improves personal health.	Student inadequately demonstrates how to breathe and how breathing maintains or improves personal health.	Student poorly demonstrates how to breathe and how breathing maintains or improves personal health.
Performance indicator 7.5.2 with infused content—Demonstrate a variety of healthy practices and behaviors, including yoga, to maintain or improve personal health.[1,p35]	Student thoroughly demonstrates three yoga positions and how they maintain or improve personal health.	Student adequately demonstrates three yoga positions and how they maintain or improve personal health.	Student inadequately demonstrates three yoga positions and how they maintain or improve personal health.	Student poorly demonstrates three yoga positions and how they maintain or improve personal health.
Performance indicator 7.5.2 with infused content—Demonstrate a variety of healthy practices and behaviors, including yoga, to maintain or improve personal health.[1,p35]	Student thoroughly demonstrates three relaxation techniques and how they maintain or improve personal health.	Student adequately demonstrates three relaxation techniques and how they maintain or improve personal health.	Student inadequately demonstrates three relaxation techniques and how they maintain or improve personal health.	Student poorly demonstrates three relaxation techniques and how they maintain or improve personal health.
Pictures (two per poster)	The two pictures on each poster are appropriate.	The two pictures on each poster are mostly appropriate.	One of the two pictures on each poster is inappropriate.	The two pictures on each poster are mostly inappropriate.
Grammar	The grammar is always correct.	The grammar is sometimes correct.	The grammar is rarely correct.	The grammar is never correct.
Spelling	The spelling is always correct.	The spelling is sometimes correct.	The spelling is rarely correct.	The spelling is never correct.

Name _____

Total possible points – 28   Your points – _____   Your grade – _____

HOW THE COORDINATED SCHOOL HEALTH TEAM HELPS STUDENTS PRACTICE HEALTHY BEHAVIORS AND AVOID OR REDUCE HEALTH RISKS

Health Education

- Teach how to identify stressors and the effect stress has on the body.
- Model healthy behaviors.
- Teach how yoga reduces stress.

Physical Education

- Promote yoga as a strategy to reduce stress.
- Model healthy ways to manage stress.

Health Services

- Model healthy ways to manage stress.
- Monitor students who exhibit stress-related physical ailments.
- Reinforce strategies to manage stress in a healthy way.

Nutrition Services

- Provide motivational posters showing students who eat healthy as a way to reduce stress.
- Create a comfortable and welcoming environment so students can relax and socialize during lunch.

Counseling, Psychological, and Social Services

- Assess student stress through the Coddington's Life Events Scale for Children[13]
- Model healthy ways to manage stress.

Healthy School Environment

- Provide health promoting activities that reduce stress.
- Create a clean and safe environment to reduce stress.

Health Promotion for Staff

- Provide professional development so staff can learn stress reduction techniques.
- Model healthy ways to manage stress.
- Encourage staff to participate in after-school yoga classes.

Family and Community Involvement

- Provide yoga classes for families.
- Plan a community fun day that includes health promotion activities.

Grades 6–8

To achieve proficiency in Standard 7, Grade 6–8 students explain the importance of assuming responsibility for personal health behaviors, demonstrate healthy practices or behaviors that maintain or improve health, and demonstrate behaviors that avoid or reduce health risks.

To teach Standard 7, explain the importance of practicing health enhancing behaviors, their effect on current and future health, why this skill is relevant to the student, and how it relates to the other national health education skills.

To achieve the standard, model the skill, provide practice time for the students, and use formative assessments while the students are learning and practicing in order to improve teaching and learning.

For example:

> Mr. Alexander includes cardiopulmonary resuscitation (CPR) and defibrillation in his healthy behaviors unit because many of his students babysit, have elderly grandparents, and play after-school and weekend sports.
>
> Last year, a middle school soccer player collapsed on the field. The coach used the automatic external defibrillator (AED) to bring her back to consciousness. That event scared many of the students, and they wanted to know what to do if they found themselves alone with someone who had collapsed. Subsequently, Mr. Alexander wrote a grant to purchase CPR training materials and taught his first section this year.
>
> He presented his students with this scenario. You are at the mall with your friends and see an elderly person collapse. What should you do? (**Table 11.8**)

To reflect, Mr. Alexander asked the following questions:

- What was the first thing Randy, Mary, and Allison did when they approached the fallen person? (PI 7.8.1) *(They checked for unresponsiveness, called 9-1-1, and ran for the AED.)*
- When Mary discovered the victim was not breathing, what did she do? (PI 7.8.2) *(She gave two rescue breaths, making sure the chest rose and fell.)*

Grades 6-8 Performance Indicators

7.8.1 Explain the importance of assuming responsibility for personal health behaviors.

7.8.2 Demonstrate healthy practices and behaviors that will maintain or improve the health of self and others.

7.8.3 Demonstrate behaviors that avoid or reduce health risks to self and others.[1,p35]

Table 11.8   Automated External Defibrillator

No.	Skill	Satisfactory	Unsatisfactory
1.	Check for scene safety.		
2.	Check patient.		
3.	Check responsiveness.		
4.	If unresponsive, open the airway.		
5.	Check for breathing.		
6.	If not breathing, deliver two breaths.		
7.	Check for carotid pulse.		
8.	If pulse is absent and arrest was witnessed, begin CPR and attach AED as soon as possible.		
9.	If pulse is absent and arrest was not witnessed, perform 2 minutes of CPR and then attach the AED.		
10.	Call 9-1-1 if not already done.		

Defibrillation:

No.	Skill		
1.	Power is turned on.		
2.	Electrodes attached to AED.		
3.	Ensure clean/dry skin surface.		
4.	Electrodes correctly applied to patient.		
5.	Clear patient.		
6.	Initiate analyze mode.		

If shock is indicated:

No.	Skill		
7.	Clear victim.		
8.	Deliver one shock.		
9.	Immediately resume CPR.		
10.	After 2 minutes of CPR, allow for re-analysis.		
11.	If a shock is indicated, repeat steps 7–10.		

If no shock is indicated:

No.	Skill		
12.	Check pulse.		
13.	If no pulse, perform CPR for 2 minutes.		
14.	After 2 minutes of CPR, allow for re-analysis.		

Evaluator:

- If the chest does not rise, what is the problem? (*Obstructed airway*)
- What should Mary do then? (PI 7.8.2) (*She needs to treat for an obstruction.*)
- How did Mary check for a pulse? (PI 7.8.2) (*She placed two fingers on the victim's Adam's apple then slid her fingers into the groove between the Adam's apple and the neck muscle and felt for a pulse for 10 seconds.*)
- When Randy returned with the AED, what was the first thing they did? (PI 7.8.2) (*Turned it on*)
- How did Mary know where to put the pads? (*She remembered from class and also the picture on the device.*)
- How do you know if the victim needs to be shocked or given CPR? (*The AED tells you.*)
- Why do people need to move away from the victim during a shock? (*Safety*)

Mr. Alexander gave the students a few more likely scenarios he thought they might encounter and provided them time to practice on the manikin. The students said they like CPR training because it makes them feel more confident.

When the students are learning the skill, provide adequate time for practice before asking them to demonstrate proficiency through an authentic assessment. While they are practicing, use formative assessments (Chapter 4) to check for understanding. Use feedback to show students how to improve performance, thereby encouraging improvement.

Once the students demonstrate the skill, teach the health content. Design a prompt that allows the students to display their knowledge of health content while demonstrating healthy behavior skills. As the students practice their content and skill, use formative assessments to redirect and encourage them.

WHAT DOES THE SKILL OF PRACTICING HEALTHY BEHAVIORS LOOK LIKE IN THE GRADE 7 CLASSROOM?

Arondale Middle School is located in the center of a large city. Most of the students and their families struggle economically and many have witnessed their parents fighting or have been a victim of their aggression.[18,p701]

Mrs. Verga, the principal, examined the most recent youth risk behavior survey (YRBS) results and discovered that 66.9% of her students have been in a physical fight, and 9.2% have been injured as a result.[12] From talking to community leaders and the police, Mrs. Verga knows that when aggressive middle school children grow up and reach the age of 19 or 20, 35% are victims of partner violence.[18,p693] She recognizes that her students are at risk and decides, with input from her staff and administrators, to implement a school-wide conflict resolution program to

help her students develop and maintain healthy relationships and learn how to deal with conflict in a healthy way.

While examining different conflict resolution programs, Mrs. Verga looked at the research and discovered that a comprehensive approach, teaching both knowledge and skill, is especially effective.[19,p3]

To begin planning, the health teacher selects specific performance indicators that address a targeted skill and content.

Standard 7—Students will demonstrate the ability to practice health-enhancing behaviors and avoid or reduce health risks.[1,p35]
> 7.8.3—Demonstrate behaviors that avoid or reduce health risks to self and others.[1,p35]
>> *Performance indicator 7.8.3 with infused content—* Demonstrate behaviors, such as conflict resolution, that avoid or reduce health risks to self and others.[1,p35]

Standard 1—Students comprehend concepts related to health promotion and disease prevention to enhance health.[1,p25]
> Performance indicator 1.8.5—Describe ways to reduce or prevent injuries and other adolescent health problems.[1,p25]
>> *Performance indicator 1.8.5 with infused content—* Describe how conflict resolution skills reduce or prevent injuries and other adolescent health problems.[1,p25]

By linking the skill and content performance indicators, the teacher has direction in planning the lessons for the healthy behaviors unit.

The first step is to think through the unit by completing the performance task template. When finished, the teacher has a good idea of the lessons that precede this culminating activity, the information and back-up materials necessary to introduce the prompt to the students, and the assessment strategies.

When distributing the prompt, include all the back-up information, student worksheets, and holistic and analytical rubrics. Distribute the rubrics with the prompt so students know how they will be assessed before working on their product. The rubrics act as a guide and help the students attain proficiency in the standards.

Designing skills-based lessons requires considerable preparation, but once the teacher distributes the information and explains the task, the students are responsible for the results. Students learn with good coaching (formative assessments) how to demonstrate proficiency in content and skill.

The following is a performance task for a Grade 7 unit on healthy behaviors that focuses on conflict resolution.

The first section, for the teacher, demonstrates how to plan for an authentic assessment of the performance indicators 7.8.3 and 1.8.5. The second, the student's, extracts information from the performance task and transforms it into the student prompt and support materials.

Standard 7 Performance Task: Grade 7—Using Conflict Resolution Skills to Improve Interpersonal Relationships

I. Which state standard(s) does this performance task address?

II. Topic: What areas of health does this project assess? Why is it important? What is the focus of the project?[3,p237]

  A. This project assesses injury prevention and safety.

  B. This project is important because:

    1. 66.9% of middle school students have been a physical fight.

    2. 9.2% of middle school students have been injured as a result of being in a fight.[12]

    3. School-based violence prevention programs are effective at all levels and across different populations.[20,p8]

    4. Improved school function reduces delinquency and antisocial behavior.[20,p10]

  C. The project focuses on using conflict resolution skills to improve interpersonal relationships.

III. Key Concepts: What basic concepts should the students know?[3,p237]

  Standard 1—Students comprehend concepts related to health promotion and disease prevention to enhance health.[1,p25]

  Performance indicator 1.8.5 with infused content—Describe how conflict resolution skills reduce or prevent injuries and other adolescent health problems.[1p25]

  A. Bystanders

    1. Likelihood of verbal disputes increases when bystanders watch because disputants feel pressure to be tough, be superior, or defend their honor.

    2. By watching violence, bystanders are sending a message that it is acceptable.[21,p57]

    3. Instead of watching conflict, get help from trusted adults when it erupts.

  B. Values

    1. Values are beliefs that are important to us and guide our decisions.[8,p37]

    2. Positive values, such as honesty, integrity, friendship, reliability, loyalty, etc., usually lead to positive behavior.

    3. Negative values, such as lying, unreliability, disloyalty, etc., usually lead to negative behavior.

  C. Avoiding conflict

    1. Some conflicts are minor and easily avoided.

    2. Encourage disputants to resolve their conflict peacefully by speaking for themselves rather than fighting.

    3. Get adult help if a conflict becomes violent.

    4. Avoid remaining where conflict becomes violent. Get help.[8,p205]

IV. Skills: Which of the seven National Health Education Standards does this performance task address?[3,p237]

  Standard 7—Students will demonstrate the ability to practice health-enhancing behaviors and avoid or reduce health risks.[1,p35]

  Performance indicator 7.8.3 with infused content—Demonstrate behaviors, such as conflict resolution, that avoid or reduce health risks to self and others.[1,p35]

(continues)

A. Take time out before trying to negotiate.
  1. Wait up to 30 minutes to cool off.
  2. Negotiate when emotions are under control.
B. Allow each person time to explain without interruption his or her point of view.
  1. Use "I" messages when explaining feelings and desires.
  2. Avoid "You" messages because they are aggressive and may escalate the situation.
  3. Do not use words or gestures that anger the other person.
C. Allow each person to ask questions of the other.
D. Brainstorm the pros and cons of three different ideas that provide a good solution for each participant.[8,p207]
E. Ask for adult help, if necessary.
  1. Check on the progress of the agreed upon solution.
  2. Check on the status of the relationship of the disputants.

V. Curricula connections: What other subject areas does this project support?[3,p237]
  English language arts
  Art

VI. Student directions and assessment criteria[3,p238]
  Prompt #1
  A. Project Description—Write and attach an engaging prompt that draws the student into the project.[3,p238]

  The lab at the Arondale Middle School contains 30 computers. They are in use before school, throughout the day, and after school until the late bus arrives.

  Jeremy's research paper is due tomorrow, and he has a lot of work to do to finish it on time. Because his computer at home is broken, he signed up to use a computer after school. When he got to his assigned station, another student was there. Jeremy told the student, "That's assigned to me. Get up." The other student refused and said, "I'm in the middle of my paper and need to finish it."[19,p5]

  Jeremy got angry and pulled the student out of the seat. The other student pushed Jeremy, and before they knew it, both were fighting.

  The computer lab monitor broke up the fight and brought the boys to the vice-principal's office. Each blamed the other, and nothing was resolved. They left school angry.

  B. Your Challenge—Provide a challenge or mission statement that describes the project.[3,p238]

  Your challenge is to help Jeremy improve his relationship with the other student by using conflict resolution to resolve their differences.

  Prompt #2
  A. Project Description—Write and attach an engaging prompt that draws the student into the project.[3,p238]

  Chris and Ralph have been friends for a long time. They have the same interests and usually spend Friday nights together.

  On Friday afternoon, another friend asked Chris to come to a party at his house that night. Chris was glad to be invited, so he said, "Yes." Later in the afternoon, Ralph told Chris that his mom had rented a movie for them to watch that night.[19,p5]

  When Chris told Ralph he was going to a party at the house of another friend, Ralph became angry. He got face-to-face with Chris and yelled at him. For the rest of the day, Ralph would not talk to Chris.

  B. Your Challenge—Provide a challenge or mission statement that describes the project.[3,p238]

  Your challenge is to help Chris improve his relationship with Ralph by using conflict resolution to resolve their differences.

(continues)

C. Assessment criteria[3,p239]

You are assessed on the following content:

Performance indicator 1.8.5 with infused content—Describe how conflict resolution skills reduce or prevent injuries and other adolescent health problems.[1,p25]

1. Describe one hazard and one benefit of bystander behavior.
2. Describe one reason why positive values help resolve conflict.
3. Describe two ways to avoid conflict.

You are assessed on the following skill:

Performance indicator 7.8.3 with infused content—Demonstrate behaviors, such as conflict resolution, that avoid or reduce health risks to self and others.[1,p35]

1. Take up to 30 minutes to cool off before trying to resolve the conflict.
2. Each person presents his point of view by using "I" messages.
3. Ask clarifying questions of the other person. Use "I" messages, not "you" messages so that the conflict does not escalate.
4. Brainstorm three solutions along with the pros and cons of each.
5. State the solution.[8,p207]
6. A peer counselor or adult follows up by checking on the progress of reaching the solution and the status of the relationship between the disputants.

Student project

1. Complete the conflict resolution worksheet for each prompt.
2. Prepare a PowerPoint presentation or a poster explaining how conflict resolution skills reduce or prevent injuries and other adolescent health problems.
3. Role-play or write a comic book showing how to resolve the conflict in the prompt by using conflict resolution skills.

Arondale Middle School

Name _____

Prompt #1

The lab at the Arondale Middle School contains 30 computers. They are in use before school, throughout the day, and after school until the late bus arrives.

Jeremy's research paper is due tomorrow, and he has a lot of work to do to finish it on time. Because his computer at home is broken, he signed up to use a computer after school. When he got to his assigned station, another student was there. Jeremy told the student, "That's assigned to me. Get up." The other student refused and said, "I'm in the middle of my paper and need to finish it."[19]

Jeremy got angry and pulled the student out of the seat. The other student pushed Jeremy, and, before they knew it, both were fighting.

The computer lab monitor broke up the fight and brought the boys to the vice-principal's office. Each blamed the other, and nothing was resolved. They left school angry.

Your challenge is to help Jeremy improve his relationship with the other student by using conflict resolution to resolve their differences.

(continues)

Prompt #2

Chris and Ralph have been friends for a long time. They have the same interests and usually spend Friday nights together.

On Friday afternoon, another friend asks Chris to come to a party at his house that night. Chris was glad to be invited so he said, "Yes." Later in the afternoon, Ralph told Chris his mom had rented a movie for them to watch that night.[19,p5]

Chris told Ralph he was going to a party at the house of another friend. Ralph was very angry. He got face-to-face with Chris and started yelling at him. For the rest of the day, he would not talk to Chris.

Your challenge is to help Chris improve his relationship with Ralph by using conflict resolution to resolve their differences.

Your project must contain the following:

1. Complete a conflict resolution worksheet for each prompt.

2. Design and present a PowerPoint or poster explaining how conflict resolution skills reduce or prevent injuries and other adolescent health problems. Each slide/criteria must contain two pictures.

3. Choose one of the prompts, then design and present a role-play, or write and read a comic book, showing how to resolve the conflict in the prompt by using conflict resolution skills.

ASSESSMENT MATERIALS

Conflict Resolution Skill Worksheet (Table 11.9)

TABLE 11.9   Grades 6–8 Conflict Resolution Worksheet

Conflict Resolution Skills

Time – Take time (up to 30 minutes or more) to cool off.

Allow – Allow each person to present his or her point of view uninterrupted. Use "I" messages to own the feelings and defuse the situation.

Let – Let each person ask the other one questions.

1. Responder should use "I" messages.

2. Avoid "you" messages because they are aggressive and may escalate the situation.

3. Do not use words or gestures that anger the other person.

(continues)

TABLE 11.9   Grades 6–8 Conflict Resolution Worksheet *(continued)*

Keep – Keep brainstorming solutions. Discuss the pros
and cons of each solution.[8,p207]

Solution #1

    Pros _____

    Cons _____

Solution #2

    Pros _____

    Cons _____

Solution #3

    Pros _____

    Cons _____

Be Open to Compromise

Solution – State the solution to which both students agree

If monitored by an adult or peer conflict counselor,
follow up by checking the:

1. Progress of reaching the solution

2. Status of the relationship

*Analytical Rubric to Assess a Poster or PowerPoint Presentation on How Conflict Resolution Skills
Reduce or Prevent Injuries and Other Adolescent Health Problems (Table 11.10)*

**TABLE 11.10   Grade 7 Analytical Rubric to Assess a Poster or PowerPoint Presentation
on How Conflict Resolution Skills Reduce or Prevent Injuries and Other Adolescent Health
Problems**

Criteria	4	3	2	1
Performance indicator 1.8.5 with infused content—Describe how conflict resolution skills reduce or prevent injuries and other adolescent health problems.[1,p25]	Student thoroughly describes one hazard of bystander behavior.	Student adequately describes one hazard of bystander behavior.	Student inadequately describes one hazard of bystander behavior.	Student poorly describes one hazard of bystander behavior.

(continues)

TABLE 11.10   Grade 7 Analytical Rubric to Assess a Poster or PowerPoint Presentation on How Conflict Resolution Skills Reduce or Prevent Injuries and Other Adolescent Health Problems *(continued)*

Criteria	4	3	2	1
Performance indicator 1.8.5 with infused content—Describe how conflict resolution skills reduce or prevent injuries and other adolescent health problems.[1,p25]	Student thoroughly describes one benefit of bystander behavior.	Student adequately describes one benefit of bystander behavior.	Student inadequately describes one benefit of bystander behavior.	Student poorly describes one benefit of bystander behavior.
Performance indicator 1.8.5 with infused content—Describe how conflict resolution skills reduce or prevent injuries and other adolescent health problems.[1,p25]	Student thoroughly describes one reason why positive values help resolve conflict.	Student adequately describes one reason why positive values help resolve conflict.	Student inadequately describes one reason why positive values help resolve conflict.	Student poorly describes one reason why positive values help resolve conflict.
Performance indicator 1.8.5 with infused content—Describe how conflict resolution skills reduce or prevent injuries and other adolescent health problems.[1,p25]	Student thoroughly describes two ways to avoid conflict.	Student adequately describes two ways to avoid conflict.	Student inadequately describes two ways to avoid conflict.	Student poorly describes two ways to avoid conflict.
Pictures	The two pictures per slide/criteria are appropriate.	The two pictures per slide/criteria are mostly appropriate.	One of the two pictures per slide/criteria is inappropriate.	The two pictures per slide/criteria are mostly inappropriate.
Grammar	The grammar is always correct.	The grammar is sometimes correct.	The grammar is rarely correct.	The grammar is never correct.
Spelling	The spelling is always correct.	The spelling is sometimes correct.	The spelling is rarely correct.	The spelling is never correct.
Creativity	The creativity is excellent.	The creativity is good.	The creativity is fair.	The creativity is poor.

Name _____

Total possible points – 32   Your points – _____   Your grade – _____

(continues)

Analytical Rubric for the Conflict Resolution Role-Play (Table 11.11)

Players – Two disputants and one adult or peer counselor who moves the process from step to step.

TABLE 11.11   Grade 7 Analytical Rubric to Assess the Conflict Resolution Role-Play

Criteria	4	3	2	1
Performance indicator 7.8.3 with infused content—Demonstrate behaviors, such as conflict resolution, that avoid or reduce health risks to self and others.[1,p35]	Student's encouragement to take at least 30 minutes to cool off is excellent.	Student's encouragement to take at least 30 minutes to cool off is good.	Student's encouragement to take at least 30 minutes to cool off is fair.	Student's encouragement to take at least 30 minutes to cool off is poor.
Performance indicator 7.8.3 with infused content—Demonstrate behaviors, such as conflict resolution, that avoid or reduce health risks to self and others.[1,p35]	Student consistently presents a point of view using "I" messages.	Student usually presents a point of view using "I" messages.	Student rarely presents a point of view using "I" messages.	Student never presents a point of view using "I" messages.
Performance indicator 7.8.3 with infused content—Demonstrate behaviors, such as conflict resolution, that avoid or reduce health risks to self and others.[1,p35]	Student does an excellent job of asking clarifying questions.	Student does a good job of asking clarifying questions.	Student does a fair job of asking clarifying questions.	Student does a poor job of asking clarifying questions.
Performance indicator 7.8.3 with infused content—Demonstrate behaviors, such as conflict resolution, that avoid or reduce health risks to self and others.[1,p35]	Student consistently uses "I" messages when talking to the other disputant.	Student usually uses "I" messages when talking to the other disputant.	Student sometimes uses "I" messages when talking to the other disputant.	Student never uses "I" messages when talking to the other disputant.
Performance indicator 7.8.3 with infused content—Demonstrate behaviors, such as conflict resolution, that avoid or reduce health risks to self and others.[1,p35]	Student accurately weighs the pros and cons of three solutions.	Student's weighing of the pros and cons of three solutions is mostly accurate.	Student's weighing of the pros and cons of three solutions has a few inaccuracies.	Student's weighing of the pros and cons of three solutions is mostly inaccurate.
Performance indicator 7.8.3 with infused content—Demonstrate behaviors, such as conflict resolution, that avoid or reduce health risks to self and others.[1,p35]	Student accurately states the agreed upon solution.	Student's statement of the agreed upon solution is mostly accurate.	Student's statement of the agreed upon solution has a few inaccuracies.	Student's statement of the agreed upon solution is mostly inaccurate.

(continues)

TABLE 11.11   Grade 7 Analytical Rubric to Assess the Conflict Resolution Role-Play *(continued)*

Criteria	4	3	2	1
Performance indicator 7.8.3 with infused content—Demonstrate behaviors, such as conflict resolution, that avoid or reduce health risks to self and others.[1,p35]	Adult or peer counselor thoroughly follows up to check on the progress of the solution and the status of the relationship.	Adult or peer counselor adequately follows up to check on the progress of the solution and the status of the relationship.	Adult or peer counselor inadequately follows up to check on the progress of the solution and the status of the relationship.	Adult or peer counselor's follow-up to check on the progress of the solution and the status of the relationship is poor.
Participation	Student participation in the role-play is excellent.	Student participation in the role-play is good.	Student participation in the role-play is fair.	Student participation in the role-play is poor.

Name _____

Total possible points – 32   Your points – _____   Your grade – _____

Analytical Rubric to Assess the Conflict Resolution Comic Book (Table 11.12)

TABLE 11.12   Grade 7 Analytical Rubric to Assess the Conflict Resolution Comic Book

Criteria	4	3	2	1
Performance indicator 7.8.3 with infused content—Demonstrate behaviors, such as conflict resolution, that avoid or reduce health risks to self and others.[1,p35]	Encouragement to take at least 30 minutes to cool off is excellent.	Encouragement to take at least 30 minutes to cool off is good.	Encouragement to take at least 30 minutes to cool off is fair.	Encouragement to take at least 30 minutes to cool off is poor.
Performance indicator 7.8.3 with infused content—Demonstrate behaviors, such as conflict resolution, that avoid or reduce health risks to self and others.[1,p35]	Characters consistently present a point of view using "I" messages.	Characters usually present a point of view using "I" messages.	Characters rarely present a point of view using "I" messages.	Characters never present a point of view using "I" messages.
Performance indicator 7.8.3 with infused content—Demonstrate behaviors, such as conflict resolution, that avoid or reduce health risks to self and others.[1,p35]	Characters do an excellent job of asking clarifying questions.	Characters do a good job of asking clarifying questions.	Characters do a fair job of asking clarifying questions.	Characters do a poor job of asking clarifying questions.

(continues)

TABLE 11.12   Grade 7 Analytical Rubric to Assess the Conflict Resolution Comic Book *(continued)*

Criteria	4	3	2	1
Performance indicator 7.8.3 with infused content—Demonstrate behaviors, such as conflict resolution, that avoid or reduce health risks to self and others.[1,p35]	Characters consistently use "I" messages when talking to the other disputant.	Characters usually use "I" messages when talking to the other disputant.	Characters sometimes use "I" messages when talking to the other disputant.	Characters never use "I" messages when talking to the other disputant.
Performance indicator 7.8.3 with infused content—Demonstrate behaviors, such as conflict resolution, that avoid or reduce health risks to self and others.[1,p35]	Characters accurately weigh the pros and cons of three solutions.	Character's weighing of the pros and cons of three solutions is mostly accurate.	Character's weighing of the pros and cons of three solutions has a few inaccuracies.	Character's weighing of the pros and cons of three solutions is mostly inaccurate.
Performance indicator 7.8.3 with infused content—Demonstrate behaviors, such as conflict resolution, that avoid or reduce health risks to self and others.[1,p35]	Characters accurately state the agreed upon solution.	Character's statement of the agreed upon solution is mostly accurate.	Character's statement of the agreed upon solution has a few inaccuracies.	Character's statement of the agreed upon solution is mostly inaccurate.
Performance indicator 7.8.3 with infused content—Demonstrate behaviors, such as conflict resolution, that avoid or reduce health risks to self and others.[1,p35]	Adult or peer counselor character thoroughly follows up to check on the progress of the solution and the status of the relationship.	Adult or peer counselor character adequately follows up to check on the progress of the solution and the status of the relationship.	Adult or peer counselor character inadequately follows up to check on the progress of the solution and the status of the relationship.	Adult or peer counselor character's follow-up to check on the progress of the solution and the status of the relationship is poor.
Creativity	The creativity of the comic book is excellent.	The creativity of the comic book is good.	The creativity of the comic book is fair.	The creativity of the comic book is poor.

Name _____

Total possible points – 32   Your points – _____   Your grade – _____

HOW THE COORDINATED SCHOOL HEALTH TEAM HELPS STUDENTS PRACTICE HEALTHY BEHAVIORS AND AVOID OR REDUCE HEALTH RISKS

Health Education

- Teach conflict resolution skills and how they reduce or prevent injuries and other adolescent health problems.
- Model conflict resolution.

Physical Education

- Teach conflict resolution skills and how they reduce or prevent injuries and other adolescent health problems.
- Model conflict resolution.

Health Services

- Encourage disputing students to manage their conflict peacefully.

- Refer disputing students to a peer counselor or a trained adult.

Nutrition Services

- Provide promotional materials that encourage students to resolve conflict in a healthy way.
- Encourage students to eat breakfast and lunch to avoid hunger and manage emotions better.

Counseling, Psychological, and Social Services

- Model conflict resolution.
- Refer disputing students to a peer counselor or a trained adult.

Healthy School Environment

- Set a school improvement goal to have a safe, violence-free school environment.[21,p59]
- Develop and implement a policy on violence prevention that enforces a protocol for responding to reports of potential violence, including protecting the reporter.[21,p59]

Health Promotion for Staff

- Provide training in conflict resolution.
- Model healthy ways to resolve conflict.

Family and Community Involvement

- Provide a 24-hour hotline to report potential school violence.[21,p59]
- Provide conflict resolution training to enhance family life and reinforce healthy behaviors.

Grades 9–12

To achieve proficiency in Standard 7, Grade 9–12 students must learn to analyze the role of the individual in enhancing health, exhibit a variety of health practices and behaviors that maintain or improve health, and demonstrate a variety of behaviors that avoid or reduce health risks.

To teach Standard 7, explain why it is important to have healthy behaviors, and how this skill relates to the other National Health Education Standards.

According to the performance indicators chosen, present and explain how to reach proficiency in the skill. Model the skill so the students can see it in action. Provide adequate time for the students to practice the skill and show proficiency through an authentic assessment. Use formative assessments (Chapter 4) to provide feedback and encouragement and improve instruction.

For example:

Shana is a junior at Gateway High School and is always tired. She sometimes falls asleep in class. Shana stays up after 11:00 p.m. to complete homework, but earlier in the evening spends too much time on the Internet and on the phone talking to friends. She is getting only six hours of sleep instead of the nine she needs.[22,p225]

Her health teacher, Ms. Tratiano, noticed that many of her students were tired. She researched the topic and found that inadequate sleep leads to stress and increases the risk of being overweight.[22,p224]

Ms. Tratiano challenged her students to record the number of hours they sleep, their academic performance and feelings, and what they eat for breakfast and lunch (**Figure 11.3**).

Ms. Tratiano then asked the students to discuss the relationship between their sleep, behavior, and food choices. When the students saw the connection, the teacher issued a challenge: "Repeat the experiment using time management skills and healthy sleep behaviors."

She recommended the students manage their time better by completing homework and socializing early. "When schoolwork is finished, put all the materials for the next day in your backpack and put the bag by the door for a quick and easy exit. Get to bed by 9:00 p.m. and get up at 6:00 a.m. so there is time for breakfast, grooming, and time with family."

The results were dramatic! The students felt refreshed, performed better in school, got along with their family and friends, and made smarter food choices!

To reflect, ask the students:

- How many hours of sleep do you need? *(Nine hours)*
- What are two consequences of not getting enough sleep? *(Stress and becoming overweight)*
- What healthy behavior changes did the students make? (PI 7.12.1, 7.12.2) *(Complete homework and socializing with friends early, pack bag and place it by the door, get to bed by 9:00 p.m., get up at 6:00 a.m., have breakfast, and spend time with family.)*

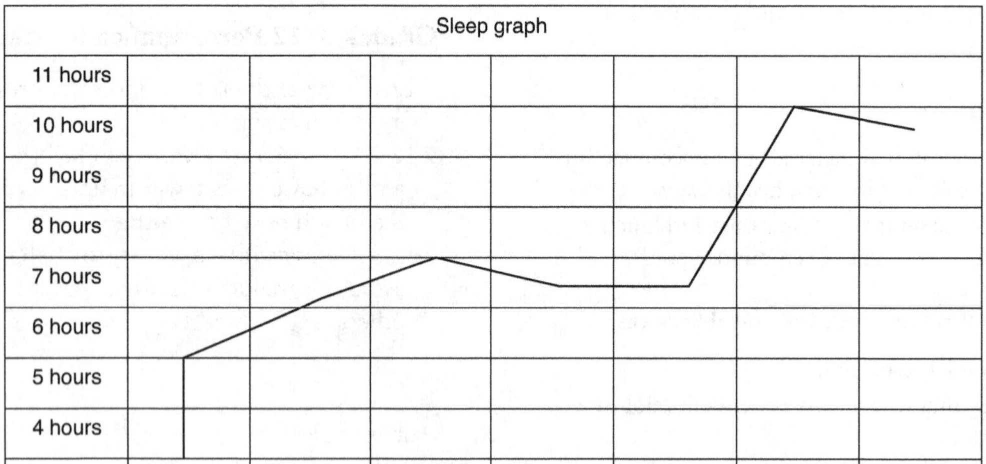

Sleep graph							
11 hours							
10 hours							
9 hours							
8 hours							
7 hours							
6 hours							
5 hours							
4 hours							
	Monday	Tuesday	Wednesday	Thursday	Friday	Saturday	Sunday
School	Grumpy.	Very grumpy.	Very tired.	Stressed and irritable.	Can't wait to go home to sleep.	Slept late.	Slept late.
	Can't concentrate. [22,p225]	Low quiz grade	Forgot homework.	Fought with friend over something stupid. [22,p225]	Don't want to do anything. [22,p225]	Feel good.	Feel good.
			Impulsively left school early. [22,p225]			Caught up with school work.	
Food log	Fast food breakfast.	Late, no breakfast.	Bagel for the bus.	Late, no breakfast.	Toast for breakfast.	Pancakes for breakfast.	Waffles for breakfast.
	Junk food snacks.	Fries for lunch.	Hamburger and fries for lunch.	Granola bar for the bus.	Grilled cheese for lunch.	Ham and cheese for lunch.	Sub for lunch.

FIGURE 11.3   One-Week Sleep Graph, Behaviors, and Food Intake

- What were the results of the changes? *(The students felt refreshed, performed better in school, got along with their family and friends, and made smarter food choices!)*

As the students are learning the skill, provide enough time for them to practice. Use formative assessments to determine the progress of learning. Motivate students by using feedback to show how performance improves.

When students demonstrate understanding of the skill, teach the content. Design a prompt that allows them to display their knowledge of health. Use formative assessments, such as white boards (Chapter 4), during content instruction to determine student understanding.

WHAT DOES THE SKILL OF PRACTICING HEALTHY BEHAVIORS LOOK LIKE IN THE GRADE 12 CLASSROOM?

Mr. Hanson, the guidance counselor at Halsey High School, works with seniors to gather all the documents needed to apply to college. Every year, seniors seem increasingly stressed about academics, family, leaving high school, peers, extra curricular activities, and responsibilities. [23,p942]

At the first coordinated school health team meeting, Mr. Hanson asked the team to design a stress management program that would help all students cope better with stress. Mrs. Barnes and Mr. Whitely, the wellness teachers, volunteered to coordinate instruction to include information about stress and stress management and then practice the skills in physical education class. They also agreed to hold before and after-school yoga sessions for students and staff.

To begin planning the practicing healthy behaviors unit, they choose the performance indicators for Standard 7 that meet the needs of the students.

> Standard 7—Students will demonstrate the ability to practice health-enhancing behaviors and avoid or reduce health risks. [1,p35]

7.12.3—Demonstrate a variety of healthy practices and behaviors that will maintain or improve the health of self and others.[1,p35]

Performance indicator 7.12.3 with infused content— Demonstrate a variety of healthy practices and behaviors, such as stress management, that will maintain or improve the health of self and others.[1,p35]

After selecting the appropriate performance indicator for the skill, Mrs. Condon chooses the performance indicator for Standard 1.

Standard 1—Students will comprehend concepts related to health promotion and disease prevention to enhance health.[1,p25]

1.12.3—Analyze how environment and personal health are interrelated.[1,p25]

Performance indicator 1.12.3 with infused content— Analyze how stressors in the environment are related to personal health.[1,p25]

By linking the skill and content performance indicators, the teacher has direction in planning the lessons for a practicing healthy behaviors unit.

The first step is to think through the unit by completing the performance task template. Thereupon, the teacher will have a good idea of the lessons that precede this culminating activity, the information and back-up materials necessary to introduce the prompt to the students, and the assessment strategies.

When distributing the prompt, include all the back-up information, student worksheets, and holistic and analytical rubrics. Distribute the rubrics with the prompt so students know how they will be assessed before working on their product. The rubrics act as a guide and help the students attain proficiency in the standards.

Designing the performance task takes considerable preparation, but once the information is distributed and explained, the students create a product by themselves or in a group. Students learn with good coaching (formative assessment) how to demonstrate proficiency in both content and skill.

The following is an example of a practicing healthy behaviors performance task for Grade 12. The focus is stress management.

The first section is for the teacher and demonstrates how to plan for an authentic assessment of the performance indicators 1.12.3, and 7.12.3. The second, the student's, extracts some of the information from the performance task and transforms it into the student prompt and support materials.

Standard 7 Performance Task: Grade 12—Using Healthy Behaviors to Manage Stress

I. Which state standard(s) does this performance task address?

II. Topic: What areas of health does this project assess? Why is it important? What is the focus of the project?[3,p237]

A. This performance task assesses the health area of mental health.

B. This topic is important because:

1. Adolescents whose strategies to cope with stress are ineffective may develop mental health problems.

2. School is rated as one of the greatest stressors for high school students.

3. Peer pressure, romantic relationships, and parents are common sources of stress for high school students.[23,p926-928]

C. The focus of the project is to help students learn how to use healthy behaviors to reduce stress.

III. Key Concepts: What basic concepts do students need to know?[3,p237]

Standard 1—Students will comprehend concepts related to health promotion and disease prevention to enhance health.[1,p25]

*Performance indicator 1.12.3 with infused content—*Analyze how stressors in the environment are related to personal health.[1,p25]

A. Stress

1. The body's reaction to everyday challenges and demands[24,p92]

2. *Eustress* is stress that results from pleasant events or conditions.

3. *Distress* is stress that results from unpleasant events or conditions.[25,p51]

(continues)

B. Stress response
   1. Alarm stage
      a. Body prepares to stand and fight or to flee.
      b. Effect on the body
         1. Muscles tense.
         2. Heart beats faster.
         3. Adrenaline is released.
         4. Breathing becomes shallow and rapid.
         5. Pupils dilate.[25,p54]
   2. Resistance stage
      a. Body tries to return to a state of equilibrium.
      b. Use stress management to return to equilibrium.
      c. Withdraw from the stressful situation.
      d. To protect self from stress, block emotional responses, deny the situation, and withdraw or isolate self from the stressor.[25,p54]
   3. Exhaustion stage
      a. The body is recovering from stress.
      b. Effects
         1. Fatigue.
         2. Cannot manage stress effectively any longer.[24,p94]
C. Effects of on-going stress
   1. Headache
   2. Weakened immune system
   3. High blood pressure
   4. Clenching the jaw
   5. Grinding teeth
   6. Digestive disorders[24,p95]
IV. Skills: Which of the seven National Health Education Skills does this performance task address?[3,p237]
   Standard 7—Students will demonstrate the ability to practice health-enhancing behaviors and avoid or reduce health risks.[1,p35]
   Performance indicator 7.12.3 with infused content—Demonstrate a variety of healthy practices and behaviors, such as stress management, that will maintain or improve the health of self and others.[1,p35]
A. Physical aspects
   1. Sleep
      a. Get nine hours of sleep per night.
      b. Go to bed every night at the same time and get up at the same time.
      c. Relax before it is time for bed by taking a bath, reading a book, or listening to calming music.
      d. Avoid caffeine and exercise before bedtime.
      e. Do not nap during the day.[25,p63]
   2. Exercise
      a. Be physically active for at least 60 minutes each day.[26]
      b. Breathe deeply during exercise to reduce stress.
      c. Endorphins released during exercise reduce stress.[25,p63]
   3. Nutrition
      a. Eat a variety of nutritious foods in the correct portion size.
      b. Drink plenty of water.[24,p101]
B. Psychological aspects
   1. Deep breathing to the count of four
      a. Breathe in 2, 3, 4
      b. Hold breath 2, 3, 4

(continues)

      c. Breathe out 2, 3, 4

      d. Relax.

   2. Progressive relaxation

      a. Assume a comfortable position.

      b. Inhale for four counts.

      c. Contract specific muscle groups (forehead to toes) to the count of four.

      d. Exhale and relax the muscle group to the count of four.[25,p66]

   3. Guided imagery

      a. Assume a comfortable position.

      b. Breathe deeply.

      c. Relax muscles.

      d. Imagine a pleasant scene.

      e. Imagine the smells, touch, taste, and sounds that go with it.[25,p67]

C. Cognitive aspects

   1. Manage time by using a planner.

   2. Set goals.

   3. Think positively.

   4. Do not procrastinate.

   5. Try not to be a perfectionist.[25,p68-69]

V. Curricular connections: What other subject areas does this project support?[3,p237]

   English language arts

   Biology

   Art

VI. Student Directions and Assessment Criteria[3,p238]

Prompt #1

A. Project Description—Write and attach an engaging prompt that draws the student into the project.[3,p238]

   Brian is still working on his senior essay for his college application. He is tired all the time and cannot seem to finish the essay.

      He works after school and on weekends and plays on the community sports teams.

      His heart frequently races and he seems to be breathing fast all the time.

      Recently, Brian is eating a lot of fast food and junk food because he is always in a hurry. He is gaining weight and he does not like it.

      Brian knows he is stressed but does not know what to do.

B. Your Challenge—Provide a challenge or mission statement that describes the project.[3,p238]

   Your challenge is to help Brian use healthy coping strategies to manage his stress.

Prompt #2

A. Project Description—Write and attach an engaging prompt that draws the student into the project.[3,p238]

   Anna is a senior and is stressed out. She argues with her parents constantly and spends considerable time at her friend's house. She wants to break up with her boyfriend without hurting his feelings. Since being accepted to college, she has let her grades slip and is afraid the college will rescind. Anna took on more hours at work and is too tired now to do her homework or study for tests.

      She has a constant headache, and her jaw hurts from grinding her teeth together.

B. Your Challenge—Provide a challenge or mission statement that describes the project.[3,p238]

   Your challenge is to help Anna use healthy coping strategies to cope with her stress.

C. Assessment Criteria[3,p239]

You will be assessed on the following content:

Performance indicator 1.12.3 with infused content—Analyze how the stressors in the environment are related to personal health.[1,p25]

(continues)

1. Name three facts about stress.
2. Describe the stress response and include two facts about how each stage affects the body.
3. List three effects of chronic stress on the body.

You will be assessed on the following skills:

Performance indicator 7.12.3 with infused content—Demonstrate a variety of healthy practices and behaviors, such as stress management, that will maintain or improve the health of self and others.[1,p35]

1. Provide three facts each about how sleep, exercise, and nutrition reduce stress.
2. Explain four facts each about deep breathing, progressive relaxation, and guided imagery.
3. Explain four cognitive things you can do to reduce stress.

Your project consists of:

1. A graphic organizer that explains stress, stress response, and the effects of chronic stress
2. A brochure that explains how to manage the physical, psychological, and cognitive aspects of stress
3. Demonstration of two stress management strategies

Halsey High School

Name _____

Prompt #1

Brian is still working on his senior essay for his college application. He is tired all the time and cannot seem to finish the essay.

He works after school and on weekends and plays on the community sports teams.

His heart frequently races and he seems to be breathing fast all the time.

Recently, Brian is eating a lot of fast food and junk food because he is always in a hurry. He is gaining weight and he does not like it.

Brian knows he is stressed but does not know what to do.

Your challenge is to help Brian use healthy coping strategies to manage his stress.

Prompt #2

Anna is a senior and is stressed out. She argues with her parents constantly and spends considerable time at her friend's house. She wants to break up with her boyfriend without hurting his feelings. Since being accepted to college, she has let her grades slip and is afraid the college will rescind. Anna took on more hours at work and is too tired now to do her homework or study for tests.

She has a constant headache, and her jaw hurts from grinding her teeth together.

Your challenge is to help Anna use healthy coping strategies to cope with her stress.

Your project consists of:

1. A graphic organizer that explains stress, stress response, and the effects of on-going stress. Each section must contain two pictures.

2. A brochure that explains how to manage the physical, psychological, and cognitive aspects of stress. Each section must contain three pictures.

3. Demonstration of two stress management strategies

(continues)

Graphic Organizer That Explains Stress, Stress Response, and the Effects of Ongoing Stress

Halsey High School

Name _____

Directions: Design a graphic organizer similar to the example below (**Figure 11.4**). Include stress, stress response, and effects of on-going stress, plus:

1. Three facts about stress

2. A description of the stress response and two facts about how each stage affects the body

3. Three effects of chronic stress on the body

4. Each section must contain two pictures.

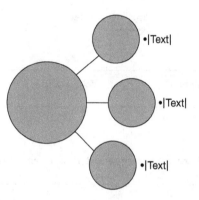

FIGURE 11.4   **Graphic Organizer that Explains Stress, Stress Response, and the Effects of Ongoing Stress**

Analytical Rubric to Assess the Stress Graphic Organizer (Table 11.13)

TABLE 11.13   Grade 12 Analytical Rubric to Assess the Stress Graphic Organizer

Criteria	4	3	2	1
Performance indicator 1.12.3 with infused content—Analyze how stressors in the environment are related to personal health.[1,p25]	Student accurately analyzes three facts about stress.	Student's analyzation of three facts about stress is mostly accurate.	Student's analyzation of three facts about stress has a few inaccuracies.	Student's analyzation of three facts about stress is mostly inaccurate.
Performance indicator 1.12.3 with infused content—Analyze how stressors in the environment are related to personal health.[1,p25]	Student thoroughly analyzes the stress response and two facts about each stage.	Student adequately analyzes the stress response and two facts about each stage.	Student inadequately analyzes the stress response and two facts about each stage.	Student poorly analyzes the stress response and two facts about each stage.

(continues)

TABLE 11.13   Grade 12 Analytical Rubric to Assess the Stress Graphic Organizer *(continued)*

Criteria	4	3	2	1
Performance indicator 1.12.3 with infused content—Analyze how stressors in the environment are related to personal health.[1,p25]	Student accurately analyzes three effects of ongoing stress.	Student's analyzation of three effects of ongoing stress is mostly accurate.	Student's analyzation of three effects of ongoing stress has a few inaccuracies.	Student's analyzation of three effects of ongoing stress is mostly inaccurate.
Picture	Student's selection of two pictures per section is appropriate.	Student's selection of two pictures per section is mostly appropriate.	One of the selected pictures is inappropriate.	Student's selection of two pictures per section is mostly inappropriate.
Spelling	Spelling is always correct.	Spelling is usually correct.	Spelling is sometimes correct.	Spelling is never correct.

Name _____

Total possible points – 20   Your points – _____   Your grade – _____

Analytical Rubric to Assess the Stress Management Brochure (Table 11.14)

TABLE 11.14   Grade 12 Analytical Rubric to Assess the Stress Management Brochure

Physical Aspects of Stress Management

Criteria	4	3	2	1
Performance indicator 7.12.3 with infused content—Demonstrate a variety of healthy practices and behaviors, such as stress management, that will maintain or improve the health of self and others.[1,p35]	Student thoroughly demonstrates three ways sleep reduces stress.	Student adequately demonstrates three ways sleep reduces stress.	Student inadequately demonstrates three ways sleep reduces stress.	Student poorly demonstrates three ways sleep reduces stress.
Performance indicator 7.12.3 with infused content—Demonstrate a variety of healthy practices and behaviors, such as stress management, that will maintain or improve the health of self and others.[1,p35]	Student thoroughly demonstrates three ways exercise reduces stress.	Student adequately demonstrates three ways exercise reduces stress.	Student inadequately demonstrates three ways exercise reduces stress.	Student poorly demonstrates three ways exercise reduces stress.

(continues)

TABLE 11.14   Grade 12 Analytical Rubric to Assess the Stress Management Brochure *(continued)*

Criteria	4	3	2	1
*Performance indicator 7.12.3 with infused content—*Demonstrate a variety of healthy practices and behaviors, such as stress management, that will maintain or improve the health of self and others.[1,p35]	Student thoroughly demonstrates three ways nutrition reduces stress.	Student adequately demonstrates three ways nutrition reduces stress.	Student inadequately demonstrates three ways nutrition reduces stress.	Student poorly demonstrates three ways nutrition reduces stress.
	Psychological Aspects of Stress Management			
*Performance indicator 7.12.3 with infused content—*Demonstrate a variety of healthy practices and behaviors, such as stress management, that will maintain or improve the health of self and others.[1,p35]	Student accurately demonstrates the four-step process of deep breathing to reduce stress.	Student's demonstration of the four-step process of deep breathing to reduce stress is mostly accurate.	Student's demonstration of the four-step process of deep breathing to reduce stress has a few inaccuracies.	Student's demonstration of the four-step process of deep breathing to reduce stress is mostly inaccurate.
*Performance indicator 7.12.3 with infused content—*Demonstrate a variety of healthy practices and behaviors, such as stress management, that will maintain or improve the health of self and others.[1,p35]	Student accurately demonstrates the four-step process of progressive relaxation to reduce stress.	Student's demonstration of the four-step process of progressive relaxation to reduce stress is mostly accurate.	Student's demonstration of the four-step process of progressive relaxation to reduce stress has a few inaccuracies.	Student's demonstration of the four-step process of progressive relaxation to reduce stress is mostly inaccurate.
*Performance indicator 7.12.3 with infused content—*Demonstrate a variety of healthy practices and behaviors, such as stress management, that will maintain or improve the health of self and others.[1,p35]	Student accurately demonstrates the five-step process of guided imagery to reduce stress.	Student's demonstration of the five-step process of guided imagery to reduce stress is mostly accurate.	Student's demonstration of the five-step process of guided imagery to reduce stress has a few inaccuracies.	Student's demonstration of the five-step process of guided imagery to reduce stress is mostly inaccurate.

(continues)

TABLE 11.14   Grade 12 Analytical Rubric to Assess the Stress Management Brochure *(continued)*

Criteria	4	3	2	1
Cognitive Aspects of Stress Management				
Performance indicator 7.12.3 with infused content—Demonstrate a variety of healthy practices and behaviors, such as stress management, that will maintain or improve the health of self and others.[1,p35]	Student accurately demonstrates four cognitive strategies to reduce stress.	Student's demonstration of four cognitive strategies to reduce stress is mostly accurate.	Student's demonstration of four cognitive strategies to reduce stress has a few inaccuracies.	Student's demonstration of four cognitive strategies to reduce stress is mostly inaccurate.
Picture	Student's selection of three pictures per section is appropriate.	Student's selection of three pictures per section is mostly appropriate.	Some of three pictures in each section are inappropriate.	Student's selection of three pictures picture per section is mostly inappropriate.
Spelling	Spelling is always correct.	Spelling is usually correct.	Spelling is sometimes correct.	Spelling is never correct.

Name _____

Total possible points – 36   Your points – _____   Your grade – _____

Analytical Rubric to Assess the Stress Management Demonstration (Table 11.15)

TABLE 11.15   Grade 12 Analytical Rubric to Assess the Stress Management Demonstration

Deep Breathing and Progressive Relaxation or Guided Imagery

Criteria	4	3	2	1
Performance indicator 7.12.3 with infused content—Demonstrate a variety of healthy practices and behaviors, such as stress management, that will maintain or improve the health of self and others.[1,p35]	Student accurately demonstrates the four-step process of deep breathing to reduce stress.	Student's demonstration of the four-step process of deep breathing to reduce stress is mostly accurate.	Student's demonstration of the four-step process of deep breathing to reduce stress has a few inaccuracies.	Student's demonstration of the four-step process of deep breathing to reduce stress is mostly inaccurate.
Performance indicator 7.12.3 with infused content—Demonstrate a variety of healthy practices and behaviors, such as stress management, that will maintain or improve the health of self and others.[1,p35]	Student accurately demonstrates the four-step process of progressive relaxation or the five-step process of guided imagery to reduce stress.	Student's demonstration of the four-step process of progressive relaxation or the five-step process of guided imagery to reduce stress is mostly accurate.	Student's demonstration of the four-step process of progressive relaxation or the five-step process of guided imagery to reduce stress has a few inaccuracies.	Student's demonstration of the four-step process of progressive relaxation or the five-step process of guided imagery to reduce stress is mostly inaccurate.
Voice	Student always spoke clearly.	Student usually spoke clearly.	Student sometimes spoke clearly.	Student never spoke clearly.

Name _____

Total possible points – 12   Your points – _____   Your grade – _____

HOW THE COORDINATED SCHOOL HEALTH TEAM HELPS STUDENTS PRACTICE HEALTHY BEHAVIORS AND AVOID OR REDUCE HEALTH RISKS

Health Education

- Teach content and skills to manage stress.
- Model stress management strategies.

Physical Education

- Provide practice time for stress management strategies.
- Offer before and after-school yoga for students and staff.

Health Services

- Monitor student stress levels and refer students to stress management, if needed.
- Model stress management strategies.

Nutrition Services

- Encourage students to eat healthy as a stress management strategy.
- Provide a comfortable, social setting during lunch so students can relax and socialize to reduce stress.

Counseling, Psychological, and Social Services

- Monitor student stress levels and recommend stress management, when needed.
- Model stress management strategies.
- Provide stress management information for students, staff, and families.

Healthy School Environment

- Provide a comfortable, safe, caring environment that reduces stress.
- Hang posters that encourage students to recognize stress and cope with it in a healthy way.

Health Promotion for Staff

- Model stress management strategies.
- Participate in school programs to manage stress.

Family and Community Involvement

- Provide information and training on stress and stress management.
- Encourage families to take time to have fun together to reduce stress.
- Urge families to take meals together and communicate.

Review Questions

1. How does Standard 7, practicing healthy behaviors, differ from the other skills standards, which also encourage healthy behaviors?

2. Give one example of an appropriate performance task for each grade span.

3. Why is it important to model healthy behaviors?

4. What is the value of formative assessment to the student?

5. When infusing content into the performance indicator, why is it important not to change the indicator?

6. Why is it important to provide statistics when explaining why a topic is important?

7. Why is it important to plan interdisciplinary performance tasks?

8. Why are the performance indicator criteria listed on the analytical rubric?

9. If a district does not have data to prove student need, what other valid and reliable data can the teacher access for planning?

References

1. Joint Committee on National Health Education Standards. (2007). *National Health Education Standards, Second Edition, Achieving Excellence.* Atlanta, GA: American Cancer Society.

2. Bektas, M. O. (2008). Effect of Health Promotion Education on Presence of Positive Health Behaviors, Level of Anxiety and Self-Concept. *Social Behavior and Personality*, 36(5), 681–690.

3. CCSSO~SCASS Health Education Project. (2006). *Assessment Tools for School Health Education, Pre-service and In-service edition.* Santa Cruz, CA: ToucanEd, Inc.

4. American Cancer Society, American Diabetes Association, American Heart Association. (n.d.). *Health Education in Schools–The Importance of Establishing Healthy Behaviors in Our Nation's Youth.* Retrieved April 5, 2010, from: http://www.ncaahperd.org/pdf/health.pdf. p. 1.

5. Scholastic. (2009). *Good Health Manners (Grades 1–3).* Retrieved April 6, 2010, from: http://content.scholastic.com/browse/lessonplan.jsp?id=601&print=2

6. Vessey, J. A. (2007). Comparing Hand Washing to Hand Sanitizers in Reducing Elementary School Students' Absenteeism. *Pediatric Nursing*, 33(4), 368–372.

7. WebMD. (2005-2010). *Drugs & Medications - Neosporin Top.* Retrieved April 6, 2010, from: http://www.webmd.com/drugs/mono-9275

8. Bronson, P. M. (2007). *Teen Health, Course 2.* New York: McGraw-Hill Glencoe.

9. Centers for Disease Control and Prevention. (April 27, 2009). *CDC Features Wash Your Hands.* Retrieved Decem-

ber 20, 2009, from: http://www.cdc.gov/Features/Hand Washing/p1

10. Centers for Disease Control and Prevention. (n.d.). *Cover Your Cough.* Retrieved April 6, 2010, from: http://www.cdc.gov/flu/protect/pdf/cdc_cough_noLogo.pdf

11. Kostenius, C. O. (2008). The Meaning of Stress from School Children's Perspective. *Stress and Health,* 24(4), 287–293.

12. U.S. Department of Health and Human Services, Centers for Disease Control and Prevention. (2005). *2005 Middle School Youth Risk Behavior Survey.* Retrieved February 7, 2010, from: www.cdc.gov/healthyyouth/yrbs/middleschool 2005/pdf/YRBS_MS__fullreport.pdf

13. Rollin, S. A. (2003). A Stress Management Curriculum for At-Risk Youth. *Journal of Humanistic Counseling, Education, and Development,* 42(1), 79–90.

14. White, L. S. (2009). Yoga for Children. *Pediatric Nursing,* 35(5), 277–283.

15. Yogaforchildren.net. (2007). *Schools and Organizations.* Retrieved April 6, 2010, from: http://yogaforchildren.net/yg/school_org/sch_org.htm. p. 1.

16. YOGAeverywhere.com. (2000-2007). *Yoga for Youth...Yoga for Children...Yoga for Kids.* Retrieved April 6, 2010, from: www.yogaeverywhere.com/youth/youth_1.html

17. American Heart Association, National Safety Council. (1999). *Heartsaver FACTS.* Sudbury, MA: Jones and Bartlett.

18. O'Donnell, L. S.-U.-S. (2006). Middle School Aggression and Subsequent Intimate Partner Physical Violence. *Journal of Youth Adolescence,* 35(5), 693–703.

19. Roberts, L. (2007). Project WIN Evaluation Shows Decreased Violence and Improved Conflict Resolution Skills for Middle School Students. *Research in Middle School Education Online,* 30(8), 1–14.

20. Hahn, P. R.-W. (2007). *The Effectiveness of Universal School-Based Programs for the Prevention of Violent and Aggressive Behavior.* Altanta: Morbidity and Mortality Weekly Report, CDC.

21. Wilson-Simmons, R. (2006). What Can Student Bystanders Do to Prevent School Violence? Percepions of Students and School Staff. *Journal of School Violence,* 5(1), 43–62.

22. Noland, M. H. (2009). Adolescents' Sleep Behaviors and Perceptions of Sleep. *Journal of School Health,* 79(5), 224–230.

23. Suldo, S. M. (2009). Sources of Stress for Students in High School College Preparatory and General Education Programs: Group Differences and Associations with Adjustment. *Adolescence,* 44(176), 925–948.

24. Bronson, P. M. (2009). *Glencoe Health.* Woodland Hills, CA: McGraw-Hill.

25. Hahn, D. B. (2011). *Focus on Health,* (10 ed.). New York: McGraw-Hill.

26. United States Department of Agriculture. (n.d.). *My Pyramid Tracker.* Retrieved March 20, 2010, from: http://www.mypyramidtracker.gov/

Teaching National Health Education Standard 8

"Students will demonstrate the ability to advocate for personal, family, and community health."[1,p26]

Standard 8

"The ability to advocate for personal, family, and community health represents an essential skill for a health literate individual. Advocacy, then, becomes an integral part of the health education process"[2,p477]

A skilled advocate promotes healthy norms and behaviors. By advocating, students can promote health-enhancing messages and encourage others to develop and maintain healthy behaviors.[1,p36]

Sample performance tasks for advocating for personal, family, and community health include:

- Creating a brochure
- Designing a T-shirt
- Writing a song or poem
- Creating a radio or magazine advertisement
- Teaching a lesson to younger students
- Performing a skit
- Designing a bumper sticker
- Sending a letter to the editor[3,p230]
- Writing and performing a skit for a video that promotes an advocacy message
- Designing and monitoring a student health advocacy portal for the school website
- Publishing an article in the school newspaper[2,p477]
- Designing a public service announcement and broadcasting it during morning or afternoon announcements
- Displaying posters from previous performance tasks
- Designing seasonal health messages and displaying them outside of class or throughout the building.

To show proficiency in this standard, students promote personal health by taking a stand on a health issue and supporting their position with relevant and accurate information. Students learn to advocate for healthy families, friends, and community; encourage peers to make healthy choices; model how to influence and support others; use social norms to develop a health message; and adjust that viewpoint and communication strategy for different audiences.[1,p36]

Teaching the Skill

According to the National Health Education Standards, Achieving Excellence, teaching and learning skills is a process. When planning, follow these steps:

I. Discuss the importance of advocating for personal, family, and community health.
- Advocating for self, family, and friends demonstrates care and respect for one's self and others.
- Advocacy results in positive health changes for self, family, and the community.

II. Explain the steps to proficiency in advocating for personal, family, and community health.
- Select performance indicators for the grade span that meet the needs of the students.
- To reach proficiency, students must demonstrate each of the performance indicators by the end of the grade span.

III. Show the students what advocacy looks like.
- Model advocacy in the classroom and school.

IV. Provide adequate time for the students to practice advocating.

V. Utilize formative assessments during practice to provide feedback and encouragement.

PreK-2

To achieve proficiency in Standard 8, PreK–2 students make requests to promote personal health and encourage their peers to make positive health choices.[1,p36]

For example:

> The students in Mrs. Lissandra's Grade 2 classroom do not have a safe place to play during recess. All grades share the same play space, and the older children play ball, tag, and other running activities. The younger children stand together because they are afraid of being injured.

> The students invited the principal to class to talk to her about setting aside a special space for them to play. They were well-prepared with facts about the importance of recess and feeling safe.

> They told her that they would like to play more during recess because it feels good to run and play, but now they stand together to avoid being hit by a ball or an older student running. They requested space where they can play with their own balls, jump ropes, and play games.

> The principal listened attentively and told them that she would speak to the other teachers and come up with a plan. A few days later, the students learned that a section of the playground had been reserved for them and the younger students. They were happy and now look forward to a recess where they can run and play without worry.

To reflect, ask the students:

- What request did the children make to promote personal health? (PI 8.2.1) *(They asked the principal for a separate space for the younger children to play during recess.)*
- What positive health choices were the children encouraged to make? (PI 8.5.2) *(Speak to the principal, run and play at recess instead of standing in groups)*

For another example, ask the students to list needs they have or see in other students. Brainstorm how to make a request to promote personal health based on those needs and discuss how to encourage peers to make positive health choices.

This example uses both performance indicators. Because the skill is not a progression, however, use the indicators independently, depending on the needs of the students.

Advocating Example for PreK–2 Students (Table 12.1)

As the students practice, assess them formatively. Provide feedback for them to improve the skill and continue instruction when students demonstrate proficiency.

WHAT DOES THE SKILL OF ADVOCACY FOR PERSONAL, FAMILY, AND COMMUNITY HEALTH LOOK LIKE IN THE PREK–2 CLASSROOM?

Mrs. Saraf wants her Grade 1 students to assume responsibility for their health and encourage other students to make positive health choices.

She started the "healthy helper" program whereby students advocate for healthy behaviors. Her helpers model healthy behaviors and urge others to make positive health choices.

Advocacy Self-Check

To reinforce the message, Mrs. Saraf shows the students a picture of a child who is making a poor health choice and asks the students, "What could you say to encourage the student to make a healthier choice?" As the students voice their opinion, signal a thumbs-up or a thumbs-down to indicate whether the response is correct.

In planning the advocacy unit, Mrs. Saraf targets the performance indicator 8.2.2.

> Performance indicator 8.2.2—Encourage peers to make positive health choices.[1,p36]
> *Performance indicator 8.2.2 with infused content*—Encourage peers to reject negative health choices and make positive health choices.[1,p36]

After selecting the appropriate skill performance indicators, Mrs. Saraf selects Standard 1 performance indicators for content.

> Standard 1—Students will comprehend concepts related to health promotion and disease prevention to enhance health.[1,p24]
> Performance indicator 1.2.1—Identify healthy behaviors that affect personal health.[1,p24]
> *Performance indicator 1.2.1 with infused content*—Identify healthy behaviors that affect personal health and can be advocated.[1,p24]

TABLE 12.1 Advocating Example for PreK–2 Students

Advocacy Issue	Request to Promote Personal Health (PI 8.2.1)	Encourage Peers to Make Positive Health Choices. (PI 8.2.2)
 1. The hand sanitizer bottles around the school are always empty.	Write a letter to the principal asking that the custodian keep the hand sanitizer bottles full so germs do not spread.	Encourage other students to write letters to the principal asking that the custodian fill the hand sanitizer bottles.
 2. The new classmate, Marcus, is in a wheelchair. He sits with his aide at lunch but would like to make friends.	Marcus asks his teacher and aide to place him in groups with his classmates and involve him in social activities.	The students who are friends with Marcus encourage other classmates to include him in social gatherings, such as those at lunch or recess.
 3. There are no healthy snacks for the students who participate in the after-school day care program.	Write a letter to the principal and food service administrator to ask for healthy snacks for the after-school program. Ask parents to request healthy snacks for the after-school program.	Encourage other students to ask for healthy snacks. Encourage other students to avoid the available junk food.

By linking the skill and the content performance indicators, the teacher has direction in planning the unit on advocacy.

The first step in planning is to think through the unit by completing the performance task template. The teacher then has a good idea of the lessons that precede this culminating activity, the information and back-up materials to introduce the prompt to the students, and the assessment strategies.

The teacher uses formative assessments while the students learn content and skill. The summative assessment occurs when students demonstrate their knowledge and skill during a class presentation.

The following is an example of a Grade 1 advocacy performance task. The first section illustrates how the teacher plans for an authentic assessment of the performance indicators 8.2.2 and 1.2.1. The second extracts some of the information from the performance task and transforms it into the prompt and support materials for students.

The students are assessed formatively during instruction and summatively through an analytical rubric.

TABLE 12.2   Advocacy Self-Check

Advocacy Self-Check

Directions – If you see the problem behavior, what healthy behavior can replace it? *(Color the positive health choice.)*

Problem	Positive Health Choice

1. My throat hurts.

Reflect – Why is your choice a healthy one?

2. I am bored watching television.

Reflect – Why is your choice a healthy one?

Performance Task Name: Grade 1—Advocating for Good Health

I. Which state standard(s) does the performance task address?

II. Topic: What areas of health does this project assess? Why is it important? What is the focus of the project?[3,p237]

    A. This performance task assesses personal health.

    B. This topic is important because:

        1. Students need to learn the knowledge and skills necessary to advocate for their own health and the health of others.[2,p479]

        2. A comprehensive PreK–12 health education program prepares students to become confident and skilled adults who advocate for personal, family, and community health.

        3. The coordinated school health program supports school and district advocacy initiatives.

        4. Administrators, legislators, and policy makers listen to advocates.[4]

    C. The focus of the project is to advocate for personal health.

(continues)

III. Key Concepts: What basic concepts should students know?[3,p237]

Performance indicator 1.2.1 with infused content—Identify healthy behaviors that affect personal health and can be advocated.[1,p24]

A. Return home from school when sick.

B. Take medicine only from a trusted adult.

C. Follow all bicycle safety rules.

D. Practice healthy hygiene.

E. Select healthy snacks.

F. Choose to be physically active.

G. Be respectful.

IV. Skills: Which of the seven National Health Education Skills does this performance task address?[3,p237]

Performance indicator 8.2.2 with infused content—Encourage peers to reject negative health choices and make positive health choices.[1,p36]

V. Curricular connections—What other subject(s) does this project support?[3,p237]

English language arts

Art

VI. Student directions and assessment criteria[3,p238]

A. Project Description—Write and attach an engaging prompt that draws the student into the project.[3,p238]

Jeffrey and his classmates are health helpers and encourage other students to make positive health choices.

The health helpers are eager to encourage all the students in the school to make healthy choices but do not know how to do it.

B. Your Challenge—Provide a challenge or mission statement that describes the project.[3,p238]

Your challenge is to help Jeffrey and the health helpers encourage other students to make positive health choices.

C. Assessment Criteria[3,p239]

You are assessed on the following key concepts: (List the concepts)

Performance indicator 1.2.1 with infused content—Identify healthy behaviors that affect personal health and can be advocated.[1,p24]

1. Choose five healthy behaviors.

    a. Place each behavior on a separate poster.

    b. Explain why each of the healthy behaviors improves health.

2. Sample behaviors

    a. Return home from school when sick.

    b. Take medicine only from a trusted adult.

    c. Follow all bicycle safety rules.

    d. Practice healthy hygiene.

    e. Select healthy snacks.

    f. Choose to be physically active.

    g. Be respectful.

2. Create a picture of the opposite unhealthy behavior.

    a. Cross out the unhealthy behavior.

    b. Explain why the behavior is not good for your health

You are assessed on the following skills: (List the skills)

Performance indicator 8.2.2 with infused content—Encourage peers to reject negative for positive health choices.[1,p36]

1. Hang posters throughout the school to encourage peers to reject unhealthy for positive health choices.

    a. Write a message on the poster that encourages peers to make positive health choices.

    b. Each poster must contain two pictures.

(continues)

2. Broadcast a public service announcement before classes start that encourages peers to make positive health choices.

Student project must include the following: (List the project components)
1. A poster
2. A public service announcement

Jeffrey and his classmates are health helpers and encourage other students to make positive health choices.

The health helpers are eager to encourage all the students in the school to make healthy choices but do not know how to do it.

Your challenge is to help Jeffrey and the other health helpers encourage other students to make positive health choices.

Your project must contain the following:

1. Five posters that you will display around the school

   a. Each poster shows one unhealthy behavior picture crossed out and explains why the behavior is not good for your health.

   b. The same poster highlights a healthy behavior and explains why the healthy behavior improves health.

   c. A message on the poster encourages peers to make positive health choices.

   d. Each poster must contain two pictures.

2. Broadcast a public service announcement before classes start that encourages peers to make positive health choices.

ASSESSMENT MATERIALS

Analytical Rubric to Assess the Health Helper Advocacy Poster and Public Service Announcement (Table 12.3)

TABLE 12.3 Analytical Rubric to Assess the Health Helper Advocacy Poster and Public Service Announcement

| | Health Helper Poster | | | |
Criteria	4	3	2	1
		Poster		
Unhealthy behaviors	Student accurately presents five unhealthy behaviors.	Student's presentation of five unhealthy behaviors is mostly accurate.	A few of the five unhealthy behaviors are inaccurate.	Student's presentation of five unhealthy behaviors is mostly inaccurate.
Explanation of why the behavior is unhealthy	Student accurately explains why the behavior is unhealthy.	Student's explanation of why the behavior is unhealthy is mostly accurate.	A few of the explanations of why the behavior is unhealthy are inaccurate.	Student's explanation of why the behavior is unhealthy is mostly inaccurate.

(continues)

TABLE 12.3 Analytical Rubric to Assess the Health Helper Advocacy Poster and Public Service Announcement *(continued)*

Criteria	4	3	2	1
Performance indicator 1.2.1 with infused content—Identify healthy behaviors that affect personal health and can be advocated.[1,p24]	Student accurately identifies five healthy behaviors.	Student's identification of five healthy behaviors is mostly accurate.	A few of the five healthy behaviors identified are inaccurate.	Student's identification of five healthy behaviors is mostly inaccurate.
Performance indicator 1.2.1 with infused content—Identify healthy behaviors that affect personal health and can be advocated.[1,p24]	Student thoroughly identifies how each healthy behavior affects personal health.	Student adequately identifies how each healthy behavior affects personal health	Student inadequately identifies how each healthy behavior affects personal health.	Student poorly identifies how each healthy behavior affects personal health.
Performance indicator 8.2.2 with infused content—Encourage peers to reject negative health choices and make positive health choices.[1,p36]	The message on the poster consistently encourages peers to make positive health choices.	The message on the poster usually encourages peers to make positive health choices.	The message on the poster rarely encourages peers to make positive health choices.	The message on the poster never encourages peers to make positive health choices.
Pictures	The two pictures per poster are appropriate.	The two pictures per poster are mostly appropriate.	One of the pictures on the poster is inappropriate.	The two pictures on the poster are mostly inappropriate.
Public Service Announcement				
Performance indicator 8.2.2 with infused content—Encourage peers to reject negative health choices and make positive health choices.[1,p36]	Student's announcement thoroughly encourages peers to make positive health choices.	Student's announcement adequately encourages peers to make positive health choices.	Student's announcement inadequately encourages peers to make positive health choices.	Student's announcement poorly encourages peers to make positive health choices.

Name _____

Total possible points – 28   Your points – _____   Your grade – _____

HOW DOES THE COORDINATED SCHOOL HEALTH TEAM HELP STUDENTS ADVOCATE FOR PERSONAL, FAMILY, AND COMMUNITY HEALTH?

Health Education

- Teach the advocacy skill.
- Provide accurate information to support the healthy/unhealthy rationale.
- Provide time to practice advocacy skills to increase self-confidence.

Physical Education

- Model how to advocate for healthy behaviors.
- Provide encouragement to student advocates.
- Hang posters that encourage students to make healthy physical activity choices.

Health Services

- Model how to advocate for health services.
- Provide encouragement to student advocators.
- Provide resources to student and staff advocates.

Nutrition Services

- Model how to advocate for healthy food choices.
- Hang posters that encourage students to make healthy food choices.

Counseling, Psychological, and Social Services

- Model how to advocate for counseling, psychological, and social services
- Hang posters that encourage students to make healthy choices.
- Provide encouragement and support for student advocates.

Healthy School Environment

- Establish a school climate that encourages students to advocate for their health and the health of others.
- Broadcast student public service announcements.
- Encourage teachers to post student advocate work in the building.

Health Promotion for Staff

- Provide professional development for advocacy skills.
- Provide a forum for staff to advocate for their needs.

Family and Community Involvement

- Provide advocacy training to parents and interested community members.
- Encourage members of the team to advocate for co-ordinated school health.

Grades 3–5

To achieve proficiency in Standard 8 Grades 3–5 students express opinions and offer accurate information about health issues as well as encourage others to make positive health choices.[1,p36]

For example:

The Grade 3 peer leaders need a project that promotes health. They must express opinions about the issue, provide accurate facts, and encourage others to make healthy choices.

The peer leaders decided to start a recycling program. One of the parents works for the town and pro-

vided paper and plastic recycling bins. To explain the program and express their opinion about the issue, the students delivered public service announcements in the morning and afternoon and placed posters around the school to encourage students to participate.

Mrs. Hannah, the peer leader advisor, organized a contest to reward the class that recycled the most paper and plastic.

To reflect, ask the students the following questions.

- How did the peer leaders express their opinion and give accurate information about health issues? (PI 8.5.1) *(The students gave public service announcements in the morning and afternoon and placed posters around the school.)*
- How did the peer leaders and the advisor encourage other students to participate? (PI 8.5.2) *(They placed posters around the school and the advisor organized a contest to reward the class that recycled the most paper and plastic.)*

In this skill, students must demonstrate how to advocate. When they exhibit an understanding of the skill, as determined through formative assessment, instruction continues with the content.

To continue the practice, ask students to list other issues they can advocate. Divide the students into groups and have them express opinions and gather facts about the issue. Challenge the students to develop a plan that would encourage others to make a positive health choice about this issue (**Table 12.4**).

As the students learn and practice the skill and content, continue to formatively assess their progress. If additional instruction is needed, provide it before moving to the performance task.

WHAT DOES THE SKILL OF ADVOCACY LOOK LIKE IN THE GRADE 3 CLASSROOM?

Mrs. Talbot is the Grade 3 teacher at Three Lakes Elementary School. She understands that if her children are to achieve academically, they must be physically, mentally, and socially healthy.

She notices that some of her students have several friends, a good sense of self-esteem, and are social and confident.[5,p341] Others are not. To help all students be social and recognize the value of having friends, she wants them to advocate for developing friendships that promote positive social behaviors.

Planning begins with selecting Standard 8 performance indicators.

Standard 8—Students will demonstrate the ability to advocate for personal, family, and community health.[1,p36]

Grades 3–5 Performance Indicators

8.5.1 Express opinions and give accurate information about health issues.

8.5.2 Encourage others to make positive health choices.[1,p36]

TABLE 12.4 Worksheet to Brainstorm Advocacy Issues

Advocacy Issue	Opinion About the Issue	Facts About the Issue	How to Encourage Others to Make a Positive Health Choice
The playground is littered with trash and broken glass.	*The playground is dirty and unsafe.*	*Four children fell and were cut.*	*Make posters for the playground that say, "Please keep our playground clean. Throw your trash in the can!"*
	The trash on the playground makes us not want to play there.	*There is only one trash can on the playground. We need more.*	*Organize committees to pick up trash. The class that collects the most trash wins a prize.* *Ask the principal to buy more trash cans.*
There are no healthy allergy friendly snacks in the vending machine.	*We need safe, healthy snacks for before and after school.*	*20% of the students have a food allergy.*	*Petition for healthy, allergy friendly snacks.* *Bring healthy snacks from home.*
There are not enough bicycle racks.	*We need more bicycle racks so we have a place to lock our bicycles.*	*Two bicycles were stolen because students could not lock them.*	*Write a letter to the principal and ask for another bicycle rack.* *Always lock your bicycle.*

Performance indicator 8.5.2—Encourage others to make positive health choices.[1,p36]

Performance indicator 8.5.2 with infused content—Encourage others to make positive health choices by considering certain facts when choosing a friend.[1,p36]

After selecting the appropriate performance indicator for the skill, choose a Standard 1 performance indicator.

Standard 1—Students will comprehend concepts related to health promotion and disease prevention to enhance health.[1,p24]

Performance Indicator 1.5.1—Describe the relationship between healthy behaviors and personal health.[1,p24]

Performance indicator 1.5.1 with infused content—Describe the relationship between healthy behaviors, such as having positive friends, and personal health.[1,p24]

By linking the skill and content performance indicators, the teacher has a clear idea of how to plan the lessons for an advocacy unit.

The first step in planning is to think through the unit by completing the performance task template. Upon completion, the teacher has a good idea of the lessons that precede this culminating activity, the information and back-up materials necessary to introduce the prompt to the students, and the assessment strategies.

When distributing the prompt, include all the back-up information, student worksheets, and holistic and analytical rubrics. Distribute the rubrics with the prompt so students know how they will be assessed before working on their product. The rubrics act as a guide and help the students attain proficiency in the standards.

Designing the performance task takes considerable preparation, but once the information is distributed and explained, the students create a product independently. They learn with good coaching (formative assessment) how to demonstrate proficiency in content and skill.

The following is an example of a Grade 3 advocacy performance task that focuses on developing friendships.

The first section, for the teacher, demonstrates how to plan for an authentic assessment of the performance indicators 8.5.2 and 1.5.1. The second, the student's, extracts information from the performance task and transforms it into the student prompt and support materials.

Performance Task Name: Grade 3—Advocate for Positive Friendships

I. Which state standard(s) does this performance task address? (Varies by state)

II. Topic: What areas of health does this project assess? Why is it important? What is the focus of the project?[3,p237]

    A. This performance task assesses personal and mental/emotional health.

    B. This topic is important because:

        1. An active social life is good for the mind and contributes to self-esteem.

        2. Socializing decreases incidences of depression.[6,p102]

        3. Adolescents who have friends are more likely to be pro-social than those who do not have friends.

        4. Friendships contribute to an increase in self-esteem.[5,p342]

    C. The focus of this project is to advocate for positive friendships.

III. Key Concepts: What basic concepts should students know?[3,p237]

    Standard 1—Students will comprehend concepts related to health promotion and disease prevention to enhance health.[1,p24]

    Performance indicator 1.5.1 with infused content—Describe the relationship between healthy behaviors, such as having positive friends, and personal health.[1,p24]

        1. Friends teach us how to:

            a. Communicate

            b. Compromise

            c. Work out problems

            d. Give support

            e. Share life

        2. Traits of a good friend

            a. Honest

            b. Trustful

            c. Caring

            d. Respectful

            e. Loyal[7,p185-186]

        3. Positive influence of friends

            a. Encourages you to make positive choices

            b. Helps you say, "No" to negative peer pressure

            c. Improves health

            d. Improves self-esteem[7,p186]

IV. Skills: Which of the seven National Health Education Standards skills does this performance task address?[3,p237]

    Standard 8—Students will demonstrate the ability to advocate for personal, family, and community health.[1,p36]

    Performance indicator 8.5.2 with infused content—Encourage others to make positive health choices by considering certain facts when choosing a friend.[1,p36]

        1. Choose friends with positive values.

        2. Join a club or organization to meet others who have the same interests as you.

        3. Reject friends who encourage you to do unhealthy or dangerous things.

V. Curricular connections—What other subject areas does this project support?[3,p237]

    English language arts

    Art

VI. Student Directions and Assessment Criteria[3,p238]

    A. Project Description—Write and attach an engaging prompt that draws the student into the project.[3,p238]

        Diana and her classmates belong to the health club and want to make their school friendlier so that all students can have fun together and help each other.

(continues)

She wants the students to know how to be a good friend and encourage everyone to choose friends who make positive health choices.

B. Your Challenge—Provide a challenge or mission statement that describes the project.[3,p238]

Your challenge is to help Diana advocate for her cause.

C. Assessment Criteria[3,p239]

You are assessed on the following key concepts: (List the concepts.)

Performance indicator 1.5.1 with infused content—Describe the relationship between healthy behaviors, such as having positive friends, and personal health.[1,p24]

1. Three things that friends teach us to do
2. Three traits of a good friend
3. Three ways friends are a positive influence

You are assessed on the following skill:

Performance indicator 8.5.2 with infused content—Encourage others to make positive health choices by considering certain facts when choosing a friend.[3,p239]

1. Three facts to consider when making a new friend

Student project must include the following: (List the project components)

1. Three public service announcements to be broadcast in the morning and afternoon that address:
   a. Three things that friends teach us to do
   b. Three traits of a good friend
   c. Three ways friends are a positive influence
2. A graphic organizer individually designed and posted around the school that shows three facts to consider when making a new friend

---

Three Lakes Elementary School

Name _____

Diana and her classmates belong to the health club and they want to make their school friendlier so that all students can have fun together and help each other.

Diana wants the students to know how to be a good friend and encourage everyone to choose friends who make positive health choices.

Your challenge is to help Diana advocate for her cause.

Your project must contain:

1. Three public service announcements broadcasted in the morning and afternoon that address:

   a. Three things that friends teach us to do

   b. Three traits of a good friend

   c. Three ways friends are a positive influence

2. A graphic organizer individually designed and posted around the school that shows three facts to consider when making a new friend (see example below)

(continues)

A Graph That Shows Three Things to Consider When Making a New Friend (Figure 12.1)

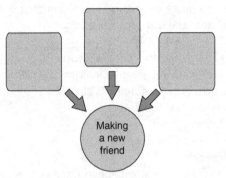

Making
a new
friend

FIGURE 12.1   A Graph That Shows Three Things to Consider When Making a New Friend

Analytical Rubric to Assess Information On a Public Service Announcement (PSA) and a Graphic Organizer

TABLE 12.5   Analytical Rubric to Assess Information on a Public Service Announcement (PSA) and a Graphic Organizer

Criteria	4	3	2	1
Performance indicator 1.5.1 with infused content—Describe the relationship between healthy behaviors, such as having positive friends, and personal health.[1,p24]	The PSA accurately describes three things that friends teach us to do.	The PSA's description of three things that friends teach us to do is mostly accurate.	The PSA's description of three things that friends teach us to do has a few inaccuracies.	The PSA's description of three things that friends teach us to do is mostly inaccurate.
Performance indicator 1.5.1 with infused content—Describe the relationship between healthy behaviors, such as having positive friends, and personal health.[1,p24]	The PSA accurately describes three traits of a good friend.	The PSA's description of three traits of a good friend is mostly accurate.	The PSA's description of three traits of a good friend has a few inaccuracies.	The PSA's description of three traits of a good friend is mostly inaccurate.
Performance indicator 1.5.1 with infused content—Describe the relationship between healthy behaviors, such as having positive friends, and personal health.[1,p24]	The PSA accurately describes three ways friends are a positive influence.	The PSA's description of three ways friends are a positive influence is mostly accurate.	The PSA's description of three ways friends are a positive influence has a few inaccuracies.	The PSA's description of three ways friends are a positive influence is mostly inaccurate.

(continues)

TABLE 12.5 Analytical Rubric to Assess Information on a Public Service Announcement (PSA) and a Graphic Organizer (continued)

Criteria	4	3	2	1
		Graphic Organizer		
Graphic organizer	The graphic organizer design is appropriate for the message.	The graphic organizer is mostly appropriate for the message.	A few of the components of the graphic organizer are appropriate for the message.	The graphic organizer is mostly inappropriate for the message.
Performance indicator 8.5.2 with infused content—Encourage others to make positive health choices by considering certain facts when choosing a friend.[1,p36]	The facts to consider when choosing a friend are appropriate.	The facts to consider when choosing a friend are mostly appropriate.	A few of the facts to consider when choosing a friend are appropriate.	The facts to consider when choosing a friend are mostly inappropriate.

Name _____

Total possible points – 20   Your points – _____   Your grade – _____

HOW DOES THE COORDINATED SCHOOL HEALTH TEAM HELP STUDENTS ADVOCATE FOR PERSONAL, FAMILY, AND COMMUNITY HEALTH?

Health Education

- Teach advocacy skills.
- Model how to advocate.
- Teach the importance of friendship and how to make good friends.

Physical Education

- Model how to advocate.
- Encourage students to advocate for increased physical education.

Health Services

- Model how to advocate.
- Support students who advocate for increased health services.

Nutrition Services

- Model how to advocate.
- Advocate for healthy school food and snacks.

Counseling, Psychological, and Social Services

- Model how to advocate.
- Support students who advocate for their special needs.

Healthy School Environment

- Encourage advocacy as a way of improving education.
- Provide an environment that supports positive student activism.

Health Promotion for Staff

- Provide professional development on how to advocate.
- Model advocacy strategies.

Family and Community Involvement

- Provide training on how to advocate for improved comprehensive health education.
- Advocate for a healthy community.

Grades 6–8

To achieve proficiency in Standard 8, Grade 6–8 students take a health-enhancing stand on a topic and support their position with accurate information. They persuade others to make a positive health choice and advocate for healthy individuals, families, and schools. Finally, students identify ways to adapt health messages and communication techniques for different audiences.

To teach Standard 8, explain the importance of advocating, how it affects current and future health, why the skill is relevant to the student, and how it relates to the other national health education skills.

To achieve the standard, model the skill, provide practice time for the students, and use formative assessments while the students are learning and practicing in order to improve teaching and learning.

For example:

Mr. Collins and Mr. Conger are collaborating on a science/health project in which students are designing an assignment book made from recycled paper and emphasizing the theme of reuse, recycle, and reduce. The goal is to excite awareness of what students can do to protect the environment and, at the same time, improve their time management skills.

Each month, a message encourages students to protect the environment in a special way: recycling paper and plastic; reusing items, such as plastic sandwich containers, forks, and spoons; and reducing the amount of trash each produces.

The teachers challenge the students to plan their projects by completing the worksheet below (**Table 12.6**). The two classes will vote on three designs to be published. Proceeds from the sale of the books will contribute to the school garden, and the food grown there will be served at lunch.

The students are excited to learn how to advocate for the environment and, at the same time, provide a time management strategy that helps their peers. Both teachers were pleased with the initial results.

To reflect, the teachers asked the following questions:

- What was the health-enhancing position the students took? (PI 8.8.1) (*"Plan your time and help the environment"*)
- What supporting facts did they present? (PI 8.8.1) (*Each person must do something to keep the environment clean and protect health. Planning your time reduces stress.*)
- Demonstrate how to influence and support others to make positive health choices. (PI 8.8.2) (*Reuse food containers and plastic grocery bags. Donate clothes*

rather than throwing them away. Place paper and plastic bottles in the recycling bins. Buy products, such as paper, made from recycled materials. Avoid using plastic plates, forks, spoons, and knives if thrown away after one use. Bring your own bag to the grocery store so you do not accumulate more plastic or paper bags. Ask your parents to buy products in bulk so there is less packaging to throw away.)

- Work cooperatively to advocate for healthy individuals, families, and schools. (PI 8.8.3) (*Science and health classes work together to design an assignment book for the school that encourages students and staff to recycle, reuse, and reduce waste.*)
- Identify ways in which health messages and communication techniques can be altered for different audiences. (PI 8.8.4) (*Students designed a special high school edition that contains slogans and pictures more appropriate for the older students.*)

When the students are learning the skill, provide adequate time for them to practice before asking them to demonstrate proficiency through an authentic assessment. While they are practicing, use formative assessments (Chapter 4) to check for understanding. Use feedback to show students how to improve performance, thereby encouraging them to improve.

Once the students demonstrate the skill, teach the health content. Design a prompt that allows the students to display their knowledge of health content while demonstrating advocacy skills. As the students practice their content and skill, use formative assessments to redirect and encourage them.

WHAT DOES THE SKILL OF ADVOCACY LOOK LIKE IN THE GRADE 8 CLASSROOM?

Students at the Franklin Middle School live in a large Midwestern city. Twenty-six percent of them consider themselves overweight, and 44% are trying to lose weight. Rather than practicing healthy weight management, 19% did not eat for 24 hours, 5% took diet pills, and 5.6% vomited to lose weight.[8]

The Franklin Middle School science, health, physical education, and math departments are collaborating to initiate experiential learning to combat these unhealthy conditions by designing and planting a school vegetable garden.

The garden enhances the study of several disciplines. Science students study the plant and insect life cycles, while health students study the nutritive value of vegetables, healthy eating, and how vegetables contribute to health. Physical education students increase their physical activity by working in the garden, and math students calculate and graph the growth of the plants.

After researching, the teachers learned that experiential learning benefits all students and disciplines by em-

TABLE 12.6 Worksheet to Plan for the Science/Health Project

State a health-enhancing position on a topic and support it with accurate information. (PI 8.8.1)	*"Plan your time and help the environment"* · *Each person must do something to keep the environment clean and protect health.[7,p158]* · *Planning your time reduces stress.[7,p158]*
Demonstrate how to influence and support others to make positive health choices. (PI 8.8.2)	***Reuse*** · *Reuse food containers, plastic grocery bags, and plastic utensils; donate clothes rather than throwing them away.[7,p515]* ***Recycle*** · *Place paper and plastic bottles in the recycling bins.* · *Buy products, such as paper, made from recycled materials.[7,p515]* ***Reduce*** · *Avoid using plastic plates, forks, spoons, and knives if thrown away after one use.* · *Bring your own bag to the grocery store so you do not accumulate more plastic or paper bags.* · *Ask your parents to buy products in bulk so there is less packaging to throw away.*
Work cooperatively to advocate for healthy individuals, families, and schools. (PI 8.8.3)	· *Science and health classes work together to design an assignment book for the school that encourages students and staff to recycle, reuse, and reduce waste.* · *Proceeds from the sale of the assignment book are used to support the school garden.*
Identify ways in which health messages and communication techniques can be altered for different audiences.[1,p36] (PI 8.8.4)	· *Students designed a special high school edition that contains slogans and pictures appropriate for the older students.*

phasizing problem-solving and critical thinking skills. It even increases standardized test scores![9,p150] Students studying English as a second language succeed here because they learn by watching and doing rather than by the language-based learning experience in the classroom.[10]

The teachers and students are excited about the project but need to advocate to school administrators, school committees, and the food service director to get approval. They also want to advocate to parents and the community to gather grassroots support.

To begin planning, the health teacher connected the project to the National Health Education Standards. She selects specific performance indicators that address a targeted skill and content.

Standard 8—Students will demonstrate the ability to advocate for personal, family, and community health.[1,p36]

Performance indicator 8.8.1—State a health-enhancing position on a topic and support it with accurate information.[1,p36]

*Performance indicator 8.8.1 with infused content—*Analyze the relationship between healthy behaviors, such as eating fresh vegetables, and personal health.[1,p25]

Performance indicator 8.8.4—Identify ways in which health messages and communication techniques can be altered for different audiences.[1,p36]

Performance indicator 8.8.4 with infused content— Identify ways in which health messages and communication techniques regarding the school vegetable garden can be altered for different audiences.[1,p36]

Standard 1—Students comprehend concepts related to health promotion and disease prevention to enhance health.[1,p24]

Performance indicator 1.8.1—Analyze the relationship between healthy behaviors and personal health.[1,p25]

Performance indicator 1.8.1 with infused content— Analyze the relationship between healthy behaviors, such as eating fresh vegetables, and personal health.[1,p25]

By linking the skill and content performance indicators, the teacher has a clear idea of how to plan the lessons for the advocacy unit.

The first step in planning is to think through the unit by completing the performance task template. When finished, the teacher has a good idea of the lessons that precede this culminating activity, the information and back-up materials necessary to introduce the prompt to the students, and the assessment strategies.

When distributing the prompt, include all the back-up information, student worksheets, and holistic and analytical rubrics. Distribute the rubrics with the prompt so students know how they will be assessed before working on their product. The rubrics act as a guide and help the students attain proficiency in the standards.

Designing skills-based lessons requires considerable preparation, but once the teacher distributes the information and explains the task, the students are responsible for the results. Students learn with good coaching (formative assessments) how to demonstrate proficiency in content and skill.

The following is a performance task for a Grade 8 unit on advocacy that focuses on school vegetable gardens.

The first section, for the teacher, demonstrates how to plan for an authentic assessment of the performance indicators 8.8.1, 8.8.4, and 1.8.1. The second, the student's, extracts information from the performance task and transforms it into the student prompt and support materials.

Standard 8 Performance Task: Grade 8—Using Advocacy to Promote the Implementation of a School Vegetable Garden

I. Which state standard(s) does this performance task address?
II. Topic: What areas of health does this project assess? Why is it important? What is the focus of the project?[3,p237]
    A. This project assesses nutrition and personal health.
    B. This project is important because:
        1. Advocacy skills promote healthy norms and healthy behaviors.
        2. Advocates target health enhancing messages and behaviors.
        3. Advocacy skills train students to encourage others to adopt healthy behaviors.[1,p36]
    C. The focus of the project is to use advocacy skills to promote the implementation of a school vegetable garden.
III. Key Concepts: What basic concepts should the students know?[3,p237]
    Standard 1—Students comprehend concepts related to health promotion and disease prevention to enhance health.[1,p24]
        Performance indicator 1.8.1 with infused content—Analyze the relationship between healthy behaviors, such as eating fresh vegetables, and personal health.[1,p25]

(continues)

A. Children 9–13 years old need 2.5 cups of vegetables each day for optimum health.[7,p113]

B. For proper growth and development, half the food at each meal should be fruits and vegetables.[7,p117]

C. Vegetables are naturally lower in fat and cholesterol, better for your heart and blood vessels, and helpful when trying to reduce calorie intake.

D. Vegetables are an important source of potassium, fiber, and folic acid, as well as vitamins A, E, and C.

 1. Potassium maintains healthy blood pressure.

 2. Fiber reduces blood cholesterol and risk of heart disease.

 3. Folic acid helps build red blood cells.

 4. Vitamin A keeps eyes and skin healthy and protects against infection.

 5. Vitamin E protects vitamin A and the essential fatty acids from cell oxidation.

 6. Vitamin C helps heal cuts and wounds and keeps teeth and gums healthy.[11,p1-2]

E. A diet rich in fruits and vegetables reduces the risk of stroke, heart disease, type 2 diabetes, and certain cancers.[11,p1]

IV. Skills: Which of the seven National Health Education Standards does this performance task address?[3,p237]

Standard 8—Students will demonstrate the ability to advocate for personal, family, and community health.[1,p36]

Performance indicator 8.8.1 with infused content—State a health-enhancing position on establishing a school vegetable garden and support it with accurate information.[1,p36]

A. School gardens, when combined with nutrition education, increase student fruit and vegetable consumption.[9,p147]

B. School gardens promote improved student health by introducing fresh food, encouraging healthier food choices, and promoting physical activity.

C. Nutrition education and programs linked to school gardens improve academic achievement.[12]

D. Students involved in environmental education programs perform better on standardized achievement tests.[9,p147]

E. School gardens enhance instruction in science, environmental studies, nutrition, and language arts.[9,p149]

F. Experiential learning, such as the school vegetable garden, emphasizes problem-solving and critical thinking that increase test performance, attention, and enthusiasm for learning while decreasing discipline problems in the classroom.[9,p150]

V. Curricula connections: What other subject areas does this project support?[3,p237]

 English language arts

 Science

 Math

 Physical education

VI. Student directions and assessment criteria[3,p238]

A. Project Description—Write and attach an engaging prompt that draws the student into the project.[3,p238]

 Robert, his classmates, and his teachers are advocating for a school garden. They decided to promote the program to several groups in order to obtain permission and funding for the project.

B. Your Challenge—Provide a challenge or mission statement that describes the project.[3,p238]

 Your challenge is to help Robert advocate for the school garden.

C. Assessment criteria[3,p239]

 You are assessed on the following content:

 Performance indicator 1.8.1 with infused content—Analyze the relationship between healthy behaviors, such as eating fresh vegetables, and personal health.[1,p25]

 1. Analyze five reasons why eating vegetables is good for personal health.

 You are assessed on the following skills:

(continues)

Performance indicator 8.8.1 with infused content—State a health-enhancing position on establishing a school vegetable garden and support it with accurate information.[1,p36]
1. Take a position on implementing a school garden.
2. Five reasons why a school garden should be approved.

Student project must include the following:
1. A presentation
    a. Present to the student body, administrators, coordinated school health committee, school advisory council, school committee, or business organizations advocating for a school vegetable garden.
    b. The presentation must contain two props and four pictures.
2. A completed planning worksheet

Adirondack Middle School

Robert, his classmates, and his teachers are advocating for a school garden. They decided to promote the program to several groups in order to obtain permission and funding for the project.

Your challenge is to help Robert advocate for the school garden.

Your project must include:

1. A presentation

    a. Present to the student body, administrators, coordinated school health committee, school advisory council, school committee, or business organizations advocating for a school vegetable garden.

    b. The presentation must contain two props and four pictures.

2. A completed planning worksheet

ASSESSMENT MATERIALS

Worksheet to Advocate for the School Garden (Table 12.7)

TABLE 12.7 Worksheet to Advocate for the School Garden

1. Are you advocating to a group or writing to the editor? *Check one box.*	☐ Student body ☐ Administrators ☐ Coordinated school health committee ☐ School advisory council ☐ School committee ☐ Business organizations
2. *Performance indicator 8.8.1 with infused content*—State a health-enhancing position on establishing a school vegetable garden and support it with three accurate reasons why a school vegetable garden should be approved and funded.[1,p36]	What is your health-enhancing position?
3. *Performance indicator 8.8.1 with infused content*—State a health-enhancing position on establishing a school vegetable garden and support it with five accurate reasons why a school vegetable garden should be approved and funded.[1,p36]	State five reasons why a school garden should be approved.

(continues)

TABLE 12.7   Worksheet to Advocate for the School Garden *(continued)*

4. *Performance indicator 1.8.1 with infused content*—Analyze the relationship between healthy behaviors, such as five reasons for eating fresh vegetables, and personal health.[1,p25]

Analyze five facts that explain why it is important to eat vegetables.

5. What two props are you using in your presentation?

1.

2.

6. Collect four pictures for your presentation and attach copies to this worksheet.

☐ Picture #1
☐ Picture #2
☐ Picture #3
☐ Picture #4

Presentation to Advocate for a School Vegetable Garden (Table 12.8)

TABLE 12.8   Presentation to Advocate for a School Vegetable Garden

Criteria	4	3	2	1
Performance indicator 8.8.1 with infused content—State a health-enhancing position on establishing a school vegetable garden and support it with three accurate reasons why a school vegetable garden should be approved and funded.[1,p36]	Student accurately states a health-enhancing position.	Student's statement of a health-enhancing position is mostly accurate.	Parts of the student's statement of a health-enhancing position are inaccurate.	Student's statement of a health-enhancing position is mostly inaccurate.
Performance indicator 8.8.1 with infused content—State a health-enhancing position on establishing a school vegetable garden and support it with three accurate reasons why a school vegetable garden should be approved and funded.[1,p36]	Student accurately presents five accurate reasons why a school vegetable garden should be approved.	Student's five reasons why a school vegetable garden should be approved are mostly accurate.	Student's five reasons why a school vegetable garden should be approved have a few inaccuracies.	Student's five reasons why a school vegetable garden should be approved are mostly inaccurate.
Performance indicator 1.8.1 with infused content—Analyze the relationship between healthy behaviors, such as five reasons for eating fresh vegetables, and personal health.[1,p25]	Student thoroughly analyzes, through five facts, the relationship between eating fresh vegetables and personal health.	Student adequately analyzes, through five facts, the relationship between eating fresh vegetables and personal health.	Student inadequately analyzes, through five facts, the relationship between eating fresh vegetables and personal health.	Student poorly analyzes, through five facts, the relationship between eating fresh vegetables and personal health.

(continues)

TABLE 12.8　Presentation to Advocate for a School Vegetable Garden *(continued)*

Criteria	4	3	2	1
Props	Student appropriately uses two props to advocate.	Student's use of two props is mostly appropriate.	One of the props used to advocate is inappropriate.	Student's use of two props is mostly inappropriate.
Pictures	Student uses four appropriate pictures to advocate.	The four pictures used to advocate are mostly appropriate.	A few of the four pictures used to advocate are inappropriate.	The four pictures used to advocate are mostly inappropriate.
Projection of voice	Student's projection of voice is excellent.	Student's projection of voice is good.	Student's projection of voice is fair.	Student's projection of voice is poor.
Grammar	The student's grammar is always correct.	The student's grammar is usually correct.	The student's grammar is sometimes correct.	The student's grammar is never correct.
Spelling	The student's spelling is always correct.	The student's spelling is usually correct.	The student's spelling is sometimes correct.	The student's spelling is never correct.

Name _____

Total possible points – 32　　Your points – _____　　Your grade – _____

HOW DOES THE COORDINATED SCHOOL HEALTH TEAM HELP STUDENTS USE ADVOCACY SKILLS TO ENHANCE HEALTH?

Health Education

- Teach advocacy skills.
- Provide time for the students to practice their skills.
- Encourage students to advocate for comprehensive school health education.

Physical Education

- Teach advocacy skills.
- Encourage students to advocate for physical activity time.

Health Services

- Advocate for health services.
- Encourage students to advocate for their personal health needs.

Nutrition Services

- Advocate for quality health services.
- Provide support for students who advocate for the school vegetable garden.

- Collaborate with teachers and administrators to use the produce from the vegetable garden to enhance the school lunch program.[9,p150]

Counseling, Psychological, and Social Services

- Model advocacy skills.
- Advocate for counseling, psychological, and social services.
- Encourage and support students who advocate for their special needs.

Healthy School Environment

- Develop and implement a school nutrition policy that requires a portion of the vegetable garden to be used in the food service program.
- Set a school improvement goal to increase the fresh vegetable intake of students.
- Provide space and resources to implement a school vegetable garden.

Health Promotion for Staff

- Provide training in advocacy.
- Advocate for the space and resources to implement a school vegetable garden.

- Offer curriculum development to connect nutrition education and curriculum standards to the educational outcomes of growing a vegetable garden.[9,p150]

Family and Community Involvement

- Provide advocacy skills training.
- Volunteer to work in the school vegetable garden.[9,p150]
- Donate materials and resources to the school vegetable garden.

Grades 9–12

To achieve proficiency in Standard 8, Grade 9–12 students must learn to use accurate peer and societal norms to formulate a health-enhancing position, demonstrate how to influence and support others to make positive health choices, work cooperatively as advocates for improving personal, family, and community health, and adapt health messages and communication techniques to a target audience.

To teach Standard 8, explain why it is important to advocate for self, family, and the community, and how this skill relates to the other National Health Education Standards.

According to the performance indicators chosen, present and explain how to reach proficiency in the skill. Model the skill so the students can see it in action. Provide adequate time for the students to practice the skill and show proficiency through an authentic assessment. Use formative assessments (Chapter 4) to provide feedback and encouragement and improve instruction.

For example:

Deidre is a junior at Minuteman High School and a member of the Student Activities Committee. The committee has decided to hold a post-prom, all-night party, to provide a safe environment for the attendees.

Two years ago, two juniors were killed in an automobile accident following the prom, and the school wanted to do something to keep the students safe.

Many of the surrounding towns have post-prom parties. Students who have friends in these communities say the parties are great fun, so Minuteman High School wants to give it a try.

The committee is planning to advocate for student, parent, and community support for the party. Members have distributed a questionnaire to all juniors attending the prom to ask what foods and activities they would enjoy. Students with the winning ideas will receive a special prize at the party.

Deidre and her committee members made a presentation to the school council asking for support and adult volunteers for the various activity and food stations. Students also asked the PTO to donate food and surprise goodie bags to encourage students to attend.

The committee sent a notice of the event home with the principal's monthly letter. To encourage student participation, they used the morning and afternoon announcements to describe the activities planned, including raffle tickets for the mystery prize. They made presentations to business and community leaders to gain their support and donations. They e-mailed students and parents to inform them of the party and to ask for encouragement.

The all-night party was a great success! The students enjoyed the many different activities, movies, and sports events, but especially the food and special prizes. The party may well become a tradition!

To reflect, ask the students:

- What societal norms caused the committee to think of a post-prom party? (PI 8.12.1) *(Many of the surrounding towns have post-prom parties and students who have friends there say the parties are great fun)*
- How did the committee demonstrate how to influence and support others to make the positive health choice of attending the post-prom party? (PI 8.12.2) *(They distributed a questionnaire to all juniors attending the prom to ask what foods and activities they would enjoy; the students with the winning ideas will receive a special prize at the party.)*
- How did the committee work cooperatively as an advocate for improving personal, family, and community health? (PI 8.12.3) *(Committee members made a presentation to the school council to ask for their support. Students also asked the PTO to donate food and surprise goodie bags to encourage students to attend.)*
- How did the committee adapt health messages and communication techniques to a specific target audience? (PI8.12.4) *(The committee sent home a notice of the event with the principal's monthly letter, described the activities planned during the morning and afternoon announcements, made presentations to*

Grades 9–12 Performance Indicators

8.12.1 Use accurate peer and societal norms to formulate a health-enhancing message.

8.12.2 Demonstrate how to influence and support others to make positive health choices.

8.12.3 Work cooperatively as an advocate for improving personal, family, and community health.

8.12.4 Adapt health messages and communication techniques to a specific target audience.[1,p36]

business and community leaders to gain their support and donations, and e-mailed students and parents to inform them of the party and to ask for support.)

As the students are learning the skill, provide enough time for them to practice. Use formative assessments to determine the progress of learning. Motivate students by using feedback to show how performance is improved.

When students demonstrate understanding of the skill, teach the content. Design a prompt that allows the students to display their knowledge of health. Use formative assessments, such as white boards (Chapter 4), during content instruction to determine student understanding.

WHAT DOES THE SKILL OF ADVOCACY LOOK LIKE IN THE GRADE 11 CLASSROOM?

Mrs. Richards, the nurse at Ridge High School, cares about the health of her students, their families, and the community. She and the coordinated school health team are interested in implementing a health fair.

Rather than taking full responsibility for the project, the team decided to challenge the juniors in the community health class to plan the health fair. Because of the scope of the project, students are assessed on their planning of this advocacy program.

To begin planning the advocacy health fair unit, the health teacher chooses the performance indicators from Standard 8.

Standard 8—Students will demonstrate the ability to advocate for personal, family, and community health.[1,p36]

8.12.1—Use accurate peer and societal norms to formulate a health-enhancing message.[1,p36]

Performance indicator 8.12.1 with infused content— Use accurate peer and societal norms to formulate a health-enhancing message to advocate for the health fair.[1,p36]

8.12.2—Demonstrate how to influence and support others to make positive health choices.[1,p36]

Performance indicator 8.12.2 with infused content— Demonstrate how to influence and support others to make positive health choices about attending the health fair.[1,p36]

8.12.3—Work cooperatively as an advocate for improving personal, family, and community health.[1,p36]

Performance indicator 8.12.3 with infused content— Work cooperatively as an advocate for improving personal, family, and community health through a health fair.[1,p36]

8.12.4—Adapt health messages and communication techniques to a specific target audience.[1,p36]

Performance indicator 8.12.4 with infused content— Adapt health messages and communication techniques to a specific target audience to promote the health fair.[1,p36]

After selecting the appropriate performance indicator for the skill, Mrs. Condon chooses the performance indicator for Standard 1.

Standard 1—Students will comprehend concepts related to health promotion and disease prevention to enhance health.[1,p24]

1.12.7—Compare and contrast the benefits of and barriers to practicing a variety of healthy behaviors.[1,p25]

Performance indicator 1.12.7 with infused content— Compare and contrast the benefits of and barriers to practicing a variety of healthy behaviors, such as attending a health fair.[1,p25]

By linking the skill and content performance indicators, the teacher has a clear idea of how to plan the lessons for an advocacy unit.

The first step in planning is to think through the unit by completing the performance task template. Thereupon, the teacher will have a good idea of the lessons that precede this culminating activity, the information and back-up materials necessary to introduce the prompt to the students, and the assessment strategies.

When distributing the prompt, include all the back-up information, student worksheets, and holistic and analytical rubrics. Distribute the rubrics with the prompt so students know how they are being assessed before working on their product. The rubrics act as a guide and help the students attain proficiency in the standards.

Designing the performance task takes considerable preparation, but once the information is distributed and explained, the students create a product by themselves or in a group. Students learn with good coaching (formative assessment) how to demonstrate proficiency in content and skill.

The following is an example of a performance task for Grade 11 advocacy unit focusing on implementing a health fair.

The first section is for the teacher and demonstrates how to plan for an authentic assessment of the performance indicators 1.12.7, and 8.12.1, 8.12.2, 8.12.3, and 8.12.4. The second extracts some information from the performance task and transforms it into the student prompt and support materials.

Standard 8 Performance Task: Grade 12—Advocating for a School Health Fair

I. Which state standard(s) does this performance task address?

II. Topic: What areas of health does this project assess? Why is it important? What is the focus of the project?[3,p237]

    A. This performance task assesses the health area of community health.

    B. This topic is important because student advocates:

        1. Enhance their self-confidence

        2. Learn to be persistent

        3. Hone problem-solving skills

        4. Increase their knowledge of a particular issue

        5. Learn to work collaboratively[13]

    C. The focus of the project is to help students plan to advocate for personal, family, and community health through a health fair.

III. Key Concepts: What basic concepts do students need to know?[3,p237]

    Standard 1—Students will comprehend concepts related to health promotion and disease prevention to enhance health.[1,p25]

    Performance indicator 1.12.7 with infused content—Compare and contrast the benefits of and barriers to practicing a variety of healthy behaviors, such as implementing a health fair.[1,p25]

    A. Benefits of implementing a health fair

        1. Community and state organizations bring expertise, information, screenings, services, and resources to the fair.[6,p690]

        2. Students learn how to access valid and reliable sources of information to enhance personal health.

        3. Collaboration with local and state health agencies may increase volunteerism or career direction.

        4. Health screenings enhance personal health.[6,p691]

        5. A health fair increases positive public relations for the school district.

        6. The health fair provides the opportunity to demonstrate the relationship between health care and learning.[14]

    B. Barriers to implementing a health fair

        1. Students are unprepared for the event.

        2. The event lacks school support.

        3. Local or state organizations do not have sufficient resources or volunteers to participate.

        4. There is a lack of volunteers, interest, and support.

        5. Local organizations are not willing to perform screenings.

        6. Media do not report the event.

        7. School and community do not acknowledge the relationship between health care and learning.

IV. Skills: Which of the seven National Health Education Standards skills does this performance task address?[3,p237]

    Standard 8—Students will demonstrate the ability to advocate for personal, family, and community health.[1,p36]

    Performance indicator 8.12.1 with infused content—Use accurate peer and societal norms to formulate a health-enhancing message to advocate for the health fair.[1,p36]

    A. Use Youth Risk Behavior Survey (YRBS) data to establish student needs. Use a health-enhancing message, based on need, to advocate for the health fair.

    B. Use social norms data to select student needs. Use a health-enhancing message, based on need, to advocate for the health fair.

    C. Survey the students and staff to determine what health promotion information and services they would like in the health fair. Use a health-enhancing message, based on need, to advocate for the health fair.

(continues)

Performance indicator 8.12.2 with infused content—Demonstrate how to influence and support others to make positive health choices about attending the health fair.[1,p36]

A. Promote the health fair with prizes.

B. Provide health promotion gifts to participants.

Performance indicator 8.12.3 with infused content—Work cooperatively as an advocate for improving personal, family, and community health through a health fair.[1,p36]

A. Engage the school nurse as a primary collaborator.

B. Ask the school administrator to advocate for students to take personal responsibility for their health.

C. Collaborate with local hospitals and healthcare professionals to provide resources for the health fair.

Performance indicator 8.12.4 with infused content—Adapt health messages and communication techniques to a specific target audience to promote the health fair.[1,p36]

A. Publicize the health fair on the morning and afternoon announcements.

B. Place health fair promotional posters throughout the school. To engage students who are learning a foreign language, use two or more languages on the poster.

C. Use e-mail to invite students, parents, and school staff to the health fair.

D. Ask the coordinated school health team to promote the health fair when they interact with students.

V. Curricular connections: What other subject areas does this project support?[3,p237]

English language arts

Foreign language

Biology

Art

VI. Student Directions and Assessment Criteria[3,p238]

A. Project Description—Write and attach an engaging prompt that draws the student into the project.[3,p238]

The juniors in the community health class are planning a school and community health fair as the final project for their course.

They must promote the benefits of the health fair and figure out ways to overcome the obstacles. They must complete several planning steps before the health fair becomes a reality.

B. Your Challenge—Provide a challenge or mission statement that describes the project.[3,p238]

Your challenge is to complete the planning for the school health fair.

C. Assessment Criteria[3,p239]

You will be assessed on the following content.

Performance indicator 1.12.7 with infused content—Compare and contrast the benefits of and barriers to practicing a variety of healthy behaviors, such as implementing a health fair.[1,p25]

A. State five benefits of implementing a health fair.

B. State five barriers to implementing a health fair.

C. Explain how to overcome each barrier.

You will be assessed on the following skills.

Performance indicator 8.12.1 with infused content—Use accurate peer and societal norms to formulate a health-enhancing message to advocate for the health fair.[1,p36]

A. Gather three statistics from the YRBS data that indicate the greatest health risks to high school students; propose a health-enhancing message to advocate for the health fair.

B. Gather three statistics from social norms data[15] that indicate the greatest, perceived health risks; propose a health-enhancing message to advocate for the health fair.

C. Gather three statistics from the school survey data to determine the most requested health promotion information and services; propose a health-enhancing message to advocate for the health fair.

Performance indicator 8.12.2 with infused content—Demonstrate how to influence and support others to make positive health choices about attending the health fair.[1,p36]

(continues)

A. Demonstrate how the five grand prizes influence students and staff to attend the health fair.

B. Demonstrate how the five items in the health fair take-home-bag influence students and staff to attend the health fair.

Performance indicator 8.12.3 with infused content—Work cooperatively as an advocate for improving personal, family, and community health through a health fair.[1,p36]

A. Explain five ways the school nurse and the planning team collaborate.

B. Explain three ways the administrators use the health fair to advocate for students to take personal responsibility for their health.

C. Explain five ways the team collaborates with local hospitals and healthcare professionals to provide resources for the health fair.

Performance indicator 8.12.4 with infused content—Adapt health messages and communication techniques to a specific target audience to promote the health fair.[1,p36]

A. Explain five ways to advertise the health fair to students and staff, including English language learners and foreign language students.

B. Explain how to use three communication techniques to advertise the health fair.

Student project must include the following:

1. A completed comparison of the benefits and barriers of implementing a health fair and the steps to overcome those obstacles

2. A completed health fair implementation plan

Ridge High School

Name _____

The juniors in the community health class are planning a school and community health fair as the final project for their course. They must promote the benefits of the health fair and figure out ways to overcome the obstacles. They must complete several planning steps before the health fair becomes a reality.

Your challenge is to complete the planning process for the school health fair.

Your project must include:

1. A completed comparison of the benefits and barriers of implementing a health fair and the steps to overcome those obstacles

2. A completed health fair implementation plan

(continues)

Worksheet to Compare the Benefits and Barriers to Implementing a Health Fair (Table 12.9)

Table 12.9 Comparison of the Benefits and Barriers to Implementing a Health Fair

Benefits	Barriers	Steps to Overcome the Barriers
1.		
2.		
3.		
4.		
5.		

Analytical Rubric to Assess the Comparison of Benefits and Barriers to Implementing a Health Fair (Table 12.10)

TABLE 12.10 Analytical Rubric to Assess the Benefits and Barriers Worksheet

Criteria	4	3	2	1
Performance indicator 1.12.7 with infused content—Compare and contrast the benefits of and barriers to practicing a variety of healthy behaviors, such as implementing a health fair.[1,p25]	Student lists five appropriate benefits to implementing a health fair	Student's list of five benefits to implementing a health fair is mostly appropriate.	A few of the five benefits to implementing a health fair are appropriate.	Student's list of five benefits to implementing a health fair is mostly inappropriate.
Performance indicator 1.12.7 with infused content—Compare and contrast the benefits of and barriers to practicing a variety of healthy behaviors, such as implementing a health fair.[1,p25]	Student lists five appropriate barriers to implementing a health fair	Student's list of five barriers to implementing a health fair is mostly appropriate.	A few of the five barriers to implementing a health fair are inappropriate.	Student's list of five barriers to implementing a health fair is mostly inappropriate.

(continues)

Criteria	4	3	2	1
Steps to overcome the barriers	Student accurately describes the steps necessary to overcome each barrier to implementing a health fair.	Student's description of the steps necessary to overcome each barrier to implementing a health fair is mostly accurate.	Student's description of the steps necessary to overcome each barrier to implementing a health fair has a few inaccuracies.	Student's description of the steps necessary to overcome each barrier to implementing a health fair is mostly inaccurate.
Spelling	Spelling is always correct.	Spelling is usually correct.	Spelling is sometimes correct.	Spelling is never correct.

Name _____

Total possible points – 16   Your points – _____   Your grade – _____

Health Fair Implementation Plan (Table 12.11)

TABLE 12.11   Health Fair Implementation Plan

	Statistics	Health-Enhancing Advocacy Message
Three statistics from the YRBS data and the corresponding health-enhancing message to advocate for the health fair. (PI 8.12.1)	1.	
	2.	
	3.	
Three statistics from the social norms data and the corresponding health-enhancing message to advocate for the health fair. (PI 8.12.1)	1.	
	2.	
	3.	
Three statistics from the school survey data and the corresponding health-enhancing message to advocate for the health fair. (PI 8.12.1)	1.	
	2.	
	3.	
Choose five appropriate grand prizes to influence students and staff to attend the health fair. (PI 8.12.2)	1.	
	2.	
	3.	
	4.	
	5.	

(continues)

TABLE 12.11   Health Fair Implementation Plan *(continued)*

	Statistics	Health-Enhancing Advocacy Message
Choose five appropriate items for the health fair take-home-bag to influence students and staff to attend the health fair. (PI 8.12.2)	1. 2. 3. 4. 5.	
Explain five ways the planning team and the school nurse collaborate. (PI 8.12.3)	1. 2. 3. 4. 5.	
Explain three ways the administrators use the health fair to advocate for students to take personal responsibility for their health. (PI8.12.3)	1. 2. 3.	
Explain five ways the planning team collaborates with local hospitals and healthcare professionals to provide resources for the health fair. (PI 8.12.3)	1. 2. 3. 4. 5.	
Explain five ways to advertise the health fair to students and staff, including English language learners and foreign language students. (PI 8.12.4)	1. 2. 3. 4. 5.	
Explain how to use three communication techniques to promote the health fair. (PI 8.12.4)	1. 2. 3.	

(continues)

TABLE 12.12   Analytical Rubric to Assess the Health Fair Implementation Plan

Criteria	4	3	2	1
Performance indicator 8.12.1 with infused content—Use accurate peer and societal norms to formulate a health-enhancing message to advocate for the health fair.[1,p36]	Student uses three appropriate statistics from the YRBS data to propose a health-enhancing message to advocate for the health fair.	The three statistics from the YRBS data used to propose a health-enhancing message to advocate for the health fair are mostly appropriate.	A few of the three statistics from the YRBS data used to propose a health-enhancing message to advocate for the health fair are inappropriate.	The three statistics from the YRBS data used to propose a health-enhancing message to advocate for the health fair are mostly inappropriate.
Performance indicator 8.12.1 with infused content—Use accurate peer and societal norms to formulate a health-enhancing message to advocate for the health fair.[1,p36]	Student appropriately uses three statistics from the social norms data to propose a health-enhancing message to advocate for the health fair.	The three statistics from the social norms data used to propose a health-enhancing message to advocate for the health fair are mostly appropriate.	A few of the three statistics from the social norms data used to propose a health-enhancing message to advocate for the health fair are inappropriate.	The three statistics from the social norms data used to propose a health-enhancing message to advocate for the health fair are mostly inappropriate.
Performance indicator 8.12.1 with infused content—Use accurate peer and societal norms to formulate a health-enhancing message to advocate for the health fair.[1,p36]	Student appropriately uses three statistics from the school survey data to propose a health-enhancing message to advocate for the health fair.	The three statistics from the school survey data used to propose a health-enhancing message to advocate for the health fair are mostly appropriate.	A few of the three statistics from the school survey data used to propose a health-enhancing message to advocate for the health fair are inappropriate.	The three statistics from the school survey data used to propose a health-enhancing message to advocate for the health fair are mostly inappropriate.
Performance indicator 8.12.2 with infused content—Demonstrate how to influence and support others to make positive health choices about attending the health fair.[1,p36]	Student's choice of five grand prizes and five items for the health fair take-home-bag to influence students and staff to attend the health fair are appropriate.	Student's choice of five grand prizes and five items for the health fair take-home-bag to influence students and staff to attend the health fair are mostly appropriate.	A few of the student's choice of five grand prizes and five items for the health fair take-home-bag to influence students and staff to attend the health fair are inappropriate.	Student's choice of five grand prizes and five items for the health fair take-home-bag to influence students and staff to attend the health fair are mostly inappropriate.
Performance indicator 8.12.3 with infused content—Work cooperatively as an advocate for improving personal, family, and community health through a health fair.[1,p36]	Student thoroughly explains five ways the planning team and the school nurse collaborate.	Student adequately explains five ways the planning team and the school nurse collaborate.	Student inadequately explains five ways the planning team and the school nurse collaborate.	Student poorly explains five ways the planning team and the school nurse collaborate.

(continues)

TABLE 12.12   Analytical Rubric to Assess the Health Fair Implementation Plan *(continued)*

Criteria	4	3	2	1
Performance indicator 8.12.3 with infused content—Work cooperatively as an advocate for improving personal, family, and community health through a health fair.[1,p36]	Student thoroughly explains three ways the administrators use the health fair to advocate for students to take personal responsibility for their health.	Student adequately explains three ways the administrators use the health fair to advocate for students to take personal responsibility for their health.	Student inadequately explains three ways the administrators use the health fair to advocate for students to take personal responsibility for their health.	Student poorly explains three ways the administrators use the health fair to advocate for students to take personal responsibility for their health.
Performance indicator 8.12.3 with infused content—Work cooperatively as an advocate for improving personal, family, and community health through a health fair.[1,p36]	Student thoroughly explains five ways the planning team collaborates with local hospitals and healthcare professionals to provide resources for the health fair.	Student adequately explains five ways the planning team collaborates with local hospitals and healthcare professionals to provide resources for the health fair.	Student inadequately explains five ways the planning team collaborates with local hospitals and healthcare professionals to provide resources for the health fair.	Student poorly explains five ways the planning team collaborates with local hospitals and healthcare professionals to provide resources for the health fair.
Performance indicator 8.12.4 with infused content—Adapt health messages and communication techniques to a target audience to promote the health fair.[1,p36]	Student thoroughly explains five ways to advertise the health fair to students and staff, including English language learners and foreign language students.	Student adequately explains five ways to advertise the health fair to students and staff, including English language learners and foreign language students.	Student inadequately explains five ways to advertise the health fair to students and staff, including English language learners and foreign language students.	Student poorly explains five ways to advertise the health fair to students and staff, including English language learners and foreign language students.
Performance indicator 8.12.4 with infused content—Adapt health messages and communication techniques to a target audience to promote the health fair.[1,p36]	Student thoroughly explains how to use three communication techniques to advertise the health fair.	Student adequately explains how to use three communication techniques to advertise the health fair.	Student inadequately explains how to use three communication techniques to advertise the health fair.	Student poorly explains how to use three communication techniques to advertise the health fair.
Spelling	Spelling is always correct.	Spelling is usually correct.	Spelling is sometimes correct.	Spelling is never correct.

Name _____

Total possible points – 40   Your points – _____   Your grade – _____

HOW DOES THE COORDINATED SCHOOL HEALTH TEAM HELP STUDENTS ADVOCATE FOR PERSONAL, FAMILY, AND COMMUNITY HEALTH?

Health Education

- Teach the skill of advocacy.
- Model advocacy.

- Advocate for personal, family, and community health by taking a major role in the implementation of the health fair.

Physical Education

- Encourage students to advocate for physical education as a part of the health fair.

- Advocate for personal, family, and community health by taking a major role in the implementation of the health fair.

Health Services

- Provide expertise and leadership as a collaborator with the health fair planning team.
- Invite healthcare contacts to participate in the health fair.

Nutrition Services

- Provide healthy snacks for the health fair.
- Explain how school food meets state and national guidelines and promotes the health of students.

Counseling, Psychological, and Social Services

- Encourage students to advocate for their personal health.
- Invite mental health contacts to participate in the health fair.

Healthy School Environment

- Provide space and resources for the health fair.
- Provide space for students to advertise the health fair.

Family and Community Involvement

- Ask volunteers to distribute information and resources at the various booths.
- Provide resources and materials to the health fair.
- Encourage the community to hold the health fair in a public space so all community members have access.

Review Questions

1. Why is advocacy such an important skill for students to learn?

2. Give an example of an advocacy performance task for each grade span.

3. What evidence is necessary for students to show proficiency in the skill of advocacy?

4. Explain how to use a formative assessment tool on each grade span to assess the student acquisition of the advocacy skill.

5. Defend the use of summative assessments in addition to the performance based analytical rubric.

6. Why is it important to research student need associated with a topic?

7. If a performance task is planned and implemented and the students do not respond, appear bored, or seem confused, what intervention should occur?

8. Explain the relationship between the skill of advocacy and leadership.

9. How can one performance indicator have two or more criteria for assessment on the analytical rubric?

10. Why is the coordinated school health committee such a significant part of the planning?

References

1. Joint Committee on National Health Education Standards. (2007). *National Health Education Standards, Second Edition, Achieving Excellence.* Atlanta, GA: American Cancer Society.
2. Tappe, M. K. (2001). Health Educators' Role in Promoting Health Literacy and Advocacy for the 21st Century. *Journal of School Health,* 71(10), 477–482.
3. CCSSO~SCASS Health Education Project. (2006). *Assessment Tools for School Health Education, Pre-service and In-service edition.* Santa Cruz, CA: ToucanEd, Inc.
4. American Heart Association. (2010). *Heart Disease and Stroke. You Are the Cure.* Retrieved April 15, 2010, from: http://www.americanheart.org/presenter.jhtml?identifier=2945
5. Dalgas-Pelish, P. (2006). Effects of a Self-Esteem Intervention Program on School-Age Children. *Pediatric Nursing,* 32(4), 341–348.
6. Meeks, L. H. (2011). *Comprehensive School Health Education, Totally Awesome Strategies for Teaching Health* (7th ed.). New York: McGraw-Hill.
7. Bronson, P. M. (2007). *Teen Health, Course 2.* New York: McGraw-Hill Glencoe.
8. U.S. Department of Health and Human Services, Centers for Disease Control and Prevention. (2005). *2005 Middle School Youth Risk Behavior Survey.* Retrieved February 7, 2010, from: www.cdc.gov/healthyyouth/yrbs/middleschool 2005/pdf/YRBS_MS__fullreport.pdf. p. 14–16.
9. Graham, M. (2005). Use of School Gardens in Academic Instruction. *Journal of Nutrition Education Behavior,* 37(3), 147–151.
10. Assadourian, E. (2003). The Growing Value of Gardens. *Encounter: Education for Meaning and Social Justice,* 16(3), 39–42.
11. United States Department of Agriculture. (2009). *Inside the Pyramid.* Retrieved April 20, 2010, from: http://www.mypyramid.gov/pyramid/vegetables_why.html
12. California Department of Education. (n.d.). *A Healthy Nutrition Environment: Linking Education, Activity, and Food Through School Gardens.* Retrieved April 20, 2010, from School Garden Program Overview–Healthy Eating & Nutrition Education: http://www.cde.ca.gov/ls/nu/he/garden overview.asp. p. 1.

13. Robinson, A. M. (2003). A National Study of Local and State Advocacy in Gifted Education. *Gifted Child Quarterly*, 47(1), 8–25.
14. Covering Kids & Families. (2007). *Planning a Health and Enrollment Fair.* Retrieved April 22, 2010, from: http://www.coveringkidsandfamilies.org/actioncenter/module_ModuleID=20.php. p. 2.
15. University of Virginia. (n.d.). *Resources.* Retrieved April 22, 2010, from NSNI National Social Norms Institute: http://www.socialnorm.org/Resources/data.php

Glossary

action research—a process whereby teachers in a school identify a problem, then collect and analyze data regarding it. They develop a prescriptive plan, implement it, and evaluate its effectiveness. Action research empowers teachers to research and resolve problems in their own classrooms and school.

anchor papers—scored examples of student work that represent ranges of student achievement from the lowest levels of performance to the highest.

authentic assessment—measures content and skill demonstrated by a student at the completion of a performance task.

Comprehensive School Health Education—a component of the coordinated school health program that provides planned instruction addressing the physical, mental, emotional, and social dimensions of health. Promotes knowledge, attitudes, and skills, and is tailored to each age/developmental level.

Coordinated School Health Model—the coordination of eight components: comprehensive school health, physical education, school health services, school nutrition services, school counseling and psychological and social services, healthy school environment, health promotion for staff, and family and community involvement to improve the health, well-being, and academic achievement of students.

criterion referenced—compares a student's performance to the content and skills performance indicators.

essential question—a broad question that stimulates inquiry of a subject.

electronic aggression—harassment or bullying that occurs through e-mail, text messaging, chat rooms, or a website.

equitable—assessing students through methods that are most suitable to them while considering their prior knowledge, cultural experience, and learning style.

exemplars—examples of student work that show a range of proficiency in meeting the performance indicator.

family and community involvement—a component of the coordinated school health program that includes partnerships among schools, families, community groups, and individuals.

formative assessment—a continuous measurement of student performance that guides instruction and enhances student learning. It is assessment for learning.

functional foods—foods that contribute to the improvement or prevention of specific health problems.

functional health knowledge—essential concepts that are accurate, reliable, and credible, and are used to assess risk, understand social norms, avoid risky situations, examine influences, make positive decisions, and build competence.

health literacy—the capacity of individuals to obtain, interpret, and understand basic health information and services and the competence to use such information and services in ways that enhance health.

health risk behaviors—the Centers for Disease Control and Prevention has identified alcohol and other drug use, injury and violence, tobacco use, poor nutrition, inadequate physical activity, and risky sexual behaviors as adolescent risk behaviors because they are the leading causes of death, disability, and social problems for youth.

healthy school environment—a component of the coordinated school health program that includes the physical, emotional, and social climate of the school. It provides a safe physical school, as well as a healthy and supportive environment to foster learning.

holistic rubric—A holistic rubric makes a judgment on the overall student product when comparing it to all the performance indicators required.

morbidity—pertains to illness or disease.

mortality—pertains to death.

norm referenced—one student's performance compared to others. For example, in the analyzing influences unit, three students earned an A; four, a B; ten, a C; five a D; and five failed.

performance indicators—statements following each National Health Education Standard that identify what the students should know and be able to do at the end of every grade span. They are the foundation of assessment for the standard.

performance task—projects that allow students to demonstrate proficiency in health knowledge and skill. Examples include role-plays, brochures, public service announcements, comic strips, etc.

physical education—a component of the coordinated school health program that provides planned, sequential instruction to promote lifelong physical activity. It develops basic movement skills, sports skills, and physical fitness, and enhances mental, social, and emotional abilities.

prompt—an open-ended question, problem, or challenge that requires students to think critically and use health content and skills to produce a solution that is demonstrated as a product or a performance.

reliable—a grade is reliable if it remains the same when retaken or the student earns the same score with a different scorer. One way of achieving reliability is by providing many tasks measuring the same outcome and having them scored by well-trained staff using clear rubrics and referring to specific anchor papers or performances.

self-efficacy—a person's belief about his or her capabilities to produce at a certain level of performance.

school counseling and psychological and social services—a component of the coordinated school health program that includes activities that focus on cognitive, emotional, behavioral, and social needs of individuals, groups, and families. It prevents and addresses problems, facilitates positive learning and healthy behavior, and enhances healthy development.

school health services—a component of the coordinated school health program that provides preventive services, education, emergency care, referral, and management of acute and chronic health conditions. It promotes the health of students, identifies and prevents health problems and injuries, and ensures their care.

school nutrition services—a component of the coordinated school health program that integrates nutritious, affordable, and appealing meals; provides nutrition education; and offers an environment that promotes healthy eating for all children.

school-site health promotion—a component of the coordinated school health program that includes assessment, education, and fitness activities for faculty and staff. It maintains and improves the health and well-being of school staff to help members serve as role models for students.

Social Cognitive Theory—describes learning in terms of the interrelationship between behavior, environmental factors, and personal factors.

summative assessment—measures student performance of standards. The results report the level of one's achievement.

targeted instruction—planning skill and content to meet a specific student need.

validity—A performance task is valid when the criteria on the rubric reflect the requirements of the performance indicator and specify the differences in quality for each score.

Index

Note: Italicized page locators indicate a figure; tables are noted with a *t*.

resisting, interpersonal communication skills used for, 226–229

underage use of, research based and theory driven curriculum and instruction on, 46–47

Alcoholism, 103*t*

health and family history of, 109*t*

Alliance for a Healthier Generation, 115

American Association for Health Education, 53, 116

American Association of Health, Physical Education, Recreation and Dance, 116

American Cancer Society, 1, 115

American Federation of Teachers, 54

American Heart Association, 115

American Lung Association, 21, 26, 115

American School Health Association, 115

Analytical rubrics. *See also* Rubrics

to assess accessing information from comic book or poster, 200–201*t*

to assess accessing information performance task, 170–171*t*, 178*t*

to assess asthma portion of PowerPoint or poster, 190–191*t*

to assess benefits and barriers to implementing of health fair, 410–411*t*

to assess bicycle helmet demonstration, 151–152*t*

to assess bullying role-play portion of interpersonal communication performance task, 223–224*t*

to assess bus safety rules poster, 125–126*t*

to assess cereal advertisement, 133–134*t*

to assess conflict resolution comic book, 371–372*t*

to assess conflict resolution role-play, 370–371*t*

to assess decision-making power, 257–258*t*

to assess decision-making process, 279–281*t*

to assess decision-making role-play, 266–267*t*, 292–294*t*

to assess demonstration of refusal skills, 239–240*t*

to assess dental health poster portion of performance task, 307–308*t*

to assess external and internal factors graphic organizers, 125*t*

to assess food allergy portion of PowerPoint or poster, 188–190*t*

to assess goal-setting role-play on personal health practices, 328–329*t*

to assess goal-setting role-play or comic book on nicotine cessation, 339–340*t*

to assess health fair implementation plan, 413–414*t*

to assess health helper advocacy poster and public service announcement, 390–391*t*

to assess multimedia presentation or poster on influence of electronic aggression and coping in a healthy way, 140–141*t*

to assess nutrition and physical activity poster, 265*t*

to assess nutrition poster, 132–133*t*

to assess peer pressure to drink alcohol, 230–231*t*

to assess poster or PowerPoint presentation on how conflict resolution skills prevent injuries and other adolescent health problems, 368–369*t*

to assess PowerPoint or poster about alcohol and marijuana, 290–291*t*

to assess public service announcement and graphic organizer on advocating for good friends, 396–397*t*

to assess recycling poster portion of performance task, 306*t*

to assess role-play of bus safety rules, 126–127*t*

to assess role-play of healthy manners, 349–350*t*, 350–351*t*

to assess role-play to principal explaining how school policies regarding electronic aggression influence health promotion, 142–143*t*

to assess rules of the road chart, 149–150*t*

to assess safety demonstration, 215–216*t*

to assess story about high school boy influenced by parents and friends to wear a bicycle helmet, 152–153*t*

to assess stress graphic organizer, 379–380*t*

to assess stress management brochure, 380–382*t*

to assess stress management demonstration, 382*t*

to assess tobacco, healthy weight loss, and eating disorder book portion of performance task, 278–279*t*

to assess validity of websites portion of PowerPoint or poster, 192*t*

to assess wellness calendar, 327–328*t*

for book portion of goal-setting performance task, 318–319*t*

to demonstrate conflict resolution skills, 240–243*t*

for My Health CD, 317*t*

for performance indicators 1.5.1 to 1.5.5, 97–98*t*

for performance indicators 1.8.1 to 1.8.9, 103–104*t*

for performance indicators 1.12.1 to 1.12.9, 109–110*t*

for stress and yoga graph portion of performance task, 359*t*

for yoga portion of performance task, 360*t*

Anaphylactic shock, peanut allergies and, 182

Anchor papers, 82

Anti-baceterial gels for hand washing, 344, 347

April Age, 20

Area of consequences, outcome expectancies and, 32

ASCD. *See* Association for Supervision and Curriculum Development

ASHA. *See* American School Health Association

Assess, meaning of word, 61

Assessments, 61–86

authentic, 77, 78

classroom use of, 62

cycle of, *61*

defined, 61

equitable, valid, and reliable, 83

formative, 62–68

grading *vs.*, 61–62

guidelines, 82–85

Health Education Assessment Project, 86

instructor review and adjustment of, 85

parents/guardians and results of, 84

performance tasks, 77–82

purpose of, 61

rubrics, 69–77

summative, 62–63, 68–69

systems of, 85–86

classroom assessment, 85

school and district assessments, 85

state assessments, 85–86

videotape and, 84

Assessment strategies, aligning with standards, curriculum, and instruction, 83

Assessment Tools for School Health Education, 43

Association for Childhood Education International, 53

Photo Credits

Chapter 4
Page 71 (tomato) © adsheyn/ShutterStock, Inc.; **(number magnets)** © Sxpnz/Dreamstime.com; **4.9 (teacher and students)** © Monkey Business Images/Dreamstime.com; **(school)** © Jesse Kunerth/Dreamstime.com; **(state outline)** © John Henkel/Fotolia.com

Chapter 7
Table 7.1 (meal) © LiquidLibrary; **(girl with soccer gear)** © Gorilla/ShutterStock, Inc.; **(girl sleeping with bear)** © LiquidLibrary; **(boy and doctor)** © Blaj Gabriel/ShutterStock, Inc.; **(girl flossing)** © Gorilla/ShutterStock, Inc.; **(boy in back seat)** © Suzanne Tucker/ShutterStock, Inc.; **(boy riding bike)** © greenland/ShutterStock, Inc.; **(boy washing hands)** Courtesy of Cade Martin/CDC; **(doctor with baby)** © AbleStock; **(girl sneezing)** © Beth Van Trees/Fotolia.com; **(ice cream)** © Kenneth Sponsler/ShutterStock, Inc.; **(bowl of cereal)** © marylooo/ShutterStock, Inc.; **(boy doing karate)** © get4net/ShutterStock, Inc.; **(girl sleeping)** © wong sze yuen/ShutterStock, Inc.; **(boy brushing teeth)** © Hughstoneian/Dreamstime.com; **(baby on driver's lap)** © Densi/ShutterStock, Inc.; **(girl rollerblading)** © Vasily Kovalev/ShutterStock, Inc.; **(children playing field hockey)** © Fancy/Alamy Images; **(boy sneezing)** © matka_Wariatka/ShutterStock, Inc.; **Table 7.2 (police officer)** © Anthony Monterotti/ShutterStock, Inc..; **(school nurse)** © Emily Behlmann/AP Photos; **(doctor with boy)** © Nyul/Dreamstime.com; **(optometrist and pharmacist)** © Photodisc; **(dentist)** © Serghei Starus/ShutterStock, Inc.; **(police station)** © TFoxFoto/ShutterStock, Inc.; **(fire house)** © Tom Fawls/Dreamstime.com; **(doctor's office)** © Frank Siteman/age fotostock; **(optometrist's office)** © Portraiture Studio/Dreamstime.com; **(pharmacist's office)** © Natalia Bratslavsky/Dreamstime.com; **(dentist's office)** © Alin Popescu/ShutterStock, Inc.; **(first aid kit)** © Mikotaj Tomczak/Dreamstime.com; **(thermometer)** © Charles Brutlag/Dreamstime.com; **(stretcher)** © Vatikaki/ShutterStock, Inc.; **(stethoscope)** © Mrsnstudio/Dreamstime.com; **(eye exam chart)** © Svetlana Larina/Dreamstime.com; **(medicine)** © Cheryl Casey/ShutterStock, Inc.; **(dentist's mirror)** © Aleksandr Ugorenkov/Dreamstime.com; **Table 7.4 (girl watching T.V.)** © Ivonne Wierink/ShutterStock, Inc.; **(doctor with child)** © LiquidLibrary; **(boy brushing teeth)** © Hughstoneian/Dreamstime.com; **(boy in car)** © olly/ShutterStock, Inc.; **(boy rollerblading)** © Elena Yakusheva/ShutterStock, Inc.; **(child sneezing)** © SaferTim/ShutterStock, Inc.; **Page 166 (pharmacist)** © Photodisc; **(stretcher)** © Vatikaki/ShutterStock, Inc.; **(optometrist's office)** © Portraiture Studio/Dreamstime.com; **(stethoscope)** © Mrsnstudio/Dreamstime.com; **(police officer)** © Anthony Monterotti/ShutterStock, Inc.; **(dentist's mirror)** © Aleksandr Ugorenkov/Dreamstime.com; **Table 7.5 (school nurse)** © Emily Behlmann/AP Photos; **(doctor with child)** © Nyul/Dreamstime.com; **(optometrist)** © Photodisc; **(dentist)** © Serghei Starus/ShutterStock, Inc.; **(police station)** © TFoxFoto/ShutterStock, Inc.; **(fire house)** © Tom Fawls/Dreamstime.com; **(doctor's office)** © Frank Siteman/age fotostock; **(pharmacist's office)** © Natalia Bratslavsky/Dreamstime.com; **(dentist's office)** © Alin Popescu/ShutterStock, Inc.; **(first aid kit)** © Mikołaj Tomczak/Dreamstime.com; **(thermometer)** © Charles Brutlag/Dreamstime.com; **(eye exam chart)** © Svetlana Larina/Dreamstime.com; **(pharmacist counting pills)** © Corbis/age fotostock; **Page 169 (meal)** © LiquidLibrary; **(ice cream)** © Kenneth Sponsler/ShutterStock, Inc.; **(bowl of cereal)** © marylooo/ShutterStock, Inc.; **(girl flossing)** © Gorilla/ShutterStock, Inc.; **(boy drinking soda)** © Phase4Photography/ShutterStock, Inc.; **(girl eating candy)** © Pavzyuk Svitlana/ShutterStock, Inc.; **(baby on driver's lap)** © Densi/ShutterStock, Inc.; **(boy in car seat)** © Suzanne Tucker/ShutterStock, Inc.; **(girl rollerblading)** © Vasily Kovalev/ShutterStock, Inc.; **(boy riding bike)** © green-

land/ShutterStock, Inc.; **(children playing field hockey)** © Fancy/Alamy Images; **Page 170 (girl washing hands)** © Brebca/Fotolia.com; **(boy sneezing)** © matka_Wariatka/ShutterStock, Inc.; **(boy washing hands)** Courtesy of Cade Martin/CDC; **(boy with doctor)** © Blaj Gabriel/ShutterStock, Inc.; **(boy blowing nose)** © Bronwyn Photo/ShutterStock, Inc.; **(children playing)** © Pavel Losevsky/Dreamstime.com

Chapter 8
8.1 © GLUE STOCK/ShutterStock, Inc.; **Table 8.1 (children talking)** © Ilike/ShutterStock, Inc.; **Table 8.2 (man in car talking to child)** © Digital Vision/age fotostock; **(car with dent)** © Soundsnaps/ShutterStock, Inc.; **(boy with mother)** SW Productions/Brand X Pictures/Getty Images; **(child running)** © Konstantin L/ShutterStock, Inc.; **(girl with mother)** © Rob Marmion/ShutterStock, Inc.; **Page 214 (man with sunglasses)** © Rob Byron/ShutterStock, Inc.; **(teacher)** © AVAVA/ShutterStock, Inc.; **(man in car)** © Photos.com; **(child holding head)** © Natalija Brenca/ShutterStock, Inc.; **(child holding bear)** © Lucian Coman/Dreamstime.com; **(children crossing street)** © Isabel Poulin/Dreamstime.com; **(older woman)** © Ryan McVay/Photodisc/Getty Images; **(man in car talking to child)** © Digital Vision/age fotostock; **(crossing guard)** © LiquidLibrary; **Page 215 (smiling girl)** © Amot/Dreamstime.com; **(boy looking scared)** © Larisa Lofitskaya/ShutterStock, Inc.; **(girl and mother)** © Studio 1One/ShutterStock, Inc.; **(shaking hands)** © raluca teodorescu/ShutterStock, Inc.; **(girl being abducted)** © Arco Images/age fotostock; **(girl and mother)** © Monkey Business Images/ShutterStock, Inc.; **(children at beach)** © Photos.com; **(girls fighting)** © Mcpics/Dreamstime.com; **(boy pulling girl's hair)** © Cheryl Casey/Dreamstime.com

Chapter 9
Page 246 (go sign) © magicinfoto/ShutterStock, Inc.; **(stop sign)** © Christophe Testi/ShutterStock, Inc.; **Page 247 (makeup)** © Tim Sulov/ShutterStock, Inc.; **(deodorant)** © Okssi68/Dreamstime.com; **(toilet cleaner)** © Picsfive/Dreamstime.com; **(pills)** © ravl/ShutterStock, Inc.; **(hair spray)** © slon1971/ShutterStock, Inc.; **Table 9.2 (smiley faces)** © VectorZilla/ShutterStock, Inc.; **(child holding pills)** © Mykola Velychko/Fotolia.com; **(child opening medicine)** © Raia/Fotolia.com; **(child holding medicine cup)** © Geo Martinez/Fotolia.com; **(spray can)** © Jakub Koštál/ShutterStock, Inc.; **(shaving cream)** © Anette Linnea Rasmussen/Dreamstime.com; **(makeup)** © rainette/Fotolia.com; **Table 9.3 (aspirin)** © James Steidl/Dreamstime.com; **(banana)** © Photodisc; **(sandwich)** © SoleilC/ShutterStock, Inc.; **(cream in jar)** © maryo/ShutterStock, Inc.; **(shampoo)** © David Kelly/

Dreamstime.com; **(bowl of cereal)** © Stephen Mcsweeny/Dreamstime.com; **Table 9.4 (girl with mouthwash)** © Beauty Photo Studio/age fotostock; **(child opening medicine)** © Renata Osinska/Fotolia.com; **(boy in medicine cabinet)** © Photodisc; **(girl drinking water)** © Amot/Dreamstime.com; **(boy brushing teeth)** © Hughstoneian/Dreamstime.com; **(girl washing hands)** © Brebca/Fotolia.com; **Page 255 (child holding pills)** © Mykola Velychko/Fotolia.com; **(girl opening medicine)** © Raia/Fotolia.com; **(makeup)** © rainette/Fotolia.com; **(spray can)** © Jakub Koštál/ShutterStock, Inc.; **Table 9.5 (aspirin)** © James Steidl/Dreamstime.com; **(bowl of cereal)** © Stephen Mcsweeny/Dreamstime.com; **(shaving cream)** © Anette Linnea Rasmussen/Dreamstime.com; **(banana)** © Photodisc; **Page 256 (boy brushing teeth)** © Hughstoneian/Dreamstime.com; **(girl drinking water)** © Amot/Dreamstime.com, **(girl opening medicine)** © Renata Osinska/Fotolia.com; **(boy in medicine cabinet)** © Photodisc; **(girl washing hands)** © Brebca/Fotolia.com; **(girl with mouthwash)** © Beauty Photo Studio/age fotostock

Chapter 11
Table 11.1 (woman smoking in car with child) © Kuttig - People/Alamy; **(girl riding bike)** © Raywoo/Dreamstime.com; **(child reaching into open bottle)** © Claus Jepsen/Dreamstime.com; **(girl eating candy)** © Pavzyuk Svitlana/ShutterStock, Inc.; **(boy watching T.V.)** © Gladskikh Tatiana/ShutterStock, Inc.; **Table 11.5 (boy sleeping on books)** © Dmitriy Shironosov/ShutterStock, Inc.; **(boy sleeping with bear)** © kavring/ShutterStock, Inc.; **(girl riding bike)** © Raywoo/Dreamstime.com; **(boy riding bike)** © greenland/ShutterStock, Inc.; **(girl holding head)** © Jacek Chabraszewski/ShutterStock, Inc.; **(girl talking to adult)** © Tomasz Trojanowski/ShutterStock, Inc.; **(girl holding throat)** © dragon_fang/ShutterStock, Inc.; **(girl doing heimlich)** © Dale Sparks/AP Photos; **Table 11.9 (hands)** © 3poD Animation/ShutterStock, Inc.; **(two girls talking)** © Photodisc

Chapter 12
Table 12.1 (hand sanitizer) © Mike Flippo/ShutterStock, Inc.; **(boy in wheelchair)** © sonya etchison/ShutterStock, Inc.; **(bananas)** © Digital Stock; **Table 12.2 (girl holding throat)** © Pzromashka/Dreamstime.com; **(boy watching T.V.)** © GeoM/ShutterStock, Inc.; **Table 12.6** © cycreation/Fotolia.com

Unless otherwise indicated, all photographs and illustrations are under copyright of Jones & Bartlett Learning, or have been provided by the author.